Francis Duncan

History of the Royal Regiment of Artillery

Vol. II

Francis Duncan

History of the Royal Regiment of Artillery
Vol. II

ISBN/EAN: 9783743313927

Manufactured in Europe, USA, Canada, Australia, Japa

Cover: Foto ©ninafisch / pixelio.de

Manufactured and distributed by brebook publishing software (www.brebook.com)

Francis Duncan

History of the Royal Regiment of Artillery

ALEXANDER DICKSON,
ROYAL ARTILLERY
ARTILLERY

HISTORY

OF THE

ROYAL REGIMENT OF ARTILLERY.

COMPILED FROM THE ORIGINAL RECORDS.

By MAJOR FRANCIS DUNCAN, M.A., D.C.L., LL.D.,

ROYAL ARTILLERY.

SUPERINTENDENT OF THE ROYAL ARTILLERY REGIMENTAL RECORDS;
FELLOW OF THE GEOLOGICAL SOCIETY OF LONDON,
AND OF THE ROYAL GEOGRAPHICAL SOCIETY.

"L'histoire de l'Artillerie est l'histoire du progrès des sciences, et partant de la civilisation."
NAPOLEON III. *Chislehurst, Nov.* 22, 1872.

IN TWO VOLUMES—VOL. II.

THIRD EDITION.

WITH PORTRAITS.

LONDON:
JOHN MURRAY, ALBEMARLE STREET.
1879.

LONDON:
PRINTED BY WILLIAM CLOWES AND SONS,
STAMFORD STREET AND CHARING CROSS

TO

HIS ROYAL H

FIELD-MARSHAL THE DU

K.G., G.C.B., K.P.,

COLONEL OF THE ROYAL REG

THIS

HIST   OF ITS

LLY, AND B

DEDICATED

PREFACE.

UNFORESEEN circumstances having arisen since the publication of the First Volume of this work, which rendered it possible that the Author might be unable to complete the narrative while holding the appointment of Superintendent of the Regimental Records, it has become necessary to modify the original plan. There were two alternatives,—either to compress the history between 1783 and the present date into one volume, sacrificing many matters of minor interest,— or to write, as fully as in the former volume, the history of a certain period later than that already treated of, leaving the subsequent years and their campaigns to be described either by the Author's successor, or by himself at some future time. After consultation with some of the senior officers of the Corps, the latter alternative has been adopted; and the addition of certain statistical tables, and of a copious index to both volumes, will, it is hoped, render the work, as far as it goes, a complete one. Unless anticipated by an abler pen, the Author does not despair of being able to avail himself at some future time of

the continued access to the
systematically arranged, wh
him by the Deputy Adjutan
with a view to compiling
the Crimea, and of the Ind

The almost unanimously
the first volume, not only by
cheering extent by his brot
Author's grateful acknowle
raged him in the labours,
now submitted to the publi
that he did not err in the
Regimental History, as a
intensifying *esprit de corps*.

	PAGE
…	vii
…	xi
…	1
…ry, Birth, and Progress of the …e Artillery	30
…uke of York in Flanders	54
…9	70
…ing of the Chestnut Troop	88
…	104
…	134
…Battalion	138
…attalion	150
…Copenhagen	158
…and Buenos Ayres	168
…th Battalion	185
…ar: Roliça, Vimiera, Corunna	195
…	223
…e Douro, Talavera	242
…Torres Vedras	262
…ajoz, Albuera	280
…go and Badajoz	307
…d Burgos	321
…San Sebastian	338
…the Peninsular War	373
…American War	392
…	412

		PAGE
APPENDIX A.—THE DUKE OF WELLINGTON, AND THE ARTILLERY AT WATERLOO		444
" B.—THE ROYAL ARTILLERY, AND THE MAGNETIC SURVEY OF 1840–8		465
" C.—TABULAR STATEMENT, SHOWING DATE OF FORMATION AND FORMER DESIGNATION OF EVERY BATTERY OF THE REGIMENT NOW IN THE SERVICE		470
INDEX		479

ERRATA TO VOL. II.

At page 141, *for* "H Battery, 11 Brigade," *read* "H Battery, 16 Brigade."
At page 282, 15th line from bottom, *delete* "7th;" and at 14th line from bottom, *for* "and 2nd Battalion 82nd, besides," &c., *read* "2nd Battalion 82nd, detachments 95th, besides," &c.

INTRODUCTION.

HAVING in the Preface stated the plan of this volume, it is incumbent on the Author now to acknowledge, with gratitude, the assistance he has received during its execution. Acting on a suggestion made by one of the reviewers of the first volume, he has noted in the margin the various authorities on which the narrative is based; and, as in many instances these are manuscript letters in the Record Office, he has given the dates of such,—to facilitate access to them by any one anxious to obtain information in detail.

Among those to whom the Author is chiefly indebted, Sir Collingwood Dickson—for the reason stated in the body of the work—stands first. Not only the Author, but the Regiment at large, is indebted to him for the generous confidence with which he entrusted the letters and journals of his distinguished father to the writer of this history. The labours of Captain G. E. W. Malet, R.A.—so visible in the tables at the end of this volume—demand the next place in the Author's acknowledgment;—and the Reader will be able to judge how great has been the value, to this narrative, of the published writings of Captain H. W. L. Hime, R.A.

Sir J. Bloomfield, Sir E. C. Warde, Sir D. E. Wood, General Burke Cuppage, Major-Generals W. J. Smythe and C. J. B. Riddell, Colonel Lynedoch Gardiner, Major H. Geary, and

Lieutenant J. Ritchie, have contributed valuable information connected with the history of the Regiment to which they belong, and have greatly facilitated the Author's labours. The assistance of the Committee of the United Service Institution; of its Librarian, T. D. Sullivan, Esq.; Sir Edward Perrott, and of Captain H. W. Gordon, C.B., is also gratefully acknowledged.

To Mr. James Browne, the author of 'England's Artillerymen,' a double debt is owing. His labour produced the Index to the first volume; and his published work has been a mine of reference, the value of which became more apparent, the more it was explored. Written without the adventitious aids at the disposal of the custodian of the Regimental Records, it is yet so exhaustive and accurate, that, when admiration of it has ceased, it is only because that feeling has passed into envy.

The admirable Index to the present volume is due to the skill, ability, and industry, eminently possessed by the Assistant-Superintendent in the Record Office, R. H. Murdoch, Esq., R.A. These talents were generously placed at the Author's disposal, with a view to this work being made as complete as possible.

The conducting a work of this description through the press,—although the last occupation in point of time,—is not the least in point of importance. Careful comparison with the MSS.,—much patient and merely mechanical labour, —and watchfulness, lest errors of style should be overlooked in the anxiety to secure rigid accuracy, or lest the latter should be sacrificed to attempts at literary embellishment,—all these are involved in the process. And all these have been displayed by one who has assisted in this operation,—the Rev. G. Martyn Ritchie, Chaplain to the Forces, whose services the Author acknowledges with gratitude.

Not unfrequently the official letter-books differ from

Kane's List of Officers in the spelling of proper names. Where the correct reading is doubtful, that found in the letter-books is given in the body of the work, and both are given in the Index.

History moves so rapidly, that even while this work has been in the press, a slight alteration in the pay of the non-commissioned officers and men of the Regiment has been made, making the rates given in the following pages as those of the year 1873, accurate only up to the 1st of October in that year. The reader can with ease make the requisite corrections.

HISTORY

OF THE

ROYAL REGIMENT OF ARTILLERY.

CHAPTER I.

REACTION.

REACTION and retrenchment followed the Peace signed at Versailles in 1783; and with them came dullness and despondency in the Regiment. Until 1787, when the state of France caused universal alarm in Europe, and preparations for possible hostilities already commenced in England, the prospects of promotion had been most disheartening. During the American War, a large number of subaltern officers had been appointed by the Generals serving with the English armies, and it was found, in 1783, that in this respect the establishment of the Regiment had been considerably exceeded. With somewhat distorted ideas of justice, it was ruled that the pay of the supernumeraries should be provided by means of stoppages from the officers of all ranks on the proper establishment, and that no new appointments should be made until all the supernumeraries had been absorbed,— an event which did not take place until the 14th February, 1786.

Dullness, therefore, reigned during these years in the Warren at Woolwich,—dullness in the Academy,—dullness in foreign stations, where the detachments were at times forgotten altogether,—and dullness the most stupendous in the offices of His Majesty's Ordnance.

Uneventful, however, as this period of the Regimental History undoubtedly was, it possesses to the student a peculiar interest. Its domestic details invite attention, as representing the transition stage of the Regiment from a past which had been glorious, to a future which was to be more glorious still,—the last act, so to speak, of a drama in which Artillery meant many things, but rarely implied mobility; and a breathing-time, which admitted of much internal organisation being perfected, which had been forgotten or overlooked in the midst of war.

In the years between 1783 and 1792 there was much to interest, much to amuse, and not a little to cause pain; but the details, although necessary to be told, are wholly domestic.

The strength of the Regiment remained until 1791 at four Service Battalions, each consisting of ten companies, and, in addition, ten companies of invalids. In March 1791, two additional companies were formed for service in the East Indies, but they belonged to no particular Battalion. The companies, which had been reduced to a minimum in 1783, were raised to a greater establishment in 1787, a year in which recruiting on a considerable scale was ordered, and never was wholly suspended until after Waterloo. The bounty allowed to each recruit was five guineas.[1]

R. A. Reg¹. Orders.

The promotion consequent on the formation of the East India Companies mentioned above was as follows:—1 Major, 3 Captains, 5 Captain-Lieutenants, and 9 First Lieutenants.

Letters to the Master-General, 1783-92.

On the reduction in 1783, all men who were eligible were transferred to the invalids, or to the out-pension list; and men who were not entitled to that privilege, but who were ordered to be discharged on reduction, received donations:—

M. S. Reg¹. Orders.

"If going to his home in Ireland, 38 days' pay; to Scotland, "28 days' pay; and if to any part of England, 14 days' "pay."

Prior to the general recruiting which was ordered in 1787,

---

[1] The Regimental Band at the date referred to in this chapter consisted of a Bandmaster at 4s. per diem, and 8 private men, who were borne on the strength of the companies at Woolwich.

a special company of artificers was raised—in 1786—for service in Gibraltar. As these men were put under the officers of Engineers, a Royal Warrant was issued on the 25th April, 1787, to define the proper position of that Corps, the name of which was then changed from the Corps of Engineers to the Corps of *Royal* Engineers. The Warrant said: " Our said
" Corps of Royal Engineers shall rank in our Army *with* our
" Royal Regiment of Artillery; and whenever there shall be
" an occasion for them to take part with any other Corps of
" our Army, the post of the Royal Corps of Engineers shall
" be on the right *with* the Royal Regiment of Artillery,
" *according to the respective dates and commissions of the officers*
" belonging to the Royal Regiment of Artillery, and the
" Corps of Royal Engineers."

The vagueness of this Royal Warrant, and the inconveniences which might arise from it, were not lost upon the officers of the senior Corps, who communicated their opinions to the Master-General through Colonel Macbean, the Commandant at Woolwich. On the 25th October, 1787, the Duke of Richmond, having taken His Majesty's pleasure, replied:
" I have received the King's commands to acquaint you that
" His Majesty only meant the said Warrant to relate to the
" circumstance when officers have occasion to parade by
" themselves *without their men*, for a funeral or any other
" military purpose; but that the directions contained in the
" said Warrant are not to be understood to authorize any
" officer of the Corps of Royal Engineers to take the com-
" mand of any detachment of the Royal Regiment of Artillery,
" although he may be senior in rank to the oldest officer of
" the said detachment, unless such officer of the Corps of
" Royal Engineers should be the senior officer of the whole
" Garrison or Command, when, by virtue of his commission,
" he would of course take the command of the Royal Regi-
" ment of Artillery with that of other troops. I am further
" to signify to you His Majesty's pleasure, that when any
" companies or detachments of Royal Military Artificers and
" Labourers are to take post, it is to be next to the Royal
" Regiment of Artillery, *and upon their left*. And the officers

Duke of Richmond to Colonel F. Macbean.

"of the Corps of Royal Engineers are on such occasions to take post and fall in with such companies or detachments of Royal Military Artificers and Labourers."

Prior to the raising of this question of precedence between the two Ordnance Corps, the general question of precedence over the rest of the Army had been raised at Gibraltar in 1783, owing to the Governor having directed the Artillery Guards to parade in the centre of the others, on general guard-mounting parades. The commanding officer of Artillery, Major Thomas Davies, having in vain protested, referred the matter to the Master-General, who ordered the four Colonels-Commandant of Battalions to assemble at Woolwich, and report to him on the origin of the privilege claimed and exercised by the Royal Artillery. The result was, that on the 1st July, 1784, the Secretary at War wrote to the Governor of Gibraltar as follows : "The Duke of Richmond "having put into my hands your letter to him of the 24th "February last, together with the papers it refers to, touching "certain claims of the Royal Regiment of Artillery, first "stated in a representation of the officer commanding that "Corps at Gibraltar ; and His Grace having desired me to "take the King's pleasure thereon, I have accordingly had "the honour of submitting them to His Majesty, and am "commanded to acquaint you, that as the privilege claimed "by the Royal Artillery of taking the right upon all parades "appears to have been acknowledged and confirmed by a "Regulation given out in public orders to the Army by His "Royal Highness the late Duke of Cumberland, when Com- "mander-in-Chief ; and, as that Regulation hath not yet been "cancelled, His Majesty considers the same to be still in "force, and is therefore pleased to direct that it shall be "adhered to on all occasions, when the compliance with it "will not be attended with material injury to the public "service."

War Office, 1/7/84, to Sir G. A. Elliott.

Next in importance to these questions of precedence, among the Regimental events contained in the period of which this chapter treats, comes the formation of a Head-quarter office for the Regiment. Prior to 1783, each

Battalion was ruled by its own Colonel-Commandant, wherever the companies might be serving; and details, which should have been under the control of the senior Artillery officer on the spot, were regulated from a distance. The Ordnance Office was, in one sense, a Head-quarter office for the Regiment; but a want existed of some *one military and regimental* channel through which the wants and correspondence of the Battalions might reach the Board. In a letter to Captain Macleod, who was the first to hold this much-needed office, the want was well expressed. "The "officers and men of different Battalions, that generally "compose commands of Artillery abroad, make the post of a "Brigade-Major obviously useful to prevent a multiplicity "of returns to different Battalions, which must often fall "short of the information required at home. The enclosed "return, for instance, will show that we have officers here "without a knowledge of what Battalion they belong to." The appointment of Captain—afterwards Sir John—Macleod was a very fortunate one. He was styled Brigade-Major, when appointed in 1783; and in 1795 the designation was altered to that of Deputy-Adjutant-General. In 1806 an Assistant-Adjutant-General was added to the office; and in 1859, a Deputy-Assistant-Adjutant-General. When Captain Macleod was first appointed, he was under the orders of the Commandant of Woolwich Garrison; but in a very short time he made himself so useful to the Master-General and the Board, and was so conversant with all those details which could not possibly be familiar to officers, who were so frequently changed as the Commandants were in those days, that most of the Regimental correspondence soon passed *direct* between him and the Board. So delicate a position required great tact, and this quality Captain Macleod eminently possessed. Appearing to act under theo rders of the Commandant, and courteously anticipating his wishes, he really was the mouthpiece of the Board in controlling the affairs of the Regiment. His correspondence is a masterpiece of courtesy, skill, and clearness. "The leading feature "of his character was the confidence he inspired in others,

<small>Officer commanding R. A., Canada, to Captain Macleod, 7 Aug., 1783.</small>

<small>Memoir of Sir J. Macleod,</small>

Marginal note: 'United Service Journal,' July 1834.

"and the unbounded trust they reposed in him; and thus, "whether called upon for counsel, or to act under unfore- "seen or sudden emergencies of service, he was ever ready "and prepared to meet its exigencies .... Of every soldier "he made himself the friend. To his equals in rank he was "a brother; to those beneath him a father in kindness and "counsel; and to the private soldiers a benefactor, ever watch- "ing over their comfort and their welfare. . . . Through- "out his long career he was never known to act with the "slightest approach to severity; and yet he never failed to "maintain discipline, to reprove fault, or to check irregu- "larity. He animated zeal, excited energy, and aimed at "perfecting discipline by always appealing to the better "and nobler feelings that prevail with the soldier's character." An office, which, with an ordinary man, would have remained always subordinate, was raised by him so as to be the very centre of the Regimental life; and although there have been times in its history, when the progress and success of the Regiment have been rather in spite, than by means of it, these occasions have been rare; and—as in the case of the commencement of the Peninsular War—were forgotten in the exertions which followed them. In a Regiment so large, and so scattered, the value of some central organiza- tion, not merely for *routine*, but also for maintaining and encouraging *esprit de corps*, can hardly be overrated.

It has been said that Captain Macleod commenced to hold the new office, as a Brigade-Major. It may be added that the ideas of a Brigade-Major's position were not exalted. From 1783 to 1790, Captain Macleod conducted all his business in one small room, shared by his clerks, two in number; but in 1790, offices having been provided for the Adjutants of the Battalions, who had hitherto been made to work together, the Brigade-Major was allowed the same privi- lege, and drew lots with the others—according to custom—for a separate apartment. In a long official correspondence, ex- tending over a long lifetime, the only irritation displayed by Sir John Macleod was at the official delays of the Board for which he laboured. But, even then, his indignation took the form of gentle irony. Whether writing, as he did in the end of the year 1786, requesting that his travelling allowances for 1783 might be sent him with as little delay as possible, or reminding the Board of a demand for stationery sent in many months before, he was never disturbed into strong language. "I hope you will forgive me," he wrote, with reference to his last-named demand, "for begging you " to *give orders for its going through the different forms* with " as much expedition as possible, the stationery of last year " being now entirely exhausted." An amusing instance of his quiet way of answering criticism from underlings at the Ordnance occurred in 1785. Many people who had assisted the troops during the American War came to England, and generally applied for Government assistance. A negro, named James Buchanan, presented himself at the Ordnance, and requested assistance, on the plea that he had been employed during the war as a labourer with one of the companies on service. The case was referred to the Brigade-Major, who replied that no such man was to be found on the rolls of the men so employed. The man, still adhering to his statement, was told to go to Woolwich and endeavour to substantiate it. On doing so, he was at once recognized by Captain Macleod as a man who had done duty with his own company; and he reported accordingly.

To B. of Ordnance, 9 Dec., 1784.

The opportunity could not be resisted; and some official of the Board wrote an offensive demand for explanation of the contradictory statements made by the Brigade-Major. With quiet sarcasm, Captain Macleod wrote: "The Board " will easily understand my inconsistency in disclaiming one " day and acknowledging the next, when I inform them that " their petitioner *has acquired the name of James Buchanan,* " *by being christened since his arrival in England.*"

The dullness at the Board, consequent on the retrenchment which had to be practised, was cheered by the genial kindness of the Master-General, the Duke of Richmond, who displayed the greatest interest in the military branch, down to the humblest individual. To the student it is also varied by exasperating anecdotes, illustrating the perfection of official doubt and criticism. The return from America of the companies, many of the men belonging to which had been in prison at various periods during the war, offered admirable opportunities for the practice of virtues which were strongly represented at the Honourable Board. To a man landing at Woolwich, the sympathy of the Ordnance took the doubtful form of a peremptory order to refund, it might be, certain moneys which had been drawn for him while a prisoner of war,—their welcome home was a disallowance. As for the Captains of the returning companies, they were allowed no peace. No consideration was given on account of their men having been scattered over a whole continent; the same minuteness of detail, the same superabundance of vouchers for every charge, was demanded, as if their companies had never left Woolwich Warren. One Captain, unable to give the exact dates and sufficient proofs of the deaths of certain men, who had been killed on distant detachments, was rash enough to question the justice of such a demand, and to point out the difficulties which compliance with it involved. Misguided, miserable man! Little did he know the system of audit, which prevailed in the year of grace 1784. Argument was inadmissible; the full pound of flesh, in the form of vouchers and authorities, was insisted on by the official Shylocks; and if circumstances rendered this an absolute impossibility, their remedy was simple. Of this wretched Captain, we read that "an order was sent to the agent " to stop his pay until the sum of 223*l*. had been " paid."

<small>Ordnance Letter-book, 1784.</small>

In the correspondence of the period, this officer's name does not appear again for some weeks,—but then in a startling manner. In a letter to the Commandant of Woolwich from the Surgeon of the 4th Battalion, we find that the ill-fated Captain "was so violent last night that I had to put a " strait waistcoat on him." Had he received notice of a fresh disallowance from his unfeeling auditors? This, indeed, does not appear; but from the fact that he had been perfectly sane before this correspondence, and recovered his sanity afterwards, it almost appears as if his reason had tottered under the admirable system of audit, which made no allowance, and would listen to no argument.

The consistency of these examiners was as admirable as their pertinacity or their indifference. They were no less reluctant to part with money except on abundant evidence, than they were determined to have it refunded unless similar evidence could be shown for its retention. From the dull pages of the Brigade-Major's letter-books we learn of a just and lawful claim made by a gunner on his return from New York. It does not appear that the claim was denied, but the line taken by the suspicious officials was to doubt the man's identity. The difficulty of proving this may be imagined from what followed. The usual evidence which the man himself could produce was, like his assertion, scornfully rejected. A certificate from an officer under whom he had served, and who was then at Woolwich, was not considered sufficient, even when followed by a second and third of the same description, and from different officers. According to their own documents, the examiners said the man had died in New York; and they would hear of no resurrection. The matter reached the Commandant, who took it up warmly. A little alarmed, but not convinced, the auditors wrote to Bath to ask General Pattison, who had commanded at New York at the date of the man's supposed death, whether it had not taken place. But they mistook their correspondent. He replied that he had no means of answering their question, but he added, "I should hope that " certificates from three respectable officers, accompanied " with a recommendation from the Commanding Officer of " the Battalion, who I am very confident would not have " offered any but on the very surest grounds, will be deemed " sufficient vouchers of the poor man's pretensions." From the subsequent cessation of the correspondence, it is presumed that the claimant's identity was at last admitted.

At no period of the Regiment's history was the paternal rule of the Board more detailed, and more inclusive of the veriest trifles. The incessant references which had to be made by the Commandant, before he could make the slightest change in the Garrison, and the constant petty collisions between the civil and military departments, picture to the student an intolerable *régime*. Nor was the overbearing of the civilian officials confined to offensive correspondence. A story is handed down of a mighty servant of the Board, rejoicing in the title of "Clerk of the Cheque," who paid periodical visits to Woolwich, and evinced his scorn for the military branch in every way. On one day, the Commandant had ordered the troops to parade for his inspection; and sentries were placed at various points to keep back the crowd of sightseers, which had assembled. Just as the Commandant came on the ground, a scuffle was observed taking place between a sentry and one of the crowd. The Garrison Sergeant-Major was sent to ascertain the cause; and on his arrival he found the Clerk of the Cheque insisting on his right to ignore any military control. The Sergeant-Major argued, but without success; the intruder said he was Clerk of the Cheque, and demanded admission. From verbal to physical persuasion was the next step; and *both* the military individuals flung themselves on their civil rival. It was without result; strong in the majesty of his office, the Clerk of the Cheque held his ground. The disturbance at length drew the Commandant himself to the spot, and he took up the discussion; and, like the Sergeant-Major, resorted to the argument of physical force. It was an awful moment; as he reads of it, the student's blood runs cold; for the battle was now condensed into a fight for the superiority of the civil over the military branch of His Majesty's Ordnance. And for the moment the Clerk of the Cheque prevailed:— pushing the Commandant on one side, he swaggered across the enclosure. But his triumph was short-lived; the matter was reported to the Master-General, who ordered the offender to proceed to Woolwich and make a public apology. Doubtless, however, he avenged the humiliation by some of the many ways of paper irritation, which he had at his disposal.

The delay in executing repairs and meeting demands was excessive. Twelve months were not considered too long a period to answer a requisition, and much longer was generally taken. A fence happened to require repair in front of the barracks, and its dangerous state was repeatedly pointed out by the Commandant. But not until years had passed, and an officer had killed his horse, and broken his own collar-bone, did any steps occur to the Board to remedy it. Even then, while they were brooding, accidents continued, coming to a climax one night, when "the Chaplain, in walking home, fell in and broke the principal ligament of his leg." <small>General Cleaveland to B. of Ordnance.</small>

A temporary chapel existed in the Warren, and, although the duties of the Chaplains will be discussed hereafter, it may be mentioned, while considering the Board's delays, that in 1783 the Chaplain applied for "a cushion and furni-" ture for the pulpit, a surplice, Bible and prayer-books, "and a few hassocks, those in use having been purchased in "1753."

After patiently waiting for *four* years, the Chaplain again sent in a demand, stating that it was *impossible* to use those he had *any longer*. <small>1787. Rev. E. Jones to B. of Ordnance.</small>

The procrastination of the Board led, as may be imagined, to many inconveniences. A company in the Bahamas was ordered to be in readiness to return to England, and no clothing was sent to it for the year 1784, as the Board promised to make immediate arrangements for its transport; but 1784 passed, and also 1785, and then 1786, and no transport was forthcoming, nor was any clothing sent for these three years. <small>Colonel Macbean to Master-General, Feb. 9, 1787.</small>

It is a relief, however, to turn from the Board and its shortcomings, and to study the purely Regimental details of the period. Tame, and uninteresting, as they may appear beside the terrible seedtime in France, where the dragon's-teeth of discord, licence, and rebellion were being scattered, to bring forth a thirty years' harvest in Europe of armed men, they cannot be passed by in any work pretending to tell the story of the Regiment. They speak of an interior economy which has utterly disappeared,—of a time which might fitly be called "the age of the Colonels-Commandant." So completely *honorary* has that rank now become in the

Regiment, that the exercise of one small piece of patronage—the nomination of the Brigade Adjutant and Quartermaster—is the only link which connects those who hold it with the active duties of the Corps.

On the 30th January, 1873, the Colonels-Commandant were invited to leave their retirement, and to meet their brother officers once again at the Regimental mess. This rare *réunion* formed a marked contrast to the days referred to in this chapter. *Then*, the Colonels-Commandant of the four Battalions were entitled to live in barracks in the Warren; and an attempt was made to place them on the same roster for duty as the Colonels. Thanks to the conscientious and far-seeing judgment of the officers who then held the rank, this order was cancelled. The following protest, submitted by them to the Master-General, will sufficiently explain the situation:—

Letter to the Master-General, Sept. 1785, from Major-Generals Cleaveland, Pattison, Brome, and Godwin.

"With respect to the proposition of the 1st and 2nd
" Colonels of the Battalion quartered at Woolwich to take
" the duty alternately of being always on the spot, and
" commanding there, we beg leave to say (if by 1st Colonel
" is meant Colonel-Commandant) that, as General Officers,
" we are under the necessity of dissenting from it. We
" wish to look up to your Grace as the guardian and pro-
" tector, under our gracious Sovereign, of the Corps of
" Artillery, as well *individually* as *collectively;* and, there-
" fore, as this measure would be derogatory thereto, we
" trust that your Grace, having condescended to ask our
" opinions, will be pleased to relinquish it. Your Grace is
" sensible that by the custom of the Army immemorially
" established, and confirmed by the Royal sanction, Colonels
" having the rank of General Officers are exempted from
" being stationary with their Regiments; and that, by a
" late regulation, even Lieut.-Colonels having the rank of
" Major-General are not required to be with their Regi-
" ments any further than they may judge necessary for
" becoming responsible for their being in good order and
" discipline, the care and command devolving upon the
" Major or senior Captain. However faint, my Lord, our

" prospects may be of deriving equal advantages with other
" General Officers, from the rank we have the honour to
" hold, we have yet every reason to believe and expect that
" the privileges annexed to it will be equally preserved to
" us. In the year 1773, the late Master-General was pleased
" to give an order, which seemed to *require* the residence of
" the Colonels-Commandant at Woolwich, whereupon the
" late Generals Belford and Desaguliers had an audience of
" His Majesty, and laid at his feet a memorial praying for
" redress, which His Majesty was graciously pleased to
" grant."

Although, however, relieved of a duty beneath their rank, the connection of the Colonels-Commandant with their Battalions remained of the closest description. No officer was allowed to be promoted, under the rank of Field-Officer, without a recommendation from the Colonel-Commandant of the Battalion in which he might be serving; nor was any exchange allowed without the consent of both the Colonels-Commandant concerned. The recruiting, clothing, and discharges of the men were under the same control; and the private affairs of the officers were also frequently the subject of their official consideration. It has been already hinted, at the commencement of this chapter, that for some reasons the period between 1783 and 1792 is a painful one to study. It is impossible to give a sufficient reason; but as to the *fact*, there is no doubt that there was then a bad spirit among some of the younger officers, which manifested itself not unfrequently in acts of open insubordination. The pages of the Ordnance letter-books of this time bristle with accounts of courts-martial on officers, an occurrence most rare before or since. Nor were they due to any stern, unforgiving discipline, visiting slight offences with heavy punishment. The offences were all of one description,—distinct and grave insubordination. Whether sufficient care had not been taken in the appointment of officers during the American War, or whether this war had engendered among some an unruly, ill-disciplined, and impatient spirit, it is impossible now to say. Nor was tragedy wanting. One case occurred, in

1785, of an officer who had been commissioned in America during the war, and who, on his return to England, had been repeatedly guilty of minor offences. A prolonged absence without leave brought matters to a crisis. He was, after some difficulty, traced to a low lodging-house in London, and, after many unavailing orders to return to Woolwich, was at last brought down by escort. A general court-martial was assembled for his trial at the Horse Guards, where all such courts were then held; and from the official registers it can be traced that he was convicted. Before, however, the sentence was promulgated, we learn from a letter in the Brigade-Major's correspondence that he was found one morning dead in his room. No explanation is given,—merely a brief report of the occurrence, leaving the reader to his own conjectures as to the manner and the cause.

But, painful as it is to come across such passages, the pain is almost forgotten in the pleasure which the same correspondence affords, when treating of the earnest fatherly interest displayed by the Colonels-Commandant in the young officers under their control. In later days, the life and progress of the Regiment have been, as a rule, in the keeping of its younger members; but, at the time now spoken of, it was emphatically the devotion of the fathers of the Corps, which tided it over the shoals of discontent, stagnation, and despair. A jealous love of their noble traditions animated them; they had all shared the toils and the honours, which had so welded the Regiment into a glorious unity; and they laboured with an unselfish love to inspire the younger members with an *esprit*, which should make them worthy channels of their own deep feelings.

They expressed in the earnestness of their lives that which was said in words by one of the Colonels-Commandant at the *réunion* in 1873, mentioned above: "The glory of our Regi-

General B. Cuppage.

ment has been in our keeping; but we are now old and passing away, and we commit it to you." How much of the noble spirit which animated the Corps in the commencement of this century was due to the unwearying teaching of the older officers at the period now treated of can never be told; but the student of the correspondence still preserved cannot but attribute to it an abundant share.

One of the duties always performed at this time by the Field-Officers of the Corps was the testing the value of new inventions. The list of such during this period is long and quaint. The inventors were both professional Artillerymen and amateurs; although it must be confessed that the latter received greater encouragement than the former. It seems hardly credible, but it is a fact, that in the year of grace 1790 the Field-Officers of Artillery were repeatedly assembled to examine into the merits of a 3-pounder *leather* gun, invented by Sir John Sinclair. Nor were rifled guns unknown at this time. One of the most persistent inventors was a Mr. Wiggins, who produced rifled guns to fire belted spherical shot. He succeeded with the smaller guns, 1 and 9-pounders; but was not successful with the larger. An 18-pounder which he produced before the Board was certainly not a success; for, on firing two rounds with common proof-charge and one shot, "on the second round it burst into a great number of pieces." Although, however, the Field-Officers were available for this duty, any interference with the manufacturing departments in the Arsenal by the Garrison officials was not allowed nor tolerated. There were repeated attempts made by successive Commandants to assume a control over the Arsenal, but without success.

Another duty which occupied the senior officers at this time was connected with the Regimental Hospital and the medical officers of the Ordnance. Complaints were repeatedly made *by* the Surgeons, and not without reason; and complaints were often made *of* them, but generally without cause. The system of making the Surgeon find medicines for the sick, out of a fixed and inadequate money allowance led to much correspondence; and attempts made to extort from the military surgeon any charges made by a civil practitioner for attendance on men on furlough led to very stormy remonstrances. On the other hand, the varying rate of stoppages made from the pay of the sick led to discontent

Inspector of Artillery to Commandant.

on *their* part. It was actually proposed by the Board to take away the whole of a man's pay when in hospital, lest the Captains of Companies should be induced to send men when in debt into hospital, and to appropriate the balance of their pay. This unworthy suspicion was resented by the Colonels-Commandant in the following dignified words:
" With regard to the temptation which might induce a
" Captain to send his men to the hospital, and keep them
" there as long as he could, in order to clear their debts by
" stoppages—we hope, and, indeed, are confident, that there
" is no Captain now in the Corps of so illiberal a mind as
" to be thus unworthily attentive to his own interest
" in preference to that of His Majesty's service; and
" should there ever be hereafter any one of such bad prin-
" ciples, a collusion must take place between him, the
" Surgeon, and the Soldier, before his base purpose could
" be accomplished."

The Regulations for the Ordnance Medical Department were embodied in a distinct form in the years 1786 and 1787, but not without much meeting of committees and examination of witnesses. Much of the labour and expense which fell upon the medical officers at Woolwich were caused by the presence in that Garrison of 150 men of the Invalid Battalion, who were incessantly under treatment. It cannot be said that men were driven out of the service in those days without every endeavour being made to effect a cure. From the lists of men recommended for discharge in the year 1791, which are deposited in the Record Office, we find that one had been " sick in the country for *four years;*" another suffered from rheumatism, loss of sight and of hearing; another had " an inveterate sore leg of many years' standing;" another was " insane, and burthensome to the Battalion;" another " hectic, and subject to fits;" another " hurt in the back, and " otherwise infirm;" while a very common epithet was " completely worn out." There were other grounds, however, for discharging men, than mere medical. One man has been handed down as having been discharged because " he was unsightly," another was " unpromising," a third

" irregular," while of a fourth the curt characteristic placed against his name is the word "thief."

History frequently repeats itself in small matters as well as large. The legislation suggested by the present Secretary of State for War, with reference to men who have occasion to go to hospital on account of their own indiscretion, was in force in Canada for many years prior to 1791,—a fine of 10s. 6d. being levied from every Artilleryman in such a position. A commanding officer, however, went to Canada who declined to enforce this fine; and the question as to the origin and duration of the custom was therefore referred to the Commandant at Woolwich. He replied: "From " the Brigade-Major I learn the custom has long been abo-" lished in Woolwich, and in other places, as tending to " induce the soldier to conceal his complaint, or apply to " quacks for a cheaper cure; both of which may be prejudicial " to his constitution."

The decisions arrived at by the Board in 1786, with reference to the medical officers, may be briefly stated. The principal medical officer at Woolwich was to be called Surgeon-General, and was to receive half-pay of 10s. per diem, while he was to be relieved of the expense of finding any medicines for the hospital. The Surgeon of the Battalion at Woolwich had to provide all the medicines for his Battalion, "excepting bark and wine," in return for which he was allowed 120*l*. per annum. The Surgeon of the Battalion detached in England remained at Woolwich with such companies of the Battalion as might be stationed there, providing the medicines required by them, and by the company in Scotland, as well as all the companies of the Battalion *when on the line of march*,—receiving in return remuneration at the rate of 12*l*. per company annually. The recruits of the Battalions abroad were also under his care, and he received 12*l*. annually for each detachment of fifty men, in return for the medicines he had to provide. So far, this Surgeon had little to complain of. But the next burden was always greater than he could bear. He had to take charge of the men of the Invalid Battalion, not merely those

Whitehall, 23 May, 1786.

at Woolwich, but also those on detachment, furnishing them with medicines, in return for the annual sum of 70*l*. When one bears in mind that no man entered the Invalid Battalion until he was completely crippled, and that his daily medicine was probably as necessary to him as the air he breathed, the inadequacy of the Surgeon's remuneration in this item becomes apparent. The Surgeons of the Battalions, to which the companies at Gibraltar and in Canada respectively belonged, went on service with these companies, and received 12*l*. per annum for each company, in addition to their pay— in return for which they had to provide all medicines " except bark and wine." The same allowance was paid for detached companies of the various Battalions to the Ordnance Surgeon on the spot. Civil artificers and labourers in the employ of the Ordnance were entitled to medical attendance and medicines, by paying at the rates of one penny and one halfpenny *per week* throughout the year to the Ordnance medical officer on the station. The rule with regard to officers was worded as follows: " It is expected that the " Surgeons of the Artillery and Ordnance at the different " places should give their attendance to the military and " civil officers without fee; but, with respect to supplying " them with medicines, it is recommended to the military and " civil officers to subscribe 2 guineas a year each, for which " the Surgeon is to supply them with medicines; otherwise " they are to pay for such medicines as they use."

Such were the regulations for the medical officers of the Ordnance,—revealing a system which was faulty and has disappeared, but which it is interesting to reproduce in a history of the Corps. But there were other non-combatants also—no longer represented in the Regiment, but who deserve to be mentioned—the Regimental Chaplains. These gentlemen, at the period treated of, did not belong, as now, to one department for general Army service, but belonged to the various Battalions of the Corps. This, however, did not imply that they did duty with their Battalions; far from it. Excellent men, they drew their pay with a punctuality worthy of all praise, but it was not among their congregations in the Warren, but away in quiet rural rectories—in fat livings which they held. They were pluralists; and they clubbed together to pay a curate in Woolwich to perform their joint duties. It is sad to have to say, also, that they did not pay their substitute very liberally. They paid him each eighteen-pence a day—a sum so inadequate that it drew forth the remonstrances of the Commandant, who wrote to the Master-General that, "considering the "reverend gentleman's constant residence and attendance, "his dress and appearance, which are always obliged to be "decent, and the disadvantage of having no surplice fees to "add to it, it will not permit him even to eat at the mess— "the cheapest and best mode of living here." The sum of two shillings and sixpence a day from each Chaplain was requested for their substitute; such as was given in other Garrisons. It will thus be seen that the system was officially recognised; and, indeed, was but one of the many vicious customs which have disappeared before public opinion. There were certain occasions when the attendance of the Chaplains was insisted upon, although they were few and far between. One such occurred in 1785, when the King announced his intention of coming to Woolwich to review the Regiment. The Chaplains were hurriedly written for, "in order," wrote the Brigade-Major, "that you may be "at Woolwich in proper time to *march by* with the Regi- "ment." One of the number replied, that on account of the distance at which he lived, and the fact of his being 86 years of age, he would be unable to attend,—which he greatly regretted, as he would have much liked to march past again before he died. The others obeyed the summons, one only protesting a little on the ground that the Battalion to which he belonged was at that time scattered in the West Indies and Canada. A few years later, in 1792, when a camp was formed at Bagshot, the Chaplains were ordered to attend and encamp with the companies; and from that time their duties ceased, more and more every year, to be so purely honorary as they had been.

Returning now to the combatant part of the Corps, there

Commandant to Master-General, Nov. 14, 1787.

are certain details connected with the dress of the officers and men, which can hardly fail to be interesting, and which find a natural place in a chapter like this. Owing to a circumstance arising out of the American War, we are fortunately in possession of very circumstantial accounts on this point. After the Convention of Saratoga, many of the officers of Burgoyne's army remained prisoners of war for nearly three years. On their return to England, they claimed compensation for loss of their equipment, &c., stating their case as follows:—" The subscribers wish to
" represent the constant and unavoidable loss they sustained
" in the mode of payment of their subsistence, as the im-
" possibility of supplying the Convention Army with specie
" laid them under an absolute necessity of drawing their pay
" at very extravagant rates, being paid by public bills, in
" the negotiation of which, from the Congress paper cur-
" rency, they suffered a discount which in the 1st year may
" be estimated at 20 per cent. . . . We beg leave to observe
" that, in conformity to the wishes of the Generals command-
" ing the troops, we were under the necessity of building
" huts at our own cost and charges, in order to take the
" more effectual care of the men, to attend to their wants
" and to alleviate their distresses. Much expense was
" incurred on this score. We have also to observe that the
" Congress at different periods obliged us to remove to most
" of the provinces in America; and in those several marches
" of at least 1500 miles, it must naturally occur that many
" and heavy charges were sustained by us. On being
" exchanged, we were unavoidably obliged to come to New
" York individually, and there being no public conveyance,
" we were necessitated to purchase horses, to transport our-
" selves and baggage, from people who took every advantage
" of our distresses." On the claims of officers on this account reaching the Ordnance, the first step was, simply, to refuse to admit them; on their being urged again in stronger terms, the next was to refer them to some one else to ascertain the truth of the claimants' statements, it being an official axiom that any one demanding money was probably

an impostor, and to be treated accordingly; and, lastly, on being satisfied of the accuracy of the claim, the invariable course was to offer something considerably less than the sum demanded. From a remonstrance made against the offer in this case we learn what was laid down by the Board of Ordnance in the previous year, 28th June, 1782, as the equipment of an Artillery Subaltern, and the cost at which it was to be valued in compensating for its loss by shipwreck, or imprisonment. It was as follows:—

		£	s.	d.
Regimentals.—1 suit of full uniform		12	12	0
1 frock suit of uniform		7	7	0
1 laced hat		2	13	0
2 pairs of boots		3	3	0
1 regimental great coat		3	0	0
1 plain hat		1	1	0
12 shirts		9	0	0
12 stocks		2	2	0
12 pairs of stockings		3	12	0
6 linen waistcoats and breeches		7	4	0
12 handkerchiefs, at 3s. 6d.		2	2	0
1 pair of pistols		4	4	0
1 regimental sword, belt, and clasp		2	12	6
1 sash		1	11	6
3 pairs of shoes		1	4	0
Camp Equipage.—Bedstead and bedding complete		12	12	6
1 pair of canteens		8	8	0
2 hair trunks		3	0	0
1 case with bottles		2	2	0
1 cask with kitchen utensils		3	3	0
Saddle and bridle		4	4	0
		£96	17	6

The contents of the knapsack of an Artillery soldier at this time were as follows; the knapsack itself being made of painted canvas:—

4 white shirts.
1 check shirt.
6 *false collars.*
1 canvas frock.
1 canvas pair of trowsers.
1 leather cap.
2 pairs of shoes.
1 pair of black cloth gaiters.
1 pair of white stockings (thread).

1 *powder-bag and puff.*
1 razor.
1 shaving-box.
1 pair of shoe brushes.
1 cloth brush.
1 twin screw and worm.
1 brush and pricker.
1 leather stock.
1 rosette.

1 pair of worsted stockings.
3 pairs of Welsh yarn socks.
1 pair of shoe-buckles.
1 pair of knee-buckles.
1 stock buckle.
1 large and 1 small comb.

The annual issues of clothing were settled by the Master-General on 17th March, 1788, to be as follows.
Each sergeant was to receive annually

1 coat.
1 white cloth waistcoat.
1 pair of white cloth breeches.
1 *frilled* shirt.
1 black leather stock.
1 pair of worsted stockings.
1 gold laced hat.
Black cloth with 3 dozen buttons for a pair of gaiters.
5s. 3d. in lieu of a pair of shoes.

The same articles were supplied to the other ranks, with the exception that while the corporal's coat had two epaulettes, the bombardier's had only one; and that the hats of the drummers were plain, instead of gold-laced. The drummers had also fur caps supplied to them when required. In the West Indies the men received white linen waistcoats and breeches, instead of cloth; and wore white gold-laced hats instead of black.

The men of the Invalid Battalion received the same articles as those of the Marching Battalions, with this exception, that their coats were lined with *red* instead of white, and their waistcoats and breeches, instead of being white, were *blue*.

So much for the clothing of the Regiment at this time; a few words must now be said as to its drills. And perhaps this can be done most easily by describing a field-day, which took place on the morning of the 9th July, 1788, before the King. On the arrival of His Majesty, a salute of 21 guns, at intervals of 8 seconds, was fired by a company, which immediately afterwards fell in on the left of the line. It was not until the preceding year that the Regiment had been ordered to fall in in two ranks, when under arms. The King having ridden down the ranks, the Regiment broke into open column, and marched past in slow and quick time.

Order by Master-General, 4 July, 1787.

The line having been reformed, and the Manual Exercise practised, the following marvellous evolutions commenced:— Two rounds were fired from *flanks to centre* of each Battalion; the line then retired one hundred yards towards the Barracks, and fired two rounds from *centre to flanks* of each Battalion; and returned to its former ground. Here it fired two rounds by grand divisions from flanks to centre of each Battalion; then one round by wings of each Battalion; and, finally, each Battalion fired a volley.

Having so rung the changes on small-arm firing, a certain number of the men were detached to man 12 field guns, the line opening to allow these guns to come up. As a contrast to modern Field Battery drill, the solemn orders issued to the officer commanding these guns may be quoted:—" Lieu-
" tenant-Colonel Walker will advance towards Woolwich
" Common with his 12 guns, 4 in front, and in three lines.
" This column will incline to the right, so that the right-hand
" gun may be near the right-hand hedge. When they have
" got about halfway between the front of the Barracks and
" the sunk fence, the 4 guns in the front line are then to
" halt, while the 4 guns in the centre line form the left of
" the front line. The 12 guns then in one line will fire
" two rounds from *flanks to centre*, then change their front
" to the left by wheeling on the centre, and in that position
" fire two rounds from *centre to flanks*. The 6 guns on the
" right will then fall in with the rear of the 2nd Battalion,
" and the 6 guns on the left will fall in with the rear of the
" 4th Battalion."

It requires the reproduction of such elephantine movements as the above, to realise sufficiently the progress made since that time in Field Artillery. This most wooden style of drill was the fashion in England; and we owe the change which followed to the wars of the French Revolution, which taught that a General, to win battles, must be something more than a drill-sergeant, and that an army must learn not merely to fight, but to move, and to move with rapidity. The only element in the field-day just described which gives the student the slightest relief, is a mention made that the Gentlemen Cadets were employed as Light Infantry towards the end of the day. Of course this was all wrong, and one would rather find that they had been employed on a public occasion like this, as Artillerymen; but it is a relief to read of anything implying rapidity of movement, after the dull, ponderous description of the line moving solemnly backwards and forwards, firing from flanks to centre, and centre to flanks.

To this style of drill our want of success in Flanders, in the campaigns shortly to be described, was mainly due. Our Generals had their brains so saturated with the drill-book, that on active service, if they encountered an enemy who violated its rules, they were utterly nonplussed. Had they won a victory by ignoring the regulations under which they had been so strictly exercised, their satisfaction would have been but a doubtful one. They had yet to learn that although drill and dogged courage are admirable qualities in troops, they will not compensate for the lack of those qualities in a General which are necessary to ensure success.

Only one or two points remain to be noticed. First, the amalgamation of the Royal Irish Artillery was contemplated as early as 1788, although it did not take place until after the Union in 1801. The delay was mainly caused by the protest of the officers of the Royal Artillery, who would have suffered greatly from supersession,—the promotion in the Irish corps having been much more rapid than in that from which it sprang. Amalgamation must always produce this supersession to a certain extent; and the Board listened to the remonstrances, and deferred the incorporation of the Irish Artillery for some years. About the same date as when this question was being discussed, a long petition was forwarded from Gibraltar, in which the officers of the Royal Artillery there stationed pointed out how much better the position had become of officers in the Royal Engineers of the same standing as themselves, than their own. The wording of the petition was faulty, and its arguments were unsound; thus giving the Master-General an opportunity, of which he availed himself, to administer a dignified rebuke to the malcontents. On one point, however, he admitted the force of their complaint. The rank of Major had been abolished in the Royal Engineers, its holders being made Lieutenant-Colonels, and thus obtaining a decided advantage over their contemporaries in the Artillery. "This difference," wrote the Master-General, "and there being no rank of Major, is, I admit, an advan- "tage in point of rank in favour of the Engineers. The "reason of the rank of Major being suppressed in the Corps "of Engineers was that there were no troops belonging to "them to be commanded in Battalions, and therefore there "could be no use for an officer of that description." In the year 1827, the rank of Regimental Major was abolished in the Royal Artillery, its holders being made Lieutenant-Colonels, but with Majors' pay; and in the year 1872, the rank of Major was substituted for that of First Captain, on account of the responsibility attached to the command of a Battery of Artillery. [Duke of Richmond, 10 March, 1788.]

It was during this period that a blow was struck at the custom, which had hitherto prevailed, of buying and selling the appointments of Adjutant and Quartermaster. On the 24th February, 1783, the Master-General ordered that no such appointment should in future be sold, with this exception, that any officer who then held an appointment which he had obtained by purchase would be allowed to sell it when he relinquished it, but must accept 100*l.* less than he gave for it; and that his successor must also sell for 100*l.* less than that purchase-money; and so on until the price should be extinguished. It was ruled, at the same time, that a Captain-Lieutenant, holding an Adjutancy, should vacate it on being promoted to a Company; and that as soon as any "warrant" of a Quartermaster should become vacant without purchase, "some meritorious non-commis- "sioned officer should be recommended for the same." [Colonel Miller, Pamph., 1868.]

A privilege which the Regiment had hitherto enjoyed was abolished, and with good reason, in 1785. Prior to that date no charge was ever made for the subsistence of either officers or men of the Royal Artillery when being conveyed by transports to foreign stations, an exemption which was not accorded to the rest of the army. Doubtless the custom arose from the fact that the Board of Ordnance, which in one capacity governed the Artillery, in another capacity hired the transports; but the case had only to be stated to ensure a remedy. On the 27th August, 1785, it was ruled that a " stoppage of 3*d*. per diem (being the same as is made " from the rest of His Majesty's troops) be made from *the* " *officers*, non-commissioned officers, and privates of the " Royal Artillery during the time they shall be on board " ship." Doubtless, the same individuals would be glad if, in the year 1873, they could continue to travel on board ship at the rate of 3*d*. per diem.

Perhaps of all the letters which the student finds in the official correspondence of the period, the following is the most amusing. It ought already to have been mentioned that when the Captain of a Company retired on his pay, awaiting a vacancy in the Invalid Battalion, his Captain-Lieutenant received certain allowances connected with the command of the Company. Apparently, the regulations were not very clear on the subject; or, as is very probable, decisions had been given in individual cases, which had not been promulgated to the Regiment—a pernicious custom which existed in the 18th century, and even since. A Captain William Houghton had retired in this way; and from his retirement the following cry of agony reached the Commandant of his Battalion :—" Ever since the day your " goodness was made known to the Regiment in getting me " leave of absence to retire from duty till provided with an " Invalid Company, I have never had a moment's peace with " my Captains-Lieutenant. Their first claim was for *one* " non-effective—I gave it; the next was for both—I gave " them; and was then told they had a right to the 6*l*. " per annum allowed for stationery—this I gave up also. " They have now demanded my share of the stock purse, " and the 20*l*. per annum granted by His Majesty's warrant, " 27th July, 1772, to the Captains of Artillery, on account " of the slowness of promotion in the Regiment. Had I

2 April, 1789.

"known these were to be the hard conditions of a little rest before death, it would have been all fair; but in that case I certainly should have remained with my Company, provided I had done duty upon crutches."

Only one point remains now to be mentioned before turning to the causes which led to sudden augmentations in the Regiment, combined with the commencement of hostilities. On the 26th August, 1792, volunteers were called for from the Companies at Woolwich, to form part of a guard ordered to attend His Excellency Viscount Macartney, who had been appointed Ambassador to the Court of the Emperor of China, and also to act as instructors in gunnery to the troops of that potentate. The strength of the party was as follows:—One sergeant, 3 corporals or bombardiers, 1 drummer, and 15 gunners, under the command of Lieutenant Parish. An advance was made to the detachment of a year's subsistence to purchase necessaries, and a second suit of clothing was given to the non-commissioned officers and men.

It has been difficult to confine this chapter to these purely domestic, although necessary, details, because, after 1787, the whole firmament of history has been lurid with the events in France, which were ripening into a state of things such as has never been seen before, or since. In 1792 it became apparent that war between England and France was inevitable. Recruiting had been brisk since 1787; in 1790 a free pardon had been offered to all deserters, who should return to their Regiments; in the first month of 1793 an augmentation to the Artillery was authorized, which will form the subject of the next chapter; and in October 1793, the following increase to the establishment was ordered, viz.:—

To each of the 40 marching Companies of the 4 Battalions . . . . .
- 30 Gentlemen Cadets.
- 1 Sergeant.
- 2 Bombardiers.
- 10 Second Gunners.
- 1 Sergeant Conductor on Sergeant's pay.
- 10 Drivers upon Second Gunner's pay.

To each of the 4 marching Battalions . . . . . 1 Surgeon's Mate.

Every officer, without exception, had been ordered to join in 1792; and, although it was not until the beginning of 1793 that the French Ambassador was dismissed from the Court of St. James's, it was evident that a sufficient *casus belli* had been found in the operations of the French army in the Low Countries, and the menace to England implied in France obtaining the control of the River Scheldt.

A sufficient *casus belli*, it has been said; but the student of history must indeed be blind who fails to see that this was but a secondary reason. A panic had seized upon the most stable European governments, a dread lest the revolutionary principles which animated the French people should spread beyond the confines of France. Nor was their fear without reason. Even England had been penetrated by Republicanism; societies were formed, ostensibly for Parliamentary Reform, and under the title of *Friends of the People*, which desired undoubtedly the overthrow of the monarchy. An Englishman, the author of 'The Rights of Man,' had been elected a member of the Assembly in Paris, on account of his advanced political opinions; and, after his trial for sedition in England, an English mob showed their sympathy by taking the horses out of his advocate's carriage, and drawing it themselves to his residence. That unfailing barometer of political disturbance—the funds—told also a tale of great uneasiness. The Three per Cents., which stood in January 1792 at 93¾, fell before December in the same year to 74; and all other Government securities were at a corresponding discount.

'Annual Register,' 1792.

The state of France was, indeed, enough to appal the most indifferent. In the powerful language of the chronicler of the French Revolution, France, roused by many causes, faced the world " in that terrible strength of Nature which " no man has measured;" and " whatever was cruel in the " panic-frenzy of twenty-five million men—whatsoever was " great in the simultaneous death-defiance of twenty-five " million men—stood there in abrupt contrast, near by one " another." France was now "seeking its wild way through " the New, Chaotic—where Force is not yet distinguished

Carlyle.

"into Bidden and Forbidden—but Crime and Virtue welter
"unseparated, in that domain of what is called the Passions."
.... "The Gospel of Man's Rights was preached abroad with
"the fearfullest Devil's Message of man's weaknesses and
"sins;" and a whole nation was drunk with revenge, and
terror, and blood.

Penetrating with different effect into every class of men
in England, the tale of the French Revolution penetrated
even the recesses of the Ordnance. Raising their eyes from
ledgers, and gazing across the Channel, even the members of
the Honourable Board were moved; and on the first day of
the New Year they resolved on a step, which should bring
Field Artillery more into accord with the era in the history
of war which was now to commence. Nor was it an hour
too soon; for in three weeks' time, on the 21st January,
1793, "there was in the streets of Paris a silence as of the Carlyle.
"grave—eighty thousand armed men stood ranked, like
"armed statues of men; cannons bristled, cannoneers with
"match burning, but no word or movement; it was as a
"city enchanted into silence and stone: one carriage, with
"its escort, slowly rumbling towards the Place de la
"Révolution, the only sound." The last of the dragon's
teeth was about to be sown, and a crime to be committed
which should bind the governments of Europe together
against France, as one man: to whom France should answer,
"The coalesced Kings threaten us: we hurl at their feet, as Danton.
"the gage of battle, the Head of a King."

Of a truth, the Honourable Board had not moved a day
too soon. Let us trace in our next chapter the development
of that portion of the Corps which dates its origin from that
terrible month of January 1793.

CHAPTER II.

THE NECESSITY, BIRTH, AND PROGRESS OF THE ROYAL HORSE ARTILLERY.

OF all the so-called Battalion Records, which were kept at the various Head-quarter offices at Woolwich up to the year 1859, and the details of which are, at the best, of the most scanty description, perhaps the most meagre and most disappointing are those of the Royal Horse Artillery.

From the well-known *esprit* of this branch of the service, it might have been expected that its earlier history would have been treated almost with effusion by those in whose custody was a book purporting to contain a record of its services. But it may be said with truth that for one item of information obtained from the written records of this brilliant arm, ten have been obtained from the traditions handed down verbally, and fondly treasured by successive generations of officers; and even a greater part of the required information has been obtained from works of general military history, and from extant official letter-books.

The first section of these old Record Books professes to treat of the circumstances of the original formation of the particular part of the Regiment concerned. In the Records of the Royal Horse Artillery this section is compressed into two lines. "The Royal Horse Artillery was formed as an "additional corps to the Regiment of Artillery on the 1st "February, 1793." Remarkable for its brevity, this account of the formation of the Royal Horse Artillery is also remarkable for its inaccuracy. It was *not* an additional corps to the Royal Artillery, but from the very commencement an essential, integral part of it. The Driver Corps, formed in 1794, *was* an additional corps to the Royal Artillery; but its officers were, until after Waterloo, drawn

CHAP. II.   *Necessity for Royal Horse Artillery.*   31

from a different source, and its men were never Artillerymen. The Royal Horse Artillery, on the other hand, was invariably officered by the Royal Artillery, and was recruited from its ranks. Of the wisdom, or otherwise, of this policy, it will be necessary to treat hereafter; but of the fact there can be no doubt. Yet again, in the brief record quoted above, are compressed other inaccuracies. The Horse Artillery did not spring into existence, as a corps, on 1st February, 1793, as the words would imply. Two troops were authorized in January of that year, but not for twelve years of straggling augmentations of staff-officers and troops, can it be said to have attained its proper maturity. The earlier wars of the French Revolution were the boyhood of the Royal Horse Artillery, as the Peninsular campaign was its glorious manhood. After Waterloo, until the Crimean War, its history was a blank page.

It is fortunate that an officer of the Regiment has been found, at once so capable and so patient in tracing out the circumstances which impressed on the world the necessity of this arm, as the author of the papers on 'The Mobility 'of Field Artillery, Past and Present.' According to this writer, England was the last among the leading nations in Europe to adopt the use of Horse Artillery. As early as 1788, the subject had strongly attracted the attention of the Master-General of the Ordnance; but, unfortunately, he referred it to a committee. The period of gestation, so to speak, in committees on military subjects is very great; in this particular instance the winter of 1792 had arrived without any result from their labours. Captain H. W. L. Hime, Royal Artillery. Proceedings R. A. Institution.

The introduction of Horse Artillery into the Prussian service dates from 1759; and in 1792 this arm was introduced into the French and Swedish armies. In other European countries improvement had been made in Field Artillery, without, however, adopting the system of *mounted detachments*; but this latter is the distinctive mark of Horse Artillery. It has been asserted, and on good authority, that Horse Artillery was used in India prior even to its adoption by Frederick the Great—and dating as far back as

1756. If the existence of an Artillery without mobility was sufficient to impress on the authorities in that country a sense of the necessity of some improvements, the argument was not wanting. In an engagement between the English and French troops near Trichinopoly in 1753, "the English, "*for more expedition*, marched without any field-pieces;" and when the infantry advanced against the French in an action fought shortly afterwards, " the *artillery, in the hurry,* "*could not keep up with the battalion.*" The advantage of a more mobile artillery must certainly have been apparent after such melancholy exhibitions.

It has already been mentioned in this work that rapidity of movement, more especially under fire, was rendered hopeless by the frequent employment of peasants to act as drivers to the batteries. The formation of the Royal Horse Artillery did not free the Field Batteries from this evil. A quaint circumstance in proof of this is narrated by the author already mentioned. "In 1798, the Commandant of "Woolwich inspected some guns manned by gunners of the "8th Battalion, R.A. The guns were each drawn by three "horses in single file, which were driven by contract drivers "on foot, hired for the occasion, dressed in white smocks "with blue collars and cuffs, and armed with long carter's "whips of the ordinary farm pattern. When this formid- "able array had been reviewed, the Commandant, General "Lloyd, and the Garrison Adjutant, expressed their joint "opinion that field artillery movements could not be per- "formed quicker." The increase of mobility over that old system—of which the above is a real, although, perhaps, exceptional illustration—which followed the introduction of Horse Artillery can best be shown by another and later instance. At the battle of Fuentes d'Onor, Bull's troop of Horse Artillery—now D Battery, B Brigade—was surrounded and cut off by the French cavalry. It was at the time under the command of the 2nd Captain, Norman Ramsay. "Guns thus dealt with are almost always lost, and con- "sequently the army ceased to think of Ramsay and his "men, except as prisoners. Presently, however, a great

"commotion was observed among the French squadrons;
"men and officers closed in confusion towards one point,
"where a thick dust was rising, and where loud cries and
"the sparkling of blades and flashing of pistols indicated
"some extraordinary occurrence. . . . Suddenly the multi- Napier.
"tude became violently agitated; an English shout pealed
"high and clear; the mass was rent asunder, and Norman
"Ramsay burst forth, sword in hand, at the head of his
"troop, his horses, breathing fire, stretched like grey-
"hounds along the plain; the guns bounded behind them
"like things of no weight, and the mounted gunners followed
"close, with heads bent low, and pointed weapons, in
"desperate career." Between the crawling peasant-driven team on Woolwich parade, and this glowing description of a Horse Artillery battery but a very few years later, there is a contrast, which shows at a glance the immense stride in the direction of mobility, which had followed the introduction of that branch of the Regiment to whose story this chapter is devoted. Much of this improvement was due to the fostering care of the Master-General, and of the Deputy-Adjutant-General, afterwards Sir John Macleod; much also was due to the encouragement of General Officers, who found to their amazement a force of Artillery, which could conform to their most rapid movements; and not a little was due to the practical school of experience opened in the Peninsula; but, to their honour be it stated, the rapid progress towards the standard of perfection attained by the Royal Horse Artillery was mainly due to the labours and the devotion of the officers belonging to it, who were inspired by the same *esprit* and the same conscientious regard for their duties, as have continued to animate the officers of that brilliant arm to this day.

While the Committee, appointed to decide the question of Horse Artillery in connection with our service, was—according to wont—babbling harmlessly and fruitlessly in the fourth year of its existence, a virtual rupture took place between England and France. The Duke of Richmond, then Master-General, immediately took the matter himself in hand; and of three schemes, very dissimilar, over which the Committee had been debating, he selected the following, as the basis of the organization of a troop of Royal Horse Artillery.

Detail.	Horses.	Drivers.	Ammunition.	Distribution of detachments.					Remarks.
				Captains.	Lieuts.	N.-C. O.'s.	Gunners.	Drummers.	Civil Lists.	
5½-inch howitzers (2)	8	4	160	1	1	2	20	..	..	4 men held the horses in action.
Waggons (2)	8	4								
3-prs. (2)	8	4	480	1	1	2	20	..	..	Ditto.
Waggons (2)	8	4								
6-prs., Col. Williams' (2)	4	2	160	..	1	2	20	..	..	Ditto.
Tumbrils (2)	4	2								
Horses for detachments	66	..	..	..	..	..	..	..	..	
2 Sergeants, Sergt.-Major, and Clerk of Stores	2	..	..	..	..	2	..	..	..	
Drummers to have bugle horns, and act as orderly men.	2	..	..	..	..	..	..	2	..	
1 forge cart	3	1	..	..	..	..	..	..	..	
1 waggon for Artificers' Stores	3	1	..	..	..	..	..	..	..	
Officers' horses not included	..	..	..	..	..	..	..	..	..	
CIVIL LIST.										
1 Commissary of horse	1	..	..	..	..	..	..	..	1	
2 Conductors of horse	2	..	..	..	..	..	..	..	2	
1 Collar-maker	1	..	..	..	..	..	..	..	1	
1 Wheeler	1	..	..	..	..	..	..	..	1	
1 Blacksmith	1	..	..	..	..	..	..	..	1	
1 Farrier	1	..	..	..	..	..	..	..	1	
Total	123	22	800	2	3	8	60	2	7	

The formation of the first two troops, A and B, took place at Woolwich, having been ordered in January 1793. The Captains were R. Lawson, afterwards so distinguished in Egypt, and the Brigade-Major of the Regiment, J. Macleod, afterwards Deputy-Adjutant-General. In these—as in the

CHAP. II. *Formation of A, B, C & D Troops.* 35

other troops subsequently formed—great care was taken to appoint none but officers of well-known ability. This fact, combined with the permission given to the Horse Artillery to select the best recruits joining the Regiment, had the immediate effect of causing the new branch to be looked on as a *corps d'élite*: as, indeed, was the case in every other country in Europe, except Austria. Whether this has proved a benefit, or otherwise, to the corps, will hereafter be considered. The *esprit* generally to be found in a *corps d'élite* was fanned by other and minor considerations. It must be remembered that the gunners of Field Artillery other than Horse Artillery, and of Garrison Artillery, were, and still are, interchangeable. But in the Horse Artillery " the men were " magnificently dressed, they were amply paid, and they " were not haunted by the constant dread of being suddenly " and forcibly torn from the Field Artillery service, which " they loved, and thrust into the Garrison Artillery service, " which was strange to them." Only 4 guns per troop were Hime. granted at first; and the establishment consisted, in addition to the officers, of 8 non-commissioned officers, 49 gunners, and 35 drivers. On the formation of C and D Troops, on R. H. A. 1st November, 1793, the armament of each troop was raised Records. to 6 guns, and the establishment per troop was 14 non-commissioned officers, 85 gunners, 45 drivers, and 187 horses.

The officers appointed to command the new troops were, E. Howorth, afterwards Sir E. Howorth, who subsequently commanded the Artillery at Talavera, Busaco, and Fuentes d'Onor, and J. M. Hadden, who afterwards became Surveyor-General of the Ordnance. The reader will continue to observe the selection always made of able officers to command the troops of Horse Artillery. In 1794, E and F Troops were formed, and the command given respectively to Captain W. Cuppage, an officer who afterwards held for twenty-six years the appointment of Inspector of the Royal Carriage Department, and to Captain J. Butler, an officer who afterwards became Lieutenant-Governor of the Royal Military College at Sandhurst.

In 1794, the number of guns per troop was augmented to

D 2

8 ; and this remained the establishment until 1804, in which year the number was reduced to 6 ; at which it continued until the reductions after the battle of Waterloo. In 1794, when the number of guns was raised to 8, the following was the establishment: 15 non-commissioned officers, 97 gunners, 71 drivers, 246 horses per troop. This was reduced in the following year very considerably, and became 15 non-commissioned officers, 85 gunners, 51 drivers, and 170 horses.

The next variation in the establishment was caused by the formation, in Ireland, of G Troop, from detachments serving in that country. The command of the new troop was given to Captain—afterwards Sir—G. B. Fisher, an officer who in 1827 was appointed Commandant of Woolwich. For two years after the formation of G Troop, the establishment of the troops was as follows : 8 guns, 16 non-commissioned officers, 96 gunners, 58 drivers, and 190 horses. An augmentation of 1 non-commissioned officer and 1 gunner per troop took place in 1803.

In 1804, the number of guns per troop having being reduced to 6, H Troop was formed at Woolwich, and the command given to Captain A. Macdonald, a smart officer, who subsequently had the good fortune to command the Horse Artillery of the Cavalry Division at Waterloo. On the reduction to 6 guns, the strength of each troop was, 14 non-commissioned officers, 75 gunners, 46 drivers, and 142 horses.

In 1805, an augmentation of four troops took place—I, K, L, and M; and the commands were given respectively to Captain W. Millar, an officer who subsequently became Inspector of Artillery, and Director-General of the Field Train Department; to Captain C. Godfrey, an officer who went on half-pay a few years later, in 1811 ; to Captain N. Foy, who died in 1817 ; and to Captain the Hon W. H. Gardner, who died as a Colonel-Commandant in 1856.

For the few years following this augmentation, the establishment remained virtually the same; but, in January 1813, 194 officers, non-commissioned officers, and men were added to act as Rocket Detachments, and also as a depôt to supply the troops on service. A depôt for the Royal Horse

Artillery has existed under various names, and in somewhat chequered circumstances. It commenced—as stated above —in 1813; it existed for many years in the form of an Adjutant's Detachment at Woolwich; in 1859 it was transferred to Canterbury; on a somewhat larger scale it was transferred to Maidstone after the amalgamation of the Royal and Indian Artilleries; for a short time subsequently, the Horse Artillery Batteries at home acted as a depôt for those serving abroad; and, at the date of the publication of this work, the last-mentioned arrangement is supplemented by the existence of two Horse Artillery Batteries in the general depôt for the Regiment.

In 1814, the various Rocket Detachments were combined, those at home becoming the 1st, and those abroad the 2nd, Rocket Troop. The officers appointed to command these were Captain W. G. Elliott, an officer who retired from the Regiment in 1828, and Captain—afterwards Sir—E. C. Whinyates, an officer whose ability, zeal, and services have hardly been surpassed in the Regiment. He ultimately—after a long and active career—became Commandant of Woolwich, where his kindly manners were long remembered. He commanded the Rocket Troop at Waterloo, where he was severely wounded.

Among the many heart-breaking reductions which exasperate the Artillery student, perhaps none are more distressing, than the reduction of the 2nd Rocket Troop in 1816. *The 1st Rocket Troop had never been out of England;* the 2nd had done good service at Leipsic and Waterloo. Neither of them had had a long existence; but one had had a stirring, glorious history. On the 16th May, 1815, the following order had been issued:—" His Royal Highness the Prince " Regent, in the name and on the behalf of His Majesty, has " been pleased to command that *the Rocket Troop of Royal* " *Artillery, which was present at the Battle of Leipsic,* be per- " mitted to wear the word 'Leipsic' on their appointments, " in commemoration of their services on that occasion." And to the same troop the reward fell, given to those who had been at the Battle of Waterloo. Yet, when the pruning-knife came to be used, the troop which had earned these honours was selected for reduction; and, as if adding insult to injury, the word 'Leipsic' came actually to be worn by the surviving troop, which had never been on active service at all! On its reduction, the officers of the 2nd Rocket Troop were transferred to the Corps of Royal Artillery Drivers.

Up to this point, we have traced the growth, *numerically*, of the Royal Horse Artillery. The conclusion of hostilities after Waterloo led to very extensive reductions. In 1816, besides the 2nd Rocket Troop, D, K, L, and M Troops were reduced, with the consequent changes of designation in the surviving troops. From a total, of all ranks, amounting to 2675, in 1815, and 2621 horses, the Horse Artillery fell in 1816 to 1181 men and 959 horses. Of the six troops in France with the Army of Occupation, the following was the establishment per troop, each troop having 6 guns:—

5 officers, 14 non-commissioned officers, 85 gunners, 56 drivers, 168 horses.

The troops on home service were allowed only 4 guns, and an establishment of 5 officers, 11 non-commissioned officers, 56 gunners, 24 drivers, 102 horses.

But this was merely a beginning. In 1819, B and G Troops were reduced; the troops in France were brought on the Home Establishment, and the number of guns per troop reduced to 2. The strength was then 5 officers, 10 non-commissioned officers, 47 gunners, 18 drivers, 36 horses, per troop; and the total strength of the Royal Horse Artillery did not exceed 616 of all ranks, and 317 horses.[1]

At this miserable establishment the troops remained for some years. In 1828, the two troops on service in Ireland were raised to 4 guns, and remained so; the relieving troops taking over 2 guns, and a suitable proportion of men, from those they relieved. In 1848, *all* the troops were raised to 4 guns, with the required increase of men and horses; and

---

[1] The Duke of Wellington, being at this time Master-General of the Ordnance, invariably selected the artillery for reductions rather than the cavalry and infantry.

CHAP. II.   *Augmentations.*   39

this lasted until 1852, when each troop was raised to 6 guns, the present establishment.

In 1847, the Rocket Troop became I Troop: and rocket carriages were added to the equipment of the whole.[1]

The 4-gun Troops in Ireland had 2 ammunition waggons, 1 forge and 1 store waggon. On the augmentation to 6 guns in 1852, there were allowed to each troop 6 waggons, 1 forge and 1 store waggon, and 1 captain's cart.   *Communicated by Sir D. E. Wood.*

The augmentations after 1847 were due to "the foresight "and determination of Lord Hardinge, who was one of the "best friends the Corps ever had, being utterly without "jealousy, and fully appreciating the value of an efficient, "and of sufficient, artillery." But he was warmly aided by one within the Corps, whose motives were as single as his arguments were sound, whose voice was ever ready to plead for the corps in which he had spent a long, pure, and illustrious life, Sir Robert Gardiner. Owing to these augmentations, 42 guns of Horse Artillery were available for service in the field in 1854: and the total strength of the Brigade stood at 1175 of all ranks, and 1054 horses.   *Sir E. C. Warde.*

Reports to House of Commons, and to Lord Panmure, by Sir R. Gardiner, in 1848, 1849, and 1856.

R. H. A. Records.

The following was the establishment of a troop of Horse Artillery when sent on active service to the Crimea in the Spring of 1854:—   *Communicated by Sir D. E. Wood, K.C.B., Captain Gordon, C.B., and Colonel G. T. Field R.A.*

Officers . . .	6	*Equipment*—Light 6-prs.	4	
N.-C. Officers .	15	12-pr. howitzers . . .	2	
Gunners . .	80	6-pr. ammunition waggons	5	
Drivers . . .	77	12-pr. howitzers . . .	4	
Trumpeters .	1	6-pr. rocket carriage . .	1	
Farriers. . .	1	Forge	1	
Shoeing smiths	4	Store-limber waggon	1	
Collar-makers .	2	Store cart	1	
Wheelers . .	2	Spare gun carriage . .	1	(not horsed).

      Horses—Officers 12
         Troop 192
          Total . . . 204

---

[1] These were withdrawn about 1861.

On the 29th November, 1855, the following was laid down as the detail of a troop of Horse Artillery with the army in the Crimea:—

Officers . . .	6		
N.-C. Officers .	20	Equipment—	4 9-pr. guns.
Gunners . .	97		2 24-pr. howitzers.
Drivers . . .	123		6 gun ammunition waggons.
Trumpeters . .	1		5 howitzer waggons.
			1 store-limber waggon.
Total .	247		1 spare gun carriage.
			1 forge.
			1 rocket carriage.
Farriers . .	1		1 store cart.
Shoeing smiths .	6		1 medicine cart.
Collar-makers .	3		2 forge waggons.
Wheelers . .	2		3 water carts.
Total .	259	Total .	28 carriages.

		No. of Horses.
Riding . . .		. . . 92
Draught . .		. . . 180
Total .		. . 272

Of the troops which had been reduced after Waterloo, B was reformed as a reserve half troop in 1855, and completed in the following year: and G and K Troops were reformed in 1857.

The highest point reached between the reductions after Waterloo, and the year 1857, was in February 1856, when the total of all ranks reached 1950, and the number of horses was 1370. The amalgamation of the Royal with the Indian Artilleries brought the strength of Royal Horse Artillery available for service to an unprecedented standard: at the present moment there are in the regiment thirty-one *service* and two *depôt* Horse Artillery Batteries. But this chapter relates solely to the *old* Royal Horse Artillery.

As yet the *numerical* variations in the Royal Horse Artillery have alone been treated. But there are many other details, mainly of interior economy, which will doubtless be interesting to the modern representatives of the arm, and which may here be briefly stated.

CHAP. II. *Precedence of Royal Horse Artillery.* 41

At first, it was directed that recruits might be taken who were 5 feet 6¾ inches in height: but before six months had passed, the standard was raised, at the urgent request of the Captains, to 5 feet 8 inches. There was often difficulty in obtaining a sufficient number of suitable recruits, and even when the troops were complete, it was customary to attach to each, when in the field, a few of the Driver Corps, with additional horses or mules. Extra pay was granted from the first to the officers, non-commissioned officers, and gunners of Horse Artillery.

Maj.-Gen. Brome to the Duke of Richmond, 6/9/1793.

Lefroy.

The exact relative *status* of the new branch of the service was speedily settled. On 21st February, 1797, the Board of Ordnance granted the same allowance for forage to the officers, as was allowed to officers of Cavalry; and so early had it been decided that the Horse Artillery should take the right of all Cavalry, that, as will be seen by the following letter, the Master-General would not in 1804 allow the point to be disputed.

"Woolwich, June 9, 1804.

" DEAR COLONEL,

" I submitted to the Master General your letter of
" the 5th instant, relating to a conversation which took
" place with General Sir David Dundas, when the Horse
" Artillery marched past with the Cavalry, on the King's
" birthday, in which Sir David, though the Horse Artillery
" *then* led, expressed doubts as to the precedence and rank of
" the Horse Artillery on such future occasions.

D. A. Gen. R.A., to Colonel Cuppage.

" Lord Chatham not being aware upon what circumstances
" Sir David's doubts have arisen, and not considering the
" communication from you in any other light than as a wish
" to know how far, as commanding officer of Artillery, you
" are justifiable in making a claim to the right for the Horse
" Artillery when paraded with Cavalry, his Lordship has
" desired me simply to say that he considers the privilege so
" well established by practice, as well as opinion, that he is
" unwilling to suppose it can be disputed.

" *His Majesty has never seen the Horse Artillery in any*

" *other place:* they were encamped on the right of all the
" Cavalry (of the Blues) at Windsor : and in all parades of
" ceremony and honour, placed on the right of the Cavalry.
"I am, dear Colonel,
" Your obedient Servant,
" J. MACLEOD."

Both by custom and regulation this precedence continued to belong to the Royal Horse Artillery until July 1869, when it was ordered that the Household Cavalry, *when the Sovereign should be present*, should have the precedence awarded to a body guard.

It was laid down as a rule, that no officer should be appointed to the Horse Brigade, who had not been on foreign service: but as this rule was occasionally broken, it was decided in July 1805 that any officers who had been appointed to the Horse Artillery, prior to having been on foreign service, should " (to avoid any officers being confined
" to one species of duty) be liable after three or four years'
" service in the Horse Brigade to be exchanged again into
" the Battalions, so that they may take their share of duty on
" foreign service, and obtain that experience which is neces-
" sary to an Artillery officer, as he advances in the Regiment."
For the information of the general reader it should here be stated, that prior to 1861, when the amalgamation of the Imperial and East India Company's armies took place, the Royal Horse Artillery never went abroad except on active service. Since 1861, however, India has opened a field of foreign service for this branch of the Regiment: and fifteen batteries of service Horse Artillery are to be found in that country, against sixteen at home.

General Orders and R. H. A. Records, and MS. Notes of General Belson, R.A., 1812.

The changes in the dress of the Horse Artillery may be gathered from the following statistics. An order dated 1st November, 1806, lays down the following rules for the dress of officers:—" Except at dress parades the blue Regi-
" mental overalls are to be worn till dinner-time in place of
" the blue pantaloons, which is to be the afternoon dress
" when at home. At all parades, whether mounted or dis-

" mounted, and during the day, the black velvet stock is to
" be worn, with an inch of shirt collar over it: no other
" white to be shown. In the evenings, it is requested that
" black silk handkerchiefs may be substituted with the same
" proportion of shirt collar over them. When officers are
" dressed for a ball, evening party, or dine out, they are to
" wear the jacket open, white pantaloons, plain white waist-
" coat (with sash over it), light sword, regulation sword-
" knot, black belt, with cocked-hat and feather. In common
" a white leather sword-knot is to be worn. Spurs with
" horizontal rowels to be worn at all times."

Prior to 1812, gaiters and knee-boots had been worn: but on the 14th January in that year his Royal Highness the Prince Regent issued the following order :—

" The officers of the Royal Horse Artillery are to wear
" jackets similar to the private men, with an aiguillette. In
" parade dress, they are to wear white leather pantaloons,
" and Hussar boots, with gold binding. On ordinary duties
" or on march, they are to wear overalls of a colour similar
" to the private men's, and a short *surtout*, which is calculated
" to be worn likewise as a *pelisse* on service. When attend-
" ing a drawing-room or levée, they may appear in long
" coats, with lappels and aiguillettes, the same as are worn
" with the jacket, but without lace on the seams: or in the
" Regimental jacket, as they may prefer. The officers of the
" Horse Artillery are likewise to wear cocked-hats, with
" the star loop, with their *dress* regimentals." -

By General Order of 5th August, 1823, leather pantaloons and Hessian boots were abolished, blue-grey overalls and Wellington boots being substituted. 1823.

By General Order of 22nd December, 1827, helmets were abolished, and chakos with tassels substituted. 1827.

By General Order of 15th March, 1831, drivers' jackets were assimilated to those of the gunners. 1831.

By General Order of 20th December, 1831, steel spurs for officers were abolished, and brass spurs substituted. 1831.

By General Order of 26th May, 1834, cross-belts were abolished, and waist-belts substituted. 1834.

1837.	In 1837 bearskin busbies were substituted for chakos. The plumes were altered in 1839.
1853.	Sealskin busbies were substituted for bearskin. The officers, however, continued to wear the bearskin until 1855, when the sable busby was adopted. The plume was shortened from 12 to 8 inches.
1854.	The officers' *pelisse* was abolished in this year.
1855.	The full-dress jacket was altered by reducing the amount of lace. A cross-belt of gold lace with pouch was instituted for the officers; as also a plain blue stable-jacket in place of the undress frock-coat and red embroidered waistcoat.
1857.	In this year booted leather overalls were instituted; and swan-neck steel spurs for all ranks were substituted for the brass spurs of the officers, and the straight steel spurs of the men.

A more important thing, however, than the dress has been the armament of the Royal Horse Artillery. Its greatest deeds have been wrought with the 6-pounder; but that was not its invariable weapon. Talking merely of the pre-amalgamation days [1]—the days which belong to *history* instead of *to-day*, when rifled ordnance was unknown in Horse Artillery—there were even then not unfrequent changes of armament. One troop, as we shall see hereafter, went on service with 12-pounders; on the eve of Waterloo, owing to the want of guns of position, three troops received 9-pounders, instead of the 6-pounders which they had brought from England; and coming to later days, at the commencement of the Crimean War, the two troops, C and I, which first left England were armed with 6-pounders; but, on reaching Varna, C Troop was ordered to exchange them for 9-pounders; and I Troop would have been left behind, for inability to do the same, had it not been that Lord Raglan yielded to the urgent entreaties of its commander, Colonel Maude, to allow it to accompany the expedition.

During the Peninsular Campaign, the armament of a troop was as follows:—2 9-pounders, or 2 heavy 6-pounders;

---

[1]. I. e. Amalgamation of Royal and Indian Artilleries.

CHAP. II. *Armament of Royal Horse Artillery.* 45

1 heavy 5½-inch howitzer; 3 light 6-pounders; 6 ammunition
waggons; 3 reserve waggons, and 4 other carriages. Com- Lefroy.
pared with the simplicity of modern Horse Artillery armament, the presence of three different guns in the same troop,
with the consequent necessity of a variety of ammunition,
seems a very complicated and undesirable arrangement.
This was frequently felt at the time; and at the change of
armament made before Waterloo, a foreshadowing of the
modern harmony of weapons might be detected in the arming
of I Troop—Bull's—with 5½-inch howitzers only. And right
noble was the service done by that troop on the 18th of June.

During the season of starvation between 1819 and 1848,
the guns attached to the skeleton troops were 6-pounders.
With the augmentations, a proportion of howitzers made its
re-appearance.

The proper armament for Horse Artillery, in the days
before the substitution of rifled ordnance put an end to the
discussion, was exhaustively treated by Sir Robert Gardiner.
His arguments are interesting even at the present day, when
the perfection of Field Batteries, and their ability to carry
more gunners into action by means of the new-pattern
carriage, have combined to make not a few question the
necessity of so expensive an arm as Horse Artillery being
retained. If we substitute the 9-pounder rifled gun for the
old 6-pounder, and the 16-pounder for the old 9-pounder, in
Sir Robert's remarks, we shall find his arguments as applicable to the later as to the former controversy. "There can Report on
" be no greater mistake than to put rivalry or comparisons, lery by
" or to expect the same results from the employment of Horse Sir R. Gar-
" Artillery as of Brigade (i. e. Field) Artillery. Though *one* 31 Mar.
" *and the same arm,* they are equipped and intended for 1848.
" totally distinct purposes. The necessary quick movements
" of the Horse Artillery could not be attained by 9-pounders;
" the telling effect of 9-pounders could not be expected from
" Horse Artillery. One is intended to act with Cavalry, and,
" from the nature of its equipment and the lightness of its
" metal, is expected to maintain at all times, and under all
" circumstances, of bad roads, of rough, hilly, or broken

"ground, the same pace as Cavalry ; and, in short, to bring
" artillery into action wherever Cavalry can act. . . . .
" I can name two instances in which, while acting with
" cavalry, any other than Horse Artillery would have been
" perfectly useless. One, the affair of Morales, in Spain ;
" the other, the movement from Quatre Bras to the position
" of Waterloo. Both were specially movements of Horse
" Artillery, and both tried the wind and speed of our horses.
" In the latter movement particularly, through a deep cross
" country, any Artillery differently equipped would have
" inevitably fallen into the hands of the enemy. In all light
" movements of the Infantry of an army, Horse Artillery is
" as indispensably necessary and as exclusively effective, as
" it is with cavalry. I have myself, in cases of reconnois-
" sance, been withdrawn from the Cavalry for the moment,
" to cover movements in which heavier Artillery could bear
" no part. . . . . On the other hand, if Horse Artillery
" has its distinct advantages over heavier guns, so likewise
" the latter have their distinct purposes, for which the
" employment of Horse Artillery would be wholly inap-
" plicable and inadequate. . . . . I have known Bri-
" gade Artillery as perfect, in its way, as Horse Artillery ;
" but no more comparison can be drawn between them than
" between Cavalry and Infantry."

Then follows a remark, which shows how the writer anticipated the changes which have come, and which have done so much to improve our Field Artillery : " Our present
" Brigades would be greatly advanced in efficiency if, like
" the Horse Artillery, or the Brigades with the Duke of
" Wellington's army in the Peninsula, they were placed
" under the command and the responsibility of their captains.
" They should also, to become effective Field Artillery, be
" placed on the same footing as the Horse Artillery, for their
" contingent share in all garrison and general duties. They
" should march to and from the outposts in relief in the same
" manner as the Horse Artillery ; they should combine, like
" the Horse Artillery, the knowledge of the duties of Cavalry
" with those of Artillery. They would thus gradually attain

Progress of Field Artillery.

"that perfection in their own distinctive service, which I
"believe to be unequalled in the few skeleton troops we
"possess of Horse Artillery."

At the time these words were penned, Field Artillery had reached a point of degradation which had hardly been surpassed even in the old days of peasant drivers. Of the six batteries or brigades nominally at Woolwich, two existed on paper, having neither men nor horses. "Two others," wrote Sir R. Gardiner, "are so little advanced in their necessary
"drill and training as to be quite non-effective for the pur-
"poses of service, or even the common movements of parade
"and review. Two only might possibly move without causing
"interruption or confusion to other troops they might be
"acting with; but that is as much as can be said of them.
" . . . . The riding and driving of our Brigade drivers
"is at this moment very bad. With the exception of the
"Brigades stationed in Dublin, where they have occasional
"opportunities of moving with other troops, they are un-
"skilful, and ignorant of Artillery movements; at Woolwich
"they are employed in *carter's work* in the civil departments
"of the Arsenal; and, of course, as long as such a system is
"pursued they can never become Artillery drivers. . . .
"The Brigades in Ireland are more efficient, and fitted to
"move with other troops, than the Brigades in England.
"But it is a delusion to say that England has a Field
"Artillery. There is not a single 9-pounder horsed in the
"British service—an astounding fact. Nor will it be believed,
"except by those who know the truth, that the English
"army has been for years without Artillery attached either
"to Cavalry or Infantry, for the common purposes of drill
"and exercise in their combined movements."

<small>Sir R. Gardiner's Report.</small>

The progress of Field Artillery to its present excellence may be said to date from 1848. Already, before 1856, the Light Field Artillery had regained what it had lost during the economical era which followed Waterloo; and since 1859, when the new brigade system put an end to the incessant change of batteries from field to garrison service, the progress has been continuous. But this progress would have been impossible had it not been that a standard of Field

Artillery excellence had been maintained, even under the most adverse and depressing circumstances, by those unequalled skeleton troops of Horse Artillery, whose officers have, by their influence and exertions, done so much to make what may be called *medium* Field Artillery the admirable service which it now is. It has been said that the influence of the Horse Artillery, during the period between 1816 and 1848, was injurious to the Field Batteries. If it were so, it was in the most indirect manner possible. Economy in our military administration being peremptorily demanded, the only alternative left to the Board of Ordnance was between a very small force of admirable Field Artillery, and a larger force of batteries starved in equipment and incapable of service in the field. The officers of the Regiment, whose position entitled them to be the advisers of the Board, were undoubtedly men whose sympathies lay with the Horse Artillery, in which they had all served; but they were also men who had seen, during the campaigns in the Peninsula, Belgium, and France, what was possible with a well-equipped Field Artillery of less mobility. In deciding on a small but perfect force, rather than a larger and indifferent one, it must be admitted that they acted wisely. The brilliant Field Artillery of the great war would have otherwise become a mere tradition, whereas, under the system adopted, it remained a reality, a model, and a standard. The adoption of the other alternative would have vitally injured the Horse, without much benefit to the Field Artillery; and it would have rendered the reorganisation of both a more difficult, and a more tardy operation. That the Field Artillery suffered terribly during the period mentioned, is too true; but dispassionate study of the Regimental history proves, not what has often been asserted, that the suffering was due to the blighting influence of a *corps d'élite*, but merely to an unwise, an unprofitable, and a singularly short-sighted economy.[1]

---

[1] It is but just to say, that much that is good in the care of the horses in the Royal Artillery in the field comes traditionally from the Horse Artillery attached to the German Hussars in the Peninsula: and the riding of the Corps was first taught by a German riding-master brought from Hanover by George III.—*Communicated by Sir D. E. Wood.*

A much larger question arises when the policy of a *corps d'élite*, as a part of a larger body on which it feeds, has to be considered. No subject has been so fruitful of discussion in the Regiment; and nowhere can a decision be more safely arrived at than in a careful study of the Regimental history. There are strong arguments in favour of, and also against, the policy which has existed since the formation of the Royal Horse Artillery; and the best way of arriving at a conclusion is to state these arguments, and to weigh their respective values.

It has been said that the existence of a *corps d'élite* produces "l'énervation de la masse au profit des groupes." In stronger language it has also been said: "The more ruth- " lessly the system of selection is carried out, the more " rapidly do the troops from amongst whom the selection is " made lose their self-respect and become at first apathetic, " and at last inefficient. The *corps d'élite*, the insatiable " parasite, must degenerate in precisely the same degree as " the body which feeds it; and the end is, that in the lapse " of a few years the whole edifice crumbles, totters, and " falls. When the oak falls, the ivy that killed it must " fall too." Trochu. Hime.

But those who apply such language to the existence, in the Royal Artillery, of a *corps d'élite* such as the Royal Horse Artillery, forget several important considerations which distinguish it from such a corps as the French *Chasseurs à pied*, of which it was said that everything that was good, everything that was efficient, everything that was soldierlike in the Infantry of the Line was seized upon with unsparing hands, and remorselessly drafted into it. In the first place, the selection for this branch of the Regiment is only made for the purpose of officering it. The field battery which rejoices in smart non-commissioned officers and men is in no dread of losing them to feed a favoured corps. From the day a recruit joins the Horse Artillery, his efficiency and his education depend on the officers of that arm; and therefore to them is the credit due if their efforts are successful.

There have been occasions when the Horse Artillery was

permitted to select from the recruits of the other battalions; but these days have passed away. No service battery of Field or Garrison Artillery has to minister to the wants of our *corps d'élite*, and therefore the language employed in another place by the able author quoted above, in reference to the Guards, the *Infantry corps d'élite* in our service, is more applicable than that used by him in reference to our Field Artillery: "The recruits are selected with care; but they "are selected from society at large, not from regiments of the "Line; and the result is that this noble body of men, the "Guards, are a source of wholesome emulation, instead of "contentious rivalry, to the rest of the army."

The whole question, therefore, may be condensed into one point—the wisdom or otherwise of *officering* the Horse Artillery from the Regiment at large. Such petty considerations as higher pay, special privileges, &c., which are apt to embitter the minds of some, must be put aside as unworthy. In a question affecting not merely the Regiment, but our whole military life as well, we cannot be too careful in clearing the ground of all but the purest argument. The opposers of the existing system have always been able to argue with great force, because there are undoubted anomalies which can easily be described in such a way as to appear ludicrous. As selection for employment in the Horse Brigade has always been conditional on previous zeal and efficiency, it follows that the reward for activity and knowledge in the performance of, it may be, Siege and Garrison Artillery duties, is often employment in a service totally dissimilar. This may be compared with rewarding an Infantry officer for skill in battalion drill, by giving him a troop of Horse! Yet, while admitting the anomaly, it is impossible to suggest a better test, if both branches of the Regiment are to be officered from the same list. The only test of efficiency which can be trusted is efficiency already proved. It must be believed that a man who has been faithful and zealous in one line of duty will display the same zeal and conscience in another; and if selection *has* to be made,—if there are many candidates for any employment, their previous history, even under very different circumstances, is the best witness for or against them.

But another argument employed against the existing system is, that an officer, who has once served in the more brilliant branch, returns with reluctance, on promotion, to the others, and is restless and dissatisfied until he·is re-appointed. In other words, that *esprit* for the particular branch drowns that for the Regiment. History is the best witness here.

Excluding the many living men, who have proved that Horse Artillery service has not affected their Regimental *esprit de corps*, let us recall the names of the men who have been most distinguished for professional talent of every description since the formation of the Royal Horse Artillery. Sir John Macleod, Sir Augustus Frazer, Sir Alexander Dickson, Sir John May, Sir Robert Gardiner, and Sir E. C. Whinyates, all served in the Horse Artillery, but never allowed themselves to be blinded, by their love of that service, to the interests of·the Regiment at large. Their letters, their very lives, are witnesses of their devotion to the whole Corps; and while serving with the Siege or Garrison Artillery, their performance of duty was inspired by the same zeal as when serving in what may be called the more attractive branch. They all saw and felt that the less showy was the more scientific, that Garrison Artillery was the backbone of the Regiment, and that, under favourable circumstances, it would dwarf, even in popularity, the mounted batteries. The Peninsular and Waterloo campaigns were conducive to the efficiency and popularity of Horse Artillery; but let Siege Artillery have as many years of such service as it went through at Sebastopol, with the mounted batteries acting merely as carriers of ammunition, and its efficiency and popularity would be quite as great.

History therefore does not support the theory that service in the Horse Brigade injures the capacity, or the *esprit de corps*, of an officer who returns to the other branches. The question at issue therefore condenses itself into a still narrower field; viz., admitting that the present system does not prevent Artillery officers from being *generally* efficient, would they not be much *more* efficient if they belonged to Field or Garrison Artillery during their whole career, without the power of interchanging their services? If ability in field battery service were rewarded by appointment to the Horse Artillery, and skill in Garrison Artillery service were rewarded, either by special employment or by appointment to some such corps as was recommended by Sir Robert Gardiner—an Artillery of the Guard—would we not have better officers of each branch than we now have? Logically, there can be but one answer; and were this the only consideration, the argument would terminate in favour of a separation of the officers of the various arms, similar to that already existing between the non-commissioned officers and men. We should then have probably *more* skilled artillerists, in point of number, in each branch; although perhaps no *individual* more skilled than those who have appeared under, or in spite of, the anomalous system which has hitherto existed.

But would the Regiment in the end be a gainer by the change? Has not the system of interchange been the best school possible for familiarising the Artillery officer with the duties and movements of other arms, and thus qualifying him for commands in the field? General Foy, in writing of the days when such a thing as a command being given to a General of Artillery was unknown, owing to jealousy of the Ordnance, said: "On a trop en horreur les avancements hors " de la règle pour permettre qu'un artilleur qui se trouverait " trop à l'étroit dans son arme s'élançât dans le service " général de la ligne. Jamais de l'école de Woolwich ne " sortira un Bonaparte." The days of the Ordnance have passed away: public opinion points more surely every day to the employment of Generals who are not merely soldiers, but scientific soldiers as well; and it would be a suicidal policy which would recommend a change which, if carried out logically, would inevitably result in the *certain* production of admirable officers of high but *narrow* professional training, and in the *impossibility* of procuring any whose experience of general service would qualify them for a mixed command. The Garrison Artilleryman who in his battery had attained a skill in his particular groove, hitherto but rare, would feel every day his association with the other arms getting less, and his consequent inability to command them getting greater. If this consideration be carefully borne in mind, even those who feel most strongly on the subject—and they are many —will hesitate ere they precipitate a result which would inscribe on the walls of the Academy the dismal prediction, " Jamais de l'école de Woolwich ne sortira un Bonaparte."

Note.—The extra rate of pay to non-commissioned officers and gunners of the Royal Horse Artillery is based on the following General Order, dated 21 January, 1793 :—

" The Master-General directs that an allowance of twopence per day, in " addition to their Regimental pay, shall be made to each non-com- " missioned officer and gunner of the Brigade of Horse Artillery, when " and so long as he continues mounted, and having the care and manage- " ment of an horse, in consideration of the extraordinary and constant " attention required of such persons for the due performance of this par- " ticular service, which must deprive them of the occasional advantages " arising from their being employed in works for which additional pay is " given.

" The dismounted non-commissioned officers and gunners of this " Brigade not being in the same circumstances, nor deprived of their share " in the works, will not be entitled to the said allowance; nor will the " drivers of this Brigade, as they are to be enlisted merely for that special " service, and will have but little of other duties to learn or perform."

Note 2.—The style of horse considered suitable for Horse Artillery at first, may be ascertained from the following instructions, dated Woolwich, March 1810 :—" The horses to be from four to six years old (when bought), " to be short-legged, open-chested, and broad-winded; not to exceed " 15 hands 2 inches, nor—four years old—under 15 hands ½ inch; to have " good bone and action, the colours to be bay, brown, and dark chestnut." The price allowed, after a month's trial, was thirty guineas.

CHAPTER III.

With the Duke of York in Flanders.

<small>Hist. R. A. Chap. i. vol. ii.

Stephen's 'Wars of the French Revolution.'

Ibid.</small>

THE *causes* of a war are to a certain extent beyond the province of a work which has mainly to deal with its history. In the present instance, allusion has already been made to the ostensible reason; but it is very difficult to arrive at the exact truth. "From the guilt and odium " of this new and disastrous conflict the ruling parties in " both nations anxiously endeavoured to vindicate them- " selves." There is no doubt that in 1792 England threatened to declare war, unless France should renounce her views of aggression and aggrandisement; or, in other words, "relinquish all her conquests, and confine herself " within her own territory." The answer given by M. Chauvelin to Lord Grenville, on the 13th January, 1793, was: "We will fight the English, whom we esteem, with " regret; but we will fight them without fear." Matters were precipitated by the execution of the French King; and on the 24th January M. Chauvelin received notice to quit England within eight days. Once again the French attempted to pacify the English Government, but without success. They therefore took the initiative—declaring war, in the name of the French Republic, against England and Holland on the 1st February, 1793; and this was followed on the 11th February by a counter-declaration on the part of England.

On the 17th February the French army took the field, resolved to carry the war into Holland; and speedily captured Breda, Klundert, and Gertruydenberg. The siege of Williamstadt was not so successful; and here good service was rendered by the Royal Artillery on board bomb-vessels. Severe reverses having befallen another French army, employed

CHAP. III.   *Battalion Guns.*   55

elsewhere in the Low Countries, the whole of the French troops were withdrawn from this first expedition against Holland. Space prevents any description of the operations between the Imperialists and the troops of the Republic—the losses and defeats of the latter under Dumouriez, and his subsequent defection. The movements of the Army under the Duke of York will be all that it is necessary to study, to ascertain the services of the Corps in this war.

Although the main Artillery force for this expedition did not embark until the 10th May, 1793, Woolwich was much disquieted after the end of February with incessant demands for battalion guns and the requisite detachments for the regiments under orders for the Low Countries. In no English war was this pernicious system of battalion guns more systematically urged and practised. Occasionally—as will be seen presently—the guns were brigaded; and during the siege operations, as at Valenciennes, the Artillery did duty by companies: but, as a rule, the guns were attached in pairs to the different battalions. Only one waggon accompanied each pair of guns; and the following was the strength of the Artillery detachment: viz., 1 subaltern, 2 non-commissioned officers, 8 gunners, 3 drivers, and 9 horses. The faults of this system have already been alluded to, but are most clearly shown in the following words:—" To prevent these "guns from impeding the movements of the infantry to "whom they belonged, their weight was reduced to an extent "which made their fire under the most favourable circum-"stances all but useless. Secondly, as a matter of fact, they "did seriously encumber their infantry. For, infantry "compelled to drag guns along with them could not be "expected to march, even on smooth and level plains, with "the same order and rapidity as infantry who marched free "from such an encumbrance ; and in a cultivated country, "intersected with ditches, hedges, and walls, the guns had to "be abandoned altogether. In this latter case they not only "failed to fulfil the very object of their existence, but left a "gap in the line which, as they were generally placed in "the centre of the battalion, might produce fatal conse-

MS. Correspondence. Brigade-Major to B. of Ordnance.

Ibid.

Captain H. W. L. Hime, R.A., on 'Mobility of Field Artillery.'

"quences. Thirdly, as it was necessary for them to take
"part in all the manœuvres of the battalion, the necessary
"time was not afforded to the gunners for placing, loading,
"or laying their guns carefully. No guns could have been
"effective under this system, which violated *both* the funda-
"mental principles of Field Artillery tactics, viz., that the
"movements of a battery in action should be minimum in
"number, and should be made at a maximum speed.
"Fourthly, their constant presence with their infantry led
"the latter to look upon the guns as necessary to the safety
"of the battalion, and thus diminished that self-confidence
"which infantry must possess to be successful. Fifthly,
"as these guns were practically useless, not only was the
"money spent on their construction wasted, but the regular
"columns or trains of Artillery were deprived of a corre-
"sponding number of guns, which might have been turned
"to good account by their own officers. In fine, this bad
"system weakened the Artillery without strengthening the
"Infantry, and raised a general prejudice against the use in
"the field of what was regarded as a complicated and useless
"mechanism."

At the special request of the Duke of York, Major—afterwards Sir William—Congreve was appointed to command
the Artillery of the expedition. He embarked in May with
the main body of his force. A party under the command of
Brevet-Major Wright left England earlier in the spring of
1793, to take part in the siege operations with which the
English share of the campaign commenced. Its strength
and the names of the officers were as follows:—

Ordnance Letter-books and Records of the 1st Battalion.	Brevet-Major Wright, in command.	
	Capt.-Lieut. Borthwick.	3 Sergeants, 7 Corporals, 4 Bombardiers.
	1st Lieutenant Thornton.	5 First Gunners, 94 Second Gunners.
	,, ,, Robe.	2 Drummers.
	,, ,, Fenwick.	
	,, ,, De Ginkle.	
	,, ,, Watson.	
	2nd Lieutenant J'ans.	Total of all ranks, 123.

Major Wright's Company, which formed the chief part of

Artillery Force embarked.

this force, was No. 2 Company, 1st Battalion, now B Battery, 1st Brigade.

The main Artillery force, which embarked at Woolwich on the 10th May, 1793, was as follows:—

Major W. Congreve, in command.		
Captain Trotter.	Surgeon, W. Smyth.	MS returns to B. of Ordnance.
,, Wilson.	Surgeon's Mate, Hearsley.	
Captain-Lieutenant Broadbridge.	Commissary and Paymaster } Captain Williamson.	
,, ,, Cookson.		
First Lieutenant Roberton (Adj.)	Commissary of Horse, Mr. Eastaff.	
,, ,, Wilson.	Clerk of Stores, Mr. Meek.	
,, ,, Hooke.		
,, ,, Depeyster.	1 Conductor of Stores.	
,, ,, Bentham.	3 Wheelers.	
,, ,, Fead.	1 Cooper.	
Second Lieutenant Rudyerd.	1 Carpenter.	
,, ,, Downman.	3 Smiths.	
,, ,, Foy.	2 Collar-makers.	
,, ,, Phillott.	1 *Farrier*.	
Sergeants 4	114 *Military* drivers.	
Corporals 5	84 Horses.	
Bombardiers 9		
First Gunners 6		
Second Gunners . . . 192		
Drummers 3		

The total of the military branch, exclusive of the drivers, was 236.

There was also an extraordinary addition to a force proceeding on active service, in the form of 21 women and 23 children.

Yet a third detachment left Woolwich for Flanders, on the 26th August, 1793, as follows:—

Major Huddlestone, in command.		
Captain Laye.	11 Non-Commissioned Officers.	
Capt.-Lieut. Boag.	232 Gunners.	
Lieutenant Lawson.	3 Drummers.	Ibid.
,, Geary.	4 Waggoners.	
,, Shrapnel.	18 *Women* and 7 *children*.	
,, Beevor.		
,, Lacy.		
,, Mann.		
,, Waller.		

Various other officers joined the Army during the war, among whom can be traced Lieutenants Schalch, Lefebure,

Boger, and Spearman. The force of Royal Artillery in Flanders reached its maximum in February 1794, when it was as follows:—

> 3 Field Officers.
> 7 Captains.
> 14 Subalterns.
> 61 Non-Commissioned Officers.
> 478 Gunners.
>
> There were also 224 *Gunner-drivers* for service with the Field Brigades, the Driver Corps having been formed in 1794 for that purpose, the men being regularly attested soldiers. Hitherto, the Drivers were generally called *Waggoners*.

An additional expedition, under Lord Moira, sailed for the Low Countries during the war; and the Artillery portion of the force comprised a field-officer in command—the 5th Company of the 4th Battalion—now B Battery, 9th Brigade—with 110 of all ranks, and also 114 sergeant-conductors and *gunner-drivers*.

MS. Returns to B. O.

The present designations of five of the companies known to have been with the Duke of York's force are—

> B Battery, 1st Brigade.
> No. 4 Battery, 5th Brigade.
> No. 4 Battery, 7th Brigade.
> B Battery, 9th Brigade.
>
> (No. 4 Company, 4th Battalion, which was also present, has since been reduced.)

The 6th Company, which was with the Army, cannot be traced with accuracy, but it was probably No. 7 Battery, 2nd Brigade. There were two bomb-vessels, the 'Terror' and 'Vesuvius,' which did good service, and on board of which were Lieutenants Suckling and Ramsay, 2 non-commissioned officers, 18 gunners, and 2 artificers, of the Royal Artillery.

MS. Returns to B. O.

The total strength of the Regiment at this time was 4857 of all ranks; and its distribution at the end of 1794 was as follows:—

> Home Stations . . 6 Troops of Horse Artillery.
> ,,   ,,   . . 18 Companies.
> Colonial Stations . 22   ,,
> Holland 6   ,,
> Toulon and Corsica. 1   ,,
>
> Total . . . 53 Troops and Companies.

Vol. i.
p. 405.

It will be remembered that the first five companies of a

new Battalion, the 5th Battalion, were raised in this year. In this estimate of the strength of the Regiment, the Invalid Companies are not included. The companies on colonial service included 2 in the East Indies, 7 in Canada, Nova Scotia, and Newfoundland, 9 in the West Indies, and 4 at Gibraltar. _{Kane's List.}

Returning to the war, it may be observed that it was at the blockade of Condé that the English troops first took the field, forming part of the Allied Army under the Prince de Cobourg. The French suffered reverses at Famars and Quiévrain; but the first occasion on which the Artillery received special mention was on the 8th May, 1793, at St. Amand, when the Brigade of Guards was engaged in support of the Prussians, and contributed greatly to the success of the day. The Battalion guns attached to the Guards on this occasion were of great service, succeeding in silencing the enemy's artillery, and so breaking his infantry that the charge ultimately made by the Guards was doubly effective. The wording of the letter to the Master-General, in praise of the conduct of the Artillery on this occasion, seems to imply that the guns were brigaded, from the fact of Major Wright's name being mentioned as in command :—

"Tournay, May 10, 1793.

" MY LORD,

" I have the utmost satisfaction in informing your
" Grace that the zeal and ability of Major Wright and
" of Lieutenants Watson and Fenwick have done them the
" highest credit. The guns commanded by these officers
" were the only ones brought into action. I was myself a
" witness of the promptitude with which Mr. Watson's were
" served, and know that they had great effect.
" I have the honour, &c.,
" JAMES MURRAY.
" *To His Grace the* DUKE OF RICHMOND, *&c. &c.*"

On this occasion the French General Dampierre was killed by a cannon-shot from the English batteries. On the following day the enemy was driven from his camp at Famars, and Valenciennes was invested by the Allies. Condé was taken three months after the commencement of the blockade. Valenciennes, having been approached in a methodical manner, according to the strictest rule, did not suffer any serious attack until the forty-first day of the siege. On the 25th July the outworks were taken, mainly through the exertions and gallantry of the English under General Abercromby; and on the following day, in answer to a second summons, the place surrendered to the English and their allies. The Siege Artillery used on this occasion was considerable in quantity, and of its effect the following extract from the Duke of York's despatch will be the best proof: " The batteries were allotted at different times to be " worked by the Royal Artillery, and every commendation " is due to Major Congreve and to the officers and men of " that Corps, who have upon this occasion fully supported the " reputation they have so long enjoyed." For his services on this occasion Major Congreve received on the 21st August, 1793, the brevet rank of Lieutenant-Colonel.

One or two minor actions took place before winter put an end to hostilities. At Lincelles, on the 18th August, 1793, the Artillery attached to the Brigade of Guards under General Lake again did good service; and on this occasion the first officer of the Corps who fell during the war lost his life—Lieutenant Depeyster. The official account of this engagement, after lauding the gallantry of the Guards, went on to say: " Equal praise is due to Major Wright and " the officers and men of the Royal Artillery attached to the " Battalions."

Ill-success followed. The siege of Dunkirk by the Duke of York proved a failure. He was badly supported by his allies, and received little or no assistance from the navy. He had therefore to retreat—certainly in good order—but leaving behind him 32 heavy guns intended for the siege. At Lannoy, on the 28th October, Lieutenant Thornton of the Royal Artillery, afterwards Sir Charles Thornton, A.D.C. to King William IV., lost an arm. It was by this time apparent to the Allies that the war, so far as they were concerned, must be a purely defensive one; and they found it extremely difficult to hold Austrian Flanders. The darkness of their situation was lit up at the end of October by a successful attack on Marchiennes, made by General Kray under the direction of the Duke of York, in which the enemy lost 12 pieces of cannon, and 2000 killed and wounded. In spite of this success, however, winter came upon the Allies, finding them in a very different frame of mind from that in which they had commenced the campaign. They did not, however, despair, but resolved and prepared to commence with greater vigour than ever the campaign of 1794.

Their united strength on the 16th April amounted to 187,000 men; but it was injudiciously divided into eight columns, to march on different points; the fourth and fifth being under the command of the Duke of York. The object of these two columns was the attack and capture of the village of Vaux, which they undertook, and in which they succeeded on the 17th April, 1794. Major-General Abercromby and Sir William Erskine commanded the columns, and Colonel Congreve in person commanded the Royal Artillery, whose well-directed fire on this day has been acknowledged by all writers. The French lost 30 pieces of Artillery. One of the companies of the Corps received on this day an honour, unprecedented in the previous or subsequent annals of the Regiment.

No. 1 Company, 4th Battalion—now No. 4 Battery, 7th Brigade—attracted the admiration of the Duke of York to such an extent by its gallantry and skill, that he made the whole army form up on the field of battle while this company marched past him. He also published a General Order, saying: "His Royal Highness desires that Captain Boag " and Lieutenant Fead of the Royal Artillery (the officers " with the company) will accept his thanks for the very " spirited and able manner in which they conducted the " battery intrusted to their care." If history is not utterly powerless, the story of the 17th April ought to stir the

MS. Records of 4th Battalion.

hearts of this battery, and make every man in its ranks strive to be not unworthy of those who proved themselves worthy of so rare and honourable a distinction. To be singled out for bravery on a day when all were brave, and to display a spirit and an ability which, amid all the confusion of battle, attracted the observation of a preoccupied commander,—surely these are traditions which should fire the most generous emotions, and awaken the most noble resolves. It is in such a belief, and with such a hope as this, that men have been found to record such tales in Regimental records, and others to transcribe them fondly from faded pages, and give to them a new life and a wider circulation.

Encouraged by the success at Vaux, Landrecies was besieged by the Allies, the English troops covering the operations towards Cambray. Twice between the 23rd and 26th April did the Duke of York's force defeat the French; and on the 26th it was mainly owing to the well-directed fire of the Royal Artillery, under Colonel Congreve, that the French were dislodged from their position in the village of Troisvilles, with a loss of 35 guns and 300 prisoners. Landrecies surrendered on the 29th April; but this advantage, even when combined with the Duke of York's successes, did not atone for the severe defeat, which had been experienced on the 26th April by the Allied Army under General Clairfayt at the hands of a French army under General Pichegru. There seems from this time to have been a want of harmony among the Allies. Their armies melted away into more isolated columns every day; and the system of incessant attack, irrespective and regardless of frequent defeat, which was pursued by the French forces, seems to have produced a nervous effect upon their opponents, under which each commander seemed to play, so to speak, for his own hand. The representatives of the old school of war were bewildered by the activity of those of the new. They found themselves fighting, confined by strict and wooden rules, by which their adversaries refused to be bound; and the consequences proved fatal.

The English army continued to achieve minor successes at Lannoy, Roubaix, and Monveaux; but met with a serious reverse on the 18th May, 1794, when Major Wright's Battery was nearly cut to pieces. The French succeeded in completely surrounding the English, who had actually to effect a retreat through the enemy's troops, in doing which Major Wright's battery, now B Battery, 1st Brigade, Royal Artillery, was charged by the French cavalry, and suffered the loss of its commander, 5 men and 31 horses killed, and 2 subalterns, Lieutenants Boger and Downman, 45 men, and 70 horses wounded. In fact, the battery was placed completely *hors de combat*, as might have been expected when guns were so hampered as to allow a charge of cavalry to be possible. Surrounded as they were on all sides by mingled friends and foes, it was impossible to come into action on the advancing hussars; and the many acts of individual bravery failed to save them from virtual annihilation.

Fortune was more favourable a few days later—on the 22nd May—when the English successfully resisted a general attack of the French under General Pichegru; and their obstinacy on this occasion was the origin of the barbarous order issued by the ruffians who held the reins of government in Paris, forbidding any quarter to be given " to the slaves " of King George." This was nobly answered by the Duke of York, who in a General Order, dated 7th June, 1794, urged his troops to "suspend their indignation, and to " remember that mercy to the vanquished is the brightest " gem in a soldier's character." In the repulse of the enemy Gen. Order. on the 22nd May the conduct of the Artillery was such that " His Royal Highness the commander-in-chief begged to " thank Captain Trotter, with the Artillery under his " command, for their great display of intrepidity and good " conduct, which reflected the greatest honour on themselves, " and at the same time was highly instrumental in deciding " the important victories of the 22nd."

From this time, however, the Allies experienced nothing but disaster. The capture of Charleroi and the battle of

Fleurus proved the increasing merits of the French army, while the welcome from the Belgian cities, which one after another, including Brussels itself, fell into the hands of the French, proved that the sympathy of the people was much more with them than with the Allies. It is difficult to overrate the value of such sympathy in war.

In the course of these disasters the Duke of York's communications with Ostend were interrupted, and the English Government, becoming seriously alarmed, fitted out the expedition already referred to, which left Southampton for the Continent, under the command of Lord Moira. After many vicissitudes this second army succeeded in effecting a junction with the Duke of York, after defeating the French at Alost and Malines. The continued advance and repeated attacks made by the French army compelled the Duke to retire across the Meuse into Holland. The surrender of the frontier fortresses followed; and then, while other French armies were detailed to pursue the Continental part of the Allied forces, Pichegru himself, with a much larger force than that under the command of the Duke of York, resolved to invade Holland, and exterminate the English. From this moment the Duke, being completely outnumbered, was compelled steadily to retire. An action took place on the 15th September, between his advanced guard and the French troops, at Boxtel, the result of which was a further retreat, and the abandonment to their own resources of Bois-le-duc, Breda, and Bergen-op-Zoom. The first-named of these places was invested by the French on the 23rd September, 1794, and surrendered on the 10th October. Without waiting to take the other two, and leaving them in his rear, Pichegru, with the energy which characterised the French armies of the Revolution, and with a contempt for the laws of war which paralyzed his opponents, pushed on in pursuit of the English, whose retreat in face of superior numbers was—it must be confessed by every one—very skilfully managed. The Duke of York was in position at Pufflech when the French came up, and on the 19th October, 1794, a severe engagement took place, which ended in the

English army being compelled to retire behind the Waal, while the French undertook the siege of various garrisons. On the 28th October, Venloo was taken; followed, on the 5th November, by the capture of Maestricht; and on the same day the siege of Nimeguen was commenced. Here gallant service was rendered by the English, and, among others, General Abercromby was wounded; but the impetuosity of the French was such that the Duke of York, finding his intercourse with the garrison cut off, retired a little farther to take up a fresh position, and, on the 8th November, Nimeguen surrendered. The Duke of York was, for many reasons, anxious to escape an engagement, and he intrenched himself strongly in the lines of Nimeguen. The French commander, however, having received peremptory orders from his Government not to desist from hostilities, notwithstanding the lateness of the season, prepared to cross the Waal, but was prevented by the fire of the Allied Artillery. He gave up the idea for the time, and confined himself to making the necessary dispositions for invading Holland in the spring;—no easy task, when one reflects on the facilities with which the whole country could have been flooded. Most fortunately for him an exceptionally severe frost set in, freezing the rivers and canals so that they could support troops and artillery. Hostilities were at once recommenced by the French, and, after taking several strong places in the end of December, fighting in a temperature lower than it had been for thirty years, on the 11th January, 1795, Pichegru, with his whole army, crossed the Waal. In the attempt made by the British to prevent this, considerable loss was met with, and, among others, two subalterns of Artillery, Lieutenants Walker and Legg, were wounded.

From this time commenced a retreat which, for misery, discomfort, and losses, has been compared with the French retreat from Moscow, although on a much smaller scale. The English Government, having resolved on the withdrawal of the army, directed it to retire on Bremen, there to embark for home. This order rendered it necessary for the troops to traverse the district called the Weluwe, a perfect desert, over which the wind was drifting the snow into almost impassable ridges—where the few scattered villages had been rendered hostile by French emissaries, and where " numbers of English soldiers perished through want and " weakness, and many were frozen to death." The hardships borne by the army did not interfere with their discipline; and they were soothed by the sympathy of all classes in England, and ultimately by a hearty welcome home. With the exception of a small force under General Dundas, which remained on the Continent until the following year, the whole army reached England in May 1795. It was on the 8th of that month that the six companies of Artillery disembarked at Woolwich, from which station they were speedily removed to Chatham and Portsmouth.

The barbarous order given by the French Government with reference to the English soldiers, which has been mentioned above, was almost atoned for by an act of chivalry on the part of the French troops at the end of the campaign. During the retreat of the English, the 87th Regiment had been left as part of the garrison of Bergen-op-Zoom. The Dutch Government, dismayed by the continued successes of the French, and urged on by a party in the country, by no means inconsiderable, which sympathised with the Republican cause, came to terms with the French Commander, and consented to the surrender of the various garrisons. Considerable anxiety naturally existed as to the fate of the 87th Regiment; "but, compromised by the " defection of an ally, it was generously permitted by the " conquerors to separate itself from the garrison, and to be " sent back to England."

One or two facts remain to be mentioned. It was during this campaign, at the affair at Boxtel, that the Duke of Wellington, then in command of the 33rd Regiment, first was under fire, and displayed the same coolness and intrepidity which afterwards characterised him. It was also during the concluding months of the war—after the resignation of the Stadtholder—that the singular military episode occurred—more singular even than that mentioned in the annals of the American War, when a fleet was defeated by a field battery—the capture of a fleet by a charge of cavalry. The Dutch fleet was lying ice-bound at the Helder—the harbour frozen over,—and was in this position captured by a body of Dragoons who had penetrated to that place in relentless pursuit of the French Royalist emigrants, who had fled thither for refuge. Vol. i. p. 372.

This chapter would hardly be complete without a short notice of an event which occurred at Toulon in 1793, and which deserves special mention, because then for the first time was the Royal Artillery brought face to face with a young French Artillery officer, who was destined to become famous, Napoleon Bonaparte. Toulon was held by the British on behalf of the royal family of France; and part of the force employed was a company of the Royal Artillery from Gibraltar, under Major Koehler, the Captain-Lieutenant of the company. Among his subalterns were Lieutenants Brady, Lemoine, John Duncan, Newhouse, and Alexander Duncan; and although in December the town had to be evacuated, this was not done until the greatest gallantry had been displayed by the British troops. The loss in the Artillery was very great; and the following order by General Dundas, dated on board the 'Victory' on the 21st December, 1793, speaks well as to their skill:—" Lieutenant-General " Dundas reports, that after a most gallant defence of Toulon, " he was under the necessity of evacuating it, from the very " great superiority of the enemy's army, and the report of " the Engineer and Artillery officers that it had become " untenable. After destroying the enemy's men-of-war and " stores in the Dockyard, the army embarked on board our " men-of-war. As the security of this operation depended " much on the protection afforded from the happy situation " of Fort La Malgere, which so effectually commands the " neck of the Peninsula, and the judicious use that should " be made of its artillery, this important service was allotted " to Major Koehler with 200 men, who, after seeing the last " man off the shore, and spiking all the guns, effected, from Browne. 'London Gazette,' 17 Jan. 1794.

"his activity and intelligence, his own retreat without loss. At Fort Mulgrave, Lieutenant Duncan of the Royal Artillery was so essentially useful that to his exertions and abilities that post was much indebted for its preservation for so long a time."

The officer last mentioned was Lieutenant John Duncan, who was promoted in the following year, and was mentioned as follows for his conduct at the capture of Bastia, in Corsica, the service in which the Toulon garrison was next engaged:—"I cannot but express in the strongest terms the meritorious conduct of Captain Duncan and Lieutenant Alexander Duncan of the Royal Artillery, and Lieutenant de Butts of the Royal Engineers; but my obligation is particularly great to Captain Duncan, as more zeal, ability, and judgment were never shown by any officer than were displayed by him, and I take the liberty of mentioning him as an officer highly entitled to His Majesty's notice." Lieutenant Alexander Duncan, who is also mentioned in this dispatch, afterwards commanded the Royal Artillery during the defence of Cadiz in 1810-12, at the battle of Barossa, and at Seville, at the last-mentioned of which places he was accidentally killed.

Admiral Lord Hood's Despatch, 'London Gazette,' 10 June, 1794.

During the service in Corsica, which resulted in its surrender by the French, the Royal Artillery did duty with Nelson's seamen,[1] and received great credit for their exertions at the capture of Bastia and Calvi. A fatal fever played havoc with the men; and it was found necessary to send an additional company from England, which absorbed the remnant of Major Koehler's. That officer was made Quartermaster-General to the forces in the island on its surrender to the English, and Major Collier was sent to command the Artillery with the title of Inspector of Artillery.

This garrison remained until the evacuation of the island by the English in 1796.

---

[1] In the year of Trafalgar, some artillerymen under Lieut. Robertson served on board the 'Victory' with Nelson, in the West Indies.

CHAP. III. *Old and New Systems of Fighting.* 69

Even thus early, and in spite of much inexperience on the part of their commanders, the French armies of the Revolution had evinced merits, zeal, and courage of no ordinary description. The new system of fighting had already defeated the old; and when organized, as it eventually was, by a master hand, Bonaparte, it was an engine before which the old system, with its pedantry, sluggish precision, and winter-quarters, was sure to go down like a house of cards. Happily for England, there were in her army in Flanders men like Wellington and Abercromby, who could see the faults of the school in which they had been trained, and at the same time not be ashamed to own the superiorities which might be possessed by an enemy,—men, in fine, who, while "conservative of glorious traditions, were fearless of " all necessary changes—endeavouring to catch the meaning " of present progress, or, with prophetic eye, reaching for- " ward to anticipate future developments." _{Major C. B. Brackenbury, R.A., at U.S. Institution.}

Without such men, the glorious stories of Egypt and the Peninsula would have been but repetitions of this futile war in Flanders.

CHAPTER IV.

1796 TO 1799.

THESE years represent a period in the history of England of which Englishmen must always be proud. Standing almost alone against the French Republic, before whose victorious armies almost every other nation in Europe succumbed, her Government and people never hesitated to protest, both by word and deed, against the unlawful ambition of the French Directorate. Blinding the French people to a sense of their hardships and their rapidly-increasing debt by the glare of military success, and attributing these same successes to the sudden development of martial spirit and liberty which followed the downfall of the monarchy, the selfish and dishonest leaders of the Republic were enabled not merely to encourage their own army, but to sow doubt and dissension in the ranks of their opponents. By flattering the people they ruled, they were enabled to sin against every rule of good government, and by creating discontent with existing authority among other nations, for which purpose they spared no labour nor expense, they brought France in 1798 to a pinnacle of greatness, to which it had never yet attained. England alone remained to defy them; and to conquer England, either by means of invasion, isolation, or by fomenting rebellion, was their fixed determination. The effect on England of suspended commerce and monetary uncertainty can be realised by the point at which the Three per Cents. stood during these years. In 1796 they fell to 66; in 1797, to $56\frac{1}{2}$; in 1798, the year of the Irish rebellion, they reached $49\frac{5}{8}$; and, after its suppression, they rose again to 55. In 1796 the Bank of England suspended payment;

Annual Registers.

and the discontent of the Navy was such as to render very probable the mutinies, which took place in the following year. The same dissatisfaction prevailed in the Army, although to a less extent; but open expression of it was prevented by the wisdom of the Duke of York in obtaining for the troops an increase of pay, and thus removing the grievance, which provoked the discontent among men, who could barely subsist on the miserable pittance that was allowed them. The Board of Ordnance made a similar increase in the pay of the two Corps under their control.; and it may be interesting to state the new rates allowed for the Artillery. The Master-General, Lord Cornwallis, prefaces his Warrant on the subject by reminding the Corps of their former good conduct and high character, to which he had often been a witness on the most arduous occasions, and to which he had often borne the most ample and honourable testimony, when he had had the honour of commanding them. He felt sure, he wrote, that it was not in the power of the most artful traitor to seduce the soldiers of the Royal Artillery from their loyalty and attachment to their King and country; and then he urged them never to prefer unreasonable requests, whose inevitable refusal might produce discontent,—but at the same time to rely upon his readiness to redress any real grievance. The improvement in the pay of the soldier may be briefly summarised from the lengthy verbiage of the Warrant. Up to 1797, in addition to the provision made for his clothing, pension, quarters, and medical assistance,—and also besides his allowance of beer, &c., provided in quarters, and of bread provided at a reduced rate when in camp,—the soldier received a daily sum of $9\frac{1}{2}d.$, besides a further daily sum of $2d.$, which under a previous Warrant had been given in lieu of certain allowances; but, under the new Warrant, an additional sum of $3\frac{3}{4}d.$ was granted, making the daily pay of the soldier $1s.\ 3\frac{1}{4}d.$ Out of this sum, however, the extra price of the bread and meat ration, which had hitherto been borne by the public, was now to be deducted; and, as this averaged $1\frac{3}{4}d.$, the net

B. O. Warrant, 27 May, 1797.

increase of pay was 2d. The pay of the various ranks after this Warrant stood as follows, viz. :—

	s.	d.		
Sergeant	2	2	per diem.	
Corporal	2	0¼	,,	
Bombardier	1	10¼	,,	
Gunner and Drummer	1	3¼	,,	each.

In the year 1873, the date of the publication of this volume, the rates of pay for the same ranks in the Corps are as follows, viz. :—

	s.	d.		
Sergeant	3	0	per diem.	
Corporal	2	4	,,	
Bombardier	2	2	,,	
Gunner	1	5¼	,,	each.

As in 1797 beer was allowed *in kind*, in addition to the daily pay, the one penny a day subsequently allowed in lieu of it has not been included in the pay of the various ranks in 1873, given above.

The increase of pay produced a feeling of contentment in the whole army; and if sedition had no chance of thriving in the Artillery before, much more had it none after. An unsuccessful attempt having been made at Woolwich in 1797 to stir up discontent among the men, we gather, from a General Order published shortly afterwards, that the non-commissioned officers and men subscribed a sum of money, which they offered as a reward for the detection of the offenders; and, further, signed voluntarily a paper declaring anew their loyalty to the King and fidelity to the country. This latter step—to modern eyes somewhat superfluous in *attested* soldiers—was doubtless called forth by certain insults to the King which had been published, and which called forth the indignation of the whole community; and also by the fact that certain soldiers serving in Ireland had been seduced from their colours by the rebels, who, under the name of United Irishmen, were traversing the whole country. The same feeling which prompted this action at Woolwich and West open. It was during this period that the great and abroad to Mr. Pitt's Loyalty Loan. It is recorded that the "officers and men of the Royal Artillery at Gibraltar, "Martinique, and St. Domingo, having, as tokens of their "love and attachment to their King and country, transmitted "to England subscriptions, as detailed underneath, the "Master-General thought it his duty to lay the same before "His Majesty, and to observe to His Majesty how rapidly the "spirit, which had so laudably shown itself in the Artillery "at home, had spread to the detachments abroad. His "Majesty, on receiving the information, was graciously "pleased to express his approbation, and to permit the "Master-General to communicate the same to the Regiment. "' The Master-General, Marquis Cornwallis, has the greatest "' satisfaction in obeying this His Majesty's command, and "' takes the opportunity of congratulating the Royal Regi- "' ment of Artillery on that zeal and alacrity which, in all "' services and in all climates and countries, have uniformly "' marked the character of the Corps.'"

Cleave-land's MSS.

B. O. 4 June, 1798.

"*Subscriptions from Gibraltar.*—Major-General Martin, "100*l.*; Field Officers and Captains, 30 days' pay each; "subalterns, 14 days' pay; non-commissioned officers and "gunners, 7 days' pay each.

"*From Martinique.*—Officers, 30 days' pay; non-commis- "sioned officers and gunners, 20 days' pay each.

"*From Cape Nicholas Mole.*—Officers and men, 10 days' "pay each."

This feeling of loyalty was general throughout the country, and was in no way affected either by temptation from without or vapouring sedition within; and to this loyal feeling, and the noble successes of her fleets, did England owe her continued maritime superiority and the salvation of her commerce. This latter had been steadily increasing; her imports and exports had risen from 27½ millions in 1784 to 49¼ millions in 1796; and, although checked and cramped by French legislation, her fleets kept the markets of the East and West open. It was during this period that the great

Annual Registers.

naval victories of Camperdown and the Nile were gained, and that Nelson's activity in the Mediterranean insured the capture of Malta and Minorca by England. Nor was any sea without the British flag. In 1799, there were in the Navy no less than 100,000 seamen, besides 20,000 marines; and both in the English seas and in the West Indies bomb-vessels, with artillerymen on board, were numerous. In the East Indies our armies were gaining renown; and in the West Indies hostilities were going on, in which the Royal Artillery took an active part, which resulted in the retention of all the English islands, and the capture from the French of St. Lucia, Martinique, St. Domingo, Trinidad, Guadaloupe, Tobago, and Curaçoa. The names of some of the officers of the Corps who were present during these operations are given by the author of 'England's Artillerymen.'[1] Consisting mainly of naval, or small detached military operations, the wars in the West Indies possess, as a rule, little but local interest. It may be mentioned, however, that they were much more fatal to our troops through the fevers and pestilence which prevailed, than the actual loss in battle.

The Board of Ordnance during this period did much good work in maturing the defences of the country, which were under its control. In 1797, the cost of the Ordnance was 1,643,056*l*.; in 1798, 1,303,580*l*.; in 1799, 1,570,827*l*.; and in 1800, 1,695,956*l*. In 1795 the Board completed the Fifth Battalion of the Regiment; and in 1799 the Sixth Battalion was added. From the very first the Sixth was a most efficient Battalion. It had as a nucleus the two companies known as the East India Detachment; and the remaining companies were composed of trained English and Scotch Militiamen, who were permitted to volunteer for service in the Regiment.

Annual Registers.

Vol. i. p. 405.

Vol. i. p. 410.

Communicated by Sir E. Perrott.

---

[1] Majors A. Du Vernet, S. D. Edwards, F. L. Deruvijnes, J. Smith; Captains J. Arbuthnot, J. Rogers, L. Newton, M. Pattison, Suckling, H. Deruvijnes; Lieutenants Mackenzie, Concannon, Brooke Young, Le Geyt, Pritchard, William Caddy, Stackpoole, Bingham, Baker, Robinson, Ommancy, Carterett, Worth, Arthur, Davers.

It will thus be seen that, during a critical time, the courage and determination of the people of England and their rulers saved the country from much national hardship and danger. But while thus facing a foreign enemy, another foe appeared in their midst. The student of this chapter in British history finds that it includes the story of the great Irish rebellion of 1798.

If ever the sins of the fathers have been visited on the children, it has happened in the case of England's connection with Ireland. The fathers ate sour grapes, and the children's teeth are set on edge. If we need a proof of the strength of history as a motive power, we cannot do better than go to Ireland. Here is a brave, a genial, a chivalrous race, shrewd and able in the affairs of life, and yet the mention of injustice done to their forefathers produces to this day such a feeling of indignation and resentment as blinds them to the fact that the descendants of those whose memory they detest are endeavouring, almost to the opposite extreme, to remove all tokens of former injustice. The history of Ireland, in its relations with England, repeats many familiar truths; it proves that national sins no more go unpunished than personal; it shows that rebellion without organisation is useless; and it tells most distinctly that reasonable demands have often been refused from want of judgment in the time and manner of urging them. It proves, also, most clearly, yet another point, for which no additional proof is required—that the passions of a people are the very best instrument with which unscrupulous men can work to obtain their own private ends; and that, by stirring these up, agitators can so blind men to the real goal which it is intended to reach, as actually to make them in time believe their own—possibly legitimate—purpose to be identical with that of their leaders, which, if presented to them in cold blood, would have made them shudder. He who doubts this needs only to study the class of men called the " United Irishmen," as they were when first organized, and as they became under

the manipulation of cunning leaders, and in the face of an
imprudent, unreasoning opposition. The Government of
England would have yielded much to the quiet reformers,
which they were bound to refuse to rebels; and it was this
knowledge that made the arch plotters fan discontent into
disturbance as quickly as possible, lest, with the satisfaction
of just demands and the removal of admitted grievances, the
discontent should disappear, and their own vocation
with it.

The story of the rebellion in Ireland in 1798 is a sorry
one; but it has its place in this history because, at some of
the more important engagements between the troops and
the rebels, such as those known as the battles of Ross,
Wexford, and Vinegar Hill, that portion of the Regiment
which had so recently been created—the Royal Horse
Artillery—was present. Two guns of A, B, and C Troops
respectively were present on these occasions. With the
exception of these, and some Battalion gun detachments, the
Artillerymen engaged during the rebellion in Ireland belonged to the national Corps—the old Irish Artillery—
whose loyalty shone undimmed during that trying time.

Although the story of the rebellion itself needs not to be
told here, certain facts connected with the Artillery arrangements will probably be found interesting.

From July 1795, care had been taken to impart some
knowledge of Artillery drills to the Infantry regiments in
Ireland, the custodians of the battalion guns being required
to instruct in each regiment at least 30 rank and file,
under a subaltern and two sergeants. At this date the
battalion guns were not *brigaded* on field-days, as was
afterwards done; but always marched past at the head of
the regiments to which they were attached. The ammunition waggons *followed* the column.

On the 20th February, 1797, battalion guns were issued
to the following regiments of Militia, viz., Donegal, Clare,
Limerick City, Antrim, Kilkenny, North Mayo, Queen's
County, and Armagh; and one " useful, well-instructed "

Marginal notes:
Now A Battery, A Brigade;
B Battery, A Brigade, and
C Battery, A Brigade.

G. O., 7 July, 1795.

General Regulations for the march of the army in Ireland, 12 Nov. 1796.

gunner from the Irish Artillery accompanied each pair of guns, which were "to be worked by soldiers of the regiments." This had been approved by the Lord-Lieutenant on the 13th February, and orders had been given for the immediate instruction in Artillery duties of over 300 Militiamen. This confidence in the loyalty of the Irish troops shows that the rebellion had but little real hold in the country, except among those with whom it will ever find a welcome, the ignorant and fanatic.

G. O., 20 Feb. 1797.

It had always been a dream of France to annex Ireland, or, failing that, to secure its independence; and the time seemed favourable for the purpose. But, owing to circumstances too long to be narrated here, the practical assistance afforded by the French was almost nothing; and the rebellion, although encouraged by French promises, received in the end but little of French performance. It would really seem, after dispassionate study, that the rebellion, in the absence of the excited opposition of the Orangemen, would never have occurred; that the removal of the disabilities of the Catholics would at first have completely gratified those who, after a time, would accept nothing but national independence; and that such removal would in all probability have been granted, had not the moderate reformers among the United Irishmen unfortunately accepted the leadership of men like Wolfe Tone and others, about whose extreme and impossible views there was no doubt whatever. The feeling of discontent was also increased by the intemperate language of the priests, who, in the heated expressions of their opponents, detected a possible future for their Church, even more gloomy than its existing state; but this last-named reason had less to do with the birth of the rebellion than the causes already stated. To panic-stricken, and therefore cruel, opposition on the part of the Protestants, and to the association of injudicious leaders with their cause, is the fact due that men, whose claims have been admitted by subsequent legislation to be just, landed in 1798 in a most unfortunate rebellion.

In even the most solemn matters there is often an element of the ludicrous; and one who is acquainted with the national character would not be surprised to find such in an Irish rebellion. The guns which were given to the Irish Militia were not at first horsed; and very great difficulty was experienced in procuring horses for the purpose. The loyal Colonel of the Tipperary Militia, Colonel Bagwell, offered to lend his own horses for the purpose, and his offer was readily accepted. A letter was then sent to the commanding officers of other Militia Regiments, inviting them to follow Colonel Bagwell's example, and offering, on the part of the Ordnance, to pay for the horses' forage, &c., during the time they should be employed. With very few exceptions the invitation was declined, and a further perusal of the official documents suggests a very natural reason for what would at first sight seem somewhat ungracious, if not disloyal. On the 27th February, 1798, a letter was addressed to the officers commanding the various districts in Ireland, pointing out that it had reached the ears of the Commander-in-Chief "that the limbers of the guns attached to bat-" talions are used for market cars, and other conveniences " for the officers and women of the regiments, and that the " horses are ridden by officers and their servants about the " country at all hours." The knowledge of this by the officers commanding the regiments would naturally make them reluctant to expose their own horses to such treatment; and a result of these irregularities was the change which took place from *battalion guns* to *brigades*, already described. It may be here stated that a considerable number of the men of the Irish Artillery were employed in gun-boats in the Shannon and elsewhere during the rebellion.

[margin: Dated "Royal Hospital," 25 Feb. 1797.]

[margin: Vol. i. p. 185, 'Royal Irish Artillery.']

The detachments of the Royal Artillery, which were present with the battalion guns attached to the regiments from England, were six in number, each detachment consisting of 1 non-commissioned officer and 9 men. The whole were under the command of Captain Henry Geary, assisted by three subalterns. The regiments to which they were attached were the Guards (three Battalions), the Queen's, 29th, and 100th Regiments. A reinforcement of two companies was asked for by General Lake, but the successes at Wexford rendered it unnecessary to meet his demand.

At this time, H.R.H. the Duke of York ordered two 12-pounder guns to be attached to each troop of Horse Artillery, and, as will be seen hereafter, these guns remained part of the armament of the troop of Horse Artillery which formed part of the expedition to the Helder, in 1799. Two guns, from four troops respectively, went to Ireland to assist in quelling the rebellion, but only those belonging to A, B, and C Troops took part in the active operations. The strength of the Horse Artillery sent to Ireland was as follows:— D. A. General to Lord Cornwallis, 28 June, 1798.

2 Captains.	2 Staff-Sergeants.	Embarkation Returns, dated Woolwich, 26 Nov. 1797.
3 Subalterns.	12 Non-Commissioned Officers.	
1 Assistant-Surgeon.	92 Gunners.	
	51 Drivers.	
	6 Artificers.	
	1 Trumpeter.	
177 horses (and 13 from Driver Corps).		
8 guns.		
15 ammunition waggons.		
N.B.—The guns were two 12-pounders, two 5½-inch howitzers, four 6-pounders.		

The total strength of Horse Artillery left in England was as follows: 968 of all ranks, 920 horses, 42 guns, and 72 waggons.

This included a reserve of 5 guns at Woolwich.

After the rebellion had been quelled, the men of the Royal Artillery, who during the operations had been under the Irish Branch of the Ordnance, returned to England; and the following table gives the distribution and strength of the Royal Irish Artillery in the succeeding year. (*See* pp. 80 and 81.)

Returning to England, the student will find not a few matters of domestic interest which occurred during this period, and which are worthy of being chronicled. A new organisation of the Ordnance Medical Department took place; and on a recommendation of a committee it was

Distribution of the Royal Irish Regiment of Artillery, October 1799.

Brigades	Station	Lieut.-Colonels	Majors	Captains	Capt.-Lieutenants	1st Lieutenants	2nd Lieutenants	Staff Sergeants	Sergeants	Corporals	Bombardiers	Drummers	Gunners	Total
East	Two at Island Bridge	1	.	.	2	2	1	1	3	3	4	2	80	99
	One Naas	.	.	1	.	2	.	.	1	.	3	.	32	38
	One Arklow	.	.	1	.	1	.	.	2	.	2	.	29	35
	One Wexford	.	.	.	.	1	.	.	.	1	1	.	22	26
North	Two Charlemont	.	1	.	.	.	3	.	2	3	5	.	73	88
	One Belfast	.	.	1	.	1	.	.	1	1	2	1	36	42
	One Omagh	.	.	.	1	1	.	.	.	2	2	.	32	38
	One Strabane	.	.	.	.	2	.	.	.	4	.	.	32	38
	One Coleraine	.	.	1	1	1	.	.	.	1	2	.	32	38
	One Dundalk	.	1	.	.	1	2	.	.	2	2	.	32	38
	One Enniskillen	.	.	.	.	.	.	.	1	.	3	.	32	39
South	One Clonmel	.	1	1	1	.	1	.	1	1	4	.	50	61
	Two Cork	1	.	1	1	2	.	1	2	5	3	1	80	97
	One Bandon	.	.	.	1	1	.	.	.	.	1	.	32	37
	One Limerick	.	.	1	.	1	.	.	1	1	1	1	32	38
	One Tarbert	.	.	.	1	1	.	.	.	1	2	.	32	37
	One Waterford	.	.	.	.	1	1	.	.	2	1	.	29	35
	One Kilkenny	.	.	.	.	1	.	.	1	2	.	.	31	37
West	Two Athlone	1	.	1	.	1	1	1	1	4	4	.	81	95
	One Galway	.	.	1	.	1	.	.	1	2	1	1	32	39
	One Carrick-on-Shannon	.	.	.	1	1	.	.	.	1	.	.	18	21
	One Castle-bar	.	.	.	.	1	.	.	.	.	2	.	16	19

CHAP. IV.   *Royal Irish Artillery.*   81

Batteries										Five Companies in West Indies						Invalid Company										Joined lately from West Indies, and not included in any of above numbers
Charlemont	Carrickfergus	Cromie Head	Tanitt	Cork Harbour	Charles Fort	Duncannon	Bantry	Tarbert	Total	Present	Sick, leave, &c.	To return to Ireland	Under orders to proceed from Ireland	Wanting	Total	On command Duncannon	On command Charlemont	Sick—absent	Employed in the Line	Serving in the Militia	At the Powder-mills	Totally unfit for any duty	In and about Head-quarters	Wanting to complete	Total	
13	9	12	10	92	15	11	21	14	1,232	399	5	1	.	4	501	12	5	1	.	1	2	2	22	7	53	19
12	7	10	9	78	12	9	16	13	1,031	340	.	.	.	75	415	10	4	.	.	1	2	22	4	.	43	11
.	.	.	.	2	.	.	.	.	8	9	.	.	.	1	10	.	.	.	.	.	.	1	.	.	1	1
1	1	1	.	2	.	.	1	.	53	15	.	.	.	5	20	1	.	.	1	.	.	1	.	.	3	2
.	1	1	7	2	.	2	.	.	49	17	.	.	.	3	20	.	1	.	.	.	.	1	.	.	2	1
.	1	.	.	1	.	1	1	1	25	4	.	.	.	6	10	1	.	.	.	.	.	.	.	.	1	4
.	.	.	.	.	.	.	.	.	2	.	.	.	.	.	.	.	.	.	.	.	.	.	.	.	.	.
.	.	.	.	.	.	.	.	.	9	.	.	.	3	2	5	.	.	.	.	.	.	1	.	.	1	.
.	.	.	.	1	1	1	.	.	26	7	2	.	1	.	10	.	.	.	1	.	.	.	.	.	1	.
.	.	.	.	.	.	.	1	.	10	5	1	1	.	.	7	.	.	.	.	.	.	.	.	.	.	.
.	.	.	.	.	1	.	.	.	11	2	2	.	.	.	4	.	.	1	.	.	.	.	.	.	1	.
.	.	.	.	.	.	.	.	.	2	.	.	.	.	.	.	.	.	.	.	.	.	.	.	.	.	.
.	.	.	.	.	.	.	.	.	4	.	.	.	.	.	.	.	.	.	.	.	.	.	.	.	.	.

N.B. The Headquarters of the Regiment were at Chapelizod.

VOL. II.   G

B. O. Proceedings, 5 May, 1797.

Cleaveland's MSS. Letters from D. A. G. Confirmed by J. C. Woollacott, Esq.

MS. by Sir W. Robe, in R. A. Record Office.

resolved, on the 5th May, 1797, that, after the 1st July following, the system of obliging surgeons to furnish the medicines for the troops out of a fixed money allowance should cease, and that one of the Ordnance chemists should be appointed Regimental apothecary. An increase of pay was also granted to the medical officers.

A change was also made in the Paymasters of the Regiment. It will be remembered that Mr. Cox had been appointed Paymaster to the Artillery in 1759. He was succeeded in 1783 by Mr. Adair, who was followed by Messrs. Meyrick. On the 1st July, 1797, the Paymastership was resumed by Messrs. Cox and Greenwood, and continued in that house (subsequently Messrs. Cox and Co.) until abolished on the 30th September, 1858, since which date they have been agents to the Corps.

In 1797 the first Regimental School was established at Woolwich for soldiers' children. On the 13th August, Captain—afterwards Sir William—Robe recommended its formation; and was strongly supported by the Commandant, General Lloyd. A building, then unfinished, and now part of the Horse Artillery Square in Woolwich Barracks, was procured for the purpose; the Duchess of York subscribed 20 guineas for the purchase of books, and this was followed by subscriptions from all the officers at Head-quarters. A sergeant, named Dougherty, was appointed Schoolmaster; and the success of the institution was so great as to induce the Board of Ordnance to undertake its management and support. The first pupil was a difficult, but very creditable subject. He was the son of a gunner in the Invalid Battalion, who lost both his arms when firing the evening gun at an out-station for his father. So remarkable was his progress at school, that it attracted the attention of the military authorities; and this, taken in conjunction with the way in which he had received his injury, obtained for him from the Board a pension for life as a drummer,—although he had never been enlisted as such.

There were a great many officers and men employed in the Bomb service during this time; and as no stoppages were

CHAP. IV.   *Artillery Officers on the Staff.*   83

made for rations while the men were employed on board the vessels, the service was a very popular one. Most of the Bomb vessels were employed in the English Channel, the Mediterranean, and among the West India Islands.   <small>Ordnance Letter-books, 20 Sept. 1797.</small>

The employment of Artillery officers on the Staff of the Army became more common than it had hitherto been; but, with great short-sightedness, it was discouraged by the Board. It was, indeed, too often made a great favour on the part of the Master-General to allow officers to be so employed. Among the names of officers who can be traced as having received the requisite permission are Major James M. Haddon, R.H.A., who was appointed Adjutant-General in Portugal, with the rank of Lieutenant-Colonel, vice Sir J. Erskine, who resigned; Lieutenant-Colonel Koehler, who was selected as Quartermaster-General in the Eastern District; and Captain Duncan, who was employed on the personal staff of H.R.H. the Duke of York. The nucleus of an appointment, which to this day has more of a Regimental than an Army nature, dates from this period. On 9th June, 1797, Lieutenant A. T. Spearman was appointed Garrison Adjutant in Woolwich. On 7th July, 1802, the title of this office was changed to Brigade-Major, the same officer continuing to hold it; and on 1st April, 1873, the title was again altered, the incumbent, Major A. T. G. Pearse, being styled Assistant Adjutant-General of the Woolwich District.   <small>D. A. Gen.'s Correspondence, and Kane's List.</small>

The Director-General of Artillery during the period treated of in this chapter was Major-General Duncan Drummond; the Commandants were, successively, Generals Farrington, Congreve, and Lloyd; and General Blomefield was Inspector of Artillery. In 1797 the Committee of Field Officers, which met periodically to consider warlike inventions, received a more permanent form than hitherto, foreshadowing the Ordnance Select Committee which subsequently came into existence,—Captain Maclean being, on the 26th February, appointed a standing Secretary to the Committee.

On the 25th December, 1798, certain augmentations in the pensions of widows of officers in the Army were granted;

G 2

and the Board of Ordnance, as was invariably the case—for in such matters the Artillery and Engineers had no cause for complaint—followed suit. It was decided that widows of officers in the Royal Artillery and Corps of Captain-Commissaries (or Driver Corps) should receive pensions at the following rates:—

<small>B. O. Letter, 13 Jan. 1799.</small>

	£
Widow of Colonel, or Colonel Commandant	80 per annum.
,, Lieutenant-Colonel.	50 ,,
,, Major	40 ,,
Widow of Captain and Captain-Lieutenant	30 ,,
,, First Lieutenant	26 ,,
,, Second Lieutenant	20 ,,
,, Chaplain	20 ,,
,, Surgeon-General	30 ,,
,, Surgeon	26 ,,
,, Assistant-Surgeon	20 ,,
,, Captain-Commissary	30 ,,
,, Lieutenant-Commissary	26 ,,
,, Quartermaster	20 ,,

These rates, as is well known, have been increased since the Warrant of 1799, although still so inadequate as to render Regimental Provident Funds a necessity; but the reader can hardly fail to be struck with the disadvantage under which the widows of non-combatant officers laboured in old times,—a disadvantage which disappeared with the introduction into the Service of what is known as *relative rank*—an arrangement which enabled non-combatant officers to acquire by length of service the same privileges as fell to the lot of their combatant brethren.

A few statistics may be appended here, as very few domestic chapters will be given between 1799 and the date at which this work comes to an end. The strength of the Regiment, at the commencement of the period embraced by this chapter, was as follows:—

<small>Return rendered to H.R.H. the Duke of York, 26 Nov. 1795.</small>

Royal Horse Artillery	1,085 of all ranks.
Marching Battalions	5,560 ,,
Invalid Battalion	505 ,,
Corps of Captain-Commissaries	1,466 ,,
Total	8,616

CHAP. IV.   *Commendation for Loyalty.*   85

These were distributed as follows :—

    6 Troops of Horse Artillery.
    52 Companies of Artillery.
    5 Companies of Driver Corps, or Captain-Commissaries.
    11 Companies of Invalids.
    1 Company of Gentlemen Cadets.

The geographical distribution of the Regiment, as far as the *combatant* companies were concerned, was as follows,— the year 1797 being selected as a year of comparative peace, *between* the two Continental Expeditions under the Duke of York :— {Kane's List.}

On Home Stations	29 Troops and Companies.
In Portugal	1 Company.
In Canada	4 Companies.
At Cape of Good Hope	2 Companies.
At Gibraltar	5 Companies.
In East Indies	2 Companies (belonging to no Battalions).
In Jamaica	4 Companies.
In Newfoundland	1 Company.
In Nova Scotia and Cape Breton	2 Companies.
In the West Indies (exclusive of Jamaica)	8 Companies.

Of these companies, as has already been stated, many men were employed on board the bomb-vessels. The companies stationed at the Cape of Good Hope deserve special notice at this time, as also subsequently did those at Gibraltar, for their loyalty at a time of mutiny among the other forces on the station. On the 4th February, 1798, the following letter was published to the Regiment by Colonel Macleod, having been transmitted to him by order of Major-General Dundas, commanding the troops at the Cape of Good Hope, who had in the first instance addressed it to Lieutenant-Colonel Yorke, who commanded the Royal Artillery on that station :— {D. A. General, R.A., 4 Feb. 1798, and Colonel Cleaveland's MS. Notes.}

                      "Castle of Good Hope,
                          "15 November, 1797.
" SIR,
      " The Corps of Artillery having had the greatest part
" of the extraordinary duty which the late disturbances on
" board the fleet have occasioned, as their alacrity in dis-

"charging their duty was no less conspicuous than on former occasions, when the Artillery have been called upon to act, I am directed by Major-General Dundas to express his entire approbation of their conduct,—honourable to themselves and to the Service.

"I have, &c.,
(Signed) "P. ABERCROMBIE,
"Major of Brigade."

Commendation of loyal conduct in time of civil disturbance is as noble a record to hoard in the story of a regiment as the chronicle of valour in the field. Military discipline is indeed a miserable weapon, if it is not found true in time of national discontent, as well as in the hour of national danger. The great lesson for a soldier to learn is obedience; and if that obedience is to be conditional on the soldier's inclination, then the nation which trains an armed force is but cherishing a possible enemy. The lesson of silent obedience is becoming every day more difficult to learn; discipline in civil life is rarer than it was, and impatience of control is almost a popular cry. What a noble mission, then, an army may follow in time of peace! To show that men with skill and power, and with a consciousness of these qualities, can yet subordinate themselves for the good of the commonwealth, instead of the individual, is surely a grand object for an army's purpose. And in the daily life of such a force a nation might read a lesson, which, if taught from the mouths of rulers or the pulpits of preachers, would fall on deaf, because doubting ears; for a suspicion dogs the heels of the mere speaker, which vanishes before the open and consistent life of the actor.

Yet a few more statistics before the chapter closes. It has been necessary to talk with disparagement of the field brigades, as distinguished from the troops of Horse Artillery in the conclusion of the last century. But if the quality of the Field Artillery was indifferent, its quantity would have satisfied an alarmist. On the 19th February, 1798, there were, in England alone, 126 battalion 6-pounder guns, besides brigades and parks of artillery, consisting of 29 12-pounders, 36 long 6-pounders, and 28 5½-inch howitzers. These were distributed in Newcastle, Hull, Woodbridge, Colchester, Warley, Canterbury, Dover, Lewes, Plymouth, and St. Austell; and there was a further reserve at Woolwich of 12 12-pounders, 30 long 6-pounders, 3 8-inch howitzers, 12 5½-inch howitzers, and 30 light 6-pounders. *the Duke of York.*

This seems a formidable force on paper, and it doubtless soothed many a terrified alarmist, and silenced many an honourable member on the Opposition benches. But, alas! both these desirable ends may often be attained by an official return, and yet the evil may not be removed. Had the House demanded that the means of locomotion for this powerful force of artillery should be produced, it is to be feared that the men would have been scarce and the horses scarcer. And yet the official return had its value. The authorities concerned always managed—it may be at great expense—to produce the necessary armament at the eleventh hour; and the balance was merely so much dust thrown in the eyes of honourable members, as a sort of Parliamentary tribute.

Official returns may be misleading, and yet the units of the force to which they relate may be worthy of all praise. Rising from the contemplation of faded pages, and the analysis of the Regimental correspondence between 1796 and 1799, the chronicler feels that there were in the Corps at that time men whose hearts were so engrossed in their work, even in this time of sad rebellion, of national depression, of uninteresting warfare, that they could truly say, with the poet who was to come in later years—and with no exaggeration, but merely in a simple expression of what was uppermost in their daily thoughts—

"I rather dread the loss of use, than fame."

CHAPTER V.

THE CHRISTENING OF THE CHESTNUT TROOP.

THE course of our narrative brings us again to the Continent of Europe. In the year 1798, an expedition was ordered from England, with a view to the destruction of the basin, gates, and sluices of the Bruges Canal, and the consequent injury to the internal navigation between Holland, Flanders, and France. The prevention of a meditated invasion of England by the French would, it was hoped, by this means also be ensured. The naval part of the expedition was under the control of Captain Home Popham, while the military force was commanded by General Sir Eyre Coote. Eight companies of the Guards, the 11th Regiment, and the flank companies of the 23rd and 49th Regiments, D.A. Gen.'s constituted the Infantry employed; and the Artillery consisted of two companies attached to a battery of four 6-pounders and three light howitzers. The Artillery officers were Captain W. H. Walker (in command), Captain—afterwards Sir Wiltshire—Wilson, Captain C. Godfrey, Lieutenants Simpson, Hughes, Ilbert, and Holcroft. The guns were carried in different vessels, and landed near Ostend. On the 19th May, at daybreak, the troops disembarked, and commenced destroying the works. In a few hours they undid the labour of five years, besides burning a number of transports, which had been collected for the conveyance of French regiments to England; but this was not effected without considerable loss. When, however, the English force attempted to re-embark, it was found to be impossible, owing to the high wind which prevailed and the heavy sea. It was therefore found necessary, after going through the empty form of summoning the citadel, to encamp for the night on the sands. The English were attacked at daybreak by the

CHAP. V.   *Expedition to the Helder.*   89

enemy in overwhelming numbers; and after a severe action, in which Sir Eyre Coote was wounded, the whole force was compelled to surrender. The conduct of the Artillery was worthy of their comrades in the battle; and their commander, Captain Walker, received wounds from which he died. Of the rest the following official mention was made:—
"Captains Wilson and Godfrey, and Lieutenants Simpson, "Hughes, and Holcroft, all of the same distinguished Corps, "after having done everything men could do, spiked their "guns and threw them over the banks at the moment the "enemy was possessing himself of them. The latter gentle- "man, Lieutenant Holcroft, when all his men were wounded "except one, remained at his gun, doing duty with it to the "best of his ability." From subsequent official correspondence we learn that the following officers were permitted, with their soldier-servants, to return to England on parole, viz., Captain Wilson, Lieutenants Simpson, Hughes, and Holcroft, Captain Godfrey remaining at Lille with the men. From a plaintive letter to the Deputy-Adjutant-General, written by the last-named officer, it would appear that the prisoners were in a very sorry plight; for he implored an advance of pay for all, as they "wanted almost everything sorely."   'London Gazette,' 21 July, 1798.

D. A. Gen., R.A., to Lieut.-Gen. of the Ordnance, 14 Nov. 1798.

Next year an expedition on a larger scale took place, although not much more fortunate. It has an especial interest to the Artilleryman, as being the first expedition in which a general officer of Artillery was considered necessary with the force, on account of the large proportion present belonging to that arm. General Pattison, who had held a command in America, did so as an *Army*, not as an *Artillery* General; and General Phillips, who also commanded in that war, was merely a regimental field officer, with army rank as General. The expedition to the Helder, in 1799, had a contingent of Artillery, consisting of one troop of Horse Artillery, and eight companies of Marching Artillery, as they were termed. The troop was A, or the Chestnut Troop, commanded by Major Judgson; and although part of it had taken a share in the suppression of the Irish rebellion, this was the first occasion on which any portion of the Royal Horse Artillery proceeded on *foreign* active service; and, as will appear, the troop had rather a rough *baptême de feu.* General Farrington was selected for the command of Artillery, receiving the following letter from the Deputy Adjutant-General, on the 8th August, 1799 :—" In " conversation yesterday with Lord Howe, he observed that " if the expedition now embarked was to be followed by " the troops and Artillery ordered to be in preparation, he " should consider it necessary for them to be accompanied " by not only an Artillery officer of experience and abilities, " but by one high in rank in the Corps ; and under that " idea I was desired to address myself to you, to know if " your health would admit of his proposing you to the " Commander-in-Chief for the command of the whole. . . ." The offer was eagerly accepted by the General, and his appointment was confirmed. He selected Captain—afterwards Sir William—Robe as his Brigade-Major, and Captain Maclean as his Aide-de-Camp.

The expedition was in two divisions : the first, under Sir Ralph Abercromby, going from Southampton, while the second, and main division, was being assembled in Kent. When united, the command-in-chief was to be assumed by the Duke of York. Sir R. Abercromby applied for Lieut.-Colonel—afterwards Sir Francis—Whitworth to command the Artillery of his division, and his request was complied with. The following was the strength of General Abercromby's Artillery, viz. : 1 field officer, 6 captains, 13 subalterns, 2 surgeons, 40 non-commissioned officers, 371 gunners, and 6 drummers. There were also present with him, belonging to the Driver Corps, 1 subaltern, 3 quartermaster commissaries, 15 non-commissioned officers, 152 drivers, 5 artificers, and 200 horses.

The main Artillery force, under General Farrington, which followed that just given, was of considerable strength, including, besides Major Judgson's Troop, Lieut.-Colonels Smith and Trotter, 9 captains, 14 subalterns, 1 surgeon, 43 non-commissioned officers, 412 gunners, and 8 drummers, besides a detachment of the Driver Corps, consisting of

CHAP. V.   *Expedition to the Helder.*   91

1 captain, 4 quartermaster-commissaries, 12 non-commissioned officers, 166 drivers, 9 artificers, and 400 horses. The strength of Major Judgson's Troop was as follows: 2 captains, 3 subalterns, 1 surgeon, 16 non-commissioned officers, 97 gunners, 58 drivers, 7 artificers, and 1 trumpeter; making a total of 185, besides 191 horses.[1] A second troop of Horse Artillery* was put under orders, but did not embark; and of

* Captain Scott's Troop, now A Battery, B Brigade.

[1] The detail of the Chestnut Troop, as it actually embarked, *exclusive of officers, officers' horses, and the attached men from the Driver Corps, included above,* was as follows :—

STATE of a TROOP of HORSE ARTILLERY as they embarked for HOLLAND in 1799.

						Gunners.				Horses.		
		Staff-Sergeants.	Sergeants.	Corporals.	Bombardiers.	Mounted.	Dismounted.	Drivers.	Artificers and Trumpeters.	Riding.	Draught.	Total.
4	Two 12-pounders and two ammunition waggons . . .	..	1	1	2	12	8	10	..	16	20	36
4	Two Royal howitzers and two ammunition waggons . .	..	1	1	2	12	8	8	..	16	16	32
6	Three 6-pounders and three ammunition waggons . .	..	1	1	2	20	12	12	..	24	24	48
1	One field-officer's waggon .	..	..	..	..	..	..	2	..	..	4	4
4	Four tilted baggage waggons	..	..	..	..	..	..	8	..	..	16	16
2	Two forges	..	..	..	..	..	..	4	..	..	8	8
	Staff-serjeants	2	..	..	..	..	..	..	..	2	..	2
	Artificers and trumpeters, as per margin*	..	..	..	..	..	..	..	8	6	..	6
	Officers' servants	..	..	..	..	..	6	1	..	..	..	..
3	Spare limbers, with ammunition	..	..	..	..	..	..	3	..	..	6	6
	Number required	2	3	3	6	44	34	48	8	64	94	158
	Spare	..	..	..	..	4	4	6	..	6	10	16
24	Total of one troop . .	2	3	3	6	48	38	54	8	70	104	174

* N.B. Artificers and trumpeters for seven guns :—3 farriers—2 mounted, 1 dismounted. 1 carriage smith mounted. 2 collar-makers, 1 mounted, 1 dismounted. 1 wheeler mounted. 1 trumpeter mounted.

a further detachment of the Driver Corps, which was held in readiness, consisting of 226 men and 400 horses, about one-half ultimately went, if not more.

The whole Artillery force which it was at first intended should be sent—including the Driver-Corps auxiliaries—amounted to 1857 officers and men and 1344 horses; and of this number certainly 1600 men and 1000 horses accompanied the expedition. Among the names of officers not yet mentioned, who accompanied the Army to the Helder, the letters of the period include the following: Brevet Lieut.-Colonel Terrot, Major Lewis, Captain Mudge, Captain—afterwards Sir Augustus—Frazer, Captain Riou, Captain Nicholls, Captain Ramsey, Captain-Lieutenant Geary, Lieutenant Knox, Lieutenant Morrison, and Assistant-Surgeon Jameson. From other sources we learn that two officers, who subsequently attained great distinction in the Corps, were also present—Sir E. C. Whinyates and Sir John Michell—both officers being then 2nd Lieutenants. Lieutenants Simpson and Eligée are also known to have been present, from the fact that both were among the wounded in the actions which took place. The reason why uncertainty prevails as to the regimental details of the Artillery force on this expedition will appear at the end of this chapter.

<small>Memoir of Sir E. C. Whinyates. Kane's List. Browne's 'England's Artillery-men.'</small>

It will be readily understood that so large a force was not collected without difficulty. But of the extent of the labour involved no one can adequately judge who has not had access to the official letter-books of the time. The expedition to the Helder proved at once the necessity of a head-quarters staff for the Royal Artillery, and the capacity of the man who had been selected as the first Deputy-Adjutant-General of the Corps. The later campaigns, in whose organization Sir John Macleod had so large a share, were undoubtedly on a grander scale; but it is questionable whether his zeal, tact, and activity were ever so prominent, as in the arrangements for this unfortunate expedition to Holland. He did everything, and made a point of knowing everything, himself: he gave himself no rest until he had accomplished his purpose; nor yet did the amount of his official labours interfere with the courtesy to all ranks for which he was so remarkable. A private letter of friendly notice always preceded the order for movement, where such intimation could be given without detriment to the Service; no unnecessary mystery attended his actions: he was almost laboriously anxious to meet the convenience of all concerned, and evinced in his letters a sympathy, such as he could not have surpassed in his dealings with his own relations. His correspondence with the various commanding officers, from under whose control he had to steal detachments to bring the companies for service up to their required strength, is a masterpiece. Never for one moment leaving the line of action which necessity and the Board had imposed on him, he yet seemed to consult and defer to the Generals whose divisions he was weakening, and to obtain by their consent what he really was taking by force. If ever a wrong system, such as the old dual government of the Artillery was, could be made less detestable, it was made so by Colonel Macleod's tact and courtesy. And it is better that the deformities of a military system should be laid bare in time of *peace*, than on the eve of *war*, when the almost inevitable confusion cannot afford to be increased by ill-timed revelations. An indifferent machine well-worked is better than an admirable one whose powers are paralysed by some temporary, but thorough disarrangement. It is not when breakers are ahead, that men speculate on the beauties of their engines: it is *then* that—be they what they may— they are expected to work to the utmost of their power. In the hands of Colonel Macleod the evils of a wrong system were reduced to a *minimum*: but the system was a wrong one still.

His exertions to perfect the force which he had to organize were as admirable as were his endeavours to remove all possible friction. There have been times in our military history when the great wheel of progress and success has—after much creaking—been set in motion by the untiring exertions of unexpected leaders, or uncomplaining heroism in the ranks, instead of the labours of those on whom the organization of the armies depended. And at such times of unexpected fortune, it has generally been found that the official flies have buzzed most loudly around the revolving wheel, as if they had been the motive power. Not so with Colonel Macleod in 1799. Nothing was beneath his notice; no exertion was spared by him which could ensure the perfection, as well as the harmony, of the machine. The same pages which reveal his consideration for individuals show also his determination to render the Artillery part of the expedition unrivalled: and the difficulties in his way were very great. In the single item of horses, he found an obstacle which seemed likely to be insurmountable; for the horses did not exist in the service, and could hardly be bought. Such animals as were procured by scouring the country were in so wretched a condition that they could barely crawl in harness. So important was every day of decent rations to the sorry brutes, that to every party marching to the port of embarkation—Ramsgate—Colonel Macleod sent orders to shorten the marches, and to delay going on board as long as possible—and at all hazards, "except," he wrote, "that of allowing it to be said, 'We are waiting for the Ordnance.'"

D. A. Gen.'s Correspondence.

Among other evils was the monotonous cry from distant colonies—not only heard in 1799, nor by one Deputy Adjutant-General—of "More men from England!" Every place was drained of every available man; even the old gunners at the Tower were drafted away, and raw recruits sent in their place: but the colonial wants were not satisfied. Militia regiments, which were embodied, were also sending daily petitions for battalion guns, followed by remonstrances and strongly-worded indignation. And Colonel Macleod, in spite of his personal opinions, was obliged to strain every nerve to meet a wish, which was still supported by our military system. His *personal* opinions, it has been said,—and truly: for the correspondence of the period reveals the fact that Colonel Macleod had commenced to detest the existing system of battalion guns. He dared not say openly what he thought; but from a private letter written at this time his opinion may be easily learnt. Writing of some detachments which had been collected under an officer's command,

he said : " I believe they are intended for the battalion guns Letter to
" of the Infantry Brigades, and I had some thoughts of Colonel—afterwards
" drawing them to Chatham, where I would have them Sir John—Smith.
" drilled to the duty expected of them—appointing 1 non-
" commissioned officer and 7 gunners to each 6-pounder, and
" accustoming them to make use of a horse to advance,
" *instead of drag-rope men*—a custom which weakens the
" battalions they are attached to without aiding the services
" of the Artillery. For, between you and I, six men are *too
" few to drag guns*, and *too many to stand with ropes in their
" hands to be shot at.*"

An incident, which occurred at this time, shows that the system of drawing lots was not confined to choice of stations or barracks at home. In a letter to the commanding officer at Newcastle—Colonel Lawson—Colonel Macleod, in calling for one of the companies under his command for service in the expedition, requested him to assemble the Captains, and make them draw lots for the duty.

It was in August 1799 that the force sailed from England; and the student, who has realised the labours of Colonel Macleod, will also be able to conceive the feelings of relief with which he despatched, at 3 A.M. on a day at the beginning of that month, a mounted orderly, to carry the intelligence from Woolwich to the Duke of York at Deal, that the last man and horse of the Artillery had embarked. It will now be necessary to follow the expedition, merely remarking here that the casualties, which speedily occurred, rendered a fresh supply of ammunition and horses necessary before many weeks had passed, and that consequently Colonel Macleod had but a brief respite from his toil.

The expedition to the Helder was intended to effect two things—the capture of the Dutch fleet, which in the hands of the French was an unmistakable danger to England, and a military demonstration in Holland, which should lead to a rising against the Republican Government. In the first of these objects the expedition succeeded; in the second it miserably failed. For an exhibition of fruitless gallantry, it has not been surpassed in the annals of the British Army.

But happily it was the closing scene in the drama of military failure, with which the last decade of the eighteenth century was surfeited. With the new century came a spirit in England's military operations, which made her campaigns by land as glorious as her successes by sea. The wars of the nineteenth century threw into the background the share taken by our armies in the wars of the French Revolution, during the period which preceded the overthrow of the Directorate in France and the virtual assumption of the supreme power by Napoleon in the winter of 1799. But the Regimental historian has to bring even fruitless and unsuccessful wars to light again, in his search for stories of individual gallantry or for the causes of failure.

England's ally in the expedition to the Helder was Russia. It had been arranged by the two governments that the land forces should comprise a Russian contingent of 17,000 men, and an English army of 13,000. England more than fulfilled her promise; for the actual force sent by her was as much as that promised as the Russian contribution. In addition, England furnished vessels to assist in the transport of the Russian troops from the Baltic, and a powerful fleet, of more than sixty men-of-war, under Admiral Lord Duncan. On the 21st August, 1799, the fleet and transports arrived off the mouth of the Zuyder Zee, and anchored off the Helder: but foul weather prevented a disembarkation until the 27th,—a delay which gave undoubted advantage to the French and Batavian troops. The enemy was at first under the command of General Daendels, but he was almost immediately superseded by General Brune; and the army, which had at first been 10,000 strong, rose in a few weeks to nearly treble that number.

<small>23rd, 27th, 29th, 55th, and 85th Regiments.</small> Abercromby's division was the first to land, and after a very severe engagement, in which the Infantry under Generals Sir James Pulteney and Coote behaved most gallantly, the Dutch were driven back, and the English took possession of the Kirkduin, and the fort of the Helder. The Artillery was not landed till after this engagement; nor was the
<small>Cust.</small> ground favourable to the use of the Dutch artillery. The.

CHAP. V.   *Action of Zyp.*   97

fleet was summoned to surrender: and the Dutch Admiral, conscious of a strong spirit of insubordination among his crews, ever since the appearance of the British flag, consented to deliver over his ships unconditionally; and he thus gave to the English the complete control of the Zuyder Zee. On this taking place, the Dutch troops retired, and took up a position in front of Alkmaar, where they were joined by General Brune and 7000 French. Abercromby occupied the ground vacated by the Dutch, and strengthened it in every way possible, being resolved to await there the arrival of the Duke of York and the Russian contingent. General Brune, however, saw the advantage of an engagement before such a junction could be effected; and therefore on the 10th September he assumed the offensive, but without success,—being totally defeated with a loss of 2000 men. The Artillery was of great service to Abercromby; and it 'London was in this engagement—known as the action of Zyp—that Gazette,' Lieutenant Simpson was wounded. The French resumed 1799. their old position in front of Alkmaar, which they greatly strengthened; and confined their operations to preventing Abercromby from advancing out of the contracted space in which he was situated.

On the 12th September the Russians arrived, and on the day following the Duke of York assumed the command, and resolved on leaving the position where the army had been stationed, and on attacking the enemy with the large force now at his disposal, numbering about 35,000 men. He divided his army into four columns: the right being under General Hermann, and composed entirely of Russians; the second, under General Dundas, consisting partly of British, and partly of Russians; the third, under Sir James Pulteney, with a large proportion of Artillery and Cavalry; and the fourth, under Sir Ralph Abercromby, consisting entirely of British troops; the last being intended to make a *détour* on the evening of the 18th September—the day before the intended battle—and to turn the enemy's right flank. The first three columns were ordered to attack simultaneously at break of day on the 19th, moving on different named points.

VOL. II.   H

These arrangements, which have been somewhat severely criticised, would doubtless have succeeded, had the Duke's orders been obeyed; but unfortunately the first, or Russian, column precipitated the engagement by attacking the enemy two or three hours before the other columns were ready to move, and drove the enemy out of the village of Bergen. General Brune brought up his reserve to recover his lost ground, and fell upon the Russian troops when in a state of intoxication from the excesses of which they had been guilty since the capture of the village. A disgraceful scene followed, ending in the tumultuous flight of the Russians with the loss of many prisoners. The Duke of York accompanied the second column, but the retreat of the Russians on his right compelled him to fall back, and to send orders to the third and fourth columns to do the same. Great success had in the meantime attended the efforts of Sir James Pulteney,—the Guards, 17th and 40th Regiments, having greatly distinguished themselves; but, owing to the change given to the whole plan by the mistake and misbehaviour of the first column, when night came the Allies occupied precisely the same ground as they held in the morning. The loss to the English amounted to 500 killed and wounded, and 500 taken prisoners;—and the Russians lost 3000 men; but an equal number of the enemy had been taken prisoners by the Allies. In this engagement, known as the battle of Bergen or Alkmaar, the loss of the Royal Artillery was as follows :—

'London Gazette,' 24 Sept. 1799.

First Lieutenant Eligée, wounded and taken prisoner;
Volunteer John Douglass, wounded;
Killed: 5 gunners; 4 gunner-drivers; and 3 additional gunners.
Wounded: 8 gunners; 6 gunner-drivers; and 4 additional gunners.
Missing: 7 gunners, and gunner-drivers.

In the interval between this engagement and the severe battle on the 2nd October,—when the event occurred which gives the title to the present chapter,—both armies were employed in strengthening their positions on shore, in obtaining reinforcements, and in arranging their respective gun-boats in such a way as to obtain from them an enfilade fire, in event of attack. The Duke of York felt the importance of making a final effort, before the season was further advanced: and his dispositions on the 2nd October were much the same as on the 19th September, except that he gave the right column to General Abercromby, whose force consisted of 8000 Infantry and 1000 Cavalry, with Major Judgson's troop of Horse Artillery. The troop was partly armed with 12-pounders,—a very heavy armament for Horse Artillery, and one never again used:—and it seems all the more unsuitable, when we find that the battalion guns, which were merely 6-pounders, were in one instance brigaded into a battery under Captain Frazer,—presenting the anomaly in the army, on this 2nd October, of a *light* field artillery, intended for rapid movements, being armed with guns of twice the calibre of those used by what should have been the *medium* field artillery, and only required to accommodate itself to the movements of infantry. General Farrington to D. A. G. 17 Sept. 1799.

The second column was composed of Russian troops, under Count Essen; the third was under General Dundas; and the fourth under Sir James Pulteney. The main interest attaches to the first column, whose duty it was to keep close to the seashore as far as Egmont-op-Zee, and thence menace the French left and rear. The other columns were to drive back the enemy's line if possible; and, at all events, so to occupy him as to prevent the left from being strengthened in such a manner as might endanger the success of the first column. The exertions of General Dundas's brigade were marvellous, and were crowned by success; but they were almost undone by the refusal of the Russians, at a critical moment, to advance against the village of Bergen, which had been laid bare by the retreat of the enemy before the impetuosity of the English troops. This refusal was never forgotten, nor was there from that hour any harmony between the allied troops. Encouraged by the impunity allowed them, the enemy resumed the offensive; but, although unable to drive them farther back, the English succeeded, although with great loss and difficulty, in holding the ground they had taken.

The first column, under General Abercromby, reached Egmont-op-Zee without difficulty; but there it found a large force of all arms, under General Vandamme, drawn up in line of battle. The engagement which followed was prolonged and bloody. Sir Ralph was at last successful; but his advantage was short-lived, for reinforcements arrived from Alkmaar in such numbers that it required all the skill of the English General, and all the undaunted courage of his men, to prevent his left from being broken before night put an end to the engagement. It was at this time that the Chestnut Troop received its baptism of fire. By some oversight on the part of the General, or possibly owing to ignorance as to the powers of this new weapon—Horse Artillery,—Major Judgson's Troop had been advanced to a dangerous distance, and left with an inadequate escort. General Vandamme observed this, and, placing himself at the head of his Cavalry, swept down upon the guns. The scene which followed was an exciting one. Taken by surprise, the gunners did not loose their presence of mind, but fired into the advancing cavalry until they were in their midst; and then, with any weapons they could lay hands on, they struggled with the troopers, who, in immense numbers, surrounded them, and sabred them at their guns. According to one account, two only of the guns were carried off by the cavalry when they retired; according to another, the whole were captured. Be it as it may, the prize was not left long undisputed, for Lord Paget, placing himself at the head of the 15th Light Dragoons—now the 15th (King's) Hussars —charged the enemy's cavalry, pursuing them for over a mile; and, assisted by the explosion of one of the captive limbers, succeeded in recovering all the guns. The story is calculated to create a friendly sympathy between the Chestnut Troop and the gallant Regiment which proved so staunch a godfather to it at this its christening, and is one to be talked over by the camp-fire in days coming on. In the order which was issued after the battle, Major Judgson

Browne.
Cust.

received special mention. "In the severe action on this day "His Royal Highness expressed his thanks to Lieutenant-Colonels Whitworth and Smith, who commanded the Artillery of reserve, and to Major Judgson, of the Horse Artillery. Captain Nicholls was wounded in this action, and is since dead." [London Gazette, 24 Oct. 1799.]

Although the Allies had not driven the enemy back as far as they had hoped, they nevertheless occupied the ground on which the French General had taken up his position at the commencement of the battle. The loss to the British was severe, 1300 having been killed and wounded, including 100 officers.

Another attempt was made by the Allies on the 7th October to drive the enemy back, and to escape from the position in which they had been cramped since the commencement of the campaign; but, although they defeated with severe loss the troops to whom they found themselves immediately opposed, the *cordon* beyond still hopelessly surrounded them. As there was no symptom of a popular rising in the country on their behalf, and as reinforcements were daily reaching the French, the Duke of York decided on opening negotiations with a view to the evacuation of Holland by the Allies. These were ultimately successful; and the only beneficial result of this campaign, which survived the negotiations, was the retention of the Dutch fleet by the English.

The conclusion of the Artillery share in this campaign had an element of the ludicrous in it. In the old letter-books, deposited in the Royal Artillery Record Office, is the following one, showing the pitiable way in which poor General Farrington, who had left with all the pomp and circumstance of war, returned to his home. Writing from Blackheath, he says:—"After a very fatiguing voyage and "journey, I am this moment arrived at my own house. "Trotter, Smith, Terrott, Robe, Maclean, Lieut. Knox, and "Dr. Jameson, came over passengers with me, and will be "at Woolwich this night, or to-morrow morning. The want "of horses keeps them back, and my anxiety of mind to [To D. A. General, Nov. 3, 1799.]

"arrive as early as possible led me to accept a passage in a post-chaise; but I have a melancholy tale to unfold. The ship in which we came passengers, mistaking the entrance into Yarmouth Harbour, ran on the sands, on which she struck with such violence as, with the first shock, to unship her rudder, and stave in her bottom; but, wonderful to tell, after keeping us in a most distressed state for an hour, she passed the sands with 4 feet of water in her hold, and, by the exertion of the boats of the fleet, every soul on board was saved—about 70 in number; and in about half an hour the ship sank in 10 or 11 fathoms of water. The cargo, such as guns, shot, and shells, may be saved; the ammunition, of course, destroyed; and *we are all reduced to our ship-dress only;* everything else lost. It has been a most providential escape, and sincerely ought we to offer up our prayers for His mercy.

"I am too unwell to wait upon Lord Howe, *nor have I things to see him in;* but if you could ride over here to-morrow, I will tell you all I can respecting the embarkation of the Artillery horses, &c., *for I have not a paper left.*"

While sympathising with the ill-fated General, the student cannot refrain from anathematising the blundering pilot, who mistook the entrance to Yarmouth Harbour, and was thus the cause of papers being lost which would doubtless have been priceless to the compiler of a narrative of the Artillery share in the campaign of 1799.

Return dated Woolwich, 5 Dec. 1799.

The following return of the losses of the Royal Artillery, *exclusive* of the Driver Corps, in this campaign, was rendered by the Deputy-Adjutant-General to the Board of Ordnance:—

Killed, and died of their wounds . . . . 25 of all ranks.
Wounded . . . . 21 ,,
Prisoners and Missing . . . . 15 ,,

Horses sent from England	910
Received in Holland from the Commissary-General's Department	200
Total	1110
Killed, dead, and left behind	654
Returned to England	456

      (Signed) J. MACLEOD,
             D.-A.-General.

CHAPTER VI.

EGYPT.

THE history of the Regiment in 1800 and 1801 has its main interest in the operations of the English Army in Egypt. In these, so glorious in a military point of view, so effective in a national,—for they were the main instrument in bringing about the Peace of Amiens—the Artilleryman finds much to interest him, and much of which he may be justly proud.

It is fortunate for the purpose of this history that the officer who commanded the Artillery in Egypt placed on record many most interesting details which the general historian would have certainly overlooked, and whose reproduction in these pages will give a far more graphic sketch of the difficulties which were encountered than could be given by the most skilful writer who had not himself been an eye-witness. The unpretending account of the means adopted to overcome the difficulties cannot fail also to inspire any officer, who may find himself in a similar position, with a resolution to yield to no obstacles.

<small>Brig.-Gen. Lawson's MSS. on Egypt, deposited in the R. A Library.</small>

The reader will remember that in the year 1800 there was a French army stationed in Egypt, which, although reduced from its original numbers, was yet too strong to be overcome by the Turks. England resolved to reinforce the Turkish army by means of an expedition from England, the military part of which was to be commanded by Sir R. Abercromby; the naval, by Admiral Lord Keith. The Artillery of the Expedition was placed under the command of Colonel Lawson, who, after much importunity, obtained from the Duke of York the rank of Brigadier-General. Officers of his own standing had obtained that rank to command brigades of Infantry on the Expedition; and Colonel Macleod, although,

as he wrote, "bewildered with orders and projects, altera- Corre-spondence
"tions and inventions," fought loyally to obtain from the of D. A.
Board a recommendation that the officer commanding the General, R.A.
Artillery should receive it also.

The strength of the Royal Artillery ordered to embark for Embarkation
Egypt under General Lawson was as follows:— Return, rendered to B. O. on 9 April, 1800.

1 Field Officer,	54 Non-Commissioned Officers,
7 Captains,	7 Lance N.-C. Officers,
12 Subalterns,	450 Gunners,
3 Surgeons,	9 Drummers,

making a total of 543, besides 38 women and 7 children. The civil branch of the Ordnance was represented by 1 paymaster, 1 paymaster's clerk, 1 commissary of stores, 1 assistant commissary and 4 clerks, 6 conductors of stores, and 19 artificers.

The names of the officers who first embarked were Colonel Lawson, Captains Thomson, Lemoine, Evans, Meredith, and Millar; Captains-Lieutenant Newhouse and Boger; Lieutenants Raynsford, 'Munro, Lawson, F. Campbell, Fauquier, Cleaveland, Armstrong, Michell, and Trelawny; and 2nd Lieutenants Kirby, Rook, and Nutt. This force was augmented in the Mediterranean from Minorca and Malta, and received a contingent, which will presently be mentioned, from Lisbon; certain changes, also, were made in it by landing at Gibraltar a company of the 6th Battalion, re- Report to ceiving one of the 5th Battalion in exchange. The battalions D. A. Gen. from Gen. actually represented in Egypt were the 1st, 2nd, 4th, and 5th, Lawson. and the companies which were present are detailed in the first volume of this work. The 3rd Battalion was at this time mainly stationed in the West Indies.

On the 5th May, 1800, General Lawson reached Portsmouth to take command of the Artillery of the Expedition, which he had been informed was on the point of sailing. He had also been informed that all necessary particulars had been communicated to him by the authorities; but in neither respect was his information correct, and the official fountain of his knowledge was found to have poured forth a somewhat muddy stream. Three weeks elapsed before he sailed—three weeks of wild, hopeless confusion—affairs having been complicated by the Government having decided on a secret expedition elsewhere, the Artillery of which was placed under the orders of Colonel Seward, then in command at Portsmouth. An interchange of companies between his force and that of General Lawson was threatened, and mutual drafts were made, as far as officers and a few men were concerned. Another company, under Major Cookson, who distinguished himself subsequently in Egypt, joined General Lawson at Portsmouth—a fact of which the student first becomes aware by finding a joint letter from the subalterns of the company, petitioning the Board, with considerable presence of mind, for an advance of pay, they "being quite out of "cash." It is presumed that their request was granted, for,

Colonel Seward to Colonel Macleod, 25 May, 1800.

on the morning of the 25th May, Colonel Seward reported the embarkation of this company "between eleven and " twelve o'clock *in high spirits.*" The whole of General Lawson's force had sailed by the 3rd June, and reached Gibraltar on the 22nd of the same month. The gallant General's existence had been embittered during the last few days of his stay in England by the masterly silence, profound as the grave, with which all his inquiries for information, reiterated daily, were received by the Board. The subsequent difficulties which he encountered were mainly due to this triumph of official reticence.

Leaving General Lawson's force at Gibraltar, let the reader return for a moment to that under Colonel Seward, which was to form part of the Secret Expedition. The Royal Artillery employed consisted of 386 of all ranks, besides that marvellous accompaniment of all expeditions in those days, whether secret or open,—22 women and 11 children. The armament consisted of 16 light 6-pounders. Three companies were taken complete, commanded by Major

Embarkation Returns, D.A. General's Correspondence.

Borthwick, Captain Salmon, and Brevet-Lieut.-Colonel Bentham; and the following officers accompanied the force: Captains-Lieutenant S. G. Adye and A. MacDonald; 1st Lieutenants W. R. Carey, E. Curry, T. Masson, R. Carthew,

S. Maxwell, D. Campbell, W. Holcombe, and L. Carmichael; 2nd Lieutenants W. Norman Ramsay, W. D. Nicolls, J. Rollo, and H. B. Lane. Major Borthwick was appointed by Colonel Seward Brigade-Major to the Artillery. Besides these three companies, drafts from almost every company in England were taken to complete them to their proper establishment, and to man the battalion guns. This heart-breaking system of robbing one company to feed the wants of another prevailed to a great and continual extent during the earlier part of this century, and its evil results show the vast improvement of the depôt system, which clothes the cadres of dwindling batteries abroad, without taking from those at home the men trained in and for themselves.

Considerable trouble was experienced by Colonel Seward in obtaining the co-operation of commanding officers of regiments in matters relating to the battalion guns; and this expedition acted as another nail, so to speak, in the coffin of that objectionable system. But infinitely greater was the trouble caused by the vacillation and uncertainty of the authorities, who, after the embarkation of the whole force, sent orders for it to disembark and encamp near Southampton, until they could arrive at some decision as to its destination. This afforded an opportunity for clerkdom to run riot. Questions as to ship rations and land rations, ship pay and land pay, poured on the ill-fated captains of companies every day; and seldom did a mail reach them without a disallowance.

At length the expedition set sail (the military part of the force being placed under Sir James Pulteney), and made an attempt on Ferrol, in whose harbour some large men-of-war were lying. The troops landed under a covering fire from the English fleet, and in the skirmish which followed they had the advantage. But, Sir James Pulteney, becoming alarmed at the strength of the Spanish works, and at the news he received of their preparations, re-embarked the troops the same evening, and sailed for Gibraltar. Here Colonel Seward transferred to Colonel Lawson many of his officers, Cust's 'Annals of the Wars.'

men, and stores; and with the remainder, and all the sick, he went to Lisbon, whence—pending his return to England—he wrote the most gloomy letters that ever crossed the threshold of Colonel Macleod's office. The transfer of his officers to General Lawson's command at Gibraltar, and the receipt of others from the companies in garrison, account for the presence in Egypt of many who did not embark with the latter from England, such as Major Sprowle, Captains Duncan and Adye, and Lieutenants D. Campbell, Sturgeon, and Burslem. One of the companies which sailed from England with General Lawson was landed at Gibraltar in exchange for Major Sprowle's; and by this means the glories of Egypt were denied to Captain Meredith and Lieutenants Cleaveland, Michell, and Nutt.

From Gibraltar General Lawson went to Minorca, which he reached on the 10th July, after a tedious passage of nineteen days. Here he landed his men to await the return of Sir R. Abercromby, who had at first started for Genoa, with all the troops he could collect from Minorca and elsewhere. While on the passage, however, Sir Ralph received a message from the Admiral, Lord Keith, informing him that the Austrians had evacuated Italy. He therefore diverted his course to Leghorn, where he remained a week, and then went on to Malta. When the citadel of Valetta in that island was given up by the French in September, and Malta passed into the hands of the English, General Lawson followed Sir Ralph, and the expedition to Egypt was in that island finally organized.

During this time the English force in the Mediterranean had been increased by the arrival of a body of 4000 men, under Lord Dalhousie, from Belleisle, where they had at first been intended to act. This reinforcement, with others which followed, brought Sir R. Abercromby's force up to 17,489 men before it finally left Malta; and an additional force of 6000 men, under Sir David Baird, was expected to meet them from India. The story of the Expedition after leaving Malta will be told in General Lawson's own words. But, in passing, it may be stated that Minorca was the residence at this time of Colonel Cuppage of the Artillery, whose correspondence with the Deputy Adjutant-General reveals the fact that he was allowed a power over the Royal Artillery in the Mediterranean of a very extensive and unusual description. As a rule, as little power as possible was allowed to commanding officers on out-stations; the movements of officers especially were carefully regulated from England; but Colonel Cuppage evidently had the power, and exercised it, of transferring officers and men from companies, even belonging to different battalions,—of appointing officers to the bomb service in the Mediterranean, and of disembarking others already appointed; and, in a word, of exercising unlimited control over that part of the Regiment which came within the area of his command. This is mentioned because such control, however advisable, was rarely permitted under the Board, which was jealous of anything approaching independence in those under its orders;— and it is impossible to avoid expressing surprise that a system which succeeded so admirably on this occasion did not receive further trial. The fact of Minorca being the residence of the Commanding Officer of Artillery must not be construed as implying that the old Ordnance Establishment and Train, which disappeared with the capitulation of Port Mahon in 1782, had been revived. His residence there was almost accidental, and mainly on account of its convenience,—previous to the capture of Malta,—as a rallying point for the naval and military forces in the Mediterranean.

One instance must be given, before entering upon General Lawson's narrative, to show how infamously the arrangements of the civil branch of the Ordnance were often conducted, after a campaign had been undertaken, and how scandalously the shortcomings of the *civil* were left to be expiated by the *military* branch. These instances will be frequent as this work proceeds, and they are reproduced with a double and deliberate purpose: first, to show under what difficulties our armies obtained their successes; and second, to remind those who are ever ready to criticise the slightest shortcoming of the same description in the present day, that in our older campaigns, whose glories are remembered when their blunders are forgotten, the faults which are deprecated so loudly to-day existed in an appalling degree.

Major Cookson's company was the first of General Lawson's force to leave Portsmouth. The earliest report of its movements is a letter written by Major Cookson from the Island of Houat, where he found 132 of the 6th Battalion, making, with his own company, a total force of Artillery amounting to 227 of all ranks. With characteristic energy he commenced, after landing his company, to improve and strengthen his position. The reader will be good enough to remember that Major Cookson's company was one of those on the equipment of which the Board had expended unusual energy; and had felt such confidence in the omniscience of their *civil* officials, that they would not even reply to the hints and prayers of the officers of Artillery, who were most deeply interested. Doubtless, then, everything will be found as it should be. Yet let us hear what Major Cookson reports.

Major Cookson, from I. of Houat, 24 June, 1800.

"I have only a moment to tell you how very much dis-
" tressed I am; and how much the Service is retarded for
" want of a *Clerk of Stores* who understands his duty.
" There is a man here who calls himself Conductor of Stores,
" but he is very far from being adequate to the situation,
" being, in the first place, *incapable of writing*. ... I have
" 16 pieces of ordnance under my charge (10 6-pounders
" and 6 howitzers), all of which I had to complete to 100
" rounds each, on board of the different vessels they were
" in, and to mount them ready to land in a *chasse-marée*,
" which was cut down and prepared for the purpose, and
" which I got done in two days; since which I have been
" obliged to land some here, and to put others from the
" 'Diadem' and 'Inconstant' on board the 'John' ordnance
" ship, and into boats. Conceive, then, how much I must have
" been in want of conductors and clerks of stores! On
" board the 'John,' when in a hurry for completing the
" ammunition, we were much annoyed to find 12-*pounder*
" *flannel cartridges for the* 5½-*inch howitzers*, and other like
" mistakes; however, I *set the women to work* and got over

" that difficulty and many others. . . . *All the camp equipage*
" *for the officers and men whom I brought out is deficient;*
" do, pray, therefore, send me out the camp equipage for
" my company .... with a hospital and laboratory tent,
" as soon as you possibly can; as also camp-kettles, canteens,
" and haversacks. The whole of the men have been un-
" commonly harassed for some days past."

This is a charming picture of official foresight, and one which we shall find painted again and again in the succeeding pages of English story. Blind to the fact that the men, who were to use them, were also the best judges of the things required, and—

"Being too blind to have desire to see,"

the civil branch of the Ordnance too often reasoned *à priori* —evolved out of its own consciousness certain ill-defined wants, which the troops might possibly have,—and, with many blunders and shortcomings, endeavoured to meet them. And then, with monotonous recurrence, came a pitiful struggle to maintain its own dignity in the face of incessant failure.

That the response to Major Cookson's appeal was not wholly satisfactory may be gathered from the following extract from a subsequent letter:—" Conceive," he wrote, " their sending
" me a common soldiers' tent for the sick, and five horsemen's
" tents *without their poles*, which to obtain here would be im-
" possible, as all the men-of-war have expended already
" every inch of wood that could be spared. You will see by
" the return that we have 50 men ill, and, I am sorry to say,
" several of them dangerously so." Major Cookson, from Houat, 1 August, 1800.

It is a relief to turn, now, to the words of a man eminently capable of removing the difficulties with which he was surrounded.

" The Expedition, under the orders of Admiral Lord Keith
" and General Abercromby, proceeded from the Island of
" Malta on the 21st December, 1800, arrived at Marmorice
" Bay, in Asia Minor, on the New Year's Day following, and
" remained there, waiting the co-operation of the Turks
" (being the time of their Ramadan), until the 20th February.
" During this period every measure was taken the situation

" admitted of to lessen the numerous difficulties expected to
" be met with in Egypt,—such as a dangerous shore to land
" upon—a country destitute of wood, water, or roads—where
" (as the Commander-in-Chief informed the General Officers,
" assembled by order) nothing was to be looked for but a
" wild waste of desert, and obstacles which the most unre-
" mitting exertions had only a chance of surmounting, inde-
" pendent of a formidable opposition from the French troops.

" Under these ideas, and the battering train (originally
" designed against Belleisle only) having joined the army
" very indifferently provided indeed for such an uncommon,
" arduous enterprise, no time could be lost. All the artificers
" were landed, and strong working parties sent into the
" woods to cut down timber for making additional spars,
" skids, and various-sized rollers, to form gangways for
" landing the heavy ordnance upon, assisting them over deep
" sandy beaches, and in crossing the canals formed for con-
" veying the rising waters of the Nile into the towns and
" cultivated spots of the country.

" The generally acknowledged difficulty of travelling by
" wheeled carriages in Egypt induced the trial of a number of
" contrivances to lessen that evil also, the first of which were
" a kind of litters, ... termed 'horse-barrows.' No wood
" growing in this country proper for such purposes, rendered
" it necessary to dig saw-pits, in order to cut the pine timber
" into long scantling (16 feet in length, and about 4 inches
" square), something near the shape of a common hand-
" barrow, preserving the grain as entire as possible. Two
" movable cross-bars, which are secured by two small bolts,
" keep these shafts at a proper interval, to admit a horse at
" each end between them. Each horse or mule had a small
" cart saddle with girth, back-band, breastplate, and crupper,
" and a halter for leading it by. These barrows were par-
" ticularly useful for narrow paths and the trenches of
" an attack, or for conveying any individual weight too
" heavy for a single horse, such as a small piece of ordnance,
" standing carriage, large casks of provisions, &c. (The
" powder and ammunition expended at the attack of Aboukir

CHAP. VI.   *General Lawson's Narrative.*   113

" Castle were mostly conveyed from the landing-place to the
" batteries in this manner.) Besides these single barrows, a
" design was formed for double ones, consisting of three
" shafts, to be carried by four horses in pairs; and also
" others upon a still larger scale for camels, but neither time
" nor materials admitted of their being put into immediate
" execution. A very considerable number of carrying-poles,
" about 9 feet long each, were formed out of the small-sized
" trees, to which rope-slings were added, for the soldiers to
" convey kegs of musket-ball cartridges, ammunition-boxes,
" or royal mortars with.

" A number of horses were purchased at Constantinople
" on the part of the English Government, and sent to Mar-
" morice, for remounting the Light Dragoons, and those
" rejected by them were turned over to the Artillery service.
" Such poor undersized animals as they were rendered it
" absolutely necessary not only to take the harness entirely
" to pieces, in order to bring it anything near fitting them,
" but also to lay aside all the heavy parts, such as neck-
" collars, chain-traces, curb-bits, &c., and replace them with
" light leather breast-collars, rope-traces, and pads formed out
" of the waggon harness, a great part of which, fortunately,
" was not likely to be otherwise called for.

" About 130 horses being thus completed with harness,
" some light pieces—guns and howitzers—were landed, and
" a small park formed, in order to drill them to the draught.
" Every reform possible was made to lighten the travelling
" of the ordnance, and it was very much wished to have
" exchanged the limber-shafts for poles also, on account of
" their weight, as well as other considerations; but no proper
" wood could then be procured—even at the Island of Rhodes
" —for the purpose. The block-trailed light 6-pounder car-
" riages had ten horses allotted to each for draught; but
" the framed ones required twelve when going over heavy
" sand or shingle.

" A few of the most useful horse-artillery manœuvres were
" also practised -here, it being the Commander-in-Chief's
" intention to establish some pieces on that principle when-

VOL. II.   I

" over horses could be procured for it. Drivers were also
" very much wanted, several of those which came out ori-
" ginally with the battering train having, with their officer,
" returned, in a very unaccountable manner, from Lisbon to
" England, after the attempt on Cadiz.

" The following considerations were submitted to the Com-
" mander-in-Chief at Marmorice Bay, on 10th Jan., 1801 :—

" 1st. As the passage of the fleet to the coast of Egypt
" may probably be short, it is humbly proposed to have the
" light field-pieces of the first division of troops conveyed
" from hence on the decks of the ships of war, so as to be
" at once lowered down altogether into the boats, having
" their Artillery detachments along with them, without the
" necessity of any other preparation after coming to anchor.

" 2nd. The ordnance ships, in which the other pieces next
" for landing are aboard, to be conducted and stationed by
" the agent himself (the masters alone not being sufficient
" at such a crisis) as near to the shore as safety will admit.
" And it will be necessary, on account of the crowded
" manner in which they were loaded in England (being taken
" upon freight), to have light vessels alongside of them to
" receive the water-casks, and articles not immediately
" wanted, in clearing away to those sought for.

" 3rd. Small vessels or decked boats, with field ammu-
" nition and musket-ball cartridges, will be required (parti-
" cularly if the coast proves shallow) still nearer in shore,
" and to be stationed opposite the centre of attack imme-
" diately after the landing of the first division of the troops,
" distinguished by Ordnance Jacks. In order to furnish the
" most speedy supply possible, a number of hand-carts and
" carrying-poles may be thrown on shore from these boats,
" for the soldiers to take off any ammunition wanting, until
" the horses can be landed.

" 4th. The flat boats and launches of the ships of war are
" wished to be employed in carrying the field ordnance, &c.,
" ashore, instead of transports' long-boats, which (as was
" experienced at Cadiz), from their want of hands and
" general size, are quite inadequate to the business.

"5th. Planks, joined together lengthways by staples and cordage, may be necessary to travel the carriages upon over the heavy sands. The French, it is said, made use of raw hides in passing the deserts with their field-pieces. Perhaps lengths of rope, about 30 feet each, with narrow netting between to receive the wheels upon, might be found as useful, and, in our situation, more readily procured.

"6th. One thousand seamen, provided with drag-ropes or harness, will be required to assist in landing and drawing up the heavy ordnance and stores.

"7th. The mode of advancing into the country will depend upon the means of draught found there; but, at all events, if a strong detachment of seamen can be procured to remain with the Artillery, it will be highly beneficial to service.

"Agreeable to these representations, application was immediately made to Lord Keith, who consented to take aboard each of the line-of-battle ships two field-pieces, which were placed on the poops ready for lowering down into the launches all together. Twenty-five seamen and officers were allotted to each piece, with fifteen of the Artillery. These 350 were all the seamen his Lordship could spare out of the 1000 demanded. Two general rehearsals of landing were then practised: the guns got ashore very readily, and *quicker than the troops could leap out of their boats.* Each ship-of-war formed its own boat's gangway; the best of them was made out of the fishing of a mast, which, being hollow, secured the wheels of the carriage from slipping, without side-pieces."

Alterations made in Carronade Carriages.—" The moving of heavy ordnance over the deserts of Egypt the French thought impracticable, and attempted no larger calibre than 8-pounders or 12-pounders. Something more, however, seemed necessary for us to make trial of against an enemy so much more formidable than any they had had to contend with, independent of the ambition of superior resource. Upon comparing all circumstances together, it appeared likely that whatever works they might have

" raised in the interior of the country since their possession
" of it could not be very solid ones, even if composed of
" masonry, for want of time to settle and the cement to
" harden sufficiently in such substances; and earth alone, in
" this climate, must soon crumble to dust or sand, and easily
" be destroyed by shells. From these considerations it was
" concluded that carronades might probably be found suffi-
" ciently powerful to breach them in either case at moderate
" distances, and be easily conveyed by the double horse or
" camel-barrow across the country if necessary. The cir-
" cumstance being suggested to Sir Ralph Abercromby, and,
" at the same time, the means proposed of altering the
" carriages for this purpose without affecting their sea-
" service in the smallest degree, His Excellency communi-
" cated the idea to Lord Keith, who immediately ordered
" several of these 24-pounder carriages (though larger
" ones were wished for) ashore from the ships-of-war, to
" undergo the necessary alteration. This operation being
" soon executed, some trials of shot and shells were made
" there, and afterwards aboard the 'Foudroyant,' in presence
" of the Admiral and the General, and much approved of."

For the information of the non-professional reader, it may here be mentioned that carronades are far lighter than guns of the same calibre. The details by which General Lawson describes, in his MSS., the modifications made by him to render the carronade-carriages suitable for his purpose, are illustrated by carefully-prepared diagrams, without which the description would hardly be intelligible. It may be stated briefly that, by certain additions to the carriage—which could easily be removed when again wanted on board ship—he produced something akin to the modern dwarf traversing platform, requiring little or no ground platform on which to be traversed. The navy officers who were present at the experiments expressed their opinion that the alteration would be very useful to their service also, for taking up posts occasionally ashore.

The MS. proceeds next to describe the arrangements made by General Lawson.

"Many mistakes, as well as loss of time, happening on
" service by the ammunition being sent into the field with
" the waggons accompanying the guns in the same state as
" lodged in the storehouses; that is, round shot, case shot,
" cartridges, and small stores, each article in separate pack-
" ing-boxes, it was thought advisable, especially on this
" occasion, where the ammunition must be mostly carried on
" camels' backs, to complete each individual box with a
" certain number of rounds (one fourth case), including small
" stores, and everything necessary to the firing of them.
" This was effected by only raising the round-shot packing-
" case about two inches higher, and the addition of a small
" board as a false bottom, which admitted of stowings as fol-
" lows, viz., for light 6-pounders, 15 rounds and 1 extra case-
" shot; light 12-pounders, 8 rounds; medium 12-pounders,
" 7 rounds. For the royal howitzer ammunition, it was
" necessary to have two packing-boxes on this principle,
" viz., one containing 9 live shells and 1 case-shot; the
" other with 2 case-shot and all the articles for firing
" 12 rounds complete. This mode was found extremely
" useful in the field, and is strongly recommended for all
" immediate occasions of service, as no possible mistake
" can then happen, either from ignorance or neglect, in
" supplying the guns or limber-boxes with the utmost
" expedition.

"The ammunition for field-service was usually conveyed
" on camels' backs, each carrying four of the altered
" 6-pounder packing-boxes, two on each side, in a sort of
" netted bag thrown over a pack-saddle; but, useful as these
" animals are generally for great weights, there are incon-
" veniences attending them in this particular service; viz.,
" when loaded (which, of course, must be daily repeated)
" they move very slowly, therefore quite unfit for Horse
" Artillery;—in order to load or unload, they must first be
" made to kneel down, which in an action they are not
" always inclined to, and sometimes become very refractory
" and unmanageable; also, whatever quantity of ammunition
" is required for the gun must always be taken equally

" from both sides at the same time, to preserve its equili-
" brium, &c.

" These reasons determined a trial of light carriages in
" their stead, first beginning with royal howitzer ammuni-
" tion, it being the most dangerous and liable to injury.
" Some of the hand-carts were selected for this purpose, and,
" in order to travel the better, converted to curricles. The
" poles were accordingly lengthened, and cross-bars fixed to
" support them in front of the horses' collars, much in the
" same manner as the 3-pounder carriages formerly used in
" the Horse Artillery, only more simplified. These carriages
" were drawn by four horses each, and went through all the
" marches of the army to and from Grand Cairo remarkably
" well, travelling very rapidly with 48 rounds of the how-
" itzer ammunition completed for immediate service, as
" already mentioned."

Light 3-pounder Carriages altered for Cavalry.—" Our
" Cavalry, from their want of proper horses, being found
" very unequal to the capitally-mounted French dragoons,
" it became necessary to aid that defect by the attachment
" of Artillery. Four light 3-pounders (brought from Malta)
" were first prepared for this service. Their original mode
" of travelling with shafts and single line of draught was
" altered to a double one by cutting off the shafts of the
" limber at the cross-bar, and introducing a pole instead of
" them, together with other improvements. (For example,
" a block of wood was fixed by two bolts to the back of the
" axletree, and the iron pintail removed from the centre of
" it to this block to receive the trail of the carriage upon.
" This was done in order to make room for a 6-pounder
" ammunition-box, to be fixed crossways in the front. The
" old side-boxes belonging to the carriage being rejected
" entirely, *their places furnished seats for two gunners.* At
" small expense an ammunition-box, containing 8 rounds,
" was made to fit in between the cheeks of the gun-carriage,
" after the French manner. *A copper tray or drawer was
" introduced under one of the gunners' seats to contain the slow-
" match, instead of carrying a lintstock.*) Four or six horses,

" with two drivers (according to the ground), drew the
" carriage. These pieces were served by four Artillerymen,
" *two on the carriage and two mounted on the off draught-*
" *horses.* They went through the service to Grand Cairo,
" and travelled much better than was expected from the
" lowness of the limber-wheels, which defect there was no
" remedy for in Egypt.

" Four light 6-pounders upon block-trail carriages, with
" two royal howitzers, were also equipped (as nearly as the
" means would admit) for Horse Artillery service. Seven
" Artillerymen and three drivers, with ten horses, were
" allotted for the service of each piece, the gunners riding
" the horses in draught, but the non-commissioned officer
" mounted single for the purpose of advancing to examine
" roads, reconnoitring the enemy, &c. These block-trail
" carriages, from their lightness, short draught, and quick
" turning, passed over the inundation dykes and desert with
" great ease, while the framed carriages with more horses
" were attended with difficulty and delay, and once in the
" desert, were obliged to be left behind.

" The success of the curricle carts (for field ammunition)
" induced a trial if something might not be done with the
" waggons also, hitherto looked upon as out of all question,
" except the local duties of the park. Some of them were
" taken to pieces, and all the heaviest parts laid aside—that
" is, the bolsters, sides, and shafts. The bottoms were then
" contracted both in length and breadth, so as just to receive
" nine or ten of the altered packing-cases only. The hoops
" were lowered, and the painted covers made to fit exactly.
" Poles were used instead of shafts, and the usual swingle
" trees reduced fewer in number. The rejected parts being
" weighed, no less than six hundred pounds appeared saved
" in the draught by this simple operation, and a larger
" proportion of ammunition conveyed by it at the same time
" with less labour. The immense weight and bulk of the
" platform and devil carriages rendered them totally use-
" less; some of these altered waggons were substituted as a
" light class of the former kind, by taking away the bottoms

"entirely, and fixing in their stead a couple of very strong "planks to each, with an interval between them resembling "the original. These light platform carriages proved very "useful in withdrawing the ordnance and stores from our "lines across very heavy sands for re-embarkation."

The next subject treated of in the MS. is "Heavy weights raised without a Gin," as follows:—

"The two-wheeled trench-cart (of which there were "luckily a number on the Expedition) is a most useful "little carriage for carrying articles of moderate bulk to a "ton in weight; indeed, even so far as 10-inch iron mortar-"beds of 23 cwt. were transported in them, but in these "cases it was necessary, of course, to make use of a gin "also. To obviate this circumstance and render the cart of "more independent utility, an inclined plane was attached "to the rear of it, and a small windlass fixed in the front, "with a rope and iron block hooked to the weight, having "rollers to ease the purchase, the weight being thus brought "up on the cart by turning the windlass. By this simple "means six men were sufficient to mount upon the cart, "and deliver at a battery any article the strength of the "axletree and wheels could bear, without making the "appearance or drawing the attention of the enemy, which "such large machines as devil carriages and sling carts "constantly do, besides taking into consideration the vast "difference, in point of weight, between these carriages in "themselves. Another considerable advantage is that this "contrivance is only occasionally applied, and the cart may "be immediately worked in its original capacity.

Narrow wheels prevented from sinking in the sand.

"It being apprehended that extraordinary heavy weights "might cause the low, narrow wheels of the trenched cart "to sink so much into the sand as to retard the draught "considerably, a contrivance was thought of to prevent "this from happening, by occasionally increasing the "breadth of the fellies. The staves of casks being strong, "and of a favourable shape for the purpose, and still more "valuable from their being easily procured at the Commis-"sary-General's store, it was proposed to cut them into

"lengths of seven or nine inches each piece, having two
"small iron staples fixed at an interval, the breadth of the
"*felly*. A rope equal in length to the circumference of the
"wheel is run through each of these lines of staples, secured
"so as not to slip out, but keep the staves parallel at one
"inch and a half asunder. They are then applied to the
"wheels, and fixed by small lashings to the spokes, to keep
"the whole from any alteration in travelling."

SOME REMARKS ON THE FOREGOING ARTICLES.

1st. "The original intention of the Expedition did not
"appear to have Egypt for its object, and for a considerable
"while was very inauspicious. In the first instance it
"proved too late to be any use to the Austrians in Italy,
"and afterwards became unsuccessful at Cadiz. Much time
"appeared to be lost before it reached the *rendezvous* at
"Marmorice Bay; and it was then thought by the Turks a
"very unseasonable part of the year for any attempt on the
"coast of Egypt, besides which it happened to be the time of
"their Ramadan, when no operations of any kind are under-
"taken by them. This last delay, however, although much
"regretted, turned out advantageous to the future proceed-
"ings of the army. Some useful arrangements were made
"then, besides the opportunity it gave of landing the sick
"after a long confinement on board ship, by which many
"recovered; and the Island of Rhodes, just in the neigh-
"bourhood, afforded hospitals for the remainder."

2nd. "All the field ordnance, which had been landed at
"Ferrol with Lieutenant-General Sir James Pulteney's
"army, and afterwards joined General Sir Ralph Aber-
"cromby, were re-embarked there in so disorderly a manner
"that no one piece was found fit for immediate service.
"This circumstance will for ever unfortunately occur, *unless
"the direction of the business is left entirely to the Artillery
"Corps*, whether navy boats and ships of war or those of
"the Ordnance only receive them. It cannot be expected
"that the navy officers are in the first place fully acquainted
"with the real importance of keeping all the parts of such

" carriages, ammunition-boxes, &c., exactly sorted together,
" or that they can bestow much consideration on the subject,
" hurried as they generally are upon such occasions."

3rd. " The turning over only rejected horses from the
" Dragoons to the Artillery services was not so well judged
" as might be expected. It would have been fortunate (the
" best of theirs bearing no comparison with the French
" cavalry) to have rendered the movement of the Ordnance
" more effectual; as it was, both corps remained insufficient;
" the effects of which were fully experienced in the action
" of the 13th March, when, had only a part of the number
" of pieces then in the field been very well horsed, the fate
" of Alexandria (it is more than probable) might have been
" decided on that day. The French, on the other hand,
" *constantly applied the very prime of their strong horses*
" *(those belonging to the officers not excepted) to the draught of*
" *their ordnance*, which were chiefly on the Horse Artillery
" establishment, with 8-pounder guns and 6-inch howitzers,
" opposed to light 6-pounders and royals only."

4th. " The disembarking of ordnance, unless in the
" instance of field-pieces let down into the boats ready
" mounted from ships of war, however regularly performed,
" is always liable to some confusion. This principally arises
" from the parts of the same natures of carriages not corre-
" sponding so correctly as they might do, particularly in the
" diameters of the wheels and arms of the axletrees, which
" should likewise be as general throughout the whole as
" possible. The waggons and carts being frequently made
" by contract, are very defective in these points, even to the
" fitting of their head and tail-boards; and, trifling as this
" may appear to a workman at home, it often occasions
" delays of consequence to the service, or credit of those
" concerned in it abroad. No nation, in point of economy
" alone, requires so much attention to the construction and
" solid stowage of its military carriages and stores as Great
" Britain does, on account of their frequent embarkations,
" the expenses of which in the course of a war are pro-
" digiously great."

5th. "The considerations submitted to the Commander-in-Chief respecting the first landing of the ordnance and stores were much approved, and happily executed with great despatch, notwithstanding some very serious impediments, arising from the manner of loading the ships by *freight* (carrying as much as possible without order), instead of being regularly assorted. The embarking troops also on board such ships is always attended with, not only great inconvenience, but considerable damage, from the quantity of water necessary to carry for them, the waste and leakage of which injures the carriages and stores considerably underneath, besides the difficulty it occasions of getting at them when required for service. In the preparations for landing at Cadiz, seventy tons of water were obliged to be first removed from one ship only. Great inconveniences were also found from the magnitude of some of the ships, which could not be brought within some miles of the shore. They should for such services never exceed 600 tons, and a moderate draught of water."

6th. "Carronades might certainly be employed in the land service to considerable advantage in many situations, particularly on the flanks or firing over the parapets of fortifications and for field-works in general. It would also be very well worth while to have some experiments tried with them in breaching walls and earthworks. The common objection made to their shortness injuring the embrasures has more of imagination than reality in it. They may be advanced the extent of any gun mounted upon a travelling carriage, and much farther than the largest garrison howitzer, with less explosion of powder. If their present carriages are found to recoil too far, it is easily checked by only laying a few filled sand-bags upon them, and in the rear, as was practised in Egypt with perfect success; or it may be checked by small iron wedges with chains, placed to receive the fore-trucks upon."

7th. "The arrangement made of the spare field-ammunition on the passage from Marmorice Bay to the coast of Egypt was very fortunate, as it proved impossible to have

" carried any quantity forward otherwise, for want of con-
" veyance, excepting a few camels taken from the enemy on
" the first landing in Aboukir Bay."

8th. " The 3-pounder light guns, patched up as they
" were, gave considerable confidence to the Dragoons. This
" calibre might be rendered very useful to Cavalry in general
" by an increase of dimensions, to $4\frac{1}{2}$ feet in length, and about
" 4 cwt. in weight, with carriages upon a quick travelling
" construction, not overloaded with ammunition, which our
" service is rather liable to.

" Foreigners frequently observe the singularity of shafts
" being preferred in the British Artillery carriages to poles,
" made use of by all other nations as being simpler, lighter,
" and cheaper; added to which the experience of having tra-
" velled over the most difficult features of Europe, and
" ground of every description with them, fully evinces their
" perfect sufficiency. A strong instance of the inconvenience
" of shafts occurred to us at Rahmanich: just as one of the
" 6-pounders was limbering up, the shaft-horse was killed
" by the enemy; much time was lost in clearing the carriage
" from him, and the harness being also damaged, rendered
" it difficult to apply another in his place.

" In the marching of the 12-pounders to Grand Cairo
" (drawn by oxen with a horse in the shafts) the want of
" double or travelling trunnion-boxes was much regretted.
" Some few carriages were formerly so constructed for the
" Horse Artillery, but why discontinued remains unknown,
" as they are undoubtedly very advantageous to a heavy
" draught or indifferent horses.

" In moving the 24-pounder guns across the country
" from the first position near Cairo (where a bridge of boats
" to communicate with the Grand Vizier's army was thrown
" over the Nile) for the attack of Gizeh, the axletrees of the
" sling-carts giving way, the medium 12-pounder carriages
" were appropriated to this purpose, the trench-carts car-
" rying the mortars, standing carriages, &c."

9th. " No carriage appears to want reform more than the
" common Artillery waggon. There is too much of it merely

" for carrying ammunition, and it is too narrow for baggage
" or bulky stores. In the alterations made for the proposed
" arrangement of spare ammunition, the boxes will require
" for hard roads to be more securely fixed than was necessary
" for travelling in Egypt."

10th. " The inclined plane, or purchase for raising weights
" upon the trench-carts, might prove very useful, upon a
" larger scale, for mounting or dismounting heavy ordnance
" without being obliged to make use of a gin, which not
" only requires a number of men to work, and a carriage to
" convey it to a battery, but when fixed there becomes a
" considerable object to the enemy besieged. This proposed
" machine being quite free from all these inconveniences
" makes it extremely well worth while to try the experiment
" for such occasions."

11th. " If the mode mentioned of preventing narrow
" wheels from sinking in deep sandy situations should have
" the appearance of possessing more fancy than judgment, it
" must be placed to the variety of obstacles which hourly
" presented themselves in Egypt, and called for every assist-
" ance the mind could catch at to surmount. And still
" perhaps the idea may lead to something useful even in a
" northern climate, passing over snow, &c."

12th. . . . " The extraordinary heavy weights of the
" iron mortars and beds proved a great embarrassment
" without any peculiar advantage derived from them.
" Indeed, where no considerable extent of range is required
" —as is the case in most attacks—brass mortars mounted
" upon proportional iron beds seem in general much prefer-
" able, at least under 13 inches in diameter. . . . ."

13th. " Flat boats are the best and most useful convey-
" ance for troops, and ordnance, possible; every means,
" therefore, should be employed to preserve them from
" injury. Though apparently slight, it is surprising what
" they can bear. In moving the stores up Lake Etcho, for
" the attack of Fort Julian, some of them were dragged three
" miles over sand and mudbank. The battering-pieces for
" this service were obliged to be landed on the open sea-

" beach, and conveyed four miles across the deserts and
" swamps to their batteries. These laborious and difficult
" operations were frequently repeated during the Expedition.
" Upwards of thirty 24-pounders were disembarked from
" the ordnance ships, conveyed by boats up Aboukir Lake,
" and landed near the head of it for the attack of Alex-
" andria. From thence twenty were returned to the ships
" in Aboukir Bay, conveyed to the mouth of the western
" branch of the Nile, disembarked and taken over that dan-
" gerous bar by *sea-jerms*, landed at Fort St. Julian, re-
" embarked there in *river-jerms*, in order to proceed up the
" Nile. Several were landed within four miles of Grand
" Cairo, and conveyed from thence twelve miles across the
" country, for the attack of Gizeh;—returned back after the
" surrender of Cairo by the same route, and exactly in like
" manner to Alexandria;—relanded there for further opera-
" tions of attacks carrying on both on the eastern and
" western side of it,—the capitulation of which concluding
" the campaign, they were again conveyed to the ships in
" Aboukir Bay.

" Besides the articles already detailed, numerous minute
" circumstances happened in the course of the campaign,
" which necessity continually urged the imagination to
" provide against. Every movement by land or water
" was attended with infinite labour and difficulties;
" added to which the violent heat of the sun, and shocks
" received by passing over the formidable cracks it oc-
" casioned in the ground (annually overflowed by the
" Nile) on the march to Cairo operated so powerfully on
" the carriages, as to require perpetual attention and daily
" repair—without the most common materials for such
" occasions, either of wood or iron, to be found in the
" country.

" N.B. The oxen drew very well upon common ground,
" but in deep sand they generally became restive. The
" large-sized mules were excellent in draught when well-
" disposed; but, from their natural obstinacy, it was found
" best to intermix them with horses."

Battle of Alexandria.

RETURN OF ORDNANCE CAPTURED IN EGYPT.

		No. of Pieces.
In the Field .	On the 8th March	5
	On the 13th ,,	3
	On the 21st ,,	2
	On the 22nd August	7
Garrisons	Aboukir Castle	11
	Fort Julian	15
	Fort Burlos	5
	Grand Cairo and Dependencies	121
	Gizeh Lines and Arsenal	530
	Alexandria Arsenal	411
	Island of Marabout	10
	Damietta and Walls of Lesbie, &c.	54
	Ships of war in the Harbour of Alexandria	77
	Total number of pieces . .	1251

N.B.—Besides the above, the French were allowed to embark 50 field-pieces from Cairo, and 10 from Alexandria.

The extremely interesting notes just quoted, although relating more to questions of *matériel* than *personnel*, still give a clear idea of the difficulties attending the movements of the Artillery in Egypt, the overcoming of which was no less honourable, if, indeed, not more so, than their marked courage in the field. In alluding to the latter, a very brief sketch of the campaign will suffice.

On the morning of the 8th March, 1801, the English army disembarked in Aboukir Bay under a heavy fire, and drove back the French with a loss of five guns. On the 13th the severe action known as the affair of Nicopolis took place, in which the French were again defeated, but not without a loss to the English of 1300, killed and wounded. Cust. The siege of Aboukir Castle followed, the bombardment being conducted by Major Cookson, and it surrendered on Browne. the 19th. On the 21st, the memorable battle of Alexandria was fought,—memorable not merely for its victorious result, but also for the irreparable loss which the English army suffered in the death of Sir R. Abercromby. The conduct of the Artillery in the battle attracted great attention; the precision of their fire was strongly commended, and, but for the wretched animals with which the guns were horsed, an advance of the army might have then taken place which would have ensured the immediate fall of Alexandria. Lieutenants H. Sturgeon, J. G. Burslem, and D. Campbell, of the Royal Artillery, were wounded. The battle had been waged mainly on the right of the English army, and before the end of the day the ammunition of both Artillery and Cavalry on the English right was all but exhausted, so much so that "on an attempt of the French to advance anew " against this flank, the soldiers of the 28th actually " pelted them with stones." Unfortunately for the modern Artilleryman, General Lawson was a very bad correspondent during the war; and when the student commences anxiously to search for his despatches to the Ordnance, he finds, instead, indignant remonstrances addressed to the gallant General for his silence. He was so occupied with overcoming the natural difficulties of the Expedition, that he had no time for writing; and he valued no words of commendation, which were spoken with regard to his services, so much as those referring to the chief engineer and himself, which formed part of a despatch written by General Hutchinson, the successor of Sir R. Abercromby :—" The skill and per" severance of those two officers have overcome difficulties " which at first appeared almost insurmountable."

The arrival of a Turkish division, 6000 strong, to support him, on the 3rd April, 1801, induced General Hutchinson, who succeeded Sir R. Abercromby in the command, to carry the war farther up the Nile, instead of waiting before Alexandria. He commenced with some detached operations : Rosetta surrendered on the 8th, and Fort St. Julian, after a bombardment, on the 19th. "On the 18th April a mortar " battery, erected against Fort St. Julian, under the direc" tion of Captains Lemoine and Duncan, fired some shells " with remarkable accuracy : one of them pitched on the " centre of the roof, and tore away the flagstaff and colours, " which the French never dared to erect again."

The great events of the campaign were the surrender of

CHAP. VI.   *Perfection of British Artillery.*   129

Cairo on the 28th June, 1801, and of Alexandria on the 2nd September. It was during the march on Cairo that the ingenuity and endurance of the Royal Artillery were most severely tried. Other writers have borne testimony—in glowing, but not exaggerated terms—to the gallantry of the other arms of the service in this campaign; and it must not be assumed that the necessary allusions to a particular corps in a work like this imply any assertion of superiority; such conduct would be at once unjust, and subversive of the main purpose of this history. There are regiments, the very-mention of whose names brings instinctively to the hearer's memory the brave story of Egypt; but, where all were brave, the special professional duties of Artillerymen obtained for those, who served in that capacity, opportunities of displaying energy and ingenuity which were denied to others. There have been campaigns where the exertions of the Infantry have dwarfed those of the other arms; there have been occasions—sung by poets, and boasted of with just pride by all Englishmen—when the honour of England was intrusted to her Cavalry, and was brought back with redoubled lustre; it is, therefore, in no spirit of depreciation of the other arms that the services of the Artillery are especially pointed out, during a campaign where the hardest work was not in battle, and in a work which hopes to hand down to their successors the merits of those who, in Egypt, were responsible for their Regiment's reputation. It is with such a hope that words like the following, referring to the siege of Alexandria, are reproduced:—" The proceedings against " Alexandria showed to what a pitch of perfection the " British Artillery had arrived. The battery on the Green- " hill opened at six o'clock on the morning of the 26th " August, and before mid-day the enemy were completely " silenced, their batteries destroyed, and their guns with- " drawn. On the west of Alexandria, the tower of Mara- " bout was bombarded from a battery commanded by Captain " Curry,¹ of the Royal Artillery. The first shot struck the

Stewart's 'Highlanders of Scotland.'

---

¹ Afterwards Sir Edmund Curry.

VOL. II.   K

"tower, four feet from the ground; every succeeding shot struck the same spot; and in this manner he continued, never missing his mark, till a large hole was in a manner completely bored through, when the building fell, and, filling up the surrounding ditch, the place was instantly surrendered."

<small>Cust.</small>

At the surrender of Cairo no fewer than 13,754 French were present, and were allowed to evacuate Egypt; and at Alexandria, where General Menou, the French Commander, was stationed,—11,000 French soldiers, exclusive of civilians, surrendered to the English. In a campaign which lasted only from March to September, the power of the French in Egypt, and even their presence, disappeared. Prior to the capitulation of General Menou, he made a strong effort to drive the English from before Alexandria. This took place on the 22nd August, and in the general orders issued after the engagement the following words appeared:—"The brunt of the day fell on the Artillery, under the command of Major Cookson, and the advance corps, who used every exertion, and showed much discipline." It is also mentioned by a writer often quoted in these pages, whose industry becomes more and more apparent the more his work is studied, that "the celerity with which the guns at the siege of Alexandria had been brought up was a remarkable instance of zeal, as they had to be carried over almost inaccessible rocks."

<small>Browne, author of 'England's Artillerymen.'</small>

Two events occurred during the campaign, which deserve mention. A contingent of troops arrived from India under Sir David Baird, including some of the East India Company's Artillery, and a troop of the Bengal Horse Artillery, commanded by Captain Jarvis Pennington,—now A Battery, C Brigade, Royal Horse Artillery. The first instalment arrived on the 10th June, and was present at the surrender of Cairo by the French; and Sir David, with the main body, arrived in sufficient time to witness the successful termination of the siege of Alexandria, and with it the conclusion of the war.

The second event involves some explanation. In 1798 a detachment of the Royal Artillery was ordered to Turkey to assist in the instruction and organization of the Turkish Artillery, and in the strengthening of their fortifications. The officer in command was Brigadier-General Koehler, who had as a subaltern attracted attention during the great Siege of Gibraltar, and who had been almost continuously employed on the Staff of the army since that time. The Artillery officers who accompanied him were Majors Hope and Fead, Captain Martin Leake, and Assistant-Surgeon Wittman. The duties of these officers, as far as can be learned from the correspondence which is extant, were of a somewhat motley order,—embracing artillery, engineering, archæology, and military organization. Their travels in Turkey, Greece, Syria, and Egypt were very extensive; and if we may judge from a quaint manuscript in the Royal Artillery Record Office, describing a journey made by them to Jerusalem, they must have travelled as royal personages. General Koehler died on the 29th December, 1800, of a malignant fever, which had carried off his wife and many of his detachment; and the regret and positive grief, which were felt by English and Turks alike, were strongly expressed in Major Hope's reports to England. After his death, Major Hope, with the remainder of the detachment, accompanied the Grand Vizier and the Turkish contingent, which went to Egypt to swell the English forces, and earned well-deserved praise before Cairo, where the union between them and the latter took place. Major Hope's abilities as an Artilleryman received favourable mention from the Grand Vizier. After the conclusion of the campaign, Captain Leake obtained special employment in the Turkish dominions, and that he attained no mean position in the scientific and literary world may be gathered from the following obituary notice:—"On the 6th January, 1860, " Colonel Leake passed from us, after a short and " sudden illness. His intellect never weakened; his " energies scarcely relaxed, notwithstanding the weight " of eighty-three years. The Greek minister, at his own " desire, followed him to the grave, expressing thereby the " gratitude of his country to one who had spared no effort on

Major Hope, R.A., to D. A. General, January 1801.

Obituary notice of Lieut.-Col. W. M. Leake,R.A., in Address of the President of the Royal Geographical Society, May 1860.

"behalf of the Greek nationality, and had done so much
" by his works towards elucidating the remarkable features
" of the land of Greece, and the scenes of her glorious
" history. In him we have lost not only a scholar and an
" antiquary, but one other link (when so few survived) that
" connected us to the politics, the literature, and the society
" of the foregone generation."

On the 16th November, 1801, an order was issued for the withdrawal of the companies from Egypt, under which Captain Beevor's company of the 3rd Battalion, and Captain Cookson's, Major Sprowle's, and Captain Wood's of the 5th, returned to England; and Major Borthwick's, Captain Lemoine's, and Captain Adye's proceeded to Gibraltar. Major Borthwick remained in command of his company during the war, although, by the records of the 2nd Battalion, to which it belonged, Captain Mudge had been posted to it some time previously, an appointment which must have been subsequently cancelled, doubtless owing to his being employed by Government on the Trigonometrical Survey of Great Britain. In this occupation he was engaged during the greater part of his life, and his admirable conduct of the survey procured for him numerous literary and scientific distinctions.

Among the officers of artillery who received special mention for their services in Egypt, besides General Lawson, were Major Cookson, who, in addition to receiving high praise in general orders and despatches, was appointed, on the 29th October, 1801, commandant of the ancient Pharos Castle and of all the Artillery in Egypt, and was presented with a gold medal by the Grand Vizier; Captains Lemoine, A. Duncan, and S. G. Adye. Major Thompson, who had received brevet rank of Colonel during the war, died of wounds received on the 9th May, 1801, near Ramanieh; and it should be mentioned that General Lawson himself was severely wounded at the battle of Alexandria.

By General orders of 31st October and 1st November, 1803, the officers, non-commissioned officers, and men of the various companies which had served in Egypt were permitted to wear the "Sphynx," with the word "Egypt" on their regimental caps; but the distinction was a *personal* one, and not to be perpetuated in the companies. In regiments of the Line the distinction is perpetuated by emblazonment on their colours. Although, however, the decoration itself was but personal, the traditions of the deeds which it commemorated are the inheritance of the batteries, whose predecessors fought under the shadow of the Pyramids. Let them treasure the memories of gallantry and of difficulties overcome, and in the hours of their own toils and dangers let them " remember Egypt."

Note.—Detachments of two, if not three companies, in addition to those named above, were present in Egypt, and will be found mentioned in the tables in Volume i.

CHAPTER VII.

To 1803.

<small>Vol. i. pp. 163 & 417.</small>

SO many important events will demand detailed notice presently, that this chapter must be confined to a bare statement of facts, necessary to keep the chain of the Regimental history complete. The circumstances, under which the Royal Irish Artillery was incorporated as the 7th Battalion of the Regiment, have already been mentioned. No sooner had the amalgamation taken place, than a questionable step was taken by the authorities at the Ordnance: they ordered the 5th Battalion to proceed to Ireland, and relieve the 7th; and the six companies of the 7th Battalion, which were serving in their native land, were promptly shipped off to the West Indies to relieve the companies of the 1st, 2nd, and 4th Battalions. This instant use of the new battalion to garrison an unpleasant station can hardly have had a conciliatory effect; and doubtless the sudden and unpleasant change of quarters awakened occasional doubts as to the value of the Union—in a military point of view, —if not occasional mental growlings on the subject of "Justice to Ireland," among those who had to exchange the pleasures of Dublin for the disadvantages of the tropics. Be this as it may, in 1802 the new battalion was ordered to the West Indies.

The arrangements of the Board for the reliefs of the companies at this time reveal a very distinct attempt to secure, as far as possible, that companies of the same battalion should serve on the same station. For example, it was decided that, in 1803, the whole of the companies at Gibraltar should belong to the 6th Battalion; that the 1st and 2nd Battalions should be collected in England; the 5th in Ireland; and that the detached commands, and the wants of Canada should be supplied by the 3rd and 4th Battalions. The scheme was marred by an occasional company of a battalion, which it was hoped to concentrate, being found to be at the Cape of Good Hope, or Ceylon; but the effort was honestly made, and with the best intentions. That it utterly failed during the tempest of war, which was so soon and so long to rage, was not the fault of those who hoped to produce a very different state of affairs; but the result of inevitable causes. The American War had proved the inconvenience of a battalion's head-quarters being on the scene of hostilities: the lesson was accepted, and the various head-quarters were located at Woolwich; and therefore, the fact having been once admitted that the necessary control could be exercised, at a distance, over an individual company, all ideas of *symmetry* had to yield to necessity: and whencesoever a company could be most readily obtained, from that station it was taken, irrespective of the battalion to which it belonged. The test of a system frequently does not occur until the system must vanish before it; and this was the case in the wars between 1807 and 1815, which proved most satisfactorily that the official dreams of the Ordnance in 1802 and 1803 were not worth the paper on which they were written. Out of the web which was so honestly spun, the company, in time of war, made its inevitable escape, and asserted yet again its right to be called the Artillery unit.

On the signing of the Treaty of Peace, at Amiens, on the 27th March, 1802, immediate reductions were ordered in the military forces of England. In the Royal Artillery they took the form of reductions in the strength of the companies; and the following was the scheme, approved by the Master General, on the recommendation of Colonel Macleod. The short-lived amity between the French and English Governments did not admit of the reductions being altogether carried out; but it is interesting to see how they were proposed to be conducted.

Proposal agreed to on 7 Dec. 1801.	—	Sergeants.	Corporals.	Bombardiers.	Gunners.	Drummers.	Non-effectives.	Total.
	Present strength of one Battalion	40	40	70	980	30	30	1,190
	Proposed strength	30	30	60	700	30	30	880
	To be reduced	10	10	10	280	..	..	310
	Total reduction in seven Battalions	70	70	70	1,960	..	..	2,170

N.B. Of the above number of men to be reduced, there were about 680 men from the Militia, who were entitled to their discharge.

This reduction left the proportion of non-commissioned officers to gunners the same as before, viz. 1 to 6. During the American War, it had been as 1 to 5; after the peace of 1783, it fell to 1 to 7; and during the earlier wars of the French Revolution it rose to 1 to 6.

The strength of the Corps of Gunner-drivers in 1802 was as follows: Seven troops, each consisting of—

1 Captain-Commissary,
2 Lieutenants-Commissary.
2 Staff-Sergeants.
4 Sergeants.
6 First Corporals.
6 Second Corporals.
6 Farriers.
3 Smiths.

4 Collar-Makers.
4 Wheelers.
150 Gunner-drivers.
25 Riding Horses.

Staff.—1 Quartermaster.
1 Veterinary Surgeon.

The gunner-drivers attached to, and doing duty with the Horse Brigade, are not included above, being by a Royal Warrant of 1st September, 1801, mustered and paid with the Troops to which they were attached. These were in number 336. There were also 18 quartermaster-commissaries awaiting absorption, having been struck off the establishment on reduction. The number of horses belonging to the Corps of Gunner-drivers at this time included 2300 draught-horses, and 178 riding-horses.

Colonel Macleod remained Deputy Adjutant-General: General Lloyd was commandant of Woolwich: General

Blomefield, Inspector of Artillery: Sir William Congreve, Comptroller of the Laboratory; and General Duncan Drummond, Director-General of Artillery.

Chevrons were put on the arms of non-commissioned officers, according to the rules of the Army generally, instead of epaulettes, in the year 1802. The Royal Artillery Band was increased from 10 to 21 in the same year.

Two allusions to methods of discharging men at this time, which are found in the official correspondence, speak for themselves. The first is an order to discharge a man for his bad conduct, and to *hand him over to the press-gang*: and the second is a reply to a request from Lord Napier, that a man might be discharged, to enable him to support his family; and is as follows: " Charles Copeland, 5 feet 11 inches " in height: a wife and *two* children. It is observed that " he would have been discharged, if he had been lucky " enough to have three." <small>Colonel Macleod to Colonel Hadden, 9 Jan. 1802.</small>

CHAPTER VIII.

THE EIGHTH BATTALION.

THE Treaty of Amiens was not destined to be carried out in its entirety by the nations concerned. Napoleon's hostility to the English could not be concealed; and the evacuation of Malta, Alexandria, and the Cape of Good Hope, which had been commenced by the latter, in accordance with the terms of the Treaty, was never fully completed. On the 13th March, 1803, Lord Whitworth, the English Ambassador, was publicly insulted by Napoleon at the Tuileries; and on the 6th May he quitted Paris. The recommencement of hostilities with France was aggravated by another insurrection in Ireland, which was happily quelled with little difficulty. But the general state of affairs was so serious that an augmentation of the military forces in England became urgently necessary, as well as renewed activity on the part of the fleet. The Government received warm and cordial support from the people, both as a body and individually. Lord Chatham, then Master-General of the Ordnance, received on the 18th July a letter from a Mr. John Bagot, to the following effect :—" Being anxious in the present awful " crisis to come forward in any line that my services can be " of use to my King and country, I beg leave to offer, for the " consideration of your Lordship, to raise a Battalion of " Artillery, of 300 men, for the war or such further period " as may be necessary, and on such terms as your Lordship " or His Majesty's Government may direct. . . . ."

Mr. J. Bagot, London, to Lord Chatham, dated 11 July, 1803.

The state of recruiting in England was, however, so favourable, that the Master-General was not compelled to have recourse to private enterprise to obtain the necessary augmentations to the Regiment. The number of non-commissioned officers and men in the Horse Brigade and Marching Battalions of the Royal Artillery on the 1st January, 1803, was 6777; on the 1st June, notwithstanding the loss of 306 men by death or discharge, the total had increased to 7119; and in two months more, it stood at 7439, besides 131 recruits in the country districts, not yet posted. The Corps of Gunner-drivers had increased in the same period by 1109 men. It was therefore resolved to increase the Regiment by another battalion, the 8th, and the first intimation of this resolution is found in a private letter from the Deputy Adjutant-General. "It is at last, I believe, "determined," he wrote, "to increase the Artillery, even "under all the disadvantages of a deficiency in officers. The "cadets are doubled; and the winter may do a good deal "for us: in the mean time we take twenty of the most "forward. Our companies will only have two 1st Lieu- "tenants: there will be hardly a 2nd Lieutenant upon the "establishment."

Mem. to Master-Genl. from Colonel Macleod, 13 Aug. 1803.

Colonel Macleod to Lieut.-Colonel Willington, dated 7 Sept. 1803.

On the 13th September seven companies were formed, and on the 6th December, three additional companies were added to the battalion. The establishment of each company was as follows:—

1 Captain.	4 Sergeants.	Lieutenant Kane to R. H. Crew, Esq.
1 Captain-Lieutenant.	4 Corporals.	
2 First Lieutenants.	8 Bombardiers (and 3 non-effective, i.e. *paper* men).	
1 Second Lieutenant.	97 Gunners.	
	3 Drummers.	

Many of the men for the 8th Battalion were obtained by calling for volunteers from the Army of Reserve; and although every obstacle was thrown in the way of this method of obtaining recruits, by the officers commanding the Reserve Battalions, which were this year called out for service, very many excellent men were thus obtained.

It is unfortunate that the Battalion record-book of the 8th Battalion has been lost since 1859, the year when Battalion Head-quarters were abolished, because, although these books were, as a rule, very meagre in the information

Lieut. J. Ritchie, Staff-Officer, Coast Brigade, R.A.

they afforded, they nevertheless supplied facts which it would have been difficult to obtain elsewhere without great labour. That labour, in the case of the 8th Battalion, has been readily undertaken by an officer at Head-quarters, and to his industry the reader is indebted for the following tables.

Unfortunately, the history of the companies of the 8th and 9th Battalions, after 1850, must be postponed until the separate work on the Crimean services of the Artillery shall be written. But these tables give the earlier history, and the various stations—down to about 1850—on which the companies served, as well as the succession of Captains: and the war services of most of the companies will be found in the subsequent accounts of the various campaigns.

No. 1 COMPANY, 8th BATTALION,

Now "H" BATTERY, 1st BRIGADE, R.A.[1]

Succession of Captains.	Stations.
1803 F. Walker.	Formed 1803, 13th Sep., Woolwich.
1803 J. Hawker.	
1803 W. Scott.	1803 Dec., Gibraltar.
1803 R. Hope.	1808 Aug., Portugal. (Expⁿ·)
1804 R. W. Adye.	1815 Feb., Woolwich.
1804 23rd Oct., A. Brodin.	1819 Feb., Dover.
1816 22nd May, J. Taylor.	1822 Feb., Mauritius.
1819 1st Feb., A. Munro.	1830 15th Dec., Woolwich.
1823 3rd July, T. Greatley.	1834 1st Feb., Jersey.
1828 23rd Nov., J. Sinclair.	1840 29th Aug., Woolwich.
1841 25th Oct., W. Greenwood.	1841 27th Nov., China.
1848 30th May, P. Ellis.	1848 4th March, Woolwich.
	1848 22nd Nov., Ireland.

[1] This Company's Peninsular services were very distinguished.

CHAP. VIII. *"H" Battery, 11th Brigade.* 141

No. 2 COMPANY, 8th BATTALION,
Now " H " BATTERY, 11th BRIGADE, R.A.

Succession of Captains.	Stations.
1803 H. Owen.	Formed 1803, 13th Sep., Woolwich.
1803 A. Macdonald.	
1803 1st Dec., C. Baynes.	1803 Dec., Malta.
1806 6th Nov., H. Hickman.	1805 Oct., Sicily. (Exp".)
1823 24th July, H. Baynes.	1807 May, Alexandria.
1826 12th Dec., A. Macdonald.	1807 Nov., Sicily.
1833 23rd May, J. A. Chalmer.	1815 May, Naples.
1841 23rd Nov., J. H. Griffin.	1815 July, Genoa.
1847 19th Sept., D. W. Paynter.	1816 Feb., Malta.
	1819 July, Woolwich.
	1823 Oct., Guernsey.
	1827 July, Woolwich.
	1827 Oct., Jamaica.
	1833 May, Woolwich.
	1838 Jan., Ireland.
	1842 Oct., Woolwich.
	1842 Nov., West Indies.
	1848 April, Woolwich.
	1849 Feb., Scotland.

No. 3 COMPANY, 8th BATTALION,[1]
Afterwards " 1 " Battery, 11th Brigade ; " 3 " Battery, 14th Brigade ; " C " Battery, 14th Brigade, and " 8 " Battery, 13th Brigade. (*Vide* vol. i. p. 441.)

Reduced 1st *February,* 1871.

1803 G. Desbrisay.	Formed 1803, 13th Sep., Woolwich.
1804 1st June, J. Dyer.	
1806 9th March, W. M. Leake.	1804 Aug., Sevenoaks.
1808 12th Feb., W. Morrison.	1804 Oct., Woolwich.
1811 31st May, G. Skyring.	1804 Nov., Gibraltar.
1820 6th Nov., J. P. Adye.	1808 9th June, Exp" under
1831 27th Oct., P. V. England.	General Spencer.

[1] Although anticipating matters somewhat, the Author cannot resist adding a few words with reference to the very distinguished services of this—unhappily

"8" *Battery*, 13*th Brigade continued*—

Succession of Captains.	Stations.
1833 3rd Nov., J. Longley. 1838 28th June, J. Pascoe. 1842 13th April, C. Gostling. 1847 5th March, T. A. Shone. 1850 28th Sept., G. Gambier.	1808 27th July, Gibraltar. 1821 10th Sept., Woolwich. 1826 7th July, Dublin. 1827 28th Sept., Ballincollig. 1828 16th April, Ionian Islands. 1836 2nd Sept., Woolwich. 1841 29th March, Ireland. 1844 9th May, Woolwich. 1844 19th October, Malta.

defunct—company during the Indian Mutiny. No. 3 Company, 8th Battalion, left Ceylon for India on the 11th June, 1857. It was commanded by the 2nd Captain, Maude: Lieutenants Maitland and Dadson were the other officers. After remaining a week in Calcutta, it proceeded on the 20th June to join the force then being formed at Allahabad under General Havelock. The strength of the company had been reduced by cholera, &c., to 51. It marched with Havelock's column to Cawnpore, fighting on the way at Futtehpore, Pandu Nuddy, Avung, and before Cawnpore. After remaining at Cawnpore a short time to recruit the energies of his force, Havelock marched across the Ganges into Oude, hoping to penetrate to Lucknow. He fought four actions, viz.: (1) Onao; (2) Basarat Gunj; (3) Basarat Gunj; (4) Boorbeaki Choki, close to Basarat Gunj, having to fall back from Basarat Gunj each time from weakness. These four actions were fought on three successive Wednesdays—the two first on the same day. He then returned to Cawnpore. Reinforcements under Generals Neill and Outram began to arrive, and during the end of August and beginning of September the force increased to 3000 men. They therefore left Cawnpore on the 18th September (leaving a small garrison), fighting at Mangalwarra and at Alumbagh, close to Lucknow, and then prepared for the great struggle of entering the city. After coming out of Lucknow, the company was reinforced by some Artillerymen from England, and by Lieutenants A. Ford and S. Brown, and remained at Alumbagh under Sir James Outram to hold the swarms of natives in Lucknow in check. During this time frequent skirmishes and two real actions took place, all ending in the natives being repulsed with loss. In March, Lord Clyde came up with a large force, and the company went to take Lucknow, forming part of the siege train, and being told off to 18-pounders, 8-inch howitzers, and 5½-inch mortars. After this, the company was engaged in a few affairs of minor importance in Oude, until the country was pacified.

If it should be the Author's privilege to write the History of the Royal Artillery during the Indian Mutiny, he is fortunately in a position to amplify the above sketch with instances of individual heroism and suffering.

CHAP. VIII. *" 7 " Battery, 12th Brigade.* 143

No. 4 COMPANY, 8th BATTALION,
Now " 7 " BATTERY, 12th BRIGADE, R.A.

Succession of Captains.	Stations.
1803 13th Sept., T. Boger.	Formed 1803, 13th Sep., Woolwich.
1803 13th Sept., C. Baynes.	
1803 1st Dec., A. Macdonald.	1804 May, Colchester.
1804 1st June, W. R. Carey.	1804 Dec., Woolwich.
1812 23rd April, W. Scott.	1805 March, Exp^n under Sir J. Craig.
1814 25th Dec., H. Pierce.	
1819 1st Feb., J. P. Cockburn.	1805 Oct., Malta.
1819 23rd Feb., C. H. Fitzmayer.	1822 April, Woolwich.
1819 22nd April, R. Douglas.	1826 Dec., Portugal.
1826 21st Dec., W. Wylde.	1828 April, Woolwich.
1839 24th Nov., E. J. Bridges.	1831 Nov., Ireland.
1842 13th April, C. H. Mee.	1838 Feb., Woolwich.
1850 16th July, C. C. Young.	1838 July, Halifax, N.S.
	1845 Nov., Woolwich.
	1847 Dec., Dover.
	1850 Jan., Woolwich.

No. 5 COMPANY, 8th BATTALION,
Now " G " BATTERY, 1st BRIGADE, R.A.

1803 13th Sept., B. Fenwick.	Formed 1803, 13th Sep., Woolwich.
1803 1st Nov., P. Drummond.	
1804 1st Dec., R. Pym.	1804 Nov., Plymouth.
1815 28th Oct., G. C. Coffin.	1805 March, Sicily. (Exp^n.)
1817 1st April, J. Maclachlan.	1807 May, Alexandria.
1825 29th July, F. Arabin.	1807 Nov., Sicily.
1832 18th July, T. Cubitt.	1810 Jan, Exped^n under Sir J. Stuart.
1836 25th May, W. E. Locke.	
1846 12th Dec., J. Hill.	1810 Sept., Sicily.
	1814 Feb., Genoa.
	1814 May, Exp^n to America.
	1815 June, Woolwich.
	1819 Feb., Dublin.
	1821 June, Limerick.
	1821 Dec., Dublin.
	1822 June, Ionian Islands.
	1828 Aug., Woolwich.
	1833 May, Ireland.

144 *The Eighth Battalion.* CHAP. VIII.

" G " Battery, 1st Brigade continued—

Succession of Captains.	Stations.
	1839 April, Halifax, N.S.
	1845 Nov., Woolwich.
	1847 Nov., Weedon.
	1848 April, Birmingham.
	1850 Jan., Woolwich.
	1850 Oct., Gibraltar.

No. 6 COMPANY, 8th BATTALION,
Now " D " BATTERY, 9th BRIGADE, R.A.

1803 13th Sept., J. S. Williamson.	Formed 1803, 13th Sep., Woolwich.
1803 1st Oct., R. Buckner.	
1808 15th May, J. S. Williamson.	1803 Nov., Canterbury.
1814 25th Dec., J. P. Adye.	1804 Feb., Chatham.
1819 1st March, J. A. Clement.	1806 July, Sicily. (Expⁿ.)
1827 31st Dec., E. Barlow.	1809 May, Sir J. Stuart's Exp^{n.}
1828 30th June, E. Cruttenden.	1809 July (about), Sicily.
1841 25th Jan., H. Williams.	1809 Sept., Zante.
1842 19th Nov., C. R. Dickens.	1811 Dec., Sicily.
1845 14th June, J. E. Dupuis.	1812 July, Spain.
1846 16th Nov., H. Pester.	1814 May, Genoa.
1847 30th Jan., F. S. Hamilton.	1816 Feb., Malta.
	1816 July, Ionian Islands.
	1822 Dec., Woolwich.
	1827 March, Portsmouth.
	1830 March, Mauritius.
	1842 March, Woolwich.
	1843 Aug., Channel Islands.
	1846 March, Woolwich.
	1847 Jan., Malta.

No. 7 COMPANY, 8th BATTALION,
Now " H " BATTERY, 8th BRIGADE, R.A.

1803 13th Sept., R. Douglas.	Formed 1803, 13th Sep., Woolwich.
1804 1st Oct., E. Curry.	
1806 1st June, R. Dickinson.	1805 Nov., Exeter.
1806 15th Sept., T. S. Hughes.	1807 May, Plymouth.

CHAP. VIII.   " 1 " *Battery, 7th Brigade.*   145

" H " *Battery, 8th Brigade continued—*

Succession of Captains.	Stations.
1808 20th June, R. Lawson.	1807 Dec., Exp" under General Spencer.
1819 1st May, F. Knox.	
1832 23rd Dec., J. H. Ward.	1808 May, Gibraltar.
1844 1st April, F. Weller.	1808 Aug., Exp" under General Spencer.
1844 24th Aug., A. R. Harrison.	
1846 16th Nov., J. W. Fitzmayer.	1808 Aug., Portugal and Spain.
1847 14th May, G. Maclean.	1814 Aug., Dublin.
	1816 Aug., Pendennis and Exeter.
	1818 Sept., Ballincollig.
	1821 July, Gibraltar.
	1822 July, Ionian Islands.
	1828 Jan., Woolwich.
	1830 March, Leith.
	1833 June, Woolwich.
	1835 Nov., Bermuda.
	1842 May, Woolwich.
	1843 Oct., Ireland.
	1846 Aug., Woolwich.
	1847 July, Ceylon.

No. 8 COMPANY, 8th BATTALION,

Now "1" BATTERY, 7th BRIGADE, R.A.

1803 6th Dec., H. Fraser.	Formed 1803, 6th Dec., Woolwich.
1815 16th May, H. B. Lane.	
1819 1st March, E. C. Whinyates.	1806 May, Warley.
1823 3rd July, J. S. Bastard.	1806 July, Malta.
1836 26th April, L. S. B. Robertson.	1809 June, Sicily.
1838 16th Nov., G. Spiller.	1809 June, Exp" under Sir J. Stuart.
1843 18th May, W. Berners.	
1845 21st May, G. Bingham.	1811 Nov., Zante.
	1814 July, Corfu.
	1822 Dec., Woolwich.
	1827 June, Guernsey.
	1829 May, Woolwich.
	1830 Feb., Cape of Good Hope.
	1842 March, Woolwich.
	1843 Oct., Leith.
	1846 May, Woolwich.
	1847 July, Ceylon.

VOL. II.   L

No. 9 COMPANY, 8th BATTALION,
Now "7" BATTERY, 17th BRIGADE, R.A.

Succession of Captains.	Stations.
1803 6th Dec., J. Vivion. 1803 6th Dec., R. W. Adye. 1804 1st Jan., R. Hope. 1804 20th July, R. T. Raynsford. 1811 18th Nov., R. W. Gardiner. 1813 23rd Jan., S. Du Bourdieu. 1813 23rd July, L. Carmichael. 1816 7th June, C. F. Sandham. * * * * * 11th Battalion Records. 1848 7th Aug., G. C. R. Levinge. 1854 A. C. L. Fitzroy. 1854 H. F. Strange. 1856 F. R. Glanville. N.B.—This Company was in the Crimea from 1854–56, and was present at the Battle of Inkerman. (11*th Battalion Records.*)	Formed 1803, 6th Dec., Woolwich. — 1806 Nov., Sevenoaks. 1807 April, Exeter. 1807 Dec., Plymouth. 1808 May, Exp^n under Sir A. Wellesley. 1808 Oct., Spain. 1809 Jan., Chatham. 1810 Sept., Exeter. 1810 Oct., Plymouth. 1811 April, Portugal, Spain, and France. 1814 May, Exp^n to North America. 1814 Oct., Jamaica. 1814 Nov., New Orleans. 1815 June, Belgium and France. 1816 Feb., Woolwich. *Reduced at Woolwich, 31st Jan., 1819.* *Reformed at Woolwich, 7th Aug., 1848.* Transferred to 11th Battalion as No. 8 Company, on 1st November, 1848. Became 7 Battery, 5th Brigade, on 1st July, 1859, and 7 Battery, 17th Brigade, on 1st Oct., 1867.

No. 10 COMPANY, 8th BATTALION.

Reduced at Woolwich on 28th February, 1819.

1803 6th Dec., R. Pym. 1804 1st Dec., P. Drummond. 1806 1st Jan., W. Millar. 1806 27th March, P. Meadows.	Formed 1803, 6th Dec., Woolwich. — 1806 Feb., Sevenoaks. 1806 Nov., Woolwich.

CHAP. VIII. *Battle of Maida.* 147

No. 10 *Company,* 8*th Battalion continued*—

Succession of Captains.	Stations.
1811 5th Sept., J. P. Eligé.	1807 July, Copenhagen.
1812 20th Jan., T. A. Brandreth.	1807 Nov., Chatham.
	1807 Nov., Woolwich.
	1807 Dec., Exeter.
	1809 March, Plymouth.
	1810 Oct., Portugal and Spain.
	1814 Aug., Shorncliffe.
	1816 July, Portsmouth.
	1816 Dec., Ireland.
	1819 Feb., Woolwich.

Between the formation of the 8th and 9th Battalions, an augmentation of five troops of Horse Artillery took place, as has been mentioned elsewhere. Very little interest attaches to this period, except that in 1806 the commencement of a garrison of Royal Artillery in Italy and Sicily took place, which remained in these countries for some years. In 1806, six companies of the Royal Artillery were stationed there; in 1807 there were five; in 1808, four; in 1809, five; in 1810, five; and in 1814, the last year of the occupation, there were four. The war in Italy, which was distinguished in 1806 by the English victory of Maida, is thus described by the officer who commanded the Royal Artillery on the Expedition. " On the 28th June (1806) I received orders " from the Commander-in-Chief to have in readiness for a " particular service a detachment of Artillery with some " light guns. In consequence I made a collection, and on " the 30th embarked with the greater part of the army, " the Commander-in-Chief (Sir John Stuart) taking the " field. On the 2nd July we anchored on the coast of Ca- " labria, near St. Eufemia, and landed immediately. After " taking a position, and reconnoitring the country, we moved " forward at daylight on the 4th to the Plains of Maida, " near where the enemy, under the command of General

Vol. ii. chap. 2.

Major Lemoine, R.A., to Brig.-Gen¹. Macleod.

" Regnier, had assembled. On our approach, he descended
" to the plains, and having formed his line, which we had
" already done, the two armies met near the centre of the
" plain, and came to immediate action, which lasted nearly
" an hour and a quarter, when the French were charged
" by our Light Infantry, and their left completely turned;
" the right also gave way shortly after. We pursued them
" the whole extent of the plain, nearly six miles, and gained
" a complete victory. The prisoners acknowledge to have
" had in action 8000 men : the British army had 4600. Our
" loss very trifling—only one officer killed, 41 men, and 253
" wounded. The loss of the enemy cannot be correctly ascer-
" tained, though we have taken and killed upwards of 2000.
" Many of their wounded got off to the mountains, and General
" Regnier among them, severely wounded. General Piegri
" was killed; General Coupère wounded, and prisoner; the rest
" of the army has retired in a confused state some distance,
" and is much harassed by the natives. Sir John Stuart,
" finding the army retiring so fast, thought it most desirable
" to return to the coast, and marched to this place (Mon-
" teloine) on the 8th, where we found 200 French, and great
" quantities of stores, which we are now embarking. There
" are also two or three other posts along the coast which
" they left in the same manner, and which are now in our
" possession. I understand that as soon as everything is
" embarked, the army will return to Messina. I have the
" honour to enclose you the General Orders of the 4th in-
" stant, and have to add that the whole of the Artillery in
" this little expedition were in the front of the action, and
" behaved in the most cool and gallant manner. Captain
" Pym, on the right of the Grenadiers, with two 6-pounders
" and a howitzer, repulsed two squadrons of cavalry in at-
" tempting to break our line. Lieutenant Bayley, with two
" 4-pounders, in front of the Light Infantry, made good use
" of his case-shot, till that corps charged, when they ran
" over his guns; indeed every officer and soldier gave me
" his utmost assistance, and I should be wanting in gratitude
" to them did I not acknowledge it; though to you, sir, I

" should be doubly wanting, did I not take the earliest
" opportunity of thanking you for having entrusted to my
" command a detachment of Artillery that have so gallantly
" distinguished themselves before an enemy nearly double
" their numbers." [1]

[1] The General Order referred to was issued by Sir John Stuart on the 6th July, 1806, and contains the following passage: " The Artillery were " well provided, and most effectually served, under the directions of Major " Lemoine, the Commandant of that corps."

NOTE.—Another event may here be chronicled, taken from the record of the services of Sir Robert Gardiner : " Captain Gardiner, in 1805, com- " manded 12 guns, with the force under Lieut.-General Don, forming the " advanced corps of the army destined to serve under Lord Cathcart in the " north of Germany, combined with the Russian army under Count Folstog. " They advanced as far as Hanover, when the result of the battle of " Austerlitz put an end to the campaign, and the army returned home."

CHAPTER IX.

THE NINTH BATTALION.

THIS Battalion of the Royal Artillery was formed in an eventful year. Whether we regard it from a political or a purely military point of view, the year 1806 had an important influence on those which followed it.

The previous year, the year of Austerlitz, had witnessed the collapse of Pitt's coalition against Napoleon, and the consequent isolation of England. But it was also the year of Trafalgar; and left England still mistress of the seas.

With 1806 came the Battle of Jena, Napoleon's triumphal entry into Berlin, and the issue of his famous declaration against English commerce, which, if obeyed to the letter, would have put England virtually in a state of blockade. It was a critical year for a country whose commerce was her very life-blood; and in this very year, those who had so long steered the ship of the State, William Pitt and Charles James Fox, were removed by death. But the country took up the gauntlet thrown down by Napoleon, and from this year conducted with sternness and determination a war which, from being one of *resistance*, became one for *existence* as well.

It was a year, too, which should be remembered fondly in the annals of the British Army—the year of the Battle of Maida, described in the last chapter, where the gallantry of the British troops against Napoleon's tried legions obtained a victory, which had a moral influence both in England and on the Continent, which is perhaps rarely realised now.

Grasping the importance of the situation, and greatly assisted by the ease of obtaining recruits, the Board of Ordnance resolved on an augmentation of the Royal Artillery to the extent of yet another battalion. The strength of the

Regiment, and its periodical increase and decrease, are ascertainable from a return which used to be furnished annually to the Board, called the "Wear and Tear of the "Regiment for the year ending," &c. From this return it would appear that during the year 1805, the number of gunner-recruits who joined the Horse Artillery and Marching Battalions was no less than 2574. But the *wear and tear* by death, transfer, desertion, &c., during the same period was 1017, so that the net increase was 1557; the Regiment rising from 10,203, at which it stood on 1st January, 1805, to 11,760, its strength on the 31st December in the same year. During the same period the Corps of Royal Artillery Drivers, and Drivers attached to the Horse Brigade, had received 489 recruits, and, allowing for the wear and tear during the year, had increased from 4897 to 4986 of all ranks, excluding officers.

It is hardly possible that this large increase to the establishment had been allowed by the Board without a motive; and it may indeed be assumed with tolerable certainty that the formation of the 9th Battalion had been to some extent contemplated during Napoleon's successes in 1805. This impression is confirmed by reference to the returns for the year 1806, which show that the increase to the Regiment during that year was only half what had taken place during the year preceding.

The increase which had been permitted during the year 1805 proved to be greater than was necessary for the wants of the new Battalion; and the establishment of the Regiment was found on the 1st May, 1806, to have been exceeded by over 400 men. This excess, however, was soon swallowed up by the year's wear and tear, which in 1806 amounted to 874 men.

The promotions consequent on the formation of the new Battalion were gazetted on 22nd May, 1806, and Major-General Thomas Blomefield was appointed Colonel-Commandant. The record-book of the Battalion, like that of the 8th, has been lost since the introduction of the Brigade system. It was permitted to accompany the head-quarters

·of the 9th Brigade, and during their frequent changes of station it has been mislaid—offering another argument, if one were needed, in favour of the centralization of all military records. As in the case of the 8th Battalion, so in the present instance the Regiment is indebted to an officer at Head-quarters for the following facts connected with the companies prior to 1850. Their present designations, and the stations in which they served, have been given, and the succession of Captains down to a certain date. The war services of some companies will be found mentioned in the succeeding narrative, and the tables will be completed, should the compilation of the separate work on the Crimea be at some future time accomplished.

Lieut. J. Ritchie, Staff-Officer Coast Brigade, R.A.

No. 1 COMPANY, 9th BATTALION,

Now "G" BATTERY, 9th BRIGADE, R.A.

List of Captains down to 1850.			Stations on which the Company has served.	
1806	Captain	J. S. Robison	1806	Woolwich.
1808	„	J. T. Cowper.	1807	Ireland.
1819	„	W. D. Nicolls.	1816	Jamaica.
1833	„	G. Durnford.	1825	Woolwich.
1842	„	R. B. Rawnsley.	1827	Ireland.
1845	„	H. G. Teesdale.	1833	Woolwich.
1846	„	R. M. Poulden.	1833	Gibraltar.
1846	„	A. J. Taylor.	1842	Woolwich.
1850	„	T. Elwyn.	1843	Ireland.
			1846	Woolwich.
			1847	Barbadoes.

No. 2 COMPANY, 9th BATTALION,

Now "E" BATTERY, 8th BRIGADE, R.A.

List of Captains who have commanded down to 1846.	List of Stations where the Company has served down to 1850.
1806 Captain J. Smith.	1806 Woolwich.
1807 „ J. W. Tobin.	1807 Ireland.
1814 „ S. Bolton.	1815 Holland and France.
1815 „ W. Clibborn.	1816 Woolwich.
1819 „ C. Wilkinson.	1822 Barbadoes.
1825 „ T. Dyneley.	1828 Woolwich.
1825 „ J. Darby.	1831 Scotland.
1827 „ C. Cruttenden.	1835 Woolwich.
1827 „ P. W. Walker.	1836 Gibraltar.
1840 „ R. Clarke.	1845 Woolwich.
1846 „ C. V. Cockburn.	1847 Guernsey.
	1849 Woolwich.
	1850 Jamaica.

No. 3 COMPANY, 9th BATTALION,

Afterwards " 8 " Battery, 11th Brigade ; then " 7 " Battery, 14th Brigade; then " G " Battery, 14th Brigade ;

Now "B" BATTERY, 14th BRIGADE, R.A.

Names of Captains down to 1843.	Stations on which the Company served down to 1847.
1806 Captain J. M. Close.	1806 Woolwich.
1819 „ H. Pierce.	1807 Plymouth.
1824 „ H. A. Scott.	1810 Ireland.
1836 „ T. G. Higgins.	1816 Jamaica.
1842 „ F. Holcombe.	1825 Woolwich.
1843 „ J. Tylden.	1828 Ireland.
	1833 Gibraltar.
	1842 Woolwich.
	1844 Ireland.
	1847 Woolwich.
	1847 Barbadoes.

No. 4 COMPANY, 9th BATTALION,
Now "6" BATTERY, 12th BRIGADE, R.A.

Captains who have commanded the Company to 1846.	Stations on which the Company has served to 1848.
1806 Captain H. Crawford.	1806 Woolwich.
1807 „ W. Lloyd.	1808 Canterbury.
1808 „ N. W. Oliver.	1809 Walcheren.
1810 „ S. Maxwell.	1809 Canterbury.
1812 „ J. Hawker.	1813 Holland.
1814 „ C. G. Alms.	1815 France.
1819 „ P. J. Hughes.	1816 Woolwich.
1825 „ W. B. Dundas.	1819 Ireland.
1833 „ C. Cruttenden.	1825 Jamaica.
1838 „ G. T. Rowland.	1830 Woolwich.
1846 „ G. Innes.	1833 Newcastle, Leeds, &c.
	1838 Woolwich.
	1840 Jamaica.
	1846 Woolwich.
	1848 Ireland.

No. 5 COMPANY, 9th BATTALION,
Now "2" BATTERY, 3rd BRIGADE, R.A.

Captains who have commanded the Company to 1846.	Stations on which the Company has served to 1849.
1806 Captain J. May.	1806 Woolwich.
1807 „ J. W. Tobin.	1809 Chatham.
1807 „ J. W. Smith.	1809 Walcheren.
1809 „ H. Stone.	1809 Chatham.
1813 „ J. Michell.	1811 Portsmouth.
1830 „ M. Louis.	1812 Peninsula and France.
1837 „ C. Otway.	1814 America.
1837 „ R. Palmer.	1815 Holland and France.
1846 „ W. H. Forbes.	1816 Woolwich.
	1819 Weedon.
	1824 Woolwich.
	1824 Jamaica.
	1830 Woolwich.
	1834 Ireland.
	1840 Woolwich.
	1841 Mauritius.
	1849 Woolwich.

CHAP. IX.   *" C" Battery, 14th Brigade.*   155

No. 6 COMPANY, 9th BATTALION,

Reduced 28th February, 1819.

Names of Captains.	Stations on which the Company served.
1806 Captain F. Griffiths. 1808 „ P. J. Hughes.	1806 Woolwich. 1808 Battle. 1810 Cadiz. 1814 Woolwich. 1816 Plymouth.

No. 7 COMPANY, 9th BATTALION.

This Company became No. 6 Company on March 1st, 1819; was called No. 8 Battery, 14th Brigade, on July 1st, 1859; its designation was again altered on January 1st, 1860, to No. 8 Battery, 13th Brigade; and on the 1st October, 1862, it became, what it now is,

" C " BATTERY, 14th BRIGADE, R.A.

Names of Captains who commanded it down to 1848.	Stations on which the Battery has served down to 1849.
1806 Captain R. Macdonald. 1806 „ H. F. Holcombe. 1807 „ G. Massey. 1812. „ J. E. Jones. 1828 „ J. E. G. Parker. 1833 „ R. Heron. 1841 „ R. L. Garstin. 1848 „ C. R. Wynne.	1806 Woolwich. 1808 Chatham. 1809 Walcheren. 1809 Canterbury. 1810 Dover. 1814 Halifax, N.S. 1826 Woolwich. 1829 Ireland. 1834 Gibraltar. 1843 Woolwich. 1845 Devonport. 1848 Woolwich. 1849 Corfu.

No. 8 COMPANY, 9th BATTALION.

Reduced on 28th February, 1819.

Name of Captain who commanded it.	Names of Stations on which the Company served down to 1819.
1806 Captain A. Munro.	1806 Woolwich.
	1807 Chatham.
	1808 Canterbury.
	1809 Walcheren.
	1809 Canterbury.
	1812 Shorncliffe.
	1814 Portsmouth.
	1814 America.
	1815 Brussels.
	1816 Canterbury.
	1816 Shorncliffe.
	1816 Dover.
	1819 Woolwich.

No. 9 COMPANY, 9th BATTALION.

This Company became No 7 Company on 1st March, 1819; and No. 8 Battery, 10th Brigade, on the 1st July, 1859. It was reduced on 1st February, 1871.

Names of Captains who commanded it down to 1850.	Stations on which the Company served down to 1846.
1806 Captain J. P. Cockburn.	1806 Woolwich.
1806 „ J. F. Ogilvie.	1808 Chatham.
1807 „ J. S. Sinclair.	1809 Portsmouth.
1808 „ T. J. Forbes.	1810 Ireland.
1823 „ C. Mosse.	1817 Barbadoes.
1831 „ W. Greene.	1827 Woolwich.
1834 „ C. Dalton.	1829 Devonport.
1834 „ J. C. Petley.	1833 Woolwich.
1837 „ A. Wright.	1834 Jamaica.
1840 „ F. Warde.	1841 Woolwich.
1842 „ B. Cuppage.	1843 Devonport.
1849 „ T. de Winton.	1845 Woolwich.
1850 „ A. T. Phillpotts.	1846 Gibraltar.

CHAP. IX. *" E " Battery, 9th Brigade.* 157

No. 10 COMPANY, 9th BATTALION.

This Company became No. 8 Company, 9th Battalion, on 1st March, 1819; and on the introduction of the Brigade system, in 1859, it became No. 5 Battery, 9th Brigade, or, as now called,

" E " BATTERY, 9th BRIGADE, R.A.

Names of Captains who commanded it down to 1842.	Names of Stations on which it served down to 1842.
1806 Captain J. Chamberlayne.	1806 Woolwich.
1810 „ R. Douglas.	1808 Chatham.
1814 „ G. Turner.	1809 Walcheren.
1820 „ A. Bredin.	1809 Chatham.
1823 „ W. Clibborn.	1810 Woolwich.
1834 „ A. B. Rawnsley.	1810 Exeter.
1837 „ A. O. W. Schalch.	1811 Plymouth.
1841 „ R. R. Drew.	1812 Peninsula and France.
1842 „ W. L. Kaye.	1814 Canada.
	1824 Woolwich.
	1827 Ireland.
	1831 West Indies.
	1837 Woolwich.
	1842 Ireland.

CHAPTER X.

THE SIEGE OF COPENHAGEN.

THE decree of the French Emperor, dated 20th November, 1806, forbidding all commerce and correspondence between the countries under his influence and Great Britain, received an alarming force from his subsequent rapid successes, culminating in the Treaty of Tilsit.

After that date it was evident that, in addition to injuring the commercial marine of England, Napoleon was resolved to make a great effort to overthrow her yet unquestionable naval supremacy. This he hoped to effect by a union of his own fleet with those of his allies and subjects; and one of the most powerful which he hoped to secure for his purpose was the Danish fleet.

The English Government resolved on a bold step, in order to defeat Napoleon's aim. They decided to request the Danish Government to hand over their fleet to England for safe keeping, and they supported their petition by the presence of a large naval and military force. This determination was arrived at on the 19th July, 1807; and before the 29th the whole force was ready to sail. The fleet consisted of 17 ships of the line, between 30 and 40 frigates, and other smaller ships of war, counting 90 pendants; together with 300 transports, having on board 20,000 troops, a number subsequently increased to 27,000. The Artillery force was as follows: Royal Artillery, 989; Royal Artillery drivers, 525; German Legion Artillery—horse, 182, and foot, 512.

Cust.

Official MS. Returns, R. A. Record Office.

The command of this large Artillery force was given to Major-General Thomas Blomefield on the 28th July, 1807, in the following terms :—

"Woolwich, 28 July, 1807.
" SIR,
"The Master-General has directed me to notify
" officially an order for your embarking upon the present
" expedition with the command of the Artillery, and that
" you place yourself under the orders of Lieutenant-General
" Burrard, or the General commanding the troops.
"I have the honour to be, Sir,
"Your most obedient humble Servant,
" J. MACLEOD,
" D.-A.-General."

" P.S.—MY DEAR GENERAL,
" Having performed the *ex officio* part, let me wish
" you every success and every happiness, and a safe return
" to Shooter's Hill, where we shall talk over all your
" performances. The ordnance is all embarked, but not a
" ship arrived as yet for the officers and men.
" Believe me
" Very truly yours,
" J. MACLEOD."

General Thomas Blomefield, who joined the Regiment on 1st January, 1759, had seen active service at the Havannah, in the West Indies, and during the American War. He had been severely wounded during the last-mentioned campaign. In 1780 he was made Inspector of Ordnance at Woolwich; and for many years held this appointment in a manner most advantageous to the country. He was a good mathematician, an excellent chemist, and most laborious in experiments in gunnery. His private character is thus described by one who knew him intimately:—" There was no display "of his merits shown in his manner; all his duties and " improvements were silently and unassumingly carried on, " with a natural reserve and undeviating correctness, so " that it was only the close observer who could duly " appreciate his value. His being generally and greatly " esteemed arose as much from his being the perfect Family MSS.

"gentleman as from the ingenuous turn of his mind, for
"there was no glare or obtrusive view, but rather a strong
"desire to improve the service with as little parade as
"possible." The marked improvement in English ordnance
while he was Inspector was tested at the very siege over
which he was to preside, and is thus alluded to by the same
writer:—"The late sieges of Copenhagen and in the Penin-
"sula, where the mode of battering assumed a rapidity of
"firing unknown on former occasions, strongly marked the
"confidence his gallant brother officers had in the weapons
"placed in their hands, and surprised the enemy, who were
"known to declare that they could not have put their iron
"ordnance of this description to such a severe test. The
"complete success of these objects of his most serious and
"careful pursuit will be duly appreciated by those capable
"of judging of their merits. To such as are not, it may
"be allowed to suggest that many gallant lives have been
"saved to their country and families by the constant and
"most anxious endeavours he at all times pursued to put
"safe and perfect machines into the hands of the brave
"defenders of His Majesty's dominions."

The following is a nominal list of the officers of the Royal Artillery who accompanied General Blomefield to Copenhagen:—

Lieutenant-Colonels Harding, Cookson, and Robe; Captains May, Cockburn, Francklin, Newhouse, Fyers, P. Drummond, Brome, and Meadows; 2nd Captains Bolton, J. P. Adye, Paterson, Unett, Whinyates, Sandham, Holcroft, and Kettlewell; 1st Lieutenants Darby, Stewart, Collyer, Orlebar, Molesworth, Cubitt, Campbell, Sinclair, Coxwell, Dyneley, Macbean, Rayner, Cairnes, Hunt, Somerville, and Lord; 2nd Lieutenants Wright, Swabey, Lyon, Wilson, Thomson, Fuller, Forster, and Maling.

Captain Fyers acted as Aide-de-Camp to General Blomefield, and Captains Drummond and Whinyates were on his Brigade Staff.

No less than 185 pieces of ordnance accompanied the Expedition. Of these, 84 were field guns, including 6, 9, and 12-pounders, and 5½ and 8-inch howitzers. The last named, although included among the field-guns, were evidently for use in the trenches. The guns taken for siege purposes were as follows:—

   20 24-pounders.   General
   5 10-inch howitzers.   Blome-
   6 68-pounder carronades.   field's
   70 mortars, of 5½, 8, 10, and 13-inch calibre. MS. Returns.

 The number of rounds of ammunition sent was 61,472; but only 11,378 were expended when the city surrendered. There was considerable difficulty in getting transports at so short a notice for the Artillery and their horses. When writing on the 28th July, the Deputy-Adjutant-General had heard of no ships at all for the purpose; but at 2.30 A.M. on the 29th, an express reached him from Gravesend, informing him of their arrival, and that the embarkation was required to take place immediately. Collecting all the boats he could find, he embarked the men at Woolwich, and sent them down to Gravesend with the tide. In writing subsequently to the Master-General, he said: "It is but fair to the officers and " men to say that, without previous notice, they were all " assembled at 9, and at the waterside by 10, in complete " order, and with all their baggage."

 The main part of the Expedition sailed from Yarmouth, and General Blomefield embarked there, on board the 'Valiant,' on the 2nd August. Lord Cathcart, who was to command the whole of the land forces, did not join until their arrival in the road of Elsineur.   Cust.

 The British Infantry numbered 15,351, and was commanded by General Burrard. The 1st Division was commanded by Sir George Ludlow, assisted by Major-General Finch and Brigadier Warde; the 2nd Division by Sir David Baird, assisted by Major-Generals Grosvenor and Spencer and Brigadier Macfarlane. The Reserve was under the command of Major-General Sir Arthur Wellesley, and included ten companies of the 95th, or Rifle Corps, besides Blomefield three other battalions. The King's German Legion, under MSS.

the command of the Earl of Rosslyn, numbered 9951 of all ranks.

At 5 A.M. on the morning of the 16th August, 1807, the Reserve of the army, under Sir A. Wellesley, landed at Webeck, about twelve miles from Copenhagen. Captain Newhouse's and Captain Brome's Light Brigades of Artillery, under the command of Lieut.-Colonel Cookson, were attached to the Reserve. No opposition was made to the landing. The remainder of the army, with the exception of General Spencer's Brigade, landed at the same place, and in the afternoon the whole moved forward in three columns towards Charlotte-lund, about five miles from Copenhagen, off which place the transports, convoyed by the fleet, anchored the same evening. On the following morning, General Spencer's Brigade landed at Charlotte-lund, and marched to the left of Sir David Baird's head-quarters, where, on the 20th, it was joined by Captain May's Brigade of 6-pounders. Captain Unett's Brigade of 6-pounders was attached to Sir David Baird's Division, and Captain Paterson's, of 9-pounders, was placed on the left of the line. The city of Copenhagen was now completely invested by the army, and the landing of guns and stores for the siege commenced. The difficulties which seem to have been inseparable from our campaigns in those days, as far as supply of stores, &c., was concerned, were present on this occasion. "We should have been " greatly distressed in the horse department if Colonel " Robe had not taken it. No Captain-Commissary or Vete- " rinary Surgeon has arrived. We are in great distress " for horses; I am obliged to send the two brigades pre- " paring, without cars. We shall want ammunition for the " 9 and 6-pounders; there are only 300 rounds per gun, and " a considerable quantity is already gone. Pray get some " more sent, and a greater supply of Shrapnel's shells: there " is a great call for them, and we have with us only 27 per " gun. . . . Pray send us a few extra subalterns; we work " day and night at unloading. Lieut.-Colonel Cookson is " advanced with the four first brigades; Lieut.-Colonel " Robe encamps the horses and carriages, which is full

" employ; and I attend unloading and supplying demands.
" General Blomefield is at head-quarters. *We are distressed
" by so many different things being put in the store-ships; the
" things at bottom are required first, in many instances, and
" we half unload the ship to get at them.*"

The operations in which the expenditure of ammunition took place—alluded to by Colonel Harding—were prior to the investment of Copenhagen, and were conducted by Sir A. Wellesley with complete success. During their progress, a very gallant Artillery officer, Lieutenant Lyon, was killed by a 3-pounder shot, from a gun which had been placed by the enemy on the Copenhagen road. On account of the facilities offered by the coast, and a continuance of fine weather, the Danish gun-boats took part in these operations. The conduct of the Royal Artillery was thus mentioned by Sir Arthur Wellesley:—" I cannot close this letter without
" expressing to your Lordship my sense of the good conduct
" of the troops. All conducted themselves with the utmost
" steadiness; but I cannot avoid to mention particularly the
" British Artillery under the command of Captain New-
" house."

<small>Sir A. Wellesley to Lord Cathcart, Kioge, 29 Aug. 1807.</small>

From the 21st August to the 1st September, the Artillery-men were employed in making and arming the batteries necessary for the bombardment. The distribution of these batteries when the bombardment commenced, on the 2nd September, was as follows:—

	No. of Guns.	Nature.	
Gun battery on the right	6	24-prs.	MS. Official Returns, and Gen. Blomefield's Diary.
On its left, and advanced	4	10-inch mortars.	
Still farther advanced	4	8-inch ,,	
In the road, on the left of the battery .	2	8-inch howitzers.	
Right mortar battery	{2 {8	13-inch mortars. 10-inch ,,	
Centre mortar battery	{2 {8	13-inch ,, 10-inch ,,	
On its left, and advanced	{2 {2	10-inch howitzers. 8-inch ,,	
Left mortar battery	{2 {8	13-inch mortars. 10-inch ,,	

	No. of Guns.	Nature.
Windmill battery	11	24-pr. guns.
	1	8-inch howitzer.
On its right, and advanced	2	10-inch mortars.
Flèche	3	24-pr. guns.
	1	8-inch howitzer.

Making a total of 20 guns, 40 mortars, and 8 howitzers.

The erection of the batteries was not carried on without molestation from the enemy; but on the 1st September they were so near completion that the city was summoned to capitulate prior to the commencement of the bombardment. The summons having been refused, the batteries opened at 7.30 P.M. on the 2nd, and the fire continued, with but little reply, for twelve hours. The city was set on fire by the first flight of shells (not *rockets*, as stated by Sir E. Cust, which would appear to have been used as a siege weapon for the first time, subsequently, at Flushing), and continued burning all night. During the afternoon of this day, another battery of eight 24-pounders had been armed by the Royal Artillery.

The expenditure of ammunition during the first night having been considered excessive, orders were given that no more than one shell per hour should be fired from each battery during the day, but that at 7 P.M. on the 3rd September, firing should commence at the rate of one shell in every three minutes, from each battery, for the space of sixteen hours. The same orders were obeyed on the night of the 4th, the city suffering terribly from fires in all parts, and no fewer than 1500 of the inhabitants having been killed. Towards 4 A.M. on the 5th, the principal steeple in the city fell, and at 8 P.M. on that day, a flag of truce was sent out, and the bombardment was suspended. On the 6th, two additional batteries were armed, and sailors were landed from the fleet to man them; but a second flag of truce having been sent from the city, Sir A. Wellesley, Sir H. Popham, and Colonel Murray went in the evening into the town, having received directions to order a continuation of the bombardment on their return, should their proposals

CHAP. X.   *Surrender of the Danish Fleet.*   165

not be accepted. They did not return until next morning, bringing, however, the intelligence that the terms of the capitulation had been agreed to. *These included the unconditional surrender of the Danish fleet.* During the evening of the 7th the citadel was taken possession of by the Grenadiers, accompanied by a detachment of the German Rifle Corps, a troop of Dragoons, and a brigade of Artillery. On the same evening the following General Order was published:—

"The Commander of the Forces cannot delay expressing Headquarters,
" his warmest thanks to all the General Officers and Staff for Hellerup,
" the great and able assistance he has received from all of 7 Sept.
" them, in their several ranks and stations. And he feels 1807
" himself, in like manner, obliged to all the officers com-
" manding brigades or regiments, and the officers and
" soldiers under their command.

" He must, however, be allowed, in a particular manner,
" to express his thanks to Major-General Blomefield and
" Colonel D'Arcy, and the officers and corps of the Royal
" Artillery and Engineers, whose laborious science and
" success, collectively and individually, have been most
" remarkable, and reflect great honour on that branch of
" His Majesty's service."

The naval stores captured were very valuable, and their weight exceeded 20,000 tons. No fewer than 3500 pieces of ordnance were also taken. By the 20th October the whole army had re-embarked, and reached England without loss. One cannot but regret that the object of the Expedition could not have been attained in a different manner; and that the means employed were not as justifiable as they were successful.

There are various points of interest connected with the services of the Artillery during the siege which seem worthy of mention. The following extracts from General Blomefield's letters to Lord Chatham speak for themselves:
" . . . . It is with great satisfaction that I have to con- Dated
" gratulate your Lordship on the fortunate issue of our 9 Sept.
" Expedition, and on the distinguished share which fell to 1807.

"the lot of our corps in accomplishing so desirable an event;
"and I should do them great injustice were I not to mention
"their exertions in the strongest manner, as well in the
"laborious task of landing and transporting the Artillery
"and stores to the batteries, from four to eight miles
"distance, as in the active and intelligent use of them
"when employed. .... I believe there are very few in-
"stances of so powerful an effect being produced in so short
"a time, and with so little loss of lives. Six thousand
"shells and carcases were thrown into the town (which is
"very spacious), from mortars, howitzers, and guns, during
"the short period of two nights and one day."

Dated 12 Sept. 1807.

Again: "I cannot sufficiently commend the conduct of the
"officers and men under my command. Your Lordship will
"observe by the enclosed sketch of the batteries, how for-
"midable the attack must have been under those three
"excellent officers, Lieut.-Colonels Harding, Robe, and
"Cookson; and nothing could resist so heavy a fire."

The satisfaction of the Master-General may be gathered from his reply:—

Lord Chatham to General Blomefield, Sept. 19, 1807.

"I received your letter of the 7th inst., and rejoiced most
"truly in the prosperous issue of the Expedition to Zealand.
"The satisfaction I derived from this event was, I assure you,
"much increased from the very highly honourable and dis-
"tinguished part borne in this enterprise by the Corps of
"Royal Artillery under your command, and whose exertions
"are the theme of general admiration. I am sincerely happy
"in communicating to you that His Majesty has announced
"his gracious intentions of conferring upon you the dignity
"of a Baronet, as a testimony of the sense entertained of
"your eminent services on this occasion. . . . . What
"a sad contrast is the miserable business of Buenos Ayres!"

On the 28th September, Lord Cathcart received a despatch from Lord Castlereagh, expressing His Majesty's high approbation of the army's performance; and this was communicated to the troops on the same evening. Lord Cathcart

Gen¹ Order, 28 Sept. 1807.

took the opportunity of thanking them again "for the
"patience, discipline, and exertions of all regiments, corps,

"and departments, to which, under the blessing of Provi-
"dence, he was indebted for the complete success of the
"Expedition, and for the most gracious approbation which
"His Majesty has been pleased to declare of the whole
"service." Military science has advanced, and may continue
to advance, with prodigious strides; but success will never
be possible without the same weapons as those to which
Copenhagen surrendered—patience, discipline, and exertion.

A long-standing right was claimed for his corps by General
Blomefield, from Lord Cathcart, after the siege. "It being
"an invariable custom in our service, whenever a place capi-
"tulates after a siege, to allow the officer commanding the
"Royal Artillery a claim of the bells in the town, and its
"dependencies, or a compensation in lieu of them,—which
"has twice occurred upon services in which I have been em-
"ployed, viz. the sieges of the Havannah, and Fort Royal
"in Martinique,—I conceive it to be my duty which I owe to
"my brother officers, as well as myself, to express my hope
"that in the present instance it will not be dispensed with."

Letter dated 12 Sept. 1807.

On the 3rd November, 1807, General Blomefield was created
a Baronet; and the story of the Expedition concludes with
the thanks of the Houses of Parliament being voted to the
army and the fleet which had been engaged. This was communicated by Sir Thomas Blomefield—now at Woolwich—to
the officers and men who had served under him, both
belonging to his own corps and to the Artillery of the
King's German Legion. In the language used by him in
addressing the former, may be detected the strength in his
bosom of that Regimental feeling which it is the main object
of this work to strengthen. "It therefore only remains
"with the General," he wrote, "to add his sincere thanks
"for their highly meritorious conduct, by which they have
"acquitted themselves no less to their own credit than to
"that of the corps in which they have the honour to serve."

NOTE.—It may have been merely accidental, but it is worthy of note that while the Master-General corresponded *directly* with General Blomefield during this service, the Deputy Adjutant-General corresponded with the Lieutenant-Colonels employed on the Expedition.

CHAPTER XI.

MONTE VIDEO AND BUENOS AYRES.

IN a letter from Lord Chatham, quoted in the last chapter, allusion is made to a campaign in South America which contrasted unfavourably with the successful siege of Copenhagen. The plan of this work requires that the reader should now turn to this unsuccessful Expedition, and see how bravely English troops endeavoured to compensate by their exertions for want of generalship in their leaders. To the Artilleryman this chapter will have a special interest,— from the fact that two of the officers who took a prominent part in the campaign were destined to become very eminent in their corps and profession—Sir Augustus Frazer, and Sir Alexander Dickson.

Letter to D. A. Gen. 12 Jan. 1806.

On the 12th January, 1806, Major Spicer, who commanded the Artillery with Sir David Baird's Expedition to the Cape of Good Hope, reported that, two days previously, Cape Town had fallen into their hands. During the operations which resulted in this important capture, the officers and men under his command behaved in a "persevering, cool, and "steady manner." The heavy surf prevented him from landing more than six 6-pounders and two 5½-inch howitzers, the whole of which were in action and did good service, although outnumbered, three to one, by the artillery of the enemy. Captains Turner and Ogilvie received special mention for their conduct on the occasion.

In the beginning of April, Major Spicer went on a tour of inspection round the outposts, leaving Captain Ogilvie—his Brigade-Major—sick at Cape Town. He had barely started when the Admiral, Sir Home Popham, resolved—on his own responsibility, and entirely without the knowledge of the English Government—to proceed with a naval and military force to South America, for the purpose of attacking the Spanish settlements, and securing the trade of the country for England. General Beresford was put in command of the military part of the Expedition; and the detachment of the Royal Artillery, which was at first ordered to accompany it, consisted of Lieutenant A. Macdonald, 1 bombardier, 1 *lance*-bombardier, 18 gunners, 1 conductor, 1 wheeler, 1 collar-maker, 1 corporal and 9 men of the Gunner-driver Corps, and 18 horses. Captain Ogilvie having offered to resign his staff appointment if allowed to accompany the force, his offer was accepted; and in a letter which he wrote from St. Helena, *en route*, he was able to announce that the detachment under his command had been augmented by an officer and 100 gunners of the St. Helena Artillery. The fleet consisted of 5 men-of-war, and the military force, in addition to the Artillery, was composed of a detachment of the 20th Light Dragoons, a few Engineers, and the 71st Regiment. The Expedition reached a point about twelve miles distant from Buenos Ayres, and on the 25th June, 1806, a landing was effected. Advancing boldly, and driving the Spanish troops before them, the English reached the city, and on the 28th June summoned the Governor to surrender—a summons to which he immediately yielded. So small, however, was the force under General Beresford's command, that he could not hold the city; and in a very short time the English troops had actually to surrender as prisoners of war. Sir Home Popham continued to blockade the river for some time; but was soon ordered home to be tried by court-martial for his unauthorized proceedings. Thus ended the first act of this unfortunate drama.

The English Government, although disapproving of the original Expedition, was compelled to take some steps to avenge the disaster to Beresford's force. The fleet, now under the command of Admiral Sterling, had already been considerably increased; and reinforcements from the Cape of Good Hope had arrived, including a few Artillerymen under Captain A. Watson, four troops of the 20th,—and two of the 21st, Light Dragoons, the 38th, 47th, and a detachment of Captain Watson to D. A. Gen. 8 Oct. 1806.

the 54th Regiment. A further force of 3000 men under the command of Sir S. Auchmuty was ordered to the River La Plata, and arrived on the 5th January, 1807; the Artillery being under the command of Captain Dickson. Captain Watson shortly after this date returned to the Cape of Good Hope, and the command of the Royal Artillery devolved for the time on Captain Dickson. Prior, however, to this taking place, Sir S. Auchmuty decided on an attempt on Monte Video, and took the place by assault on the 3rd February, 1807. The conduct of the Artillery on this occasion may be ascertained from the following extract from the General Order, which was published immediately after the capture of the town:—" The established reputation of the Royal Artil- " lery has been firmly supported by the company under my " orders; and I consider myself much indebted to Captains " Watson, Dickson, Carmichael, and Wilgress, for their " zealous and able exertions." On this occasion Captain Wilgress, who acted as Adjutant to the Artillery, was wounded.

'London Gazette,' 13 April, 1807.

On the 2nd June, an additional force of 4200 men, under General Craufurd, arrived at Monte Video from England; and the command of the whole army devolved upon a most incapable officer, General Whitelocke. With this last rein- forcement came a troop of Horse Artillery, now C Battery, B Brigade, under Captain A. Frazer, who, being senior to Captain Dickson, now assumed command of the Artillery, and retained it until the active operations were over, when he was relieved by Lieut.-Colonel Schalch, who reached Monte Video on the 26th July, 1807.

General Beresford's force still remained prisoners of war —some remaining at Buenos Ayres, the others divided in small detachments among the various villages in the neigh- bourhood. General Linières, the French commander of the Spanish forces, was most kind and courteous to the prisoners, and did all he could to promote their comfort; but the feeling of the people, more especially of the Roman Catholic clergy, was very bitter against the English, and led to a painful occurrence. On the 14th January Captain Ogilvie, while riding with Colonel Pack of the 71st Regiment—who was also a prisoner of war—was assassinated; and his companion with difficulty escaped. Captain Ogilvie had been severely wounded at the first attack on Buenos Ayres, and his loss was deeply regretted. The command of the captive Artillery now devolved upon Lieutenant Alexander Macdonald, who had received two wounds in the attack on Buenos Ayres, and who had been recommended by Captain Ogilvie as a most deserving and zealous young officer.

General Whitelocke decided on a second assault on Buenos Ayres; having first, and unsuccessfully, attempted to persuade General Linières to release his prisoners. The failure of his attempt on the city will, perhaps, be more readily understood, if a few words of description of Buenos Ayres, as it was in 1807, precede the narrative.

The city extended for nearly three miles along the banks of the Rio de la Plata, and its breadth at the widest point was about a mile and a half. The population, including the suburban villas or *quintas*, was about 70,000. Like most modern cities in the United States and Canada, it had been built on a fixed plan, not left to the distorted tastes of individual proprietors—as is not unfrequently the case in England. Its streets and squares were large, broad, and convenient; and although the individual houses did not always harmonise, and were rarely impressive, they did little injury to the general effect. Most of them were two-storeyed, and built in Moorish fashion, in the form of a square, with one large entry, the different apartments on the ground floor opening into the square, and the roof flat, and occasionally terraced. The Fort, or Citadel, was a miserable work, with a parapet of little more than two feet in height. In many places it was incapable of resisting artillery fire, and, at the best, was of little use save in overawing a mob, or as a receptacle for the city treasure and the public records. The most important public buildings were the Cathedral, and the churches of St. Francisco, St. Domingo, St. Michael, and the Jesuits—all imposing enough externally, but with gaudy interiors, which offended the sober taste of English travellers.

Major Nicolls' 45 Regiment, MS. Journal in R. A. Record Office. Captain Frazer's and Capt. Dickson's Letters to D. A. Gen.

There was also a large civic hall, known as the Cabildos; and the Plaza de Toros, where the passion of the inhabitants for bull-fighting was gratified, was a very striking place. The Custom-house, Arsenal, and theatres were small and unimposing.

For many reasons Buenos Ayres was admirably adapted for defence against an enemy whose attack should develop itself in the form of street fighting. The barracks were scattered over the city in low, retired squares, and the houses were like so many small fortifications. Their shape rendered each perfectly distinct, and not easily assailable save from a neighbouring roof. This one weak point led to the passing of a law, which might have led at times to embarrassing results, under which the proprietor of one house was permitted to *fire at any stranger whom he might detect on the roof of an adjoining one.* The gates and doors of the houses were very strong, made of wood several inches thick, and heavily bolted and barred; the windows had strong iron railings outside, and heavy wooden shutters with iron fastenings within; and the flat roofs were very useful, both for offence and defence. Altogether it was as awkward a city to take in the way unhappily chosen by General Whitelocke as can be imagined.

In most of the squares enclosed by the larger houses there were wells; but the water was brackish, and the inhabitants preferred the water from the river, which was sold in the streets, and which, although somewhat muddy, became clear when allowed to stand, and, with the addition of a little alum, was believed to have peculiar virtues for clearing and strengthening the voice. The river, between Buenos Ayres and Colonia, was about thirty miles in breadth; and it should be mentioned that the latter place had already surrendered to a force of 800 English troops, under Colonel Pack of the 71st, who had made his escape from Buenos Ayres shortly after the assassination of Captain Ogilvie. The Artillery with this force was commanded by Captain Wilgress, who had recovered from the wound he received at Monte Video only to receive a second and more severe injury at Colonia. His detachment manned two light 6-pounders and two light 3-pounders; and he had in addition eight Spanish 16-pounders, with which it was intended to arm the defensive works proposed to be erected at Colonia. Had these last-mentioned guns, and the siege ordnance left at the village of Reduccion and at Monte Video, been brought against Buenos Ayres with a view to its bombardment, there is no doubt that the city, whose streets proved a tomb to the attacking forces, would have been their prize.

The country round Buenos Ayres was well wooded, and the land in the immediate vicinity rich and singularly productive. Thanks to the inquiring minds of General Beresford's force, it was ascertained that beef, mutton, fowls, and river fish were cheap and abundant, bread excellent, and the markets filled daily soon after sunrise with wild-fowl, quails, and partridges in abundance. The last-named birds must have resembled the Canadian tree partridge, as they were caught with ease, even in the immediate suburbs, by means of a noose at the end of a stick. There was abundance of larger game in the country, both four-footed and winged, and " vultures and birds of that class, luckily very common too, " otherwise the air would be infected by the quantity of " carrion left after the men, dogs, and pigs had been " satisfied . . . . . . Bullocks are here what the cocoa-trees " are in India. They turn them to the following uses: food, " fuel, shoes, ropes, trunks, sacks, covering for houses, beds, " bridles, saddles, bird-cages, drinking-cups, &c. . . . . . . " Their horses are the accidental breed of the country, de- " scended from those originally brought by the Spaniards. " They are undersized, but show some blood, are very tract- " able, and hardy. Each proprietor affixes his mark on his " droves, makes geldings of them, and they run wild till " required for use or sale. They are driven in now and " then for inspection. The King of Spain is a proprietor; " his mark is the tip of the left ear cut off. They are of " very trifling value in the drove—not more than half a " dollar each. It is not uncommon for a traveller whose " horse is jaded to catch another and leave his own. The

<small>Major Nicolls' Diary.</small>

"Peons, or country people, who have more Indian than
"Spanish blood in them, are very expert horsemen. They
"tame a wild horse in a few hours, but by severe treatment.
"Their bridles are those used by the Mamelukes, and they
"use stick and spur without reluctance."

The chief exports from Buenos Ayres were hides, tallow, skins of valuable animals, bark, coffee, and spices; the imports were cloths, wearing apparel, glass, earthenware, cutlery, &c. So extensive was the trade of the place, and so keen were the inhabitants for its development, that it is not to be wondered at that, in the first flush of short-lived conquest, the English commanders dwelt on its possible advantage to Great Britain in terms which the hope of justifying an unauthorized expedition may possibly have made somewhat fervent.

The moral aspect of Buenos Ayres in 1807 seems to have been very uninviting. Immorality of the grossest description prevailed in both sexes and in all classes; indolence and intemperance characterized the lower orders, and the whole community was priest-ridden to an intolerable extent. The Bishop, in particular, tyrannized over all ranks and classes; and when he went anywhere in state, every one knelt to him, the guards even presenting arms to him kneeling. During the short time that General Beresford commanded, the Bishop demanded the same ceremony from the English troops; but it was refused, and he never forgave it. He was a very crafty man, and to the last he affected good-will to the English; but by his orders every pulpit was used for fulminating threats against them, and for inventing and exaggerating tales of English atrocity. To such an extent was this carried, that the better class of the inhabitants did not dare to make any advances to the English officers, or show them open kindness, although they always welcomed them to their houses if they came uninvited. The revenue of the Bishop was very great, and included a fourth part of all sums paid as fees at births, marriages, and funerals, the amount of which varied with the will and ability of the parties concerned, or their friends. Another fourth went to the King, and the

CHAP. XI. *Dual Government of Artillery.* 175

remainder to the canons of the church in which the necessary ceremony was performed. The clergy of Buenos Ayres were very numerous, and their private life was said to be most immoral. As regarded the people generally, Major Nicolls wrote: " With respect to religion, they appear to attend pretty " regularly to its exterior forms, especially the women, who " attend mass daily, in which, however, the men do not show " so much zeal. Since, however, vice of every description " follows, it does not appear likely that forms of this nature " would be very useful, either in this world or as a prepara-" tion for that to come. On General Beresford's taking the " city, many thousands of indulgences and remissions of all " kinds were found, which have ever proved a source of re-" venue and power to the Roman Catholic clergy, and are " here made the tools of Government.[1] The Bishop amuses " the high and low every week with some pompous procession " or ceremony to make the great remember that there is such " a thing as religion. To the sick he holds out forty days' " plenary indulgence for going to mass and giving alms; " and the poor are governed by a promise that their sins " shall be forgiven. On our landing, the Bishop induced the " people to swear they would defend the place to the last, " for which their sins should be forgiven."

Against this city General Whitelocke resolved to move the greater part of his force, leaving small garrisons in Monte Video and Colonia. Before describing the Expedition, an anecdote is worthy of mention, as showing, what has so frequently been shown already, the evil effects of the dual government of the Artillery which existed in the days of the Board of Ordnance. There is deposited in the Royal Artillery Record Office the original order to Captain Frazer, signed by General Whitelocke, desiring him, as commanding officer of Artillery and representing the Ordnance Department, " to pay the sum of *forty pounds* sterling for every " field-piece that may be captured from the enemy during

Dated Monte Video, 6 June, 1807.

---

[1] The Bishop was a leading member of the Royal Council.

" the approaching service at Buenos Ayres, according to
" the established usage of the service in such cases."

In the same office is a correspondence in which Captain Frazer is *forbidden* by the Board to make any such payment. The question for consideration is not whether the General or the Board was right in the interpretation of the Regulations. The error of the system was that the officer who received an order from the General, under whom he was immediately serving, was made the channel for conveying to that General an intimation that his order was wrong, and was not to be obeyed. The marvel is that, under such a system, harmony was *ever* possible between the commanding officer of Artillery and his General; and, certainly, if tact could have been imparted to a cadet at the Academy, along with his mathematics, he would probably have found it the more useful accomplishment of the two in his after career.

The arrangements made by Captain Frazer for the transport and service of the Artillery were admirable and exhaustive. In General Whitelocke's report of the subsequent operations, he used the following terms of commendation:—

'London Gazette' extraordinary, 13 Sept. 1807.

" I cannot sufficiently bring to notice the uncommon exer-
" tions of Captain Frazer, commanding the Royal Artillery,
" the fertility of whose mind, zeal, and animation, in all cases
" left difficulties behind." That Captain Frazer was staunchly supported by the officers and men under his command is apparent from his letters. Captain Dickson, whom he had superseded, and under whom, singularly enough, he was destined to serve in the Peninsula, was most loyal in his exertions, and earned the following acknowledgment:—" I
" have met with so much assistance from Captain Dickson,
" whom I found in command of the Artillery on my arrival,
" that it is at once my duty and my inclination to report
" to you the sense I entertain of his valuable assistance.
" But it is unnecessary for me to mention more than the
" name of a brother-officer who is at once so highly and so
" deservedly valued." And again, after the conclusion of the campaign: "If, in my several letters to you, I have not
" mentioned Captains Hawker and Dickson, you will, I trust,

Captain Frazer to D. A. Gen. 21 June, 1807.

CHAP. XI. *Artillery at Attack on Buenos Ayres.* 177

"impute this to the real cause—a delicacy in venturing to express an opinion of officers of equal standing in the Regiment with myself, and with whom, in many cases, I should feel myself flattered to be compared."

Captain Frazer had urged the propriety of heavy artillery accompanying the army, with a view to a bombardment of the city, prior to an assault; and in answer to an argument employed—that Monte Video would be left unprotected—he drew out a detailed statement showing that no less than 145 guns, mortars, and howitzers would be left mounted in that city, besides 270 dismounted. He further showed that there was an abundance of ammunition for these guns; and he detailed three officers to remain behind, of whom he was afterwards able to say: " Colonel Brown, Commandant of "the Garrison of Monte Video, has expressed to me his high " sense of the exertions of Captain Durnford and Lieutenants " England and Stopford, whose exertions were unremitting " during our temporary absence." But his appeal was to no purpose. General Whitelocke had determined to land at a place about thirty miles from Buenos Ayres, called Enfinada de Barragon, and thence march over the swamps which intervened, and which would have made the movement of heavy artillery very difficult. With great difficulty, Captain Frazer obtained permission to take three 24-pounders, two 12-inch Spanish mortars, and two 5½-inch howitzers as a reserve, in addition to his field guns; but these, which would have been so useful in the subsequent attack, were not allowed to proceed farther than the village of Reduccion, where the first encounter with the enemy took place. The following was the detail of the Royal Artillery which actually took part in the attack on Buenos Ayres, on the 5th July, 1807 :—

Captain Frazer to D. A. G R A.

1st Brigade—Captain A. S. Frazer. 2nd Captain W. D. Nicolls. Lieutenant Lloyd Dowse.	98 N.C. officers and men. 4 6-pounder guns. 2 3-pounder „	MS. Returns in R. A. Record Office.
2nd Brigade—Captain James Hawker. 2nd Captain Henry Lane. Lieutenant Thomas Trotter.	100 N.C. officers and men. 5 4-pounder guns. 1 5½-inch howitzer.	

VOL. II. N

| 3rd Brigade—Captain Alexander Dickson. Lieutenant J. Mackonochie. „ Falkner Hope. | 100 N.C. officers and men. 3 12-pounder guns. 4 6-pounder „ 2 5½-inch howitzers. |

Captain Frazer erred rather in being too minute in his arrangements, than the reverse; he wrote his orders with his own hand, and knowing the nature of the country which the men would have to traverse after disembarkation, he issued the most detailed instructions before leaving Monte Video, as to dress, diet, horses, &c. These are too long for reproduction, but some are quaintly amusing, and one suggests a new use for foot-straps to a gunner dismounted. " The men " will land with one great coat and blanket each, with a " flannel waistcoat, brush, comb, razor, and shaving-brush " rolled up in the blanket; and with such proportion of " cooked provisions as may be directed. *Every man to have* " *shoe-straps tied round his shoes to keep them on in boggy* " *ground;* the men's hair to be plaited up behind, not tied " in a queue; the great coats and blankets to be rolled up " so as to leave them as much as possible the full and free " use of their limbs."

To each Brigade of guns was attached a cart containing long troughs, which were laid over very swampy ground or across ditches, and in which the gun-wheels were made to travel, which otherwise would have sunk to the axletrees. In fact everything which ingenuity could devise to lighten the difficulties of the operation was thought of by Captain Frazer. That he was rewarded by success is apparent by the following extract:—" During the advance the Artillery " exerted themselves to the admiration of the whole army; " the Artillerymen pulling at the drag-ropes up to their " waists in water.... In the most difficult ground they " were continually obliged to restrain their zeal, lest they " should outmarch the army, whose repeated intimations of " ' Easy the Artillery!' were most gratifying." Of the services of his own troop of Horse Artillery, Captain Frazer wrote: " The conduct of the officers and men was admirable, " yet it were better that the praise due to Quartermaster-

"Sergeant Hay and the men of the Horse Artillery should come from any other pen than mine; but their gallantry and intelligence have ensured the respect of the whole army. It would be injustice not to mention in terms of the most unequivocal commendation Quartermaster-Sergeant Hay, in whom the valuable qualities of clear arrangements and undaunted courage are joined to the greatest zeal; this man is cast in no ordinary mould."

On arrival at Buenos Ayres, after two engagements at Reduccion and Passo Chico, in which the English were successful, General Whitelocke completely invested the city. The plan of attack on which he decided was to enter the place in separate columns by totally different entrances and streets; each column to march "along the street directly in its front, till it arrived at the last square of houses next the River La Plata, of which it was to possess itself, forming on the flat roofs, and there wait for further orders. No firing was to be permitted until the columns had reached their final points and formed." The reader, who has already been informed of the size of Buenos Ayres, and the style of the houses, will at once see the madness of such a method of attack; but the extraordinary thing to be noted is that General Whitelocke employed, as an argument for the course he adopted, the very circumstance which should have forbidden him to hazard his troops in the dangerous and unsatisfactory occupation of street fighting. "The knowledge," he wrote, "that the enemy meant to occupy the flat roofs of the houses gave rise to the plan of attack."

'Gazette,' 13 Sept. 1807.

The guns accompanied the columns; but "the detachments of the Horse Artillery were not mounted, and of the Cavalry only two squadrons had their horses." The attack took place on the 5th July, and if endurance and courage among the troops could have redeemed their General's blunder, this would have been done. At the end of the day no fewer than 2500 men were killed, wounded, or prisoners. The battle was just what might have been foreseen. In General Whitelocke's own words, "The nature of the fire to which

" the troops were exposed was violent in the extreme.
" Grape shot at the corners of all the streets, musketry,
" hand grenades, bricks, and stones from the tops of all the
" houses; every householder with his negroes defended his
" dwelling, each of which was in itself a fortress, and it is
" not, perhaps, too much to say that the whole male popula-
" tion of Buenos Ayres was employed in its defence."
General Whitelocke's subsequent conviction by court-
martial for incapacity might have been assured on his own
testimony.

The only real gain to the English army at the end of the day was the possession of the Plaza de Toros: and its situation was such, that, if fortified, it would have commanded the town, and perhaps compelled the inhabitants to insist on a surrender. Captain Frazer urged this without success: he pointed out that with some guns captured that day from the Spaniards he could construct a battery of 26 guns, immediately serviceable, and strengthen it by unspiking 10 other pieces of ordnance which had been for a time rendered unserviceable by the enemy, prior to their capture: he assured the General that there were not less than 600 barrels of powder, captured that day in the Arsenal of Buenos Ayres, and an apparent abundance of every requisite for the service of a battery; and he reminded him that each gun which they had brought from Monte Video was provided with 200 rounds: but all was to no purpose. A loop-hole for an escape without utter disgrace, as he thought, was opened to General Whitelocke, of which he availed himself, and which he thus described in his official report:—"On the morning of the 6th inst. General
" Linières addressed a letter to me, offering to give up all
" his prisoners taken in the late affair, together with the
" 71st Regiment and others taken with General Beresford,
" if I desisted from any other attack on the town, and with-
" drew His Majesty's forces from the River Plata, intimating
" at the same time, from the exasperated state of the
" populace, he could not answer for the safety of the
" prisoners, if I persisted in offensive measures. Influenced

" by this consideration (which I knew from better authority to be founded on fact), and reflecting of how little advantage would be the possession of a country the inhabitants of which were so absolutely hostile, I resolved to forego the advantages which the bravery of the troops had obtained, and acceded to the annexed Treaty, which I trust will meet the approbation of His Majesty."

It may be here mentioned that the Treaty was carried out; the English army returning to Monte Video, and thence to England. But as, fortunately, an immense number of private and unpublished papers on this subject had been accumulated by Sir A. Frazer, and ultimately reached the Royal Artillery Record Office with a view to embodiment in some such work as this, it seems desirable to analyze the conduct of General Whitelocke at this crisis, and to ascertain, as far as is practicable, whether any other course would have been successful. *MS. Narratives of Captains Hawker and Nicolls, and Lieut. Trotter, relative to attack on Buenos Ayres.*

First, the threat of murdering the prisoners should have been dismissed from General Whitelocke's mind at once. With his powers of retaliating after any such atrocity, —being, as he was, in possession of part of the town,—the threat was an empty one; and between civilized communities most unlikely of execution, even if the control of the General had been weak. But, as a matter of fact, General Linières' power and popularity among the inhabitants at the time were very great;—a rumour of his having fallen during the day produced a profound depression, which made the reaction of joy the more intense when it was found that he was uninjured. That such a crime against humanity would have been allowed by one who was admitted by all to be chivalrous in the extreme, is utterly improbable; and the use of the threat merely showed that he found it necessary to make use of every argument, real and unreal, to secure his purpose;—that his position was not sufficiently strong to dictate terms to an enemy, even in the first hour of his discomfiture;—and, possibly, that he measured the man with whom he had to deal, and acted accordingly. *Major Nicoll's Diary, and Official Report. Captain Frazer's Diary, &c.*

Secondly, the very eagerness of General Linières to let the

troops go, and his ready permission to let them take all the guns, &c., which they had captured, should have suggested to General Whitelocke that these were not the characteristics of a General confident in his own strength, and in his enemy's inferiority.

And, thirdly, *were* the inhabitants so bitterly hostile to the English as General Whitelocke assumed? Doubtless they were not likely to evince much amiability while having to fight for their lives and homes; but, had a different mode of attack been adopted—blockade with a threatened bombardment, followed by the occupation in force of one or two commanding points—would it not have been possible so to foster English trade with the inhabitants as to ensure a thoroughly friendly feeling? This was evidently believed by those whose written opinions are extant—opinions formed in the city, and after careful inquiry. They said that had the Bishop been strictly watched, and warned that he would be sent to Europe, should he be detected in any political conspiracy, or countenancing any irregularity;—had all the Spanish officers and regular troops been sent to England immediately, and all the arms and ammunition of the inhabitants removed;—had the chief public officers been removed, but no injury done to the private inhabitants, and had honesty and uprightness been displayed in the English administration, the country might have been easily retained as a very useful appendage to Great Britain. The presence of an English army would have raised the price of nearly every commodity, and at the same time the system of ready-money payment would have benefited the local trade, and would have given the stock-owners a very strong interest in the presence of the English. The people of all ranks in Buenos Ayres were fond of copying English fashions in dress and furniture, and the facilities for comparing these would have been favourable to the invaders. The people born in the country, who were despised by the Spaniards, would have been raised to a degree of consideration unknown to them previously; and it would have been politic to place many of them in the situations of which the Castilians had been deprived. As for the Indians, the gain to them would have been immense, for their furs and hides would have met with a ready sale at an increased price. Commercial intercourse between England and Buenos Ayres once established, every vessel that sailed between their ports would have spun another thread in the web which bound them together, until what at first might have been a mere commercial alliance would have ended in a firm friendship and union.

All these possibilities were frustrated by the ignorance of a General. His landing so far from the city was one great blunder: his sub-division of his army, leaving part at Reduccion and part at Colonia, was another: his dispensing with siege artillery was a fatal error; and his crowning folly was the employment of a trained soldiery in street fighting, thus depriving them of the opportunity of exercising the qualities which a disciplined army possesses, and compelling them to meet an enemy under the very circumstances which that enemy would himself have chosen. General Whitelocke had sufficient troops to prevent the entry of supplies into the city if he had chosen;—or he might have entered Buenos Ayres two days before, when there was nothing but the wildest confusion within;—or he might have confined the attack to the side of the Ritoro, and approached the Citadel by regular parallels, using the streets to a great extent for that purpose, and ending by an assault which would have certainly been successful.

But he took the very course which was certain to be fatal; and the army he commanded, after performing useless prodigies of valour, had to succumb to terms which were openly talked of at Monte Video, while the army was awaiting embarkation for England, as disgraceful.

And with this irritating consciousness of failure, there came among the troops, when at Monte Video, not a little demoralization. Crime was general; desertions frequent; insubordination not unknown; and capital punishment was resorted to to enforce discipline. It is with pride that the Artilleryman learns from Captain Frazer's letters, that not a single desertion occurred from the ranks of the Royal Artillery,

The possible consequences of a General's incapacity ought to stir every officer to a determination to master his profession. The thought that his ignorance may some day be the cause of unnecessary slaughter, or may neutralise the bravest efforts of his men, and tarnish his country's honour, ought to make a man afraid of being found wanting when called upon. In the success of a great General, the officer who loves his profession traces means and maxims which he himself may study; and in the failures of an incapable commander, he searches for blunders which he may avoid. The study of both will be found useful to the man who may some day have to lead others, and would fain lead them to victory.

The last letter written by Captain Frazer from Monte Video was one imploring that he and his troop might be attached to any portion of the army which might be on active service. He seemed eager to drown the recollection of failure in the excitement of successes under some more able leader. And, as this history will show, he was not disappointed. The time was near when England was to draw the sword on behalf of suffering Spain, nor to sheathe it again until the invader had been driven from Spanish soil, albeit at a terrible cost to herself of life and treasure. But with all their attendant sufferings and cost, those were days to gloat over; now, alas! is it not too often found that—

> " . . . . Man is parcelled out in men
> Even thus :—because for any wrongful blow
> No man not stricken asks, 'I would be told
> 'Why dost thou strike:' but his heart whispers then,
> 'He is he, I am I !' By this we know
> That the earth falls asunder, being old."
>
> ROSETTI.

CHAPTER XII.

THE OLD TENTH BATTALION.

IT is necessary to distinguish this battalion as above, because it was reduced after Waterloo, and another 10th Battalion added to the Regiment subsequently, in 1846. As, however, there was no connection between the two in any way, not even a battalion head-quarters, or a company cadre, however small, left of the old 10th, this chapter differs from all the preceding histories of the battalions, in being merely a sketch of a part of the Regiment, whose traditions can be handed down to no lineal descendant, and are the property of the Corps at large.

In the year 1807 the Regiment consisted of 12 troops of Horse Artillery, 90 marching companies, and 12 companies of invalids, besides the Riding-house establishment, the last-named of which had been formed in 1806. There were also 10 companies of the Driver Corps. The Board of Ordnance decided on augmenting the Regiment by another battalion of 10 companies; and this was the last augmentation of this description which took place during the great wars with France. The *second* 10th Battalion, as has been stated above, was not formed until 1846; and the others as follows: 11th[1] and 12th Battalions in 1848; 13th Battalion in 1854; and 14th Battalion in 1855. All the augmentations which took place between the formation of the *old* 10th and the Battle of Waterloo were in the form of additional numbers to the ranks of the existing troops and companies.

The receipt in Woolwich, in the winter of 1807, of 1000 stand of arms, was followed in February 1808 by the formation of a new battalion of 10 companies, in every respect Colonel Macleod to R. H. Crew, Esq., B. of Ordnance.

---

[1] The 11th Battalion was formed of the 9th Companies of the eight senior existing battalions.

MSS. R. A. Record Office.

like those already existing. The staff of the brigade was as follows :—

Colonel-Commandant	Robert Lawson.
Colonels	{ John Schalch. { Henry Hutton.
Lieutenant-Colonels	{ G. A. Wood. { R. Dickinson. { Thomas Charlton.
Major	William Dixon.
Adjutant	1st Lieutenant William Wylde.
Quartermaster	Samuel Barnes.

The officers appointed to the various companies on their formation were as follows :—

	Captains.	Second Captains.	First Lieutenants.
No. 1 Company	J. Maclachlan.	Wm. Butts.	E. Sheppard.
			G. M. Graham.
No. 2 „	W. J. Lloyd.	H. Scott.	F. Wells.
			F. Strangways.
No. 3 „	J. Addams.	W. Green.	G. Mathias.
			J. T. Ellison.
No. 4 „	R. Dyas.	R. Cairnes.	E. Seward.
			H. Wyatt.
No. 5 „	W. Shenley.	J. Mallett.	R. Godby.
			S. Wyatt.
No. 6 „	W. Roberts.	Hon. H. Gardner.	W. Dunn.
			E. C. Vinicombe.
No. 7 „	J. Fead.	J. Marlow.	W. H. Hill.
			J. H. Frere.
No. 8 „	R. H. Birch.	L. Carmichael.	A. W. Hope.
			W. A. Gordon.
No. 9 „	B. T. Walsh.	F. Bedingfeld.	G. M. Baynes.
			D. Patullo.
No. 10 „	W. M. Leake.	W. Millar.	G. F. Roberts.
			J. O. Burton.

There were no 2nd Lieutenants appointed to the companies on their first formation.

The following changes took place among the Captains during the short but eventful existence of the battalion :—

No. 2 Company,	Brevet Lieut.-Col. Power,	vice Lloyd :	29th July, 1815.
No. 4 „	Captain (Sir A.) Dickson,	vice Dyas :	1st June, 1808.
„ „	„ Taylor,	vice Dickson :	1st April, 1815.
„ „	Brevet-Major Bredin,	vice Taylor :	1st June, 1815.
No. 5 „	Captain Chester,	vice Shinley :	6th Oct., 1813.
No. 9 „	Brevet Lt.-Col. Thornhill,	vice Walsh :	1st Jan., 1810.
„ „	Captain Gilmore,	vice Thornhill :	6th June, 1815.
No. 10 „	„ Cobbe,	vice Leake :	1st May, 1815.

CHAP. XII.   *History of the Companies.*   187

The history of each company may be shortly stated :—

No. 1 *Company.*—This company formed part of the Expedition to Walcheren in 1809, returning the same year. Its next foreign service was during the second American War. It embarked at Plymouth in March 1814, and landed at Quebec on the 3rd June, accompanied by the whole of its officers. On the 5th June it left Quebec, in boats, and arrived at Fort George, on the Niagara River, in the end of the month. On the 3rd July the Americans crossed the river into Canada; and on the 5th, part of the company, with Captain Mackonochie and Lieutenants Shipperd and Hunter, was in action with the enemy at Chippewa. For his conduct on this occasion Captain Mackonochie was mentioned in despatches by General Riall. On the 10th July, part of the company, with two field guns, under Lieutenant Tomkyns, was engaged with the enemy near Fort George; and was thanked in General Orders. On the 25th July, the whole company was engaged with the Americans near Niagara Falls, and Captain Maclachlan was severely wounded, losing the use of his right arm. He, Captain Mackonochie, and Lieutenant Tomkyns were specially mentioned by General Drummond in his despatches. On the 13th and 14th August, the company, with its three subaltern officers, was engaged in the batteries at Fort Erie; and on the 15th August, at the assault on the same place. From the 16th August to 16th September, they were engaged in the batteries at Fort Erie; and on the 17th September, assisted in repulsing a *sortie* made from the Fort by 5000 Americans. On the 30th September, the company, with its subaltern officers (both Captains being sick in hospital), was engaged in repulsing a general attack on the British lines on the Chippewa; after which the Americans, having completely failed in obtaining possession of Upper Canada, recrossed the Niagara River into the United States. In October the company took part in fresh operations at Fort George and Fort Niagara; and Lieutenant Tomkyns, with two 6-pounders, was attached to the 37th Regiment, when sent to drive a strong party of

Captain J. Maclachlan.
2nd Capt. J. Mackonochie.
1st Lieut. Shipperd.
1st Lieut. G. Hunter.
2nd Lieut. R. Tomkyns.
'Annual Register,' 1814.

Ibid.
General Drummond's Despatches, 27 July, 1814.
Ibid.
15 Aug. 1814.
Ibid.
17 Sept. 1814.

Americans out of the country, who had remained on the British side, plundering the inhabitants in the neighbourhood of Turkey Point, on Lake Erie. In the spring of 1815, the company was sent to Amherstburg; on the 23rd July, 1817, it returned to England; and on the 31st of the same month it ceased to exist.

No. 2 Company.—This company, under Captain Lloyd, and with 2nd Captain Marlow, 1st Lieutenants Baker and Wells, and 2nd Lieutenant Manners, took part in the Expedition to Walcheren in 1809. Its next foreign service was very important. It embarked at Plymouth on 14th January, 1815, and sailed for Cork to join the fleet destined for the American Coast: after remaining there ten weeks it proceeded to sea; but the second day after doing so, it received counter orders to proceed to Ostend, where it arrived in the end of April.

The company, with Captains Lloyd and Rudyerd, and Lieutenants Wells, Phelps, and Harvey, was engaged against the French on the 16th, 17th, and 18th June, commencing at Quatre Bras and ending at Waterloo. During these engagements, Captain Lloyd was mortally wounded, and died at Brussels on the 29th July following; and Lieutenant Harvey lost his right arm. To any one familiar with the story of the Artillery at Waterloo, the subsequent reduction of this gallant company seems almost a crime. It accompanied the army into France, where it remained until March 1816; returning then to England, it disembarked at Ramsgate, and proceeded to Woolwich, where, on the 28th April, 1817, it fell a victim to the reductions which economy rendered necessary, but which the Artilleryman must always bitterly regret.

No. 3 Company.—This company, with Captain Adams, 1st Lieutenants Otway and Moore, and 2nd Lieutenant Weston, took part in the Expedition to Walcheren in 1809.

On the 16th March, 1814, the company, with Captains Adams and King, 1st Lieutenant Day, and 2nd Lieutenant Pickard, embarked at Portsmouth for North America, and disembarked at Quebec on the 30th May. In the July following Captain King and Lieutenant Pickard, with part of the company, were ordered to march to Chambly, where they were attached to a battery of 6-pounder field guns, for duty with that part of the army serving under Major-General De Rottenburg. In the beginning of August, this detachment, with two 6-pounders, and one $5\frac{1}{2}$-inch howitzer, was ordered to the frontier to act with the army under the command of General De Watterville; and on the 4th September it moved forward with the army commanded by Lieut.-General Sir George Prevost to Plattsburg, at which place it was removed from its field guns, and posted to a battery of two 8-inch mortars, for service against the American lines and gun-boats. From this place the army retreated on the 11th September. No part of the company was engaged subsequent to this date; and the head-quarters remained at Montreal, under Captain Adams. On the 17th June, 1817, it embarked at Quebec for England, landing at Woolwich on the 23rd July. On the 31st of the same month, the company was reduced.

No. 4 Company.—If regret is unavoidable when one reads of the reduction of the companies already mentioned, a much stronger feeling inspires the Artilleryman—a feeling of righteous indignation,—when he finds that this, Sir Alexander Dickson's own company, shared the same fate. Just as its Captain—in his position of confidential adviser to the Duke of Wellington—raised the position of an Artillery commander on service, so did the company, under its gallant 2nd Captain, Cairnes—who was killed afterwards at Waterloo—contribute no mean share to the meed of glory, and work well done, which attached to the representatives of the Corps in the Peninsular campaigns. What battery is there now in existence but would give a great price to be able to say that the following records of No. 4 Company, 10th Battalion, were its own property by right of uninterrupted descent? And yet, perhaps, it is well that praise, earned in such words as recognized the labours of Sir Alexander Dickson's company, should be viewed as a regimental, instead of a battery inheritance. Let the record be briefly stated.

In February 1810, the company embarked at Woolwich on board the troop ship 'Alert,' and disembarked at Cadiz on the 1st April. The officers of the company present with it were Lieutenants Woolcombe, Raynes, and Talbot; 2nd Captain Cairnes joined it in June 1810, and Lieutenant Bridges in September 1811. It was stationed at the Isla de Leon during the siege of Cadiz, taking its tour of duty in the advanced batteries. The blockade continued from April 1810 to August 1812. In the beginning of 1811, 30 non-commissioned officers and gunners, with small arms, were told off under Lieutenant Mainwaring, Acting Quartermaster, as an escort to the ammunition accompanying the expedition under Lieut.-General Graham, which resulted in the battle of Barossa, on 5th March, 1811. This detachment was present at that battle, as were also Captain Cairnes and Lieutenant Raynes, who were attached to Major Roberts' brigade of guns; and Lieutenant Woolcombe, who acted as Adjutant to Major Duncan, who commanded the Artillery. Lieutenant Woolcombe was mortally wounded, and died on the following day.

In the month of September 1812, Colonel Skerrett was ordered to join Lord Wellington's army with 4000 men of the Cadiz division. Captain Cairnes with the whole of the company marched from the Isla de Leon on the 12th September, and on their arrival at Seville they were posted to a brigade of 9-pounders. Captain Cairnes, having been severely wounded by the explosion of a powder-mill near Seville a few days previously to the march of the division, was left behind. The brigade, under the command of Lieutenant Raynes, marched from Seville on the 30th September, and joined the army under Lieut.-General Hill at Val de Moros. On 30th October it was present at the affair of Puente Largo, near Aranjuez, but was not engaged. At the close of this year's campaign, the brigade was stationed at Val de la Mula, on the Portuguese frontier. Here it was rejoined by Captain Cairnes, and shortly afterwards moved to Pena ma Cor.

On the 6th June, 1813, the brigade joined the 7th Division of the army at Villalba, the following officers being present with it: Captain Cairnes, Lieutenants Raynes, Bridges, Talbot, and James, and Assist.-Surgeon Kenny. It was present at the battle of Vittoria, and received the following mention in orders :—

Extract from Division Orders by the Earl of Dalhousie.

"Camp in front of Vittoria,
"22 June, 1813.

" The Lieut.-General desires to express his high admi-
" ration of the conduct of the 1st Brigade, and of Captain
" Cairnes' brigade of guns yesterday. Nothing could surpass
" the steadiness and bravery of the men and officers. To
" Captain Cairnes, the officers, and men of the brigade of
" guns, the Lieut.-General offers his warmest acknowledg-
" ments for the steadiness and excellence of their fire at the
" different points where Captain Cairnes brought it to bear
" during the day.

(Signed) " F. D'OYLEY, A.-A.-G."

The brigade was afterwards employed in the blockade of Pampeluna in conjunction with the Spanish troops. On the 27th July, the right wing being driven back from Roncesvalles, after a series of actions commencing on the 25th, Captain Cairnes' brigade was ordered to take up a position on the heights near the village of Oracain, commanding the high road to Pampeluna. On the 28th July, the Artillery of the 6th Division not having arrived, Lieutenants Raynes and James were detached with two guns to the support of that division; and during the action Lieutenant Talbot joined with another gun. General Packe, who commanded the division, stood near the guns, and afterwards was pleased to say: "The guns were brought up at a most critical moment, " and served with all that gallantry for which the Corps is " remarkable." On the 29th July, this detachment rejoined Captain Cairnes, who was ordered to take up a fresh position, and on the following day an action commenced at daybreak. The enemy had previously endeavoured to surprise the advanced posts, but was soon driven back. The brigade was heavily engaged from daybreak till noon, when the enemy, driven back at all points, retreated. These two actions of the 28th and 30th July formed part of what are known as the "Battles of the Pyrenees." The brigade remained in the neighbourhood of Pampeluna until the 1st November, when the place surrendered.

On the 10th November, the brigade was present at the battle of Nivelle—held in reserve. On the 20th of the same month, it was ordered to the rear and cantoned near Fuenterabia, where it remained during the winter. In consequence of a deficiency of horses for the pontoon train, those belonging to the brigade were given up for that service.

On the 11th February, 1814, Captain Cairnes having been appointed to the Royal Horse Artillery, the command of the company fell to Lieutenant Raynes. On the 19th February, it marched to St. Jean de Luz, to take charge of rockets to be given over to Captain Lane.

On the 22nd February, Lieutenant Raynes received the following order:—

"Lieutenant Raynes with three non-commissioned officers
" and 4 gunners, with spikes, will cross with the first party,
" and spike the guns of the battery at the mouth of the
" Adour; which being accomplished, Lieutenant Raynes will
" return to the left bank of the Adour, and take charge of
" the rocket detachments on that side, which will have been
" previously told off as follows, viz.:

" One-half to be employed against the 'Sappho' frigate:
" for this duty, Lieutenant Bridges.

" The other half against the enemy's vessels, should any
" attempt to come down the river: for this post, Lieutenant
" Elgee.

" The parties under Lieutenants Bridges and Elgee to
" accompany the 18-pounders on their march. Lieutenant
" Raynes to accompany the pontoons.

(Signed) "A. G. FRAZER, Lieut.-Colonel.

" 22 February, 1814."

On the 23rd February, the passage of the Adour took place. The company remained before Bayonne until 8th March, when it was ordered to Reuterix (Spain) to assist in preparing the battering-train for the proposed siege of Bayonne.

On the 11th June Captain Close joined and took command of the company; and on the 20th of the same month it embarked for England,—disembarking on 12th July at Woolwich, and proceeding to Chatham.

It should have been mentioned that when the company was not actively employed, its officers often volunteered for other services. For example, from October 1811 to February 1812, Lieutenant Raynes was employed with another company at the siege of Tarifa. Lieutenants Bridges and Talbot, also, took part in the Expedition to Carthagena.

The company went from Chatham to Ireland, and was reduced, while serving in that country, on the 31st May, 1817.

No. 5 Company.—This company embarked at Woolwich on 28th February, 1810, for Cadiz, and landed at that place on the 1st April. The officers who accompanied it were Captain Shenley, 2nd Captain Mallett, 1st Lieutenants Maitland and Godby, and 2nd Lieutenant Cator. The company was employed in the batteries and lines in the defence of Cadiz until June 1812, when the French abandoned the siege. On the 16th August, 1814, it embarked at Cadiz for England, and landed at Woolwich on 27th September, 1814. On the 28th February, 1818, it ceased to exist.

No. 6 Company.—This company embarked at Gravesend on 28th February, 1810, for Cadiz, and landed there on 1st April. The company was employed in the batteries and lines in the defence of Cadiz until the abandonment of the siege by the French in June 1812. The officers with the company were Captain Roberts, 1st Lieutenants Dundas and Cozens. During the siege Lieutenant Cozens lost a leg. Part of the company, under Captain Roberts, was detached in February 1811 on an expedition to Algaziras, and afterwards was present at the battle of Barossa.

Second Captain Gardiner joined the company in 1811, but exchanged shortly afterwards.

On the 9th August, 1812, part of the company, under Captain Roberts, with Lieutenants Raynes, Maitland, and Brett attached, embarked at Cadiz with a brigade of 6-pounders under the command of Colonel Skerrett, and was present at the taking of Seville on the 27th of the same month. Here Lieutenant Brett was killed, and Lieutenant Maitland so severely wounded that he died a few weeks after. From Seville the detachment returned to Cadiz, where on the 16th August, 1814, they embarked for England with the whole company, arriving at Woolwich on the 27th September, 1814. The company was reduced after Waterloo on the 31st March, 1817.

No. 7 Company.—This company served in Gibraltar from March 1810 to April 1817. On its return to Woolwich, it was reduced,—on 31st May, 1817. Its reduction dislocated no traditions.

No. 8 Company.—The history of this company tallies, even to the dates of embarkation, with that of No. 7.

No. 9 Company.—This company served at the Cape of Good Hope from March 1811 to August 1817. It was reduced at Woolwich on 31st December, 1817.

No. 10 Company.—This company served in Malta from December 1810 to March 1817. It was reduced while in Malta, the men being transferred to the 1st Battalion, to a company which is now called A Battery, 11th Brigade, Royal Artillery.

The battalion head-quarters and Adjutant's detachment were reduced on 28th February, 1818.

This summary of the history of the old 10th Battalion companies should be read in connection with, and in amplification of, the chapters on the Peninsular and Second American Wars.

CHAPTER XIII.

PENINSULAR WAR—ROLIÇA, VIMIERA, CORUNNA.

"Saw
Time, like a pulse, beat fierce
Through all the worlds."
Rossetti.

THE history of the Regiment between 1808 and 1814 is concentrated in the Peninsular campaigns,—with the one exception of the Expedition to Walcheren. As the war in Spain drew to a close, the Second American War, which had in the meantime arisen, increased in importance, reaching its culminating point in 1814.

It is proposed in this chapter to treat of that section of the wars in the Peninsula which terminated in the sad but glorious victory of Corunna. After a diversion on the subject of the Walcheren Expedition, the Peninsular narrative will be resumed, and be continued uninterruptedly to its close.

The reader will doubtless remember that in the spring of 1808 the Spaniards rose as one man to resist the schemes of Napoleon, who had placed his brother Joseph on the throne of Spain. The English Government, always ready to assist any country which defied the French emperor, placed a force of 9000 men under the command of Sir Arthur Wellesley, who sailed for Portugal on the 12th July, to co-operate with the Spanish forces. This force was subsequently increased to nearly 30,000; but the conflicting instructions given by Government, and the utter ignorance of the real state of affairs in Spain, prevented the possibility of harmony of action among the English forces, and had

2 o

ultimately much to do with the abrupt and mistaken Convention of Cintra. Portugal had recently suffered dismemberment at the hands of Napoleon as a penalty for its friendship with England; the English Expedition had therefore a double motive,—the delivery of Portugal, and co-operation with the Spaniards. How terrible the errors of the English Government were in organizing this Expedition can only be realised by a study of the celebrated and standard history of the war; and such a study is necessary to enable one fully to realise the marvellous genius of Wellington, and his determined vigour. It is sufficient for the purpose of this work to show that, if the Royal Artillery shared the glories of Wellington, they also from the very first shared his difficulties—which were certainly not lessened in their treatment by the Ordnance. The conflicting instructions given by Government to Sir Arthur Wellesley were matched by the total absence of any information from the Board to Colonel Robe, who had been appointed to command the Artillery of the Expedition. A man full of zeal—one of the best practical Artillerymen whom the Regiment has ever produced— he naturally sought by every means in his power to ensure the completeness in every respect of the equipment of the force under his control. How completely he was foiled by the masterly silence of the Board will be seen by the following letters written by him after his arrival in Portugal. That, in spite of all his difficulties, he succeeded in earning the warm commendations of a chief who was rarely guilty of many words of praise, is merely another instance of the truth of the saying of a recent writer: "The student who reads " the history of the Royal Artillery can hardly fail to be " struck by proof after proof that the progress of the Regi- " ment has been due to the energy and manly courage of " individual officers within its ranks in spite of the wither- " ing cold of officialism. . . . So it must be, and ever will be. " Boards and clerks will bind chains in peace round the " men of talent, who will either break them when a crisis " comes, or die in the effort to do so."

The correspondence was as follows :—

<small>Napier, vol. i., book i., chapter iii.</small>

<small>'Times,' 13 Jan. 1873.</small>

"'Kingston' Transport,
"Mondego Bay,
"July 30, 1808.

". . . I shall therefore take the liberty of mentioning to you some points which it may be essential should on future occasions be put right on the embarkation of Artillery. [Lieut.-Col. Robe to Brig.-Gen. Macleod.]

". . . It appears to me necessary that the officer appointed to command Artillery on any expedition should know something more of the nature of the service intended than I did, and that he should not be made to take upon trust that everything necessary for his service will be found on board his ships. Our equipment is not yet arrived at the state of perfection to render such a mode efficient; and if it is practised, the commanding officer of Artillery will find, as I have, that his brigades will be wanting in articles extremely necessary, and be very short indeed in stores intended for repair or for keeping them in good order. He will perhaps find also, as I have, that intrenching tools, and even platforms, are sent with the Engineer's department for a species of service for which he has not a gun, nor a mortar, nor a round of ammunition. I do not make this a matter of complaint to you. I complain not of anything, because I can go no further than use to the best of my ability the means put into my power; but I confess it would have been much more satisfactory to me had I been permitted an opportunity of stating before I embarked what might have been sent with me for the real benefit of the service, and I don't think it would have occasioned an hour's delay to the embarkation, or have added a shilling of expense to the country, because the essential articles, if not supplied, *must* be purchased. I have so often mentioned *horses* that I ought perhaps to apologise for again recurring to that subject; and perhaps it may be said that I have no reason to mention them, having the horses of the Irish Commissariat ordered to be turned over to me on landing. Fortunate, indeed, I think myself to have even *them*. I know not what figure we should have cut without them; but when you learn that

" they are acknowledged to be *cast horses from the Cavalry*
" turned over to the Commissariat, you will readily think
" that we are not likely to make a very capital figure with
" them. I have been also fortunate enough to obtain with
" them a promise of shoes |from that branch, sufficient,
" with the *one hundred sets* supplied to me, to shoe them on
" first going off. Future service must be supplied as it can,
" and I shall not let it go unsupplied." . . . . .

This letter was written by Colonel Robe before he had realised the whole of his wants, and how admirably the Honourable Board had succeeded in proving their ability "How not to do it." The truth dawned on him very soon, and his language of remonstrance became stronger. His next letter is dated the 7th August, 1808, from the camp above Lavos, Mondego Bay, and contains the following passages:—

Lieut.-Col. Robe to Brig.-Gen. Macleod.

" I now deem it my duty (which were I to neglect I should
" be highly culpable) to point out to you in the strongest
" manner the impolicy of sending Artillery to a foreign
" country without horses. Even the horses we have now,
" old, blind, and casts from the Cavalry as they are, we find
" superior to what we can obtain from the country. The
" latter are good of their kind, but small, and not of sufficient
" weight for our carriages. Three hundred good horses would
" have cost the country no more for transport than as many
" bad ones, and what we shall do for the brigade now to be
" landed remains to be decided. . . . I must also mention
" the proportion of general stores which you, sir, know
" Artillery cannot do without, and which ought to be sent
" out with every embarkation. Had I been made ac-
" quainted with what was to have been embarked, I should
" not have gone on board ship till the proper proportion
" had been furnished. *I did everything in my power to obtain*
" *the information from the Board, and was referred to Mr.*
" ———, *who himself at the time was not furnished with any*
" *information.* I did at hazard request Mr. Spencer to put

CHAP. XIII. *Errors of the Board of Ordnance.* 199

" on board one hundred sets of horse-shoes and some nails,
" thinking them an addition to what would be provided
" for us. *These are all I have had for the horses of three
" brigades;* and had I not obtained some more from the
" Commissary-General, belonging to the horses delivered
" to us, the horses must have taken the field *barefoot*. I
" have made demands for some, and for such things as are
" most immediately required, and what may be wanted in the
" meantime must be purchased here.

" I write this to you officially, and must not be considered
" as individually complaining or making difficulties. My
" people of all classes exert themselves, and I am determined
" to get on; but I know that, engaged in a department
" where much is expected, I am doing my country greater
" service by pointing out what may render that department
" as complete as it is supposed to be, than if I were to
" remain for ever silent on the subject."

Then followed the battles of Roliça and Vimiera, to be alluded to hereafter, and merely mentioned here to show that before the date of his next letter Colonel Robe had been able to form a very practical opinion of the Board's shortcomings. Writing after Vimiera, on the night of the 21st August, 1808, he says: " My men are staunch, and the
" admiration of the army; and had they been properly sup-
" plied with horses and with stores, as artillery *should have*
" embarked from England, Europe would not have produced
" a more efficient artillery. I shall have occasion to write
" to you and to the Board on the latter subjects, as soon as
" I can obtain time; but give me leave to say now that
" never more will I leave England taking my provision of
" Artillery upon trust, and coming upon an army burthened
" with cast horses, or no horses at all, or with brigades
" unsupplied with any one store to make repair, and scarce
" a shoe to put on horses when I could beg them. This may
" be strong; but I have reason to use the expressions after
" suffering the inconveniences occasioned by the want of
" these supplies."

Lieut.-Col. Robe to Brigadier Macleod.

<small>Lieut.-Col. Robe to Colonel Harding.</small>

On the 1st September, 1808, Colonel Robe pointed out to Colonel Harding, who had arrived to take command of the Artillery in Portugal, that "not less than two hundred and " fifty horses would be required to render that Artillery " efficient for taking the field for a length of service. Those " received originally from the Irish Commissariat were old " cast horses of Cavalry, and many of them blind. They " now fall off very fast."

<small>Board of Ordnance to Lieut.-Col. Robe.</small>

The reader will be eager to learn how the Board explained its shortcomings, and what reparation it proposed to make to the brave officer who had gained honour for his Corps in spite of official blunders. For calm, cool assumption, perhaps, the reply sent by the Board is unsurpassed. It bears date the 6th October, 1808, after the news of the English successes, and the gallantry of the Artillery under Colonel Robe had reached England, and after Colonel Robe had been twice specially mentioned by Sir A. Wellesley in his despatches. It was written, let the reader remember, on behalf of a Board whose errors were not confined to those quoted above; which had actually sent guns without their ammunition, and ammunition which would have been useless, had not Colonel Robe succeeded in borrowing suitable guns from the navy. It was addressed to an officer who had been straining every nerve, night and day, to remedy the defects due to official ignorance, or to what is much the same, official affectation of omniscience;—to an officer who, in spite of the remonstrances which had been extorted from him by his discovery of the Board's incapacity, had never attempted to shelter himself behind the faults of others, but had, instead, toiled to remedy them. Let the reader bear these facts in mind, as he attempts to realise the feelings with which Colonel Robe must have perused the following lines:—
" In reply to the parts of your public correspondence in
" which you have so very warmly complained of some
" omissions and deficiencies, particularly in the Light Bri-
" gade of Artillery shipped at Plymouth, I am to say that
" his Lordship has, upon inquiry, ascertained that there *were*

" *some irregularities* in the embarkation, and that he has, in
" consequence, expressed his displeasure through the Board
" to the parties concerned, in a manner to make a lasting
" impression. His Lordship has, besides, issued such orders,
" and made such regulations, as must effectually preclude
" every plea or excuse for irregularity or omission in future.

" The Master-General, in desiring me to give you the
" above information, has directed me to add that, although
" he is willing to ascribe much of the style and many of the
" expressions in the letters to your known zeal for the service,
" and the anxiety attending an officer during the moments
" of preparation for the field, yet his Lordship cannot but
" regret that, instead of forwarding a complaint, which it
" would be the wish and the interest of the Ordnance to
" attend to, you should have allowed yourself to arraign,
" with such improper and unmerited asperity, the conduct
" of the Ordnance Department in general."

The old, old story! Officialism, on being detected in error, hurriedly, and with attempts at dignity, assumes an air of injured innocence, and neither forgives nor forgets the unhappy soldier who is the means of revealing its shortcomings. What a contrast does Colonel Robe's dignified and soldierlike acknowledgment of this reprimand present! Having first acknowledged the congratulations of the Master-General on the conduct of the Artillery at Roliça and Vimiera, which he had caused to be read to the men on parade, and entered in all the order-books, thereby, as he wrote, "awakening
" every joyful feeling that could arise in the breasts of
" soldiers," he proceeded as follows:—" The latter part of Lisbon,
" your letter is indeed a great source of grief to me, and 1809.
" has hurt me more than I can express. I had hoped to
" have obtained for my whole conduct the approbation of his
" Lordship the Master-General and the Board of Ordnance.
" I set out with the most earnest desire to fulfil, to the
" extent of my abilities, every duty I might be honoured
" with, and to abide in the strictest manner by their orders,
" for which purpose I applied for instructions and such
" information as the very limited time prior to my departure

"would admit. The shortness of that time, our expected
"destination (which, as you know, we had reason to believe
"was far more distant than it proved afterwards to be[1])
"certainly produced in me an anxiety that the branch of
"service entrusted to me should be supplied in the manner
"most conducive to the end for which it was sent out. This
"anxiety may have caused a warmth of expression not
"deemed advisable in public correspondence, however good
"the intention. And that an unfavourable impression has
"been received in His Lordship's mind I, with pain, per-
"ceive, and submit in the most respectful manner to the
"animadversion you have received His Lordship's commands
"to make. . . . . . . Whatever the warmth of my feelings
"might have been which impelled me to the remarks that
"have caused His Lordship's displeasure, I entreat that
"they may be ascribed to the peculiar situation in which I
"was placed. My letter to you was written on the ground
"of, and almost during, the action, and, consequently, that
"degree of coolness was not attended to which ought to
"have been manifested."

The difficulties of the campaign of August 1808 were increased by the insincerity and disunion of the Spaniards, the feebleness of the Portuguese support, and the extraordinary conduct of the English Government in sending General after General with conflicting instructions. The supersession of Sir Arthur Wellesley at a critical moment, uncalled for and undeserved, would have paralysed a less determined commander. To his resolution, his singleness of purpose, and his tact in dealing with the Portuguese authorities, is the fact due that, brief as the campaign was, it was marked by two brilliant engagements, and established already the military reputation of the English troops. The British army in Portugal, in 1808, was gathered from the four winds of heaven, without harmony either in instructions or management, and destitute of adequate equipment or supplies. The

---

[1] The force had originally been destined for South America.

CHAP. XIII. *The King's German Artillery.*   203

main body, which sailed from Cork, had been intended for South America; the contingent brought by Sir John Moore had been sent in the first instance to Sweden, on an errand rendered fruitless by the obstinacy of the Swedish monarch; and the rest of the army was gathered in instalments from Gibraltar, Madeira, and various parts of England. The annexed table, prepared from the embarkation returns, shows the method in which the Artillery portion of the army was collected :—at first destitute of horses, and, later, embarked with so much precipitation, that in many instances the horses died from long confinement on board ship; and in others it was found that animals had been hurriedly purchased, and embarked afflicted with fatal and infectious diseases, which spread rapidly among those which were healthy. The horses which were purchased in the country were small, and unfitted for Artillery work. The roads round Lisbon, and in the district traversed by Sir A. Wellesley's force, were of the worst description; and Colonel Robe and his successor, Colonel Harding, wrote to the Board, expressing their thankfulness that, for the three brigades engaged at Roliça and Vimiera they had been able to procure *oxen* to draw the guns, with horses as leaders! The remonstrances of Colonel Robe and his successors succeeded in procuring from England, as the annexed table will show, a suitable supply of horses as the year advanced; but the honours gained by the Corps had been earned before these arrived (*see* p. 204).

In addition to the companies (Captain Geary's and Captain Raynsford's) which embarked with Colonel Robe to form part of Sir A. Wellesley's force, 161 of the King's German Artillery were also detailed. The services of this Corps during the Peninsular and Waterloo campaigns were of the highest order. The head-quarters of the Corps were at this time at Porchester, and the strength in 1808 was as follows :— [Now 3 Battery, 2 Brigade, and 7 Battery, 17 Brigade.]

Field officers, 4; staff officers, 6; staff sergeants, 3. Two troops of Horse Artillery, consisting in all of 372 officers and men, and 186 horses. [Muster-Rolls of K.G. Artillery, 1808.]

RETURN of the OFFICERS and MEN of the ROYAL ARTILLERY, and of Officers' or Draught Horses, or others under the Ordnance, which were sent from various Stations to Spain or Portugal during the Year 1808, with the Dates of their respective Embarkations.

Date of Embarkation.	ROYAL ARTILLERY.					R. A. DRIVER CORPS.						General Total.	Horses.
	Officers.	N.C. Officers.	Gunners.	Drummers.	Total.	Officers.	N.C. Officers.	Drivers.	Trumpeters.	Artificer.	Total.		
Embarked with Sir A. Wellesley — June, 1808	10	27	204	4	245	2	18	143	2	10	175	420	..
Embarked with General Spencer from Gibraltar for Cadiz — June 13, 1808	3	6	53	1	63	..	1	13	..	..	14	77	..
Embarked with Sir J. Moore for Sweden, and then for Spain — April 30, 1808	24	62	406	8	500	3	18	276	2	30	329	829	360
Embarked with Generals Ackland and Anstruther — July 23, 1808	10	29	187	4	230	3	13	178	2	14	210	440	300
Embarked from Gibraltar by order of Sir H. Dalrymple — Aug. 13, 1808	8	27	186	3	224	..	..	..	..	..	..	224	..
Embarked from Madeira for Portugal with General Beresford — Aug. 17, 1808	3	14	94	2	113	..	..	..	..	..	..	113	..
Embarked with Sir D. Baird from Cork — Sept. 23, 1808	8	26	205	3	242	2	20	181	2	16	221	463	300
Embarked with Sir D. Baird from Woolwich — Sept. 22, 1808	10	26	200	2	238	2	20	181	1	15	219	457	300
Embarked from Woolwich: Horse Artillery — Oct. 5, 1808	12	28	160	..	200	..	..	109	2	14	125	325	296
Embarked from Portsmouth: Horse Artillery — Nov. 18, 1808	10	26	161	..	197	..	..	108	2	14	124	321	304
Embarked from Portsmouth — Dec. 8, 1808	2	..	1	..	3	4	28	213	3	19	267	270	600
Total embarked for Portugal or Spain in the year 1808	100	271	1857	27	2255	16	118	1402	16	132	1684	3939	2460

N.B. The return given by Napier in vol. i. p. 590, of his 'History,' neither includes the R. A. drivers, nor the officers and N. C. officers of the R. A. of several of the detachments mentioned above, but merely the gunners. It, however, does include the King's German Artillery, which is not shown in this purely regimental return.

Four marching companies, in all 714 officers and men—with 67 horses.

One of these companies was stationed in the Mediterranean. An addition to Colonel Robe's force of a doubtful value was received from Gibraltar. Lieut.-Colonel George Ramsey was ordered from Gibraltar with three companies to meet the Artillery expected from England, and a *car brigade* of guns, as it was termed, was issued from the Ordnance stores, for the service. Two of the companies, and Colonel Ramsey, were sent back to Gibraltar immediately on their arrival in Cadiz:—only one, Captain Morrison's[1] being allowed to proceed in charge of the guns. Colonel Ramsey, however, had time to inspect the car brigade which had been issued to him, and his official report on it was not complimentary to the store-keepers. A similar brigade, it would appear, had been sent to Sicily, a few weeks before; and the clerk of stores had hopelessly confused the two. The shafts for the howitzers had been sent with the 6-pounders; seven gun-wheels had been put on board for use with the waggons,—although not interchangeable,—and one waggon was entirely useless. The stores were inadequate and unsuitable; and there was neither a commissary, nor an artificer, with the detachment. A little further vacillation on the part of the authorities led to two companies leaving Gibraltar for Portugal immediately after the return of those under Colonel Ramsey; and one of these, Captain Skyring's, had the good fortune to join Colonel Robe in time for the battle of Vimiera.

To D. A. G. from Cadiz, 21 July, 1808.

Now 1 Battery, 6 Brigade.

Colonel Robe's force anchored in Mondego Bay on 28th July; and on the following day Sir Arthur Wellesley, who had preceded the army, and had been engaged in diplomatic as well as military duties, arrived, and gave orders for the disembarkation. The French withdrew from the coast, and the inhabitants showed symptoms of co-operation with the English, which were, however, sadly neutralised by the conduct of their rulers; while Sir A. Wellesley pressed forward, on the 9th August, to Leiria, hoping to cover the dis-

---

[1] Afterwards 8 Battery, 13 Brigade, but reduced on 1 Feb. 1871.

embarkation of the additional troops which he now knew were on their way from England, and perhaps at the same time to strike an effective blow, as near to Lisbon as possible, with the force under his command. This would have the effect of inspiring the Portuguese with courage; of asserting the right of the English to control the military operations of the Allies; and of disarranging the plans of the French. The English army was augmented at Lavos on the 6th August by General Spencer's contingent; and was divided into six brigades, under Generals Hill, Nightingale, Crawford, Bowes, Ferguson, and Fane. A demi-battery of Artillery was attached to each brigade; howitzers being attached to the 1st, 2nd, 5th, and 6th Brigades, and the 9-pounders being kept in reserve. On the line of march, the Artillery always moved in front of the brigades to which they were attached, and the Artillery of the reserve followed the Infantry.

G. O. dated Lavos, 7 Aug. 1808.

The advance of Sir Arthur Wellesley was perfectly successful; he succeeded in cutting the line of communication between Generals Loison and Laborde, and in inducing the French Commander-in-Chief, Junot, to quit Lisbon, and take the field with the reserve. The cowardice and self-interest of the Portuguese leaders robbed him, however, at a critical moment, of several thousand troops; so that in his first engagement with the enemy he had the assistance of no more than 1650 Portuguese. That engagement was the one known as the combat of Roliça—fought on the 17th August, with superior numbers on the side of the English, but against a General, Laborde, who was not only very able, but also occupied a position of great natural strength.

The attack of the English, who, with the Portuguese, numbered 14,000, was made in three columns, the left commanded by General Ferguson,—the right composed of the Portuguese,—and the centre, consisting of three brigades, commanded by Sir Arthur in person. The Royal Artillery had 18 guns, one-half of which came into action to cover the advance of the Infantry. So determined was that advance, and so critical did General Laborde's position become, as the left column, under General Ferguson, closed in upon his

CHAP. XIII. *Losses of the English and French.* 207

right, that he fell back to a new and parallel position, on the heights of Zambugeira. The steep heights, and dense brushwood, which had to be traversed in the advance of the English, rendered the attack of this new position a more difficult and costly one, and the losses of the 9th, 29th, and 82nd Regiments were especially heavy. The ardour of the troops was, however, irresistible; and Laborde again fell back, handling his troops with the utmost skill. In a very short time, after one or two attempts to make a stand, the French were in full retreat—"leaving three guns on the field "of battle, and the road to Torres Vedras open to the victors." Napier.

The loss of the French was admitted by themselves to be 600 killed and wounded; but it was probably much greater. Sir Arthur Wellesley, writing on the following day, said the loss had been reported to be 1500; and Colonel Robe, in his despatch to the Ordnance, said that the loss of the French far exceeded that of the English, which amounted to 479 killed and wounded. The loss of the Royal Artillery on this occasion was, as Colonel Robe wrote, irreparable. Captain Henry Geary, an officer of great promise and experience, was killed. "He was, by his own desire, and as "senior Captain, in charge of guns with the Light Brigade, "and was killed while pointing his gun within one or two "hundred yards of the enemy. I regret him as an officer, "for he was invaluable; and as a friend and old fellow-"campaigner, by no means less. His loss to his family "cannot be appreciated; but it will always be a comfort "that he died as he had lived, in the very act of doing his "duty to his country, and a true Christian." The force of Artillery under Colonel Robe's command at Roliça numbered 660 of all ranks. Wellington Supplementary Despatches, vol. vi. p. 116. Col. Robe to D. A. Gen., R.A. 18 August, 1808. Napier, vol i. p. 591.

The next engagement between the French and English forces took place under singular circumstances. Sir Arthur Wellesley had been reinforced by the brigades under Generals Ackland and Anstruther,—thus bringing his force up to 16,000 men, besides 660 Artillery, and 240 Cavalry,—exclusive of the Portuguese under Colonel Trant. The greatest number which Junot could bring against this army could—

it was known—hardly exceed 14,000. Further English reinforcements being known to be on the way, Sir A. Wellesley decided on assuming the offensive. Unfortunately, Sir H. Burrard, one of the three Generals sent out by the English Government to assume the command, arrived on the night of the 20th August, and Sir A. Wellesley was obliged to wait on him for orders. No arguments that he could employ could persuade Sir H. Burrard to attack before the arrival of the expected reinforcements; and Sir Arthur parted from him with feelings of the most bitter disappointment. Fortunately for him, and for the army, Junot, who by this time had reached Torres Vedras, resolved himself to assume the offensive; and to attack the English in their position near the village of Vimiera. The battle commenced at seven o'clock on the morning of the 21st August, and deserves a special mention in this work. For at Vimiera, for the first time, as Napier and Cust show, did the French realise the difference between the English forces and those with whom they had hitherto been contending;—for the first time did they appreciate those qualities with which they were so soon to be familiar: "the stolid firmness and resolute thrust of the Infantry, and the wonderful skill and precision of the Artillery." No chronicler of this battle fails to speak of the "murderous fire of Robe's Artillery;"—a fire which told with admirable effect at the most critical periods of the engagement. The number of guns present was small,—only 18, as at Roliça; but on this occasion all were engaged,—the reserve as well as the divisional Artillery being brought into play.

The right wing of the English army consisted of the 1st Brigade, under General Hill; the centre, of the 6th and 7th, under Generals Fane and Anstruther; the left, of the 2nd, 3rd, 4th, and 8th, under Generals Ferguson, Nightingale, Bowes, and Ackland; and the reserve was composed of the 5th Brigade, under General Crawford.

The attack of the French was made with great gallantry, in spite of many difficulties caused by the broken and wooded nature of the ground, and was directed against the English

centre in the first instance, and mainly against General
Fane's brigade. That officer, wisely availing himself of a
discretionary power granted him, and seeing that the position
was a favourable one for the employment of his Artillery
against the advancing columns, brought up the guns of the
reserve at once, and with those of his own division formed
a battery, which played on the advancing foe with " such a Cust.
" shower of shell and grape as might have been sufficient
" to stop any troops;" and although the French troops *did*
reach the summit of the hill on which the English stood,
they were, as Napier writes, so " shattered by the terrible
" fire of Robe's Artillery," that they fell an easy prey to the
gallant charges of the 50th Regiment. At another part of
the line, where skirmishing between Anstruther's brigade
and the French was going on, the Artillery played an equally
important part. A column of Grenadiers had been sent
forward by Kellermann to share in this part of the battle,
and "coming at a brisk pace, these choice soldiers beat Napier.
" back the advanced companies of the 43rd Regiment; but
" to avoid Robe's artillery, which ransacked their left, they
" dipped a little into the ravine on the right, and were
" immediately taken on the other flank by the guns of the
" 4th and 8th Brigades; then, when the narrowness of the
" way, and the sweep of the round shot, were crushing and
" disordering their ranks, the 43rd, rallying in one mass,
" went down upon the very head of the column, and with
" a short but fierce struggle, drove it back in confusion."
Yet again : in the attack upon General Ferguson's brigade
made by Solignac, who expected to find a weak force on
the left to oppose him,—but found it strengthened with the
same forethought and skill as marked, in days coming on,
the tactics of Wellington at Waterloo,—we read of the
" powerful artillery which swept away their foremost ranks."
As the reader finishes the account of this battle, and reads
of the French retreating in confusion, leaving thirteen of
their guns on the field, he can scarcely realise that the
whole Artillery force of Sir A. Wellesley was little more
than the captured guns represented. How much of the

VOL. II. P

effect of this force, small as it was, was due to the individual exertions of all ranks may be gathered from the following extract from Colonel Robe's despatch to the Ordnance :—

<small>Col Robe to D. A. Gen. Vimiera, 21 Aug. 1808.</small> "Never was man better supported by his officers and soldiers than I have been. I would not change one of them, "from the Major to the youngest subaltern, for anything "in the world; and only regret my son was not with me. "My men are staunch and the admiration of the army." It may interest the professional reader to know that great part of Colonel Robe's report after Vimiera was occupied with praises of Shrapnel's spherical case, of which he begged large additional supplies. He concludes with a sentence which proves the *entente cordiale* which existed between himself and his superiors. "Nothing but the unexampled "assistance and attention of Sir A. Wellesley, and the "general officers, could have brought this artillery into the "field in an efficient manner; and I am proud to say they "have never yet stopped an hour for us."

Sir H. Burrard, with the chivalrous courtesy which has so often been repeated in the annals of the English army, did not interfere with Sir A. Wellesley's command during the battle, but at its termination he declined to accede to the proposal of the latter to undertake an energetic pursuit, which would doubtless have ended in an unconditional surrender of the French troops. Of Sir Arthur's bitter disappointment,—of the further complication caused by the arrival of yet another General to supersede Sir H. Burrard—Sir Hew Dalrymple, —of the singular Convention of Cintra, which while it certainly succeeded in procuring the evacuation of Portugal by the French, did so on terms which were very disproportionate to the success of the English arms,—and of the indignation in England which followed the news of this marvellous treaty,—it is beyond the province of this work to treat. The state of affairs in Portugal—the absence of <small>Wellington Supplementary Despatches, &c., vol. vi. p. 129.</small> all harmony of plan or action, was such as to call from Sir Arthur Wellesley the expression, "Considering the way in "which things are likely to be carried on here, I shall not "be sorry to go away."

The recall of Sir Hew Dalrymple, Sir H. Burrard, and Sir A. Wellesley to England, on account of the Court of Enquiry ordered to investigate the circumstances under which the Convention had been agreed to, left the command of the English forces in Portugal with Sir John Moore. An army of 28,000 men was concentrated at Lisbon under that General. The command of the Artillery, which had been considerably reinforced, had been given to Colonel Harding, who endorsed every complaint which had been made by Colonel Robe, but who seems to have been somewhat more of an optimist than that officer; for in one of his letters, describing his field artillery, he wrote that " four " oxen and two horses bring along a gun famously." On his arrival at Lisbon, he found that he had to arrange for the proper equipment not merely of his own batteries, but also of the artillery of a force of 4000 Spaniards at Lisbon, whom the Convention had set free, and who, when armed and equipped, marched for Catalonia. Sir John Moore decided on taking the field in October 1808, but being misinformed as to the state of the roads, he decided on breaking up his army, so as to march by different roads, and to unite at Salamanca with another army under Sir David Baird, which had landed at Corunna. The Artillery was ordered to march through the Alemtejo and by Badajos to Talavera, and was arranged by Colonel Harding as follows. He himself, Lieut.-Colonel Wood, Major Viney, with the following companies, Thornhill's, Drummond's, Wilmot's, Raynsford's, Crawford's, Carthew's, and Skyring's, went with the army; the guns being four brigades of light 6-pounders, and one of 9-pounders. He was unable to take a brigade for each company, for lack of horses. Colonel Robe was left in command at Lisbon, with Major Hartmann and three companies of the King's German Artillery, Captain Bredin's company of the Royal Artillery, and half a company of the same under Captain Lawson. The guns to which these were attached consisted of a 12-pounder brigade, three brigades of light 6-pounders, a few howitzers, and the car brigade of 3-pounders from Gibraltar, mentioned above. The

Colonel Harding to D.-A.-Gen.

P 2

force of Artillery with Sir David Baird's army, which had landed at Corunna, was commanded by Colonel Sheldrake, and consisted of four companies and a proportion of drivers. The guns used by this force, and by the Horse Artillery under Colonel George Cookson, which arrived—also at Corunna—on the 8th November, 1808, were as follows: —One 9-pounder brigade and three brigades of light 6-pounders, which moved on to Betanjos: one 9-pounder brigade, and one of light 6-pounders, which remained at Corunna; and one light 6-pounder brigade, and a brigade of mountain artillery, for service with the Cavalry, as soon as horses and mules could be obtained.

Colonel Cookson to D.-A.-Gen. Corunna, 9 Nov. 1808.

Of all the difficulties encountered in the winter campaign of 1808 by the Royal Artillery, the scarcity of horses was the greatest. The table given in a former part of this chapter shows that after the first gross omission in the case of Colonel Robe's force, the Ordnance Department endeavoured, as far as numbers were concerned, to send an adequate supply of horses to ensure that mobility without which field artillery is a sham. But that the simplest precautions as to quality and soundness were overlooked is too evident from the monotonous protests of all the officers who found themselves in a position of responsibility. Colonel Harding, writing from Lisbon, reported that he had obtained permission to sell the Artillery horses he had received from England, as useless and worn out, and to purchase those of the French army, which was then embarking under the provisions of the Convention of Cintra. Colonel Cookson had not reached the Downs ere he had to report the appearance of glanders among the horses entrusted to him; and Colonel Robe had to report the death, immediately after landing, of 75 out of 300 horses—more than half occasioned by the same complaint. The officer in charge of the drivers attached to the Artillery under the command of Colonel Sheldrake, reported that "all his horses " were in dreadful order when they embarked, that he had " lost many, and that he attributed it in a great measure to " the horses being a great many very old." Mules were difficult to obtain—the horses of the country were few and of small size; and in spite of the plaintive appeals from successive officers that "it cost no more to the country to "keep a good horse than a bad one," shipload followed shipload of cripples from England, and nothing but superhuman exertions on the part of all on the spot enabled the Artillery to move at all. The desperate state of affairs may be gathered from a report of Colonel Robe's, in which he described the means left to him for horsing the brigades in his charge, after Colonel Harding's force had left Lisbon with Sir John Moore. With 52 field-guns, liable to be demanded at any moment by Colonel Harding, he had only 500 men; but this number was lavish compared with that of his horses. "The following," he wrote, "is a state of "the horses left with me on the departure of the army for "Spain:— Col. Robe to D.-A.-Gen. 1 Nov. 1808.

	Horses.	Mules.
"Effective	15	3
"Sick or lame	49	4
	64	7
"Since died of general decay, or destroyed for glanders	7	1
"Remaining	57	6

"The sick of these are reported to be in a very bad con-"dition; and nearly the whole of them to be at present "unserviceable, from lameness, age, and sore backs."

So great was the scarcity of horses, that when the Horse Artillery landed at Corunna, the officers' horses were taken on repayment—without their consent, and they were left to purchase any animals they could find in the country. That Colonel Robe had good reason to fear a demand being made on his small depôt may be seen from the following account of the number of horses, which the state of the roads between Lisbon and Spain had rendered absolutely necessary for the brigades which had marched with Colonel Harding. Every artillery carriage, of whatever description, had 6 horses; the long 6-pounder gun had 8, and the 12-pounder Official Return to Sir H. Burrard, Nov. 1, 1808.

had 10. Besides this, horses were required for the officers, non-commissioned officers, and for park duties; and the ammunition waggons, for conveyance of such as could not be carried on the limbers, were drawn by a motley collection of horses, mules, and oxen. Six days after this return was prepared, Colonel Robe's supply had decreased to 40, and the demands from the front were such that he declared no less than a reserve of 600 horses would be required to meet them.

<small>Colonel Robe to D.-A.-Gen. 6 Nov. 1808.</small>

There is a danger, in perusing the noble story of the Peninsular War, lest all the reader's admiration should be given to the courage and endurance of the men, or the skill of the leaders. But there were men who would infinitely rather have endured bodily suffering than the charge which neglect or ignorance at home had thrust upon them. To feel in all its terrible reality the starvation of equipment, without which no adequate results can be expected either from skill or courage;—to know that if that equipment is not in some way forthcoming, the disgrace of failure or consequent disaster will be transferred from those to whom it is due, and will be visited on themselves;—and at the same time to be certain that any responsibility which they may assume is at their own peril, and can only be exercised with a halter round their neck of possible disallowances, reprimands, and suspicion,—all these produce in men a state of mind beside which danger or bodily hardship seems almost repose: and it was in such a condition that many of England's best soldiers had to live during the war in Spain —enduring more than has formed the theme of song and story—and yet bearing it without sympathy, without acknowledgment.

No one can thoroughly understand Sir John Moore's campaign in Spain without bearing in mind the boasting and lying of the Spanish Generals, with whom it was intended that he should co-operate, and the yet more extravagant falsehoods of the Spanish Government. Deluded by these, Sir John Moore, even after he had heard of the surrender of Madrid to Napoleon, pressed on to Majorga in the hope of effecting a junction with the Marquis Romana, and of receiving Sir David Baird's reinforcement from Corunna. With an English army of 25,000 men he pressed still farther on to Sahagan, where for the first time he heard the whole truth, and realised the strength of the French armies which were being directed against him, under Napoleon himself. With every Spanish General already beaten in detail, Madrid in the hands of the enemy, and greatly superior forces hurrying to meet him, he commenced a retreat which has become famous,—the first step of which is thus described by Colonel Harding :—" We fully expected to have engaged "the enemy on the 23rd, about five leagues from Sahagan; "the army was in full march at 8 o'clock on the night of "the 23rd, and hoped to have fallen in with them early in "the morning of the 24th. An intense hard frost, and the "whole of the roads one sheet of ice from the snow thawing "during the day, was much against the march of Artillery, "as we had not time to rough all the horses. The march "of the troops was stopped an hour after they marched off; "some of the troops, particularly Downman's troop, were "out till 2 in the morning. The General received some "information immediately after the troops marched off, "which caused their sudden return. We now seem to be "pointing towards Corunna, and forming depôts that way. "Our movements have lately been so intricate and unex- "pected, that if I had had time to write to you, I could give "you little information. . . . Lieutenant-Colonel Cookson "has the command of the three brigades on the right of the "line, Evelegh's, Bean's, and Wilmot's. Lieutenant-Colonel "Wood has charge of those on the left of the line, Down- "man's, Drummond's, and Carthew's. Four reserve brigades "with the park are Raynsford's (9-pounders), Crawford's, "Brandreth's, and Wall's (light 6-pounders) brigades. The "park, stores, and ammunition are under Major Thornhill. "The depôts advanced are under Captain Skyring. There "is a brigade of mountain guns somewhere, which I hope "will not join us, but return to Corunna. We have lately "received 59 prize horses, which, although not good, are a "great help to us, from our great loss."

Colonel Harding to D.-A.-Gen. Majorga, 25/12/1808.

English troops are apt to become demoralized during a retreat; and in the retreat to Corunna, irregularity was increased by the intense cold, suffering, and hardship which the men had to endure. The conduct of the rear-guard and of the Cavalry was, however, beyond all praise; and was due in a great degree to the constant presence of Sir John Moore himself, whose skill, firmness, and powers of persuasion never shone more clearly than at this time. But, even when irregularity was greatest, it vanished when an engagement appeared probable: it was at such times as these that perfect discipline prevailed. The Artilleryman reads with pleasure that while 2627 men strayed from the English army during the retreat, not one belonged to his corps; and that Sir John Moore himself was so struck by this fact and by their general conduct, that he wrote, " The Artillery consists " of particularly well-behaved men." These words are the more gratifying as the strength of the Artillery was considerable—eleven brigades of guns,—and the duties of the men were very arduous.

<small>Cadell.</small>

Several affairs of small importance took place between the two armies, but the English came in sight of Corunna without any general engagement. The dismay which seized every one on learning that the transports had not yet arrived may be imagined; fortunately it was short-lived, as they soon made their appearance.

The story of the Artillery at the end of the retreat, and during the battle of Corunna, may be summarised from Colonel Harding's reports. On the 11th January the army took up a position about five miles from Corunna; but on the 14th, being unable, with their reduced numbers, sufficiently to occupy this ground without danger of being outflanked, they withdrew to a position about three miles nearer the town, leaving their original ground to be occupied by Soult, before the battle. On the 12th all the Artillery, except the brigades required for outpost and rearguard duties, was ordered by Sir John Moore to be embarked; and at the same time a magazine containing 12,000 barrels of powder, situated about four miles from Corunna, was blown

CHAP. XIII.   *The Story of the Artillery.*   217

up with great skill, under the supervision of Colonel Cookson. This was not done, however, until some 400 barrels had been carried for the use of the Artillery, along dreadful roads, for a distance of four miles, on the shoulders of the Artillerymen; while at the same time serviceable arms were issued from the stores to all the troops, in exchange for those which had become useless during the retreat. A supply of ammunition at the rate of 70 rounds per man was also given out. These measures had the double effect of destroying valuable stores which must have inevitably fallen into the hands of the enemy, and of giving an advantage to the English army in the battle which ensued, which was denied to their opponents, whose arms and ammunition had suffered greatly during the harassing marches of the preceding days.

All the Artillerymen, who could be spared from the embarkation of guns and stores on the 14th and 15th, were employed in the destruction of the guns and mortars on the sea front of Corunna (which would otherwise have been used against the English fleet, on the occupation of the town by the French), and also of those mounted on a small island in the bay. Upwards of 50 heavy guns and 20 mortars were dismounted, spiked, and thrown over the precipice, and their carriages and beds destroyed. In this the men were assisted cheerfully by the inhabitants, although, as Napier points out, they were aware that the English army would ultimately embark, and that they would incur the enemy's anger for having taken part in any military operations. This conduct, so inconsistent with the insufficient defence made by the Spaniards as a nation, drew forth from the historian a remark, which the events of 1873 have strangely justified : " Of proverbially vivid imagination and quick re-" sentments, the Spaniards feel and act individually, rather " than nationally."

The Artillery of the outposts, on which the brunt of the action of the 16th fell, was commanded by Major Viney, and consisted of 145 officers and men of the Royal Artillery, and 94 officers and men of the Royal Artillery Drivers. Official MS Return, signed by Colonel Harding.

The guns employed were seven light 6-pounders, one 5½-inch howitzer, and four Spanish 8-pounders.

The names of the officers serving under Major Viney's command were as follows: Captains Truscott, Wilmot,[1] Godby, and Greatley; Lieutenants Sinclair and King; and Assistant-Surgeons Price and Hutchison. The officers of the Royal Artillery Drivers were Lieutenants Abercromby and Read.

A slight affair of picquets took place on the 15th; but even as late as noon on the 16th, Sir John Moore told Colonel Harding that he did not think the enemy meant to attack, and therefore he continued the embarkation. Most of the horses and appointments belonging to Downman's and Evelegh's troops of Horse Artillery had been lost during the retreat; and their guns, and those of several of the other brigades, had been placed on board ship; so that many of the Artillerymen, who had been present during the retreat, and were under fire on the 16th, were without their guns on that day, and were employed in bringing up ammunition for the army. The Artillery of the outposts, although lightly armed, did good service; but the ground was not calculated for the manœuvring of guns, either on the side of the French or of the English.

On Monday the 16th, at 3 P.M., Soult advanced with all his army in three columns, his cavalry and artillery remaining on the heights to cover his formations. Two divisions of the English army, under General Hope and Sir David Baird, occupied the most advanced ground on their side, with their left to the Bay of Corunna; a third division, under General Frazer, was posted on some heights to the right—more retired—commanding the approaches to Corunna from the Vigo Road. Captain Gardiner wrote: "The action became general about 3 o'clock, and an uninterrupted fire of cannon and musketry was kept up till one hour after dark. They evidently pushed for our right, which was our weakest

To D.-A.-G. 23 June, 1809. N.B. Capt. Gardiner was Brigade-Major to the R. A.

---

[1] Captain Wilmot was in command of the Company which is now D Battery, 4th Brigade.

"point, but the firmness of our line was in no way to be
" shaken. At one time I feared they would outflank us from
" their numbers; but this was prevented by the movements
" of the reserve under General Paget. At a little after
" 6 o'clock Soult retired, leaving us masters of the field,
" and in possession of a village he occupied in the morning."
This village, Elvina, had been to the battle of Corunna
what Hougomont and La Haye Sainte were afterwards to
that of Waterloo. The battle, at various periods of the day,
raged fiercely round it. Here Sir David Baird received the
wound which compelled him to leave the field; and it was
when watching the attack by the English reserve on the
French troops in possession of this village late in the day,
that Sir John Moore received the wound which proved fatal.
Its retention by the English at the close of the day was
therefore a distinct proof of victory.

But it was not a victory, as General Hope well said, Despatch
which could be attended by any very brilliant consequences to Sir D. Baird.
to Great Britain. The utmost that could be hoped for was
the embarkation of the army without molestation. Thanks
to the defeat of the French, their want of ammunition, and
the friendly courage of the inhabitants of Corunna, the
whole army, with the exception of the rear-guard, was embarked with perfect order during the night of the 16th.
The incessant rumble of wheels over the field denoted the
gathering of the wounded, and their conveyance in the artillery carts and waggons to the beach. The guns which
had been engaged during the day were taken for embarkation to a sandy bay, south-west of Corunna, but, as Colonel
Harding wrote, " The weather would not permit it: the
" guns were spiked; the carriages destroyed; and the
" whole thrown over a precipice into deep water."

The rear-guard had been detailed by Sir John Moore
himself, to assist the Spaniards in manning the guns on
the land front of Corunna,—to keep possession of the small
island in the bay,—and to cover the embarkation of the
troops from the citadel. The Artillery attached to it was
commanded by Major Beevor, assisted by Major Thornhill,

Captains Truscott, Beane, Brandreth, and Greatley, and Lieutenants Maling, Wright, and Darby. There were 36 non-commissioned officers and 253 men. The whole of the rear-guard was embarked, but with difficulty, on the evening of the 18th and morning of the 19th. The voyage to England was tempestuous in the extreme. Many officers and men died on the passage; many others, including Colonel Harding himself, only survived their hardships a few months. The whole army landed in England at various ports in such a state of destitution, that the whole nation was shocked, and could not believe it possible that the story of the final success was true. These skeleton regiments, starved and half-clothed, had not the appearance of an army fresh from victory; and for many years the skill displayed in the retreat upon Corunna, and the subsequent success, received little, if any, credit from the people.

So ended Sir John Moore's campaign in Spain;—and with it—his life. A type of the same individuality of which the Duke of Wellington was the perfection,—in which a sense of duty rises above every other feeling,—he yet possessed charms of character, denied to his great comrade, which won for him the love, as well as the confidence, of his troops. A disciplinarian, indeed, he was—what leader can be great who is not?—but, with all his strictness, there was something so winning in his disposition, that even after a lapse of fifty years, the writer of these pages has seen tears in the eyes of a man who had served under him, at the mere mention of his name.

The many letters from the various officers, whose correspondence with the Ordnance is extant, tell in simple words the worth of the leader who fell at Corunna. "You *Colonel Harding to D. A. Gen.* "have heard," writes one, "of our terrible loss: we could *Captain (afterwards Sir R.) Gardiner to D. A. Gen.* "not believe he was dead." Another writes: "General "Hope's despatches will acquaint you with our affecting "loss. You will imagine how severely I felt it. I saw him "after he received the wound, but he was talking with such "firmness, that I did not apprehend the danger he was in." General Hope's words cannot be too frequently read. "The

"fall of Sir John Moore has deprived me of a valuable
"friend, to whom long experience of his worth had sincerely
"attached me. But it is chiefly on public grounds that
"I must lament the blow. It will be the consolation of
"every one who loved or respected his manly character,
"that after conducting the army through an arduous retreat
"with consummate firmness, he has terminated a career
"of distinguished honour by a death that has given the
"enemy additional reason to respect the name of a British
"soldier. Like the immortal Wolfe, he is snatched from
"his country at an early period of a life spent in her
"service: like Wolfe, his last moments were gilded by the
"prospect of success, and cheered by the acclamation of
"victory: like Wolfe, also, his memory will for ever
"remain sacred in that country which he sincerely loved,
"and which he had so faithfully served."

Despatch to Sir D. Baird, 18 Jan. 1809.

There is a pathos about these words which is not surpassed even in the lines which have given an eternal place in English verse to the battle which has just been described. But all the regret of friends, all the eloquence of admirers, all the hymns of poets, fade into nothing beside the simple words of the dying chief,—who uttered with his last breath no appeals for praise, no boastings of difficulties overcome, no chidings against those who had disappointed or deceived him, but the quiet, confident expression of a soldier whose duty is done: "I hope that my country will do me justice."

The following return shows the strength of the Royal Artillery left in Portugal, after the evacuation of Spain by Sir John Moore's army. It also shows the number who had returned at various times from the Peninsula, prior to 27th February, 1809, having proceeded thither with the various contingents detailed in the preceding table. (*See next page.*)

TABLE showing the NUMBER of OFFICERS, NON-COMMISSIONED OFFICERS, GUNNERS, and DRUMMERS of the ROYAL ARTILLERY; and also of the OFFICERS, NON-COMMISSIONED OFFICERS, DRIVERS, TRUMPETERS, ARTIFICERS, and HORSES belonging to the Royal Artillery Drivers, relanded from Spain or Portugal before the 27th February, 1809.

	ROYAL ARTILLERY.					ROYAL ARTILLERY DRIVERS.						General Total.	Horses.
	Officers.	N.C. Officers.	Gunners.	Drummers.	Total.	Officers.	N.C. Officers.	Drivers.	Trumpeters.	Artificers.	Total.		
Relanded in Great Britain and Ireland, fit for service	64	178	1,215	16	1,473	14	105	1,116	14	97	1,846	2,819	764
In Portugal, per return of 1st January .	31	84	556	11	682	2	7	219	2	28	258	940	
Total	95	262	1,771	27	2,155	16	112	1,335	16	125	1,604	3,759	764

N.B. There had been purchased, or otherwise obtained, in Portugal, and still remained effective, 146 horses and 78 mules; but as they had not been sent from England they are not included in the above table.

CHAPTER XIV.

WALCHEREN.

AN Expedition has now to be described to whose conception and partial execution justice has not been done by historians. Remembered, if at all, for its miserable termination, it is not unfrequently classed among the military operations which an Englishman had better forget. And yet there was a strategic value in the idea, which was proved even by its incomplete realisation; and there was a determination, and an uncomplaining suffering among the English troops, worthy of note in military story, which have been ill repaid by the nameless graves which crowd the island of Walcheren, and by the national forgetfulness of the Expedition.

To an Artilleryman the Walcheren Expedition has an interest which well repays him for turning his eyes and thoughts from the Peninsula to this strange island in the Northern Sea. Here no less than seventeen troops and companies of his Corps were present; and so important was their duty considered, that the Master-General, Lord Chatham, who was also Commander-in-Chief of the forces employed, requested the Deputy Adjutant-General, Brigadier Macleod, himself to accompany the army in command of the Artillery. And on this island, so baneful to our troops, and yet so beautiful, a singular historical question connected with the Regiment was settled, which will receive detailed notice in this chapter.

Forming the right bank of the West Scheldt at its mouth, the islands of South Beveland and Walcheren, now united by a railway embankment, present to the traveller the most singular appearance. Rich and fertile beyond measure, they are yet only saved from submersion by the sea by means of costly dykes, kept efficient by incessant labour. In most places the island of Walcheren, especially, is many feet below the level of the sea; and even its highest points, the towns of Middleburg and Flushing, have frequently suffered great injury from the inroads of the ocean. One such inundation had occurred in 1808, and tended to make the autumn of 1809 exceptionally unhealthy. Dykes now not merely surround the island itself, but also the individual villages and farmhouses on its surface, giving a singular and fortified appearance to the whole.

Flushing and Antwerp, in the hands of Napoleon, strongly fortified, and offering protection and anchorage to his fleets, were a strong and perpetual menace to England, and gave an appearance of probability to his threats of invasion, both in the eyes of the English people and their Government. One of the strongest arguments against the Walcheren Expedition has always been that it was a dissipation of England's military resources, which, if concentrated on the Peninsular campaign, would have produced infinitely greater results. But it is easy to argue thus with the wisdom which follows the fact. The danger which was involved in the fortifications of Antwerp and Flushing was very present to the English people; and immunity in that respect seemed then more desirable than victory at a distance, even although that victory might, in the end, have been a more serious blow at Napoleon's power. And the importance of Flushing, armed as it was, may be now better realised by imagining it in the hands of a powerful Continental dynasty, —not dismantled and disarmed, as it has been since the siege to be treated of in this chapter,—but with batteries sufficiently strong to protect the anchorage in front, and with a fleet riding there within a few hours of the English coast. Were such a thing ever to occur again—and it is by no means impossible—Englishmen would perhaps confess that there was more wisdom in the Expedition of 1809, which rendered Flushing harmless, than has generally been allowed.[1]

Much of the unpopularity attending it, and all the incompleteness of execution, were due to a want of harmony between the naval and military commanders, which has never yet been satisfactorily explained, but which undoubtedly was the main cause of the first part of the scheme—the capture of Flushing—being the only part that was executed. Lord Chatham would appear to have been much to blame in the matter; but there has been a mystery connected with it all which cannot be cleared up. Of that nobleman's military incapacity there is, however, no doubt; nor is the reader surprised to find that his name disappeared, soon after this Expedition, from the list of the Masters-General of the Ordnance.

The troop of Horse Artillery which accompanied the force was that commanded by Captain A. Macdonald, and is now D Battery, A Brigade. The sixteen companies will be found enumerated in the various tables of the battalions. General Macleod took Captain—afterwards Sir Robert—Gardiner as his Brigade-Major; and it is from the private diaries of these officers that the main Regimental incidents connected with this Expedition have been obtained. Captain Drummond was the General's Aide-de-camp. The field officers who accompanied the Artillery were Colonel Terrot, Lieut.-Colonels Dixon, Francklin, Cookson, and Wood, and Majors Griffiths, Dixon, and Waller. The immense battering train included 70 guns and 74 mortars; and we learn that not merely was a large supply of Congreve's rockets taken for employment as siege weapons, but also that every man in the Regiment who had been trained to the use of rockets was ordered to embark with the army.

Sir J. T. Jones's 'Sieges.'

A.-A.-Gen. to Colonel Neville, 18 July, 1809.

The name of nearly every Artillery officer with the Expe-

---

[1] The Infantry force with the Expedition numbered 33,096
The Cavalry 3,015

Sir J. T. Jones, from whose work these numbers are taken, gives only the *field* and not also the *siege* Artillery companies.

dition will appear in the course of the narrative. In the meantime the following numerical return of the force under General Macleod's command will be found worthy of perusal. (*See opposite page.*)

The Second Division of the army, which General Macleod accompanied, sailed from the Downs on Saturday, the 29th July, 1809, and anchored the same evening in the Stein Diep. On the following day they weighed anchor, and moved into the Room Pot, where they found the First Division, and where orders were at once given for the troops to land in light marching order. At 4 P.M. the first six battalions landed, without opposition, at the Bree Zand, and during the night the remainder of the troops, under the command of Sir Eyre Coote, continued to disembark, with the several brigades of Artillery attached to them,—the last named being under the command of Colonel Terrot. The following detail shows the Artillery attached to this part of the army:—

Captain Marsh's Light 6-pr. Brigade, attached to Lieut.-Gen. Frazer.
  ,,   Webber Smith's   ,,   ,,   Major-Gen. Graham.
  ,,   Massey's   ,,   ,,   Lieut.-Gen. Lord Paget.

There was also a Heavy Brigade under Captain S. Adye.

About 3 P.M. the reserve, under Sir John Hope, proceeded to South Beveland (immediately adjoining Walcheren), accompanied by Captain Wilmot's Light 6-pounder Brigade.

On Monday, the 31st July, Ter Veer, a village at the opposite end of the island of Walcheren from Flushing, was invested, two guns of Captain Macdonald's troop and two 8-inch mortars having been landed to assist; and it surrendered the following day. Until the fall of Flushing, Ter Veer was employed as a landing-place and depôt for ordnance stores,—the Balaclava of the Walcheren Expedition. The army then advanced across the island, and proceeded to invest Flushing. During the siege, frequent reinforcements of the French garrison took place, their troops being transported by sea from Cadsand, and the weather being such as to render it very difficult for the English fleet to intercept them. The defence made by the French was very gallant, although the wretched

Numerical Return of Artillery.

ARTILLERY EMBARKED for the SCHELDT EXPEDITION, under the EARL OF CHATHAM, in 1809.

Number of Troops and Companies, with Drivers attached; also Ports of Embarkation.	ROYAL ARTILLERY.								ROYAL ARTILLERY DRIVERS.					(General Total.)	Horses.
	Field Officers.	Captains.	Subalterns.	Surgeons.	N. C. Officers.	Gunners.	Drummers.	Total.	Officers.	N. C. Officers.	Drivers.	Artificers and Trumpeters.	Total.		
PORTSMOUTH.															
Eight companies	4	16	24	4	104	800	16	968	2	10	90	8	110	1,078	150
RIVER THAMES.															
One troop: Royal Horse Artillery (now D Batt., A Brigade)	..	2	3	1	13	81	..	100	..	..	54	8	62	162	162
Eight companies	4	16	24	4	104	800	16	968	7	41	308	37	393	1,361	515
With the battering train	..	..	..	..	..	..	..	..	7	54	500	42	603	603	1,000
Total	8	34	51	9	221	1,681	32	2,036	16	105	952	95	1,168	3,204	1,827

N.B. A few casualties occurred prior to the sailing of the Expedition. About 50 additional horses were embarked, and rather more than 100 men were left behind sick, and for other causes; but these are the numbers prepared from the official returns, both in Record Office and United Service Institution.

inhabitants were the main sufferers during the bombardment. By Napoleon's positive order, and notwithstanding the remonstrances of the French Commandant, one of the dykes near Flushing was partly cut, and the sea poured into the English trenches to a considerable extent, increasing the discomfort and difficulties which the heavy and almost incessant rains had already produced.

The English army was drawn up against Flushing as follows: General Graham's division on the right, General Grosvenor's next; then Lord Paget's at West Zouberg, and General Houston's at Oust Zouberg. Six batteries were formed, five of which were manned by the Royal Artillery, and one by seamen. The former were numbered and armed as follows :—

No. 1 Battery.—[1] 1200 yards from the town.

13 24-prs. . . . . ⎫
2 8-in. howitzers . ⎬ This was evidently No. 5 Battery, according to the numbering of the Engineers;
6 8-in. mortars . ⎭ vide Jones's 'Sieges.'

No. 3 Battery.—2200 yards from the town.

6 10-in. mortars . { This was evidently No. 1 Battery in the Engineers' catalogue.

No. 4 Battery.—1600 yards from the town.

4 10-in. mortars.
10 24-pounders.

No. 5 Battery.—1600 yards from the town.

2 10-in. howitzers. { This was evidently No. 7 Battery in the Engineers' catalogue.

No. 6 Battery.—1700 yards from the town.

3 24-pounders.
4 10-in. howitzers.

N.B.—Two additional batteries, Nos 7 and 8, were afterwards armed: No. 7 with 2 10-inch mortars, No. 8 with 6 24-pounders.

These batteries were opened on the 13th August, at 1 P.M. At early morning on the 15th August Flushing surrendered. Including the ammunition expended by the sailors from

---

[1] The armament and numbering of these batteries differ from those given in Sir J. T. Jones's 'Sieges;' but as they are taken from Captain Gardiner's MS. diary—written in his own hand—they must be correct. Probably they show the armament of the batteries when the bombardment *commenced;* and Sir J. Jones may give the armament when at its maximum.

No. 2 Battery, which was armed with six 24-pounders, and opened on Sunday, the 14th August, the following was the expenditure of ammunition, other than rockets, during the short siege:—

	Rounds.
24-pr. guns	6582
10-in. mortars	1743
8-in. „	1020
10-in. howitzers	269
8-in. „	380
Total	9994

N.B.—Sir R. Gardiner's MS. agrees exactly in this particular with Sir J. T. Jones's 'Sieges.'

Rockets had been used before the opening of the batteries, and continued to be employed in great profusion, and with fatal effect. Great part of the city, including the Hôtel de Ville, was burnt to the ground, and hundreds of the inhabitants were killed. To this day shot may be seen in the walls of many of the houses,—handing down from one generation to another the traditions of the siege.

The chief labour and hardship, however, to the English troops preceded the opening of the batteries. It was during their construction that the energies of officers and men were most severely tried. The roads between Ter Veer and the trenches became almost impassable with constant traffic and rain; the landing of the guns and stores was attended with great difficulty; it was impossible to procure cattle in sufficient quantities for purposes of draught; and many of the horses intended for the later operations had to be landed at Walcheren to draw the stores from Ter Veer. As for the trenches themselves, a few extracts from Sir R. Gardiner's diary will enable the reader to realise the conditions under which the Artillerymen worked:—

"August 10th. Ascertained, by the saltness of the water,
" that the dyke had been cut. . . . . . . The water making
" great progress in the communication from the right to
" West Zouberg. The cross-roads very deep and bad; great
" difficulty in drawing the guns from the park to the several
" batteries.

"August 11th. A violent thunder-storm and incessant
" rains during the night precluded all work the greatest
" part of it. The water rose in the gun-battery on the left
" about six inches.

"August 12. The roads much worse, and the water
" rose very high in the trenches. The water-gauge showed
" the rising of the water to be 4 inches. The magazine
" of No. 1 Battery on the right was filled with water
" during the night from the heavy rains, and it was feared
" would not be ready to receive the ammunition. *The
" exertions of the men, however, overcame every obstacle.*"

Three companies, commanded by Captains Drummond, Campbell, and Fyers, had landed at Ter Veer on the 8th August, and proved of great service in the batteries at Oust Zouberg; but the Artillery before Flushing had been weakened the previous day by the removal of the detachments of Captains Buckner's[1] and Brome's companies, with Captains Adye and Light, under the command of Colonel Cookson, to join the force in South Beveland, in consequence of a letter received from Sir John Hope. There was considerable anxiety in South Beveland. The forts had, certainly, been occupied by the English; and Captain Wilmot had succeeded in unspiking and rendering serviceable almost all the guns which they found; but there were many reasons for disquiet. Provisions were not so easily obtained as had been expected in such a country; the inhabitants, without exhibiting actual hostility, were decidedly cool and unfriendly; rumours were spread, which magnified every hour, announcing large reinforcements, not merely to Antwerp, but to every Dutch garrison, and describing swarms of French troops being pushed forward in waggons and boats to form a large army at Bergen-op-Zoom, or some such place, with a view to assuming the offensive; the drains made on their resources by the army in Walcheren alarmed the military chiefs; and the disagreement between the Admiral and Lord Chatham as to the

---

[1] Now No. 3 Battery, 3 Brigade, R.A.

method of conducting future operations had already ceased to be secret. It does not, therefore, surprise the reader to find that when, after the fall of Flushing, all the troops and horses which had been originally intended for the second operation, as the design on Antwerp was termed, were about to return to South Beveland, a decided hesitation manifested itself among the authorities, which ended in a suspense from further action. Before the end of August, the whole of the Horse Artillery, Cavalry, and all the horses of the battering train had returned to England;— Captains Wilmot's, Buckner's, and Brome's companies were ordered to follow, after dismantling the forts in South Beveland;—on the 2nd September, Lord Chatham's headquarters were moved to Middleburg, in Walcheren;—on the 3rd, the embarkation of much of the ordnance, stores, &c., for England commenced;—on the 10th, Lord Chatham announced that he had received the King's commands to return home; and on the 14th, accompanied by his staff, including General Macleod, he sailed from Flushing.

The much-vaunted Expedition was therefore at an end; and with the exception of the garrison of Walcheren, the army returned home by instalments. But in the successful part of the campaign,—the capture of Flushing, there is more than a crumb of comfort for the Artilleryman who is in search of incidents creditable to his corps. The words penned after the siege by Lord Chatham, who was observant, although incapable, are worthy of a high place in the Regimental records. "It is *impossible*," he wrote, "for me to do sufficient justice to the distinguished conduct of the officers and men of the Royal Artillery, under the able direction and animating example of Brigadier-General Macleod." And in a letter presently to be quoted, the reader will see that in the duller work of dismantling the works, under circumstances of great difficulty and sickness, the men of the Royal Artillery earned noble words of commendation. *Lord Chatham's Despatch announcing the surrender of Flushing.*

Walcheren has been remembered for the sickness which

scourged the English army in 1809, when it has been forgotten as to everything else;—and the sickness certainly was fearful; although perhaps due more to exposure, injudicious diet, and inefficient hospital arrangements, than to any local influences, such as were conceived by superstition and fear. The former, it is known, *did* exist; and their results have been seen in later days, during the first winter of the war in the Crimea, much as they were in Walcheren. But the latter,—the mysterious local fevers, which were believed to be indigenous to this island,—seem to have marvellously disappeared, or to be innocuous, as far as the healthy, contented, and long-lived inhabitants of its beautiful villages are concerned. Be that, however, as it may; the sickness among the English troops in 1809 was very great. On the 30th August there were 5000 sick; on the 3rd September the number increased to 5745; on the 5th September it rose to 8000; and on the 8th it was no less than 10,948, with fresh cases occurring every hour. The sickness in the Artillery may be gathered from a return which is extant. On the 27th September there had been left in Walcheren a total strength of 1089 officers and men belonging to the Royal Artillery and Royal Artillery Driver Corps. Before the 16th October,—in less than three weeks,—255 had been sent sick to England, 396 were sick at Walcheren, and 109 were in their graves. From a return of the officers who were invalided to England, we find the names of many not yet mentioned, including Captains Oliver, Monro, Parker, Wallace, Greene, and Scott; and Lieutenants J. Evans, Parker, Dalton, Pringle, Grant, Chapman, and Drawbridge. The names of others, who remained to the date of the evacuation of the island, will be mentioned presently.

After Lord Chatham's departure, it was intended at first to strengthen the island for defence in the event of a French attack. Napoleon being, however, as he said, perfectly satisfied that the English should die in Zealand without any assistance from him, and the continued sickness appalling the authorities, it was decided to dismantle the

Dismantling of the Batteries.

newly-armed batteries with a view to the evacuation of the place. This was done under the control and supervision of Major William Dixon, R.A., assisted by the remnants of the twelve companies, left as part of the garrison of the island. On his arrival in Woolwich, with these companies, he made a report to the Deputy Adjutant-General, which cannot fail to be interesting. "It would be of no use now, "sir," he wrote, "to enter into a detailed account of the "state of defence in which Walcheren was placed at the "moment the order came to withdraw; but, in justice "to the officers and men I had the good fortune to com- "mand, you will permit me to state that, up to the 15th "November, every possible exertion was made to withstand "an attack in the field, or a siege in the fortified places. "All the Dutch mortars and many of the guns were ex- "changed for English; the extra foreign ammunition sent off "to England; Flushing, Veer, and Rammekens completed; "the coast strengthened by batteries mounted with heavy "ordnance; the field brigades distributed to the different "corps of the army; and depôts of ammunition established "throughout. These labours were effected without any "assistance from the troops of the Line, and under cir- "cumstances peculiarly trying;—the companies diminished "by sickness to one-third of their original strength, and "even then jaded and worn by an oppression and feeling "from climate which I cannot describe, but which actually "did not amount to disease. Yet, sir, notwithstanding "this, I am happy to say they performed every part of their "duty without a murmur, and obeyed every order with "zeal and alacrity.

"It will be plain to you, sir, that as we had risen to this "state of defence, so in proportion were our labours in- "creased when we came to dismantle. All that was done "had to be undone; and every article of guns, ammunition, "and stores throughout the island, to be embarked in the "least possible time. The same diligence was continued, "and within the given period not a trace remained in the

Major Dixon to D.-A.-Gen., 3 Jan. 1810.

" works of the ordnance with which they had been de-
" fended. . . . Without meaning to take at all from the
" general report of the good conduct of the officers and men
" employed in the island of Walcheren, but as you are aware
" that, from various causes, there are degrees even in ex-
" cellence itself, I hope I shall not be considered as acting
" inconsistently when I recommend the following officers
" as more particularly deserving your approbation. To
" Captains Maitland and Light I am greatly indebted for
" their activity and zeal in completing the defences of
" Walcheren. To Captain Adye I owe everything for the
" assistance he gave in dismantling the works, and embark-
" ing the guns, ammunition, and stores; and to his name,
" which, in every respect, deservedly stands first, I beg
" leave to add those of Captains Rawlinson, Maitland, and
" Macartney, in the same undertaking. The whole of the
" subalterns went through every part of the duties imposed
" on them with zeal and goodwill, even in serving on board
" the *shutes* with parties of gunners to load and unload
" these vessels. I could place no reliance on the Dutch who
" navigated them, but was thus compelled to ensure their
" services by guarding against their escape. The navy, I
" presume, could not (for they certainly *would* not) grant us
" any assistance. Nautical skill we were not supposed to
" possess, but necessity, at length, helped us to find it. I
" shall conclude, sir, by recommending to your favour
" Lieutenant Anderson, the acting Adjutant, whose zeal
" and activity neither sickness nor fatigue could arrest, and
" I cannot hesitate in pronouncing him one of the finest
" young men I ever met in my life."

The amount of ordnance and stores captured in the islands of South Beveland and Walcheren, and either sent to England or destroyed, was very considerable. Summarised, according to date of capture, the following is a list of the guns and mortars which were taken.[1]

---

[1] From MS. return found among Sir A. Dickson's papers.

List of Captured Ordnance.

Date.	Place.	Guns.	Howitzers.	Mortars.
g. 1, 1809.	Action on landing	4 6-prs. 1 3-pr.	..	..
g. 1809	Fort Haak	4 24-prs. 3 12-prs. 5 18-prs (iron) 2 ,, (brass)	.. .. 3 7¼-in. howitzers 1 5½-in. howitzer	3 coehorn. ..
g. 1, 1809.	Camp Veere	9 24-prs. 6 12-prs. 14 6-prs. 3 brass wall-pieces	.. .. .. 1 8½-in. howitzer	 8
g. 1809	Camp Veere Arsenal	2 swivel guns 1 18-pr. ,, 4 8-pr. ,, 4 6-pr. ,, 4 18-pr. ,,	.. ..	 1
g. 4, 1809.	Fort Rammekens	6 12-pr. ,, 3 6-pr. ,, 3 2-pr. ,,	.. .. ..	.. .. ..
g. 1, 1809.	Coast Batteries, Walcheren	12 26-prs. ,,	..	7
g. 1809	Fort Bathz, S. Beveland	15 24-prs. ,,	3 8-inch 8 6 inch	4
g. 1809	Waarden Battery, S. Beveland	12 24-prs. ,,	..	...
	West Borselin Battery	12 24-prs. ,,	..	..
	East Borselin Battery	8 24-prs. ,,	..	..
	Barland Battery	12 24-prs. ,,	..	..
	Ounderskirk Battery	6 24-prs. ,,	..	..
g. 16, 1809	Flushing	96 brass guns 70 iron ,, 122 ,, carronades	22 howrs. (brass)	56 mortars (brass). .. ..

There were, in addition to the ordnance mentioned above, very large supplies of ammunition and stores of every description, of which the islands were denuded on their evacuation by the English.

The embarkation of the troops from Walcheren was conducted under circumstances of great difficulty. The weather was unfavourable, and for many days after the men were on board, the wind was so adverse as to prevent the ships from sailing. A rear-guard had been left on shore to guard against any attack from the enemy, whose vessels had been accumulating for some weeks in the neighbourhood; and the troops on board the English ships were held in readiness for immediate disembarkation, should the expected attack take place. Some reinforcements which reached the island from England during the embarkation, including two companies of Artillery under Lieut.-Colonel Gold and Major Carncross, were not required to land, but their arrival had a moral effect in ensuring a peaceable evacuation of the place. From Colonel Gold, who landed for a few hours, a graphic description of the state of Walcheren was forwarded to General Macleod in Woolwich. Major Dixon had previously boasted of the thoroughness of his measures in destroying the fortifications. "I am most happy," he wrote, "to say

<small>Major Dixon to D.-A.-Gen., 4 Dec. 1809.</small>

" that not an article in point of honour or value will be
" found in the island when the enemy again takes possession:
" never was there a clearer sweep (I mean in a military
" point of view); and I am satisfied that he will not for years
" be enabled to use the Bason for the purposes of the navy.
" All the parapets are also thrown down, and not a vestige
" is to be seen of gun, ammunition, or store throughout the
" island." This picture was confirmed and completed by

<small>Colonel Gold to D.-A.-Gen., 10 Dec. 1809.</small>

Colonel Gold, who wrote as follows: " I arrived just in time
" to witness the destruction of the Arsenal, which is com-
" pletely effected; the entrance to the Bason, in which the
" French navy were sheltered last winter, is entirely choked
" up by blowing up the pieces of the flood-gates. Never
" was a scene of greater *public mischief*. On putting foot on
" shore I found Macartney in the midst of a wreck of car-
" riages, and, at Flushing, Pilkington and Dixon surrounded
" by their own conflagrations; while Middleburg presented
" the most pacific appearance, and even at a church in
" Flushing, immediately opposite to the scene of destruction,
" divine service going on as if nothing unusual had oc-
" curred. .... I have been across the island to-day, and
" although, from the many good descriptions I had heard,
" I was fully prepared, I could not have conceived any
" country so intolerably bad for military operations; and

Failure of Supply.

" that you (General Macleod) made your batteries and got
" your guns into them is surprising."

From these extracts, it will be seen that the first object
of this much-abused Expedition was completely effected, and
Walcheren rendered innocuous, as a means of menacing
England. That this was mainly owing to the energy and
perseverance of the troops has, it is hoped, also been made
apparent. Alas! that the story of this Expedition, as of so
many others from England, would be incomplete without the
mention of failures in the supply departments of the army.
Three months after the fall of Flushing, the troops were
still suffering from want of necessary comforts. " It will
" be doing us a very great favour," wrote Major Dixon, " if
" you can by any means expedite the arrival of the *bedding*.
" It is now miserably cold, and I am convinced that much
" of our indisposition arises from the want of necessary ac-
" commodation and comfort. By a letter from the Honour-
" able Board (two packets ago) I expected bedding for the
" whole of the Ordnance Department, but nothing of the
" kind has yet appeared." From complaints like these the
reader cannot fail to suspect that much of the exaggerated
abuse of the climate of Walcheren was employed to shield
those departments, whose members, in this as in other wars,
have evinced a belief that the army exists for them, not they
for the army.

Dated Flushing, 14 Nov. 1809.

It only remains to tell the singular story, whose conclusion
has affected the regimental privileges of the Royal Artillery
from the fall of Flushing to this day. Mention has been
made several times in this work of a custom, which placed
the bells of a captured city, or an equivalent, at the disposal
of the commanding officer of the Artillery of the besieging
force. The privilege—as the reader will remember—had
been exercised so recently as at the siege of Copenhagen.
After the surrender of Flushing, General Macleod preferred
the usual claim. The Mayor and Corporation replied through
the Commandant that they acknowledged with due respect
a right established by custom immemorial that the bells
belonged to the commanding officer of the Royal Artillery,

Lieut.-Col. Mosheim to Lieut.- Colonel Wood, 4/9/ 1809.

if he thought proper to enforce his claim, but that they were persuaded he would grant consideration to their already sufficiently distressed condition, and not deprive the unfortunate town of its bells, which they would be as incapable of replacing as they felt unable to tender any compensation for them. On the following day General Macleod replied that, in consideration of the destruction brought upon the town of Flushing by the system of defence which the French General had thought proper to adopt, he had no wish to add to the misery of the inhabitants by seizing the bells, or by demanding a strict compensation to the full amount of their value. In consenting, however, to sacrifice to a great extent his own rights and pretensions, he could not, he said, in any degree compromise those of the Corps. He must, therefore, demand a modified sum in order specifically to mark the transaction, and to enable him at the same time to contribute to the comforts of the officers and men who had partaken in the artillery duties of the siege.

Valuing the bells at 2000*l.*, General Macleod expressed his readiness to accept 500*l.* This offer was communicated by the French commandant to the Mayor of Flushing, but was received with indignation :[1] "On nous a rapporté," wrote the Mayor, " que Messieurs les officiers de l'Artillerie
" Royale persistoient dans leur demande à ce que la ville de
" Flussingen leur offrît un compromis en indemnité des
" cloches, qui—suivant une ancienne coûtume Anglaise—
" leur reviendroient, comme une récompense de leur service
" contre une place assiégée, qui s'étoit rendue par capitu-
" lation aux troupes de sa Majesté Britannique, et qu'ayant
" supposé les dites cloches à 2000*l. sterling* ils avoient fait
" grâce à la ville, en considération de son malheur, des trois
" quarts de cette somme, et se contentoient par conséquent
" d'un quart, montant à 500*l. sterling.* Vivement pénétré
" du sentiment de la situation malheureuse à laquelle la

M. Becker to Lieut.-Colonel Mosheim, 6 Sept. 1809.

---

[1] The Dutch Mayor's French petition is peculiar; but it is given as in the original.

" ville de Flussingen et ses pauvres bourgeois sont réduits,
" nous ne cessons cependant pas d'être nés descendans des
" anciens Hollandais, et tous les désastres que nous avons
" éprouvés ne nous ont pas tellement enlevé cet esprit franc
" et sincère, qui caractérise notre nation, et qui rivalise en
" ce point avec la nation Anglaise, que nous ne sentirions
" pas l'offense qui nous est faite, et que nous n'oserions
" l'exprimer.   Oui, Monsieur! malgré tout ce qui puisse
" nous en arriver, nous ne pouvons que regretter l'offre
" qui nous est faite. . . . Nous avons de la peine à nous
" persuader que la demande qu'on nous a faite a été au-
" torisée par le Commandant en chef. Comment, Mon-
" sieur? La ville de Flussingen, ses malheureux habitans
" qui excitent la compassion de tout le monde, qui sont
" ruinés, sans ressource, qui n'ont pas de quoi pouvoir dans
" leur propres besoins ; cette ville de Flussingen, ces habi-
" tans, qui à plus d'un titre méritent la considération par-
" ticulière du Gouvernement Anglais, et qui, nous n'en
" doutons pas, deviendroient les objets de sa moralité!
" Cette ville, et ces habitans, disons-nous, seroient-ils,
" après avoir passé par tous ces malheurs, réduits à cette
" extrémité de voir laisser enlevé ses cloches, faute de moyen
" de représenter la valeur supposée ? Non, Monsieur, il est im-
" possible que le Gouvernement Anglais autorise une pareille
" demande envers la ville de Flussingen, et nous sommes
" fermement résolus de lui emporter nos plaintes, en cas
" que Messieurs les Officiers de l'Artillerie persistent dans
" leur demande contraire à l'équité et à la capitulation ; et
" nous ne doutons pas que l'âme généreuse de sa Majesté
" Britannique n'y fasse droit. Vous-même, Monsieur, qui
" connaissez la situation de Flussingen, qui savez qu'une
" somme de 5500f. de Hollande est au-dessus de nos forces,
" et qui avez déjà montré compassion à nos maux, ne man-
" querez pas—nous nous en flattons—d'employer vos efforts
" auprès de Messieurs les Officiers de l'Artillerie pour qu'ils
" désistent de leurs prétentions. Nous prenons la liberté de
" vous adresser un double de notre lettre, vous priant
" de l'adresser à son Excellence *My Lord* Chatham, et

"d'appuyer auprès de son Excellence nos réclamations "raisonnables."

Dated Middleburg, 8 Sept. 1809.

This appeal was answered by General Macleod to the effect that he could not, under any consideration, relinquish the rights of his Corps: that he persisted in his claim, which had received the perfect approbation of Lord Chatham; but that, in consideration of the representations made by the magistrates, he again renounced the idea of deriving emolument to himself at the expense of the distresses of the inhabitants, but would persist in the right of his Corps, unless the magistrates should consent to pay the still further reduced sum of one hundred guineas in establishment of the right;—"to be disposed of in charity to the soldiers' "wives and widows of the Royal Artillery, as may be "thought proper hereafter."

As General Macleod was on the eve of leaving Walcheren for England, he transferred the correspondence to Colonel Terrot, with the intimation that he himself would have no objection to an appeal to the English Legislature, should

Dated Middleburg, 9 Sept. 1809.

the magistrates of Flushing insist on it; but "in that case," he wrote, "it is to be understood that the appeal is for the "*whole* of the bells, or for the full amount of their value. "The appeal leaves no room for generosity on either side."

The magistrates were obstinate, and the appeal was forwarded to England. On the 12th November intimation was sent to Major Dixon, in Walcheren, now in command of the Artillery, that the decision was unfavourable to the claims

Dated Doctors' Commons, 26 October, 1809.

of the Corps. The following extract from the decision, addressed by Sir Charles Robinson to the Earl of Liverpool, explains the grounds on which it was based. "With re- "spect to the bells of the church, the demands of the "Artillery are, I conceive, altogether unsustainable. It "is apparently not supported on the part of the Prize Com- "missioners, since they do not advert to this claim in their "letter of the 4th of October. Anciently, there prevailed "a law of pillage, which assigned to different corps and to "different individuals a privileged claim to particular ar- "ticles. Whether this was a privilege of the Artillery

" under the ancient custom of England, as described in the
" Petition, I am not informed; but in the modern usage of
" respecting property and public edifices, and more par-
" ticularly those set apart for divine worship, such a demand
" cannot, I conceive, be sustained. What the custom may
" be,—whether deserving of any compensation in the division
" of what is properly *prize*, or from any other quarter,—may
" be a subject of consideration according to circumstances.
" But I am of opinion that the demand ought not to be
" enforced against the town."

From subsequent correspondence which is extant, and which passed between General Macleod and Sir Anthony Farrington, it is evident that the former felt much regret that an old Regimental privilege should have disappeared during operations in which he had occupied so prominent a place; but the reader will admit that no one could have conducted the cause of the Corps in a more unselfish, chivalrous, and yet resolute manner.

N.B.—The comments of an officer of the sister corps, on the conduct of the Artillery at the siege of Flushing, were very favourable. Two extracts from Sir J. Jones's work may be given.

" The guns of the batteries on the right of the attack were more par-
" ticularly directed to enfilade and take *en écharpe* the rampart of the
" western sea-line, in order to silence the fire of its artillery on the fleet,
" now preparing to force the passage of the Scheldt. This they accom-
" plished very effectually, by disabling or very severely wounding many
" of the traversing platforms and their carriages, and much injuring the
" guns themselves."

Again:

" Discharges of carcasses and shells from the mortar batteries, with
" powerful flights of rockets intermixed, were kept up throughout the
" night on the devoted town, and frequently large portions of it burned
" with fury."—Jones's ' Sieges,' vol. ii. pp. 269—271.

CHAPTER XV.

PENINSULAR WAR RESUMED.—PASSAGE OF THE DOURO, AND TALAVERA.

"The deliverance of the Peninsula was never due to the foresight and "perseverance of the English ministers, but to the firmness and skill of the "British Generals, and to the courage of troops whom no dangers could "daunt and no hardships dishearten, while they remedied the eternal errors "of the Cabinet."—NAPIER.

IN resuming the story of the Peninsular War, it will be seen that the narrative has to go back to an earlier date than that of the expedition described in the last chapter,—Sir Arthur Wellesley having returned from England to Lisbon, to take command of the army, so early as the 22nd April, 1809. But it has been thought better to clear the ground, so to speak, of the Walcheren Expedition, and thus to enable the reader to follow uninterruptedly the story of the operations, which terminated in the glorious victory of Talavera, and the subsequent withdrawal of the English troops from Spain to Portugal.

The British Government still resolved that the English army in Spain should be merely an auxiliary one, and remained still undeceived as to the real state of the Spanish forces. Perhaps it was as well, therefore, that the army entrusted to Sir Arthur Wellesley was not a larger one; for the difficulty he encountered in obtaining provisions and transport from the Spaniards would have been insurmountable, had the forces under his command been more numerous.

Merida, 25 Aug. 1809.

" I do not think," wrote Sir Arthur to Lord Castlereagh, " that matters would have been much better if you had sent " your large expedition to Spain instead of to the Scheldt. " You could not have equipped it in Galicia, or anywhere in " the north of Spain. If we had had 60,000 men instead of " 20,000, in all probability we should not have got to Tala-

"vera to fight the battle, for want of means and provisions. But if we had got to Talavera, we could not have gone farther, and the armies would probably have separated for want of means of subsistence, probably without a battle, but certainly afterwards." The campaign of 1809, from beginning to end, was marked by obstinacy on the part of Spanish Generals, and faithlessness on the part of the Spanish Government; by inadequate supplies of money from England, and by difficulties with the Portuguese troops, not the less annoying because they were often petty; as well as by hardships which tried the discipline of the English troops quite as much as the retreat to Corunna, and which drew from Sir Arthur Wellesley the bitter words: "We are an excellent army on parade, an excellent one to fight; but we are worse than an enemy in a country; and, take my word for it, that either defeat or success would dissolve us." The success which he almost dreaded came: the 27th and 28th July witnessed as gallant an exhibition of English courage as has ever been seen; but in a few days Sir Arthur wrote: "A starving army is actually worse than none. The soldiers lose their discipline and spirit; they plunder even in presence of their officers. The officers are discontented, and are almost as bad as the men; and, with an army which a fortnight ago beat double their numbers, I should now hesitate to meet a French corps of half their strength.". The administration which has so often marked our campaigns with passages like this cannot be too distinctly held up to view as a perpetual warning. No troops, as Sir Arthur wrote, can serve to any good purpose unless they are regularly fed; and yet it is in this very point—the question of supply—that our military history abounds with failures.

<small>To Lord Castlereagh, dated Abrantes, 17 June, 1809.</small>

<small>To Marquis Wellesley, dated Deleytosa, 8 August, 1809.</small>

The army which had landed in England from Corunna was speedily organized, and sent back to Portugal. Sir J. Cradock commanded the troops at Lisbon, some 14,000 in number; Marshal Beresford had been appointed to the command of the Portuguese forces, and was assisted in his task of organizing them by several British officers. All arrangements were made for taking the field; and this was done immediately on the arrival of Sir Arthur Wellesley, who was appointed Marshal-General of the united armies. Colonel Robe had remained in command of the Artillery in Portugal during the interval between Corunna and Sir Arthur's arrival; but he was now superseded by Brigadier-General—afterwards Sir E.—Howorth. The number of troops and companies in the Peninsula in 1809 was only seven. There were, in addition, five at Gibraltar, five in Italy, and three in Malta.

The Artillery officers first appointed for duty with Marshal Beresford were Captain—afterwards Sir J.—May and Captain Elliot, of the Royal Artillery, and also Captain Arentschild, of the King's German Artillery. Lieutenant Charles was attached to the Portuguese force raised by Sir Robert Wilson; and Captain P. Campbell and Lieutenant Wills were employed with the Spanish troops at Seville and Cadiz respectively.

General Howorth, on his arrival in Lisbon in the beginning of April, arranged, with Colonel Robe's assistance, the equipment of five brigades of guns, to take the field with the army, viz., one brigade of heavy 6-pounders, three of light 6-pounders, and one of 3-pounders. These were all he could equip; and, notwithstanding the opportune arrival, from Ireland, of 170 drivers and 298 excellent horses, he yet complained of the want of mobility from which they suffered, mixed as they were with the horses of the country, mules, and oxen. However, like Colonel Harding, he took a cheerful view of matters, and pronounced the mules to be very fine animals, and "the oxen, though slow, a steady, good draught." The development of the Field Artillery during the Peninsular War, from the wretched batteries employed at its commencement to those which attracted such admiration at its close, will appear in the course of this work. Suffice it, at present, to remind the Artilleryman, by way of contrast, while the picture of the batteries of 1809 is yet fresh in his recollection, that before the conclusion of the Peninsular War, it was admitted by the artillerymen of the country with which England was engaged in hostilities,

*To D.-A.-G.
Lisbon,
8 April,
1809.*

Affair at Algabaria.

that "the English *matériel* might have been taken as a 'Le passé
"model by any nation in Europe;"—that, shortly before et l'avenir
Waterloo, Marshal Marmont remarked that the equipment of lerie,'
the English Field Artillery was in every respect very su- tom. v.
perior to anything he had ever seen; and that the French p. 64.
Committee appointed in 1818 to compare the Artillery of
the various countries represented in the review held that Hime.
year in Paris, expressed unqualified delight with that of
England.

On Sir Arthur Wellesley's arrival in Lisbon, he found that
Soult was in possession of Oporto, and Victor in Estremadura. He promptly resolved to attack them in detail; and,
making Lisbon the base of his operations, he requested the
Spanish General, Cuesta, to watch Victor's movements, while
he himself should march to the north against Soult. The
moral effect of driving the French out of Portugal would,
he felt, be very great—all the more so as his arrival had
produced a sudden hopefulness among the Portuguese, which
it was desirable not to disappoint.

Accordingly, on the 1st May, he moved his head-quarters
to Pombal and Coimbra, and found himself in command of
an army which, after deducting the sick and absent, numbered 20,653 rank and file, with 30 guns. On the 9th he Napier.
left Coimbra with the main body, and arrived on the Douro,
opposite Oporto, on the 12th, after a march of eighty miles
over infamous roads. "But," wrote General Howorth, To D.-A.-G.
"neither difficulty nor danger impedes Sir Arthur: he is all Oporto,
"fire, and establishes confidence in the troops." 14 May, 1809.

On the 10th, the left column of the army, which marched
from Aveiro, fell in with the enemy at Algabaria Nova. A
slight affair ensued, in which the Artillery and Cavalry were
chiefly engaged; and the enemy was repulsed with the loss
of a gun. On the 11th, the right column, which marched
on the Vouga, came up with the French between Algabaria
Nova and Grijon, and an engagement followed which lasted
two hours, ending in the retreat of the enemy. On the
arrival of the English at Villa Nova, opposite Oporto, it was
found that the French had destroyed the bridge across the

Douro, and removed every available boat to their own side of the river. It was of the utmost importance that the English troops should cross, so as to co-operate with Marshal Beresford, who, having crossed the river higher up, was now menacing the left and the rear of Soult's army. The crossing was effected in a gallant, and yet singular and romantic way, the details of which, too long for reproduction here, render the passage of the Douro one of the most interesting episodes in the Peninsular War. Wellesley saw a building on the other side of the river—here three hundred yards wide —called the Seminary, surrounded by a walled yard, capable of containing two battalions. Close to where he himself stood was a rock, called Serra, from which artillery would well command the passage of the river, and where he therefore desired General Howorth to place eighteen guns. The guards on the other side seemed few and negligent. Soult expected no danger on the part of the river above the town, and had posted himself to the westward; if, therefore, boats could but be obtained, Wellesley resolved to cross. A small skiff was found, and Colonel Waters, a staff officer, crossed, and found three large barges, which he towed back to the Villa Nova side of the river. The men were ordered to embark, and, in the face of an army of ten thousand men, the passage was effected. Very few, however, had crossed ere the alarm was given, and the French troops poured down upon the Seminary. The alarm acted in one respect favourably to the English; for some of the citizens hastened to unmoor some boats, and cross to Villa Nova, thus facilitating the embarkation and passage of the troops. All this time the fire of the Royal Artillery from the Serra told with great effect; and, as it completely swept one side of the Seminary, it soon limited the attack to the other. The gallantry of the Infantry was unrivalled. General Sherbrooke had crossed the river a little lower down, and was now in possession of the town of Oporto, and pressing, with the Guards and 29th Regiment, on the rear of the French troops as they poured out towards the Seminary. The Buffs and their comrades in the enclosure rained showers of bullets on the disorganized French; and in a short time they were in full retreat, "the artillery, from the Serra, still searching "the enemy's columns as they hurried along." General Howorth, in describing the battle, said that he never saw anything like the gallantry of the English troops. Their firmness was irresistible; nor could the French make any impression; and, from the position which he occupied, he was able to form a good opinion, as he could see everything. Sir Arthur, in his despatch announcing the victory, after enumerating the various officers who had especially distinguished themselves, said, in describing the services of the regiments engaged: "I had every reason to be satisfied with "the Artillery." That his satisfaction was also extended to the previous operations and to the severe march of eighty miles over most difficult country may be gathered from General Howorth's words: "I have reason," he wrote, "to "believe that Sir Arthur is perfectly satisfied with the "Artillery; and, it must be owned, never was Artillery put "to such trial." The French ordnance captured at the recovery of Oporto included 56 brass guns and 3 brass howitzers. A considerable supply of ammunition was also taken. *[margin: Napier. To D.-A.-G. 14 May, 1809. To Lord Castlereagh, dated Oporto, 12 May, 1809.]*

The pursuit of Soult's army was undertaken by Sir A. Wellesley with as little delay as possible, although not with sufficient promptness to satisfy the demands of certain military critics, who are ready to find fault, but slow to acknowledge difficulties in the way of armies. That it was sufficiently prompt to ensure the success of the English General's purpose, may be gathered from the fact that on the 18th May Soult and his army crossed the frontier into Spain, having been driven out of Portugal with the loss of artillery, stores, and baggage, and of no fewer than 6000 men; while of those who remained, many were without arms and accoutrements, the majority without shoes, and all utterly exhausted and miserable; and, further, that the English army did not delay in the pursuit from any effeminate ideas of comfort or luxury may be gathered from the following letter from General Howorth: "The extraordi- *[margin: Napier.]*

To General Macleod, dated Oporto, 24 May, 1809.

"nary rapidity of events in this country, which have been accompanied by a succession of the most triumphant operations against the enemy, left me no leisure to communicate them as they occurred. However, I am at last returned here, after passing eight days in continued marches over the worst roads I ever saw, through incessant rain, a depopulated country, quartered in uninhabited houses, and with no supplies whatever, but what was scantily provided by the Commissariat Department. During the greater part of this march the luxury of a bed, or a change of clothes, which were always wet, was unknown to me. . . . . . We pursued to Montalagree, where the enemy turned short to the left, over the mountains, and took the shortest way into Galicia."

During the pursuit, the English overtook Soult at Salamonde, and his rear-guard being in a confined space, some guns were brought to bear on them with fearful effect.

Napier.

"Man and horse, crushed together, went over into the gulf; and the bridge, rocks, and the defile beyond were strewed with mangled bodies." The furious peasantry also turned on the French troops, and rendered their retreat—which has been compared with that of the English on Corunna—infinitely more horrible.

Wellington Despatches.

As Soult sacrificed artillery and baggage in order to move more rapidly, it was but natural that he should outmarch an army which had not so disencumbered itself. But this pursuit has an importance to the Artilleryman in being a text on which much useful argument was hung by General Howorth and others, in favour of greater mobility than had yet attended the brigades of Field Artillery employed in the Peninsula. The 3-pounder brigade was the only one which was able to march with the army during its more rapid movements; and therefore General Howorth made a demand for additional brigades of that nature, suggesting, with the assistance of Colonel Robe, various improvements in the equipment. Among other changes, he recommended double instead of single draught, both for guns and waggons; and that the brigades should be of four guns instead of six,

Dated Oporto, 24 May, 1809.

the howitzers being dispensed with, and a liberal supply of spherical case being issued for the guns. Another very suggestive recommendation was made by him : "to have a " small forge with each brigade of four guns ; the forge to " be placed on the frame of a small limber waggon ; *it can* " *then follow the brigade, which is not the case with the present* " *one.*" The absence of a forge on the line of march must at times have sadly crippled the batteries. He also suggested that the span of the wheels should be narrowed to 4½ feet, and (to prevent liability to upset from this cause) that the gun should be lowered on its carriage by adopting *a bare iron axletree.* His next recommendation reveals a starvation of equipment which would account for almost any shortcomings on the line of march. He urged the authorities "to have spare shafts, wheels, axles, spokes, felloes, " and pintails supplied, *none having been sent with the* " *present brigades*, and now much needed !" He also made suggestions which would ensure greater mobility to the heavier brigades of 6-pounders. The Artilleryman may therefore date to the campaign of the Douro some of the most valuable lessons taught in the Peninsular War, and can trace to it that change in the opinions and experience of the military authorities which resulted in so extended a use of Horse Artillery in the Peninsula, and in so marked an improvement in the brigades of Field Artillery before the conclusion of the war.

Marshal Victor, on hearing of the disastrous termination of Soult's operations, fell back on Almaraz and Torremocha; so that Sir A. Wellesley, who had commenced his southward march through Traz-oz-Montes, resolved to halt at Abrantes, and to commence a thorough reorganization of his army, now sadly undisciplined. The correspondence of Sir Arthur at this time reveals what one is apt to forget in reflecting on the glories of the Peninsular campaigns. The military genius of the Duke of Wellington and the courage of English soldiers are too often considered to have been the only necessary causes of success; but a study of the appeals made by him at Abrantes to officers and men,—of the strict

Wellington Despatches and Supplementary Despatches.

orders, on even the smallest matters, which he found it necessary to issue,—and of the letters to ministers and friends, in which he never failed to tell the truth about the army, however unpalatable,—reveals another most necessary element in the success which attended him in all his operations. As the first thought in his own mind always was *duty*, so the first and last thing which he held before his troops, as that without which they would be worse than useless, was *discipline*. The arguments he used have a value for all time, and a special value for England at a time when she possesses an armed force of Volunteers, who might possibly consider that drill, instead of discipline, is the chief end of a soldier's life; but whose discipline, on the other hand, if thorough, would be nobler than that of regular troops, in being more self-imposed, and less dependent on a penal code. As for the Duke of Wellington's remarks on the discipline of the Spanish troops, they apply in a singularly exact way to the armies of Spain in the anarchy of 1873. "In Spain," he wrote, " the business of an army is little understood. They " are really children in the art of war; and I cannot say " that they do anything as it ought to be done, with the " exception of running away and assembling again in a " state of nature. . . . . . The Government have attempted " to govern the kingdom in a state of revolution by an adherence to old rules and systems, and with the aid of what " is called *enthusiasm*; and this last is, in fact, no aid to accomplish anything, and is only an excuse for the irregularity with which everything is done, and for the want of " discipline and subordination of the armies. People are " very apt to believe that enthusiasm carried the French " through their Revolution, and was the parent of those " exertions which have nearly conquered the world; but if " the subject is nicely examined, it will be found that enthusiasm was the *name* only, but that *force* was the instrument which brought forward those great resources, under " the system of *terror*, which first stopped the Allies." In his correspondence with Marshal Beresford, who found great difficulty in organizing the Portuguese troops, he laid down

To Lord Castlereagh, dated 25 Aug. 1809.

what may be considered a military creed. "They want the *habits*," he wrote, "and the spirit of soldiers,—the habits of command on one side, and of obedience on the other— mutual confidence between officers and men: and, above all, a determination in the superiors to obey the spirit of the orders they receive, let what will be the consequence; and the spirit to tell the true cause, if they do not." Poor Marshal Beresford had, indeed, need of support and sympathy in his task. Long habits of disregard to duty, and of consequent laziness, made it impossible for the senior officers to pay any regular or continued attention to the duties of their situations, and neither reward nor punishment would induce them to bear up against fatigue. By replacing these by younger officers, or English officers detached from the various regiments, he ultimately succeeded in making the Portuguese contingent a most valuable force; but this was only done by impressing on them the necessity of discipline and unhesitating obedience. More than sixty years have passed away, and the same lesson, though more difficult to learn, is not the less vitally necessary. The spirit of criticism spreads with the growth of education, and considerably out of proportion with it. The reasoning obedience which a soldier should yield is, perhaps, confused with an obedience which requires to know the reason of an order, instead of that which is readily yielded in the belief that what may be unintelligible in detail is necessary for the general plan. That such obedience is not easy always to give may be true enough. The possession, with a strong will, of but pigmy power, is undoubtedly trying; but the self-denial which is demanded stands among the highest of all military virtues, as it is the very alphabet of all military training. He only is fit to rule who has first learned to obey.

Reference has been made to the association of English officers with the Portuguese forces. The appointment of Captain—afterwards Sir Alexander—Dickson, to the Portuguese Artillery, which took place after the Douro campaign, was productive of so important results that it deserves

margin notes: Dated Badajoz, 8 Sept. 1809.

Supplementary Despatches of Duke of Wellington, vol. vi. p. 362.

detailed notice. As Captain Dickson, he had acted as Brigade-Major to General Howorth during the recent operations. He had, however, come to Portugal with the intention of obtaining employment in a higher local rank with the Portuguese Artillery, and had only been deterred by difficulties which had arisen as to the *status* and pay of officers so attached. On the 4th June, he quitted Oporto with General Howorth, who had been indisposed for some time, and proceeded to Abrantes to join the army, and also to speak to Marshal Beresford on the subject of employment with the Portuguese troops. Fortunately, on his arrival, he found that Captain May, then in command of a division of Portuguese Field Artillery, was on the point of resigning, in accordance with instructions from England; and Marshal Beresford readily appointed Captain Dickson as his successor,—Captain May, in exchange, assuming the duties of Major of Brigade. So far all was well; but Captain Dickson soon found that he had no pleasing position. The local rank of Major, which had been conferred on his junior officer, Captain Arentschild of the King's German Artillery, was refused to him by Marshal Beresford, who had been irritated by contradictory orders from the English and Portuguese Governments; so that he found himself under the orders of his junior. The Portuguese officers were also very jealous of their English comrades; and the seniors, without incurring any risk themselves, made every difficulty in their power when any suggestion was made which they disliked. Letters from the British to the Portuguese officers on official matters, and all applications for supplies, were left unanswered; and yet "these same men," wrote Captain Dickson indignantly, "are embracing you as often as they meet!" He would gladly have given up his new appointment had he not felt bound by his promise to Lord Chatham to retain it; so he set to work, in a true soldier-like spirit, to perfect the two 6-pounder Portuguese batteries which had been placed under his charge, and of which, even at the beginning, he was able to write in terms of the warmest approbation. As this narrative will show, he was rewarded for remaining at his post. The local rank was given to him ultimately; and by its means he found himself commanding many brother officers, much senior to himself regimentally, and ultimately at the head of the Artillery of the armies of the Duke of Wellington, while only a Captain in his own Corps.

It is now necessary to follow the movements of Sir Arthur Wellesley. The English Government continued to overrate the value of the Spanish armies; and the pressure brought to bear upon the English General was such as he could not resist. He therefore proposed to the Spanish General, Cuesta, to co-operate with his army against Victor's forces, and ultimately against Madrid. Cuesta, whose treatment of Sir Arthur Wellesley was, on all occasions, of the most obstinate and boorish description, had an army of 33,000 men. Sir Arthur's army, when he quitted Abrantes, numbered 20,997 men of all arms, with 30 guns. The advance of the united armies against Madrid by the valley of the Tagus had been foreseen by Napoleon, and he had ordered Soult, at the head of a powerful army, to concentrate his forces in such a manner that, on the advance of Wellesley, he could pass by his left rear, and cut him off from the base of his operations,—Lisbon and its surrounding country. The English General was far from correctly informed either of the strength or position of Soult's army; he was urged by the English representative, Mr. Frere, and by his own Government, to take the offensive; the vacillation of Joseph Buonaparte tempted him to march on Madrid before further union could be effected among the French armies; he was further assured of the courage of the Spanish armies, the enthusiasm of the peasantry, and the abundance of supplies. On the 27th June, therefore, he broke up his camp at Abrantes, and marched towards Oropesa, to effect a junction with Cuesta. The farther he advanced, the more doubtful did he become of the sincerity of the Spaniards—a doubt which exhibited itself in the pertinacity with which he demanded from Cuesta and the Junta solemn promises to keep the English army supplied, during any farther advance, with the

Napier.

requisite transport and supplies. The reader does not require to be reminded how shamefully these promises were broken;—how thwarted Wellesley was, alike by the intrigues of the Junta and the conceited obstinacy of Cuesta;—nor how faithful he was, amid all his difficulties, to the duty which England had imposed upon him. Standing beside Cuesta like a better angel,—and receiving the treatment not unfrequently bestowed on such,—calm under insult, his judgment never heated by an indignation which would have been righteous,—he ultimately succeeded in placing the united armies in the very position in front of Talavera which he had selected, when he saw that a general action with the combined forces of Victor and Sebastiani was inevitable, if not, indeed, desirable. But not until the morning of the 27th July, nor until Cuesta's folly and rashness had courted and received, at Alcabon, a well-deserved defeat, did the English General succeed in placing the Spanish forces in the position he had chosen. The quiet irony of the memorandum of Sir Arthur Wellesley on the battle of Talavera cannot be seen without remembering the defeat just mentioned, and a disgraceful panic which seized on the Spanish troops at the appearance of some French cavalry, on the afternoon of the 27th, when 10,000 Infantry and all their Artillery fled, terror-stricken, to the rear. Part of these were recovered before the following day; but the Spanish contingent was weaker by the greater part of its Artillery, and 6000 of its Infantry. With such troops as allies, no wonder that Sir Arthur wrote: " The position of Talavera " was well calculated for the troops that were to occupy it. " The ground in front of the British army was open; that " in front of the Spanish army was covered with olive-trees, " intersected by roads, ditches, &c." In other words, the offensive part of the battle was to fall on the British, while a masterly and imposing inactivity was reserved for the Spaniards.

Gurwood's Despatches: Selections, p. 278.

The battle of Talavera was fought on the 27th and 28th July. The loss of the Spanish Artillery in the panic mentioned above was very serious, as the English had only

30 guns, very badly horsed and of small calibre, to oppose to 80 guns, admirably served by the enemy. Fortunately, the few guns of the Spanish Artillery, which *were* brought into action, were gallantly fought; and of those of the Royal and King's German Artillery, both the officers present and all military historians speak in the highest terms. At the defeat of the 4th French Corps by Campbell's division, the British Artillery, as Napier wrote, played vehemently upon their masses:—at the critical moment, later in the day, when the English centre was almost broken on account of the injudicious advance of the Guards, and of the confusion which seized the King's German Legion, the marvellous effect which followed the arrival of the 48th Regiment, moving, amid all the confusion, with the steadiness of a parade, was greatly heightened by the conduct of the Artillery, which, as the same historian says, " battered the enemy's " flanks without intermission." Sir Arthur Wellesley, in addition to an expression of his satisfaction with the Corps in the General Order after the battle, made use of the following expression in his despatch to Lord Castlereagh: " The Artillery, under Brigadier-General Howorth, was also, " throughout these days, of the greatest service."

Compared with the loss of the other arms, that of the Artillery was but small. On the 27th, only two men were wounded; on the 28th, the loss was as follows:—

> Royal Artillery.—1 officer and 7 men killed; 3 officers and 21 men wounded.
> King's German Artillery.—1 sergeant and 2 men killed; 3 sergeants and 27 men wounded.

The officer who was killed was Lieutenant Wyatt; those who were wounded were Lieut.-Colonel Framingham, and Captains Baynes and Taylor. In reporting the severe wound of Colonel Framingham, and applying for a pension, General Howorth said: " If it were possible that any testimony or " praise of mine could add to the weight of this application, " or to the merit and brilliancy of Lieut.-Colonel Fra- " mingham's gallant conduct in the action of the 28th July, " at Talavera, I should most freely have bestowed it; but, as

To D.-A.-G. Dated Badajoz, 20 Oct. 1809.

"he distinguished himself on that occasion by a most skilful
"discharge of his duty, I have only to wish him sincerely a
"reward equal to his merits." On the retreat of the army
from Talavera, Captain Taylor, whose wound prevented his
removal, fell into the hands of the French, and remained a
prisoner to the end of the war.

There are several points connected with the battle of
Talavera which stand out prominently, and seize the attention of the student at once. The weakness of King Joseph
in playing into the hands of the English General, and allowing him to fight under the terms most advantageous to
himself;—the hard, honest fighting, as Napier calls it, of the
English troops, who, for hours, were closely engaged with a
force of double their own numbers;—the watchful tactics of
Sir A. Wellesley, who never missed a point during the whole
engagement, and was always ready at critical moments with
the necessary remedies; and the heavy losses on both sides—
over 6000 being killed and wounded on the side of the English, and more than 7000 on that of the French;—these are
points which cannot escape the most superficial reader. But
to the soldier there are several precious instances of steadiness and discipline among particular regiments which
shed a glow over this well-fought field,—the 45th and
5th Battalion of the 60th being conspicuous for these qualities on the 27th, and the "stubborn old 48th" on the 28th.
Napier's pages glow with the enthusiasm of a soldier as
he describes the movements of the last-mentioned regiment
on the occasion referred to above. "At first," he writes,
"it seemed as if this regiment must be carried away by the
"retiring crowds; but, wheeling back by companies, it let
"them pass through the intervals, and then, resuming its
"proud and beautiful line, marched against the right of
"the pursuing columns, and plied them with such a
"destructive musketry, and closed upon them with such
"a firm and regular pace, that their forward movement was
"checked."

Wellington Despatches.

The changes which have become necessary in the art of
war, owing to the improvement in fire-arms, may have

forbidden the use in battle of the line which the gallant 48th showed at Talavera; but, in whatever form troops may be called upon to fight, the qualities which animated that regiment will still, if present, entitle their possessors to the same epithet, and the perfection of their drill and discipline will still claim the words, " proud and beautiful."

The horrors of a battle-field, when the deadly encounter is over, were aggravated at Talavera by a fire which caught the dry grass, and which licked the ground where the dead and wounded were lying, adding a new agony to the sufferings of the latter, and hideously scorching the bodies of those whose pain was for ever at an end. This incident gives a ghastly element to the recollection of a field on which English courage was so ably proved.

On the 29th, Wellesley's army was strengthened by the arrival of Crawford's brigade, consisting of the 43rd, 52nd, and 95th Regiments, with Captain Ross's, "The Chestnut," troop of Horse Artillery,[1] which, in their eagerness to reach the field of battle, and undeterred by the lies of the flying Spaniards, had marched no less than sixty-two miles in twenty-six hours, in the hottest season of the year, and in heavy marching order. But news reached the English General which determined him to fall back, and to have done with the assistance of Spanish troops, whose worthlessness he had now thoroughly tested. Hearing that Soult was pressing on by rapid marches, and with increased forces,— had already gained possession of one of his most important communications with Portugal, and was threatening the others,—he resolved to leave his wounded at Talavera, and to fall back into Portugal. He did so by means of rapid marches; but he still conducted them so as to show no appearance of flight, such as would have injured the reputa-

---

[1] The officers of the Chestnut Troop on its arrival in the Peninsula, were Captain—afterwards Sir H. D.—Ross, 2nd Captain G. Jenkinson, Lieutenants G. J. Belson, A. Macdonald, and Smith, and Assistant-Surgeon O'Brien. The following is a copy of the Embarkation Returns. *See next page.*

EMBARKATION RETURN of a TROOP of ROYAL HORSE ARTILLERY, commanded by Captain H. D. ROSS.

Ships' Names and Masters.	Captain.	Second Captain.	Lieutenants.	Assistant Surgeon.	N.-C. Officers.	Trumpeters.	Artificers.	Gunners.	Drivers.	Total.	Women.	Children.	Officers'.	Troop.	Total.	6-pounders.	5½-in. Howitzers.	Ammunition Waggons.	Baggage Waggons.	Wheel Carriage.	Forge Cart.	Baggage Cart.	Total.
'Rodney'—G. Bowes	1	:	1	1	3	1	3	19	8	37	:	:	7	26	33	:	:	:	:	:	:	:	:
'Phœnix'—R. Oswell	:	1	2	:	3	:	2	15	9	32	2	:	7	24	31	:	:	:	:	:	:	:	:
'Amphitrite'—R. Stevenson	:	:	:	:	2	:	:	10	13	25	:	:	:	32	32	:	:	:	:	:	:	:	:
'Jane'—J. Jackson	:	:	:	:	2	:	1	15	10	28	:	:	:	30	30	:	:	:	:	:	:	:	:
'Ruby'—S. Chapman	:	:	:	:	2	:	1	13	12	28	:	:	:	34	34	:	:	:	:	:	:	:	:
'Ganges'—J. Nisbett	:	:	:	:	:	:	:	2	2	4	:	:	:	2	2	:	:	:	:	:	:	:	:
'Blessing'—R. Armstrong	:	:	:	:	1	:	:	7	:	8	1	:	:	:	:	5	1	6	3	1	1	1	18
Total . . .	1	1	3	1	13	1	7	81	54	162	3	:	14	148	162	5	1	6	3	1	1	1	18

(Signed) H. D. Ross, *Captain Commanding R. H. A.*

Ramsgate, 8th June, 1809.

CHAP. XV.   *Sickness in the Artillery.*   259

tion of his army in the eyes of the Spaniards—a most important consideration. General Howorth, in alluding to the retreat from Talavera, emphasises this point. "We made a retrograde movement," he wrote, "with a dignified "deliberation perfectly suitable to the gravity of Spanish "deportment." The whole of his brigades of Artillery returned from Talavera complete, with the exception of one 6-pounder gun which had been damaged in the battle of the 28th, and which, the General wrote, had been *privately buried*, perhaps out of consideration for Spanish deportment also. But all the spare ammunition and stores had to be abandoned, as the carts were required to carry the sick. No less than 150 carts were so employed; for the sickness during the retreat, and even after the troops went into cantonments at Merida, was very great. The well-known sickness in the Chestnut Troop, which so nearly led to its return to England, took place at Merida after the retreat. So severely did it suffer, that, in sending in his returns of available Artillery force at this time, General Howorth wrote: "I have one troop of Horse Artillery, Bull's,[1] and "half a one, Ross's. The latter has suffered severely by "sickness and death of men and horses." The sickness was aggravated by a dearth of medical officers; and the unfortunate Chestnut Troop, which required medical assistance to an extraordinary extent, was robbed of its own surgeon in an inglorious manner. "Poor Doctor O'Brien," wrote General Howorth, "of Ross's troop, died last night, owing to his "servant's getting drunk, and giving him too strong a dose "of opium, which destroyed him." Ere many weeks passed, the attempt to cope with the havoc made in the troop was almost abandoned. Two guns and their waggons were sent into store, from want of men and horses to work them; and orders were given that, on the arrival of another troop (Lefebure's) from England, the surviving men and horses of the Chestnut Troop should be handed over to it, and Captain Ross and his officers return to England to organize a new

To D.-A.-G. Dated Badajoz, 26 Oct. 1809.

---

[1] The gallant Norman Ramsay was 2nd Captain of Bull's troop.

troop. Luckily for him, Captain Lefebure's troop suffered so much from a storm on its way to the Peninsula that, on its arrival, it was little more efficient than the one it was meant to relieve; so, to Captain Ross's delight, he had his vacancies completed from the new arrivals, and Captain Lefebure had, instead, the duty of rebuilding his troop.

Memoir of Sir H. D. Ross.

The head-quarters of the English General, on whom the title of Lord Wellington was bestowed after Talavera, were at Badajoz until the end of 1809. He devoted himself to the strengthening of his position, with the double motive of ensuring to himself the possession of Lisbon and the Tagus, and of securing the unmolested embarkation of his troops, should reverses render it necessary. The lines of Torres Vedras, which were to play so important a part in the campaign of 1810, were matured in the winter of 1809. Lord Wellington had given up all hope of succeeding by means of the Spaniards; but he by no means despaired of offering an effectual resistance to the most powerful French attacks by means of the combined English and Portuguese army under his command. He felt confidence in his troops. As he boasted to a correspondent, "I command an unanimous " army." Supplies in Portugal were better arranged than in Spain; and, with the remembrance fresh in his mind of Talavera, which he himself pronounced " the hardest-fought " battle of modern days, and the most glorious in its results " to the English troops," he looked forward to the next campaign with quiet confidence, and displayed during the winter an industry in strengthening his position which, at all events, deserved success.

Lord Wellington to Colonel Malcolm, Badajoz, 3 Dec. 1809.

NOTE.—Although the Peninsular War eclipses in point of interest any other operations in which the Royal Artillery was engaged in 1809, it would be a great omission were no allusion made to the services of the Corps, in the beginning of 1809, during the operations in the West Indies under General Beckwith and Sir George Prevost, which resulted in the capture of the French colonies of Cayenne and Martinique. Over 500 officers and men of the Royal Artillery were present under the command of Brigadier-General Stehelin, and the value of their services may be ascertained from the following extract from the General Order issued at the termination of the campaign :—

"To Brigadier-General Stehelin, commanding the Royal Artillery, for his regularity in all interior arrangements, and especially for that order and system established in this distinguished Corps, which led to those eminent services rendered by them during the bombardment, and which brought the siege to an early and glorious termination. . . the Commander of the Forces is anxious to renew all those assurances of public and individual consideration, to which from their distinguished services they are fully entitled, and he requests, as an old soldier, that he may live in their remembrance and friendship."

G. O. Dated 8 March, 1809.

The officers of the Royal Artillery who were present during these operations were—in addition to Brigadier-General Stehelin—Captains Blaney Walsh, Unett, Phillott, St. Clair, Cleeve, Story, Du Bourdieu, Clibborn, Butts, and Rollo; and Lieutenants Spellen, Bell, Gordon, Lewis, Mathias, Tucker, Turner, Heron, Scriven, Simmons, and F. Arabin.

B. G. Stehelin to D.-A.-Gen. 23 March, 1809.

CHAPTER XVI.

BUSACO AND TORRES VEDRAS.

IT may not be uninteresting to the reader, before resuming the consideration of the Peninsular War, to study some statistics connected with the Regiment in the year 1810, the period to be treated of in this chapter. The number of troops and companies remained as before, 112—exclusive of the invalid battalion. They were distributed as follows:—
16 in the Peninsula, 5 in Italy and Sicily, 56 on home stations, 4 in Canada, 3 at the Cape of Good Hope, 3 in Ceylon, where they had been engaged on active service during the previous year, 6 in Gibraltar, 4 in Jamaica and 6 in the rest of the West Indies (these ten companies being actively engaged in the defence of the colonies), 1 in Madeira, 4 in Malta, 1 in Newfoundland, and 3 in Nova Scotia and Cape Breton.

<small>Kane's List.</small>

The following tables show the strength of the battalions, and the proportions of the various ranks. They also show the pay of the various ranks, *less* the charges for agency, which are not deducted in the pay-tables published in 'Kane's List.' But, in addition to the strength of the Royal Artillery, the reader will find detailed statements of the other corps which swelled the total Artillery force of Great Britain. It is hoped that, by publishing these tables in this form, reference will be easier, and lengthy description may be dispensed with. It cannot be too often repeated that the services in the Peninsula of the King's German Artillery, the detail of which is given in the annexed tables, were of the most gallant description, unsurpassed by those of the corps to which they were attached. The active service of the corps, named the Royal Foreign Artillery, was chiefly in the West Indies.

CHAP. XVI. *Artillery Forces of Great Britain.* 263

STATEMENT OF THE ARTILLERY FORCES of GREAT BRITAIN IN THE YEAR 1810—ACCORDING TO THE ESTABLISHMENT LAID DOWN IN THE KING'S WARRANT—WITH THE VARIOUS RATES OF PAY, LESS AGENCY CHARGES. *From MS. Returns in Library of the Royal United Service Institution.*

I.—ROYAL ARTILLERY.

a. STAFF.

Rank.		Pay per diem.		
		£.	s.	d.
1 Master-General	} No pay on the			
1 Lieutenant-General	} establishment.			
10 Colonels-Commandant	each	2	14	4
20 Colonels	,,	1	6	0
30 Lieutenant-Colonels	,,	0	17	11
10 Majors	,,	0	16	9
1 Deputy-Adjutant-General		1	0	0
10 Adjutants	each	0	8	6
10 Quartermasters	,,	0	7	10
1 Chaplain		0	9	11
10 Sergeant-Majors	each	0	3	7¼
10 Quartermaster-Sergeants	,,	0	3	7¼

b. COMPANY OF GENTLEMEN CADETS.

		£.	s.	d.
1 Captain		1	4	7¾
1 Second Captain		0	13	0
2 First Lieutenants	each	0	6	10
1 Second Lieutenant		0	6	10
200 Gentlemen Cadets	each	0	2	0
1 Drum-Major		0	2	4
1 Fife-Major		0	2	4

c. TEN BATTALIONS, CONSISTING EACH OF

		£.	s.	d.
10 Captains	each	0	11	0
10 Second Captains	,,	0	11	0
20 First Lieutenants	,,	0	6	10
10 Second Lieutenants	,,	0	5	7
40 Sergeants	,,	0	2	5¼
40 Corporals	,,	0	2	3¾
90 Bombardiers	,,	0	2	1¾
1240 Gunners	,,	0	1	5¾
30 Drummers	,,	0	1	5¾

1490 being the total for each battalion, and therefore 14,900 for the ten.

Royal Artillery, continued.

d. INVALIDS.

Rank.		Pay per diem.
		£. s. d.
1 Colonel-Commandant		2 14 4
2 Second Colonels	each	1 0 0
2 Lieutenant-Colonels	„	0 19 9
3 Second Lieutenant-Colonels	„	0 17 11
1 Major		0 16 9
1 Adjutant		0 9 0
1 Quartermaster		0 7 10
2 Staff Sergeants	each	0 3 7½
12 Captains	„	0 11 0
12 First Lieutenants	„	0 7 10
12 Second Lieutenants	„	0 5 7
48 Sergeants	„	0 2 5¼
48 Corporals	„	0 2 3¾
108 Bombardiers	„	0 2 1¾
100 First Gunners	„	0 1 9¾
620 Second Gunners	„	0 1 5¾
12 Drummers	„	0 1 5¾
48 Non-effectives	„	0 1 5¾

e. ROYAL HORSE ARTILLERY.

1 Colonel-Commandant		2 19 3
2 Colonels	each	1 12 0
3 Lieutenant-Colonels	„	1 6 9
1 Major		1 2 8
1 Adjutant		0 16 6
1 Quartermaster		0 10 9
1 Regimental Staff Sergeant		0 3 9½
1 Regimental Sergeant (for Staff)		0 2 7½
2 Farriers and Carriage Smiths	each	0 3 5½
1 Collar-maker		0 3 5½
1 Trumpet-Major		0 2 3¾
12 Captains	each	0 15 11
12 Second Captains	„	0 15 11
36 First Lieutenants	„	0 9 10
24 Troop Staff Sergeants	„	0 3 9½
36 Sergeants	„	0 2 7½
36 Corporals	„	0 2 3¾
72 Bombardiers	„	0 2 1¾
480 Gunners mounted	„	0 1 5¾
528 Gunners dismounted	„	0 1 5¾
720 Drivers	„	0 1 5¾
12 Farriers and Shoeing Smiths	„	0 3 5½
12 Carriage Smiths	„	0 3 5½

CHAP. XVI. *Artillery Forces of Great Britain.*   265

Royal Horse Artillery, continued.

Rank.		Pay per diem.
		£. s. d.
24 Shoeing Smiths	each	0 2 3¾
24 Collar-makers	,,	0 2 1¼
12 Wheelwrights	,,	0 2 1¼
12 Trumpeters	,,	0 2 1¾

f. RIDING-HOUSE TROOP.

1 Captain		0 15 0
1 Lieutenant, at		0 15 0
1 ,, at		0 13 0
1 ,, at		0 11 0
1 Quartermaster		0 7 10
2 Staff Sergeants	each	0 3 2
3 Sergeants	,,	0 2 2
3 First Corporals	,,	0 2 0
3 Second Corporals	,,	0 1 10½
1 Trumpeter		0 1 11¼
1 Farrier		0 3 2¾
1 Collar-maker		0 1 10¾
44 Riders	each	0 1 3¼

II.—FIELD TRAIN.

1 Chief Commissary.	1 Foreman.
5 Commissaries.	7 Smiths.
24 Assistant Commissaries.	6 Collar-makers.
113 Clerks of Stores.	7 Wheelers.
115 Conductors.	2 Carpenters.
13 Military Conductors.	1 Painter.

III.—ROYAL ARTILLERY DRIVERS.

1 Major		1 1 0
2 Adjutants	each	0 10 0
8 Veterinary Surgeons	,,	0 8 0
11 Captain-Commissaries	,,	0 15 0
55 First Lieutenants	,,	0 9 0
11 Second Lieutenants	,,	0 8 0
55 Staff Sergeants	,,	0 3 2
165 Sergeants	,,	0 2 2
165 First Corporals	,,	0 2 0½
165 Second Corporals	,,	0 1 10½

Royal Artillery Drivers, continued.

Rank.		Pay per diem.
		£. s. d.
22 Rough-riders	each	0 1 3¼
55 Farriers	,,	0 3 2¾
165 Shoeing Smiths	,,	0 2 1¼
110 Collar-makers	,,	0 1 10¾
110 Wheelers	,,	0 1 10¾
55 Trumpeters	,,	0 1 11¼
4950 Drivers	,,	0 1 3¼

IV.—ROYAL FOREIGN ARTILLERY.

1 Major.
4 Captains.
4 Second Captains.
12 Lieutenants.
6 Sergeants.

4 Corporals.
17 Bombardiers.
124 Gunners.
8 Drummers.

V.—ARTILLERY OF THE KING'S GERMAN LEGION.

Officers.

1 Colonel Commandant.
1 Lieutenant-Colonel.
2 Majors.
8 Captains.
8 Second Captains.
16 First Lieutenants.
16 Second Lieutenants.
1 Captain Commissary.
1 Paymaster.
1 Adjutant.
1 Quartermaster.
1 Surgeon.
3 Assistant Surgeons.
1 Veterinary Surgeon.

Sergeants and Rank and File.	Horse Artillery.	Foot Artillery.
Staff Sergeants	4	3
Sergeants	6	14
Corporals	8	18
Bombardiers	14	23
Trumpeters	8	
Farriers	2	

Artillery of the King's German Legion, continued.

Sergeants and Rank and File.	Horse Artillery.	Foot Artillery.
Smiths	6	
Collar-makers	4	
Wheelers	2	
Gunners	186	 372
Drivers	116	Drummers .. 9

DRIVER CORPS.

Sergeants and Rank and File.

4 Sergeants.   8 Collar-makers.
8 Corporals.   5 Wheelers.
4 Farriers.   189 Drivers.
9 Smiths.

The recruiting for the Regiment during the year 1809 had been successful, no fewer than 1820 gunners and 868 drivers having been enlisted. The establishment just given was nearly maintained, and even occasionally exceeded, during 1810; and the usual decrease, caused by the discharge of men by purchase, did not occur during that year, all such discharges being forbidden. A falling off in the strength of the Regiment became apparent, however, in the winter of 1810.

The "wear and tear" among the horses of the Royal Horse Artillery and the Royal Artillery Driver Corps had been excessive during the year 1809, owing to the Peninsular Campaigns and the Scheldt Expedition. No fewer than 2786 had either died or been destroyed; and 3367 had to be purchased to compensate for these losses, and to meet the ever-increasing demand. Very large numbers were sent to Portugal during the year 1810; and, owing to the consequent increase in the numbers of the Driver Corps attached to Lord Wellington's armies, it was decided to appoint a field officer to command them. This duty, with cavalry pay, was given to Colonel Robe.

MS. 'Wear and Tear' Returns for 1809, to B. of Ordnance

D.-A.-Gen. to Gen. Howorth, 28 Oct. 1816.

The numerical force of Artillery, serving under General Howorth in the Peninsula, in the end of 1809, was as follows.

MS. Returns, compiled from the Monthly Returns, dated Woolwich, 17 Dec. 1809.	Royal Horse Artillery .	{ 187 of all ranks, besides a contingent of drivers attached to the Troops, numbering 106.
	Foot Artillery	627 of all ranks, with 545 drivers.
	King's German Artillery.	322 of all ranks, with 100 drivers.

The total being 1957, of whom 821 belonged to the Driver Corps. Of this number 357 were returned as sick; and there were in addition 39 prisoners of war.

The number of horses attached to the Artillery in the Peninsula was 951, of which 256 were returned as sick; and there were 132 mules, chiefly attached to the brigades of field and King's German Artillery.

MS. Returns, Dated Woolwich, 11 Sept. 1810.

The following tables will show that before a year had elapsed a very considerable increase to this force had taken place; and are also useful, as showing the companies which were present, and the names of the senior officers. (*See opposite page.*)

It is difficult, without a study of the correspondence of this period, to realise the energy with which General Macleod endeavoured to meet the wants of the Regiment abroad. Unfortunately, there was not similar energy in the other public departments. Large reinforcements, both of men and horses, were ready early in the summer of 1810; but no ships could be found for their conveyance until the end of December. From the nature of these drafts, and from various remarks in General Macleod's letters, it was clear that the remonstrances made by the various officers concerned on the subject of the want of mobility of the field brigades had produced their effect, and the rapid increase in the force of Horse Artillery in the Peninsula which took place between 1810 and 1814 was the consequence. Anticipating that Lord Wellington would prefer a complete troop of Horse Artillery to more of the sluggish field brigades, General Macleod suggested that the remnant of Captain Lefebure's troop, which was under orders for England, should remain in Portugal; and he despatched men and horses to complete it in that country. At the same time he did everything in his power to improve the field brigades in the point of mobility, by sending out large numbers of horses. No fewer than 500 were embarked in the first week of January 1811.

CHAP. XVI. *Artillery Force in the Peninsula.* 269

Stations.	Date of Last Returns.	Colonels, Field Officers, and Captains of Companies.	Battalions and Corps.	Colonels.	Field Officers.	Captains.	Subalterns.	Surgeons and Asst.-Surgn.	N.-C. Officers.	Gunners.	Drivers.	Artificers.	Drummers & Trumpeters.	Total.	Horses.	Mules.
Portugal.	1st July, 1810.							5						9		
		Brig.-Gen. Howorth	H. B.	1	1			2	12	81			1	3		
		Lieut.-Col. Framingham	1		1	2	3	1	13	45	73	7	1	180	157	
		Lieut.-Col. Robe	3		1	2	3	1	13	81	10	5	1	80	70	
		Lieut.-Col. Fisher	10		1	2	3	1	14	107	75	8	1	164	156	
		Major Hartmann	K.G.A.			2	3		14	109			2	127		
		Captain Bull	H. B.			2	3		14	105			1	130		
		Captain Lefebure	H. B.			2	3		13	99			1	125		
		Captain Ross	H. B.			2	3		13	117			2	118		
		Captain May	1			1	4		6	26	53	6	1	137	60	57
		Captain Glubb	5			2	4		14	80	30	5	2	39	7	
		Captain Thompson	7			2	4		13	80	37	6	2	159	107	7
		Captain Bredin	8			1	4		13	80	221	25	4	136	218	50
		Captain Lawson	8			1	3		31		318	33	4	144	330	72
		Detachmt. of British Art.	K.G.A.			2	4	1	35					286		
		Captain Heise	K.G.A.											395		
		Captain Gesenius	K.G.A.													
		Captain Arentschild	R.A.D.													
		Captain Turner	R.A.D.													
		Captain Lane														
		Total in Portugal		1	4	25	47	11	218	1010	817	95	24	2252	1105	186
Cadiz.	1st July, 1810.	Major Duncan	6		1	1		3	7	53			2	4		
		Captain Campbell	2			2	3		14	98			1	64		
		Captain Owen	5			2	3		13	100			2	119		
		Captain Hughes	9			2	3		13	98			1	118		
		Captain Dickson	10			2	3		12	99			1	117	218	
		Captain Shenley	10			2	3		12	97			1	116		
		Captain Roberts	10				2		12		134	10		159		
		Lieutenant Wilkinson	R.A.D.													
		Total in Cadiz			1	11	20	3	84	545	134	10	8	816	218	

MS. Returns, Dated Woolwich, 19 Nov. 1810.

The numerical division of the Regiment for home and foreign service in the year 1810 was as follows:—

	At Home. All ranks.	Abroad. All ranks.
Horse Brigade (including drivers)	1499	433
Marching Battalions	8235	5940
Invalid Battalions	822	39 [1]

MS. Returns, Dated Woolwich, 11 Sept. 1870.

The force in the Mediterranean garrisons, which was considered available in event of sudden demands from the Peninsula, appears in the following tables (*see pp.* 271 and 272), which also show the names of the senior officers. With these the statistics for the year to be treated in this chapter will terminate, and the consideration of the campaign be resumed.

The campaign of 1810 in the Peninsula was, in one sense, the least active of any during the war. Napoleon certainly made a great effort to completely subdue the country, and to expel the English armies. For this purpose, Marshal Massena was placed in command of the French troops; but the duty proved to be beyond his powers. It is doubtful if in any period of the Duke of Wellington's military career he displayed more ability, more patience, more foresight, than he showed during the first nine months of the year 1810. Not merely had he to contend with local influences, but he failed to secure the requisite support from the English Government. There was at home a fear of losing power, which led English statesmen to commit unworthy actions, and to display a nervousness in administration which demoralized such of their agents as were not above the ordinary standard. The wisdom of publishing the private letters of a great man is certainly questionable; but once published, they become the historian's legitimate property. From the letters of the Duke of Wellington we have a graphic picture of the Government in 1810. "What," he wrote to Admiral Berkeley, "can be expected from men who are beaten in the House of Commons three times a week?

Gurwood's Despatches of the Duke of Wellington.

---

[1] It will be observed that, as before stated, the Regiment had, before the end of 1810, fallen below the establishment shown at pages 263-265.

CHAP. XVI. *Artillery in Mediterranean Garrisons.* 271

Stations.	Date of last Returns.	Colonels, Field Officers, and Captains of Companies.	Battalions and Corps.	Colonels.	Field Officers.	Captains.	Subalterns.	Asst. Surgs. Surgeons and	N.-C. Officers.	Gunners.	Drivers.	Artificers.	Drummers & Trumpeters.	Total.	Horses.	Mules.	Remarks.
Gibraltar	1st July, 1810.	Major-General Smith	3	1	:	:	:	2	:	:	:	:	:	5	:	:	
		Lieut.-Colonel Ramsay	2	:	1	:	:	:	:	:	:	:	:	:	:	:	
		Lieut.-Colonel Wright	5	:	1	:	:	:	:	:	:	:	:	:	:	:	
		Captain Godby	1	:	:	1	3	:	14	87	:	:	2	107	:	:	N.B. At Ceuta, 1 captain, 1 subaltern, 3 N.-C. officers, and 11 gunners.
		Captain Dodd	2	:	:	1	2	:	17	117	:	:	4	141	:	:	
		Captain Smyth	4	:	:	2	2	:	11	83	:	:	2	100	:	:	At Turifa, 1 subaltern, 6 N.-C. officers, and 61 gunners included in the general total.
		Captain Morrison	8	:	:	2	2	:	13	86	:	:	2	105	:	:	
		Captain Birch	10	:	:	:	3	:	13	102	:	:	2	120	:	:	
		Captain Fead	10	:	:	2	3	:	13	101	:	:	1	120	:	:	
		Total in Gibraltar	:	1	2	8	15	2	81	576	:	:	13	698	:	:	
Malta.	1st June, 1810.	Colonel Bentham	7	1	:	:	:	1	:	:	:	:	:	3	:	:	A detachment of 1 subaltern, 2 N.-C. officers, and 25 gunners belonging to these companies serving in Sicily, and not included in the general total.
		Lieut.-Colonel Harris	2	:	1	:	:	:	:	:	:	:	:	:	:	:	
		Captain Vivion	2	:	:	2	3	:	13	93	:	:	2	113	:	:	
		Captain Reynell	5	:	:	2	3	:	13	88	:	:	2	108	:	:	
		Captain Carey	8	:	:	2	2	:	10	71	:	:	1	86	:	:	
		Total in Malta	:	1	1	6	8	1	36	252	:	:	5	310	:	:	

Stations	Date of last Returns	Colonels, Field Officers, and Captains of Companies	Battalions and Corps	Colonels	Field Officers	Captains	Subalterns	Asst. Surgs. and Surgeons	N.-C. Officers	Gunners	Drivers	Artificers	Drummers & Trumpeters	Total	Horses	Mules	Remarks
Sicily	1st May, 1810	Lieut.-Colonel Lemoine	5	..	1	1	..	4	..	..	..	..	..	6	..	..	At Zante, 2 captains, 2 surgeons, 13 N.-C. officers, and 80 gunners included in the general total.
		Lieut.-Colonel Dickinson	10	..	1	..	2	..	13	99	..	..	1	116	..	..	
		Captain Gamble	6	..	..	2	3	..	14	98	..	..	2	119	..	..	
		Captain Williamson	8	..	..	2	3	..	14	98	..	..	2	119	..	..	
		Captain Fraser	8	..	..	2	2	..	13	99	..	..	1	117	..	..	
		Captain Pym	8	..	..	2	2	..	14	99	..	..	1	118	..	..	
		Captain Hickman	8	..	..	..	1	..	2	25	..	..	..	28	..	..	
		Detachment of Artillery from Malta	..	..	..	2	4	1	16	105	39	6	2	175	..	..	
		Captain Bussman	K.G.A.	..	..	..	1	..	5	..	32	2	..	40	..	..	
		Lieut. G. Smith	R.A.D.	..	..	..	..	..	..	..	..	..	..	..	109	45	
		Total in Sicily	..	..	2	11	18	5	91	623	71	8	9	838	109	45	

"A great deal might be done now, if there existed in England less party, and more public sentiment—and if there was any Government." Again, in pleading his inability to carry out certain operations, he urged, in a letter to the Right Hon. H. Wellesley, that he would have been able to do so "if the Government possessed any strength, or desire to have anything done but what is *safe* and *cheap*." The same hands that applauded the conqueror at Talavera strove, in timorous anxiety, to drag him back from any further operations. The terror of the French armies, which had obtained possession of the Portuguese Government and people, seems to have reached London. The Government despatches to Lord Wellington breathed nothing but advice to guide him *when he should be expelled from Portugal*. While *he* was ensuring in a masterly manner the safety of Lisbon, *they* were urging on him the claims of Cadiz. Their letters and the tone of the public press swelled the despondency, the presence of which in Portugal Lord Wellington lamented; and his protests, assuring the Government that he had left nothing undone,—whether the event should be defeat or victory,—were treated as idle words, or as the heated expression of a mere soldier's hopes. Had Wellington been a weaker man, the lines of Torres Vedras had been got ready in vain, the battle of Busaco had never been fought, and the unpaid arrears of the French troops would have been liquidated by the plundering of Lisbon and Oporto.

_{Gurwood's Despatches of the Duke of Wellington.}

But his difficulties were not confined to the chilling advice of the Government. At a time when he required the best men in the army to aid him, the exercise of home patronage inflicted on him the most incapable assistants. Not merely did he suffer from useless subordinate staff officers, but even his general officers were not always what he wished. "Really," he wrote to Colonel Torrens, "when I reflect upon the characters and attainments of some of the general officers of this army, and consider that these are the persons on whom I am to rely to lead columns against the French Generals, and who are to carry my instructions into execution, I tremble; and, as Lord Chesterfield said

_{Supplementary Despatches, vol. vi. p. 582.}

" of the Generals of his day, 'I only hope that when the
" ' enemy reads the list of their names, he trembles as I do.'"
And at the very time that these men were being sent out to
him, he was debarred from offering reward, in the shape of
promotion, to any one under his command whose gallantry
might seem to him to have earned it. No subject is more
frequently alluded to in his letters than this. The Government would gladly make political capital out of his successes,
—would greedily gather votes by making appointments to his
army, but declined to strengthen him by trusting his military
knowledge, or increasing his legitimate authority.

But the aggravation to which he had to submit in 1810
did not cease here. While the French were advancing into
Portugal, and the English Government as little realised the
strength of the lines which Wellington had prepared for his
troops as Massena himself, the cry was always to embark,—to
quit Lisbon,—to devote his energies to Cadiz; yet when
strategical reasons and absolute necessity compelled him to
leave Ciudad Rodrigo to its fate, the same voices, in querulous
terror, remonstrated with him on his inaction. When he
gained the victory of Busaco, the first idea with the Government was, not recognition of his merits, but political capital.
And when, after a fruitless and self-destructive residence
before the lines of Torres Vedras, Massena was obliged to
retire from Portugal, who so loud in their cries for pursuit
as the very men who had scoffed at the bare possibility of
offering resistance to the French invaders?

The year 1810 was, however, not merely a year which
tested the marvellous ability and patience of Wellington;—it
was also the year which placed on the Portuguese troops the
seal of ability to face their dreaded French enemies. At
Busaco, the courage of the Portuguese, under English discipline, was nobly manifested,—and the value of this discovery
was beyond expression at that most critical time. As Lord
Wellington said, the battle had the best effect in inspiring
confidence in the Portuguese troops; it removed an impression, which had been general, that the English intended
to fight no more, but to retire to their ships; and it gave

Supplementary
Despatches,
vol. vi.
p. 606.

the Portuguese a taste for an amusement to which they were not before accustomed, and which they would not have acquired in a position less strong than that of Busaco. Had the battle been productive of no other gain than this, it ought to have found favour with a Government whose members desired that their successes might be "*cheap.*"

When the campaign commenced, the head-quarters of the English army were at Celorico; and Almeida and Ciudad Rodrigo were organized for defence. The latter city, which was defended by Spaniards, capitulated on the 10th July, after a month's siege; and Almeida, a small place with a Portuguese garrison, followed suit on the 28th August. During the siege of the latter place, the combat of the Coa, as it was termed, took place; and, as the Chestnut Troop took part in it, it deserves some notice. Crawford, who commanded the Light Division, and had the outpost duties to perform, had retired before the French, after the fall of Ciudad Rodrigo, under the walls of Almeida. The position which he took up was very dangerous. The river Coa, crossed by a single bridge, was in his rear, and an open country in front. He had been ordered to cross this river on the approach of the French, but had foolishly remained— with a small force of 5000 men and one battery of Artillery, the Chestnut Troop—awaiting the arrival of Ney's force, of more than three times the number. Regardless of the fire from the guns of Almeida, Ney availed himself of Crawford's blunder, and attacked him with vehemence. The crossing of the bridge, now absolutely necessary, was most difficult, and could not have been effected but for the gallantry of the regiments, and the precision of the fire of the Chestnut Troop, which had been sent across the bridge early in the affair to occupy some rising ground, and to cover the retreat of the other troops. The bridge was crowded by the retiring columns of the English, so as to be almost impassable; and when, ultimately, the whole had succeeded in crossing, the pursuing columns of the French blocked the passage in a similar manner, and, under a heavy fire, were reduced into heaps of killed and wounded, level with the parapet of the bridge. A

Cust.	tremendous storm of rain, which set in, flooded the pans of the French muskets, and put an end to the engagement, which, in point of losses, had been on both sides very severe. Of the Artillery on this occasion, Napier wrote that it played on both sides across the river and ravine, the sounds repeated by numberless echoes, and the smoke, slowly rising, resolving itself into an immense arch, spanning the whole chasm and sparkling with the whirling fuzes of the flying shells. Cust, in his 'Annals of the Wars,' describes the Chestnut Troop, from the high ground, sending well-directed shot over the heads of the skirmishers. The gallant officer who
'Memoirs of Sir H. Ross,' pp. 11, 12.	commanded the troop wrote as follows: " General Crawford " ordered a retreat. Lieutenant Bourchier, of the Artillery, " brought me the order to retire, as rapidly as in my power, " across the bridge, and to get my guns into position on the " opposite heights. At this time we had five guns in action. " . . . . . . Our fire was excellent, and broke them two or " three times." Captain Ross's brother, an officer of Engineers, who was serving with the army, writes of this combat of the 24th July: " Hew's guns did their duty." The loss on the English side during this engagement was over three hundred killed and wounded; that of the French was over a thousand.
	But a battle on a larger scale has now to be mentioned: Lord Wellington retreated towards Coimbra, followed by Marshal Massena on the north bank of the Mondego. The English General resolved to make a stand on the Sierra de Busaco, a high ridge which extends from the Mondego in a northerly direction about eight miles. In the battle which followed, Lord Wellington displayed an ignorance of Artillery tactics, from the results of which he was happily saved by the intelligence and gallantry of the representatives of that arm. This want of knowledge, which he never overcame, was the cause of a not unfrequent irritation against Artillery
Capt. T. B. Strange, R.A., on Practical Artillery.	as an arm, and a tendency to depreciate its value. At Busaco, instead of massing his Artillery in reserve until the attack should develop itself, the guns were placed, as a rule, in the easiest parts of the position, where it was supposed

the French *would* attack; and they were massed in these positions so as to form an excellent mark for the enemy's fire. This was more especially the case with Major Arentschild's 6-pounder and 9-pounder brigades of Portuguese Artillery. Fortunately, the Artillery was well served, and, as Sir John Burgoyne wrote, " the guns had great effect." Captain Thompson's company of the 7th Battalion—now D Battery, 11th Brigade, Royal Artillery, was of essential service, although it was broken up into divisions during the battle. Captain Lane, who was 2nd Captain of the company, thus describes the conduct of one division : " My men " did their duty. Lieutenant F. Bayley's conduct was ad- " mirable. It was the first time he had been in action, and " no old soldier could have acted better. The French Vol- " tigeurs (37th Regiment) came close to the guns; and one " was killed only eight paces off. An immense column " showing themselves in the ravine, we, with three cheers, " gave them a few rounds of case and round-shot together, " at about seventy paces distance, which drove them back." The same officer, who was quoted above as alluding to the services of his brother's troop at the Coa, wrote of Busaco: " I will venture to assert that the greatest loss the enemy " sustained was by our Artillery ; and the guns that had " the most duty, and, I believe I might say, that were best " placed for effect—even if nothing is said of the admirable " manner in which the guns were fought—were those of " Hew's troop. . . . . . Several officers who remained on " the field the day after the retreat, among others General " Crawford himself, were convinced, more than those who " only looked on it from the heights, of the immense " slaughter the enemy sustained from the Shrapnel shells " thrown from my brother's guns, aided for a short time " by those of Captain Bull's troop." This opinion, which, coming from a brother, might perhaps be considered more indulgent than just, was confirmed by the great historian of the war. In the resistance offered to the attack of Loison's division, Napier says that Ross's guns were worked with incredible quickness, and their shot swept through the ad-

'Life of Sir J. Burgoyne,' vol. i.

MS. Letter among Cleaveland's MSS.

'Memoirs of Sir H. D. Ross.'

vancing columns. The attack having failed, Crawford's Artillery, with which was the gallant Chestnut Troop, was equally useful against the attack of Marchaud's division, which followed. "It heavily smote," writes Napier, " the " flank of Marchaud's people in the pine-wood; and Ney, " who was there in person, after sustaining this murderous " cannonade for an hour, relinquished that attack also."

Lord Wellington to Lord Liverpool, dated Coimbra, 30 Sept. 1810.

Well might Lord Wellington say, "I am particularly in-" debted to ...... Brigadier-General Howorth and the " Artillery."

Ibid. dated Pero Negro, 3 Nov. 1810.

The force under Lord Wellington's command on this occasion did not exceed 50,000, and extended over a distance of eight to ten miles. The French are estimated by Napier to have been 65,000 in number; but Wellington considered that they exceeded that number by 5000 men. The French loss amounted to 4500 killed and wounded, while that of the Allies was under 1300, the English having lost 631, and the Portuguese 622. The absence of Artillery on the side of the French, who overrated the difficulties of the ground, and the great activity shown in the use and service of the guns of the Allies, accounted for the great difference in the number of casualties. Much of the efficacy of the fire of the Royal Artillery was due to the use of Shrapnel's spherical case-shot,—a projectile which was daily increasing in favour,—with no one more than with Lord Wellington him-

Dated Sabugal, 23 Feb. 1812.

self. "At the battle of Busaco," wrote Major May to Colonel Shrapnel, "your shells were of the utmost use, and their destruction plainly perceived from the heights."

Marshal Massena, finding it impossible to cross the Sierra de Busaco by either of the two direct roads, while such an enemy lined the heights, but being resolved to press on to Coimbra, turned the position by its left flank,—Wellington continuing the retreat which he had varied by so noble an episode. Massena reached Coimbra just as the English rearguard quitted it; and his troops were there guilty of the grossest licence. The English army continued slowly to retire to the lines which its prudent commander had prepared for it; and when Massena came up he found it in a position which was almost impregnable, while his own communications were interrupted, and his flanks and rear annoyed by levies of Portuguese Militia. The lines of Torres Vedras were a masterpiece of military sagacity and of engineering skill. Seated behind them the Allied Army received a training which proved fruitful in the campaign of the following year; the Portuguese contingent was made more efficient; and the folly of the Portuguese Government received repeated rebukes from the mouth of a General whose prudence and determination were never more clearly shown than in the history of Torres Vedras and Busaco. Croakers, as he wrote, might include the latter among useless battles; but an encounter, which made each Portuguese soldier feel himself a match for a Frenchman, was the best assistance which fortune could throw in Lord Wellington's way. Having realised the value of this beforehand, his next task was to ensure it *independently* of fortune.

CHAPTER XVII.

BAROSSA, BADAJOZ, AND ALBUERA.

LEAVING Massena in front of Torres Vedras, the reader is requested to turn towards Cadiz. Here Spanish pride had long resisted offers of English assistance, hoping without foreign aid to raise the siege of the city; but here the English Government thought it very desirable that some demonstration should be made. In 1810 the presence of a British contingent was at length tolerated; and the Artillery element has been detailed in the preceding chapter. Major Duncan and the companies under his command had originally embarked for Gibraltar; but the opening in Cadiz led to their proceeding to that city instead. Their arrival having been reported, steps were immediately taken by General Macleod to equip them for service in the field; and with this view, three batteries of six guns each, with the necessary equipment, were despatched from England, and a small supply of horses, seventy-four in number,—to form a nucleus of a larger establishment.

It had been intended that Colonel Framingham should be the officer to command the Artillery at Cadiz, as soon as the Spaniards should deign to admit any. Fortunately for Major Duncan, it was found impossible to spare that officer from the head-quarters of the army; and at the urgent request of General Graham, who commanded the English troops at Cadiz, the command of the Artillery with his force was left in Major Duncan's hands, and remained so until 1812, when he was accidentally killed by the explosion of a powder-mill at Seville.

In the records already given of the services of the companies of the 10th Battalion, reference has been made to the duties of the Royal Artillery at Cadiz. In this chapter it

Vide page 269.

General Macleod to Major Duncan, dated 23 April, 1810, and 8 May, 1810.

D.-A.-Gen. to Major Duncan, 13 May, 1810.

is proposed to describe a battle which was fought by General Graham's force, and in which,—it has been said, the Artillery covered themselves with glory. The gallant General stated that Artillery had never been better served; but it may be added that it had never been better handled than by him. His contingent was but small—ten guns—but it was never idle, and always in the right place. The circumstances which led to the battle of Barossa may be summarised as follows:—An attempt had been resolved upon by the Anglo-Spanish leaders in Cadiz to raise the French siege, the opportunity being favourable, as the besieging force did not at the time exceed 12,000 men. The English had 4200, and the Spaniards nearly 10,000. To facilitate matters, General Graham consented to serve under the Spanish General La Pena, although the event proved that there never was a man less fitted to hold a command. The plan of action was to transport the allied force to Tarifa, disembark there, and effect a junction with another Spanish force; and then countermarch the whole on the rear of the besieging force at Chichlana. Inclement weather prevented the first part of the scheme from being carried out; and the landing was effected, not at Tarifa, but at Algesiras. The whole army, however, effected a junction at the former place on the 28th February, 1811, and, driving the French before them, reached a place known as the Vigia de la Barrosa, or Barossa, at noon on the 5th March. Here they were encountered by the French Marshal, Victor, who had been warned of the expedition, and who promptly availed himself of the numerous openings which the blunders and incompetency of the Spanish General offered. The tale of these is too long to reproduce in a merely Regimental history; suffice it to say that, owing to them, General Graham found himself in an extraordinary and embarrassing position. Having been ordered to march from the height of Barossa, which was the key of the whole position, and to proceed to Bermeja through a difficult pine-wood, he obeyed, but with regret. Assuming that the important point he had just quitted would be occupied by the Spaniards, he left his

General Graham to Lord Liverpool, 6 March, 1811.

Cust's Annals.

baggage with a small guard. To his amazement, he soon learned that no such precaution had been taken; that the French Marshal, detecting the omission, was already ascending the height; and that his own baggage-guard was in extreme and imminent danger. Retracing his steps as rapidly as the nature of the wood would admit of, he arrived in time to see the enemy in complete possession of the height,—himself face to face with the French, and utterly unsupported by the Spaniards. By what has been called by Napier an inspiration—but such an inspiration as never comes to the short-sighted or ignorant—he realised that retreat would be folly, and that his only hope of success lay in immediately assuming the offensive. Massing his Artillery, he desired Major Duncan to keep up a powerful fire, while he organized his force into divisions for the attack. Of this fire Napier writes that it ravaged the French ranks. As soon as the Infantry had formed, General Graham advanced his Artillery to a more favourable position, whence, as he afterwards wrote, it kept up a most destructive fire on the French columns now advancing. The right division of the English, under General Dilkes, and the left, under Colonel Wheatley, encountered respectively the French divisions under Generals Ruffin and Laval. The Infantry regiments engaged were the Guards, 28th, 7th, 67th, and 87th,—the flank companies of the 1st Battalion 9th Foot, 2nd Battalion 47th, and 2nd Battalion 82nd, besides part of the 20th Portuguese Regiment. Where all behaved with gallantry, it may seem invidious to select any particular regiment for notice; but, at a most critical moment, the defeat of General Laval's division was completed by a magnificent advance of the 87th Regiment. Both the French divisions were borne backwards from the hill; and, uniting, attempted to reform and make another attack. But their attempt was frustrated by the fire of the Artillery, which from being terrific, as Napier termed it, became now "close, rapid, and murderous, and rendered the attempt "vain." Marshal Victor, therefore, withdrew his troops from the field, and the English, having been twenty-four

Napier, vol. iii. p. 446.

hours under arms and without food, were too exhausted to pursue.

In this battle, which only lasted one hour and a half, over 1200 were killed and wounded on the side of the English, and more than 2000 on the side of the French. Six guns and 400 prisoners also fell into the hands of the conquerors. Of the conduct of his troops generally, General Graham wrote to Lord Liverpool that nothing less than the almost unparalleled exertions of every officer, the invincible bravery of every soldier, and the most determined devotion to the honour of His Majesty's arms in all, could have achieved this brilliant success, against such a formidable enemy so posted. Sir Richard Keats, the Admiral on the station, who had superintended the transport of the troops to Algesiras, wrote that the British troops, led by their gallant and able commander,—forgetting, on the sight of the enemy, their own fatigue and privations, and regardless of advantage in the numbers and situation of the enemy,—gained by their determined valour a victory uneclipsed by any of the brave achievements of the British army. ^{To Admiral Sir C. Cotton, dated Cadiz, 7 March, 1811.}

The special expressions used by General Graham in his despatch with reference to the services of the Royal Artillery on this occasion are well worthy of a place in the records of the Corps. " I owe too much," he wrote, " to Major Duncan and the officers and corps of the Royal Artillery, not " to mention them in terms of the highest approbation: " *never was artillery better served.*" He recommended Major Duncan for promotion, and the brevet rank of Lieutenant-Colonel was accordingly conferred upon him.

The losses of the Artillery at Barossa were as follows:—

Died of his wounds, Lieutenant Woolcombe.

Wounded: Captains Hughes and Cator, — Lieutenants Mitchell, Brereton, Manners, Maitland, and Pester.

Three rank and file killed, and 32 wounded: besides of the Royal Artillery Drivers, 1 sergeant, 2 rank and file, and 18 horses killed: 1 sergeant, 7 rank and file, and 22 horses wounded.

The ordnance captured from the French was as follows:—

Major Duncan to General Graham.

Two 7-inch howitzers, 3 heavy 8-pounders, 1 4-pounder, —with their ammunition waggons, and a proportion of horses.

The fruits of the battle of Barossa might have been very considerable, had the Spanish General been capable of understanding even the rudiments of his profession. As he was at once ignorant and proud, General Graham found it necessary to return with his force to Cadiz; the object of the expedition had failed, for the siege was not raised,— but Marshal Victor had received a check which alarmed him considerably, and which led to eager demands for reinforcements. In his conduct, both in the action of the 5th March, and in his withdrawal to Isla de Leon on the following day, when he separated from the Spaniards, General Graham received the warmest support from Lord Wellington, to whose movements the reader is now invited to return.

After an inactivity of five months before the lines of Torres Vedras, Massena commenced to evacuate Portugal. He had no siege artillery with which to attack the fortifications behind which his enemy was securely sheltered; and his supplies were becoming every day more difficult to obtain; he therefore had no other alternative. As he retired, he was closely followed by the English army, and many smart affairs took place between the advanced guards of the latter and the rear-guard of the French army, in which the Royal Horse Artillery did good service. The limits of the largest work and the patience of the most enduring reader would be exhausted were these minor actions given in detail. Suffice it to say, that the Artillery engaged on these occasions included the troops commanded by Captain Ross and Captain Bull,—that the names of the various actions are given in the first volume of this history at pages 396 and 401, and that the way in which they performed their duty may be gathered, in the first place, from Lord Wellington's despatches, and, in the second, from the exhaustive narrative of Napier. In writing of the actions of the 11th, 12th, and 13th March, 1811, at Pombal, Redinha, and Cazal Nova,

Lord Wellington said that the troops of Horse Artillery under Captains Ross and Bull particularly distinguished themselves. At the affair of Foz d'Arouce, on the 15th March, he also wrote that the Horse Artillery, under Captains Ross and Bull, distinguished themselves. Later, in the affair which took place on the 7th April, during a reconnaissance, in which the English, under Sir W. Erskine, drove a division of the French army before them across the Turones and Dos Casas, Lord Wellington wrote that "Captain's Bull's troop of Horse Artillery did great execution on this occasion." *To Lord Liverpool, dated 14 March, 1811. Ibid. dated 16 March, 1811. Ibid. dated 9 April, 1811.*

At the celebrated engagement of Fuentes d'Onor,[1] the dashing affair mentioned in an early part of this work took place, in which Captain Norman Ramsay, of Bull's troop, so greatly distinguished himself. On this occasion the losses of the Artillery were as follows:— *Vol. ii. chap. ii.*

Royal Horse Artillery—1 rank and file and 3 horses killed: 1 rank and file, and 3 horses wounded.

Royal Foot Artillery—1 sergeant, 4 rank and file, and 9 horses killed; 1 captain, 2 subalterns, 18 rank and file, and 21 horses wounded.

The officers wounded were Captain Thompson,—whose brigade did as good service as it had done at Busaco, and by its practice attracted universal admiration,—Lieutenant Martin, and a subaltern of the same name as the officer who fell at Barossa, Lieutenant Woolcombe. The total casualties on the side of the Allies amounted to 1786: those of the French to 2665. The battle resulted in the evacuation of Portugal by Massena, and the capture of Almeida by

---

[1] The Artillery of the Allies at Fuentes d'Onor was as follows:—

Royal Horse Artillery	12 guns.
Royal Artillery	12 „
Portuguese Artillery	18 „
	42

Sir A. Dickson's MSS.

the English, although, unfortunately, not until the garrison had made its escape.

During these continued successes, Lord Wellington was afflicted by a want of adequate supplies and money,—and by discouraging letters from England. With a temerity such as few commanders would have displayed, he did not hesitate to point out to the Government how weak and mistaken their vacillating, timorous policy was. Still undeceived as to the worthlessness of Spanish promises, the English rulers urged upon Wellington to make Spain the theatre of his operations, and yet declined to make him independent of the Spanish authorities. His protestations, also, in favour of Portugal as a base of operations fell on doubting and unwilling ears. English statesmen seemed to live in a fools' paradise: and from their dreams it seemed impossible to wake them. On the 23rd March, 1811, Lord Wellington had actually to write, beseeching the Government to forego an intention which appeared to have been formed of withdrawing the troops from Portugal on account of the expense of the war. He had already urged on them the folly of starving an expedition in the hope of securing popularity for their party; and he now boldly asserted that if they carried out their intention, and freed the French from the pressure of military operations in the Continent, they must prepare to meet a French army in England. "Then," he wrote, "would commence an expensive contest;—then would " His Majesty's subjects discover what are the miseries of " war, of which, by the blessing of God, they have hitherto " had no knowledge." It was a difficult task which Lord Wellington had to perform,—not merely to fight his country's battles under difficulties and discouragement,—not merely to be exasperated by advice, the folly of which was glaring,— but also in his few moments of leisure to have to take up his pen, and teach her senators wisdom. The superiority of England's greatest General cannot be realised without a careful study, not merely of his campaigns, but also of his correspondence.

It is necessary now to turn to Marshal Beresford's force,

with which was Major Dickson, now serving in command of the Portuguese Artillery. It had been hoped that this army would reach Badajoz in sufficient time to raise the French siege of that city; but a slight delay in Beresford's movements, combined with undoubted treachery on the part of the garrison, frustrated this hope, and rendered it necessary to prepare for a siege of the city with its now French garrison. From this time, the reader will enjoy an advantage which cannot be overrated, and which appears now for the first time in any narrative of the Peninsular War.

Sir Alexander Dickson was not merely a great Artilleryman, but also a most methodical and industrious collector and registrar of details which came under his notice. During the various sieges in the Peninsula which were conducted by him, he kept diaries mentioning even the most trifling facts: and on his return to England he procured from General Macleod the whole of the long series of letters which he had written to him between 1811 and 1814. The mass of information which he thus possessed was arranged, and at his death the whole passed into the hands of his son, Sir Collingwood Dickson. In the hope that the papers of the most prominent Artilleryman of the Duke of Wellington's armies would be useful in framing a history of the Corps in which he spent his life, Sir Collingwood kindly placed them at the disposal of the author of this history. Priceless under any circumstances, they are even more so from the fact that several of the letter-books of the Deputy-Adjutant-General's department during the Peninsular War have been mislaid;— and these refer chiefly to the periods covered by the manuscripts of Sir Alexander Dickson. On the latter, therefore, the narrative of the period between 1811 and 1814 will be chiefly based: and it is hoped that the reproduction of the opinions and statements of one, so able to express the former with confidence and the latter with authority, will be a welcome addition to the literature of England's wars in the Peninsula.[1]

---

[1] In his notes on the various sieges in the Peninsula, Sir A. Dickson frequently differs from Sir J. Jones's well-known work. But as the latter

On the 9th April, 1811, Marshal Beresford advanced from the Guadiana and invested Olivença. When he reconnoitred the place, Major Dickson pointed out an inclosed lunette in front of the gate of San Francisco, from which he knew, by a former visit to Olivença, that the curtain could be battered in breach. Approving of the suggestion, Marshal Beresford despatched Major Dickson to Elvas that night to bring up the siege artillery. This consisted of six heavy brass 24-pounders, each provided with all necessary stores, and with ammunition at the rate of 300 rounds per gun. To move this battery and equipment from Elvas to Olivença 104 pairs of bullocks were required, and a company of Portuguese Artillery attended as escort. On the 13th April the guns arrived at the camp before Olivença, and immediately proceeded to the neighbourhood of the point of attack. The breaching battery for four 24-pounders had been got in complete readiness, and an attempt was accordingly made at once to put the guns in battery. It was found, however, impossible to effect this on that day, on account of the dreadful state of the roads, and the circuit which the guns were obliged to take. By the night of the 14th, the communications had been made practicable, and four guns were placed in the battery, with ammunition and stores, in readiness to open fire at dawn. Two field batteries of the King's German Artillery were also placed so as to keep the enemy's fire in check. The field-pieces employed by these were five 6-pounders and one 5½-inch howitzer.

The breaching battery did not open fire until 8 A.M. on the 15th, the point aimed at being the curtain to the left of the San Francisco gate, and the distance being about 340 yards. At 11 A.M. the enemy showed a flag of truce, which occsioned a cessation of fire; but nothing definite resulting, it was resumed, and after a few more rounds the enemy

---

had more to do with engineering details, and as Sir A. Dickson's MSS. contain occasional marginal notes of later date, saying that his statement is correct, and Sir J. Jones's wrong, it has been decided to accept his account, when differing from the latter work.

CHAP. XVII. *First Siege of Badajoz.* 289

surrendered at discretion. Major Dickson was much pleased with the practice made by the young Portuguese Artillerymen under his command. Only 320 rounds had been fired in the four hours, and yet the breach was almost practicable. A brisk fire from five or six guns had been kept up by the enemy against the breaching battery, and had inflicted some slight loss; but the field guns of the German Artillery did much to moderate it, firing about sixty rounds a gun.

On taking Olivença the following ordnance was secured:— *Mounted.* Brass, one 8-pounder and two 4-pounders; iron, five 12-pounders, two 8-pounders, and two 6-pounders. *Dismounted.* Brass, one 8-pounder; iron, two 12-pounders.

<small>Sir. A. Dickson's MSS.</small>

On the 17th April, Major Dickson waited on Marshal Beresford at Zafra, and received orders to proceed to Elvas to make preparations for the siege of Badajoz. On the 20th Lord Wellington arrived at Elvas, and issued instructions for the carrying on of the siege to Marshal Beresford, Colonel Fletcher of the Engineers, and Major Dickson, the last-named officer being appointed to direct the Artillery department of the operation. From the 21st April to the 10th May, the greatest exertions were made, both at Elvas and around Badajoz, to prepare the necessary ordnance and stores for the siege, transport them, and make and arm the batteries. The following shows, in a tabulated form, the nature and distribution of the ordnance employed:—

TABLE A.[1]

FIRST SIEGE OF BADAJOZ.

April 23, 1811.—Ordnance selected for the Siege :—

    Sixteen brass 24-pounder guns.
    Eight   „   16-pounder „
    Two 10-inch brass howitzers.
    Six 8-inch „   „

<small>Prepared from various returns among Sir A. Dickson's MSS.</small>

The ammunition to be at the rate of 800 rounds per gun, and 400 rounds per howitzer.

[1] *Vide* note at Table B, p. 299.

First Siege of Badajoz, continued.

The following distribution of ordnance was determined on for the first operations of the siege, on the 8th May, 1811:—

1. For the attack of St. Cristoval:

    24-pounders .. .. 3 ⎫ 5
    8-inch howitzers .. .. 2 ⎭

2. For the false attack on Pardaleras:

    24-pounders .. .. 3 ⎫ 4
    8-inch howitzer .. .. 1 ⎭

3. For the false attack on Picurina:

    24-pounders .. .. 3 ⎫ 4
    8-inch howitzer .. .. 1 ⎭

On the 9th May, the following additional ordnance was sent from Elvas for the St. Cristoval attack, viz.:

    24-pounders .. .. 2 ⎫ 3
    8-inch howitzer .. .. 1 ⎭

Four brass 12-pounders were at the same time ordered from Elvas to enfilade the bridge of Badajoz. Four guns for the attack of St. Cristoval were replaced on the 11th May—having been damaged—by three heavy 12-pounders and a field howitzer.

On the 12th May, four 24-pounders were sent from the great park to the Cristoval attack.

On the 13th May the siege was ordered to be raised, as will hereafter be shown.

Badajoz was invested on the right bank on the 8th May, and on the morning of the 11th the breaching battery against San Cristoval opened. Being, however, totally unsupported, and having to resist a very heavy fire from that fort and the Castle, the young Portuguese Artillerymen proved unequal to the contest. Their practice, after a few rounds, became very uncertain; and in the course of the morning the battery was silenced, all the pieces being disabled except one howitzer.

CHAP. XVII.   *Failure of the Siege.*   291

On the night of the 11th, the battery intended to enfilade the bridge was armed, and the disabled ordnance in the breaching battery exchanged. Captain Hawker, commanding a 9-pounder field brigade of the Royal Artillery, lately arrived from Lisbon, was directed to place himself under the orders of Major Dickson, although regimentally senior to that officer, and was placed in charge of the Artillery operations against San Cristoval.

The commencement of the siege was very disheartening. On the day before the solitary battery opened fire, the Allies had met with a severe loss during a sally made by the garrison; and now, in a few hours their one battery was silenced. Beresford was also disquieted by rumours which reached him that Soult was on his way to raise the siege, and that he would certainly arrive before the city could be taken. He therefore sent for Major Dickson late on the night of the 11th, and desired him not to bring forward any more ammunition or stores from Elvas, and to be in readiness to remove at the shortest notice what had already arrived. Colonel Fletcher also was ordered not to break ground that night against the Castle. In event, however, of the operations proceeding, it was arranged that four 24-pounders should be moved from the south attacks to that of San Cristoval, and that they should be replaced by six additional guns of the same calibre from Elvas.

On the morning of the 12th intelligence reached Beresford which led him to doubt the accuracy of the reports which had reached him on the previous day, and he ordered active operations to recommence at once. Additional guns were therefore sent forward from the park at Elvas, and at night ground was broken for the batteries against the Castle. The new activity, however, was but short-lived; for positive information was received at midnight as to the enemy's movements. On the morning of the 13th the siege was ordered to be raised, and Major Dickson directed to send the heavy ordnance, ammunition, and stores back to Elvas. This duty was admirably performed. As many pieces of ordnance were at once despatched as the means of conveyance would permit; and in the first instance it was thought sufficient to take the pieces across the flying bridge, and to park them in a situation not visible from Badajoz. On the Cristoval side the guns were removed from the battery on the night of the 13th; and at the same time the battery in the false attack against Picurina was dismantled. The 14th May was spent in carrying away the ordnance and stores in such a way as to conceal from the enemy the fact that the siege was being raised; and by noon on the 15th the whole of the besieging artillery and ammunition from the great park had been sent across the river, and the flying bridge removed, while the park of the Cristoval attack had been taken back to the vicinity of Elvas.

The investing troops on the south bank were then withdrawn; but a corps remained on the north bank to cover the removal of the heavy artillery to Elvas. Of the duty performed by Major Dickson on this occasion, under Marshal Beresford's orders, Napier writes that " the arrangements " for carrying off the stores were admirably executed; . . . . " and that the transactions were so well masked by the 4th " Division, which, in concert with the Spaniards, continued " to maintain the investment, that it was only by a sally on " the rear-guard, in which the Portuguese piquets of the " 4th Division were very roughly treated, that the French " knew the siege was raised."

The same author visits the failure of this siege, and the heavy losses attending all the subsequent sieges carried on by the British in Spain, on the absence of any properly-equipped corps of Sappers and Miners to assist the officers of Engineers. The want of such a corps, with the necessary implements, rendered, according to Napier, the British sieges a mere succession of butcheries. But Sir Alexander Dickson was ready to accept part of the responsibility of this failure for his own department. In his diary of the first siege of Badajoz he wrote: " Every praise was due to the Portuguese " Artillery for the activity, zeal, and willingness they dis- " played in this service. Indeed, nothing could exceed their " personal exertions; but, from their professional inexperience,

Sir A. Dickson's MSS.

" Major Dickson has great doubts whether a satisfactory result
" would have been obtained without the assistance of a pro-
" portion of better-trained Artillerymen." At the same time, [Dated Elvas, 22 May, 1811.]
however, he distinctly stated, in a letter to General Macleod,
that his wish was not to begin the fire from any one battery
until the whole attack should be more advanced, and that
the Cristoval attack should be supported from other points.
He added that the battery against the Picurina, although
well placed as an auxiliary for general attack, afforded no
support to that against San Cristoval. In these points, he
wrote, " my opinions coincide entirely with those of Colonel
" Fletcher (R.E.), with whom it is a pleasure to serve." .

Marshal Beresford was brave, but was better as an admini-
strator in peace than as a General in war. No praise can exceed
his deserts in reference to the organization and training of
the Portuguese army, or his fidelity to Wellington; but his
abilities as a commander in the field were feeble, and the success
of his troops in the battle which followed the raising of the
siege of Badajoz was won in spite of, rather than by him.
Albuera was one of the fiercest battles of the Peninsula;
with it the name of Beresford will always be associated; but
its chronicler will always have to register with the stories of
its gallantry that of his incapacity. The policy of fighting
the battle at all—a question which lies with a General alone
—was more than doubtful; but, even admitting that it was
wise, his tactics were extremely faulty, and the errors were
expiated only by the courage and losses of his men. With
a General like Soult against him, the arrangement of his
army on the morning of the 16th May revealed a childlike
innocence, which, in a General charged with the lives of
men, was criminal. Part of his army was still at Badajoz,
and could not possibly reach his position in time for the battle;
—part had barely succeeded in doing so on the eventful
morning;—he had, on the previous day, allowed the French
to occupy a wood on the other side of the Albuera River,
where they could conceal their intentions;—and, with marvellous blindness, he had allowed them to secure a hill in
the immediate front of his own right, behind which they

organized the famous attack, which so nearly proved fatal.

On the afternoon of the 15th, Major Dickson, having completed his duties at Badajoz, proceeded to Albuera, where the army had taken up its position, and resumed the command of his two brigades of Portuguese Field Artillery. About the same hour on the morning of the 16th as that on which General Cole's division happily succeeded in joining Beresford's army, the enemy showed himself in force. The first appearance was the advance of seven or eight squadrons of cavalry, some light infantry, and a troop of horse artillery, from the wood towards the bridge of Albuera by the Seville road. This was a feint, but not immediately recognized as such by Marshal Beresford. They drove in the English piquets, and formed in the plain, where they opened an artillery fire towards the village of Albuera, a small place, which, with the exception of its church, was almost in ruins, and which was without inhabitants. This fire was answered by some of Major Dickson's and of the German Artillery, which directed their practice against the cavalry. At first Major Dickson thought it was merely a reconnoissance; but it was soon seen that the real attack was intended against the right, which was composed of Blake's Spanish troops. Beresford sent orders to Blake to throw back the right at right angles to the line; but the command was not obeyed until he went in person to enforce it, by which time the French were upon them, harassing them, as they wheeled, with a murderous fire. From the position occupied by Major Dickson near the bridge, which was opposite the centre of the line, he first saw a column of infantry advancing to the bridge by the same road as had been taken by the cavalry, on which a brigade of General Stewart's division was at once sent to the village to support Baron Alten, who commanded there. Very soon afterwards, however, he saw another column moving through the wood in the direction of the Allied right, and as, at the same time, the column approaching the bridge first halted, and then commenced to retire, it was evident that the real French effort would be made against the right. Stewart's British brigade, therefore, at once marched from the village to the right, followed by the rest of the division, and Cole's division formed up in support.

By this time a heavy shower of rain had commenced, which greatly favoured the approach of the French columns against the Spaniards on the right, and during which they passed the river, and advanced upon and came round the height which the latter occupied, and on which they were then, in great confusion, wheeling into a new position. In describing the conduct of the Spanish troops at Albuera, Major Dickson, referring to this particular episode in the battle, wrote to General Macleod as follows: " The fact is, "the Spaniards, once in line, could not be moved—I mean, " could not manœuvre—and the Marshal was obliged to use " the British, that knew how to move, or else our flank " must have been completely turned." <small>To D.-A.-G. dated 22 May, 1811.</small>

This quite corroborates Napier's account of the battle. It was on the hill occupied by the Spanish that the contest was decided; it was there that the gallantry of the French Cavalry and the heroism of the English Infantry were manifested; there a murderous artillery fire of grape at close range was maintained incessantly on both sides; and it was there that the grand final episode took place which was described with poetic fervour by the great historian. " The <small>Napier.</small> " Fusileer battalions of Cole's division advanced in gallant " line, but, struck by the iron tempest, reeled and staggered " like sinking ships. But, suddenly and sternly recovering, " they closed on their terrible enemies; and then was seen " with what a strength and majesty the British soldier " fights. . . . . . Nothing could stop that astonishing in- " fantry. No sudden burst of undisciplined valour, no " nervous enthusiasm, weakened the stability of their order ; " their flashing eyes were bent on the dark columns in their " front, their measured tread shook the ground, their dread- " ful volleys swept away the head of every formation, their " deafening shouts overpowered the dissonant cries that " broke from all parts of the tumultuous crowd, as, slowly

" and with a horrid carnage, it was pushed by the incessant
" vigour of the attack to the farthest edge of the height.
" .... At last the mighty mass gave way, and, like a
" loosened cliff, went headlong down the steep. The rain
" flowed after in streams discoloured with blood; and
" eighteen hundred unwounded men, the remnant of six
" thousand unconquerable British soldiers, stood triumphant
" on the fatal hill!" Before this final charge took place
Beresford thought the battle was lost, and commenced
arrangements for a retreat. He ordered the withdrawal
of Alten's Germans and Major Dickson's guns from Albuera bridge. This was strongly asserted by Napier,
although denied by one of his critics; and it is confirmed
by a passage in one of Major Dickson's letters. "The Marshal himself, for a moment, thought he was defeated, as I
" received an order to retreat, with my Artillery, towards
" Valverde, and Baron Alten absolutely, by order, quitted
" the village for a moment. All this was, however, soon
" countermanded and rectified." To Colonel Hardinge was
due the credit of ordering the final and successful advance.

To D.-A.-G. 22 May, 1811.

The Artillery force at Albuera, on the side of the Allies, comprised :—

Sir A. Dickson to General Napier, dated 16 Dec. 1830, and to Lord Beresford, dated 19 March, 1831, in correction of the former.

Captain Lefebure's Troop of Royal Horse Artillery, consisting of 4 6-pounders.
Captain Hawker's Brigade of Royal Artillery, now No. 4 Battery, 7 Brigade, R.A., consisting of 4 9-pounders.
Captain Cleeve's Brigade, King's German Artillery, consisting of 5 6-pounders and 1 5½-inch howitzer.
Captain Sympher's Brigade, King's German Artillery, consisting of 5 6-pounders and 1 5½-inch howitzer.
Captain Braun's Brigade, Portuguese Artillery, consisting of 6 9-pounders.
Captain Arriaga's Brigade, Portuguese Artillery, consisting of 6 6-pounders.
Spanish Artillery, consisting of 6 6-pounders.

No explanation is given in any of the Regimental records why Captain Lefebure had only four guns; it may, however, be assumed that his troop had not yet recovered the drain on its resources which was made on its arrival in the Peninsula, when it was called upon to fill up the vacancies in the Chestnut Troop.

A detailed statement of the services of the Artillery at

Albuera was forwarded by Major Dickson to General Howorth, for transmission to England, but, unfortunately, was lost. The student has, therefore, merely a private letter from Major Dickson to General Macleod to rely upon, whose details are, of course, less ample than could be wished. In it he mentioned that the cannonade on both sides was tremendous during the whole battle, and that probably on few such occasions had there been more casualties from artillery fire. Major Hartmann was in command of the British and German Artillery; Major Dickson of the Portuguese. The latter behaved admirably. Captain Lefebure's troop also distinguished itself, one gun having been for a short time taken, but afterwards recovered. Captain Hawker's brigade, from Major Dickson's personal observation, did great execution. General Cole spoke in the highest terms of Captain Sympher's brigade; and Captain Cleeve's guns went through a number of vicissitudes. Being placed on the hill, where the great attack was made, the whole of them fell into the enemy's hands, but were afterwards recovered, with the exception of one howitzer. They were admirably served until the French were actually amongst them; and then retreat was impossible, the enemy's cavalry having swept round the hill, and taken them in rear.

Modern battles may dwarf those of the Peninsula in point of the numbers engaged; but it is questionable if the British courage displayed at Albuera, and the proportionate losses to the number engaged, have ever been surpassed. The severe fighting lasted about four hours; and in that time nearly 7000 of the Allies, and over 8000 French, were killed or wounded. On the side of the Allies, over 4000 of the casualties were among the British troops, only 1800 of the total number engaged being untouched. Major Dickson, in describing the scene, said that every one declared they had never seen such a field; that on the hill where the great struggle had been, in the space of from 1000 to 1200 yards, there were certainly not less than 6000 lying dead or wounded. Napier's description of the field after the battle is characteristically graphic, and leaves an indelible impression on the reader's mind. Such was the crippled and famished state of the Allies, that, had the French attacked again on the 17th, resistance would have been impossible. Fortunately, Soult resolved to retire; and Lord Wellington, reaching Albuera on the 19th, sent Beresford to watch his movements, while he himself proceeded to reinvest Badajoz. The order issued by Marshal Beresford, after the battle, included the following paragraph :—" To Major Hartmann and Major " Dickson, and to the officers and soldiers of the British, " German, and Portuguese Artillery, the greatest praise is " due, and the Marshal returns them his best thanks." In forwarding to the Ordnance a copy of this order, Major Dickson, with soldier-like generosity, added : " The Marshal's " orders are not strong enough in favour of the Fusileer " Brigade, who really saved the day." In Lord Wellington's letter to Admiral Berkeley, dated 20th May, 1811, he said that he considered the battle of Albuera one of the most glorious and honourable *to the character of the troops* of any that had been fought during the war. In Marshal Beresford's report to Lord Wellington, dated 18th May, 1811, he said : "I have every reason to speak favourably of the manner " in which our Artillery was served and fought. Captain " Lefebure's troop of Horse Artillery did great execution."

On the 19th May, 1811, Lord Wellington, Colonel Fletcher, and Major Dickson arrived at Elvas, from Albuera, to make preparations for resuming the siege of Badajoz. Colonel Framingham had joined at head-quarters, and assumed command of the Royal and other Artillery; but Lord Wellington expressed a wish that Major Dickson should continue to direct all the arrangements for the siege, and communicate directly with himself. This distinction caused no jealousy in Colonel Framingham's mind; on the other hand, that officer spoke of Major Dickson to Lord Wellington in the highest terms, and during the siege assisted him in every way. This was the beginning of a confidence between Lord Wellington and Major Dickson, which only increased as the war went on; and it is interesting to find, even thus early, the latter officer speak of his great chief as follows :

Marginalia: To D.-A.-G. dated Elvas, 29 May, 1811.

CHAP. XVII.   *Second Siege of Badajoz.*   299

" I have transacted business with many Generals, but never
" such an one as Lord Wellington, both for general know-
" ledge, and attention to reason and suggestion."

To D.-A.-G.
dated
Elvas,
29 May,
1811.

The story of the second unsuccessful siege of Badajoz, as of the first, may be prefaced by showing in a tabular form some of the more important Artillery statistics connected with it. These have been extracted from the voluminous diary and almost daily correspondence of Major Dickson, on which the summary, given afterwards in the form of narrative, is also based.

TABLE B.

SECOND SIEGE OF BADAJOZ.

May 22, 1811.—The following was the appropriation of ordnance determined upon for the siege:—

CRISTOVAL ATTACK.		SOUTH, OR CASTLE ATTACK.	
24-pounders (brass)	12	24-pounders (brass)	14
16-pounders	4	10-inch howitzers	2
10-inch howitzers	2	8-inch howitzers	4
8-inch howitzers	4		
	22		20

In reserve : 24-pounders (brass) 4

Detail of men for siege artillery :—

1st Regt. Portuguese Artillery : officers and men				100
2nd ,, ,, ,, ,,				100
3rd ,, ,, ,, ,,				300
Royal Artillery ,, ,, ,,				110
				610

Many of these guns were replaced during the siege, as may be gathered from the following table :—

	24-pounders.	10-in. howitzers	8-in. howitzers.	
Disabled by the fire of the enemy	3	..	3	
Disabled by the effects of their own fire	15	2	1	
Total	18	2	4	= 24.

Second Siege of Badajoz, continued.

The expenditure of ammunition during the siege was as follows :—

No. of rounds.	24-pr. round shot.	24-pr. grape shot.	16-pr. round shot.	Shell 10-in.	Shell 8-in.
North, or San Cristoval Attack ..	5950	200	1134	62	989
South, or Castle Attack	8419	441	..	640	1090
Total	14369	641	1134	702	2079

N.B.—The totals given above, and in the first table (Table A), agree with those given by Sir J. Jones; but the details here are more minute. It was but natural that Sir J. Jones, being an Engineer officer, should devote more space and detail to the labours of his own corps; but his artillery details in most sieges in the Peninsula were obtained from Sir A. Dickson and Sir J. May, and generally agree with the MSS. of the former.

On the 10th June Lord Wellington determined on raising the siege.

On the night of the 30th May the trenches were opened on both attacks, and great progress was made. The whole of the guns for the batteries were also set in movement, with ammunition at the rate of 300 rounds per gun.

Captain Rainsford's company (now No. 7 Battery, 17th Brigade) having arrived from Lisbon, the Artillerymen were divided as follows :—

ATTACK AGAINST THE CASTLE.

Major Dickson commanding.

Officers' Names.

Royal Artillery	55 officers and men.		Captain Rainsford.
1st Reg. Portuguese Artillery	100	,,	Captain Latham.
2nd ,, ,,	100	,,	Lieut. Saunders.
3rd ,, ,,	50	,,	Lieut. Willis.
Total ..	305		

ATTACK AGAINST SAN CRISTOVAL.

Captain Cleeves, (K.G.A.), commanding under Major Dickson.

Officers' Names.

Royal Artillery	55 officers and men.		Lieut. Hawker.
3rd Reg. Portuguese Artillery	250	,,	Lieut. Connel.
Total ..	305		

CHAP. XVII. *Second Siege of Badajoz.* 301

This gave but a very small relief; and Lord Wellington remarked, after the raising of the siege, that some of the Royal Artillery were indefatigable, and had never quitted their batteries. <small>Lord Wellington to the Earl of Liverpool, dated</small>

Captain Latham was the 2nd Captain of Captain Hawker's Field Brigade, and was lent for the service of the siege train. Of him Major Dickson afterwards said: "I assure you the assistance I derived from his professional knowledge and activity can never be forgotten by me." Instances like this, and others hereafter to be mentioned, when even Horse Artillerymen served in the trenches, are arguments against the necessity of any *complete* divorce between the Field and Garrison branches of the Artillery service. Of Captain Rainsford's company—now 7 Battery, 17th Brigade —Major Dickson wrote: "It was of wonderful assistance; it is an uncommon fine one." <small>13 June, 1811.</small>

<small>To D.-A.-G. dated 13 June, 1811.</small>

<small>Ibid.</small>

On the 1st June the batteries on both sides were in a very forward state, and two on the north side received their armament. On the south side several guns were brought into the parallel, ready for mounting on the following night, when the batteries should be prepared for them. By half-past 8 o'clock on the morning of the 3rd everything was ready; and on the south side a fire was commenced with fourteen guns against the point which it was intended to breach. The fire was most vigorous, and, although well replied to, gave considerable hopes of success. Two of the guns became disabled from the effects of their own fire,—a casualty whose recurrence during the siege was most monotonous. On the north side No. 1 Battery was partly employed to breach San Cristoval, and partly to enfilade the Castle front; No. 2 to breach San Cristoval; No. 3 against the defences of the same fort; and No. 4 to keep in check the tête de pont and enfilade the bridge. The breach in San Cristoval was begun in the shoulder to the right of the work, where it formed a dead angle; and in firing at this from a battery on the north side, a gun, on the very first night, became disabled by muzzle-drooping. These incidents will prepare the reader for the verdict of condemnation <small>To D.-A.-G. 26 June, 1811.</small>

which was unanimously passed on the armament of the Allied siege trains in the earlier Peninsular operations.

The howitzers were used as mortars, by taking the wheels off the carriages and inventing means of elevating them. Major Dickson had carefully tested what was the extreme elevation at which they could be used with safety, and found the *maximum* was an angle of 30°. Righteous, therefore, was his indignation when he learnt that, in spite of his own and Captain Cleeves' positive orders, an officer on duty on the north side, whom he tersely stigmatised as "a brute of a Por-" tuguese Captain," had thought proper to elevate them to 40° or 42°, with a charge of 2½ lbs. to 3 lbs., the result being that both carriages were rendered entirely unserviceable, without any means of replacing them.

On the 4th June, the fire from the south side continued, but with less effect, the shot entering the wall without bringing down any part of it worthy of mention. On this day another gun was disabled at the vent by the effect of its own fire; and one was rendered unserviceable by that of the enemy. On the 4th very considerable progress was made in the breach at San Cristoval. During the night a new battery was opened in the south attack, and the guns from No. 1 Battery removed to it.

The 5th of June was a very disheartening day. The progress in the breach of the south attack was little more hopeful than on the 4th; and before afternoon the batteries were reduced—principally by their own fire—to nine serviceable guns. Major Dickson, therefore, proceeded to Lord Wellington, and obtained his permission to bring six *iron* 24-pounders from Elvas to the south attack. The breach in San Cristoval made by the north attack made apparent progress, but was not yet deemed practicable. Here, also, one or two of the guns showed symptoms of giving way.

On the 6th June, Lieutenant Hawker of the Royal Artillery was killed in the north attack:—a gallant young officer, of whom Major Dickson wrote, " He has never been " out of No. 1 Battery from the commencement of the fire." In the south attack, a steady fire was kept up from the nine

serviceable guns during this day, and more progress was made
in breaching the wall, than had been effected during the two
preceding days. Before night, the breach was practicable for
a single person. In the evening, the breach at San Cristoval
was also considered practicable for an assault, which accordingly
was ordered, but was repulsed. The enemy had previously
cleared the breach, leaving a certain portion of the wall
standing perpendicular: and their fire was so warm that the
troops could not face it at the breach for any time. Attempts
were made to escalade at one or two other points, but the
ladders were too short; so the party had to retire with a
loss of 130 men.

On the 7th June, another battery of the south attack,
No. 3, was completed; and the iron guns, having arrived
from Elvas, were mounted during the night. The breach on
this side was a little improved, but the resistance of the
wall was far in excess of Major Dickson's expectations.

On the 8th June, under a fire from 16 24-pounders in
the south attack, the breach on that side seemed large
enough to admit several persons abreast. On the north side,
the fire continued, but the breach was not yet deemed again
practicable. During the night of the 8th, grape-shot was
fired from the south side, but the Portuguese grape was
extremely bad, and the enemy was successful in clearing
away all the rubbish from the breach, in spite of the fire,
leaving to view a considerable height of wall yet uninjured.
A quantity of 3-pounder shot was therefore brought up
from Elvas, which, when tied up in bags containing eight or
ten each, formed a better description of grape. Various
guns in both attacks showed symptoms of distress during
this day.

On the 9th June, there were only twelve or thirteen guns
left serviceable on the south side after the day's firing,
but the breach was decidedly larger, and grape was fired
all night to prevent the enemy working at it. On the north
side, there were only eight or nine guns left undisabled in
in the evening, but the breach at San Cristoval was pronounced practicable; and another attempt was made, at

9 o'clock, to carry it by assault. It was, however, again repulsed; for it was found that, notwithstanding the appearance of the breach, there was a perpendicular wall about 6 or 7 feet high still standing, which had been concealed from view by the counterscarp: and the enemy had taken every precaution to keep it clear of the *débris* of the breach. The gallantry of the assailants was as great, as the defence of the French was resolute. The ladders were thrown down, —grenades thrown among the stormers in great abundance, and masses of stone hurled down upon them. With the loss of 150 men, the assailants were obliged to retire.

<small>Major Dickson to D.-A.-G. 26 June, 1811.</small>

On the following morning it was found that the grape-shot from the south attack had been successful in preventing the enemy from working at the breach, and preparations for resuming the battering had been ordered, when Major Dickson received a summons from Lord Wellington. He met him with Colonel Fletcher on the north side: and they were informed that he had decided on raising the siege. He mentioned his reasons; but he particularly pointed out the impossibility of getting possession of San Cristoval without advancing to the crest of the *glacis*;—the still difficult situation of the main breach on the south side;—the imprudence of attempting it, even when practicable, without first having Cristoval;—the strong entrenchments which the enemy had had time to construct within the breach;—and finally the approach of the enemy in such force that prudence would not allow him to be caught by them in the midst of a siege.

<small>Dickson's MSS.</small>

Soult was at this time in force at Llerena, and Drouet's corps was reported as having joined him; while the Northern French army under Marmont was also in motion.

<small>Major Dickson to D.-A.-G. Elvas, 13 June, 1811.</small>

Major Dickson immediately set to work, and by the evening of the 12th the whole of the guns, stores, and ammunition were either in Elvas again, or at such a distance as to be in perfect safety in all circumstances.

" Thus," wrote Major Dickson to General Macleod, " ended " this siege, in which everything that artillery could do was " done, considering our miserable means; and this Lord " Wellington was good enough to express, both to Colonel

"Framingham and myself. The brass guns could not stand
"the necessary fire, and their destruction, I am of opinion,
"was considerably occasioned by the lowness of the shot,
"which generally had so much windage that you could put
"your fingers in between the shot and the bore. . . . .
"On the whole I have to observe that our batteries were
"too far off. . . . . The whole principle of the attack was
"founded on the supposed weakness of the Castle wall, which
"it was thought could be beat down at a distance. On
"discovering the difficulty of this, the batteries were thrown
"forward as far as they could, at the same time avoiding the
"fire of the modern fronts, nor could they be advanced
"farther until Cristoval was in our hands. Indeed, if that
"had been carried, I think we should have got the place.
". . . . Lord Wellington was good enough to say that every-
"thing that could be done on our parts had been done."

The casualties among the Artillery during the siege were as follows :—

		Killed.	Wounded.
Officers, Royal Artillery	Lieut. E. Hawker, killed. Lieut. W. Saunders, wounded.		
Officers, Portuguese Artillery	Captain Barreiros, wounded. Lieut. Lopez, wounded dangerously.		
N.-C. officers and men, Royal Artillery		0	4
" " Portuguese Artillery		6	28
Total		6	32

The total loss of the Allies amounted to 118 killed, and 367 wounded and taken prisoners.

In his despatch to Lord Liverpool, announcing the raising of the siege, in addition to expressing his great satisfaction with the Corps, Lord Wellington said that the British service had derived great advantage in the different operations against Badajoz from Major Dickson's zeal, activity, and intelligence.

The subsequent sieges of Ciudad Rodrigo and of Badajoz, which took place in 1812, were in marked contrast to those described in this chapter; and the rapidity with which the breaches were then made was mainly due to the employment of iron ordnance from England, instead of the miserable brass Portuguese guns which were employed in the sieges of 1811.[1] Of these guns, Lord Wellington truly said that they were very ancient and incomplete, and that their fire was very uncertain. It had at first been intended to fire at the rate of 120 rounds a gun *per diem:* but that was soon found to be impossible with the wretched brass pieces at the disposal of Major Dickson. It was therefore reduced to 80 rounds; but even with this limited expenditure the guns were repeatedly disabled by the effect of their own fire.

<small>To Lord Liverpool, 13 June, 1811.</small>

The Peninsular sieges cannot be thoroughly understood without two points being borne in mind. First, the besieged cities belonged to, and were inhabited by, the allies of England, and the war was only with the garrison. The Artillery fire, therefore, was confined to breaching, and dismounting the ordnance in battery,—not used for bombardment. Secondly, the sieges were mere episodes in Wellington's general operations, not goals to which these operations tended. Hence, in 1811, the raising of sieges, without hesitation, after but a brief continuance; and hence, also, in 1812, the rapidity and loss of life with which he stormed cities, rather than complicate his plans by indulging in siege operations of a longer and, perhaps, more regular description.

---

[1] In answer to an inquiry from General Macleod about these guns, Major Dickson, writing from Oporto, on 27 Aug. 1811, said : "They were "brass Portuguese guns of the time of John IV. and his son Alfonso, "bearing dates 1646, 1652, and 1653, &c.; also some Spanish guns of "Philips III. and IV.—dates 1620, 1636, &c."

CHAPTER XVIII.

CIUDAD RODRIGO AND BADAJOZ.

THE enemy approaching in force, after the raising of the second siege of Badajoz, the Allies crossed the river on the 17th June, 1811, and on the 19th encamped between Elvas and Campo Maior. Elvas had been put in a state of siege, and a position had been marked out behind Campo Maior, in case the French should show any inclination to attack. The bold front which Lord Wellington here showed deceived the two French Marshals, Marmont and Soult, who had now united their armies, and entered Badajoz in triumph, congratulating its gallant governor, Philippon. They concluded that he must have received great reinforcements; and although they crossed the Guadiana with a great body of cavalry supported with infantry, and one or two small affairs with the outposts took place,—they declined a general engagement. A want of *entente cordiale* between Marmont and Soult led soon to a separation,—the latter moving towards Seville, whither Wellington despatched Blake's Spanish troops,—and the former marching away by the valley of the Tagus towards Almaraz. Thus relieved of their presence, Lord Wellington took up his quarters at Pontalegre, and allowed his army to have some repose after its recent exertions.

This seems a favourable moment for placing before the reader a tabular return (*see next page*) which shows the gradual increase in the Artillery element of Lord Wellington's army in the Peninsula. Prepared from the monthly returns, it shows the numbers at different periods, distinguishing between the Royal and Foreign Artilleries. The point which will doubtless strike the reader most is the steady increase in the force of Horse Artillery and Artillery drivers, which took

Marginal notes: Major Dickson to D.-A.-Gen. dated 26 June, 1811. Cust.

RETURN of the ROYAL BRITISH and GERMAN ARTILLERY attached to the ARMY under the Command of the DUKE OF WELLINGTON in the PENINSULA and FRANCE at the undermentioned periods.

(*Extracted from the Monthly Returns.*)

	1811.		1812.			1813.		1814.	
	March.	May.	January.	April.	May.	July.	December.	January.	April.
1. General, Field, and Staff Officers, not included on Company Rolls	8	8	9	10	11	11	9	10	8
2. Royal Horse Artillery	495	499	699	728	926	998	1,016	1,007	1,012
3. Royal Foot Artillery	884	1,111	996	1,327	1,876	1,862	1,950	1,985	1,966
4. Royal Artillery Drivers	777	858	1,040	1,159	2,154	2,150	2,683	2,719	2,734
5. Ordnance Medical Staff	9	10	13	18	27	26	29	29	29
6. Field Train or Commissariat Department of the Ordnance	84	86	129	121	130	128	153	154	148
General Total of Royal British Artillery	2,257	2,572	2,891	3,363	5,124	5,165	5,840	5,904	5,897
King's German Artillery	421	412	449	434	450	446	439	439	412

N.B.—The Field Train Department attached to the Engineers is not included, as it did not appear in the Monthly Returns of the Artillery.

place; marking the growing recognition of that which had hitherto been overlooked to a great extent,—the value of mobility in Field Artillery.

General Howorth vacated the command of the Artillery in the Peninsula in July 1811, being obliged to return to England on account of ill-health,—and was shortly afterwards succeeded by General Borthwick. This officer was wounded at Ciudad Rodrigo, and returned to England,—a coolness having sprung up between him and Lord Wellington, which recurred with one of his successors, and continued until the command of the Artillery devolved upon his favourite, then *Colonel* Dickson, a few months after the siege of Burgos.

On the 19th July, 1811, Lord Wellington sent for Colonel Fletcher, Colonel Framingham, and Major Dickson, and informed them that it was his intention to attempt the siege of Ciudad Rodrigo; and after a little conversation as to the means of transport, &c., he desired Major Dickson to proceed to Oporto, to superintend the conveyance of the English battering train up the Douro to Lamego, and thence by land to Francoso, whence it would also be conveyed by land to its final destination. This battering train had arrived in Lisbon in the first instance, and had been carried secretly to Oporto, with a view to the proposed siege of Ciudad Rodrigo, its ostensible destination being Cadiz.[1] Two new companies of Artillery which had arrived in Lisbon were now ordered to Oporto to assist Major Dickson. In all these arrangements Lord Wellington underrated the strength of the French army in the north of the Peninsula.

Major Dickson reached Almeida, on his way to Oporto, on the 28th July, and arrived at the latter place on the 3rd August, where he found Captain Bredin's and Captain Glubb's companies—now H Battery, 1st Brigade, and 5 Battery 5th Brigade—waiting his orders. Before the 13th the

Major Dickson to D.-A.-Gen. dated Castello Branco, 23 July, 1811.

To D.-A.-G dated Oporto, 27 Aug. 1811.

---

[1] This battering train consisted of 78 pieces, according to Sir J. T. Jones, but, as will be seen presently, only 64 pieces went up the country with Major Dickson from Oporto.

whole of the train had been embarked in boats, about 160 in number, and despatched to Lamego; but the work and the climate proved too much for Major Dickson, and before he could follow the train he was struck down with a violent fever, accompanied by delirium. When first attacked, he requested Lord Wellington to send some one to take up his duties, and, accordingly, his friend Captain May was sent, and superintended the movement of the train until the 5th September, when the gallant Dickson, only half recovered, and travelling in a litter, arrived at Lamego. Here he found that all the guns and stores had marched for Villa da Ponte, and that Captain May was on the point of following them. On the 8th Major Dickson left Lamego, and reached Villa da Ponte on the 10th, where he fell an immediate victim to a relapse of fever, which lasted acutely several days. Captain Bredin's company had, in the meantime, been recalled to the head-quarters of the army, to take over the brigade of guns from Captain Thompson's, which was almost *hors de combat* from sickness.[1] The troops left with the battering train were therefore reduced to Captain Glubb's company of Royal Artillery, about 250 Portuguese Artillery, and from 1200 to 1400 Portuguese Militia, intended to assist on the march. Captain Holcombe's company of Royal Artillery was hourly expected. That company is now No. 4 Battery 2nd Brigade.

<small>Major Dickson to D. A. Gen. dated Villa da Ponte, 13 Sept. 1811.</small>

<small>Ibid. 20 Sept. 1811.</small>

On the march, the battering train had been arranged by Captain May as follows:—It was arranged, as far as the ordnance was concerned, in five divisions; each gun marched with 350 rounds, and each howitzer and mortar with 160 rounds. An officer was placed in charge of each division, and each division marched separately. The remaining stores and ammunition requisite to furnish a total of 800 rounds per gun, and 400 for each howitzer and mortar, were under the charge of the Commissary and other officers, and marched in rear.

---

[1] Captain Thompson's company—now D Battery, 11th Brigade—was afterwards employed in the operations on the east of Spain.

CHAP. XVIII. *Battering Train moved to Almeida.* 311

While at Villa da Ponte, awaiting orders from Lord Wellington for a further advance, Major Dickson's correspondence was of a nature which reveals to the reader more of the personal element, than his letters, as a rule, allow to become visible. The alternate hoping and despairing as to orders for advance,—the *ennui* produced by enforced idleness,—the impetuous way in which he would fling himself into professional discussions with General Macleod, merely to occupy his leisure,—the spasmodic fits of zeal in improving the arrangement of the immense train,—all unite to present to the reader a very vivid picture of him whose hand, so long still, penned these faded letters. His recurring attacks of fever—followed by apologies like the following: " The " fact is, when I am well I forget all, take violent exercise " at all times and seasons, and knock myself up; but I am " determined to be more careful in future "—followed by an inevitable relapse, in proof of the failure of his good resolutions,—combine to bring before the reader a very lovable picture of a very earnest man. It is by such study alone that the Artilleryman can realise the characters of the great among his predecessors in the Corps, and by such links that he can bind them to himself with that almost family tie, of which the Regimental union is but an expansion.

The extent of the battering train under Major Dickson's command was as follows:—34 24-pounders, 4 18-pounders, 16 iron 5½-inch howitzers, 2 8-inch howitzers, and 8 10-inch mortars; and much of his leisure at Villa da Ponte was devoted to improving and renewing the somewhat shattered carriages of this ordnance. On the 16th November he received an order from Lord Wellington to commence moving the battering train to Almeida; and by the 21st the last division, spare carriages, &c., had left. The march was most successful. No fewer than 1100 bullocks were employed for the divisions alone, apart from the reserve of stores; and in no case did the march occupy more than six days, although the country was very mountainous; nor did a single accident occur. The bringing up the reserve of ammunition and stores was delayed by want of means

To D.-A.-G. dated 27 Sept. 1811.

Ibid. 22 Nov. 1811.

Ibid. 4 Dec. 1811.

of conveyance; and pending its arrival, Lord Wellington requested Major Dickson to superintend the unspiking of the ordnance in Almeida, and the placing the batteries in a state of defence. In this occupation the reader is requested to leave him while he returns to the movements of Lord Wellington, which were now assuming an active form.

The English General had moved northward, with the view of besieging Ciudad Rodrigo; and a summary of his movements may be given from some admirable MS. letters, written by Captain May on his return to the headquarters of the army. On the 23rd September the enemy's advanced guard was near Ciudad Rodrigo. The French army was under Marmont and Dorsenne, and numbered 60,000 men, including 6000 cavalry. On the 24th, the whole of this cavalry had crossed the Agueda, about 10,000 infantry remaining on the other side. On the 25th the enemy advanced, and Wellington disputed the ground, retiring gradually to the position at Fúente de Guinaldo. In this advance the enemy's cavalry and artillery were principally engaged; and on the side of the Allies, the Cavalry, Portuguese Artillery, and Cole's and Picton's divisions of Infantry. During this forward movement the enemy, by a charge of cavalry, gained possession of five Portuguese guns, which, however, were speedily recaptured by the 5th Regiment of Foot, in a most gallant and intrepid manner. On the 26th, the Allies remained all day in the position of Guinaldo, which extended from the right and front of the town for four miles towards Ituero, the woods being occupied by two Infantry brigades from the right down to the Agueda. Thus posted, they witnessed the arrival of the whole French army, the last of which did not arrive until sunset. On satisfying himself as to their numbers, and bearing in mind the great extent of country to be watched, Lord Wellington determined to retire in the evening to a more favourable position for concentration and battle. The army, therefore, began its march to the rear at 10 P.M., and next day, the 27th, everything was in the neighbourhood of the new position, which

occupied a length of about six miles. The left was near
Rendon, on the Coa, and the right in the rear of Çouta,
resting on the mountains. When daylight revealed to the
enemy the masterly retreat which had taken place, some
cavalry and infantry were pressed forward, and the Allied
piquets were driven in; but Wellington, suddenly assuming
the offensive, drove them back from Alfaites to Aldea da
Ponte, his troops occupying the latter village. After sunset,
however, the enemy advanced in such force, in front and
also on the flanks of the village, that the officer commanding there wisely withdrew his troops to Alfaites. This
final advance of the French was made to cover a retreat
which had now been determined on. On the morning of the
28th nothing could be seen of them; and on the 29th it
was learnt that they were moving back on Ciudad Rodrigo.
After they had thrown provisions into that city, they continued to retire, and went into cantonments in the neighbourhood of Salamanca. The British army did the same
between the Coa and the Agueda, Lord Wellington, with his
head-quarters at Freneda, keeping watch on the city which
he had determined to take.

The only brilliant affair which took place between this
time and the successful sieges, which will now have to be
mentioned, was the surprise of Girard's division by General
Hill, at Arroyo de Molinos. As, however, the Artillery with
Hill's force was Portuguese,—Major Hawker's 9-pounder
brigade of Royal Artillery having been unable to get up on
account of the state of the roads,—its further notice in this
work will be unnecessary.

Taking advantage of the French troops being scattered in
their cantonments, and having ascertained that large reinforcements from Marmont's army had been detached to
Valencia, Lord Wellington resolved on a short, sharp siege
of Ciudad Rodrigo. In the end of December he sent for Major
Major Dickson, and directed him to move forward the bat- Dickson to D.-A.-Gen.
tering train and stores from Almeida, Galegos being made 1 Jan.
the intermediate depôt. To the latter place the army 1812.
head-quarters were moved on the 7th January.

The main interest to the military reader in the sieges of Ciudad Rodrigo and Badajoz, in 1812, attaches to the gallantry of the Infantry. The monotonous, albeit shortlived, work in the batteries is drowned in the recollection of the scenes of valour at the final assault. In these pages, therefore, the Artillery share in the sieges will assume, of necessity, the form of a few dry statistics.

The Artillery present at the siege included 185 of the Royal Artillery and 370 of the Portuguese. The names of the officers of the Royal Artillery who were present were General Borthwick, Major Dickson, Captains Holcombe, Thompson, Power, Dundas, and Dyneley; Lieutenants Bourchier, Love, Johnstone, Ingilby, Smith, and Grimes; and Captain May, Brigade-Major.

The batteries opened in the afternoon of the 14th January, 1812, the guns having narrowly escaped being spiked in the morning of that day. On the night of the 19th, the breaches were pronounced practicable, and Wellington announced in orders, "Ciudad Rodrigo *must* be stormed this "evening." Except on the 16th and part of the 17th, the weather was clear and admirably suited for artillery practice, and the batteries were in action daily for an average of eight and a half hours.

The guns employed were as follows:—On January 14th, 20 24-pounders and 2 18-pounders; on January 15th, 23 24-pounders and 2 18-pounders; on January 16th and 17th, the same; on January 18th, 30 24-pounders and 2 18-pounders; and on January 19, 30 24-pounders.[1]

The expenditure of ammunition during this short siege was as follows,—the total number of guns in battery having been 34 24-pounders, and 4 18-pounders :—

24-pr. guns : Round shot, 8950. Rounds expended per gun, 263.
18-pr. guns : Round shot, 565. Rounds expended per gun, 141.

---

[1] According to Sir J. Jones, the guns in action on the 19th were 29 24-prs. and 1 18-pr.; but Sir A. Dickson, who was in charge of the Artillery, says as above. The difference is, however, infinitesimal.

CHAP. XVIII.   *Losses of the Artillery.*   315

The absence of mortars and howitzers from this siege was explained by the increased amount of transport required for shell, compared with shot, and by the fact that Lord Wellington had resolved on an assault the moment a breach was practicable, without any other siege operations. Shot were, therefore, all that was necessary, except for keeping the enemy from working at the breach.

The following extract from a letter written by Major Dickson after the siege, is interesting:—"Lord Wellington <small>To D.-A.-G. dated 29 Jan. 1812.</small>
" has certainly made a most brilliant *coup*, and, I am con-
" vinced, astonished the enemy by the rapidity of his opera-
" tions. They intended to relieve the place and raise the
" siege about this day (29th January). We were certainly
" favoured by the most delightful weather—excessively cold,
" but perfectly dry. It was not even necessary to put the
" powder under the laboratory tents, which I was enabled
" to spare to keep the poor fellows from the pinching frost;
" for we were nearly without cover. . . . . . . I am hard
" pressed for time, but I must say a word in favour of our
" fine fellows of the Corps. They were (Portuguese and all)
" at relief and relief, off and on; but nothing could exceed
" their zeal and activity, and their work speaks for itself.
" *Never was better practice made.* I had only 430 Artillery-
" men of both nations,—about 130 British, and the rest
" Portuguese. We had somewhere more than 50 Artillery-
" men killed and wounded, but no officer materially hurt.
" The latter days, to make it up, I had some help from our
" own field Artillery:—part of Lawson's company was one
" day in the trenches, and part of Sympher's German com-
" pany another."

The actual number of killed and wounded between the <small>MS. Return dated 26 Jan. 1812.</small>
14th and 19th January,—while the siege lasted,—was as follows (excluding Portuguese Artillery):—[1]

<small>Captains Dyneley and Power, wounded.
Captain Glubb's company, now 5 Battery, 5th Brigade; 2 gunners died of their wounds; 2 gunners wounded slightly.</small>

---

[1] Sir J. Jones's statement *includes* the Portuguese Artillery.

Captain Holcombe's company, now 4 Battery, 2nd Brigade; 1 gunner killed; 17 non-commissioned officers and men wounded.
Captain Lawson's company, now H Battery, 8th Brigade; 1 gunner died of his wounds; 2 gunners wounded.
Captain Sympher's company (K.G.A.); 1 gunner killed; 3 gunners wounded.

The ammunition expended was:—8950 rounds from 24-pounders, and 565 from 18-pounders.

To Lord Liverpool, dated 20 Jan. 1812.

In Lord Wellington's despatch, announcing the successful termination of the siege, he—after extolling Major Dickson's conduct of the Artillery operations—proceeded to say: " The rapid execution produced by the well directed fire " kept up from our batteries affords the best proof of the " merits of the officers and men of the Royal Artillery, and " of the Portuguese Artillery, employed on this occasion; " but I must particularly mention Brigade-Major May, and " Captains Holcombe, Power, Dyneley, and Dundas, of the " Royal Artillery."

General Borthwick's name is not mentioned, either in the despatch or among the wounded; but he appears in 'Kane's List'—generally most accurate in its details—as having been in command of the Artillery, and also as having been wounded, during the siege.

Ciudad Rodrigo had hardly fallen before Lord Wellington resolved to attempt a third siege of Badajoz,—now that he had suitable ordnance. He ordered Major Dickson to proceed on the 30th January to Setubal, calling at Elvas to make some necessary arrangements. From Setubal he was directed to send 16 24-pounders of a new battering train, which had arrived, to Elvas,—as well as 20 guns of the same calibre, which were to be furnished from the navy. The whole of these guns were to travel on block carriages. The difficulty of sending the heavy guns of the train at Almeida to Elvas led to this arrangement: but it was decided to send the 24-pounder howitzers, as being much lighter, and also a number of 24-pounder carriages, which were stored at Almeida. By this means it was hoped to have speedily equipped at Elvas a new battering train of 36 iron 24-pounder guns, and 16 24-pounder howitzers,—an armament

Third Siege of Badajoz.

very different from the brass Portuguese guns which had assailed the stronghold of Philippon twice before.

So incessant was the work which now devolved on Major Dickson that he had no time for correspondence, and there is a great blank, where the student had hoped to find much that was interesting. From other sources, therefore, the Artillery details of a siege, which can never be forgotten, must be procured. As at Ciudad Rodrigo, the Infantry share in the operations dwarfs all other;—but it dwarfs it to even a greater extent. The story of the storming of Badajoz is one which will thrill the heart of every Briton for all time; which will bind together by sacred memories the regiments which were so nobly represented on that day; and which will impress on all, who study it, the truth of Napier's words, that "a British army bears with it an "awful power." The scene on the night of the 6th April, 1812, was one before which the energy, zeal, and proficiency of the Artillery on the preceding days pale away into nothingness; and the chronicling of their humble statistics seems almost an impertinence. For, the night of the 6th was, indeed, one in which "many died, and there was much Napier. " glory;" it was one in which death took many and hideous forms,—" the slain dying not all suddenly, nor by one " manner of death; some perishing by steel, some by shot, " some by water, some crushed and mangled by heavy " weights, some trampled upon, some dashed to atoms by " fiery explosions;" and yet it was a night in which the most cruel death was fair to look on,—because hallowed by marvellous courage and rare devotion.

The breaches, which were rendered famous by this combat Tables " so fiercely fought, so terribly won," were virtually made published by an between the 30th March and the 6th April. On the 30th officer of March 8 18-pounders were in action for purely breaching in 1819. purposes; on the following day, this number was increased, by 12 24-pounders, and 6 18-pounders, to 26 guns; and these remained in action, for 13 hours a day, until the storming of the place. Of round shot, alone, no fewer than 18,832 24-pr., and 13,029 18-pr., were expended during the short siege; besides 1163 24-pounder grape shot, and 496 of the same from the 18-pounders. Of the round shot, 23,896 were employed in forming the three breaches. Besides the breaching guns, there were 10 24-pounder and 18-pounder guns, and 16 5½-inch howitzers, employed for enfilading and other fire. From the last mentioned, 507 common shell and 1319 spherical case were fired during the siege.

<small>Tables published by an officer of Artillery in 1819.</small> The three breaches were rendered practicable from a distance of between 600 and 700 yards; and the curtain breach was made in one day, the day of the assault. To the rapidity of the making of this breach was much of the success in the final storming due; because, had several days been required, measures would have been adopted by the defenders during the intervening nights to render it wholly impracticable. In making this curtain-breach, 14 guns were employed, with an expenditure of 3514 rounds.

Colonel Framingham commanded the Allied Artillery during the siege, but Major Dickson virtually directed the operations. From a rough MS. diary in the Record Office, in the handwriting of the latter officer, it would appear that the strength of the Artillery was as follows:—

	N.-C. officers and men.
Captain Holcombe's company	110
Captain Gardiner's ditto[1]	110
Captain Glubb's (commanded by Captain Power) company	78
Captain Rettberg's (King's German Artillery) ditto	30

There were also 377 of the 3rd Regiment, and 249 of the 2nd Regiment, of Portuguese Artillery.

<small>To Lord Liverpool, 7 April, 1812.</small> In his despatch, after the storming of the city, Lord Wellington said: "Major Dickson conducted the details of "the Artillery service during this siege, as well as upon "former occasions, under the general superintendence "of Lieut.-Colonel Framingham, who, since the absence of "Major-General Borthwick, has commanded the Artillery

---

[1] Now No. 7 Battery, 17th Brigade R.A., Captain Gardiner having been posted *vice* Raynsford.

"with this army. I cannot sufficiently applaud the officers and soldiers of the British and Portuguese Artillery during this siege, particularly Lieut.-Colonel Robe, who opened the breaching batteries, Majors May and Holcombe, Captain Gardiner and Lieutenant Bourchier, of the Royal Artillery; Captain de Rettberg, of the King's German Artillery; and Major Tulloh, of the Portuguese. Adverting to the extent of the details of the Ordnance Department during this siege, to the difficulty of weather, &c., with which Major Dickson had to contend, I must mention him most particularly to your Lordship." Besides the officers named in the despatch, there were present in the batteries Captains Power, Latham, Dundas, and Dansey; and Lieutenants Weston, Connel, Grimes, and Love.

The loss of the Royal Artillery during the siege was as follows:—

Killed: Captain Latham, Lieutenant Connel, and 23 non-commissioned officers and men.
Wounded: Captain Dundas, Lieutenants Grimes and Love, and 48 non-commissioned officers and men.[1]
Major Tulloh, an officer of the Royal Artillery attached to the Portuguese, was also wounded.

The troops of Horse Artillery commanded by Majors Bull and Ross were present at the investment and siege of Badajoz; and although not included in the detail made out by Major Dickson for duty in the trenches, it is evident that they must have taken part in the operations, for Major Ross was severely wounded by a grape-shot. But his name does not appear in Lord Wellington's lists. *Major Ross to Sir H. Dalrymple, 8 April, 1812.*

The losses in the other arms of the service employed in the siege were very great. No fewer than 5000 officers and men fell during the siege, and of that number 3500 fell on the night of the 6th April. Sixty officers and upwards of seven hundred men were slain on the spot.

---

[1] These numbers, which differ from those given by Napier, are taken from the official MS. Regimental Returns prepared immediately after the siege, which include all, even *slightly* wounded. Doubtless many such were not included in the Army returns.

Napier.

No wonder that, " when the extent of the night's havoc " was made known to Lord Wellington, the firmness of his " nature gave way for a moment, and the pride of conquest " yielded to a passionate burst of grief for the loss of his " gallant soldiers."

The recollections of such a night are among the greatest treasures which an army can cherish. Even the reaction after success, the irregularities and licence displayed by the troops in the captured city, while certainly dimming, could not permanently injure the glory of the marvellous assault. Such traditions are a weapon for discipline, which only a soldier can estimate. Inspired by them, men will feed the lamp of their present lives with the oil of past glory, and strain every nerve to make the flame burn pure and clear.

Perhaps one of the highest motives, which can influence a soldier, is the desire to be worthy of his predecessors, and true to the reputation which they have earned for their corps. It carries him at once out of himself, and introduces an unselfish element even into his own ambition and aims. Only those who have served long in a regiment which they love can understand the fond jealousy for its honour, which will inspire its members. Its history never dies; the deeds of the years that are gone are the living possession of all; the valour which may have been exhibited in former days lives again in the breasts of those who hunger for an opportunity of similar display; and the men who, by their courage and skill, may have earned honour for their corps, still haunt in no shadowy form the dreams of the young aspirant, and the memories of the old.

NOTE.—In alluding to the services of the two scientific corps at this siege of Badajoz, Sir J. Jones wrote that "as an engineer and artillery " operation, it succeeded to the utmost letter."

CHAPTER XIX.

SALAMANCA AND BURGOS.

AFTER the fall of Badajoz, Lord Wellington decided on marching northward, and carrying the war into Spain. In the meantime, however, he directed General Hill to storm the forts at Almaraz, a great French depôt,—and so weaken the chance of union between the armies of the North and South. Colonel Dickson[1] was detailed as commanding officer of the Artillery for this service, which consisted of a brigade of 24-pounder howitzers, horsed by the mules of one of the Portuguese Field Brigades, and manned by Captain Glubb's company of the Royal Artillery, and a Portuguese company. The ammunition, which was carried in Spanish mule carts, comprised 600 24-pounder round shot, 300 5½-inch common shells, 240 5½-inch spherical and 60 5½-inch common,—case shot. Six pontoons accompanied the guns on this expedition,.which was perfectly successful; and in which General Hill was pleased to say that he found the exertions of Colonel Dickson, and his officers and men, to be unwearied. *To D.-A.-G. dated Elvas, 6 May, 1812.* *General Sir R. Hill to Lord Wellington, dated 21 May, 1812.*

Before turning to Lord Wellington's movements in the north, which culminated in the battle of Salamanca, and the temporary occupation of Madrid, a statement of the strength of the Artillery force of England during this eventful year may possibly be found interesting. Two dates have been chosen, and it will be seen that the numbers—already large in the beginning of the year—continued to increase; more especially in the item of

---

[1] The rank of Lieut.-Colonel had at first been conferred on him by the Portuguese government. He received the same—by brevet—from the English Government on 27th April, 1812.

drivers for the brigades in the Peninsula. These tables give one an idea of the strain on the resources of England which was caused by the Peninsular War. No fewer than 1811 recruits had joined the Artillery alone in the previous year, and over 1200 became non-effective from various causes during the same period.

MS. 'Wear and Tear Return' of the Regiment for 1811.

RETURN of the ARTILLERY FORCES OF ENGLAND on the 25th June, 1812, distinguishing the ROYAL ARTILLERY from the ROYAL HORSE ARTILLERY, and specifying the Numbers serving at home and abroad.

	AT HOME.		ABROAD.		TOTAL.	
	Officers.	N.-C. Officers and Men.	Officers.	N.-C. Officers and Men.	Officers.	N.-Com. Officers and Men.
Royal Horse Artillery . .	49	1,417	21	696	70	2,113
Royal Artillery . . .	391	8,812	331	6,599	722	15,411
R. A. Drivers	63	3,521	24	1,950	87	5,471
King's German Artillery .	21	430	28	587	49	1,017
Royal Foreign Artillery .	6	158	15	327	21	485
General Total . .	..	..	..	..	949	24,497

RETURN of the ARTILLERY FORCES of ENGLAND on 25th Dec. 1812, &c.

Royal Horse Artillery . .	51	1,452	19	733	70	2,185
Royal Artillery	405	8,723	333	6,817	738	15,540
R. A. Drivers	70	3,554	25	2,305	95	5,859
King's German Artillery .	21	392	27	638	48	1,030
Royal Foreign Artillery .	7	123	15	348	22	471
General Total . .	..	..	..	..	973	25,085

The year 1812 was the most eventful in the Peninsular War. Already marked by the successful sieges described in the last chapter, it was to be distinguished by events, both in Spain and elsewhere, destined to have a great effect on subsequent hostilities. The English General — who opened the year with an unexpected attack on Ciudad Rodrigo—was destined, ere it should be much more than half over, to defeat his enemy in a pitched battle, drive him ignominiously before him, and enter the capital of Spain in triumph. These successes were to be further heightened by Soult raising the long-continued siege of Cadiz, in alarm at the intelligence of the French disasters in the north. Scarcely, however, were these advantages to be realised, ere the whole picture should change. The conqueror at Ciudad Rodrigo and Badajoz should find himself fretting hopelessly before the castle of Burgos; and the General, who entered Madrid in triumph at the head of a victorious army, should lead that same army—in disorder and semi-mutiny—from Salamanca to Portugal, in retreat. The light and shade in the military operations of the Peninsula were also to be intensified by news from without, which should mightily affect the powers whose armies had faced one another for so many years. Another war should be thrust upon England's preoccupied people;—her own children in America should seize the opportunity of gratifying a seemingly undying jealousy;—while, away in the colds of Russia, the greatest army that even Napoleon had ever commanded, should dissolve, as utterly as the snows amid which they died should melt before the strengthening sun.

It was, indeed, a year of great events: but of these the two in which this history has most interest were the battle of Salamanca and the siege of Burgos.

Colonel Dickson, with the brigade of howitzers which he had commanded at Almaraz, left Elvas on the 5th June to join Lord Wellington's army in the north. Passing the Tagus at Alcantara, he joined the army at Salamanca by way of Zarza, Fuente Guinalda, and Ciudad Rodrigo. Wellington was engaged at this time, with very limited means, in endeavouring to reduce the French Fort St. Vincent at Salamanca, a strongly entrenched work, having a large convent as its stronghold, and mounted with 36 pieces of

Colonel Dickson to D.-A.-Gen. dated Orbada, 30 June, 1812.

ordnance. The Allied siege Artillery—previous to Colonel Dickson's arrival—consisted of only 4 18-pounder guns, and a battery of long 6-pounders, under Lieut.-Colonel May.[1] That officer had performed his duty, with inadequate means, in a manner which called forth universal admiration; and Colonel Dickson, when he arrived with his howitzers to assist him, expressed the great satisfaction it afforded him to be able now to repay, in a small degree, the many acts of kindness and co-operation, which he had enjoyed at Colonel May's hands. Several points of the defence were breached by the fire of the Allied Artillery, but the whole work was so strong, and the defences so connected, that no assault could be attempted on the body of the work. An assault made on two outworks failed at first, but the gorge of one of them having been subsequently breached, they were carried with little or no loss a few hours before the surrender of the chief fort. The means at their disposal being very small, Colonels May and Dickson employed hot shot from the howitzers against the Convent, and succeeded, after firing 260 rounds, in setting fire to it, and destroying the whole of the enemy's provisions. The surrender followed almost immediately. These operations had been mainly conducted by General Clinton, under the supervision of Lord Wellington; and, in his despatch, Lord Wellington reported that that officer had mentioned in strong terms Lieut.-Colonel May, who commanded the Royal Artillery under the direction of Colonel Framingham, and the officers and men under his command. The capture of the forts was delayed until the 27th June, it having been necessary to send to the rear for more ammunition, a step which caused a delay of six days. As soon as they fell, the French army commenced to retire, pursued by the Allies.

Despatch dated Fuente la Pena, 30 June,

The loss of the Royal Artillery at the siege of these forts was as follows:—

Killed: Captain Eligé, and 9 rank and file.

Wounded: 1 lieutenant (Love), and 25 rank and file.

---

[1] Appointed Brevet Lieut.-Colonel on 27th April, 1812.

In the various movements of both armies between the 27th June and the 22nd July, 1812, on which day the great engagement known as the battle of Salamanca was fought, no use appears to have been made of the Artillery, with the exception of the Horse Artillery attached to the Cavalry division. In one affair, on the 18th July, at Castrejou, when the troops under Sir Stapleton Cotton were attacked, Lieutenant Belson, an officer in the Chestnut Troop, was wounded. For honest, conscientious hard work, and staunch performance of his duty, this officer was unsurpassed by any in the Regiment. On reference to his record of service, it appears that between the 3rd August, 1809, and 14th April, 1814, Lieutenant Belson was present in no fewer than thirty-three engagements. Beside such services, which received but little official recognition, those of men in more recent campaigns, who have received lavish, although merited, rewards, sink into insignificance.

It is impossible, without exceeding the limits of this work, to describe in detail the services of the Horse Artillery in the Peninsula,—the branch of the regiment to which young Belson belonged. The tables at the end of the preceding volume give some idea of what these services were, but are totally inadequate. The history of some of the individual troops would alone fill a volume; and the writing of such a history will doubtless be undertaken by some officer, who may find himself in the proud position of commanding one. Their active duties were incessant; even during the sieges, when they ostensibly formed part of the armies of investment or observation, they were ready to volunteer at all times to do additional duty in the trenches. At San Sebastian, as will be seen shortly, their services in the sieges, as siege artillerymen, were invaluable. The details of their services in the great battle now to be described are, unfortunately, not given in any of the documents in the Record Office. The fact of the presence of three troops, Ross's, Bull's, and Macdonald's, is known, but little more. They were included in the general mention of the Corps, by Lord Wellington, after the battle, when he said that "The Royal and German Artillery under Lieute-"nant-Colonel Framingham distinguished themselves by "the accuracy of their fire;" but no further details are given. From another pen we learn that the whole of the troops and batteries were more or less engaged during the eventful day; but this general statement is neither satisfying, nor quite exact. In a letter from Colonel Dickson, written three days after the battle, he mentions that one of his heavy brigades was not ordered up, but was kept in the rear, ready to move in case of retreat. Possibly this brigade may have been manned by Portuguese, and the howitzer brigade, which he commanded during the battle, may have been manned by Captain Glubb's company, which was under his orders;—in which case the author referred to would be right; but it is extremely rare in Colonel Dickson's correspondence to find him alluding to any action, in which he commanded men of his own Corps, without particularizing some by name. On the other hand, it must be admitted that Napier describes Colonel Dickson's howitzers as being manned by British and Portuguese brigaded together.

Lord Wellington's letters show that he was by no means anxious for a general action at this time, if it could have been avoided; and this fact was apparent to those around him. When it was inevitable, he found that the enemy had a better position than himself; and but for the unexpected opening given by Marmont, in the over extension of his left, it would have been a very doubtful issue. "I "really believe," wrote Colonel Dickson, "that Lord "Wellington fought against his inclination, and that if "Marmont by his manœuvres had not pushed him so hard, "he would quietly have fallen back, and relinquished "Salamanca to the French. The audacity of the enemy "was such, however, that British honour required it should "be checked; and most severely Marshal Marmont has "been punished for playing tricks with such a leader as "Lord Wellington. When at last his Lordship determined "to attack the attacker, his dispositions were splendid, and "his operations rapid and overpowering. I can compare

"the close-fighting part of the battle more to one of those
"battles between the French and Spaniards, of which there
"have been so many, with always the same result, than to a
"contest between armies equally powerful. It was a rapid
"succession of overthrows, with some failures, but none
"that for a moment impeded the grand result."

There were two hills on the left of the Allied line, called Dos Arapiles or Los Hermanitos, situated within easy artillery range of one another. The French had obtained possession of the loftier of these, and by this means had acquired an undoubted advantage. But this advantage was modified by the artillery fire on the left of Lord Wellington's line, which was very effective. It was here that Colonel Dickson's howitzer brigade was in action, taking part in an Artillery duel, which is mentioned in the correspondence of several Artillery officers who took part in it. Major Macdonald, who commanded a troop of Horse Artillery on the occasion, said that the French artillerymen were driven from their guns on the hill opposite, and prevented from returning, by the destructive fire of Shrapnel shell from the English guns. In another letter, from an officer who was also present, the same statement is endorsed; and the reader learns that the brigades of Artillery chiefly engaged were Ross's, Bull's, and Macdonald's troops, Colonel Dickson's and Captain Douglas's brigades, and Major Sympher's of the King's German Artillery. From the same sources it is ascertained that in the staunch final advance of the enemy against the village of the Arapiles, the fire of Shrapnel shell from the howitzers of the English Artillery produced great effect; and that, on another important occasion during the battle, a battery of the enemy's guns was disabled by the same means. It will be in the recollection of the military student that Marmont's extension and weakening of his left sprang from a desire to cut off the retreat of the Allies on Ciudad Rodrigo, while he should yet retain the strong position on his right, afforded by the possession of the hill already mentioned. The division Thomières was selected for the flank movement, and against it Pakenham's division was

[margin notes: To Colonel Shrapnel, dated 9 May, 1813. Lieut. Sinclair, R.A., to Colonel Shrapnel, dated 22 Oct. 1814.]

despatched by Lord Wellington, accompanied by 12 guns. The service performed by these guns was most valuable. Being placed in a commanding position, they suddenly took the French troops in flank, and aided materially in ensuring a victory, which Lord Wellington's quick judgment and military skill had placed in the way of his troops. Then followed the stern battle all along the line, which resulted in the "beating of forty thousand men in forty minutes;" the French seeing General after General fall, and fighting at times in bewilderment, for want of orders;—the English fighting with all the courage of their race, and all the confidence which a General like Wellington inspired,—who seemed to be always at the right place at the right time:— then the French falling back from their first position only to make a new effort; and then the utter rout and confusion, redeemed but by the coolness and skill of the brave Foy, who with his rear-guard strove to cover the headlong flight of the others.

The strength of the Allied army at Salamanca was 46,000, that of the French 42,000; but the superiority in point of numbers on the side of the Allies was caused by the presence of some utterly useless Spanish troops. The French had 74 guns on the field, the Allies only 60. These, according to Napier, were as follows:—

Royal Horse Artillery. Three troops	18 guns.
Royal Foot Artillery. Two 9-pounder brigades ..	12 ,,
Royal Foot Artillery. Two 12-pounder ,, ..	12 ,,
King's German Artillery. One 9-pounder ,, ..	6 ,,
Portuguese and British brigaded together	6 24-pr. howitzers.
One Spanish battery	6 guns.
Total	60 pieces.

There would certainly appear to be an error in this statement. In none of Colonel Dickson's manuscripts can it be traced that there were more than five 24-pounder howitzers with his brigades; it would therefore seem that the strength of the Allied Artillery at Salamanca was even more disproportionate than that given, and that Lord Wellington had only 59 guns against Marmont's 74.

The losses on both sides at Salamanca were very heavy. The Allies lost 1 General, 24 officers, and 686 men killed; and 5 Generals, 182 officers, and 4270 men wounded. The loss of the French has never been exactly stated. They lost 7000 prisoners alone, besides 11 guns and other trophies. An approximation to their real loss has been obtained by taking General Clausel's statement of the army on the 18th of the following month. He had succeeded Marshal Marmont in the command, on the latter being wounded; and on the 18th August he reported that the army, which had been 42,000 strong on the 22nd July, had fallen to 21,800, with 50 instead of 74 guns. Much of the loss may have occurred during the pursuit after the battle, but the whole was virtually attributable to the contest of the 22nd. Cust's 'Annals of the Wars.'

Important as the results of the victory were, they would have been more so had not the retreat of the French across the Tormes been facilitated by a blunder of the Spanish General, Espana, who left the bridge of Alba open to them. This enabled Clausel to get as far as Peneranda with far less punishment than an army so beaten as his was should have received from his pursuers.[1] Wellington followed him to Valladolid, but failed to overtake him; so, while Clausel continued his flight to Burgos, Wellington, after a pause of some days, turned towards Madrid, to free the capital from the presence of Joseph Buonaparte and his army.[2] He

---

[1] "A few days after the battle of Salamanca, the troop of Horse Artillery, under Captains Lefebure and Whinyates (which was on the Tagus with Hill's force), distinguished itself in a brilliant affair, resulting in the total defeat of the French cavalry at Ribera. Major-General Long, who commanded, spoke in the highest terms of all the troops under his command, particularly the Horse Artillery, who displayed great activity in their movements, and rapidity in their fire."—BROWNE.

[2] "On the 10th August an engagement took place with a body of the enemy's cavalry which had been sent forward to watch the movements of the Allies. This force was driven in by General D'Urban, but made another attack. General D'Urban ordered the Portuguese cavalry, with

entered it in state on the 12th August, Joseph having quitted it without waiting for the Allies ; and he remained there until the 1st September, receiving from the Spaniards a perpetual ovation, and learning from England how valuable his services were deemed, by their further recognition in the form of a Marquisate.

Affairs in the Peninsula forbade longer repose, nor was Wellington the man to risk his army finding a Capua in Madrid. Soult, alarmed at the news from the north, raised the siege of Cadiz, and let Seville fall into the hands of the Allies, while he moved northward himself. An expedition from Sicily landed in the east of Spain, to co-operate with Lord Wellington, of which it must suffice here to say that the Royal Artillery accompanying it was commanded by Captain—then Brevet Lieut.-Colonel—Holcombe, the same officer whose company had been at the sieges of Ciudad Rodrigo and Badajoz. And, lastly, the French General, Clausel, had reorganized his army, and was taking the offensive against the Allied troops left in the north. Of the operations of Wellington to check this General, and to defeat him again before Soult's army could join him from the south, it is proposed to select one, as being a specially Artillery subject—the siege of the Castle of Burgos.

Dickson's MSS.

After the fall of the forts at Salamanca, the heavy Artillery employed there continued to be attached to the reserve Artillery under Colonel Dickson, and followed the movements of the army during the campaign. It consisted of three 18-pounder guns on travelling carriages, and five 24-pounder howitzers, to which were attached Captain Glubb's company of the Royal Artillery, commanded by Captain Power, and a company of Portuguese Artillery,

---

" which was Captain Macdonald's troop of Horse Artillery, to charge.
" Before reaching the enemy they were seized with panic and fled, leaving
" Macdonald's guns, which had been moved forward in support, utterly
" unprotected. The exertions of the troop got the guns moved off, but
" owing to the state of the ground, three got damaged and fell with
" Captain Dynely and their detachments into the enemy's hands."—
BROWNE.

commanded by Major Arriaga, with some additional detachments of the Artillery of both nations. After the battle of Salamanca, the whole eight pieces were brought forward to the neighbourhood of Madrid, preparatory to the attack of Fort la Chine, which was still occupied by the French, but which ultimately surrendered without a contest. On the 1st September, Lord Wellington quitted Madrid, to proceed to Arevalo, where the 1st, 5th, 6th, and 7th Divisions were ordered to assemble preparatory to a movement to the northward; and Colonel Dickson, with his 18-pounders and howitzers, was ordered to accompany this corps.

Previous to this movement, measures had been taken to bring forward from Ciudad Rodrigo the following proportion of ammunition, viz.—

24-pr. round shot 600
18-pr ,, ... 800
with powder, and all necessary small stores.

On the 9th September, this small siege-train arrived at Valladolid, and on the following day continued its march towards Burgos. On the 19th, the Castle of Burgos was invested, the Artillery park being formed near Villa Toro.

That Lord Wellington undertook this siege with wholly inadequate means has been well known; but how inadequate these means were will appear from the following statement. First, as regards *personnel*: how many Artillerymen had he to carry on the duties in the batteries against a place which held a commanding situation, and was powerfully armed? He had merely

	No. of men.
Capt. Glubb's company, under Capt Power ..	45
Lieut.-Col. May's company under Lieut. Elgee	45
Major Arriaga's company of Portuguese Artillery	57
Total	147

As mentioned above, he had only eight guns; and the following was the total ammunition of all sorts, including the additional supply from Ciudad Rodrigo.

24-pr. round shot	.. 900	18-pr. round shot	.. 1306
24-pr. common shell	208	18-pr. spherical case	.. 100
24-pr. spherical case	236		

To swell this amount, Colonel Dickson offered a reward for bringing in any shot fired by the enemy. He found that the enemy's 16-pounder shot fitted his own 18-pounder guns, and that his 8-pounder shot would fit the 9-pounders of the English field brigades. Before the end of September, about 1400 shot were brought in, in this way. Colonel Dickson also obtained detachments from the Horse and Field Brigades occasionally, to give his siege artillerymen relief; but the duties of the Field Artillery were so active at this time round Burgos that men could with difficulty be spared.

The names of the officers of the Royal Artillery engaged in the siege were as follows:—

Lieutenant-Colonel Robe, commanding.
Lieutenant-Colonel Dickson, in immediate charge of the operation.

Captain Power
Lieutenant Robe
Lieutenant Pascoe } Present during the whole operation.
Lieutenant Elgee
Lieutenant Hough

Captain Greene
Captain Dansey
Captain Gardiner } Belonging to Field Brigades, but occasionally employed.
Lieutenant Monro
Lieut. Johnstone

Captain Blachley, joined 1st October.

Of the Royal Artillery, small in numbers, the casualties were very great in proportion. Fifteen men were killed, and forty wounded, during the siege, and in the operations immediately attending or succeeding it. The officers who were wounded were Colonel Robe, Captains Dansey and Power, Lieutenants Elgee and Johnstone.

After severe loss, a hornwork in front of the castle had been carried by assault on the night of the 19th September, and on the following night a battery for five guns was commenced. This battery was armed on the night of the 22nd with two 18-pounders and three 24-pounder howitzers, in readiness to open on the inner lines, in the event of an assault, which had been determined on for that evening on the outer line, proving successful. At the same time, a second battery for six guns was commenced to fire against the keep of the castle. The assault, which was premature, failed; and its leader was killed. On the night of the 24th, the two 18-pounders were taken out of No. 1 Battery, and drawn along a trench, part of the way towards No. 2, being replaced in the former by howitzers. On the 25th, the five howitzers in No. 1 Battery opened a fire to destroy some palisades, which were used to flank the works of the castle. The fire was not successful; the howitzers were found to be very deficient in precision when firing round shot; and the result was inadequate to the expenditure of ammunition,— 141 rounds,—a consideration of some importance under the existing circumstances.[1] Lord Wellington, conscious of the deficiency of his guns, worked now by means of mining; and on the night of the 29th September, a mine was sprung which threw down part of the outer wall. An assault was immediately ordered; but from the darkness of the night the detachment missed its way, and those who were leading— having gained the top of the breach—were driven down again for want of support. The whole, therefore, returned to the trenches.

On the 30th September, the howitzers in No. 1 Battery were of essential service. About 10 A.M. they opened fire, with the addition of a French 6-pounder gun, taken in the hornwork, to demolish a stockade upon the top of a tower in the outer line a little to the enemy's right of the breach, from which the French with musketry annoyed the English in the sap,—the fire being so close that every man, who exposed himself in the slightest degree, was sure to be hit.

---

[1] "The total, expenditure of ammunition during the siege was as "follows:—

" 920 24-pr. round shot   288 French 4-pr. round shot.
1854 18-pr. ,,   203 24-pr. common shell.
333 French 8-pr. round shot. 182 ,,   spherical case.
90 ,,   6-pr. ,,   192 French 6-pr. shot."
—JONES's 'Peninsular Sieges.'

The stockade was strengthened by sand bags, &c., but, after three hours' firing, it was utterly destroyed. The ammunition expended for this purpose was 136 rounds;—90 24-pounder shot, 40 6-pounder French shot, and 6 5½-inch common shell. It was on this day that Captain Dansey, who had volunteered for service in the trenches, was wounded.

The next episode in the Artillery portion of the siege was the moving the three 18-pounders into a breaching battery so close to the outer wall, that the guns of the upper work could not bear on them. The French commander, Dubreton, lost no time, however, in bringing down a howitzer and a light gun from the upper work, followed by others as quickly as he could; and as the breaching battery was very slight, the result was serious. "The defences of the battery were "quite demolished, two of the gun-carriages were disabled, "a trunnion was knocked off one of the 18-pounders, and the "muzzle of another was split." A second, stronger, breaching battery was then formed, but the plunging fire from the castle was too severe; the guns which were yet serviceable were therefore removed back to No. 1 Battery, on the hill of San Michael. From this position, on the morning of the 4th October, they opened again on the old breach; and a mine having been exploded with great effect in the same evening, another assault took place,—the fourth during the siege. This was more successful, and a lodgment was effected; but on the following evening, a large body of the enemy charged down upon the guards and workmen, and got possession of the old breach, besides killing and wounding 150 men, and destroying their works. On the 7th, the besiegers, who had continued their advance, and were now close to the wall, were again charged with fatal effect by the garrison; and the guns from San Michael, although effecting a great breach in the second line, suffered severely from the artillery fire of the enemy,—another 18-pounder losing a trunnion. Guns were, however, too few and too valuable to be considered unserviceable, even after so serious an injury as this; and the ingenuity of Colonel Dickson produced a species of carriage, from which the damaged ordnance could fire with reduced charges. Between the 7th and the 10th October, the San Michael guns continued to make breaches in the works; on the 10th, some ammunition arrived from Santander; on the 18th, another breach was pronounced practicable, and Wellington ordered a fifth assault. This also was unsuccessful; the Allies lost 200 men killed and wounded; and the siege was at length raised—on the 20th—by Lord Wellington, who had received alarming intelligence of the approach of a French army to relieve Burgos, and of the movements of Soult.

The siege of Burgos is a blot on the military reputation of the Duke of Wellington; and revealed an ignorance of what artillery could and could not do, which every now and then manifested itself in his military operations. If Sir Hew Ross was correctly informed, the error made by Lord Wellington was almost criminal, as there was no necessity for attempting such a siege with so inadequate a siege-train. " Why he should have undertaken the siege of such a place," wrote Major Ross from Madrid, " with means so very inadequate appears very extraordinary, *especially as there was " little or no difficulty in augmenting it to any extent*, either " from the guns and ammunition found here, or the ships at " St. Andero." That Sir Hew wrote with reason seems all the more probable from the fact that, while the last assault was actually taking place, two 24-pounders sent from Santander by Sir Home Popham had passed Reynosa on their way to Burgos. But it may be urged that the responsibility of undertaking a siege with insufficient Artillery lay not with the General, but with the Artillery commander. Those who are familiar with the character of the Duke of Wellington, as shown in the various narratives of the Peninsular War, will not make use of this argument. It was not his wont to allow his plans to be altered by the representations of his subordinates, nor was he addicted to the habit of consulting them. Besides, in this particular instance, he officially relieved the Artillery and Engineer officers of the responsibility. " The officers," he wrote, " at

[margin: Sir Hew Ross to Sir Hew Dalrymple, dated Madrid, 18 Oct. 1812.]

[margin: Napier.]

To Lord Bathurst dated Cabeçon, 26 Oct. 1812.

"the head of the Artillery and Engineer departments, "Lieut.-Colonel Robe and Lieut.-Colonel Burgoyne, and "Lieut.-Colonel Dickson, who commands the reserve Ar- "tillery, rendered me every assistance; and the failure of "success is not to be attributed to them." The Duke of Wellington believed in the bayonet beyond any other weapon; and if a legitimate belief became occasionally credulity, it is hardly to be wondered at, when one reflects on the gallantry of the Infantry which it was the Duke's good fortune to command. What seemed to be impossibilities, when ordered by him, were proved possible in the result; and the consequently increased belief in the power of the bayonet seems but natural. But his creed was supported at a terrible cost. When we find Napier himself,—Wellington's idolater,—pronouncing his sieges a succession of butcheries, the criticism of a more temperate student may be excused. Doubtless, the want of adequate ordnance was often severely felt by the Duke of Wellington, and compelled him to an exaggerated use of the other arms; but this fact was hardly an excuse for neglecting its employment, when available in sufficient quantities, and obtainable with moderate exertions.

Nor was the fact that he—as he justly complained—*never* had a proper amount of Artillery with his armies any excuse for his making occasionally but an indifferent use of that which he had. Fortunately, the Duke of Wellington had merely to encounter Napoleon's Marshals in Spain: had he had to meet their master, it is probable that the creed which he believed and practised might have received some rude assaults. If one could free oneself of all but purely professional considerations, one would wish, for the sake of the student in the art of war, that Napoleon, instead of Marmont and Clausel, had faced Wellington in the campaign of 1812. The result would, doubtless, have been the same; but the ways and means would have been very different. As it happened, Wellington's sole encounter with Napoleon took place on ground chosen by himself, and under circumstances which yet further assisted his military creed, by

CHAP. XIX. *Results of the Siege of Burgos.* 337

testing yet again that which he had so often extravagantly proved, the marvellous endurance, discipline, and courage of the British Infantry.

The results of the mistaken siege of Burgos are curtly described by Sir J. T. Jones, in his ' Journal of the Sieges in ' the Peninsula.' "By its means," he writes, "a beaten " enemy gained time to recruit his forces, concentrate his " scattered armies, and regain the ascendancy." The same author writes, with regard to the service of the Royal Artillery during the siege: "It is a pleasing act of justice " to the Artillery officers, employed in this attack, to state " that they vied with each other in their exertions and " expedients to meet the hourly difficulties they encoun- " tered, and that no set of men could possibly have drawn " more service than they did from the limited means at " their command."

CHAPTER XX.

VITTORIA AND SAN SEBASTIAN.

<small>Despatch to Lord Bathurst, dated 26 Oct. 1812.</small>
THE threatening appearance of the various French armies in Spain, which compelled Lord Wellington to raise the siege of Burgos, compelled him ultimately to withdraw into Portugal for winter-quarters, In leaving Burgos he found the activity of the commanding officers of Artillery very beneficial. It enabled him to carry off all his serviceable guns and stores in a single night; but the absence of cattle prevented his removing the few French guns which he had captured in the storming of the hornwork. During the retreat, the services of the Horse Artillery, under Major Downman, were of a high order, and called forth the commendation of Lord Wellington. The troop which most distinguished itself was Major Bull's, commanded by Captain Norman Ramsay, Major Bull having been twice wounded,—on one occasion so severely,—when in advance with the Cavalry at Torquemada on the night of the 12th September, 1812,—that he was obliged to be invalided. He does not reappear in the story of his gallant troop until the battle of Waterloo.

The retreat terminated on the 24th November, and the troops went into cantonments, the head-quarters being stationed at Frenada, and the Artillery at Malhada Sourda, three miles distant.

An old friend reappears, in the winter of 1812-13, to the burrower among Artillery records. Captain—now Brevet-Major—Frazer, who last was mentioned in this work in the account of the operations at Monte Video and Buenos Ayres, arrived to take command of Major Bull's troop during that officer's absence. His own troop being on home service, he more easily obtained permission to assume this duty. He had not been many weeks in the Peninsula before he received a more important command,—that which had hitherto been held with such distinction by Major Downman,—the command of the Royal Horse Artillery with Lord Wellington's armies. Although a reserved man in public, and fond of solitude, he was almost diffuse in his correspondence. Happily for those who have succeeded him in the Corps, his letters from the Peninsula have been collected and published by one who served in his troop for seven years,— General Sir Edward Sabine. These letters, and the unpublished letters of Sir A. Dickson, give together a most graphic picture of the operations of 1813, 1814, and 1815, which cannot but lose by the necessary condensation of the historian. Sir A. Frazer's Letters, page 89.

In the beginning of 1813, Lord Wellington proceeded to Lisbon to make the necessary arrangements for the coming campaign. The intelligence of the French disasters in Russia had reached him; rumours also came that Soult and many of the best troops in the French Peninsular armies had gone to France; and, from his preparations at Lisbon, it is evident that he had already resolved on offensive operations, which should, if possible, have the effect of driving the French out of the Peninsula. That he succeeded is well known to the reader; it remains to single out, in this and the following chapter, some of the more salient points in the campaign.

Colonel Dickson had been ordered to Lisbon, to consult as to some means of making the Portuguese Artillery more available for service than it had as yet been; and while there, he was sent for by Lord Wellington, who had also arrived, and was directed to superintend the equipment of a pontoon train of thirty-four large pontoons, which was to be sent by river to Abrantes, and there handed over to the master-pontonier, for use in the coming operations of the army. This train was destined to be a sore grievance to the Artillery. It had always to be horsed *first*, even at the expense of the Artillery brigades; and its possible wants in that respect haunted, like a nightmare, the commanding Colonel Dickson, to D.-A.-G. Lisbon, 16 Jan. 1813. Ibid. dated Lisbon, 30 Jan. 1813.

officer of the Corps. At this interview Lord Wellington also expressed considerable anxiety about the brigade of 18-pounder guns, which, he said, he was determined to have early in the field, as the French were understood to be fortifying positions everywhere. Some new 18-pounders were expected daily from England; and, on their arrival, he desired that they should be sent up the Tagus to Abrantes. This was safely effected; and bullocks were ordered to bring them thence to head-quarters, at Malhada Sourda.

<small>Colonel Dickson to D.-A.-G. dated 24 Feb. 1813.</small>

They were ultimately manned by Captain Morrison's and Captain Glubb's companies of the Royal Artillery; and the number of carriages in the brigade was no less than 57, viz. :—

<small>Ibid. dated 18 April, 1813.</small>

6 18-pr. guns on travelling carriages.	18 ammunition (limber) waggons.
2 spare carriages.	3 store waggons.
6 platform waggons.	20 bullock carts.
2 forges.	

N.B.—Ammunition was carried at the rate of 150 rounds per gun.

The guns, and nine of the ammunition waggons, had horses in addition to their bullocks; the remaining carriages were drawn by bullocks only.

<small>Ibid. dated 24 Feb. 1813.</small>

About the same time as the 18-pounders arrived from England, another troop of Horse Artillery, under the command of Captain Webber Smith, also reached Lisbon. A change in the armament of the troop, from 6-pounders to 9-pounders, was immediately ordered by Lord Wellington,—a change which, on more than one occasion, and in more than one campaign, has been ordered in the armament of the Royal Horse Artillery. At this time, also, a recognition was made by the Portuguese Government of the services of the Artillery,—Colonels Robe and Dickson being made knights of the Tower and Sword.

<small>Ibid. dated 28 March, 1813.</small>

The old difficulty as to horses reappeared in the beginning of 1813. The sickness among these animals during the winter had been excessive; and the difficulty of purchasing any in the country seemed daily to increase. This led to many changes. Among others, Lord Wellington reduced the whole of the Portuguese Artillery for service in the field to three brigades,—one 9-pounder and one 6-pounder brigade to be with Sir Rowland Hill's force, and one 9-pounder brigade to be attached to the general Artillery reserve of the army. These three were made very efficient by this means, and the purchase of a considerable number of horses avoided.

The campaign of 1813 was distinguished by a feature of considerable importance. Lord Wellington was now Commander-in-Chief of all the *Spanish* armies, and all necessary correspondence came direct to him, instead of through Cadiz. The assistance of the Spanish regular troops was never of much value, even under the new system, except at the subsequent combat of San Marcial and at the Bidassoa; but the part taken by the Partidas, or irregular forces, during the campaign was not unimportant, and increased the difficulties of the French troops.

The French commenced to fall back from Salamanca towards Burgos, and in the beginning of April had not above a thousand men in the former place. At the same time, supplies were arriving from England weekly, and were disembarked in the northern ports of the Peninsula, with a view to the advance of the English army. An organization of the Allied troops was taking place, superior to anything which had yet been witnessed; and the Corps, whose history is treated in these pages, improved with the other arms in this respect. It seems a suitable time to touch on the improvement in the Field Brigades which had already taken place; and, at the risk of wearying the reader, to place before him a specimen of these in the spring of 1813.

Colonel Dickson to D.-A.-G. dated Corilhaa, 4 April, 1813.

The brigade, *i.e.* battery, which it is proposed to describe belonged to the 10th Battalion, and was commanded by the 2nd Captain, R. M. Cairnes, a gallant officer, who afterwards fell at Waterloo. It was pronounced by various inspecting officers to be the best field brigade with the army; but Captain Cairnes in his correspondence declined to accept this honour, as he considered others equally efficient. It may, therefore, be accepted as a fair type. From a letter written by Captain Cairnes himself, the following particulars are obtained; and they exhibit a startling contrast to the oxen-draught brigades of the commencement of the Peninsular War. His system was based on that of the Horse Artillery, now universal in field batteries, in which each officer was wholly and solely responsible to the captain for his division, whether in matters of men or *matériel*. He declined to allow the officer of the Driver Corps, who commanded the drivers attached to the brigade, to have any control over his men, except as far as their pay and subsistence were concerned; and by thus giving his own officers complete responsibility, he received the reward which such conduct generally ensures, and was able to say, " My subalterns, Raynes, Bridges, James, and Talbot, are " all most excellent, full of zeal, activity, and intelligence; " they run before me in everything I can desire concerning " their respective charges, and are never more happy than " when in stables." The chief difficulty in field brigades had always been in the divided allegiance of the men of the Driver Corps. The solution of this difficulty, which was adopted by Captain Cairnes, gradually obtained favour, and ended in a most natural manner,—the abolition of the Driver Corps and the absorption of the drivers into the Regiment. It took, however, some years to educate the authorities up to this point; and not until 1822 was the corps actually abolished. Another point in Captain Cairnes' system to which he attached great importance, and which he said had been generally adopted in the other brigades, was that of having promotion among the non-commissioned officers to go, not by *battalion*, but by *company* seniority; and of waiving even the question of seniority in the presence of undoubted superiority. There were faces in Woolwich which grew very long, and fossil old gentlemen whose remaining hairs stood on end, at such a perversion of the old order of things; but Lord Wellington supported the captains of companies in a measure which on service gave them a powerful engine for discipline. So, time after time, does the reader find the real Artillery unit asserting itself.

The artificers with a brigade were 2 wheelers, 2 collar-

CHAP. XX.   *Improvements in Field Brigades.*   343

makers, 1 farrier, 1 jobbing smith, and 4 shoeing smiths. The non-commissioned officers of the Driver Corps attached to a 9-pounder brigade were, 1 staff-sergeant, 2 sergeants, and 6 corporals, one of whom acted as forage sergeant, under the acting storekeeper of the brigade (a *company*, not *driver* non-commissioned officer), who, again, was under an assistant commissary-general attached to the brigade (under the immediate orders of the Captain commanding). This officer was responsible for the rations and the supply of corn, for which purpose he had a number of forage mules, at the rate of one mule to two horses.

Sixteen round tents and two horsemen's tents were carried; and, for the convenience of the artificers, two store waggons accompanied the brigade. The other extra carriages were the forge waggon, spare wheel carriage, and the captain's cart. The brigade itself consisted of 6 guns and howitzers, 6 ammunition waggons, and 2 reserve ammunition waggons. The proportion of ammunition carried was as follows:—

For each 9-pr. gun: 70 round shot, 34 spherical case, and 12 common case. Total 116 rounds.
For each 5½-in. howitzer: 44 spherical case, 8 common case, and 32 common shell. Total 84 rounds.
In each reserve ammunition waggon there were 57 round shot, 21 spherical case, and 6 common case. Total 84 rounds.

The number of drivers with a brigade was one hundred. Five of the spare carriages were drawn by mules; those being selected which were the least likely to go under fire.

This was altogether a most desirable command for a young 2nd Captain to have on active service; and keenly did Captain Cairnes enjoy it. His dismay may therefore be imagined, on receiving, on the 5th May, 1813, a letter from Colonel Fisher, then commanding the Artillery in the Peninsula, announcing that Lord Wellington had decided to take away the horses of his brigade for the service of the pontoon train, leaving him to the chance of any horses which might hereafter come from Lisbon. He was not allowed any time to brood over his troubles, but was ordered

to meet the pontoons at Sabugal in three days' time, and hand over to the Engineer the whole of his stud. Colonel Fisher's letter, which was a private communication, sent a few hours in advance of the official order, held out hopes of a speedy restoration (which fortunately took place) of the equipment of his brigade for the field.[1] Captain Cairnes' reply to this letter was so soldierlike, that it is well worthy of a place in the records of his Corps. "I return you," he wrote, " my dear Colonel, my sincere thanks for your com-
" munication of yesterday's date, anterior to the arrival of
" any *order*, which would, I think, have set me perfectly
" *crazy*. As it is, I have read your letter over twenty times,
" and am yet very unwilling to understand it. Lord
" Wellington having fixed on this brigade, I trust we shall
" be entitled to every consideration, when it is recollected
" that a junior one in all respects is within a league of the
" same distance from Sabugal as this place. The pain of
" urging anything prejudicial to my valued friend Parker
" is superseded by the promise held out to us of a speedy
" re-equipment. . . . I know, my dear Colonel, that you
" cannot avert the blow from us, and that the necessity of
" the service has forced Lord Wellington to this measure;
" therefore, however sorely affected and hurt we may now
" feel, you will assure yourself that the whole shall be given
" over to the pontoons in as complete and efficient a manner
" as if they were going to be put to our own carriages. I
" am full of dread and alarm that our new equipment of
" horses and harness will not come up in time to march with
" the army; and that (without being so extravagantly
" sanguine or conceited as to *build on* future successes and
" good fortune) we shall be too late for the golden oppor-
" tunity that a few days will probably offer to other
" brigades."

This allusion of Captain Cairnes to the other Artillery

Dated 6 May, 1813.

---

[1] As will be seen, on reference to the chapter on the Old Tenth Battalion, Captain Cairnes had also to give up to the pontoon train his *second* supply of horses in the end of this year.

brigades with Lord Wellington's army suggests the propriety of placing before the reader their distribution at the opening of the campaign of 1813. This would appear to have been as follows :—

With 1st Infantry division : Captain Dubourdieu's Brigade, R.A.
„ 2nd „ „ Captain Maxwell's „ „
„ 3rd „ „ Captain Douglas's „ „
„ 4th „ „ Major Sympher's K. G. Artillery.
„ 5th „ „ Captain Brandreth's Brigade, R.A.
„ 6th „ „ Major Lawson's „ „
„ 7th „ „ Major Gardiner's Troop, R.H.A.
„ Light Division : Major Ross's „ „
1st Division of Cavalry : Major Frazer's (Bull's) Troop, R.H.A.
2nd „ „ Captain Beane's „ „
Reserve .. .. .. {Captain Webber Smith's Troop, R.H.A.[1]
Captain Cairnes' Brigade, R.A.
Captain J. Parker's „ „

In the middle of May the plan of the campaign was arranged. The army was ordered to move in two columns, the head-quarters to leave Frenada on the 22nd May. One column was to cross the Douro at the mouth of the Coa, and to advance by Miranda de Douro ; the other was to go by Ciudad Rodrigo. Lord Wellington was to accompany the latter column, which consisted of Sir Rowland Hill's corps, the Light Division, Cavalry, &c. The other column, composed of the rest of the army, was under Sir T. Graham ; and with it went the pontoon train. It was decided to lay the pontoon bridge across the Douro, near Miranda, and thus unite the two columns ; this operation to be followed by the siege of Zamora, which, when concluded, would leave the Allies masters of the Douro. Following the head-quarters, the reader finds that they moved to Ciudad Rodrigo on the 22nd May, to Tamames on the 23rd, and to Matilla, about six leagues from Salamanca, on the 25th. On the way, Lord Wellington inspected the Portuguese Division, commanded by General Silveira, and found the men better

Colonel Dickson to D.-A.-G. dated 19 May, 1813.

Ibid. dated Matilla, 25 May, 1813.

---

[1] It would appear from Sir A. Frazer's letters that Webber Smith's troop was for a time attached to the Hussars, but ultimately to the 7th Division, in lieu of Captain Gardiner's troop, which joined the Hussar Brigade.

equipped than they had ever yet been. The brigades of Artillery with them were commanded by Colonel Tulloh, an officer of the Royal Artillery, whose zeal and ability were repaid by the efficiency of the men under his control. The whole of the reserve Artillery of Lord Wellington's army, with the exception of the brigade under Captain. Cairnes, which was now re-equipped, had gone with the main body, under Sir T. Graham.

Colonel Dickson was now in command of the Artillery, although junior to many in point of regimental rank; and as the way in which he obtained the command is not so generally known in the Regiment as the fact, it seems desirable to state it. While he was at Corilhaa, preparing the reserve Artillery for the coming campaign, Colonel Fisher, who had succeeded to the command of the Artillery after Colonel Robe was disabled at Burgos, but who had not held the command as yet in the field, wrote to him, requesting his attendance at head-quarters without loss of time. On his arrival, he ascertained that a misunderstanding had arisen between Lord Wellington and Colonel Fisher, which had ended in the latter's requesting permission to resign, and return to England. Lord Wellington inquired of Colonel Dickson whether he was senior to Colonel Waller, who had just arrived in Lisbon, and on learning that he was not, he said, " Colonel Dickson, then, will take the command of " all the Artillery in the field, both British and Portuguese; " and Colonel Waller and General Roza, as commandants of " the Artillery of the two nations, will remain at Lisbon for " the purpose of forwarding supplies." He then desired Colonel Fisher to give such explanations of the state of affairs as would enable Colonel Dickson to enter on his charge.

There would seem to have been considerable hastiness and injustice on the part of Lord Wellington in this matter. Colonel Dickson himself, while naturally flattered, could not but say, " I am convinced, if Lord Wellington had known " Colonel Fisher's talents and abilities, he would never have " allowed any such circumstance to take from him such an " officer; and I hope you will forgive my thus presuming to

To D.-A.-G. dated 25 May, 1813.

"discuss in so particular a manner the merits of a superior,
"which I am only induced to do in order that you may better
"know the merits of an officer I love and esteem; and I am
"sure every man of sense or ability in the Corps of Artillery
"in the Peninsula will subscribe to what I now state."

The honour paid to Colonel Dickson was an embarrassing one. Although his Portuguese rank placed him over all officers under the rank of Colonel, many such were senior to him regimentally. This fact demanded great tact from him in the execution of his duty. Fortunately, he met with ready, soldier-like co-operation from all; and one, who had commanded him on service before, in writing to his friends on the subject, expressed the general feeling when he said: "I shall get on very well with Dickson; "he was second to me in the South American Expedition, "and then obeyed my orders with the implicit readiness "which I shall now transfer to his. He is a man of great "abilities and quickness, and without fear of any one." And again: "Colonel Fisher left us the day before yesterday, "sincerely regretted by all. I hope Dickson's reign may "be long for the sake of the service, but the times are "slippery." Yet once more: "Dickson showed me yester- "day a very sensible, plain letter, which he had written to "Colonel Waller, and was just going to send off. Dickson, "too, feels himself awkwardly off, but will bear his honours "well. There is an open, manly simplicity about Dickson "very prepossessing. I hope and trust he will long enjoy "the confidence of the Marquis; and this I should desire "for the sake of the service, independently of any regard "I might have (and I have a very sincere one) for Dickson."

Letters of Sir A. Frazer, page 101.

Ibid. page 106.

Ibid. page 110.

To return, however, to the movements of the army. On the 26th May the head-quarters moved forward in the direction of Salamanca, on approaching which place columns of the enemy's infantry were observed, halted at each side of the town, a part of their cavalry being, however, on the left bank of the river to watch the movements of the Allies. As the latter advanced, the cavalry retired across the bridge into Salamanca, but the infantry for a considerable time

Colonel Dickson to D.-A.-G. dated 6 June, 1813.

remained unmoved. In the meantime, Sir Rowland Hill's Cavalry and Captain Beane's troop of Horse Artillery were ordered to push for the ford of Santa Martha, a little above the town. As soon as the French saw these troops approach the river, they moved off with their whole force, which included about 2500 infantry, two or three squadrons of cavalry, and three or four guns. General Fane, who was in command of Sir R. Hill's Cavalry, passed the river in a moment, and came up with the French before they had gone three miles from Salamanca. They were retiring *by squares* along the Arivalo road, which leads up the Tormes by Aldea Langua; and, on overtaking them, the Horse Artillery opened upon their squares with considerable execution. The pursuit was thus continued for five or six miles, the Horse Artillery cannonading them from every available point. The Artillery fire was interfered with by the repeated interposition of the Cavalry between the guns and the enemy; but was nevertheless very efficient. According to Colonel Dickson,—of 400 killed, wounded, and prisoners, lost by the enemy,—100 were victims to the Artillery fire alone; and the squares were so shaken by it, that, if the regiments moving on the flank had pushed on, the whole force might have been captured. Lord Wellington, however, seeing that the pursuing Cavalry was somewhat exhausted, desisted from further pursuit. The head-quarters halted at Salamanca on the 27th May, and orders were issued for their transfer to the other army, north of the Douro. On the 28th, therefore, the head-quarter staff proceeded to Almeida, and on the 29th to Miranda, crossing the Douro at a ferry near the latter place. Lord Wellington, himself, remained one day later at Salamanca; and on the 29th proceeded the whole distance to Miranda. On the 30th the head-quarters were moved to Carvajales, and on the same evening the Esla was reconnoitred, and preparations made to cross it on the following morning. Small parties of the enemy were seen on the opposite bank with two guns. Early on the morning of the 31st, the Hussar Brigade, Gardiner's and Webber Smith's troops of Horse Artillery, and two regiments of

Infantry crossed,—upon which the French parties immediately retired. The Infantry found the greatest difficulty in crossing,—the river being both deep and rapid,—and several men were drowned. A pontoon bridge was therefore made in a couple of hours, over which the rest of the army passed, with the exception of the Cavalry, Artillery, and waggons, which forded the river. A special pontoon bridge was made for the 18-pounder brigade, over which it passed with safety. On the 1st June head-quarters proceeded to Zamora, and the army completed the passage of the Esla,—the French evacuating Zamora as the Allies approached.

"Thus," wrote Colonel Dickson, "we succeeded in our "manœuvre of turning the Douro, and getting possession "of that river without sustaining the smallest loss. It has "been a bold one; but, by his Lordship's rapidity in moving "the army, and transferring himself from one point to the "other, I think the French did not succeed in discovering "our real intention until it was too late for them to hinder "it. Otherwise, we found the Esla such an obstacle, that "if they only had had ten or twelve thousand men on that "river, the passage of it would have been a serious opera-"tion to us, and could not have been effected without either "great loss of time or of men, and probably both."

On the 2nd June, the French abandoned Toro, and Wellington's head-quarters proceeded there,—remaining over the 3rd, on which day, and on the 4th, the force which had advanced by Salamanca, under Sir R. Hill, crossed the Douro. On the 4th, the army moved forward in three columns,—the right, under Sir R. Hill, in the direction of Valladolid; the centre upon La Mota, and the left under Sir Thomas Graham towards Rio Seco. The head-quarters proceeded to La Mota on the 4th, to Castro Monte on the 5th, and to Ampudia on the 6th; the French abandoning Valladolid, as the Allies advanced, and retiring upon Palencia and Duenas. The armies continued to keep within a day's march of one another: indeed, when the Allies reached Palencia, on the 7th June, the rear-guard of the enemy was clearly visible from the high ground. On the 12th (the pursuit still going on steadily, and Wellington continuing this, his greatest, march in the most persevering, relentless manner) the French army had reached Monasterio and the neighbourhood of Burgos,—but indicated no sign of discontinuing its retreat. Warned by past experience, Wellington had decided to take no active measures against Burgos, but merely to blockade it with part of the Spanish army, leaving the English troops undiminished. In the meantime, Sir Thomas Graham, with the left column of the army, inclined to his left in the direction of the upper part of the Ebro; with the view, it was believed, of turning or crossing that river. The events of the next few days, however, modified matters very much. On reaching Villa Diego, Lord Wellington ascertained that the Castle of Burgos had been blown up by the French, and was in utter ruins. Sir Richard Fletcher, of the Engineers, accompanied by Colonels Dickson and May, and Major Frazer of the Artillery, penetrated into the place, although the French rear-guard was still close at hand, and brought back the report. Joseph Buonaparte had meditated taking up a position at Burgos, but it having been pronounced unwise, he continued to retire on Vittoria. His army—which was known to be *en route* for France—was embarrassed with huge convoys of spoils,—and crowds of followers, male and female, who were unwilling to be left in Spain, unprotected by the French troops. Lord Wellington now executed a very brilliant strategical manœuvre,—the crossing of the Ebro. The route by which he abruptly moved his army was unfrequented and considered impracticable. The descent to the river by the Puente de Arenas was by a very narrow and steep pass, opening into a small but fertile valley, entirely surrounded by high mountains, with the river running through it. The *sortie* from the valley of Puente de Arenas was by a road running for a considerable distance close to the river, with stupendous rocks overhanging on either side. Had this movement been foreseen, a very small body of the enemy could have impeded the passage of the army. The advantages of this manœuvre were many. The

[margin: Colonel Dickson to D.-A.-G. dated 19 June, 1813.]

CHAP. XX.   *The Crossing of the Ebro.*   351

French communications with the coast were cut off, and <small>Cust's 'Annals of the Wars.'</small>
a new base was opened for the operations of the Allies.
The English fleet entered Santander, and commissariat communication was opened with the coast. Wellington was also in a position to threaten the communications between Vittoria and the Pyrenees, and the French found the English already in rear of their right. An engagement took place between Sir Thomas Graham and the French General, Reille, who had been detached to protect the communications between the French army and their own country; and the Light Division—with which Lord Wellington himself was— <small>Colonel Dickson to D.-A.-G. 19 June, 1813.</small>
succeeded in surprising General Maucune's division on the march,—killing a good many, dispersing one brigade, and capturing an immense quantity of baggage, and 300 prisoners. But these were merely the preliminaries to a battle, which, in its results, was unsurpassed in the whole narrative of the Peninsular War. Writing on the evening of the 19th June, from Subijana de Morillas, three leagues south-west of Vittoria, Colonel Dickson said: "We can see "the whole French army on their march to Vittoria;—the "column is not more than six or seven miles off. To-"morrow we expect to move forward upon Vittoria, which, "I think, must lead to something."

In proceeding to discuss the share of the Royal Artillery at the battle of Vittoria, it has unfortunately to be premised that the most valuable letter on the subject has been mislaid, or lost. In writing to General Macleod after the battle, Colonel Dickson said: "I know Frazer has given you <small>Dated 23 June, 1813.</small>
"some account of it, so I will not enter into further details "at present, except on our own matters." And in two subsequent letters, he said: "Frazer's letter will have explained "everything." Now, in the published letters of Sir Augustus Frazer, this letter is not to be found; nor is there much in his allusions to the battle in his other letters to assist the Artilleryman in tracing the services of his Corps. The loss of the letter is, to a certain extent, compensated by details given in subsequent letters from Colonel Dickson, but still remains irreparable.

It would be beyond the province of this work to describe the battle of Vittoria, as a whole. In the pages of the *general* military historian such a description can be found. In these, the regimental statistics alone need be reproduced. The general plan of the battle is, doubtless, familiar to all:—the plain in front of Vittoria, into which—as into a trap—Joseph Buonaparte poured all his troops and convoys;—the one road available for the retreat of his forces to France, which was menaced—but not with sufficient decision—by Wellington's left;—the confusion in the space between the French army and the town of Vittoria, where mobs of terrified fugitives were mingled with heaps of vehicles and stores;—the three-handed assault of the Allies, advancing with steadfast purpose from three quarters at once;—the frequent Artillery duels, in which the Artillery on both sides so greatly distinguished themselves;—the grand final effort of the French artillery,

Napier. when "more than eighty guns, massed together, pealed with "such a horrid uproar, that the hills laboured and shook, "and streamed with fire and smoke, amidst which the dark "figures of the French gunners were seen, bounding with a "frantic energy;" and then the wild rout, the headlong flight of an army leaving its guns and everything behind it;—the shrieks of women, the terror of men, rising so vividly before his mind as he wrote, that Napier exclaimed, "It was the wreck of a nation!" But no such ambitious description is required in detail from the mere regimental historian. What is demanded from him is the narrative, from old records that have never seen the light, of the share taken by his corps on this eventful day.

Official Report to the Master-General, dated 23 June, 1813.

Let the distribution of the various troops and brigades of Artillery at Vittoria first be given. Colonel Dickson was in command, assisted by the following field officers:—

Lieut.-Colonel Hartmann, K.G.A., commanding the reserve Artillery.
Major Carncross, with Sir Rowland Hill's column.
Major Buckner, with column of 3rd and 7th Divisions.
Major Frazer, commanding the Horse Artillery.

The troops of Royal Horse Artillery were distributed as follows:—

Captain Webber Smith's, with the Reserve.
Major Ross's, with Light Division.
Captain Beane's, with General Fane's Cavalry.
Major Gardiner's, with the Hussars.
Captain Ramsay's, with the Cavalry Division.

The Field Brigades were distributed as follows:—

Major Lawson's, with 5th Division.
Captain Douglas's, with 3rd Division.
Captain Maxwell's, with 2nd Division.
Captain Dubourdieu's, with 1st Division.
Major Sympher's (K.G.A.), with 4th Division.
Captain Cairnes', with 7th Division.
Captain Parker's, with the Reserve.
Lieut.-Colonel Tulloh, R.A., commanded two Portuguese brigades with Sir R. Hill's corps, and Major Arriaga commanded the Portuguese Reserve Brigade.
Lieut.-Colonel May acted as Assistant Adjutant-General, and Lieut. Woolyear acted as Brigade-Major. Lieutenants Ord, Harding, and Pascoe, were employed as staff officers by Colonel Dickson.

The number of guns, exclusive of the Spanish, which were brought into action by the Allies at Vittoria was ninety; but the French had considerably more. There happened in this battle, on the 21st June, 1813, what rarely happens,— *every* brigade of Artillery was brought into action. In his official report, Colonel Dickson said that he had reason to be satisfied with the conduct of the officers and men of the Royal Artillery on this occasion; that their skill and bravery were highly conspicuous, as were their exertions in bringing forward the Artillery through a difficult and intersected country, both during the attack and the pursuit. "In short," he added, "I can safely assert that artillery could not be "better served; and, to the credit of the officers, I have to "add that from the beginning of the day to the last mo-"ment of the pursuit, it was always to be found where it "was wanted." In his private letter to General Macleod, Colonel Dickson particularised some of the officers who had especially distinguished themselves; and the following extract deserves publication: "I cannot close this letter with-"out mentioning the valuable assistance my friend Frazer "afforded during the whole business. I may truly say he

Dated 23 June, 1813.

"flew from one troop to another,—accompanying them into action and attending to their supply, or looking out for roads for them to move. You, who know Frazer so well, can easily anticipate what he would be on such an occasion."

The massing of the English Artillery was effected at Vittoria to an unprecedented extent, and with most happy results. It might at first be assumed that the admirable use made of this arm on that occasion is a sufficient reply to any insinuations against Lord Wellington's knowledge of Artillery tactics. Unfortunately for him, a letter has survived which proves, on the best authority, that to accident alone was this artillery display due. "The nature of the country," wrote Colonel Dickson, "and want of roads, was the means of throwing a large proportion of our Artillery together, away from their divisions, which I availed myself of, and by employing them in masses, it had a famous effect. This was adjoining to the great road to Vittoria; and the French brought all the artillery they could to oppose our advance, so that the cannonade on one spot was very vigorous. In none of our Peninsular battles have we ever brought so much cannon into play; and it was so well directed that the French were generally obliged to retire ere the Infantry could get at them. There were few or no instances of the bayonet being used during the day."

Considering the duration of the battle, the casualties among the Artillery were singularly few. They were as follows:—

MS. Official Return to D. A. Gen.

Staff.—*Wounded:* Colonel May, and Brigade-Major Woodyear (died of wounds).

	Killed.	Wounded.	Missing.
Royal Horse Artillery	4	36	2
Royal Artillery	8	19	..
Horses of R. H. A.	28	23	8
Horses of R. A.	15	2	..

Ibid.

The number of guns captured from the enemy was no less than 151, besides 415 caissons. Of gun ammunition 14,249

CHAP. XX. *Results of the Battle of Vittoria.* 355

rounds were taken, besides 40,668 lbs. of gunpowder and 1,973,400 musket ball-cartridges. The other spoils were countless; and it is difficult to conceive a more complete defeat.

Lord Wellington's account of the battle contains the following short, but satisfactory, allusion to the services of the Artillery:—"The Artillery was most judiciously placed by "Lieut.-Colonel Dickson, and was well served; and the army "is particularly indebted to that Corps." During the pursuit of the enemy after the battle, Colonel Dickson kept the Artillery well up,—and was rewarded, as will be seen from the following anecdote:—"In the pursuit after Vittoria, " in the bad roads, Lord Wellington saw a French column " making a stand, as if to halt for the night. 'Now Dick- " ' son,' said he, ' if we had but some Artillery up!' 'They " ' are close by, my Lord.' And in ten minutes, from a hill " on the right, Lieut.-Colonel Ross's Light Division guns " began; and away went the French two leagues farther " off." The same author from whom this quotation is made says: "Dickson, though only a Captain in the Royal Regi- " ment of Artillery, now conducts the whole department " here, *because he makes no difficulties.*"

During the pursuit, the only remaining guns—two in number—taken away by the French from the field, were captured,—one being disabled by the fire of the Chestnut Troop, and the other being taken within a league of Pampeluna, in which direction the French had retreated.

The results which followed the battle of Vittoria are summarised by Napier in his description of the campaign, in which that battle was the chief incident. "In this cam- " paign of six weeks," he wrote, " Wellington, with 100,000 " men, marched 600 miles, passed six great rivers, gained " one decisive battle, invested two fortresses, and drove " 120,000 veteran troops from Spain." The fortresses referred to were Pampeluna and San Sebastian; and it is now proposed to treat of the double siege of the latter, as an episode of essential importance in the history of the Regiment, and one concerning which Sir Alexander Dickson left

To Lord Bathurst dated 22 June, 1813.

Extract from the private Journal of F. S. Larpent, Esq., Judge-Advocate-General to the British forces in the Peninsula. Published by Sir G. Larpent, page 142.

Lord Wellington's Despatch, dated 24 June, 1813.

'Memoirs of Sir Hew Ross,' page 41.

2 A 2

much valuable information, yet unpublished. Before doing so, however, there are two incidents which deserve to be mentioned.

In the *brevet* which followed Vittoria, Majors Frazer and Ross were made Lieut.-Colonels, and 2nd Captain Jenkinson (of the Chestnut Troop) was made Major. Captain Jenkinson's brevet promotion was the first which had been received by a 2nd Captain of Artillery. In the beginning of the year 1813, the 2nd Captains serving in the Peninsula had memorialised Lord Wellington on the subject. The memorial having been referred to England, a favourable reply was given, and Captain Jenkinson's promotion was the first fruits. In addition to the somewhat scanty recognition of the Artillery in this *brevet*, a boon was granted, which is described in the following extract from a letter written by the Master-General of the Ordnance, Lord Mulgrave, to Colonel Dickson:—" On receipt of your letter, addressed to
" Major-General Macleod, I did not fail to bring under the
" consideration of the Prince Regent the very striking and
" unexampled circumstance of the whole of the British
" Artillery having been brought into action at the battle of
" Vittoria, and the whole of the enemy's Artillery having
" been captured in the glorious victory which crowned the
" exertions of the Allies on that ever-memorable occasion.
" His Royal Highness has been graciously pleased—in con-
" sideration of the peculiar circumstances above stated—to
" mark His Royal Highness's approbation of the particular
" and successful activity of the Corps of Royal Artillery
" under your orders, by granting severally to the officers
" intrusted with the command of divisions or brigades an
" allowance for good service in the following proportions:—
" To the officers commanding divisions, each 10s. per diem;
" to the officers commanding brigades, each 5s. per diem;
" and to yourself a similar allowance for good service of 20s.
" per diem."

Better, far better, that these words had never been penned, and that the generous thought had died in its conception! For the day was to come when a reference to this precedent after Vittoria should call forth from him under whom the representatives of the Corps had so often and so bravely fought, a letter as cruel and unjust to those of whom it treated, as it was unworthy of him who penned it. _{Vide Appendix A.}

The other incident is one which has become a household word in the Regiment. If there is one name more familar than another to the Artilleryman, it is that of Norman Ramsay. From public orders and the pages of history his gallantry and professional skill may be learnt; but it is from the pages of private correspondence that one ascertains how lovable he was. He joined the Regiment in 1798, and he fell at Waterloo; and yet in that short space of seventeen years he had gained the love of his brother officers without exception, the devotion of his men, and the admiration of all. A man *sans peur et sans reproche*, he reminds one of the knights of Arthur, whose pleasure was to

> "Live pure, speak true, right wrong, follow the king."

A thorough master of his profession, he earned the respect as well as the love of those whom he commanded: and the love of men for their commander must have that element in it to make the gift worth having. The personal qualities of an officer may attract the affection of his men; but if he is deficient in knowledge of his profession, there will be in their love an element approaching pity, which will be fatal to their confidence in the hour of trial. It will be like the love for a child,—pure, warm, and sincere,—but not such as will demand from the soldier, in the day of battle, blind confidence and unhesitating obedience. In Norman Ramsay were combined all the virtues which compel affection, and all the skill which demands respect. But there was more: he possessed that professional enthusiasm which hallows the dullest tasks, and gilds the severest hardship. His pride in his troop made its men strive to be worthy of his good opinion; and it is in this way that a commander can with certainty generate *esprit de corps* among his men. Let him but place before them a standard of perfection, even although unattainable, and, in their voluntary efforts to reach it, they will rise far higher than if driven by order, or goaded by fear of punishment.

Successful in all his aims, Norman Ramsay was yet so fortunate as to escape jealousy. The letters of his brother-officers,—written for private eye alone, but subsequently published,—show this to a singular extent. Sir Alexander Dickson, Sir Augustus Frazer, Sir Hew Ross, Major Cairnes, and others,—all men of different characters and disposition,—rarely wrote without a loving word or kind inquiry about Ramsay. If his troop distinguished itself, they all rejoiced as if it had been their own; if he met with any grief, they longed to share it; and if sorrow came upon themselves, their first instinct was to confide it to him. In October, 1813, a distinguished Artilleryman, Sir Howard Douglas, lost in action a brother whom he deeply loved. Older than Ramsay, one yet finds without surprise that it was to him he went, "bitterly lamenting his loss." So also when any of them came within his reach at any time, the letters always speak alike,—as if every one would readily understand the writers' longings—"I *must* go and see Ramsay."

[marginal note: Sir A. Frazer's Letters, page 314.]

In these pages, later on, the story will have to be told how, in the midst of the din of battle, there seemed to fall a silence like a pall, as he, the brave and much-loved, met with a soldier's death; but the grief was then that of his friends. The incident now to be told tells of a grief which was his own,—which never quitted him while he lived, and which was said by many who knew him to have led him to court unnecessary exposure on the day in which he died. At Vittoria, Bull's troop, commanded by Ramsay, had done special service. On the following day, during the pursuit, "Lord Wellington spoke to Ramsay as he passed; desired "him to take his troop for the night to a village near, add- "ing that if there were orders for the troop in the course of "the night, *he would send them.*" No orders came; but at 6 A.M. an Assistant Quartermaster-General arrived, and ordered him to join the brigade to which he belonged. The

[marginal note: Published Letters of Sir A. Frazer, page 183.]

troop at once marched, but was shortly afterwards overtaken by a written order from General Murray, the Quartermaster-General of the army, directing "Captain Ramsay's troop to "rejoin General Anson's brigade." The troop halted, while Ramsay rode on to discover the road; and at this moment Lord Wellington rode up, and called repeatedly for him.

Published Letters of Sir A. Frazer, page 186.

" His Lordship," wrote Sir Augustus Frazer, "then called for
" Dickson, whose horse being unable at the instant to clear
" a wide ditch over which we had just passed, I rode up to
" mention the circumstance to Lord Wellington, who ordered
" me to put Captain Ramsay in arrest, and to give the com-
" mand of the troop to Captain Cator. This I accordingly
" did. . . . . It appears that Lord Wellington had intended
" that Ramsay's troop should not have moved that morning
" till he himself sent orders, and his Lordship declared that
" he had told Ramsay so. This Ramsay affirms he never
" heard or understood; and his Lordship's words, repeated
" by Ramsay, young Macleod, and a sergeant and corporal,
" all at hand when his Lordship spoke to Ramsay, are pre-
" cisely the same, and do not convey such a meaning. I
" spoke instantly to Lord Fitzroy Somerset on the subject,
" who, together with every other individual about head-
" quarters, was, and is, much concerned at the circumstance.
" Nay, two days afterwards, when the despatches were
" making out, every friendly suggestion was used by several
" that Ramsay might be mentioned as he deserved; but I
" have reason to believe that he is not. There is not, among
" the many good and gallant officers who are here, one of
" superior zeal or devotion to the service to Ramsay, who
" has given repeated proofs of spirit and good conduct.
" Admitting, contrary to all evidence, that he had mistaken
" the verbal orders he received, this surely is a venial
" offence, and one for which long-tried and faithful services
" should not be forgotten. . . . . . Few circumstances have
" engaged more general attention, or occasioned more regret.
" It has naturally been expected that after the first moment
" was over, a deserving officer would, at least, have been
" released from a situation most galling to a gallant spirit.

"... . I trust this will soon be the case; but . . . . I am "at a loss to account for the delay in a point so easily "settled. In the meanwhile, Ramsay bears up with great "fortitude, although he deeply feels." Writing on the same subject, some weeks later, Sir Hew Ross said: "Norman "Ramsay is at present with his troop in this neighbourhood, "and we are much together. He is quite well, and bears "his unjust treatment, and consequent disappointment, in "the manly and proper way that might be expected of him." For a considerable time he was kept under arrest; and the numerous applications on his behalf, including a very urgent one from Sir Thomas Graham, seemed to have the effect of irritating Lord Wellington. The consciousness of having done an unjust act is rendered more difficult to bear, when the victim has been one for whom affection has been entertained; and it was believed in the army that, as far as his undemonstrative nature would allow, Lord Wellington had a strong liking for Norman Ramsay. There was no doubt of the devotion of the latter for his great chief; and the keen suffering caused by injustice from a person whom one loves must be realised to be fully understood. He was happily released from arrest in time to carry his brave troop through the many actions, with which the war concluded; and he received a *brevet* promotion for these services; but he was never the same man. At Waterloo, on the morning of the battle, as the Duke rode along the line, he saw Ramsay at the head of his troop for the first time since his arrival in Flanders. He accosted him cheerfully as he passed. Ramsay merely bowed his head sadly, until it nearly touched his horse's mane, but could not speak. In a few hours he was where sorrow and injustice are unknown.

It is necessary now to turn to the siege of San Sebastian. Pampeluna was blockaded and ultimately starved into submission; but stronger measures were adopted with San Sebastian, into which place Marshal Jourdan had thrown a garrison of between 3000 and 4000 men. On the land side, it was invested by the left wing of the Allied army, under Sir Thomas Graham; and on the sea side it was blockaded

CHAP. XX. *Officers present at Siege of Sebastian.* 361

by a squadron under Sir George Collyer. On the 4th July, 1813, Lord Wellington wrote as follows to Colonel Dickson: "From what I have heard of San Sebastian, I am inclined "to form the siege of that place, and I shall be very much "obliged to you if you will send an officer to Bilbao to order "the train from thence to Passages."[1] The order was immediately obeyed, and Captain Morrison's 18-pounder brigade was also directed to proceed to Passages for the same purpose. On the 12th, Lord Wellington reconnoitred San Sebastian, and on the 14th, he departed to join the army on the field, leaving Colonel Dickson to conduct the Artillery part of the siege. Lord Wellington's operations in the field were at this time of a very delicate nature. The Allied army in the east of Spain had failed, and had raised the siege of Tarragona; while, in his front and on his right, there were menacing French armies. French garrisons in Pampeluna and San Sebastian also weakened his available force, by demanding troops to watch them.

Dated Lanz, 4 July, 1813.

Colonel Dickson to D.-A.-G. dated 10 July, 1813.

Before entering on the details of the double siege, the following list of artillery officers, who were present, may be interesting.

LIST OF OFFICERS of the ROYAL ARTILLERY employed in the SIEGES of ST. SEBASTIAN under LIEUT.-COLONEL DICKSON, commanding the Artillery under the MARQUIS OF WELLINGTON.

MS. Returns dated 12 Sept. 1813.

	First Operation.	Second Operation.
Lieut.-Colonel May, A. A. General	1	0
,, Frazer, R. H. Artillery	1	1
Major Buckner	0	1
,, Dyer	0	1
,, Webber Smith, R. H. Artillery	1	1
Captain Morrison	1	1
,, Douglas	0	1
,, Dubourdieu (killed)	1	0
,, W. Power	1	1
,, Green	0	1
,, J. B. Parker	1	1
,, Deacon	1	1
Carried forward	8	10

[1] Passages de la Calçada.

List of Officers of the Royal Artillery, continued.

	First Operation.	Second Operation.
Brought forward	8	10
Captain Dansey	1	0
,, C. Gordon	0	1
,, A. Macdonald, R. H. Artillery	1	0
Lieutenant J. W. Johnstone	1	1
,, Henry Blachley, R. H. Artillery	1	1
,, R. H. Ord	1	1
,, W. Brereton, R. H. Artillery	1	0
,, J. Wood	0	1
,, Basil Heron	1	1
,, G. Mainwaring	0	1
,, R. Hardinge	1	0
,, R. Harding, R. H. Artillery	1	1
,, R. F. Phillips	0	1
,, J. Pascoe	1	1
,, R. Manners	0	1
,, W. Dennis	0	1
,, Hugh Morgan	0	1
,, C. Shaw	1	1
,, H. Stanway	1	1
,, R. Story	1	1
,, H. Slade	0	1
,, H. Hough	0	1
,, F. Monro	1	0
,, H. Hutchins	0	1
,, John Bloomfield	1	1
,, H. Palliser	0	1
,, T. G. Williams	1	1
,, A. Macbean	1	1
	25	33

Lieut. England's name also appears in some of the Journals of the First Operation, and in Jones's 'Sieges,' and should be included above.

Total, exclusive of King's German Artillery, present at St. Sebastian:

First Operation.—Colonel Dickson and 25 officers of the Royal Artillery.
Second Operation.—Colonel Dickson and 33 officers of the Royal Artillery.

Extract from a letter dated Passages de la Calçada, 12 Sept. 1813:

"These officers vied with each other in their endeavours to forward the "object in view in the most indefatigable manner."—COLONEL DICKSON to GENERAL MACLEOD.

The story of San Sebastian divides itself into three parts,— viz. : the first siege, terminating in an unsuccessful assault;

Siege of San Sebastian.

the blockade; and the second and successful siege. The *matériel* at the disposal of the Artillery at the first siege was inadequate, even when supplemented by field guns, and guns borrowed from the navy; but during the second siege the supply was ample, and the fire most efficient. In sieges, the association of the Artillery with the breach made by them ceases when the assault commences; but this was not so in the second siege of San Sebastian, when the assault would certainly have failed but for the powerful fire maintained by the Artillery over the heads of the assailants. Of this, however, more hereafter.

San Sebastian is built on a neck of land jutting out into the sea; and the first point which it was necessary to secure on the land side was a place which had been fortified,—the convent of St. Bartholomew. This was taken, after four days' vigorous cannonade, by assault, on the 17th July, 1813. The guns employed against the convent and the adjoining redoubt were placed in the batteries of the left attack, numbered 1 and 2, and were four 18-pounders and two 8-inch howitzers. Before the assault, however, Sir Thomas Graham, who had been left by Lord Wellington in command, directed as many field guns as possible to be brought into play in support. This was done; and they were found to be of material assistance, and were served with great effect during the assault. The number of rounds expended against the convent and redoubt was 3000: a large quantity of hot shot was employed; and in his despatch announcing the success of the assault, Sir Thomas Graham said: "I cannot conclude this report without expressing " my perfect satisfaction with all the officers and men of " the Royal Artillery, both in the four-gun battery employed " for three days against the convent, and on the opposite " bank of the river, whence several field-pieces were served " with great effect." *[Colonel Dickson to D. A. G. / Colonel Dickson's Diary; and Jones's 'Peninsular Sieges.' / Sir Thomas Graham to Colonel Dickson, dated 15 July, 1813. / Jones's 'Sieges.' / To Lord Wellington, dated 18 July, 1813.]*

The batteries against the town had been in course of preparation during the bombardment of the convent; and the following tables extracted from Sir A. Dickson's letters and returns will show at a glance much that would otherwise occupy much space in description. The numbering of the batteries differs from that of the Engineers; but where possible, *both* have been shown.

The batteries were divided into those of the right and left attacks. Lieut.-Colonel May assisted, during the first siege, under Colonel Dickson; the left or detached attack was under Colonel Hartmann, K.G.A., and the batteries were armed, manned, and superintended as follows :—

RIGHT ATTACK.

No. 1 Battery (No. 11 in Jones's 'Sieges') { 2 24-pr. guns / 4 8-in. hows. } { Against the Mirador and castle, and to enfilade the land fronts.

No. 2 Battery (No. 12 in Jones's 'Sieges') 2 24-pr. guns { Against defences: only used two days.

No. 3 Battery (No. 13 in Jones's 'Sieges') 4 24-pr. guns For breaching.
No. 4 Battery (No. 14 in Jones's 'Sieges'[1]) 12 24-pr. guns For breaching.

No. 5 Battery (No. 15 in Jones's 'Sieges') { 4 68-pr. carronades. } { Against breach, and to annoy defences.

No. 6 Battery (No. 16 in Jones's 'Sieges') { 4 10-inch mortars } { Against land front and castle.

Total .. .. 32 pieces.

Major Webber Smith, R.H.A., was in charge of Nos. 1, 2, and 6 Batteries.
Lieut.-Colonel Frazer, R.H.A., was in charge of Nos. 4 and 5 (the breaching) Batteries.
Major Arriaga, Portuguese Artillery, was in charge of No. 3.

The officers in the various batteries were as follows :—

No. 1 Battery.—Captain Macdonald, and Lieutenants Brereton, Heron, and Williams.

No. 2 Battery.—Captain Deacon and Lieutenant England.

No. 3 Battery.—Captain Rosières and Lieutenant Costa (Portuguese).

No. 4 Battery.—Captains Dubourdieu and Parker, and Lieutenants Harding and Bloomfield of the Royal Artillery, and Lieutenants Silva and Judice of the Portuguese Artillery.

No. 5 Battery.—Captain Dansey and Lieutenant Johnstone.

No. 6 Battery.—This was not manned at first.

---

[1] Jones's 'Peninsular Sieges' would appear to err here :—and to show one gun less than the real number in No. 4 Battery.

Siege of San Sebastian.

LEFT ATTACK.

No. 1 Battery	..	4 18-prs.	Against the convent up to 17 July, 1813.
No. 2 Battery	..	2 8-inch hows.	Ditto. ditto.
No. 3 Battery	..	6 18-prs.	To annoy defences of land front, and support attack. Doubtless these included the guns from Nos. 1 and 2 Batteries.
No. 4 Battery	..	2 8-inch hows.	

The officers of the Royal Artillery engaged in the left attack, were—

Captain Morrison.	Lieutenant Oldham.
„ Power.	„ Story.
Lieutenant Shaw.	„ Stanway.

The strength of the companies of Artillery before San Sebastian, on the 18th July, 1813, was as follows :—

Captain Morrison's (18-pr. brigade)	162 of all ranks.
Major Lawson's	57 „
Captain Dubourdieu's	66 „
Captain Parker's	68 „
Detachment	17 „
Portuguese Artillery..	107 „
Total	476

The ammunition expended during the first siege amounted to 27,719 rounds, and, as the batteries did not open until the 20th July, and the assault took place on the morning of the 25th, the rapidity of fire must have been excessive. In alluding to this, General Jones says: "The expenditure "from the breaching battery alone, on the 22nd July, "amounted to 350 rounds a gun, expended in about 15 "hours of daylight. Such a rate of firing was probably "never equalled at any siege, great accuracy of range being "at the same time observed." Captain Dubourdieu of the Royal Artillery was mortally wounded in the batteries on the first day; and the total loss of the Corps and the Portuguese Artillery during the first operation was 12 *killed*, and 44 *wounded*.

On the morning of the 24th July, two breaches were deemed quite practicable, but the assault which was first intended to take place on that day was postponed until the 25th at 5 A.M. It completely failed: a certain amount of gallantry was shown by the attacking troops, but there was a feeling of depression among them, which seemed to have arisen from exaggerated ideas of the difficulty of the task. Sir Thomas Graham, while giving due credit for the courage which was shown, and which was proved by the list of casualties, felt that his troops were not in the same mood as those who stormed Badajoz. In a letter to Colonel Dickson on the night of the assault, he said: "It is evident to me "that *the troops here* never will carry this breach, unless " every annoyance but the castle fire (which is not come- " at-able at present) be removed. . . . The approach to the " breach is certainly very unfavourable, and does not admit " of attemping to feed or renew the attack, as all must go in " one narrow column over rough, slippery stones,—and *that*, " with an enfilading and flanking fire, occasioned the com- " plete failure; nor would it have been possible at last to " get any other fresh men from the trenches to have ad- " vanced." Further than keeping up a fire which would not interfere with the attacking party, the Artillery had nothing to do with the assault; but Sir Thomas Graham in reporting the failure took the opportunity of referring to their services on the preceding days, in the following gratifying terms :—
" The conduct, throughout the whole of the operations of " the siege hitherto, of the officers and men of the Royal " Artillery and Engineers, never was exceeded in inde- " fatigable zeal, activity, and gallantry; and I beg to " mention particularly to your Lordship Lieut.-Colonels " Dickson, Frazer, and May, and Major Webber Smith, of the " Royal Artillery ". . . .

To Colonel Dickson, dated 8 p.m. 25 July, 1813.

To Lord Wellington, dated 27 July, 1813.

Colonel Dickson to D.-A.-Gen. dated 12 Aug. 1813.

Lord Wellington came in person to look at the state of affairs, and as it was not deemed prudent to repeat the assault, and the ammunition of the Artillery was nearly expended, the operations against the place were brought to a close;—greatly to the disappointment of many. After the failure of the assault, Lord Wellington ordered, for security, that all the guns, with the exception of a few pieces, should be removed from the batteries, and a blockade substituted for a siege. The forward movement of Soult's army, which will be discussed hereafter, produced a further order to embark the guns and stores. On the French being driven back, Colonel Dickson received orders to land them again; the batteries also were repaired, new ones constructed, and everything put in readiness for a second siege as soon as ammunition should arrive from England. The arrival of this was, however, delayed beyond the endurance of Sir Thomas Graham, who was not so familiar with the dilatory habits of the Civil branch of the Ordnance as Colonel Dickson was. In one of his numerous letters to the latter during this period, he wrote: " It is too provoking to think " of such mistakes and delays at home, where they have " nothing else to do or think of but the execution of de- " mands made at an early enough period to give full time " for preparation.". Sir Thomas Graham's correspondence shows at this time a feverish, almost fretful, anxiety about the preparations for the second siege, which was not unnatural in a General anxious to wipe out the recollection of failure. The reader of his letters cannot resist a wish to have seen his face when the incident occurred, described by Napier: " With characteristic negligence, this enormous " armament (*i.e.* two new battering trains) had been sent out " from England with no more shot and shells than would " suffice for one day's consumption." At length everything was in readiness, and the batteries opened on the 26th August, 1813. Before entering on the narrative of the siege, a list of the batteries with their respective armaments will be given, extracted not merely from Sir A. Dickson's official returns, but also from private letters written at the time,—with all the necessary information at his hand.

Dated 7 Aug. 1813.

To commence with the *Left Attack*. The only batteries used before the storming of the city on the 31st August were those numbered 5 and 6,—containing 7 24-pounders, 2 8-inch howitzers, and Captain Morrison's brigade of six

18-pounders. Others will be given, hereafter, which were used at the bombardment of the castle. The object of the fire of the left attack was to breach the right face of the left demi-bastion, and the curtain over it; also, the face of the left demi-bastion of the hornwork, and generally to annoy the defences. Lieut.-Colonel Hartmann, K.G.A., again commanded the left attack.

The *Right Attack* was under the command of Lieut.-Colonel Frazer, and consisted of the following batteries, according to Colonel Dickson's numbering :—

No. 1 (evidently No. 11 in Jones's 'Sieges') containing 2 8-inch howitzers.

No. 3 (evidently No. 13 in Jones's 'Sieges') containing { 1 12-inch Spanish mortar, and 5 10-inch mortars.

No. 4 (evidently No. 14 in Jones's 'Sieges') containing { 5 8-inch howitzers. 4 68-pr. carronades. 6 24-pr. guns.

No. 5 (evidently No. 15 in Jones's 'Sieges') containing 15 24-pr. guns.
No. 6 (evidently No. 16 in Jones's 'Sieges') containing 4 10-inch mortars.
No. 7 (evidently No. 17 in Jones's 'Sieges') containing 6 10-inch mortars.

The breaching batteries were Nos. 4 and 5, but more especially the latter. Field officers were detailed for duty alternately in these two batteries, while the firing was going on : Majors Dyer and Webber Smith being in No. 4, and Majors Buckner and Sympher, K.G.A., in No. 5.

According to Sir J. Jones, the batteries opened with a general salvo from 57 guns;—according, however, to Colonel Dickson, only 48 were in action. The whole commenced by signal, and as Sir Thomas Graham wrote to Colonel Dickson,

Dated 26 Aug. 1813.
" Nothing could be more imposing than the opening of your " fire this morning." The guns in the left attack were found to be too distant for the effect required; but the fire from the batteries of the right attack was so destructive,

Colonel Dickson to D.-A.-G. 1 Sept. 1813.
that in the course of five days, from the 26th to the 30th, the demi-bastion was demolished, a breach made in the curtain behind it, the towers on each side of the former breach laid down, and the wall laid open which connected the curtain with the left of the first breach. The batteries of the

left attack laid open a hornwork; and four guns having been brought forward into a battery (No. 7) which was much nearer the works, they breached the right face of the demi-bastion, and greatly assisted in bringing down the end of the curtain.

About 11 oclock A.M. on the 31st August, the column for the assault, which had now been ordered, moved forward, and arrived at the breach with comparatively little loss. The defence of the French was such, however, that no lodgment could be effected,—more than one attempt having been repulsed; and as the enemy occupied a higher position than his assailants, he was able to fire down upon them and inflict great loss. It was at this time that Sir Thomas Graham ordered the Artillery to commence a fire, which has received the greatest praise at the hands of historians, and of which the following graphic description, from Colonel Dickson's pen, cannot fail to interest the reader:—"The " great body of our cannon, howitzers, and carronades fired " upon the great curtain and behind it—over the heads of " our own men (*only a few feet perpendicular lower down*), " with a vigour and accuracy probably unprecedented in the " annals of artillery. It was the admiration and surprise of " Sir Thomas Graham, and Marshal Beresford, and all who " beheld it. No one could say there was a single error to " the disadvantage of our own people; and the force of the " fire entirely prevented the enemy making any effort along " the rampart to drive us from the breach. I must say " the enemy stood with great firmness, firing over the " parapet as well as they could, notwithstanding numbers " had their heads taken off by our round shot. In short, on " this occasion, our artillery was served in such a manner " that I would not have believed it had I not seen it."

Sir J. Jones says of the Artillery fire at this time, that it was admirable, and occasioned no casualties among the assailants; and Napier describes the stream of missiles, like a horrid tempest, in its fearful course strewing the rampart with the mangled limbs of the defenders. It was a critical time; and a want of precision on the part of the Artillery

<small>Dated Oyarzun, 1 Sept. 1813.</small>

would have produced a fatal panic among the assailants. In his despatch to Lord Wellington, announcing the success of the assault, Sir Thomas Graham admitted that, prior to the Artillery coming into action on this occasion, the state of the attack was desperate; and he described the fire (which after consultation with Colonel Dickson he ventured to order) as having been "kept up with a precision of practice beyond "all example." The ultimate success was almost accidental. A large number of shells and combustible materials had been accumulated above the breach to throw down on the storming party. This was fortunately ignited by the fire of the Allied Artillery, and a great explosion followed, killing many of the French, and producing a disorder which enabled the troops to establish themselves on the curtain, which they fought from traverse to traverse. Some additional troops having entered the town by another breach near the Towers, the curtain was abandoned, and the fighting confined to the streets; but very soon the French were driven into the castle, which alone remained in their hands at the end of the day. The Allies lost 500 killed, and 1500 wounded in this assault.

<small>Colonel Dickson to D.-A.-G. dated 12 Sept. 1813.</small>

To ensure the surrender of the castle, a bombardment from mortars was kept up, until two batteries were made ready in the left attack (Nos. 9 and 10), which were armed with 17 24-pounders,—and 2 24-pounders with 1 8-inch howitzer, respectively. No. 9 was to breach the Mirador and Battery de la Reyna, and No. 10 to operate against the lower defences of the castle, and to enfilade the back of the hill. On the morning of the 8th September, the preparations being complete, the whole of the batteries opened on the castle. Colonel Dickson describes the bombardment as having been conducted in beautiful style, and carried on so vigorously, that in two hours the enemy hoisted a flag of truce. Sir J. Jones says that the fire was so extremely rapid and well directed, and of so overpowering a nature, that the castle scarcely returned a single shot. The terms of the capitulation having been agreed to, two batteries of the castle were delivered up the same evening, and on the next day the garrison marched out with the honours of war, and laid down their arms. Colonel Dickson was one of the three officers detailed to arrange the terms of the capitulation.

The sufferings of the garrison, and of the prisoners in the castle, during the bombardment, were excessive, as may readily be imagined when one learns that "they had not a "bomb-proof in it except for powder."[1]

The siege of San Sebastian has an especial interest for the Royal Artillery,—more especially for that part of the Regiment the duties of which are confined to the use of heavy ordnance. This episode was selected by an able and dispassionate historian, as one reflecting especial honour on the Corps. "It offers," he wrote, "an example of precision " of aim, and absolute coolness on the part of the gunners, " never surpassed. . . . Such services as these were rendered " thirty years ago by no other artillery in the world; and " as the same spirit still prevails which prevailed then, in " the magnificent corps of which we are speaking, it cannot " be doubted but that when the opportunity offers again, " they will prove themselves worthy of the renown that " attaches to them."

Colonel Dickson to D.-A.-G. 12 Sept. 1813.

Gleig's 'Military History.'

These words corroborate what has been so frequently urged in this work, that a regimental history differs essentially in its aim from all others. The glow which it endeavours to throw over past events is not meant to conceal defects, or to distort facts, but to awaken the spirit of emulation;—the boastful way in which special honours are recounted, and distinctive triumphs sung, is not egotistical pride, or aggressive conceit, but merely the fond treasuring of a glory which has been gained by others, and transmitted to their successors for safe keeping;—and the anxious gleaning among the fields of former action is but to find herbs which in

---

[1] "The number of rounds expended during the second operation was "43,112. The strength of the Artillery (including 187 Portuguese) was "681. The casualties amounted to 7 *killed* and 31 *wounded*."—JONES's 'Peninsular Sieges.'

times of peace shall brace the gleaner for coming days of work or danger. The more truly a soldier knows and values the deeds and honours of those who have gone before him in his corps,—the more certain will he be to emulate them. There is no jealousy of the dead. Admiration of their qualities passes unconsciously into a love for their memories; and this love inspires a longing not to be unworthy. It may seem to some but a poor ambition, to use the weapons well which have been given to us,—to sacrifice one's will unmeaningly,—and never to be downcast by discomfort or failure; but it is the highest ambition to which a soldier can aspire. Nor is it easy for him to conceive a higher. Cheerful obedience and conscientious zeal imply most of the higher qualities of humanity; and a perfect soldier must possess both. The great poet of England in these days has been the noblest preacher to whom her army has ever listened. As he places before his readers the ideal of a true knight, the soldier sees a standard which he should never cease to gaze upon. He sees, it may be for the first time, that diverse virtues should not rebel, but mingle; and that such should be found in himself as

> " Utter hardihood, utter gentleness,
> And loving, utter faithfulness in love,
> And uttermost obedience to the king."

And, once realising this,—with the knowledge, possibly, in his heart that there have been in his corps before him men who approached even the standard of Arthur's knights, —he must, as he reads of their deeds, long

> " To sweep
> In ever-highering eagle-circles up
> To the great sun of glory, and thence swoop
> Down upon all things base, and dash them dead."

CHAPTER XXI.

CONCLUSION OF THE PENINSULAR WAR.

THE absence of Colonel Dickson from the head-quarters of the army during the sieges of San Sebastian has had the effect of leaving the Artillery share in the operations known as the battle of the Pyrenees unwritten. He did not rejoin head-quarters until the 17th September, 1813: the period, therefore, between the battle of Vittoria and that date is, as far as the operations of Lord Wellington's army are concerned, almost ignored in his correspondence. In the chapter on the Old Tenth Battalion, in this volume, some allusion to the services of the Artillery at this time will be found; and one or two facts are mentioned in Sir Hew Ross's memoir; but, really, the chief work fell upon the Infantry during these operations. Soult had been sent to take command of the army of Spain, with orders to assume the offensive at once; which he did, with the ostensible view of relieving the blockade of Pampeluna. This he failed to do, and that city ultimately surrendered on the 31st October, 1813, relieving Lord Wellington of a great drag on his movements. The mountainous country, in which the combats which constituted the battle of the Pyrenees were fought, was unsuited to the movements of Artillery; and the Chestnut Troop, which may be taken as a sample of those engaged, had its carriages completely shaken to pieces. Soult, having failed to relieve Pampeluna, made an attempt to raise the siege of San Sebastian; and, on the very day when the city was stormed, the 31st August, he attacked the Spanish forces on San Marcial for this purpose, but was defeated with loss. The conduct of the Spanish on this occasion was much commended by Lord Wellington; and it was a singular and happy coincidence that this engagement,

Colonel Dickson to D.-A.-G. dated 18 Sept. 1813.

Lord Wellington to Lord Bathurst, 1 Nov. 1813.

'Memoirs of Sir H. Ross,' p. 45.

374   *Conclusion of the Peninsular War.*   CHAP. XXI.

[margin: To Lord Bathurst, dated 2 Sept. 1813.] so creditable to the Spanish troops, was the last fought on Spanish soil. Soult withdrew his forces across the frontier, and assumed the defensive. For six weeks Lord Wellington remained inactive, pending intelligence from the Allies in the north, who were then concentrating their forces against Napoleon, and would shortly demand from Lord Wellington a diversion in the south.

During these six weeks, much was done to render the equipment of the Artillery suitable for a rough and winter campaign; measures were taken to expedite the arrival, from Lisbon, of some additional horses which had been sent from England; and, in the meantime, the troops and [margin: To D.-A.-G. dated 3 Oct. 1813.] brigades were, as Colonel Dickson wrote, "kept above water" by the purchase of mules and French horses.

On the 7th October, Lord Wellington made a forward movement into France by crossing the Bidassoa. This has always been considered one of the ablest movements made [margin: Colonel Dickson to D.-A.-G. dated 10 Oct. 1813.] by the great English General. The passage was effected as follows. The 5th Division and two 9-pounder brigades forded at Fuentarabia. The 1st Division, and General Wilson's brigade, with one 9-pounder brigade, and Webber Smith's Troop of Horse Artillery, crossed at Irun; the Artillery of this column being commanded by Major Dyer. The passage of the 1st Division column was covered by the 18-pounder brigade and a troop of Horse Artillery. General Freire's Galician army passed at two fords higher up, covered by a 9-pounder brigade, Bull's troop of Horse Artillery, and a brigade of Spanish Artillery. The passage of the river was effected, and the French position carried with great ease. The most difficult duty fell upon the Spaniards, who behaved well. The French, on the other hand, behaved ill. The 18-pounder brigade was especially useful in covering the passage of the troops.

The attack upon the Puerto de Vera was made by the Light Division and General Giron's Spanish reserve army, supported by the 4th Division, who were successful in getting possession of the pass and adjoining heights; but not until the 9th October did the French quit the Montagne de la Rhune.

The night prior to the crossing of the Bidassoa had been very stormy, and aided in concealing the movements of the Allies. But Soult never imagined such a thing possible as " the astonishing hardihood of passing columns by fords Cust. " where the tide rose 16 feet, and where the sands were " half a mile broad, to force such a river as the Bidassoa at " its mouth." In his description of the crossing of the Bidassoa, Sir Augustus Frazer mentions that, when he reached Irun with Ramsay's troop and Michell's (late Parker's) brigade, he found 400 Infantry waiting to pull the guns over the mountain to the places from which they were to cover the crossing of the army. "But," he adds 'Frazer's with pride, "*Bull's* (*Ramsay's*) *horses never want assistance*; Letters,' p. 290. " they were soon posted on a height with some Spanish " Horse Artillery." From a subsequent official return to Dated the Master-General, it appears that the 9-pounder brigade Vera, 10 Oct. which accompanied the 1st Division was Captain Dansey's; 1813. and that the 9-pounder brigade which accompanied the 5th Division was Lawson's, commanded by the 2nd Captain, —Mosse. Captain Morrison still commanded the 18-pounder brigade; and Lieut.-Colonel Ross's troop of Horse Artillery was held in reserve, moving from one point to another as most required. Including Major Arriaga's Portuguese brigade, and the other troops and brigade already mentioned, there were 48 British and Portuguese guns engaged at the passage of the Bidassoa; and the Master-General was informed that the fire of the Artillery on the occasion was well directed, and that the exertions made by the officers in bringing forward their respective brigades to the point of attack were most satisfactory. Lieut.-Colonel May was Assistant Adjutant-General to the Artillery, Lieutenant Ord was Brigade-Major, and Lieutenant Pascoe Adjutant. Lieut.-Colonel Hartmann was in charge of the artillery in position, and Lieut.-Colonel Frazer and Major Dyer superintended the bringing forward of the guns.

Further inaction followed the passage of the Bidassoa, until the fall of Pampeluna, already mentioned, set Lord Wellington free for a further advance. During this time, attempts were

376   Conclusion of the Peninsular War.   CHAP. XXI.

Colonel Dickson to D.-A.-G. dated 17 Oct. 1813.

made to supply mountain batteries for the coming service. Marshal Beresford brought a few 3-pounders from Lisbon; but it was found almost impossible to procure mules for them. Three guns of the same calibre, which had been taken from the French, had been temporarily equipped for single draught, and placed under the command of Lieutenant Robe, the son of the gallant officer who commanded at Roliça and Vimiera. This young officer subsequently fell at Waterloo,

Ibid. 24 Oct. 1813.

having seen more battles than years. A medley equipment was found for the guns brought from Lisbon,—the Artillerymen being Portuguese, but the drivers and mules being British. These guns were carried on the backs of the mules, and three of them were added to Lieutenant Robe's command. A detachment for rocket-service was also sent from England, but received by Lord Wellington with very mixed feelings, as he had rather a horror of the rocket as

Ibid. 31 Oct. 1813.

a weapon of war. The Chestnut Troop, and Douglas's and Sympher's field brigades were also got over the mountains to Vera, for outpost duty, and to be in readiness to support the attack on the enemy's position, which Lord Wellington had decided to make as soon as Pampeluna should surrender. The difficulty in getting these guns over was very great, and was aggravated by the tempestuous weather which prevailed;

Ibid. 7 Nov. 1813.

but it was effected without accident. When the news arrived from Pampeluna, which should have set the army free for forward movement into France, the weather had become such that movement was impossible. At Roncesvalles, the fall of snow was so heavy and unexpected, that three of Captain Maxwell's guns had to be abandoned in a redoubt, —the guns being buried under ground and the carriages concealed under the snow. Ross's, Douglas's, and Sympher's guns had, however, been advanced still farther to support in the meditated attack on the position of Sarre; Robe's mountain guns were attached to the 6th Division, and the Portuguese 3-pounders to the Light Division and Giron's army; while no fewer than 54 guns had been attached to the left of the army under Sir John Hope,—Colonel Hartmann being in command. It will thus be seen that all necessary arrangements had been made, as far as the Artillery department was concerned.

The attack—which is known as the battle of La Nivelle—took place on the 10th November, and resulted in the enemy's entrenched position being carried at every point, from St. Jean de Luz to the front of the Puerto de Maia; and in the capture of 51 French pieces of ordnance, and 1500 prisoners. The following was the distribution of the Artillery during the battle; and it will be seen that the greater part remained on the left of the army,—the nature of the country rendering it extremely difficult to move Artillery, except by the high road from Irun :— *[Official Report to Master-General, dated St. Pé, 14 Nov. 1813, and Letter from Colonel Dickson to D.-A.-G. of same date.]*

With Sir Rowland Hill's corps—
    Lieut.-Col. Tulloh's Portuguese brigades {One of 9-prs.
    {One of 6-prs.

With the 6th Division: Lieutenant Robe's mountain guns.

To support the attack of the 4th and (Lieut.-Col. Ross's troop, R.H.A.
7th Divisions on the redoubts and {Major Sympher's brigade of 9-prs.
position of Sarre.' (Captain Douglas's brigade of 9-prs.

With General Giron's Spanish reserve: a half brigade of Portuguese 3-prs.

With the Light Division: a half brigade of Portuguese 3-prs.

With Lieut.-General Sir John Hope's corps—
    Lieut.-Col. Webber Smith's troop, R.H.A.
    Captain Ramsay's troop, R.H.A.
        „   Carmichael's brigade of 9-pounders.
        „   Mosse's brigade of heavy 6-pounders.
        „   Greene's brigade of 9-pounders.
        „   Cairnes' brigade of 9-pounders.
        „   Michell's brigade of 9-pounders.
    Major Arriaga's Portuguese 9-pounders.
        „   Morrison's 18-pounders.

There was also a brigade of Spanish Artillery with General Freire's army.

The Artillery with Sir John Hope's column was but little engaged, as its advance depended on the success of the right; but it kept up a heavy and successful cannonade, and met with a few casualties. The Artillery on the right, in support of the attack on the redoubts, was, however, of essential service; and was skilfully handled by the field officers in charge, Lieut.-Colonels Frazer and Buckner. They opened a vigorous fire on the first redoubt, while the 4th Division was moving forward to assault it, and the effect of the fire was such as to compel the enemy to abandon the redoubt without waiting for the assault. At this time the Chestnut Troop distinguished itself especially. " I must particularly notice," wrote Colonel Dickson, " the gallant " manner in which Lieut.-Colonel Ross's troop was moved " to an advanced position, when it reopened its fire at the " distance of 350 yards from the work, and covered the " approach of the others. In this operation Lieutenant " Day was severely wounded." As soon as the enemy quitted the first redoubt, the guns moved forward to support the 7th Division in the attack of the second, but after a few rounds it also was abandoned. In the subsequent operations on the right, the Artillery were unable to take much part, on account of the difficulty in moving the guns. The frightful state of the roads also aided the ultimate escape of the enemy without pursuit. To use Sir Augustus Frazer's words, the ground over which the battle of La Nivelle was fought was " so rugged, that it would be difficult to attempt a sketch " of it.' You must fancy rocks, and hills, and woods, and " mountains, interspersed with rough heaths and rivers, and " everything but plain ground." The casualties in the Artillery were as follows :—

[margin: Cust.]

[margin: Frazer's 'Letters,' p. 342.]

> Lieut.-Col. Ross's troop—
>   Killed : 1 man, and 1 horse.
>   Wounded : 1 officer, 10 non-commissioned officers and men, and 4 horses.
> Lieut.-Col. Smith's troop—
>   Killed : 1 man, and 2 horses.
>   Wounded : 6 non-commissioned officers and men, and 7 horses.
> Major Bull's (Ramsay's) troop—
>   Killed : 1 man, and 1 horse.
>   Wounded : 2 non-commissioned officers and men.
> Captain Michell's brigade—Wounded : 3 gunners.
> Captain Carmichael's brigade—Wounded : No officers or men. 1 horse.
> Lieutenant Robe's brigade—Killed : 1 mule.
>   Total—Killed : 3 men, 4 horses, 1 mule.
>   Wounded : 1 officer, 21 non-commissioned officers and men, 12 horses.

The entire losses of the Allies at La Nivelle amounted to 2694 killed and wounded. The conduct of the Artillery during the battle was such as to excite the following comments: "Flattering compliments were paid by all on the undoubted service of the three batteries of Artillery on this occasion, *i.e.* the attack on the redoubts." "I beg you will further state to the Master-General," wrote Colonel Dickson, "that I have every reason to be satisfied with the conduct of all the field officers, officers, non-commissioned officers, and men, employed on this occasion; as also of Lieut.-Colonel May, and the officers of the Artillery Staff." In his private letter to General Macleod, Colonel Dickson wrote: "The attack of the first redoubt at Sarre it was expected would be a very obstinate operation, and for that reason all the eighteen guns were brought up against it; however, their fire was so active and well directed, and Frazer pushed the guns up so close, that the enemy could not stand it." In another report, Colonel Dickson said that the mountain guns under Lieutenant Robe, and the Portuguese guns of similar calibre, were most active and useful, accompanying their respective corps during the day, and supporting the advance of their light troops. Captain Ramsay's troop and Captain Carmichael's brigade, with Sir J. Hope's force, were especially mentioned;—the former for having repeatedly silenced the guns opposed to him, and dismounted one in the redoubt in front of the 12th and 16th Dragoons; and the latter for having repeatedly driven back the enemy's skirmishers, silenced their guns, and dismounted one in the redoubt opposite the 1st German Regiment of Infantry. Lord Wellington, in his despatch, said: "The artillery which was in the field was of great use to us; and I cannot sufficiently acknowledge the intelligence and activity with which it was brought to the point of attack, under the direction of Colonel Dickson, over the bad roads through the mountains, at this season of the year."

The success of the Allies on the right obliged the enemy to abandon the works at St. Jean de Luz, but any further

Frazer's 'Letters,' p. 335.

Official Despatch, 14 Nov. 1813.

Dated St. Jean de Luz, 21 Nov. 1813.

Major Dyer to Lieut.-Col. Hartmann, 12 Nov. 1813.

To Lord Bathurst, dated St. Pé, 13 Nov. 1813.

immediate advance was forbidden to Lord Wellington by the incessant rain which fell for some days. During this period of compulsory inactivity, every endeavour was made to generate confidence among the French inhabitants, and although rendered difficult by the irregularities committed by the Allied troops, the attempts were ultimately successful. Writing on the 5th December, 1813, Colonel Dickson, after his usual announcement that it had never ceased raining, and that the country was quite impassable, went on to say: " The inhabitants continue to return to their homes, " and we are the best friends possible." The dulness of the weather at St. Jean de Luz, and the inactivity which Colonel Dickson abhorred, were cheered by an announcement that the Portuguese Government had been pleased to promote him to the rank of Colonel in their service, in recognition of his recent services.

Colonel Dickson to D.-A.-G. dated 28 Nov. 1813.

The weather having at length sufficiently moderated to admit of further operations in the field, Lord Wellington forced the passage of the Nive at Ustaritz and Cambo, on the 9th December, with the view of extending his right towards the Adour. On the 10th, Soult made an attack on the Allies' left, near Biarritz, and on the Light Division near Arcangues; but he failed in both. The services on this occasion of Captain Ramsay's troop, and of a division of Captain Mosse's brigade, were very conspicuous. A similar attempt was made on the 11th, in which the French were again repulsed; Captain Ramsay's troop, and the whole of Captain Mosse's brigade, again rendering most valuable assistance in the defence of the position. Marshal Soult, being thus disappointed in his hopes of making an impression on the Allied left, drew the greater part of his force back to Bayonne on the night of the 12th December, and in the early morning of the 13th, made a determined attack with great force on Sir Rowland Hill's corps, which was in position on the right of the Nive. His attempts were, however, vigorously repulsed, and he had eventually to retire into his entrenched camp, with great loss. The Artillery with Sir Rowland Hill consisted of the Chestnut

Lord Wellington to Lord Bathurst, dated 14 Dec. 1813.

MS. Return to the Master-General, dated 15 Dec. 1813.

Colonel Dickson to General Macleod, dated 15 Dec. 1813.

Troop and Colonel Tulloh's Portuguese brigades. With reference to their conduct, Colonel Dickson wrote: "Nothing "could be stronger than the manner in which Sir Rowland "expressed to me his satisfaction at the conduct of both "these corps." Colonel Tulloh was wounded on this occasion. At the same time as the passage of the Nive was forced, Sir John Hope's corps on the left reconnoitred Bayonne. General Hay, who commanded the 5th Division with this corps, wrote as follows with reference to two guns of Captain Ramsay's troop, which were attached to him. "I take the first spare moment to mention to you how "much I was pleased, on the 9th instant, with the very "gallant, zealous, and skilful conduct of Captain Cator, who "commanded two guns of Captain Ramsay's troop of Horse "Artillery attached to me on that day, which were of the "greatest use in assisting me to dislodge a very superior "body of the enemy opposed to me." <small>General Hay to Colonel Dickson, dated 12 Dec. 1813.</small>

The attacks made on the 13th by Soult were admirably planned, but the dogged courage of the five Infantry brigades, which was the whole force which Sir Rowland Hill had at first to oppose to him, was invincible. Although driven back into his intrenchments, his position was one which was most objectionable to the Allies. His attacks were like *sorties* from a fortress,—which he could make in great force upon any point, and if he failed, his retreat was short and easy. It was resolved, therefore, to strengthen the position occupied by the Allies,—to fortify one or two salient points, —and to place some guns of position. The army then went into cantonments,—the Spaniards recrossing the Bidassoa for that purpose,—but, as may be imagined, winter quarters in front of an enemy, known to be very active, did not conduce to any sense of repose among the commanders. The conduct of the Artillery at the action of the 13th December was thus noticed by Lord Wellington: "The British "Artillery under Lieut.-Colonel Ross, and the Portuguese "Artillery under Colonel Tulloh, distinguished themselves." In the same despatch, the name of Norman Ramsay appears, as having been favourably mentioned by Sir John Hope. <small>Colonel Dickson to D.-A.-G. 15 Dec. 1813.</small> <small>To Lord Bathurst, 14 Dec. 1813.</small>

Like that brave General, Ramsay had also been twice wounded during the operations on the Nive.

During the few weeks which preceded the resumption of hostilities in 1814, the mortality among the Artillery horses exceeded anything that had yet been witnessed.[1] An accident, which occurred to a supply sent from England to reinforce them, by which many were killed on board the transports during a storm, was particularly ill-timed. And, to crown the evil, Lord Wellington, having decided on the passage of the Adour, ordered the pontoon train to be increased, and horsed without delay. There was no alternative but to take the horses from one of the Artillery brigades; and the unfortunate Captain Cairnes was again the victim. Luckily for him, the promotions consequent on the formation of the Rocket troops had just been notified from England; and as Norman Ramsay received his promotion to the rank of 1st Captain, and returned to England, the command of his troop was given to Captain Cairnes.

The movements in the spring of 1814 were important, and on a considerable scale. In the end of January, the enemy showed considerable activity on the Adour, and fitted out several gun-boats to keep the navigation open, and to annoy the posts of the Allies. Against these Lieutenant Robe's mountain brigade was first employed, but it was soon found necessary to supplement it with guns of a heavier calibre. But in the following month, a change in the weather—from rain to frost—induced Lord Wellington to commence the execution of operations, which he had been quietly designing for some weeks. These included the passage of the Adour near its mouth,—a feat deemed by Soult impossible,—and a simultaneous attack on the left of the French army to conceal his real intention from Soult. Colonel Dickson was sent to assist Sir John Hope in the

Colonel Dickson to D.-A.-G. dated 30 Jan. 1814.

---

[1] In the end of January 1814, after giving over the horses to the pontoons, 460 were deficient for the Artillery, and 200 others were sick or worn out. To meet this deficiency, 500 had been promised, and were to leave England in February.

former operation, which the reader knows was well and skilfully executed. While the covering fire of the Artillery at the passage of the Adour was generally effective, that of the now famous 18-pounder brigade was especially so. Lord Wellington superintended the operations on the right; and as his numbers were now superior to his enemy's, he was able without risk to carry out both parts of his scheme at the same time, and to drive Soult's forces back from their position. The various operations, which culminated in the battle of Orthes, are too long to reproduce in a work of this description; suffice it to give an account of the services of the Artillery at that great battle. Colonel Dickson being away, the command of the Artillery with the right of the army fell to Major Carncross. Colonel Frazer had been ordered to go with Sir John Hope's army to the Adour, in charge of Captain Lane's rocket detachments, which did good service during the passage of the river. It may here be mentioned, that during the operations prior to the investment of Bayonne, which followed the passage of the Adour, Colonel Frazer was wounded. Although, however, Major Carncross was senior officer of Artillery on the field, yet, being with Sir Rowland Hill's column, he did not participate in the action so much as Major Dyer, who was with Marshal Beresford's column, and from whose reports the services of the various batteries can more readily be traced. On the morning of the 27th February, the 3rd, 4th, 6th, 7th, and light divisions of Infantry, Colonel Vivian's and Lord Edward Somerset's brigades of Cavalry, Ross's and Gardiner's troops of Horse Artillery, and Maxwell's, Sympher's, Turner's (late Douglas's), and Michell's brigades of Field Artillery, had crossed the river Pau, over which a pontoon bridge had been placed during the night. Colonel Ross was no longer with the Chestnut Troop, he having returned to England on leave, and given the command to his 2nd Captain, Major Jenkinson. The enemy was found to be in full force on a strong height near the villages of St. Marie and St. Boe's, and his left covering Orthes, and the fords between Depart and Biron. The battle commenced early in the day, and ended after

Major Jenkinson, R.H.A., to Colonel Frazer, dated 4 March, 1814.

'Memoirs of Sir Hew Ross,' p. 55.

Major Jenkinson, 4 March, 1814.

severe fighting, and a loss to the Allies of 2200 killed and wounded, in the total defeat of the French, with a loss, which—if the numerous deserters be included, who came over afterwards—has been estimated at no fewer than 14,000. Although the verdict of Lord Wellington might satisfy the most fastidious Artilleryman, "The conduct of " the Artillery throughout the day deserved my entire ap- " probation,"—a few extracts from the correspondence of the officers present at the battle cannot fail to be interest- ing;—and the opinions of Generals of division must be deemed valuable. Taking the latter first, it is recorded that Sir Thomas Picton expressed himself in terms of the highest praise with reference to Captain Turner's brigade; and Sir Lowry Cole did the same in regard to Major Sympher's. The last-named officer, who had done such good and con- tinuous service in the Peninsular War, was killed at Orthes, at the very commencement of the action. Major Jenkinson wrote in general terms, that "all the General Officers speak " in high terms of the services of Ross's and Gardiner's troops, " as also of poor Sympher's brigade." Major Dyer, in his report, wrote: " I had the satisfaction about one o'clock to " get Lieut.-Colonel Ross's and Gardiner's troops of Horse " Artillery, and the German brigade of Artillery attached " to the 4th Division, into position opposite the enemy's " strongest columns: the fire from their guns was tremen- " dous, and, being admirably served, soon caused the enemy " to retire. The brigades then took up separate positions " and annoyed the enemy. About 4 o'clock the guns ceased " firing, the enemy retreating in great confusion, leaving " some pieces of cannon on the field. I have to regret the " loss of Major Sympher and many valuable Artillerymen." In his official report to Marshal Beresford, Major Dyer wrote: " I should really feel that I omitted a duty imposed " upon me if I did not recommend to your Excellency's " notice the conduct of Major Sympher, Major Gardiner, " and Major Jenkinson on that brilliant day." Captain Beane's troop of Horse Artillery was with Sir Rowland Hill's force, under Major Carncross; and that officer was able to speak with pride of the steady, well-directed, and destructive fire kept up by it, although exposed to a very severe fire of musketry. On the 2nd March, Sir Rowland Hill's force came up with the enemy, and Captain Beane's troop performed services for which it was specially mentioned in orders. Four guns belonging to it were brought into action with great effect; and one of them, under Lieutenant Brereton, after a few rounds, silenced two of the enemy's, and forced them to retire. On this day, Captain Macdonald, of Captain Beane's troop, distinguished himself in leading on the Portuguese troops, who had been forced back; and received Sir Rowland Hill's thanks in public orders on the following day. Sir Rowland took the opportunity of assuring Major Carncross that, on the several occasions on which the troop had been recently engaged, he had been much satisfied with the officers, non-commissioned officers, and men composing it.

Major Carncross to Colonel Dickson, dated 10 March, 1814.

A period of inactivity followed the battle of Orthes; and not until April did Wellington resume active operations; but in the meantime Marshal Beresford, with a considerable force, proceeded to Bordeaux, and was received with great delight. Louis XVIII. was proclaimed, and the badges of the Empire were doffed by the magistrates. During this time Colonel Dickson's life had become a burden to him. Innumerable accidents and delays occurred to the horses which were on the way to reinforce his brigades; and at the same time the drain on his resources to meet the wants of the pontoon train daily increased. " The pontoon equip-
" ment," he wrote, " has become such a *sink* of horses under
" the stupidity, inability, and inactivity of the Driver officers,
" that I have been obliged, in consequence of the continued
" observations of Lord Wellington, to place Artillery officers
" to superintend the care of the horses, until the arrival of
" the Alicante army, when officers and men of the Royal
" Artillery are to be posted to the pontoon train, by which
" the bridge department will revert to the Corps it always
" belonged to. The bad state of the concern in its mode
" of organization enabled me to convince his Lordship of

To D.-A.-G. dated 2 April, 1814.

" the benefit that would arise by having it under one head
" and managed by the same officers. *He was ignorant of its
" having formerly been an Artillery concern; and he added
" that he did not know how it had got into the hands of the
" Engineers at first.*"

To return, however, to the movements of the army. Marshal Soult, having learnt what had taken place at Bayonne, commenced to retire upon Toulouse, and Wellington followed in pursuit, but very leisurely. The Allies had 40,000 bayonets and 60 guns to oppose to Soult's 28,000 and 38 guns; but a reinforcement was expected by the latter in the shape of Suchet's army from the east of Spain; and the position at Toulouse, on which he was retreating had been strengthened by gradual intrenchments during the past few weeks. In the commencement of Soult's retreat, one or two smart actions had taken place between divisions of the Allies and the French, but without any result other than perhaps increasing the rapidity of Soult's movements. Toulouse was an important strategic post for the French; it commanded the passage of the Garonne; a number of roads met there, which would enable Soult to carry out many different schemes; and it was the chief military arsenal in the south of France. Here, if ever, something might be done to improve the fast-failing fortunes of the French Emperor, whom the Allies in the north were hunting relentlessly to his doom. When Wellington reached the Garonne, his first intention was to cross it above Toulouse; but this was found so difficult that the idea was given up, and a flank march having been made on the 3rd April to a convenient situation about a mile above Grenade, and below Toulouse, the pontoon bridge was laid early in the morning of the 4th, and three divisions (the 3rd, 4th, and 6th) with their artillery, as also six regiments of Cavalry with Major Gardiner's troop of Horse Artillery, crossed without opposition. During this operation, however, the river rose considerably, owing to the rains which had fallen during the previous night; and at last the further passage of troops was suspended. Heavy rain fell again on the night of the 4th, and the river increased so much that the pontoons were obliged to be drawn into the banks, and the army was thus divided into two parts. Strangely enough, Marshal Soult did not avail himself of this circumstance, although it was the morning of the 8th before the river was sufficiently low to admit of the bridge being relaid. The Spanish corps, Colonel Arentschild's Portuguese Artillery, and the headquarters staff passed over on that day. The bridge was then moved a little farther up the river, and early on the morning of the 10th April the Light Division crossed. On this day was fought the battle of Toulouse. The offensive was taken by Lord Wellington, who attacked a strong position which the enemy had fortified to cover the city of Toulouse, and succeeded in obtaining entire possession of it after an obstinate resistance. In consequence of this defeat, Soult evacuated Toulouse during the night of the 11th, retiring by the route to Carcassone. The distribution and services of the Artillery of the Allies were as follows. The Portuguese Artillery, consisting of ten 9-pounder guns, under Colonel Arentschild, covered the attack made by the Spaniards on the left of the enemy's position. This Artillery was warmly engaged during the best part of the day, and distinguished itself greatly by its firmness and correct firing. A German brigade, under Captain Daniel, and Captain Brandreth's 9-pounder brigade—both being under Major Dyer, were for some time employed in covering the movements of Marshal Beresford's column in its attack on the right of the position; and on that being carried, they moved up to higher ground, and assisted in taking the remainder of the position, and also in moderating the fire of the enemy from the opposite side of the canal, across which the French were ultimately driven. The enemy's fire from that point had greatly annoyed the Allies; and Colonel Dickson expressed himself highly satisfied with the counter-effect produced by the fire of Captain Brandreth's and Captain Daniel's guns.

Major Gardiner's troop of Horse Artillery was at first employed in supporting the left of the Spanish attack, and afterwards moved to the ridge carried by Marshal Beresford, where Colonel Dickson reported that it was "of infinite

MS. Official Despatch to the Master-General, dated Toulouse, 13 April, 1814.

service." While these operations were going on, the 3rd and Light Divisions were employed in threatening the enemy's position along the canal, towards the point where it joined the Garonne. In this service, Captain Turner's (late Douglas's) brigade was engaged. Captain Bean's troop and Captain Maxwell's brigade (now No. 4 Battery, 7th Brigade) were on the opposite side of the river with Sir Rowland Hill's corps, engaged in the attack made upon the tête de pont. The officers on the Staff of the Artillery at the battle of Toulouse were Lieut.-Colonel May, Lieut.-Colonel Frazer, and Lieutenants Ord and Bell. From these officers Colonel Dickson reported that he had received every assist-

MS.Return to B. O.
ance. The casualties among the Artillery engaged amounted to 1 officer (Lieutenant Blumenbach, K.G.A., killed) and 58 non-commissioned officers and men killed and wounded. Among the horses, 28 were killed and 13 wounded. The casualties among the Royal Horse Artillery engaged amounted to 8 men and 4 horses; and among the Royal Artillery brigades to 29 men and 23 horses. The remaining casualties occurred among the Germans and Portuguese.

Colonel Dickson to D.-A.-Gen. 13 April, 1814.
Early in the morning of the 12th, the Allies took possession of Toulouse, and the white flag was hoisted. Lord Wellington was received by the corporation at the Town Hall, and addressed them, pointing out the necessity of weighing well the step which they were about to take at a moment when a congress was sitting possibly for the purpose of making peace with Napoleon. *Vive le Roi!* however, was heard from every lip, and every one mounted a white cockade. In the evening of the 12th, a messenger arrived from Paris with the intelligence of Napoleon's abdication, and the restoration of the Bourbons. The intelligence was very welcome to the inhabitants of Toulouse, who could not but feel rather nervous after the step which they had taken. The same messengers carried to Marshal Soult the news of the Allies entering Paris, and of the official dethronement of Napoleon by the Senate; but he would give them no credence. How faithfully Napoleon was served by his Lieutenants, and how devotedly they clung to his cause, must be

CHAP. XXI. *Devotion of Napoleon's Lieutenants.* 389

apparent to the most superficial reader of his history. In him, who has been called the incarnation of war in all its bad as well as good attributes, they saw but one who was *facile princeps* in the profession which they loved;—seeing this, they clung to his cause to the bitter end; and with a hungering in their hearts for his leadership, even while serving another prince, they turned to him, after his escape from Elba, with an enthusiasm more like the love of a woman than the cold, reasoning affection of a man. Soldiers, indeed, have many of the qualities of the other sex. Once let them believe in a leader, and no disasters, no slanders will upset their creed; and from a leader, whom they love, even many harsh words will be forgotten in the presence of one word of kindness. There are those who think that a soldier's mind is like a blank page, on which their own views and wishes may with ease be inscribed. And in one sense they are right. Let skill and courage once be visible in a commander, and the obedience and enthusiasm of his men will be his; and if he supplement these qualities by thoughtful consideration, by kind words, by ready participation in hardships, he will earn from them a love which shall pass even the love of woman. But the kind words will not win it without the skill, nor the consideration without the courage.

On Soult's refusing to credit the intelligence from Paris, Lord Wellington made arrangements for moving forward with the army. On the 16th, however, a French officer arrived from Paris with despatches for Marshal Soult; and this was followed by an officer arriving from the French army to treat with Lord Wellington. Had the despatches been received a little sooner, a loss of life would have been saved at Bayonne. A *sortie* was made from that city, on the 14th April, which, although unsuccessful, resulted in the death of General Hay and not a few brave officers, and in the capture of that most brave and chivalrous leader, Sir John Hope.

The war was now over; but, before closing this chapter, let a word be said with reference to the services of an officer

Colonel Dickson to D.-A.-Gen. dated Toulouse, 18 April, 1814.

of the Corps who commanded with distinction the rocket detachments attached to the Allied army at Leipsic in 1813, and who met a soldier's death many years after at the battle of Inkermann—Thomas Fox Strangways. At Leipsic he commanded, from the circumstance that his Captain, Bogue, fell early in the day. He was then but a subaltern; but ere he left the field, at the head of his brigade he received the personal thanks of the Allied sovereigns; and the Emperor of Russia, taking from his breast the order of St. Anne, placed it upon that of the young officer whose services had been so eminent on that day. In recounting the story of the battle, Sir Edward Cust says that such was the fearful effect of the rockets, that a whole brigade surrendered after enduring their fire for a few minutes; and it has also been recorded, on the best evidence, that, at a most critical time of the battle, the Crown Prince of Sweden rode up to him, and implored him to advance his brigade, as nothing else would save the day. To his exertions at Leipsic was the subsequent organization of regular rocket troops due; and on this taking place the command of the brave men, who had distinguished themselves at Leipsic, passed into the hands of one both able and brave,—one who had done noble service in the Peninsula, which he was to repeat at Waterloo,—gentle and yet enthusiastic,—the late Sir E. C. Whinyates.

From a Letter written by Lady Fox Strangways.

In closing this narrative of the services of the Artillery in the Peninsula, it is impossible to avoid feeling that it has fallen immeasurably short of the narrative to which these services are justly entitled. It is felt that the attempt to place before the reader the chivalry, courage, and endurance of those who represented the Corps in the great wars with France has been defeated by considerations of space, as well as by the writer's inexperience. To realise these qualities thoroughly, it will be necessary for the reader to clothe these skeleton pages with the noble drapery of Napier.

But if these qualities, which are matter of history, have failed to receive adequate description, how much greater has been the shortcoming in endeavouring to picture those virtues, which can only be detected in the intimacy of private friendship, or the study of private correspondence! It is only from the latter that the student is now able to see how almost brotherly was the relationship between the officers of the Corps in Lord Wellington's army. For example:—on hearing of Colonel Dickson's promotion by the Portuguese Government, in the winter of 1813, what were the words of the man whom he had superseded, and who was as able as himself? "I wish," wrote Sir Augustus Frazer, "that he were a General; he fully deserves all that can be given him either as honour or reward." And as he felt, so did all. In the letters, also, announcing the Artillery losses at the various battles in that war, of which it has been said that the Allies "left 40,000 of their own number dead on "the plains and mountains of the Peninsula," how fervently does the loving, brotherly spirit appear! Each good quality in the dead is fondly dwelt upon; and as one gazes on the loving words, written on pages now so faded by hands so long still, there rises a picture of a Regimental unity which it were a sacrilege now to disturb by internal differences. It is, indeed, well at times to close our eyes to the present, and to look back at the past;—a standard is often to be found there which shall dwarf that which we may have set up in our self-esteem, and thought colossal. Possibly, never in the whole history of the Regiment has there been a time of such intellectual life among its members as at the present day; but as the great school of experience, which in the beginning of this century made giants of our Artillerymen, is not now open, it may be that there is almost a danger in this mental activity, unless it be tempered by the study of comrades, who in days gone by were the embodiments of duty, courage, and hardihood. Thus history may furnish to the student a stability which shall allay present restlessness.

Cust.

CHAPTER XXII.

THE SECOND AMERICAN WAR.

THE Canadian incidents in this war have been glanced at in the chapter on the Old Tenth Battalion; and the actions, in which the various Companies were engaged, have been given in the tables of the Battalions to which they belonged. No allusion has, however, been yet made to the disastrous chapter in the history of the war, in which the scene was laid at New Orleans; and, as the largest Artillery force together during the campaign was with the army on that service, it is proposed in this chapter to devote the chief space to the incidents connected with it.

The story of the second American War may be summarised as follows. On the 18th June, 1812, the Government of the United States declared war against Great Britain. It is not uncharitable to repeat what is matter of history, that the United States have always found their grievances against the mother-country more intolerable when that country has happened to be engaged in war. It was so in 1812; and the dream of annexing Canada, which has haunted American statesmen for nearly a century, seemed likely to be realised. But, then, as since, the United States underrated the loyalty of the Canadians; and their attempted invasion in 1812 proved a ludicrous failure. Their first attempt was made with a force of 2500 men under a General Hall, who invaded Upper Canada, but was successfully resisted by a force of Regulars and Militia under a British General, Brock, and had to retire to the American side of the St. Lawrence, where he took shelter in Fort Detroit. Here he was followed by General Brock, to whom he surrendered on the 16th August. A similar fate awaited the second attempt made by the United States. A force of

1400 men, under General Wadsworth, crossed into Canada, near Niagara, in October 1812. The reception he met was a warm one; the American fort at Niagara was captured by the English; and after a few minor operations, in which, unfortunately, General Brock was killed, the American General surrendered himself, with 900 men, to General Sheaffé, who had succeeded to the command on the death of General Brock. A third invasion, on a larger scale, was then decided on. One detachment crossed the frontier between Chippewa and Fort Erie, but was repulsed with loss; while the main body menaced Montreal. Such, however, were the preparations made by the English General, Prevost, at the latter place, that the Americans withdrew into their own country without an engagement.

The operations during the year 1813 were on a larger scale, and success was not always on the side of the British. The year commenced with the defeat of the Americans at Fort Detroit by a mixed force under Colonel Procter; but was followed by the capture of York, the capital of Upper Canada. The lakes became the scene of very active hostilities. A severe engagement took place at the rapids of the Miami, a river flowing into Lake Erie, in which the English were successful, but could not maintain their position. The loss of Fort George, at Niagara, by the English followed; and this became for a time the American General's head-quarters. Disasters on the lakes, which ensued, made the English position in Upper Canada very feeble; but affairs brightened in the autumn with the discomfiture of the Americans in their attempted invasion of Lower Canada. Operations were therefore ordered to be resumed in the west with vigour; and it having been found that the Americans had evacuated Fort George and set fire to many Canadian villages, the English followed them across the frontier, and took Fort Niagara and Buffalo, setting fire to the latter city in retaliation for the injury done to the Canadian settlements.

The attempts made by the Americans in the beginning of 1814 to invade Lower Canada were so unsuccessful, that the war was now limited to the more western districts, where they had the advantage on the lakes. The commencement

Russell.

of the campaign in the west was favourable to the Americans, but the arrival of reinforcements from the Duke of Wellington's army in France speedily gave a change to the aspect of affairs. While the British troops were retreating in good order before the Americans, they were joined by General Drummond, with these fresh troops, and had hardly formed up before they were attacked by the enemy, and the combat known as the battle of Lundy's Lane followed. It was a very fierce engagement, and lasted till midnight; and so closely was it fought, that "several of the British Artil-"lerymen were bayoneted at their guns;" but it ultimately resulted in the precipitate retreat of the Americans. This part of the enemy's force was subsequently cooped up in Fort Erie, which was invested by General Drummond during the rest of the war. The strength of the Royal Artillery in Canada had increased in 1814 to eight companies, under the command of Major-General Glasgow.

The commanding officers of Artillery at the various affairs which took place during the war in Canada, hardly worthy of the name of battles, were as follows:—

At Detroit: Lieutenant Felix Troughton.
At Queenstown : Captain Holcroft.
At Fort Erie, in Nov. 1812 : Lieutenant King, who was wounded, and subsequently died of his wounds.
At Frenchtown, in Jan. 1813: Lieutenant Troughton:—wounded.
At Fort George, in 1813 : Major Holcroft.
At Black Rock, in July 1813 : Lieutenant R. S. Armstrong.
At Christler's Farm, in Nov. 1813: Captain H. G. Jackson.
At Fort Niagara: Captain Bridge.
At Fort Oswego, 1814 : Captain Edwin Cruttenden.
At Lundy's Lane, 1814 : Captain Mackonochie.
At Fort Erie, 1814 : Major Phillott, assisted by Captain (now Sir Edward) Sabine.
At Moose Island, 1814 : Captain W. Dunn.
At Hamden, 1814 : Lieutenant Garstin.
At Castine, 1814 : Major G. Crawford.
At Machias, 1814 : Lieutenant J. Daniel.

It had been decided by the English Government to carry the war into the enemy's country in another direction, and the energy of the officer who commanded the expedition against Washington—Major-General Ross—was a marked contrast to the nervous indecision of Sir George Prevost, in the opera-

CHAP. XXII. *The New Orleans Expedition.* 395

tions of the latter against the States from Canada. General Ross's force came from France, and the companies of Artillery were those commanded by Captain—afterwards Sir John—Michell, Captain Carmichael, and Captain Crawford. Some rocket detachments, under Captain Deacon, formed part of the force. The engagements in which this army was engaged were the battle of Bladensburg, the capture of Washington, and the battle of Baltimore; on all which occasions—as in the previous operations in Canada—the Artillery earned the commendations of the Generals under whom they served.[1] In one despatch it was said, that "the "Royal Artillery, in the laborious duties they performed, "displayed their usual unwearied zeal." It is pleasant to find how often, in various campaigns, the services of the Corps are alluded to in almost these words. Courage is expected from every soldier; but a zeal, which no labour can weary, is a nobler, and as necessary a quality.

The next episode in the war is one which it is intended to treat at somewhat greater length,—the New Orleans expedition. On the 25th November, 1814, a squadron arrived from England, with a body of troops under the command of Major-General Keane, and cast anchor in Negril Bay, Jamaica. Here the force, lately commanded by General Ross, who had been killed at the battle of Baltimore, was also assembled; and General Keane, as senior officer, assumed command of the whole, viz. :—

MS. Journal of the operations against New Orleans by Major Forrest, A. Q.-M.-Gen.

		No.
1 squadron 14th Light Dragoons	.. ..	160
Royal Artillery	.. ..	320
Captain Lane's Rocket Brigade	.. ..	40
1st Brigade, Major-Gen. Keane { 93rd Regiment	.. ..	907
1st West India Regiment	.. ..	0
5th „ „	.. ..	648
2nd Brigade, Colonel Brooke, 44th Regiment { 4th Foot	.. ..	893
44th „	.. ..	647
21st „	.. ..	995
Carried forward	.. ..	4605

[1] In alluding to General Ross's expedition, Jomini, in his 'Précis de l'Art de la Guerre,' says that it was "une enterprise qui peut être rangée "parmi les plus extraordinaires;" and that it produced results "dont on "chercherait vainement un autre example dans l'histoire."

		No.
	Brought forward	4605
Advance, Colonel Thornton, 85th Regiment	85th Light Infantry	456
	95th Rifles	488
	Total	5549

It will be observed, that the numbers of the 1st West India Regiment are not given. This is because at the date of both forces uniting, only seventy men of that Regiment had yet arrived.

Some modifications in the strength of the Royal Artillery took place during the campaign, but it may be as well to anticipate matters, and to give now the exact details of the force as it ultimately stood, on Christmas Day, 1814.

The information is obtained from the MS. official returns of that date; and those shown as "on board ship" were those who had not landed in time for the engagement on the 23rd December. They were landed immediately after the arrival of Colonel Dickson on the 25th December, which is mentioned hereafter.

ROYAL ARTILLERY.	Officers.	N.-C. O. and men.	ROYAL ARTILLERY DRIVERS.	Officers.	N.-C. O. and men.
Effective present	14	224			
„ Rocket Brigade	2	96		2	62
Total present	16	320	Total present.	2	62
On board ship	1	114	On board ship	0	184
General Total	17	434	General Total.	2	246

NOMINAL LIST OF OFFICERS, ROYAL ARTILLERY.

Major Alex. Munro.
„ J. Michell.
Captain L. Carmichael.
„ H. B. Lane.
„ Charles Deacon.
„ Adam Crawford.
„ W. C. Lemprière.
1st Lieutenant John Crawley.
„ Charles Ford.
„ R. A. Speer.

1st Lieutenant Francis Weston.
„ Benson E. Hill.
„ Alexander Ramsay.
„ Frederick Bayley.
„ James Christie.
„ Henry Palliser.
2nd Lieutenant T. G. Williams.
„ B. L. Poynter.
„ Henry Williams.

The fleet sailed from Jamaica on the 27th November, 1814, General Keane and the Admiral, Sir A. Cochrane, having preceded the others to make the necessary arrangements.

On the 24th December, a frigate from England joined the fleet, having brought out Major-General Sir Edward Pakenham, as Commander of the Forces, accompanied by Colonel Dickson and Colonel Burgoyne, as commanding officers, respectively, of Artillery and Engineers. On their arrival they learnt that—certain difficulties in the way of a passage to New Orleans through the lakes having been removed—the army had landed at a creek at the head of Lake Borgne on the 24th December. Being very anxious to join them, Sir Edward Pakenham and his staff pushed on in a boat without delay, for a distance of forty miles, through a number of dismal reed-covered islands, reaching the 'Britannia' transport at 10 P.M. Here they learnt that General Keane had landed on the morning of the 23rd with 2000 men at the upper part of a creek called Bayou Catalan, at the head of Lake Borgne;—that he had advanced to the bank of the Mississippi, and on the evening of the same day had been attacked by a strong force of the enemy, which he had repulsed, but not without considerable loss;—that the army had not yet moved farther forward, but was waiting for more troops to join,—only 2000 having been landed at first, and the remainder having gone up the creek in schooners, many of which had gone aground. By rowing all night, and adding thirty miles to the journey already made, Sir Edward Pakenham and his staff reached the headquarters of Sir Alexander Cochrane, which were established in a few fishermen's huts,—the only habitations that existed for miles round in that most melancholy and unhealthy district. By 11 A.M. on the 25th December, they succeeded in reaching the landing-place at the head of the creek; and ascertaining that the army head-quarters were only 2½ miles farther on, they proceeded to join them. The road which they traversed was merely a wretched marshy footpath along the bank of a little canal or *bayou*, which extended from the

Sir A. Dickson's MSS.

creek almost to the Mississippi, and was navigable for canoes to within 1000 yards of that river. On arriving at headquarters, they found the army on the ground on which they had fought on the 23rd; the number of men landed having been increased to 3500. The Artillery, which had been landed and equipped, was as follows:—

>   2 9-prs. with 110 rounds per gun.
>   4 6-prs. with 120   „
>   1 heavy 5½-inch howitzer, with 60 rounds.
>   1 light   „   „   „
>   4 light 3-prs. with 150 rounds per gun.
>
>   Total 12 guns.

Captain Lane's rocket equipment, with 150 field rockets.
Three 5½-inch mortars (brass) under Captain Lawrence, of the Marine Artillery, with 20 rounds each.

The officers and men who had already landed were as follows:—

> Royal Artillery: 16 officers, and 320 non-com. officers and men.
> R. A. Drivers   2   „   and 61   „   „
> Sixty-four horses had also been landed.
> The Marine Artillery numbered 1 officer and 26 men, and they were assisted by 3 naval officers and 39 seamen.

The guns were distributed as follows:—

> 2 9-prs. } Major Michell.   2 6-prs.   } Capt. Carmichael.
> 2 6-prs. }   1 light 5½-inch how^r.   }
> 4 light 3-prs.: Captain Deacon. 1 heavy 5½-inch how^r. : Capt. Crawford.

The first duty which Colonel Dickson had to perform was to place what guns he had in battery, to destroy a 14-gun corvette, which lay in the Mississippi, and annoyed the camp. The gallant Colonel had a weakness for hot·shot, and having made the necessary arrangements, placing all his guns on the levée (as the river embankment was called), except his 3-pounders, which were sent on with the advanced guard, he opened fire at 8 A.M. on the morning of the 27th December. He fired hot shot from his 9-pounders and shell from the other guns. He got the exact range almost at once, and the practice was excellent. The enemy returned a few random shots, and then the crew made for the shore; and until half-past 10, when the vessel blew up, not another shot was fired from it. The number of rounds expended in destroying this corvette was 191.

The army now prepared to advance against New Orleans; but, from want of horses, Colonel Dickson was obliged to leave two 6-pounders and a light howitzer behind; and as it had been resolved to make the ground which was their first head-quarters a sort of depôt for stores, &c., Captain Crawford was also left behind to superintend the forwarding of the necessary ammunition, &c., for the Artillery. The cold was so intense that the men of the West India Regiments suffered greatly, many dying from its effects, and all being more or less torpid. It seems superfluous to inform the reader that no change had been made in their dress or equipment, on leaving the West Indies, to prepare them for the change in temperature and the continued exposure.

On Sir E. Pakenham's arrival, a rearrangement took place among the troops of the divisions. Major-General Gibbs was placed in command of the 4th, 44th, 21st, and 1st West India Regiments; and Major-General Keane in command of the 85th, 93rd, 95th, and 5th West India Regiments. The Artillery was distributed, as follows, for the advance :—Captain Deacon's 3-pounder brigade and half the rocket equipment under Lieutenant Crawley, were to advance with General Gibbs's brigade by a road leading through the fields to the main piquet-house of the enemy, against which they were to be employed to drive the enemy from the post, and to cover the advance of the column. The small mortars, and the other half of the rocket equipment, under Captain Lane, were attached to General Keane's brigade, ordered to advance by the chief road, running along the bank of the river. Major Michell's two 9-pounders and heavy howitzer, and Captain Carmichael's two 6-pounders, were to be in reserve, and to move with General Keane's column. The guns left behind with Captain Crawford were placed in battery on the river, to prevent boats or vessels passing up or down.

On the morning of the 28th December, at daybreak, the army moved forward; but the results of the day's operations were far from favourable. General Gibbs's column marched against the enemy's piquet-house, known as La Ronde's, and the 3-pounders and rockets having opened on it, it was soon evacuated by the American troops. Both columns then pressed on, and suddenly, at a turn of the road, found themselves within 700 or 800 yards of the enemy, whose force was drawn up behind an entrenchment flanked on either side by the river and a wood. A corvette was at anchor in the stream, to assist the American troops. A brisk cannonade was immediately opened against the English, and, although heartily replied to, the advantages of the enemy's position were such that it was found advisable to withdraw to a distance of about 2200 yards from the enemy's line, and to take up a position parallel to that of the Americans, and flanked by the river and the wood. Captain Carmichael's 6-pounders had been disabled by the enemy's fire, and were therefore exchanged for those left behind at the depôt. Entrenchments were thrown up in front of the 9-pounders, and a battery commenced in which it was proposed to place two 18-pounders which had been brought from the ships, transported on bullock-waggons originally intended for the conveyance of sugar hogsheads. This battery was at the angle of a field adjoining the high road to New Orleans, which ran parallel to the river. It was placed under the command of Lieutenant Speer, with a detachment of twenty gunners; and, as might have been expected from Colonel Dickson's well-known proclivities, it was speedily supplied with the necessary apparatus for heating shot.

As Sir Edward Pakenham had decided on deferring any assault on the enemy's position until some effect had been produced by heavy artillery, every exertion was used to land 18-pounder guns and 24-pounder carronades from the ships, and to draw them as far as La Ronde's house, to remain there until the batteries should be got ready. Ammunition was also landed; but it was found necessary to take all the made cartridges to pieces and make fresh quantities, for which purpose all the available cotton and sheeting were taken from the houses in the neighbourhood, and all the regimental tailors were employed in making cartridges. The want of any artillery machines for the transport or placing of heavy ordnance was severely felt; the necessary guns however having been brought up on the 31st December, and ammunition having been prepared at the rate of 68 rounds per gun and 40 for each carronade, Sir Edward Pakenham directed that batteries should be made and armed that evening, as follows,—their position being where the army had penetrated when the first encounter with the enemy behind his entrenchments took place—about 800 yards distant from the American line:—

1. On the high road, and immediately adjoining the river, two 18-prs., with 50 rounds a gun, to fire upon the enemy's defences on the right: officer in charge, Captain Lemprière. This battery was the most advanced of all.
2. A little in rear, and to the right of No. 1, was a battery of three 5½-inch mortars, with 30 shells each, under Captain Lawrence. A little in front of this battery, Captain Lane with the rocket battery was stationed.
3. To the right of the rocket battery a 7-gun battery was erected for Major Michell's two 9-prs. and one heavy howitzer, and Captain Carmichael's three 6-pounders (one of the disabled 6-prs. having been repaired) and his light howitzer. This battery was to be employed against the enemy's guns, and the centre of his line.
4. On the centre road, which was parallel to the river and main road, and at right angles to the enemy's entrenchments, there was a 10-gun battery, consisting of six 18-prs. under Captain Crawford, R.A., and four 24-pr. carronades under Captain Money, R.N. These guns were to be employed in the first instance against the enemy's artillery, and afterwards to break down the entrenchment a little to the left of the centre.
5. To the right of the 10-gun battery was a second rocket battery under Lieutenant Crawley.

As these batteries had to be erected between 8.30 P.M. on the 31st December, 1814, and 5.45 A.M. on the following day, they could not be very strong. They were constructed of sugar casks filled with earth *not* rammed, one cask in thickness, and backed up. They were only one cask in height, and, as the platforms were also a little raised, it followed that the gunners, when standing erect, were head and shoulders above the parapet. The platforms were very ill-laid, uneven, and unsteady.

The night was very dark, and the working parties were not collected without much difficulty; but on Sunday morning, New Year's Day, 1815, at daylight, all was ready. A heavy fog, however, came on at 4 o'clock, and not until 9 o'clock was it possible to see the enemy's works. During the interval, the columns of Infantry moved to their respective posts to be in readiness for the assault.

On the fog clearing away, the English batteries opened vigorously, and at first a little confusion was apparent among the Americans. This soon disappeared, however; and, as their batteries were strong, and the embrasures strongly constructed with cotton bags, they soon served their guns admirably, and their heavy shot, penetrating the slight English batteries, caused a considerable number of casualties. After about three hours' firing, the ammunition in the 10-gun English battery was nearly exhausted, the 7-field-gun battery had been silenced, a cheek of the heavy howitzer carriage was shattered, and several other injuries to the gun-carriage had been received. The heavy guns had, fortunately, received no injury; but want of ammunition soon compelled them to be silent also, to the great delight of the enemy. Even, however, if the ammunition had not failed, the nature of the batteries was such that the men could not have gone on much longer. The Americans fired from ten to twelve guns in their lines, and from four to five on the other side of the river, many of them being heavy guns—32-pounders and 24-pounders;—and although several of them had been dismounted by the fire of the English, the remainder were as active at the last moment as at any time during the day. The casualties among the Royal Artillery were as follows :—

> Lieutenant Alexander Ramsay : mortally wounded.
> 12 Artillerymen killed.
> 13   „   wounded.

Owing to the uneven and loose state of the platforms, the

ship carriages were found to be very awkward and unmanageable, so that the fire did not attain the necessary precision, nor could it be kept up with the rapidity necessary to silence the enemy's guns. The carronades recoiled off the platform every round. The insufficient strength of the batteries, and the fact of the men being so unprotected, also tended to make the fire less active, and to prevent its silencing guns which were protected by good and solid cover. Colonel Dickson, in his report, said that if he had had heavy ordnance on proper travelling carriages, he was convinced that, with the same quantity of ammunition, he would have silenced or dismounted every gun in the American lines. It has been urged, and with reason, that it was a mistake to commence with so small a quantity of ammunition; but it must be remembered that there was no immediate certainty of a further supply, and the necessity of doing something had become every hour more urgent, as the Americans were busy daily in strengthening their position.

In consequence of the failure on the 1st January, Sir Edward Pakenham resolved to defer further action until the arrival of some reinforcements which he knew to be on the way, and in the meantime to withdraw the guns from the batteries, and the troops from the advanced position which they had taken up. The removal of the guns was not effected without great difficulty. The rain, which was falling continuously, had made the batteries and roads knee-deep with mud; but, thanks to the energy of Sir Edward himself, the whole was effected before daylight on the 2nd.

Although superfluous, it will confirm what has been so often said in the course of this history, with reference to the supply department of the Ordnance, if a few words written by Colonel Dickson be now quoted, with reference to the expedition against New Orleans, which had begun so unfortunately, and was to end so disastrously. "With respect," he wrote, " to our own ammunition and stores, great quan-
" tities of articles have been sent that are perfectly un-
" necessary and never have been demanded, whereas others
" greatly required have never been sent, although demanded

"in the most urgent manner." In this respect the narrative of the services of the Royal Artillery is singularly monotonous.

On the 3rd January, General Lambert arrived at headquarters, and on the following day the 7th and 43rd Regiments marched in. The attack, which was now decided upon, cannot be understood without some preliminary explanation. It must be borne in mind that the Americans did not content themselves with remaining idly behind their entrenchments. They had erected flanking works at each end of their line, and had also made and armed batteries on the other side of the river, which were useful both for direct and enfilade fire. It was therefore resolved to send a column across the river, to attack and, if possible, capture the batteries there, prior to the general assault on the enemy's main work. To do this it was necessary to obtain boats: and a canal was dug from the head of the lake to within a few yards of the river, up which forty-two ships' boats were brought, ready to be launched in the river on the night of the attack. Considerable changes were made in the position and armament of the English batteries. In order to support the attack on the other side, the following guns were placed so as to command the river and fire at the enemy's batteries on the right bank:—

  4 18-prs. manned by R. A. } Under the superintendence
  2 „   „ seamen } of Lieutenant Speer.
  2 24-pr. carronades, manned by Marine Artillerymen.
  4 field-guns, under Captain Carmichael.

The batteries against the main entrenchment on the left bank were two in number, containing four 18-pounders and four 24-pounders. It was first intended that Captain Michell's brigade of heavy howitzers and 9-pounders should be sent across the river, if the attack on that side should prove successful; but this plan was subsequently altered, and Captain Michell's brigade, with Captain Deacon's, was employed in the main attack on the enemy's line.

The attack took place on the morning of Sunday, the 8th January. As soon as it was dark on the previous night, the

CHAP. XXII. *Fatiguing Nature of the Work.*   405

operation of carrying the boats from the canal to the Mississippi commenced, but was found to be more difficult than had been anticipated. There was scarcely any water in the opening which had been cut in the *levée*,—and between that and the stream the water was shallow, and the mud very deep. The greater part of the night was spent in getting the boats afloat. At 3.15 A.M. only thirty boats had been launched into the deep water, and the 85th Regiment alone had been embarked. The fatiguing nature of the work passed description, and the exertions made by all to overcome the difficulties were beyond praise. Many of the working parties were obliged to stand in mud which almost reached their waists; and yet there was not a word of complaint. Had the determination of the troops in the battle of the 8th been equal to that displayed on the night preceding, a painful chapter in English history need never have been written. The difficulties experienced in getting the force under Colonel Thornton transported across the river were almost equalled by those experienced in getting the batteries ready for the main attack. The ground over which the guns had to be transported was very heavy, and intersected with ditches: and at 4.30 A.M. the batteries were not yet half finished. The reader will bear in mind that it was necessary to defer the erection and armament of these batteries until the night preceding the engagement, in order to deceive the enemy.

When Sir Edward Pakenham quitted his quarters at 5 A.M. on the 8th, he was surprised to hear that Colonel Thornton's party had not yet crossed the river; and, as it was so nearly daylight, he hesitated as to the wisdom of letting them go, as there would not be time for them to get possession of the works on the other side, and to bring up artillery to enfilade the enemy's line in support of the general attack, which was to take place at daylight. Still, bearing in mind that, at the worst, Colonel Thornton's movements would operate as a timely diversion, he sent to inquire how many men had been embarked: and, having been informed that the 85th Regiment, with some Marines—amounting in all to 460—had been put on board, and that there was room for 100 more,—

he ordered that additional number to be embarked, and the whole to cross without delay.

Too literal obedience to orders is often fatal. Had the officer superintending the launching of the boats made use of a smaller number, and made more frequent trips with them across the river, there is little doubt that he would easily have succeeded in transporting the whole force in sufficient time. But, having received orders to launch forty-two boats, he obeyed his orders to the letter; nor did the unexpected difficulties which he encountered suggest to him the propriety of consulting Sir Edward Pakenham, with a view to modifying his orders, and bringing them into accord with the altered circumstances. The hurried embarkation at the end, and the smaller force employed, produced the alteration already mentioned in the disposition of the Artillery intended to accompany Colonel Thornton's force. Major Michell, without his guns, and Captain Lane's rocket detachments alone crossed the river.

<small>MS. Journal of Sir A. Dickson.</small> At 5.30 A.M. Sir Edward proceeded to the front. Colonels Dickson and Burgoyne followed him; and the description of the battle may be summarised from the voluminous account of the former officer. Day was fast breaking, and, as they passed the house known as La Ronde's, a rocket was fired, which, they afterwards learned, was a signal for the advance of the columns to the attack. They had not proceeded much farther when the fire of musketry commenced, followed by that of artillery; and, as they proceeded to a point about 600 yards distant from the enemy's line, they observed the reserve troops moving forward by a road on their flank. It was evident that the attack should have been made a little earlier in the morning, as the Americans could not have directed their fire with such certainty against the English columns, which, as Colonel Dickson rode forward, he perceived must be distinctly visible from the enemy's lines. At first the musketry fire was scattered along the line; it then became more general, although not so incessant as might have been expected. The fire of artillery was heavy, and kept up with the utmost vigour; but as Colonel Dickson

advanced, he observed the infantry fire to be slackening,—
heard that Sir Edward Pakenham was badly wounded,—and
met the troops coming back in great confusion, the 1st
Brigade, however, which had been in reserve, continuing to
advance in good order. Seeing the field Artillery on his left
slowly retiring, Colonel Dickson rode up, and ascertained
from Captain Carmichael that he had moved forward according
to order, taken up a position, and opened as soon as the musketry fire commenced; but that he had scarcely fired five
rounds a gun when the attacking columns broke at the head,
and such numbers of men came in front of his guns that he
was obliged to cease firing; and being under a most heavy
fire, without the power of returning it, he had thought it
best to fall back. One 3-pounder gun had been dismounted,
both gun-wheels having been shot away. It was soon apparent that the attack had entirely failed; but the sight of
the 1st Brigade continuing to advance, and the 2nd commencing to re-form, gave some hopes of its renewal. These
were, however, soon dissipated; the artillery and musketry
fire of the enemy continued unslackened; and the 1st
Brigade, followed by the other troops, was soon observed to
move to the right towards the wood, and to lie down under
cover. During the whole of these events, the fire from the
Royal Artillery batteries, under Major Munro, was kept up
with the greatest vigour. Colonel Dickson then moved the
brigades of Artillery, and formed line for action on the road.
While doing this, he heard that both General Gibbs and
General Keane were wounded,—the former mortally. "A
" little afterwards," he wrote, " I heard of the death of Sir
" Edward Pakenham, who perished in a noble effort to re-
" establish the confidence of the troops, which had halted
" from panic just as they were arriving at the line of the
" enemy,—a panic which no exertion could restore, and
" which occasioned their total repulse and defeat. Major
" Macdougal, Sir Edward's aide-de-camp, informed me that
" at the moment the column of General Gibbs' brigade
" stopped they began firing front and rear, and Sir Edward,
" who was at some distance behind to observe the operation,

MS. Journal of Sir A. Dickson.

" immediately galloped up to the head of the column,
" exclaiming, 'Lost from want of courage!' and was trying
" to encourage the troops on, which he succeeded in doing
" for a few yards, when he was wounded in the thigh, and
" his horse killed. Major Macdougal having extricated and
" raised him from the ground, he was in the act of mounting
" Macdougal's horse when he was hit again, and fell into
" Macdougal's arms, ejaculating a few words, which were the
" last he spoke. He expired just as he was conveyed to
" General Gibbs' house, thus falling a sacrifice to the mis-
" conduct of his troops, by which Great Britain lost one of
" her ablest and bravest soldiers, and myself one I must ever
" regret both as a commander and a friend."

The troops advanced until very near the enemy's line; but, the enemy's fire becoming extremely heavy, they stopped, and began firing; and, confusion taking place, nothing could induce them to advance farther; so that, after losing a great number of officers and men, they fell back. A party, consisting of the light companies of the 7th, 43rd, and 93rd Regiments, with one hundred negroes, under the command of Lieut.-Colonel Renny, 21st Regiment,—taking with them a spiking party of Artillery, under Lieutenant Ford,—attacked the advanced work on the right of the enemy's line, which they succeeded in carrying, but not without great loss, Colonel Renny and many officers and men being killed. They kept possession of the outwork for some time, and at last were obliged to leave it, in consequence of the heavy fire from the main work. This force was the advanced part of General Keane's column, which consisted of the 93rd Regiment, with two companies of the 95th. It had been arranged that, in the event of Colonel Thornton succeeding in capturing the works on the other side of the river, General Keane's column should press after Colonel Renny's force, and endeavour to turn the right of the enemy's line through the small outwork. Unfortunately, the delay in sending Colonel Thornton's force across caused Sir Edward Pakenham to alter this plan; and General Keane's column was ordered to join the left of the 2nd Brigade in the main attack. What

CHAP. XXII. *Retreat of the English Army.* 409

was the result? General Keane complied with the new order, and attacked the line to the left of the 2nd Brigade; but the ditch was found to be too deep at this place, and, after the most gallant exertions, his attack was repulsed with heavy loss. Had Colonel Renny's force, on taking the outwork, been followed by the 93rd Regiment, it is extremely probable that, by means of the open communication between it and the main work, the latter might have been entered and carried.

In the meantime, Colonel Thornton's force, which had crossed the river without opposition, advanced rapidly, and carried everything before them. They turned and captured with great gallantry the whole of the enemy's entrenchments, becoming possessors of the flanking batteries, which it had been decided, if possible, to secure and silence before the main attack commenced. These batteries contained sixteen guns and howitzers; and on one of the latter was found the inscription, ". Taken at the surrender of York Town in 1781." Major Michell's conduct during this attack was thus described in Colonel Thornton's despatch: " Major " Michell of the Royal Artillery afforded me much assist- " ance by his able direction of the firing of some rockets, " it not having been found practicable in the first instance " to bring over the artillery attached to his command." Had the attack on the left bank of the Mississippi been as well carried out as that on the right, the defeat of the Americans would have been certain. As it was, General Lambert, to whom the command fell on the death of Sir Edward Pakenham, seeing how desperate the state of affairs was, and bearing in mind that no fewer than 2000 men had been killed or wounded, decided on withdrawing the army to its old encampment, which was to be strengthened to prevent surprise—should the enemy adopt the offensive. He also recalled Colonel Thornton's force from the other bank, but not until that gallant officer had demolished the captured batteries and spiked their guns. He then decided on abandoning the expedition;—levelling the batteries which had been thrown up;—and rendering the heavy ordnance

Major Michell to Colonel Dickson, 8 Jan. 1815.

unserviceable. The boats were removed from the river and placed in the canal, and the wounded were sent away as rapidly as the limited boat accommodation would permit. In answer to some proposals made by General Lambert, the Americans agreed that all prisoners should be returned on both sides; and promised that the wounded in their possession should be sent down the river to the English ships.

The retreat of the English army towards the landing-place, where they were to re-embark, was admirably conducted in the face of great difficulties. The design was so effectually concealed from the enemy, that by the 18th January the whole army, with its field artillery and stores, had moved, and the bridges in its rear had been destroyed, without attracting the enemy's notice. It may interest the reader to know that the rocket detachments acted as the Artillery of the rear-guard. On the evening of the 28th January the whole of the army had embarked on board the fleet. In the despatch from General Lambert reporting the re-embarkation of the army, he wrote: " Lieut.-Colonel " Dickson, Royal Artillery, has displayed his usual abilities " and assiduity: he reports to me his general satisfaction " with all the officers under his command, especially Major " Munro, senior officer of the Royal Artillery previous to " his arrival, and the officers commanding companies."

'London Gazette,' 8 March, 1815.

Before the news of the Peace, which had been concluded between England and America, reached the army which had been discomfited at New Orleans, a successful affair for the English arms took place. General Lambert had now proceeded with his force against Fort Bowyer, Mobile, and, after deliberate approaches by the Engineers, and the erection of powerful batteries, the fort was summoned. After a short parley, its Governor surrendered: begging, however, to be permitted to defer its evacuation until the following day, *as so many of his men had got drunk*. This was agreed to: but the gate of the fort was immediately given over to a company of British Infantry, and the British flag was hoisted. On the 12th February, the garrison marched out; and on the 13th, the arrival of the news of the Peace, which had been signed at Ghent, put an end to further operations.

The Second American War was unjustifiable in its commencement,— was unpopular with the majority of the Northern States,— and failed to effect either of the two great objects desired by the Americans—the annexation of Canada, or the coercion of embarrassed England into their own terms. Sixty years have passed away; and the first of these dreams is as visionary as it ever was. The loyalty of Canada is undimmed; and her power for self-defence is marvellously increased. She remains a Naboth's vineyard in the eyes of American Ahabs: but their power for gratifying their lust is diminishing yearly with the development of Canadian resources, and the political manhood of the Canadian people. What is to be said of the second of the two objects which inspired the men who declared the war of 1812? For nearly three years—while they were fighting obscure and petty battles in the north and west, in which the combatants were numbered by hundreds only — the country, which they had attacked so wantonly while bearing her Titanic burden of war, was writing on the pages of history tales of conquest in Europe, which shall never die. Not until her hands were free again did England suffer the disaster at New Orleans: as if the fates grudged her unfilial sons their wish to strike with disaster the parent country, while in the agony of another struggle. And ere they obtained this one solace from New Orleans, the hand of the invader had reached the American capital.

But what better description of the uselessness of this war can be given than the words used by a modern historian in describing the Peace agreed to between the two countries? "*No notice whatever*," he writes, " was taken of the circumstances which occasioned the war." Russell's 'History of Modern Europe.'

CHAPTER XXIII.

WATERLOO.

THE year, with which this narrative must for the present be brought to an end, was an eventful one. The same year which witnessed the great battle of Waterloo was the hundredth of the Regiment's existence. How marvellous was the development of England's Artillery between 1716 and 1815, cannot be better seen than in contrasting the two struggling companies of the former year with the magnificent force of Artillery collected in Belgium in 1815, of which its commander, Sir George Wood, wrote: "I do believe there never was in the world such a proportion of Artillery so well equipped. The result must be felt by Europe."

<small>To D A. G. dated Brussels, 16 May, 1815.</small>

The growing importance of the arm is apparent from the following statistics. The proportion of guns per 1000 men in the British armies at Marlborough's three famous battles was as follows: Blenheim, 1·2; Ramilies, 2; and Malplaquet, 1·1. In the Peninsula, the proportion was somewhat higher: at Corunna, 3; Talavera, 1·2; Albuera, 1·2; Salamanca, 2; Vittoria, 1·3; Nivelle, 1·3; Orthes, 1·3; and Toulouse, 1·2. But during the whole of the Peninsular War, the Duke of Wellington complained that he was inadequately supplied with Artillery; and as soon as war was inevitable in 1815, he urged upon the Government at home to send him a large proportion of that arm. The result was that in the British army at the battle of Waterloo the proportion of guns per 1000 men was no less than 3·7.

The circumstances, which led to this great battle, must first be briefly stated. It will be in the reader's recollection that in February 1815, Napoleon quitted Elba; and on the 20th March entered the Tuileries. As he had foreseen, the army rallied round him; but to his mortification he found

Napoleon's Plans.

coldness and even mistrust on the part of the Chambers, and a decided apathy on the part of the civil population. He beheld also the whole of continental Europe resolving to arm against him,—to stamp out the man, who had so audaciously violated the solemn Convention of Paris; while England—to compensate for the weakness of her military contingent—furnished money to the other Powers, and a General whose name was in itself a host. No uncertain sound came from the European council, which sat at Vienna; and Napoleon saw before him a stern and growing resolution for war to the bitter end. He was not sorry. If he could win battles, he knew that he would have found a cure for all coldness at home :—the army, which had again placed him on the throne, would, if victorious, consolidate his power, and make him independent of all who distrusted him. He commenced, therefore, to reorganize and equip a force which should sweep all before it. He hastened his preparations, in the hope of encountering his enemies in detail, before they should have effected that concentration of their armies along the entire eastern frontier of France, which he knew they contemplated. It will be seen, hereafter, that on more than one occasion during this last of Napoleon's campaigns, he was guilty of unaccountable lack of energy; but no one can fail to admire the spirit and ability with which in the short spring of that fatal year he organized the army, which was to ensure his complete success, or witness his utter ruin.

To realise his difficulties, one must bear in mind the state of the country which he governed. "France had exhausted Hooper. " her vigour in the unrestrained indulgence of her passion " for military glory. Her blood was impoverished,—her " muscles relaxed, her nerves unstrung, her moral force " debilitated by twenty-three years of almost uninterrupted " warfare. The laurels gathered in a hundred battles were " poor compensation for a paralyzed industry and a crippled " commerce,—for desolate corn-fields and half-cultured vine- " yards. She was 'la belle France' no longer;—she had " used her prime in the debauch of war!" And yet from this country, Napoleon, before the middle of June, had raised the effective force of the regular army to no less than 276,000 men; besides having 200,000 other and inferior troops.

He determined to carry the war first into Belgium. For concentrating an army with this view, the line of fortresses on the French frontier to the north-east offered special advantages. And, on crossing it in force, he hoped to defeat the Prussians and English separately,—to make by this means the war and the Government unpopular in England,— and to detach from the Allies some whom he believed to be but half-hearted in their opposition to him. Another and important reason for selecting Belgium as the theatre of his operations, was the undoubted presence in that country of many who on his first success would flock to his standard.

On the night of the 14th June, Napoleon had collected on the French side of the frontier an army ready to march on the following morning, consisting of 128,000 men, and 344 guns. Of this number, 22,000 were cavalry; and the whole force was divided into five corps d'armée, besides the Imperial Guard, and four corps of reserve cavalry. On that night he slept at Avesnes, which he made his head-quarters, and from which he issued a characteristic address to his troops. Leaving him there,—with the great mass of his army "gathered, so to speak, to a head at Beaumont," and pointing directly upon Charleroi,—the reader is invited to turn to the English army, and examine its constitution and disposition.

A force of Artillery had been in Holland for some time with Sir T. Graham,—under the command of Sir G. A. Wood; and this formed the nucleus of the contingent of that arm in the Duke of Wellington's army in Belgium. Many names familiar to the reader re-appear in the lists of those who fought at Waterloo. Colonel—now Sir Alexander—Dickson was still in America; but arrived in time for the battle. Others, who had received honours for their Peninsular services, were also there: Sir Augustus Frazer, Sir John May, Sir Hew Ross, and Sir Robert Gardiner. Norman

Ramsay, transferred to another troop in order to be present, had also joined; and was already, as Sir Augustus Frazer wrote, "adored by his men:—kind, generous, and manly, he "is more than the friend of his soldiers." Other names will appear, as the narrative proceeds; suffice it at present to say that it is doubtful if ever in one field, or even in one generation, the Regiment has had so many able men gathered together. Frazer's Letters, p. 532.

Sir George Wood was enthusiastic, and revelled in his command. His enthusiasm, while not forbidding him to point out his wants, aided him in remedying or bearing them. They were at first but two in number; but they were rather important to a force, for they were officers and men. Fortunately for him and the Corps, General Macleod was still Deputy Adjutant-General of the Royal Artillery, and was indefatigable in supplying Sir George Wood's demands. As fast as the companies and drivers arrived from America, they were sent to Belgium; but the demand still exceeded the supply. Only six days before the battle, it is recorded that no fewer than 1000 drivers were wanting. This had been partly caused by the Duke of Wellington insisting on the formation of three brigades of 18-pounders, to be placed under the command of Sir Alexander Dickson; and partly by the demands of the small-arm ammunition trains. He would neither hire nor enlist Belgian drivers, saying that he placed too much consequence on his Artillery to trust it to such a crew; and he ordered Sir George Wood to write to General Macleod, requesting that four companies of foot Artillery might be sent out to act as drivers. It was not often that the Duke tried to coax the Board, or honoured it with his reasons; but on this occasion he did. He said that he was well aware that it was not the particular duty of Artillery soldiers to take care of horses, but he was confident that should the Master-General be pleased to allow that duty to be performed by gunners for the present, the service would receive much greater benefit,—"the "Artillery officers having more power over their own men, "than any given number from the Line;" and that in the Sir G. Wood to D. A. G. Brussels, 9 June, 1815.

case of a siege they might do their Artillery duties in the trenches, as at Antwerp in 1814.

It was on the 4th April, 1815, that the Duke of Wellington reached Brussels. Less fortunate than Sir George Wood, he found that his demands, at first, were merely made excuses by the authorities at home for the exercise of official patronage. He at last ironically suggested to them that it would be well, before sending him any more Generals, to send him some men for them to command. The local arrangements, as far as the Artillery was concerned, are graphically described in Sir A. Frazer's letters, and in General Mercer's journal of the Waterloo campaign. The historian must, however, draw his information from a less sparkling stream, —the official letters of Sir George Wood and others. From these it is ascertained that Ostend was the principal port of disembarkation for artillery and stores: that Sir George Wood himself, and afterwards Sir A. Frazer and Lieutenant-Colonel S. G. Adye, superintended the arrival of these at Ostend, and their removal to various places; and that in these matters they were assisted by a man whom all united to pronounce marvellously able, Mr. Commissary Stace.

Sir G. Wood to D. A. G. Ostend, 1 May, 1815.

It appears that the urgent demands for more Horse Artillery came from Sir A. Frazer, who was appointed to the command of that branch; whereas the Duke himself at first seemed more anxious to get drivers for the brigades, and foot Artillerymen for the garrisons of Mons, Oudenarde, Ghent, and Ath. As early as the beginning of May, the Duke almost broke Captain Whinyates's heart by deciding on changing his rocket troop into an ordinary troop: nor was it without much difficulty and pleading that Sir G. Wood succeeded in obtaining permission for him to carry

Mercer's Journal, vol. i. p. 166.

a proportion of 12-pounder rockets with his guns. The Duke's prejudice against rockets was unmistakable; and his unofficial language on this occasion was somewhat unfeeling; but the official reason he gave was that when he

Sir G. A. Wood to D. A. G. 1 May, 1815.

had a proper proportion of Artillery attached to his army, as all other nations had, then he would bring the Rocket Corps into play; but that he thought, situated as he was, the

CHAP. XXIII. *Admirable Horsing of Batteries.* 417

gun a superior weapon. The argument, which had most weight in support of the request to retain a proportion of rockets, was thus stated by Sir G. Wood: "The Duke was "determined at first to place the rockets in depôt, but after "the good appearance of our friend Whinyates's troop, and the "plan and mode he suggested to his Grace, he has permitted "him to take into the field eight hundred rounds of rockets "with his six guns, which makes him very complete." To D.-A.-G.
8 May,
1815.

The horsing of the Horse and Field Batteries during the Waterloo campaign was admirable; but the Field Artillery excelled in this particular to such an extent, that Sir George Wood wrote: "the Horse Artillery are really jealous of "their appearance." The Duke had inspected the 9-pounder Field Brigade, commanded by Captain C. F. Sandham, and had been so pleased that he desired General Maitland to write to that officer as follows: "The Duke of Wellington "has desired me to communicate to you (and I have to "request you will do so to the officers, non-commissioned "officers, and soldiers under your command), his *unqualified* "*approbation* of the appearance of the brigade. I feel "gratified in being able to assure you that he commented "on the horses, appointments, and every part of it, with "peculiar approbation." This company, which was No. 9 of the 3rd Battalion, and fired the first shot at Waterloo, was—alas!—reduced in 1819. In forwarding a copy of the above complimentary letter to the Ordnance, Sir G. Wood said: "All the other brigades are equal, if not better, in "horses." What a contrast to the Field Brigades of Egypt, and the first years of the Peninsula!—how staunchly had the lessons taught by the experience of the latter been studied and accepted! Ibid.

On the 12th May, the Duke desired Sir G. Wood to write to the Ordnance, requesting that two troops of Horse Artillery, in addition to the six already in Belgium, should be sent out; stating, as his reason, the deficiency of Field Brigades, and the impossibility of getting drivers in sufficient numbers. He would gladly have taken 1000 drivers over his actual artillery wants, for service with the small- Sir G.
Wood
to D.-A.-G.
Brussels,
12 May,
1815.

VOL. II. 2 E

arm ammunition waggons, which he had succeeded in horsing in the country. Sir H. Ross's, the Chestnut Troop, and Major Beane's, were accordingly despatched; and arrived, the former at Ghent, on the 9th June, and the latter on the 10th, at Ostend.

<small>Frazer's Letters, p. 530-533.</small>

Constant changes in the armament of the troops of Horse Artillery in Belgium had been suggested with a view to increasing the weight of metal, and some of a tentative description were made in the beginning of May. On the 16th of that month, the following armament was finally decided upon:—

<small>M.S. Return to D.-A.-G. with Letter from Col. Adye, 30 May, 1815, and Sir G. Wood, to D.-A.-G. 2 June, 1815.</small>

	Guns.				Ammunition Carriages.				
	9-prs.	Light 6-prs.	Hvy. 5½-in. how.	Total.	9-prs.	Light 6-prs.	Hvy. 5½-in. how.	Caissons.	Total.
Sir H. D. Ross's Troop	5	..	1	6	7	..	2	..	9
Sir R. Gardiner's „	..	5	1	6	..	7	2	..	9
Lt.-Col. Webber Smith's „	..	5	1	6	..	7	2	..	9
Captain Mercer's (G) „	5	..	1	6	7	..	2	..	9
Major Ramsay's „	5	..	1	6	7	..	2	..	9
Major Bull's „	..	..	6	6	..	..	9	..	9
Captain Whinyates's „	..	5	1	6	..	5	1	6	12
	15	15	12	42	21	19	20	6	66

N.B.—Major Beane's Troop, when it arrived, was armed like Sir H. Ross's.

This change of armament proved very beneficial at Waterloo; but the credit of introducing it seems to have been ascribed, without reason, to the Duke of Wellington. Writing two days after the battle, Sir A. Frazer said: "I "must be allowed to express my satisfaction, that, *contrary* "*to the opinion of most, I ventured to change* (and under dis- "couraging circumstances of partial want of means) *the* "*ordnance of the Horse Artillery.*" And again: "I bless my

<small>Frazer's Letters, 551.</small>

"stars that I had obstinacy enough to persist in changing "the guns of the Horse Artillery." The forethought was certainly more consistent in one who was an able and enthusiastic Horse-Artilleryman, than in one who, like the Duke of Wellington, knew little of Artillery details or tactics.

The arrangement and constitution of a troop of Horse Artillery at Waterloo are given with minuteness by General Mercer in his Diary. Taking the troop, which he commanded, although only its 2nd Captain,[1] as a sample of those more heavily armed, it appears that each gun, and the howitzer, were drawn by 8 horses, and each waggon by 6. Each of the six mounted detachments required 8 horses; 5 were required for the staff-sergeants and farriers; 18 for the spare-wheel carriage, forge, curricle-cart, baggage-waggon, &c.; 17 horses for officers, and 6 mules, and 30 spare, additional horses. This gave a total of 226 per troop. There were 23 non-commissioned officers, artificers, and trumpeters; 80 gunners, and 84 drivers. On parade, the 5½-inch howitzer was the right of the centre division of the troop. It was of this troop that Blücher said, at the review near Grammont on the 29th May, that "he had never seen anything so superb in his life;" concluding by exclaiming, "Mein Gott! dere is not von orse in dies batterie wich is "not goot for Veldt-Marshal!"

There is in the official correspondence of May and June 1815, a collection of quaintly amusing letters from various 2nd Captains of Artillery in Belgium, who, prior to the war, had been left in undisturbed command of their batteries, —their 1st Captains being specially employed—and who now wrote begging that the latter should not be allowed to join, and thus rob them of their chances of distinction and preferment. One of these—Captain Napier—wrote direct to the Master-General, protesting against the appointment of Captain Bolton to command his battery; which, he wrote,

Mercer's Diary, vol. i. p. 160.

Ibid. p. 217.

---

[1] Sir A Dickson, being only *regimentally* a 1st Captain, had been appointed to the command of G Troop, on Sir A Frazer's promotion; and in his absence in America, Captain Mercer held the command. At Waterloo, Sir A. Dickson was otherwise employed.

"hurt him much." Little did he think as he wrote that a mightier hand than the Master-General's was in a very few days to cancel the appointment, and that ere the first battle should be over, he should resume the command, vacant by his senior's death! Pages might be filled with instances of this resentment at the presence of a 1st Captain; nor were they confined to attempts to prevent the seniors from joining. One 2nd Captain, whose commanding officer was wounded at Quatre Bras, wrote off immediately, begging the Master-General to appoint no one in his place, but to leave the command in his hands.

When the Allies were ready, as far as equipment was concerned, Brussels remained the head-quarters of the Duke of Wellington, and the army was scattered through the country, in a way which has excited much criticism among continental writers. Napoleon, when he fought the battles of Ligny and Quatre Bras, had hoped to find the English army still in its cantonments; but he was disappointed, for it had quitted them, and commenced to concentrate on the 13th and 14th June. His intention had been to defeat the Prussians, and compel them to retire on the base of their communications and supplies, and to compel the advanced part of the Anglo-allied army to retire from Quatre Bras on Brussels. In neither particular were his hopes fulfilled. He certainly compelled the Prussians, after their defeat at Ligny on the 16th June, to retire; but they quitted the main road to Namur, along which Napoleon expected that they would continue their retreat, and marched to Wavre by a road parallel to that occupied by Wellington between Quatre Bras and Brussels. This brilliant movement was unsuspected by Napoleon, whose remissness after Ligny and during the early part of the 17th was unaccountable. Disappointed in his plans with regard to the Prussians, he failed also in his purpose against the English. Marshal Ney with two corps attacked part of the Allied force at Quatre Bras, a place in front of the village of Genappe, where two main roads—from Genappe to Charleroi, and Namur to Nivelle—cross one another. The endurance of the Allies was tried to the

Sir G. Wood to D.-A.-G. 24/6/15.

utmost by having to wait the arrival of reinforcements, and to fight against superior numbers, but it was rewarded by a complete, although costly, victory. The first attack was received by the Belgians; but Picton's English division, over 7000 strong, soon came up, followed by over 6,500 Brunswickers and Germans. The battle commenced at 2 P.M. on the 16th; and at 4 o'clock the Duke of Wellington came on the field with a brigade of foreign cavalry, and assumed the command. Later in the evening, the 1st British division, under Generals Cook and Maitland, with its artillery, arrived from Enghien, having marched for a period of fifteen hours;[1] and with the approaching darkness came the retreat of the French on Frasnes. This defeat ruined the French Emperor's plans, and paved the way for the greater defeat of the 18th. *Cust.*

The following field-officers, troops, and brigades of Artillery were present at the battle of Quatre Bras:— *Sir G. Wood to D.-A.-G 24/6/15.*

Lieut.-Colonel S. G. Adye, commanding the Artillery of the 1st Division.
„ Sir A. Frazer, commanding Royal Horse Artillery.
„ Sir J. Hartmann, commanding King's German Artillery.
„ Sir J. May, Assist. Adjutant-General.
„ Sir A. Dickson.

Captain Sandham's Brigade, R.A. } Attached to the 1st Division.
Major Kuhlmann's Troop, K. G. L. }

Major Lloyd's Brigade, R.A. }
Capt. Cleeve's „ K. G. L. } „ 3rd Division.

Major Roger's „ R.A. „ 5th Division.

Major Heise, with Captain Rettberg's brigade of Hanoverian Artillery, was also engaged.

The Horse Artillery and British Cavalry did not come up until after the battle; and the want of the latter was severely felt during the day, the French being very strong in that arm.

Major Lloyd's and Major Rogers' batteries were warmly engaged at Quatre Bras. Two guns belonging to the former were lost, but were afterwards recovered. The troop of German Horse Artillery was of great service, sustaining *Sir A. Frazer's Letters, p. 541.*

---

[1] In recent times, the most remarkable march made by Artillery was on one occasion during the Indian Mutiny, when a battery of R.H.A. marched 78 miles in 24 hours, and continued marching, elephants carrying the forage. *Communicated by Sir D. E. Wood, K.C.B., &c. &c.*

the reputation which that corps had earned in the Peninsula. But the losses among the Artillerymen were small in proportion to those among the regiments of Infantry. Of 3750 British killed and wounded at Quatre Bras, only 28 belonged to the Royal Artillery. The losses were, however, very severe among the horses, and crippled the batteries very much. In Sir George Wood's despatch announcing the battle, he wrote: "I beg you will be pleased to mention to " his Lordship, the Master-General, the good conduct " of that part of the Artillery which was engaged on " the 16th. They were warmly engaged, being several " times charged by the French Cavalry,—and tended much " to the success of the day." The merits of Quatre Bras, as a scene on which English courage and endurance were nobly displayed, are too often forgotten in the recollections of the greater battle, by which it was so speedily followed.

Sir A. Frazer's Letters, p. 540.

To D.-A.-G. 24 June, 1815.

In consequence of the Prussians moving on Wavre, it became necessary for the Duke of Wellington to fall back also; and orders were given on the 17th for the army to retire to Mont St. Jean, not far from the village of Waterloo. This position had been carefully selected and examined by the Duke, with a view to the event which was now at hand. The retreat through Genappe was effected with the greatest order, and was covered by the Horse Artillery and Cavalry. Captain Mercer's and Captain Whinyates's troops were the last to retire, the former officer having been detailed for that duty—the latter having exceeded his orders, and remained behind, hoping to come in for some fighting.[1] For the Horse Artillery and Cavalry, the retreat was no bed of roses. The heavy rains had made the roads and fields almost impassable. Genappe is in a hollow; and as the Horse Artillery mounted

Mercer's Diary, vol. i. p. 270.

---

[1] This statement is based on Mercer's diary, but it seems possible that he refers to the retreat of the centre of the army, to which he was attached. Sir Robert Gardiner, who was on the extreme left, always believed that his troop was the last to retire. Certainly, the army retreated from the right, and Sir Robert's troop, on the left, had to make a very hurried retreat through the fields to the east of the Genappe and Brussels road.

the slopes towards La Belle Alliance, pursued by the French
Cavalry, they had to move at a gallop through fields, which
would have tried them even at a walk. Sir Robert Gardiner's troop was especially taxed in this way; and he used
frequently to say that it was fortunate that his 6-pounder
armament had not been exchanged for the heavier nature;
for his guns would certainly have been captured had this
been done. The nature of the ground which was traversed
may be gathered from the fact that not a horse in Sir
Robert's troop reached Mont St. Jean without losing at least
one shoe. The whole night of the 17th was spent in shoeing *Commu-*
the horses, and getting the troop ready for the work of the *nicated by Colonel*
following day. *L. Gar- diner,*

On the morning of the 18th June, the French army was *R.-H.-A.*
drawn up on the south side, and the Allies on the Brussels
side, of a long hollow, which common *parlance* has inaccu-
rately named the "field of Waterloo." The strength of the
French army, according to the industrious Siborne—checked
by later writers—was, in round numbers, 72,000; that of
the Allies, about 68,000. The French had, in addition,
Marshal Grouchy's force of 33,000 men, fourteen miles away,
on a blind chase after the Prussians, who were already six
miles nearer Waterloo than their pursuers; and Wellington
had a division of 18,000 men on detachment to his right,
towards Hal, at a distance of ten miles. This extra precaution—this strange nervousness about his right—has been
much and justly condemned by critics. When one reflects
of what value that force would have been at different times
during the 18th, one cannot but feel that if the Allied information to the right had been as carefully procured as it had
been to the left of the army, the whole of these 18,000 men
might have been drawn in to the main body. However,
even admitting this to be a blunder, the French were nevertheless utterly outmanœuvred. Napoleon's remissness on
the night of the 16th, and his idleness on the morning of
the 17th, were now to receive the punishment which such
qualities in the face of an enemy always deserve, and
generally get.

Sir George Wood to D.-A.-G. 24 June, 1815.

The Artillery engaged on the side of the Allies was as follows:—

Sir G. A Wood commanding.
Lieut.-Colonel Sir A. Frazer, commanding R. H. A.
„ S. G. Adye, „ Artillery of 1st Division.
„ Gold, „ „ 2nd Division.
„ Williamson, „ „ 3rd Division.
„ Sir J. Hartmann, „ King's German Artillery.
„ A. Macdonald, „ {Six troops of H. A. attached to Cavalry.
Major Drummond, „ Reserve Artillery.
Lieut.-Colonel Sir A. Dickson.

The troops of Horse Artillery attached to the Cavalry were those commanded by—

Lieut.-Colonel Webber Smith,
Lieut.-Colonel Sir R. Gardiner,
Major R. Bull,
Major N. Ramsay,
Captain Mercer, and
Captain Whinyates.

The divisional Artillery was as follows:—

Captain Sandham's Brigade, R.A. } 1st Division.
Major Kuhlmann's Troop, K.G.A. }
Captain Bolton's Brigade, R.A. } 2nd Division.
Major Sympher's Troop, K.G.A. }
Major Lloyd's Brigade, R.A. } 3rd Division.
Captain Cleve's Brigade, R.A. }
Major Rogers' Brigade, R.A.   5th Division.

The reserve Artillery—the whole of which came into action early in the day—consisted of—

Lieut.-Colonel Sir H. D. Ross's Troop, R.H.A.
Major Beane's „ „
Captain Sinclair's Brigade, R.A.

Major Heise, and two brigades of Hanoverian Artillery, were also engaged.

It will thus be seen that the number of troops and brigades of the Royal Artillery engaged at the battle of Waterloo was thirteen, or a force of 78 guns, exclusive of the German and Hanoverian Artillery. Some companies of the regiment were also present with the small-arm ammunition for the army.

Captain Baynes acted as Brigade-Major to the Artillery;

and Captain Pakenham, Lieutenants Coles, J. Bloomfield, and W. Bell, acted as staff officers.

The description of the battle which will now be given will be brief; as it will be necessary subsequently to enter with more detail into the services and conduct of the Artillery during the day. *Vide* vol. ii. Appendix A

The battle of Waterloo was—as Sir James Shaw Kennedy expresses it—a drama in five acts. The first was the attack on Hougomont at 11.30 A.M., many precious hours having been wasted by Napoleon; the second was the attack by the French on La Haye Sainte, at half-past 1; the third was the celebrated succession of cavalry attacks on the Allied line between Hougomont and La Haye Sainte, commencing at 4 o'clock; the fourth was the successful attack by Marshal Ney on La Haye Sainte, at 6 o'clock,—an event which, if properly used by Napoleon, might have had a very grave effect on the result of the battle, for it caused a great gap in the very centre of the Allied line; and the fifth was the celebrated attack on the Allied centre made by 12 battalions of the Imperial Guard, strengthened by the co-operation of other divisions, and supported " by a powerful Artillery, and " what remained of the Cavalry." Kennedy.

In the attack on Hougomont, the battery which most distinguished itself was the famous old I Troop—now D Battery, B Brigade, R.H.A.—under Major R. Bull, whose Peninsular history rivals that of the Chestnut Troop. It was armed with howitzers; and cleared the wood in front of Hougomont of the French troops,—firing shell with wonderful accuracy over the heads of the English Infantry; an operation so delicate, as to make the Duke remark to Sir Augustus Frazer, who ordered it, that he hoped he was not undertaking too much. But Sir Augustus said that he could depend on the troop; and the event proved that he was right: for after ten minutes' firing, the French were driven out of the wood. Webber Smith's troop was also hotly engaged during this first attack, and suffered during the day very severely, not merely—as all did—from the French skirmishers, but also from having been on one occasion enfiladed by one of Prince

Frazer's Letters, p. 556.

Jerome's batteries. Captain Bolton's field brigade, which was to have so great glory at a critical period in the day, was in action at the first attack on Hougomont; and when subsequently moved more to the centre of the Allied line, its place to the left of Hougomont was taken by Norman Ramsay's troop. It has already been mentioned that the first shot fired by the Allied Artillery at Waterloo was fired by Captain Sandham's brigade. This was in reply to the first attack on Hougomont; and during the day no fewer than 1100 rounds of ammunition were fired by this single brigade.[1] Although beyond the province of this work to enter into the Infantry details of the battle, it must yet be said that, even in a day when the British Infantry showed a valour and endurance which have never been surpassed, their defence of Hougomont shines with especial lustre. Knowing its value, as strengthening the right of his line, the Duke had taken precautions on the previous night by loopholing the walls to render its defence more practicable. Although set on fire, and attacked repeatedly by superior numbers, it was never lost; its defenders showing a tenacity and courage unexampled almost in the annals of war.

In the second act of the drama—the first attack on La Haye Sainte—Captain Whinyates's troop and Major Rogers' field brigade were first engaged; and it is important to remember, with a view to the argument, which is to come, that it was during this act that the Artillery of the reserve was brought up. Sir Hew Ross's and Major Beane's troops suffered at this time great loss. Among the officers alone, Major Beane was killed, and both 2nd captains and two subalterns wounded.

Vide Appendix A.

The third act, the charges of the French cavalry, will be fully discussed in the argument, which will be found in the Appendix. Suffice it to say, at present, that they were preceded by clouds of skirmishers, and by a tremendous artillery fire; and that at no period of the day were the

---

[1] Many of the guns at Waterloo actually became unserviceable *from incessant firing.*

losses among the Artillery more severe. Among those who fell then was Norman Ramsay; and it was the lot of his dearest friend to witness and to tell the circumstances. "In "a momentary lull of the fire," wrote Sir Augustus Frazer, "I buried my friend Ramsay, from whose body I took the "portrait of his wife, which he always carried next his "heart. Not a man assisted at the funeral who did not "shed tears. Hardly had I cut from his head the hair "which I enclose, and laid his yet warm body in the grave, "when our convulsive sobs were stifled by the necessity of "returning to renew the struggle." Two days later, the same hand wrote: "Now that the stern feelings of the day "have given way to the return of better ones, I feel with "the bitterness of anguish not to be described, the loss of "my friend Ramsay. Nor for this friend alone, but for "many others, though less dear than poor Norman." And yet again, writing from Paris, Sir A. Frazer said: "I cannot "get Ramsay out of my head; such generosity, such ro- "mantic self-devotion as his, are not common." It was written of Ramsay, "Sibi satis vixit,—non patriæ;" and it is difficult to conceive a nobler eulogy. A man who never tampered with temptation, but trampled on it instead,—he left behind him the story of a life, which is a model for his successors in the Corps to imitate. There is a Waterloo going on daily in a soldier's life: his enemies are more skilled than Napoleon—they are as relentless as death: they come dressed in many garbs, but their names are sloth, ignorance, and vice; and the weapon by which alone they can be overcome is an earnest and conscientious performance of duty. This weapon must be grasped most firmly, and wielded most mercilessly, when the duties to be performed are monotonous or uninviting; but its unfailing use, even through a life of uninteresting routine, will earn for the soldier, when the night comes, the same words as were spoken of Norman Ramsay, "Satis sibi vixit,—non patriæ."

Frazer's Letters, p. 548.

Nivelle, 20 June, 1815.

Dated 6 July, 1815.

The fourth act of the drama witnessed, at 6 o'clock, the capture of La Haye Sainte by the French, after a magnificent defence by Major Baring and part of the King's German

Legion, which only failed from want of ammunition. There seems little doubt that the Duke of Wellington had underrated the importance of this position; indeed, he is said in later years to have admitted it. Fortunately, Napoleon did not sufficiently note the advantage he had gained; and contented himself with using its now friendly cover in preparation for his great final effort.

The Prussians had by this time arrived, and were in force on the French right. At the village of Planchenoit, they were already in such numbers that the French General, Loban, required 16,000 men to keep them in check. On the extreme left of the English, at Papillote, the advanced parties of another Prussian column had also arrived; and, all fear for his left being now at an end, the Duke of Wellington was enabled to strengthen his centre, and his right centre, by moving Vivian's and Vaudeleur's Cavalry Brigades from the left, accompanied by Sir Robert Gardiner's troop of Horse Artillery.

The necessity of a great final effort was now apparent to Napoleon; and the curtain rose on the fifth act of the drama at half-past 7 o'clock. It is a point which the Artilleryman should never forget, that, in this majestic advance of the Imperial Guard, its head was broken and thrown into confusion by the fire of Captain Bolton's guns, before the 52nd Regiment, and the Guards, did their celebrated work. It was at this time that Captain Bolton was killed, and that the Duke personally gave his orders to Captain Napier,— the 2nd Captain,—as the French approached, to load with canister.

While the advancing columns of the enemy were in the hollow, their artillery carried on a cannonade over their heads, more terrible than had been witnessed during the day. The following description of Mercer's battery at the end of the day will give the reader an idea of the murderous fire to which the Allies were exposed. "Of 200 fine " horses," he wrote, "with which we had entered the battle, " upwards of 140 lay dead, dying, or severely wounded. Of " the men, scarcely two-thirds of those necessary for *four*

[marginal note: Mercer's Journal, vol. i. p. 331.]

"guns remained; and these so completely exhausted, as to
"be totally incapable of further exertion. Lieutenant
"Breton had had three horses killed under him; Lieutenant
"Hinks was wounded in the breast by a spent ball;
"Lieutenant Leathes on the hip by a splinter; and although
"untouched myself, my horse had no less than eight wounds.
"Our guns and carriages were all together in a confused
"heap, intermingled with dead and wounded horses, which
"it had not been possible to disengage from them." And
this was but typical of most of the batteries engaged.

As for the Infantry, words cannot paint too highly their
endurance on that long day. One regiment had 400 men
killed or wounded, before they were allowed to fire a round;
and all suffered heavily. Yet there was not a word of
distrust as regarded their great commander. They pined
with all their hearts for permission to attack, instead of
lying where they often were—being shot by scores; but
discipline was stronger than desire. Even at the worst
times, a word from the Duke, or a report that he was coming,
sufficed to produce a silence and a steadiness, as perfect as if
on parade in a barrack-square. For those who were present,
Waterloo was thus a double victory,—over their enemies,
and over themselves. True discipline is a succession of such
victories.

With the noble charge of the 52nd, followed by the
general advance of the whole line, the French retreat
became a rout,—the most disastrous, as has been said, on
record: but the record referred to did not include the
Titanic battles of the last few years. The Prussians took
up the pursuit, and the Allied Army bivouacked on the field
of battle.

So much detail connected with the services of the Artillery
at Waterloo must of necessity be given in the Appendix,
that it has not been thought advisable to anticipate it here.
But there are several interesting Regimental matters connected with the battle, for the insertion of which this seems
the most suitable place.

In the first place, the names of the officers belonging to

the troops and brigades, which were present, may be given.

TOTAL NUMBER OF ALL RANKS of the following TROOPS and BRIGADES present at WATERLOO, according to MS. RETURNS to BOARD OF ORDNANCE, dated Paris, 18th September, 1815.

R.H.A.

Major R. Bull's Troop, now "D" Battery, B Brigade.

	No.
2nd Captain Brevet-Major R. M. Cairnes .. Lieutenant Louis .. ,, Smith .. ,, Townsend	168

Lieutenant Colonel Webber Smith's Troop, now "B" Battery, B Brigade.

| 2nd Captain E. T. Walcott ..
 Lieutenant Edwards..
 ,, Forster ..
 ,, Crawford.. | 167 |

Lieutenant-Colonel Sir Robert Gardiner's Troop, now "A" Battery, B Brigade.

| 2nd Captain T. Dyneley ..
 Lieutenant Harding
 ,, Swabey
 ,, Ingilby | 174 |

Captain Whinyates's Troop (reduced in 1816).

| 2nd Captain Dansey..
 Lieutenant Strangways
 ,, Wright ..
 ,, Ward
 ,, Ord | 194 |

2nd Captain Mercer's Troop, now "C" Battery, B Brigade.

| 2nd Captain Newland
 Lieutenant Leathes ..
 ,, Hinks
 ,, Breton | 164 |

Major Ramsay's Troop, now "D" Battery, A Brigade.

| 2nd Captain A. Macdonald ..
 Lieutenant Brereton..
 ,, Sandilands
 ,, Robe | 173 |

Lieutenant-Colonel Sir H. D. Ross's Troop, now "A" Battery, A Brigade.

| 2nd Captain and Brevet-Major Parker ..
 Lieutenant Hardinge
 ,, Day ..
 ,, Warde
 ,, Onslow .. | 159 |

CHAP. XXIII.   *Officers present at Waterloo.*   431

Total Number of all ranks present at Waterloo, &c., continued.

R.H.A.

Major Beane's Troop (reduced in 1816).

	No.
2nd Captain Webber..	
Lieutenant Maunsell	
„ Bruce	109
„ Cromie	

R.A.

Captain C. F. Sandham's Brigade (reduced in 1819).

2nd Captain Stopford	
Lieutenant Foot	
„ Baynes	105
„ Jago	

This and all the other Field Brigades were armed, each with five 9-pounders and one 5½-inch howitzer.

Captain Bolton's Brigade, now "E" Battery, 8th Brigade.

MS. Returns, dated 30 May, 1815.

2nd Captain Napier	
Lieutenant Pringle	
„ Anderson	
„ Spearman	101
„ Sharpin	
„ B. Cuppage	

Major Lloyd's Brigade (reduced in April, 1817).

2nd Captain S. Rudyerd	
Lieutenant Phelps	97
„ Harvey	

Captain Sinclair's Brigade, now "4" Battery, 3rd Brigade (Captain Gordon being absent).

2nd Captain F. Macbean	
Lieutenant Wilson	
„ Poole	104
„ Burnaby	

Major Roger's Brigade, now "7" Battery, 13th Brigade.

Lieutenant R. Manners	94
(*Other officers' names not given.*)	

These were the only troops and brigades which were engaged. There were others, which were in the vicinity, but not present at the battle; and there were also detachments of other brigades present with small-arm ammunition. Lieutenants E. Trevor, W. Lemoine, J. Bloomfield, E. W. Wood, G. T. Maule, G. T. Hume, and others already named, were present on staff or unattached duty.

Of the officers named above, the following were killed or wounded at the battle of Waterloo :—

Sir George A. Wood to Master-General, 24 June, 1815.

Major W. N. Ramsay, R.H.A,		..	Killed.	
„ R. M. Cairnes	„	..	„	
„ G. Beane	„	..	„	
„ J. B. Parker	„	..	Severely wounded : leg amputated.	
„ R. Bull	„	..	Slightly wounded.	
Captain Whinyates	„	..	„	
„ Dansey	„	..	„	
„ Macdonald	„	..	„	
„ Webber	„	..	„	
Lieutenant Strangways	„	..	„	
„ Brereton	„	..	Severely, not dangerously.	
„ Robe	„	..	„ (since dead).	
„ Smith	„	..	Slightly wounded.	
„ Cromie	„	..	Severely : both legs amputated.	
„ Forster	„	..	„ not dangerously.	
„ Crawford	„	..	Slightly wounded.	
„ Day	„	..	„	
Major H. Baynes	R.A.	..	Slightly wounded.	
Captain Bolton	„	..	Killed.	
Major Lloyd	„	..	Severely wounded (died).	
Captain Napier	„	..	Severely wounded.	
Lieutenant Spearman	„	..	„	
„ R. Manners	„	..	Severely (since dead).	
„ Harvey	„	..	„ right arm amputated.	
„ Poole	„	..	„ not dangerously.	

Dated 24 June, 1815.

The numerical losses, as shown by Sir George Wood in his official return to the Ordnance, were as follows : —

	Officers.	Sergeants.	Rank and File.	Horses.
Royal Horse Artillery—				
Killed	3	1	31	229
Wounded.. ..	14	8	107	59
Missing	0	0	7	21
Total ..	17	9	145	309
Royal Artillery—				
Killed	1	0	19	80
Wounded	7	4	61	34
Missing	0	0	2	12
Total	8	4	82	126

CHAP. XXIII. *Killed and Wounded at Waterloo.* 433

	Officers.	Sergeants.	Rank and File.	Horses.
King's German Legion Artillery—				
Killed	1	1	10	47
Wounded	6	1	47	44
Missing	0	0	1	3
Total	7	2	58	94
General Total	32	15	285	529

There were two field brigades, which formed part of the Duke of Wellington's army, but which were not brought up in time for the battle, although they were of great importance during the subsequent siege operations against the fortresses. Their armament was the same as that of the others; and one of them, Captain Brome's, would appear to have been in position, although not engaged;—possibly detached at Hal. The officers with these, and their numbers, were as follows :— *Vide* 'Hist. R.A.' vol. i. p. 221.

	Total of all Ranks.
Captain Brome's Brigade, now 2 Battery, 13th Brigade, R.A.	
2nd Captain J. E. G. Parker	
Lieutenant Saunders	
„ Cater	106
„ Molesworth	
Major G. W. Unett, now 3 Battery, 7th Brigade, R.A.	
2nd Captain Browne	
Lieutenant Lawson	106
„ Montagu	

These brigades received the boon service granted for the battle of Waterloo under a Horse Guards' decision, which was promulgated in Paris on the 5th September, 1815, including among Waterloo men all troops, which had on the 18th June been employed either in the village of Waterloo, or had been detached to the right to prevent the advance of the enemy towards Brussels by Hal.

The companies which were present with small-arm ammunition, or which furnished detachments for that service, will be found in the chapters on the various battalions.

VOL. II.   2 F

The commendations passed on the corps generally for its services at Waterloo will be found in Appendix A, in support of the argument therein contained. But it may be interesting to the friends or descendants of individual officers, who were present, and who specially distinguished themselves, to read extracts from the reports sent to the Ordnance. These will be given without comment. "I feel," wrote Sir George Wood, "that I should particularly mention that I wish "Lieutenant-Colonel Sir John May may succeed to one of "the vacant troops; and I do assure you the conduct of "Major Lloyd was conspicuous to the whole army. This "officer and Captain Mercer[1] are candidates for the other "vacant troop. Captain Mercer was the senior second "captain in the field, and behaved nobly. I must also "mention that Lieutenant Louis commanded Major Bull's "troop for some time. Lieutenant Sandilands was the only "officer left with the command of poor Major Ramsay's "troop, the rest of the officers being wounded. I beg to "mention him to your protection, as well as Lieutenants "Coles and Wells, whom I have appointed to do duty with "the Horse Artillery, and I beg you will use your interest "with the Master-General that they may be confirmed. . . . "I shall certainly give in the name of Captain Macdonald "for brevet promotion; it was with great difficulty that he "could be made quit the field when severely wounded,—as "well as Lieutenant Brereton, who remained in the field of "battle until Lieutenant-Colonel Macdonald ordered him to "the rear, to have his wounds dressed. . . . Although "Lieutenant-Colonel Gold was in command of a Division of "Artillery in the field, I beg you will mention to the "Master-General that I have received great benefit from "his advice and zeal, during the time I have commanded "the Artillery in the Pays-Bas. . . ·. I beg leave to mention "that Lieutenant Bloomfield was both days in the field with "me; and should he wish at some future time to be posted

Dated
Le Cateau,
24 June,
1815.

---

[1] The casualties at Waterloo promoted Captain Mercer to the rank of 1st Captain.

CHAP. XXIII. *Commendation of Officers and Men.* 435

" to the Horse Brigade, I hope he will not be forgot." In
another despatch to General Macleod, Sir George Wood
wrote as follows : " I must call your particular attention to
" the officers who attended me personally in the field, whose
" merits I beg to recommend to the consideration of His
" Lordship the Master-General." These officers were
Lieutenant-Colonel Sir A. Frazer, Lieutenant-Colonel
Sir J. Hartmann, Lieutenant-Colonel Sir A. Dickson,
Lieutenant-Colonel Sir J. May, Captain Baynes, Brigade
Major, Lieutenants Coles, Bloomfield, Bell, and Meölmann—
all of whom were mentioned by name.

Lieutenant-Colonel Macdonald thus described the services
of his Adjutant : " In justice to the conduct of Captain Paken-
" ham, who acted as my Adjutant in the battle of the 18th,
" I feel it a duty I owe this most promising officer to state
" to you that he made himself equally conspicuous by his
" coolness and bravery, and the precision with which he con-
" veyed my orders to the troops of Horse Artillery I had the
" honour to command on that occasion." Sir Augustus
Frazer spoke in equally favourable terms of his Adjutant :
" I beg to submit my hope that, in the promotion which
" may be expected, the Horse Artillery may not lose the
" services of Lieutenant Bell, who, both here and in the
" Peninsula, has acted as Adjutant of Horse Artillery, and
" is an officer of much professional merit, whose judgment,
" intelligence, and unceasing application to the duties of his
" office, have rendered him very valuable."

To Sir G. A. Wood, 24 June, 1815.

Ibid. 23 June, 1815.

Major Bull thus described the conduct of his gallant
troop, now D Battery, B Brigade, Royal Horse Artillery :
" I consider it a duty I owe equally to the officers, non-
" commissioned officers, gunners, and drivers, to say that,
" throughout the day, and in every situation, nothing could
" exceed their coolness, intrepidity, and strict attention to
" orders ; and as a proof of their zeal in the service, at one
" period of the evening when we were short of ammunition,
" and H Troop " (Major Ramsay's) " on our left rather short
" of gunners, on an application for assistance, several of my
" men volunteered joining their guns, until our ammunition

Major Bull to Sir A. Frazer, 19 June, 1873.

2 F 2

"came up; and as far as was prudent or necessary, I
"granted their request. I must also beg leave to say that,
"from Major Cairnes having unfortunately fallen very early
"in the action, I received the greatest assistance through-
"out the day from Lieutenant Louis's activity; and it is
"but justice to this officer to add, that, when I was under
"the necessity of quitting the field for half an hour, in con-
"sequence of my being wounded, he commanded the troop
"during my absence in a manner that did himself great
"credit, and gave me perfect satisfaction at a very arduous
"period of the action."

<small>To Sir G. A. Wood, dated 15 July, 1815.</small>

General Colquhoun Grant, in writing of Captain Walcott, said: "I beg to recommend this gallant and meritorious
"officer to your attention." He added: "I have great
"pleasure in embracing this opportunity to mention my
"entire and full approbation of the conduct of Lieut.-
"Colonel Webber Smith, and the officers and men of his
"troop" (now B Battery, B Brigade, Royal Horse Artillery),
"during the whole of the period they have been attached
"to the brigade under my command."

<small>Ibid, dated 16 July, 1815.</small>

Lieutenant-Colonel Macdonald,—an enthusiastic Horse Artilleryman—in addition to the letter quoted above, wrote as follows: "In addition to the names of the various officers
"belonging to the six troops of Royal Horse Artillery,
"attached to the Cavalry, whose lot it was to command
"troops on the memorable day of the 18th June, it has
"occurred to me to be no less my duty to express to you
"my admiration of the cool and determined conduct of
"Captain Walcott, who was some time detached from his
"troop on that day; and who, in the handsomest manner,
"after the whole of his ammunition was expended, volun-
"teered to take charge of some of the guns of Major
"Ramsay's troop, after it had suffered much by the loss
"of officers. It is also highly satisfactory to me to report
"to you the equally gallant conduct of Captain Dansey, of
"Captain Whinyates's Rocket Troop, which I also had an
"opportunity of witnessing; and who was wounded when
"detached with rockets in the *chaussée*, which crossed the

" centre of the position. You are already aware, from your
" own observation, how much all the officers of these troops
" distinguished themselves on the occasion, and what a noble
" example they set to the non-commissioned officers and men
" by whom it was so gallantly imitated. Words are indeed
" inadequate to express my sense of the conduct of all, where
" the reputation, which the Horse Artillery had before ob-
" tained, was so nobly sustained, if not even surpassed; and
" which I must plead as my excuse for extending the limits
" of this communication beyond my original intention, viz.,
" that of drawing your attention to the merits of Captains
" Walcott and Dansey."

In reporting the death of Major Lloyd, from his wounds, Sir George Wood wrote: "I can, without hesitation, affirm " that a braver, or more zealous officer, never entered a field " of battle; and who did his duty on the 16th and 18th to " the satisfaction of every General officer." A few days later, in enclosing a letter from Lieutenant Brereton, Sir George said: "I have received from every commanding " officer the handsomest testimony of the conduct of Lieu- " tenant Brereton, both in the Peninsula and at the battle " of Waterloo; and I have it from General Byng to say that, " on the battle of the 16th (the Horse Artillery not being " engaged on that day), he proffered his service to act as " aide-de-camp, which service he performed to the great " satisfaction of the General." At a subsequent date, in forwarding an application from Major Percy Drummond, Sir George Wood said: "I have ever found Major Drummond " a most active, zealous, and attentive officer, having been " under my command on several occasions, particularly in the " battle of Waterloo." In acknowledging a letter from Major Rogers, Sir George said: "Your company at all times " did you every justice, and proved it under your command " at the battle of Waterloo, in which your brigade bore a dis- " tinguished feature." Almost every officer who served in the Artillery at Waterloo received from his gallant commander some official commendation; and, by this means, many Regimental incidents connected with the battle have been handed

Dated Paris, 3 Aug. 1815.

Ibid. 17 Aug. 1815.

Ibid. 8 Oct. 1815.

Ibid. 26 Jan. 1816.

down. In writing, for example, about an officer who lived to be a revered General in the Corps, Sir George Wood said: "Lieutenant William Anderson has conducted himself in every situation as a good and zealous officer. On the 18th June,—on many occasions during that day,—he carried my orders, and brought off some disabled guns under a severe fire. Having my horses shot, I was forced to dismount him."

Dated Valenciennes, 29 Feb. 1816.

At the battle of Waterloo, the Artillery expended 10,400 rounds of ammunition. The amount fired by one battery, Captain Sandham's, has already been stated; and it may be mentioned here that Captain Whinyates's troop fired 309 shot, 236 spherical case, 15 common case, and 52 rockets.

Sir George Wood to Gen. Macleod, dated 3 July, 1815. Memoir of Sir E. C. Whinyates, p. 3.

The subsequent operations of the English army during the year, in which this history comes for the present to an end, will merely be glanced at. The main body of the army marched at once towards Paris; and the damage suffered by the Artillery during the battle was so quickly repaired, that Sir George Wood was able to take every gun with him that had been on the field, with four 18-pounders in addition; making a total of 123 pieces of ordnance, and over 20,000 rounds of ammunition, with which the army marched on Paris. The collapse of any opposition, and the ultimate occupation of that city by the Allies, are facts well known to the reader. There were, however, some Artillery operations against the French fortresses, in which some brigades of Artillery, under Sir Alexander Dickson, were engaged. Maubeuge surrendered on the 12th July, and was taken possession of on the 14th, after three days' open trenches, and firing. Landrecy surrendered on the 21st, and was taken possession of on the 23rd July, after two days' open trenches, and about two hours' firing. Marienbourg surrendered on the 28th, and was taken possession of on the 30th July, after one day's open trenches and heavy bombardment. Philippeville was taken possession of on the 10th August, having surrendered on the 8th, after one day's open trenches and heavy bombardment. Sir Alexander Dickson spoke in the highest terms of the officers and men under his command; he attributed to their energy the fact that at every place he

Sir George Wood to D.-A.-Gen., dated 3 July, 1815.

Sir A. Dickson, to D.-A.-G., dated 12 Aug. 1815.

CHAP. XXIII. *Operations subsequent to Waterloo.* 439

was able to collect, previous to commencing operations, sufficient ordnance and ammunition to have reduced it, as he said, by main force. At Maubeuge, he had 60 guns—30 of which were 24-pounders,—20,000 round shot, and 26,000 shells. At Landrecy he had 60 guns, 24,000 round shot, and 22,000 shells. At Marienbourg, he had 15 mortars, with 3000 shells; and 6 24-pounders arrived, just as the place surrendered. At Philippeville, he had 66 pieces of ordnance, with 17,000 round shot, and 23,000 shells. During these operations, the Artillery was attached to a corps of the Prussian army, by which the sieges of the fortresses were conducted. The terms on which the duties were performed were somewhat peculiar. "Our line of duty," wrote Sir A. Dickson, "is to move the battering-train, keep it in order, "fix the shells, fill the cartridges, and, in short, do every "individual thing except fighting the guns: which my "instructions neither authorize me to do, nor would it be "pleasant to do, if they did; for we should not get the "credit we ought, when working in competition with the "Prussian Artillery: whereas, as the duty is conducted now, "every fair and just credit is allowed for our exertions, and "the service goes on with the utmost cordiality. Prince "Augustus of Prussia is chief of the Artillery of that "kingdom, and he takes into his own hand very much the "application of the artillery; which is very pleasant for me, "as I receive all the arrangements and instructions direct "from his Royal Highness. An application is given in every "morning at the park during a siege, expressing the "ordnance and ammunition required for the next day; and "in the evening the Prussian Artillery come to receive their "demands. I have, however, a few officers and men of the "Royal Artillery in the trenches, to afford any assistance "when required; and also to watch the practice, report "about the fuzes, &c." <small>Sir A. Dickson to D.-A.-G., dated 12 Aug. 1815.</small>

After the fall of Philippeville, Major Carmichael's company, with the advanced division of the battering-train, consisting of thirty-three mortars and howitzers, reached a point near Rocroy, on the 15th August:—followed by Major Michell's <small>Ibid. dated 22 Aug. 1815.</small>

and Major Wall's companies with ten 24-pounders, and a large supply of ammunition. The Prussians opened the trenches on the night of the 15th, and batteries were prepared for twenty-one mortars and howitzers. With such effect were these opened on the morning of the 16th, that before 9 A.M. Rocroy capitulated. After this event, Prince Augustus expressed himself highly satisfied with the exertions of the British Artillery attached to the battering-train; and orders reached Sir Alexander Dickson from the Duke of Wellington to bring the second battering-train, which was at Antwerp, to Brussels, and to land it forthwith. The next operation of any importance was against the town of Givet, against which no fewer than one hundred guns were collected. Before the bombardment commenced, however, the Governor consented to give up the place, and retire into Charlemont; which he did on the 11th September.

A force under Sir Charles Colville had been sent against Cambray, immediately after Waterloo, and the place—after a short siege—was carried on the 25th June. Of the conduct of the Artillery on this occasion, Sir Charles wrote: "The "three brigades of Artillery under Lieutenant - Colonel "Webber Smith, and Majors Unett and Brome, under the "direction of Lieutenant-Colonel Hawker, made particularly "good practice." The services of Major Unett's brigade (now 3 Battery, 7th Brigade) received special mention in a report from Sir Charles Colville to Sir George Wood; and the following extract from a letter written by its gallant commander may interest the officers and men now serving in the battery. "My brigade, being in reserve, had not an "opportunity of witnessing the late glorious battle of "Waterloo, but it afterwards proceeded with the 4th Division "of the army for the purpose of reducing the fortress of "Cambray; and, in justice to my officers, I must be per-"mitted to say that my three subalterns, never having been "under fire before, deserve much praise for their cool and "steady behaviour at their guns (within four hundred yards "of the curtain of the citadel, in an open field), and which "was clearly evinced by the uncommon good practice made,

To the Duke of Wellington, 26 June, 1815.

Sir George Wood to D.-A.-G., Paris, 4 Sept. 1815.

Major Unett to Sir G. Wood, dated 3 Aug. 1815.

"which so completely silenced the enemy as to cause (by
"driving them from their guns and ramparts) a most
"trifling loss to our Infantry when they stormed the place."
The French king entered Cambray on the day after it was
taken : and on the same day, Peronne was taken by General
Maitland and the Guards.

Arrangements for concluding hostilities, and entering
upon a treaty, were soon made in Paris. One of the
conditions inflicted on the French people was that an army
of occupation should be left in France for five—afterwards
reduced to three—years; and considerable difficulty was
found in apportioning the various arms in the English contingent of that army.

The Duke of Wellington decided on reducing the Artillery
share to a point far below what Sir George Wood thought
desirable ; and the latter urged his views very strongly, but,
as he said, "What can a Lieut.-Colonel do against a Field-
Marshal?"[1] However, his importunity succeeded in obtaining
an addition of two companies to the Artillery force which
was at first intended to remain in France.

The following was the number ultimately decided upon :—

1 Colonel . . . . .
1 Assistant Adjutant-Gen.
1 Brigade Major . . .
} for duty as the Regimental Staff of the Royal Artillery in the Army of Occupation.

MS. Return to B. of Ordnance, dated Paris, 10 Dec. 1815.

Three troops of Royal Horse Artillery to be attached to the Cavalry, and to amount to 542 of all ranks, with 516 horses.

Seven brigades of Foot Artillery, having a company of Artillery to each; six of which were to be attached to the three divisions of the army, and one to be in reserve. The total of all ranks, with these brigades, amounted to 790 ; and there were in addition 599 officers and men of the Royal Artillery Drivers, and 770 horses.

For duty with the small-arm ammunition brigades for the three divisions of the army, there were three officers of Royal Artillery ; 150 non-commissioned officers and men of the Royal Artillery Drivers; and 210 horses.

There was also a company of Royal Artillery in reserve, numbering 111 of all ranks.

One Lieut.-Colonel and one Major were attached to the Royal Horse Artillery.
Two Lieut.-Colonels and one Major were attached to the Royal Artillery.
And one Lieut.-Colonel was attached to the Royal Artillery Drivers.

---

[1] Although a Colonel in the army, Sir George Wood was only a Regimental Lieutenant-Colonel in 1815.

The following were the five troops of Horse Artillery selected to return to England, when the above establishment was decided upon:—

MS. Return to B. of Ord. dated Paris, 10 Dec. 1815.

	Strength.	Horses.	R. A. Drivers attached.
Lieut.-Colonel Sir R. Gardiner's troop	179 of all ranks.	198	22
„ Webber Smith's „	176 „	197	20
„ Sir H. D. Ross's „	189 „	219	30
Major Whinyates's „	223 „	219	nil.
Captain Mercer's (late Beane's) „	176 „	196	26
Detachment R. H. A.	59 „	156	83

Orders for the shipment of the battering-train also arrived in the end of 1815, with a view to its return to England; and, as Sir Alexander Dickson's active duties on the continent then ceased, it seems but justice to the memory of one whose name has occupied so prominent a place in these pages, to quote a passage from a letter written by Sir George Wood, proving that his exceptional Peninsular honours had not unfitted him for serving, when required, in a subordinate position:—" You may expect Sir A. Dickson in the course of the next week at Woolwich. I have found him the same good officer and man, as you well know him."

To D.-A.-G., R.A., dated Cambray, 2 April, 1816.

The reductions which followed the battle of Waterloo have been frequently alluded to in these volumes. They would furnish but a gloomy topic for the historian, for the pruning-knife was used without regard to sentiment, and some of the best companies in the regiment were the victims. It is more pleasant to close this story in 1815, when the Corps was at the greatest strength attained since its birth, —a hundred years before. Suffice it to say that from 114 troops and companies in that year, it fell before 1819 to 79, and even these were mere ghosts or skeletons of their former selves. For nearly thirty years, after 1819, the history of the Regiment was almost a blank page, and hopelessness and depression weighed heavily on its members.

Kane's List.

But 1815 is the year in which this narrative ends; nor is it meant to close it with any gloomy foreshadowing of those years of inaction and despondency, which rolled on with dismal monotony, until the Regimental firmament was lit by the lurid fires of the Crimean struggle. In 1815 the military reputation of England was at a maximum. She possessed an army which had graduated with honours in the sternest school, and a General to whose words the Sovereigns of Europe listened with deference. Determination, single-mindedness, and an exalted sense of duty were the qualities which had animated the Duke of Wellington through his whole career. Their reward was found in his successes; and his successes were crowned in Paris. Imperfections exist in the most able, and even in the most conscientious; and England's greatest General was certainly no exception to this rule. But, if we allow for the irritation caused by frequent and injudicious interference,—and for occasional hastiness, which led him to speak without always testing the accuracy of his information,—we must admit the Duke of Wellington to have been the most perfect type of an English soldier ever presented in the pages of our history. When, however, the Artilleryman seeks for something that is genial and lovable in the soldiers of that victorious age,—he turns from the cold and undemonstrative Chief, and dwells fondly on the men who had by their exertions raised Artillery, as a science, to an unprecedented point, and had elevated with it the Corps they loved. The researches of a recent writer have brought Hime. to light words spoken by a chivalrous enemy, which should be emblazoned in the records of every battery, and impressed on the mind of every Artilleryman:—"Les canonniers General " Anglais se distinguent entre les autres soldats par le bon Foy. " esprit qui les anime. En bataille leur activité est judi- " cieuse, leur coup d'œil parfait, et leur bravoure stoïque." Of the latter three qualities, two may be ensured by diligence in peace, and the third is tested by the difficulties and dangers of war: but the history of the great and the good in the Corps must indeed have been feebly written, if it do not strengthen among its living members that which exists now, as of old, " le bon esprit qui les anime."

APPENDICES.

APPENDIX A.

THE DUKE OF WELLINGTON, AND THE ARTILLERY AT WATERLOO.

<small>Jones's Sieges, vol. i., p. 222.</small> IN the first volume of Sir J. T. Jones's 'Sieges in Spain,' edited by Lieutenant-Colonel H. D. Jones, the following passage occurs: "It becomes the duty of the Editor to "remove the very injurious and unmerited censure cast upon "the officers of Engineers who were employed at the Siege "of Badajoz, and which is contained in a letter from the "Earl of Wellington to Major-General G. Murray, a copy "of which is published in the collection of the Despatches "of the Duke of Wellington."

The Editor then proceeds to prove, most clearly and successfully, that the hasty language used with reference to the Engineers was not only injurious, but also unmerited.

The same great General is also convicted by his admirer, Napier, of hasty inconsistency in his private correspondence. It was of the very same troops, and referring to precisely the same time, that the Duke of Wellington wrote in one <small>Napier's 'Peninsular War,' vol. vi., p. 166.</small> letter: "The soldiers are detestable for everything but "fighting; and the officers are as culpable as the men:" and in another, "that he thought he could go anywhere, and do "anything with the army that fought on the Pyrenees."

Well might Napier say that the vehemence of the censure in the former of the quotations is inconsistent with the latter, and now celebrated, observation.

APP. A. *The Duke and the Artillery at Waterloo.* 445

It now becomes the painful, and yet necessary, task of the chronicler of the services of the Royal Artillery, as of the member of the sister corps already quoted, "to remove a very "injurious and unmerited censure" cast upon the Regiment, in a private letter, written by the Duke of Wellington, with reference to its conduct at the battle of Waterloo. Of this letter's existence the world was ignorant until the year 1872, when it made its appearance in a volume of 'Supplementary Letters and Despatches of the Duke of Wellington,' published by his son. The sensation which it was certain to produce was foretold by one of the reviews, and was anticipated by the noble Editor. As, however, his object was to tell the truth, the whole truth, and nothing but the truth, the present Duke did not feel justified in withholding from publication any letter which was found among his father's papers, merely because it might wound the feelings of its readers, or give a new interpretation of historical events. And although the indiscriminate publication of a man's private correspondence is a doubtful tribute to his memory, and a severe test of his reputation, it is, on the whole, fortunate for the Royal Artillery that this letter made its appearance while officers were yet alive who had taken a part in the battle referred to in its pages, and clearly remembered its details. 'Athenæum.'

The original letter was written by the Duke of Wellington to Lord Mulgrave, then Master-General of the Ordnance, on the 21st December, 1815. The published letter was from a copy, or draft, of the original which was found among the Duke's papers. The hope that perhaps there may have been modifications in the original, which did not exist in the draft or copy, disappears before the fact that Lord Mulgrave's answer was also found among the Duke's papers, expressing his amazement at the letter he had just received. The harsh statements in the published draft or copy were doubtless, therefore, left in the original when forwarded. The circumstances under which the letter were written were as follows. The field officers of the Royal Artillery, who had been present at Waterloo, applied to the Master-General of the Ordnance for the same pensions for service as had been given after Vittoria. The indignation with which the Duke of Wellington had heard of the Vittoria pensions was well known in the Regiment: nor can one avoid sympathising with him. Discipline must suffer if the power of rewarding, or recommending for reward, be independent of the commander of the forces as a channel. The special interference of the Ordnance on behalf of the Corps, which was their *protégé*, was not merely a breach of discipline, to which a man like the Duke of Wellington was not likely tamely to submit, but must have had an irritating effect on the rest of the army. When, therefore, the field officers of Artillery present at Waterloo resolved to apply for the same reward as had been given after Vittoria, they had the alternative before them of making their request through the Duke, basing it upon a precedent which was detestable in his eyes, or of availing themselves of the dual government under which they served, by making a direct application to the Ordnance. Of these alternatives, the former would have been the more soldier-like, but was not likely to succeed: the latter, therefore, was unfortunately adopted.

The application was not couched in a very official form, nor was it officially pressed by Sir George Wood. The only reference to it which can be traced in that officer's correspondence is in a letter announcing Major Lloyd's death, in which he writes:—" Should Lord Mulgrave, in his goodness, be inclined to grant pensions to field officers and captains commanding brigades, similar to the battle of Vittoria, I hope and trust that the late Major Lloyd's family may receive the benefit his service deserved." The precedent of Vittoria was not quite a parallel case to that of Waterloo: in the former every brigade with the army had been in action; while, in the latter, some had been detached. It seems to have been on this distinction, mainly, that Lord Mulgrave based his refusal to grant the reward. To justify himself, he referred the matter to the Duke of Wellington, who approved of the refusal, as might have been expected, but did so in terms which reveal an inaccuracy, and a hastiness unparalleled in his Grace's correspondence. He wrote as follows:—

"TO THE EARL OF MULGRAVE.

"*Paris, 21st December*, 1815.

"MY DEAR LORD,

"I received yesterday your Lordship's letter of the 10th, regarding the claim of the field officers of the Artillery present in the battle of Waterloo, to the same measure of favour granted to those in the battle of Vittoria.

"In my opinion you have done quite right to refuse to grant this favour, and that you have founded your refusal on the best grounds. I cannot recommend that you should depart from the ground you have taken. To tell you the truth, I was not very well pleased with the Artillery in the battle of Waterloo.

"The army was formed in squares immediately on the slope of the rising ground, on the summit of which the Artillery was placed, with orders not to engage with artillery, but to fire only when bodies of troops came under their fire. It was very difficult to get them to obey this order. The French cavalry charged, and were formed on the same ground with our Artillery in general, within a few yards of our guns. In some instances they were in actual possession of our guns. We could not expect the artillerymen to remain at their guns in such a case; but I had a right to expect that the officers and men of the Artillery would do as I did, and as all the staff did, that is, to take shelter in the squares of the Infantry till the French cavalry should be driven off the ground, either by our Cavalry or Infantry. But they did no such thing; they ran off the field entirely, taking with them limbers, ammunition, and everything: and when, in a few minutes, we had driven off the French cavalry, and had regained our ground and our guns, and could have made good use of our artillery, we had no artillerymen to fire them; and, in point of fact, I should have had no Artillery during the whole of the latter part of the action if I had not kept a reserve in the commencement.

"Mind, my dear Lord, I do not mean to complain; but what I have above mentioned is a fact known to many; and it would not do to reward a corps under such circumstances. The Artillery, like others, behaved most gallantly; but when a misfortune of this kind has occurred, a corps must not be rewarded. It is on account of these little stories, which must come out, that I object to all the propositions to write what is called a history of the battle of Waterloo.

"If it is to be a history, it must be the truth, and the whole truth, or it will do more harm than good, and will give as many false notions of what a battle is, as other romances of the same description have. But if a true history is written, what will become of the reputation of half of those who have acquired reputation, and who deserve it for their gallantry, but who, if their mistakes and casual misconduct were made public, would not be so well thought of? I am certain that if I were to enter into a critical discussion of everything that occurred from the 14th to the 19th June, I could show ample reasons for not entering deeply into these subjects.

"The fact is, that the army that gained the battle of Waterloo was an entirely new one, with the exception of some of the old Spanish troops. Their inexperience occasioned the mistakes they committed, the rumours they circulated that all was destroyed, because they themselves ran away, and the mischief which ensued; but they behaved gallantly, and I am convinced, if the thing was to be done again, they would show what it was to have the experience of even one battle.

"Believe me, &c.,

(Signed) "WELLINGTON.

"P.S.—I am very well pleased with the field officers for not liking to have their application referred to me. They know the reason I have not to recommend them for a favour."

In discussing this letter, it is proposed to examine what may be termed the internal and external evidences of its inaccuracy, commencing with the former.

In his despatch of the 19th June, 1815, announcing the

victory, the Duke wrote: " The Artillery and Engineer departments were conducted *much to my satisfaction* by Colonel Sir George Wood and Colonel Smyth." Evidently, then, the fact "known to many" of the Artillerymen running off the ground had not been known to him when he wrote his despatch, or he could hardly have described the Artillery department as having been conducted much to his satisfaction. Nor does the fact, even when made known to him, seem to have produced the effect upon his Grace's mind, which misconduct among the troops under his command, in the face of an enemy, would at any other time have instantly created. Were not the genuineness of the letter beyond all question, some of the contradictions and inconsistencies in it would have justified the reader in pronouncing it a forgery, invented to throw discredit on the reputation of England's greatest General. Was it the Duke of Wellington who, after writing the words, " They ran off the field entirely, taking with them limbers, ammunition, and everything," proceeded to say, " The Artillery, like others, behaved most gallantly "? Was it the Iron Duke who, after saying, " In " point of fact, I should have had no Artillery during the " whole of the latter part of the action if I had not kept a " reserve in the commencement," went on, with the resignation of a martyr, to say, " Mind, my dear Lord, I do not mean " to complain "? The inconsistency with his known character is astounding.

After describing the disappearance of his Artillerymen, and the straits to which he was consequently reduced, he proceeds in this letter to say: " It would not do to reward a " corps under such circumstances." If he were correctly informed as to these circumstances, there would not have been a single individual in the whole of his army who would have differed from him as to his conclusion. But, unfortunately for him, he endeavoured to prove too much. Not content with giving, as a reason for withholding rewards, an assertion which, if accurate, would have more than justified him, he must needs strengthen an already overwhelming case by a mysterious insinuation in the postscript of the letter, respecting some other unexpressed ground of his displeasure, with which the field officers must be familiar as a cause for his refusing to recommend them for reward. Was there not, in this piling of Pelion upon Ossa, some consciousness of the necessity of self-justification?

But these are merely striking self-contradictions and inconsistencies in style. It is when the truth of the statements made by the Duke in this letter is inquired into that one stands astounded at the inaccuracy of his informants, and the hasty assumptions of the writer himself. The letter is so involved,—so confusing in its mixed references to the Artillery and to the army generally,—so laden with marvellous didactic sentences as to the propriety of writing a history of the battle of Waterloo,—that it is not always easy to ascertain the connection between argument and conclusion. So slovenly, indeed, is the style at the end of the letter, that it reads as if the whole army ran away! Let two sentences be reproduced: "The fact is, that the "army that gained the battle of Waterloo was an entirely "new one, with the exception of some of the old Spanish "troops. Their inexperience occasioned the mistakes they "committed, the rumours they circulated that all was "destroyed, because they themselves ran away, and the "mischiefs which ensued; but they behaved gallantly." . . . One rises from a perusal of these words with a bewildered feeling that gallant behaviour among troops is identical with running away;—and that the whole army, with the exception of some of the old Spanish troops, exhibited their gallantry in this singular manner. But, as the statement that the army was entirely a new one is used apparently in the first instance to account for the Artillery running off the field, it may be interesting to glance at the troops and brigades, whose inexperience seemed—in the Duke's mind as he wrote—to have made their flight almost natural.

Of the eight troops of Horse Artillery present at the battle of Waterloo, five were the old tried troops of the Peninsula, whose gallant services had been recorded year after year by the Duke's own hand: Sir Hew Ross's, Sir Robert

Gardiner's, Colonel Webber Smith's, Major Beane's, and Major Bull's. A sixth, Captain Whinyates's, was the famous Rocket Troop of Leipsic; and of the other two, one had fought at Buenos Ayres, and the other in Walcheren. It was to one of these latter and more inexperienced troops, Captain Mercer's, that the victory at one period of the day was due. With regard to the field brigades of this new army, it would seem that Major Rogers's company had been engaged for two years past in the operations in Holland, and had been in the Walcheren Expedition previously; that Captain Sinclair's brigade had been at Copenhagen, Corunna, and Walcheren; Captain Sandham's at Copenhagen and Walcheren; Major Lloyd's at Walcheren; and that Captain Bolton's, the only brigade without war service, happened to be the one whose effect in breaking the head of the columns of the Imperial Guard has become historical,— and whose inexperience would therefore hardly appear to have been very detrimental. From this statement it is evident that the Artillery element in the Duke's army at Waterloo was veteran rather than new;—for, if the troops and brigades possessed such records as are given above, much more did the majority of the field and staff officers present deserve the title of veterans. <small>Battalion Records of the Royal Artillery.</small>

But the next inaccuracy is more unpardonable; and the informants of the Duke on the subject were guilty of errors for which there was no excuse. "In point of fact," wrote the Duke, "I should have had no Artillery during the whole " of the latter part of the action if I had not kept a reserve " at the commencement." Fortunately for the exposure of this grave inaccuracy, there is no point on which there is more full and official information both in Sir George Wood's and other despatches, and more detailed notice in private correspondence, than on the subject of the Artillery reserves at Waterloo. As stated in the last chapter of this volume, it was composed of Sir Hew Ross's and Major Beane's troops of Horse Artillery, and Captain Sinclair's Field Brigade. So far was this force from being kept in reserve, and being brought forward providentially at the end of the action to replace the runaways, that it was actually in action —every gun—almost at the *commencement of the day*, and suffered the heaviest losses before half-past one. By a happy coincidence, the Artillery, which must have been represented to the Duke as his reserve, is mentioned by Sir Augustus Frazer: "Some time before this—*i.e.*, the " massing of the second line *during the cavalry attacks*—the " Duke ordered me to bring up all the reserve Horse Ar- " tillery, which at that moment were *Mercer's* and *Bull's* " *troops*." But, instead of these troops being a reserve kept, as the Duke's letter says, " from the commencement," —they also had both been in action from the beginning of the day, and Bull's troop had actually been sent to the centre of the second line "to refit and repair disabled " carriages ! "

<small>Frazer's Letters, p. 559.</small>

<small>Ibid. p. 557.</small>

The importance of this inaccuracy in the letter cannot be overrated. If the Artillery, which the Duke admits having had at the end of the day, was not the reserve, which he had kept in hand,—and it certainly was not,—what was it ? The asserted flight of the gunners with their limbers and ammunition hangs upon the truth, or otherwise, of there having been reserves in hand to replace them. But the fact of these reserves having been in action from the beginning of the day is incontestable; and is proved by the correspondence of Sir Hew Ross, who commanded one of the reserve troops, as well as by the official and semi-official correspondence of others. It is possible that the arrival of Sir Robert Gardiner's troop, with Vivian's and Vandeleur's brigades, from the left of the line, at the end of the day, may have deceived the Duke's informant, and led him to imagine that it was fresh Artillery from the reserve. That it was not so, however, but merely moved with the division to which it was attached, is a matter of fact; and at no time in the day was this troop ever in reserve. Therefore, in a vital point, the Duke's letter is unquestionably inaccurate.

The next statement in the letter which demands scrutiny is the following : " The Artillery was placed with orders " not to engage with artillery, but to fire only when bodies

"of troops came under their fire. It was very difficult to
"get them to obey this order." Sir John Bloomfield, who
was on Sir George Wood's staff, carried this order to all the
troops and brigades, and is confident that, with one exception, it was rigidly obeyed. He remembers that the Duke
saw a French gun struck by a shot from one of the English
batteries,—and, under the impression that it came from
Captain Sandham's brigade, he sent orders to have that
officer placed in arrest. This was not done, some satisfactory
explanation having been given,—relieving Captain Sandham
of the disobedience. Singularly enough, the offender was
never discovered, until, in 1870, with the publication of
General Mercer's Diary, came the confession of the crime.
"About this time, being impatient of standing idle, and
"annoyed by the batteries on the Nivelle road, I ventured
"to commit a folly, for which I should have paid dearly had
"our Duke chanced to be in our part of the field. I ven-
"tured to disobey orders, and open a slow, deliberate fire at
"the battery, thinking, with my 9-pounders, soon to silence
"his 4-pounders." As Captain Mercer's troop was placed
near Sandham's brigade at this time, it is evident that this
occurrence, and that mentioned by Sir John Bloomfield, are
identical. Sir John, whose duties carried him to all parts of
the field, and whose recollection of the day is as clear as
possible, asserts positively, that in no other instance was the
order disobeyed; and it will be seen from accounts, both
French and English, to be quoted hereafter, that the order
to fire upon bodies of troops approaching was literally obeyed
with the most marked results. Was it, then, quite worthy
of the Duke of Wellington to reason from the particular to
the general, and to visit the disobedience of one officer
upon a whole corps? As has been well said by the son of
one of the bravest Artillery officers on the field, Sir Robert
Gardiner: "If a Regiment of Infantry had run away, and
"all the others had behaved splendidly,—would the whole
"arm have been similarly condemned? Would it not have
"been more just to reward those who deserved it?"

The mention of reward suggests the next amazing incon-

'Mercer's Diary,' vol. i. p. 301.

Colonel Gardiner, R.H.A.

sistency in the Duke's letter,—and makes it almost certain that it was written on receiving some subsequent information from another source,—not from his personal observation. In this letter, dated six months after the battle, he wrote: "It " would not do to reward a corps under such circumstances;" and again : " The field officers know the reason I have not " to recommend them for a favour." How are these sentences to be reconciled with the following extract from the 'London Gazette,' which immediately followed the battle, and was issued while all its details must have been fresh in the Duke's recollection ?

Dated Whitehall, 22 June, 1815.

" His Royal Highness the Prince Regent has further been " pleased to nominate and appoint the undermentioned offi- " cers to be Companions of the said most Honourable Military " Order of the Bath, *upon the recommendation of Field Mar-* " *shal the Duke of Wellington, for their services in the battles* " *fought upon the* 16*th and* 18*th of June last :*

>   Lieut.-Colonel S. G. Adye, Royal Artillery.
>   Lieut.-Colonel R. Bull,   ,,
>   Lieut.-Colonel C. Gold,   ,,
>   Lieut.-Colonel A. Macdonald,   ,,
>   Lieut.-Colonel J. Parker,   ,,
>   Major T. Rogers,   ,,
>   Lieut.-Colonel J. W. Smith,   ,,
>   Lieut.-Colonel J. S. Williamson,   ,,
>   Colonel Sir G. A. Wood, Kt.,   ,,

This list includes the very field officers of whom the Duke wrote afterwards, " *They know the reason I have not to re-* " *commend them for a favour.*" Was it no favour to be recommended for the Order of the Bath ?

Again : "It would not do," wrote the Duke in December, 1815, " to reward a corps under such circumstances." Let the reader glance at the following picture of an unrewarded corps.

Out of thirteen troops and brigades, with the requisite staff, the following officers obtained rewards, in addition to the nine appointments to the Order of the Bath, quoted above. It must be remembered that the number eligible excluded subalterns, and was further reduced by the death of Majors Beane, Lloyd, Ramsay, Cairnes, and Captain Bolton.

Brevet promotion, for service at Waterloo :

Major R. Bull to be Lieut.-Colonel, dated 18th June, 1815.
Major J. Parker   ,,   ,,   ,,
Captain E. Whinyates to be Major   ,,
Captain T. Dynely   ,,   ,,
Captain A. Macdonald   ,,   ,,

Brevet promotion for services at Waterloo was also conferred in January 1819 on

Captain C. Napier,
Captain W. Webber,
Captain W. Brereton,
Captain R. H. Ord, } Subalterns at Waterloo.

At the request, also, of the Duke of Wellington, Sir George Wood obtained permission to accept a knighthood of the Order of Maria Theresa, from the Emperor of Austria ; and, a few days later, the Order of St. Wladimir, from the Emperor of Russia. _{Dated Paris, 2 Aug. 1815. Ibid. 21 Aug. 1815.}

Yet again, at the request of the Duke of Wellington, the following officers obtained permission to accept from the Emperor of Russia the Order of St. Anne, " in testimony " of His Majesty's approbation of their services and conduct, " particularly in the late battles fought in the Netherlands :" _{Ibid. 8 Oct. 1815.}

Lieut.-Colonel Sir J. May, K.C.B., R.H.A.
Lieut.-Colonel Sir H. Ross,   ,,   ,,
Lieut.-Colonel Sir R. Gardiner, ,,   ,,
Lieut.-Colonel R. Bull,   ,,   ,,
Major A. Macdonald,   ,,   ,,

It is unnecessary to add that the boon service granted for the battle of Waterloo, and the Waterloo medals, were given to the Artillery present, without exception. It would, therefore, appear that for a corps which did not deserve to be rewarded, it did not fare badly; and that its merits were only called in question when pensions based on an unpopular precedent were asked for. It is also impossible that the Duke could have been so generous in his original recommendations had he known, of his own personal observation, that which he stated in his letter of the 21st December, and which must now receive grave consideration; the asserted flight from the field of battle of many of the Artillerymen with their limbers, &c.

In ascertaining the unmistakable inaccuracy of this cruel and hasty assertion, which must have been made by the Duke of Wellington on the most worthless evidence, the advantage of the late publication of the letter has become apparent. Much of the evidence, which will be adduced to rebut it, was not written with the view of meeting such an accusation, but is merely extracted from the simple narrative of a battle, in which the facts are stated without any idea of their being questioned. Had the Duke's letter been published while the writers of many of the letters to be quoted were alive, their answers would not have had half the historical value they now possess, for they would have been regarded as the pleadings of interested defendants. The statements of disinterested historians will conclude this brief argument.

When the celebrated charges of the French cavalry at Waterloo took place, the English guns lined the crest of the position, and the Infantry was formed in squares in their rear. The order given by the Duke was that the Artillerymen should stand to their guns as long as possible, and then take refuge in the Infantry squares; and that *the limbers should be sent behind the squares.* This order was carried to the various batteries by Sir John Bloomfield, and was obeyed to the letter. "The idea of six limbers," writes Colonel Gardiner, "with six horses in each limber, going into a square of Infantry, was of course an impossibility, and never contemplated." The gunners had cartouche-bags slung round them, containing ammunition, and invariably,

Communicated by Sir J. Bloomfield.

with the exception of those of Captain Mercer's troop, took refuge in the adjacent squares, or under the bayonets of the kneeling ranks. When the cavalry retired, on each occasion the gunners ran out, and, as a rule, the guns were in action against the retreating cavalry before they had gone sixty yards. The delay of a few moments occurred once or twice, while shot were being brought from the limbers; and Sir John Bloomfield remembers an expression of impatience escaping the Duke on one of these occasions. Nor was it unnatural. "To lose," writes Colonel Gardiner, "an opportunity of "inflicting destruction on the French cavalry, directly they "turned their backs, and before they could get out of the "range of canister, must have been very tantalizing." But that the delay ever exceeded a few moments, or that a single limber ever left the ground, Sir John Bloomfield is confident is an utter delusion. Such an occurrence as is described in the Duke's letter could not have happened without being well known. The Duke himself said, "It is known to many;" and yet Sir John lived for three years with the head-quarter staff in Paris, and never heard even an insinuation on the subject. Another Waterloo survivor writes on this point:
"I never did hear, nor any one else, of the artillery mis- *General B.*
"behaving at Waterloo. Sir Alexander Dickson took me *Cuppage,*
"with him into Brussels after the battle. We saw every *Author.*
"officer who came in, and the action was in every part the
"constant theme of conversation, both in our private, as well
"as more general moments. Had anything bearing such a
"term taken place, it would certainly have been canvassed.
"I was in daily conversation with our wounded in the town.
"Surely I may say, but that the Duke of Wellington says
"it, it is as cruel as it is unjust."

If known to many, it could hardly have escaped the commanding officer of the corps most interested. The fact that Sir George Wood did not write his despatches to the Ordnance until the 24th June,—that during the six days' interval since the battle he had been constantly with the Duke,—and yet that he could write as follows, proves most clearly that the Duke himself cannot then have been aware of what he afterwards wrote to Lord Mulgrave, and that his letter must have been based on subsequent malicious and worthless testimony. The wording of Sir George Wood's letters have an almost providential bearing on the point at issue; and could not have been used, had there been even a doubt as to the conduct of the Corps.

<small>Dated Le Cateau, 24 June, 1815.</small>
"I beg leave," he wrote, "to call the attention of His " Lordship the Master-General to the skill and intrepidity " so eminently displayed by the British and German " Artillery. The accompanying return of their loss will " show how much they participated in the action, and I can " assure His Lordship the Master-General, that, notwith- " standing their being outnumbered by the Artillery of the " enemy, *their merits never shone more conspicuous* than on " this occasion. It now remains for me to express with " much pleasure and satisfaction that *every officer and man* " *in the field of battle did their duty.*"

With his despatch, Sir George wrote a private letter to General Macleod, in which the following passage occurs:
<small>Ibid.</small>
" I do assure you, I have not words to express the extreme " good conduct of the Corps. All exerted themselves, both " officers and men, and such a conflict of guns never was in " the memory of man."

But there are recorded, also, the opinions of the Generals of other arms, under whose immediate command various troops and brigades served: and who would have known had any misconduct occurred among them, better than the Duke himself, on account of the more limited field of their observation. General Colquhoun Grant's complimentary
<small>Vide p. 436.</small>
order with reference to Colonel Webber Smith's Troop has already been quoted. The following order was issued by
<small>Dated Nivelle, 20 June, 1815.</small>
Lord Hill: "The highly distinguished conduct of the " 2nd Division, and Colonel Mitchell's Brigade of the " 4th Division, who had the good fortune to be employed in " the memorable action, merit His Lordship's highest appro- " bation; and he begs that . . . . Colonel Gold, command- " ing Royal Artillery of the 2nd Corps, ... Major " Sympher, commanding a troop of Horse Artillery, King's

APP. A.   *and the Artillery at Waterloo.*   459

" German Legion, Captain Napier (to whose lot it fell to
" command the 9-pounder Brigade, 2nd Division, on the
" death of Captain Bolton), will accept his best thanks for
" their exemplary conduct, and will be pleased to convey
" his sentiments to the officers, non-commissioned officers,
" and men under their command."

The following extract from the 5th Division orders, by
Sir James Kempt, speaks equally favourably of another
brigade: " The British Brigade of Artillery commanded by
" Major Rogers, and the Hanoverian Brigade commanded by
" Major Heisse, were most nobly served, and judiciously
" placed; and these officers and men will be pleased to
" accept of his—*i.e.* the Major-General's—particular thanks
" for their service." Dated 19 June, 1815.

References to the services of other brigades, and of the
Horse Artillery, by the officers of the Corps under whom
they served, have already been quoted; and in every case
commendation of the warmest description was passed upon
them. The following quotation from Sir Augustus Frazer's
correspondence is interesting here, as asserting what was
denied by the Duke in his letter to Lord Mulgrave, that the
men took shelter in the squares. " The repeated charges of
" the enemy's noble cavalry were similar to the first: each
" was fruitless. Not an infantry soldier moved; and, on
" each charge, abandoning their guns, our men sheltered
" themselves between the flanks of the squares. Twice,
" however, the enemy tried to charge in front; these
" attempts were entirely frustrated by the fire of the guns,
" wisely reserved till the hostile squadrons were within
" twenty yards of the muzzles. In this, the cool and quiet
" steadiness of the troops of Horse Artillery was very
" creditable." This was written two days after the battle; Frazer's Letters, p. 559.
and no man had better opportunity of seeing the conduct of
his Corps than the writer. Every historian of the battle
endorses this version: and the testimony of an impartial
historian always represents the carefully sifted testimony of
many. Sir Edward Cust, the laborious military annalist,
writes thus: " Suddenly some bugles were heard to sound,

" and all the Artillerymen, abandoning their guns and
" tumbrils, ran back into the infantry squares. . . . In a
" moment, the Artillery gunners quitted the protection of the
" squares, and running up to their guns, which were most
" of them ready loaded, opened heavily with grape and with
" every species of projectile. . . . . . The cavaliers again
" mounted the plateau; again the gunners abandoned their
" guns, and took refuge within the squares." Creasy writes:
" As the French receded from each attack, the British
" Artillerymen rushed forward from the centre of the
" squares, where they had taken refuge, and plied their
" guns on the retiring horsemen." The same is the account
given by every historian of the battle. Were they all
dreaming? or were they in some conspiracy to conceal the
truth? And if so, did the Duke himself join it? In the
thirty-seven years of his life after Waterloo, he never
contradicted the numerous accounts of the battle, all of
which agreed in their statement of the eminent services of
the Artillery. Was it consistent in one who professed
belief in an occurrence "known to many," and who gave
that belief as a ground for the refusal of favours,—to allow
such passages as the following to be published without
contradiction, unless indeed he had subsequently ascertained
the worthlessness of his information?[1] "There," wrote

'Battle of Gleig, "every arm did its duty; the Artillery from the
Waterloo,': " beginning to the close of the day." Again: "In the
by G. R.
Gleig, " course of the day every battery was brought into action;
Chaplain-
General. " and not even the records of that noble Corps can point to
Ibid. " an occasion in which they better did their work." Sir
James Shaw Kennedy, in summing up his description of the
Sir J. S. battle, says: "Full scope was thus given for the British
Kennedy's " Cavalry and Artillery to display their surpassing gallantry
'Waterloo,'
p. 179. " and excellence; and they did not fail to display these
" qualities in an eminent degree."

But it has been admitted that Captain Mercer's troop was
an exception to the others; that his men did not take

---

[1] This seems the most probable solution of the difficulty.

shelter within the Infantry squares. Let him tell his own story. "Sir Augustus, pointing out our position between "two squares of Brunswick Infantry, left us with injunc- "tions to remember the Duke's orders (to retire within the "squares) and to economise our ammunition. The Bruns- "wickers were falling fast . . . . these were the very boys "whom I had but yesterday seen throwing away their arms "and fleeing, panic-stricken, from the very sound of our "horses' feet. . . . . Every moment I feared they would "again throw down their arms and flee. . . . . To have sought "refuge amongst men in such a state were madness; the "very moment our men ran from their guns, I was convinced, "would be the signal for their disbanding. We had better, "then, fall at our posts than in such a situation." He accordingly made his men stand to the guns, until the cavalry were within a few feet of them; and on each occasion the havoc he wrought among them—as he drove them back—was frightful. The immense heap of dead, lying in front of Mercer's guns, was such that Sir Augustus Frazer said that, in riding over the field next day, he "could plainly distin- "guish the position of G Troop from the opposite height by "the dark mass, which, even from that distance, formed a "remarkable feature in the field."

Mercer's 'Diary,' p. 312.

Ibid. p. 343.

Captain Mercer's men, therefore, were those who did not obey the Duke's order. It was a fortunate act of disobedience, and it saved the Brunswickers; but Captain Mercer was severely punished for it. He was not recommended for brevet rank; and, on his appointment by Lord Mulgrave to a vacant Troop, he was deprived of it by the Duke of Wellington, who got it summarily reduced in 1816. Did, however, the limbers of Captain Mercer's battery ever leave the ground? That they did not, can be shown most clearly. In his Diary, he describes the state of his Troop after a heavy fire, to which it was exposed *after* the charges of the French cavalry. In the description, he says: "The guns came to- "gether in a confused heap, the trails crossing each other, "and the whole *dangerously near the limbers* and ammunition "waggons." The same description also proves that the

Ibid. p. 313.

Ibid. p. 326.

frightful losses suffered by the troop took place during the very time when, according to the Duke's letter, the men and limbers would have been off the field. In going to take up the position, they moved at a gallop, and in so compact a body, that the Duke cried out: "Ah! that's the way I "like to see Horse Artillery move!" In a short time, such was the havoc committed among men and horses, that Captain Mercer wrote: "I sighed for my poor troop; it was already " a wreck."

With regard to the insinuation as to the lack of artillery at the end of the battle, it is shown clearly by Siborne, in his model of the battle as it was at a quarter before 8 P.M., that thirteen Troops and Brigades of the Royal Artillery were in action, when the final attack took place; *this being the entire number with the army.* Of these, some were so crippled by losses—as Mercer's was—that they were unable to join in the pursuit; and possibly some recollection of this fact may have been in the Duke's mind when he wrote. That the artillery fire, however, at the end of the day was slack from the cause stated in the Duke's letter is an utter mistake; nor do the French seem to have found it very slack, as will presently be seen.

One word before appealing to a few other historians. If such conduct had taken place as is described in the letter under consideration, it would have been bruited over the whole army. Concealment, or collusion, would have been impossible; inquiries would have been officially instituted. To believe that such an occurrence could have been kept quiet requires a considerably greater stretch of credulity than to believe that the Duke of Wellington was misinformed. In fact, that such unanimity of testimony to one version, and such a general agreement to be silent to another should be possible, unless the former were true, and the latter imaginary, would be nothing short of a miracle. One or two miracles of this description would demolish all belief in history.

In the earliest and most detailed account of the Battle of Waterloo, the tenth edition of which was published in 1817, and which is called ' The Battle of Waterloo, also of Ligny, and Quatre Bras, described by the series of accounts published by authority, by a near observer ;' edited by Captain G. Jones, the following passage occurs : " No account " yet published of the battle, seen by the Editor, has mentioned in adequate terms the effect of our artillery at " Waterloo—no *English* account at least. *The enemy felt* it, " and in their manner of expressing themselves have passed " the greatest compliments. A French account, given in " our preceding pages, says : ' The English artillery made " ' *dreadful* havoc in our ranks.' . . . ' The Imperial Guard " ' made several charges, but was constantly repulsed, " ' *crushed by a terrible artillery, that each minute seemed to* " ' *multiply*.' [1] These invincible grenadiers *beheld the grape-* " *shot make day through their ranks ;* they closed promptly " and coolly their shattered ranks." . . . " In proportion as " they ranged up the eminence, and darted forward on the " squares, which occupied its summit, *the Artillery vomited* " *death upon them, and killed them in masses.* . . . In an " account given by an officer of the ' Northumberland,' of " Napoleon's conversation on board that ship, he says : ' Bona-" ' parte gives great credit to our Infantry and Artillery.' " Again : " The artillery on both sides was well served, but " Bonaparte had upwards of 250 pieces in the field. Not-" withstanding our inferiority in this arm, which was still " more apparent from the size of the enemy's guns (being " 12-pounders, ours only 9 and 6), than from their numbers, " ours were so well fought, that I believe it is allowed by " all they did equal execution. . . . See also the account of " Captain Bolton and Napier's Brigade of Foot Artillery, " from which it appears the Artillery had turned the enemy, " previous to the advance of the Guards. The French dis-" played the greatest rage and fury ; they cursed the English " while they were fighting, and cursed the precision with

---

[1] At this time, according to the Duke's letter, he had nothing but his reserve Artillery, the rest having quitted the field !

" which the English grape-shot was fired, which ' was neither
" ' too high nor too low, but struck right in the middle.' "

From the many writers who have done credit to the exertions and courage of the Artillery at Waterloo, three more extracts will be made.

In proof of the activity of the Corps at the end of the day, the following quotation, from an author already mentioned, is given. In describing the reception given to the French Imperial Guard, he says : " The English gunners once more " plied their trade. It was positively frightful to witness " the havoc that was occasioned in that mass." Sir James Shaw Kennedy also describes the strength of the British artillery fire at the end of the day.

<small>Gleig.</small>

<small>Kennedy, p. 142.</small>

In a Paper on ' The Campaign of Waterloo,' which appeared in the ' United Service Journal,' in 1834, the following passage occurs : " If we admit that, during this arduous " and terrible day, the British Infantry acted up to the " right standard of soldiership, which their long career of " victory had established, it must be added that *the Artillery* " *actually surpassed all expectation*, high as, from their pre- " vious conduct, that expectation naturally was. In point " of zeal and courage, the officers and men of the three " arms were of course fully upon a par; but the circum- " stances of the battle were favourable to the Artillery ; " and certainly the skill, spirit, gallantry, and indefatigable " exertion which they displayed, almost surpasses belief."

Only one more witness will be called from the ranks of historians. Hooper, in his work on Waterloo, to which he devoted eight years, and in the compilation of which he used every known authority on both sides, made use of words which appropriately close this argument : " The Artillery, " so devoted and effective, gathered another branch from the " tree of honour."

APPENDIX B.

THE ROYAL ARTILLERY AND THE MAGNETIC SURVEY OF THE GLOBE.

AFTER the peace of 1815 officers of Royal Artillery had little opportunity for active employment or staff duty. Among other officers who turned their attention to employments out of the ordinary routine were General Sir Edward Sabine and the late Colonel Colquhoun. The latter officer made a voyage to the Arctic Seas as an amateur whaler, took employment in connection with a South American Mining Company, and, before his appointment to the Carriage Department, in which he did most excellent service for many years—till nearly the date of the Crimean war—commanded the Artillery of Sir de Lacy Evans's Spanish Legion, and was employed with the naval expeditions sent to Spain and to the coast of Syria.

Sir Edward Sabine began a long scientific career by accompanying the late Sir Edward Parry to the North Polar Seas in 1819-20, as the scientific observer of his expedition. His interest in scientific pursuits, and especially in the determination of the figure of the Earth and in the science of terrestrial magnetism, has continued to the present date. He filled the office of Secretary of the Royal Society from 1828 to 1829, that of Foreign Secretary from 1845 to 1850, and that of Treasurer from 1850 to 1861; and he was President from 1861 to 1871, when he retired from office. In 1839, the Royal Society and British Association procured the sanction of the Government for a naval expedition to the Antarctic Seas, and for the establishment of four fixed magnetic and meteorological observatories at four stations widely apart, namely, Hobarton, in Van Diemen's Land, Cape Town, St. Helena, and Toronto. The station at

Hobarton was undertaken by the Admiralty, and given to officers of the late Sir James Ross's Antarctic expedition. The establishment of the other observatories was, under the authority of the Master-General and Board of Ordnance, entrusted to Royal Artillery officers, with non-commissioned officers as assistants, who were employed under the orders of the Deputy Adjutant-General and of Sir Edward (then Major) Sabine, as an ordinary staff duty. The officers successively employed were Lieutenants (now Major-Generals) F. Eardley-Wilmot, W. J. Smythe, J. H. Lefroy, C. J. B. Riddell, and H. Clerk; Lieutenant (now Colonel) Younghusband and the late Colonel H. J. Strange.

The magnetic instruments employed, of singular elegance and precision, were designed by the Rev. Humphrey Lloyd (now Provost) of Trinity College, Dublin, by whom the officers were instructed in their manipulation at the Magnetic Observatory in the College grounds, the only one then existing in the United Kingdom. The discovery which had been made of the simultaneous manifestation of magnetical disturbance over a wide extent of the globe rendered it desirable that the observations at all the stations should be taken at the same moment of absolute time; and, in compliment to Professor Gauss, to whom magnetic science was so deeply indebted, Goettingen time was universally adopted. Observations of the three elements—Declination, Horizontal Force, and Vertical Force—were made every two hours, day and night, and with such strictness that, if by any accident the right moment was lost, the observation was entered in red ink, with a note of the number of seconds elapsed. Once a month, on what was called "Term Day," the observations were prosecuted at intervals of a few minutes for twenty-four hours uninterruptedly, and a similar course was adopted whenever a magnetic storm declared itself, and persevered in until the storm passed away, a period, occasionally, of as much as thirty hours.

The observatories were established originally for three years, but were continued, in the case of the Cape and St. Helena, for a second term of the same length, and in that of Toronto for three terms. At the conclusion of these terms the St. Helena observatory was discontinued, and the remaining observatories were taken over by the local governments.

Lieutenant Clerk commenced his magnetic employment by a cruise in the Antarctic Seas for a magnetic survey. Lieutenant Lefroy carried out a magnetic survey of a considerable portion of the Hudson's Bay territories, and Lieutenant Eardley-Wilmot a survey of the Cape Colony.

The observations made at the Ordnance and Naval Observatories have been published under the direction of Sir Edward Sabine, who has had an office for the purpose at Woolwich, which has been subsequently removed to the Kew Observatory. [In November, 1871.]

The brief summary given above of the operations which earned for so many Artillery officers the blue riband of Science,—Fellowship of the Royal Society,—would establish to a great extent that which its most distinguished officers have always sought to secure for the Regiment,—a scientific reputation. But in the career of Sir Edward Sabine, so briefly alluded to, there has been one continued proof of the possibility of a soldier attaining the highest eminence in the world of science. Although personally unknown to many of his brother officers, his fame has been the pride of all; and has been felt to reflect a lustre, unprecedented in the profession, upon the Corps of which he is a member. Many readers of these pages will remember the reception given to him when, with the other Colonels-Commandant, he was persuaded during the present year to revisit the head-quarters of the Regiment. In the enthusiasm with which he was greeted by old and young, there was an unmistakable evidence of an *esprit de corps*, which, while admitting the claims of the scientific world at large upon their distinguished comrade, yet determined that it should be known to him that his honours were doubly dear to them because he was one of themselves.

In the sketch of the Magnetic Survey of the Globe given above, there would be a great omission if it were not stated how much the employment of Artillery officers in these operations was due to the previous labours and successes of Sir Edward Sabine. It was in 1817, two years after the conclusion of the war, that the first Polar Expedition was prepared. The Admiralty, to whom the preparations were entrusted, applied to the President and Council of the Royal Society to recommend a person who should be competent to conduct the researches in Physics and Natural History. General Mudge—already mentioned in this work—was then at the head of the British Trigonometrical Survey, and was a member of the Council of the Royal Society. It may be here mentioned, in passing, that in those days the Artillery and Engineers had the alternate direction of the Trigonometrical Survey, now apparently vested exclusively in the latter. Sir Edward Sabine was already favourably known, not merely to General Mudge, but also to other leading members of the Council of the Royal Society, such as Young, Kater, Wollaston, and Davy,—on account of some works which he had written, one being on the Birds of North America, in which country he had served during the war of 1812-14. After passing a severe examination, with great credit, Sir Edward Sabine's appointment to the Polar Expedition was sanctioned by Lord Mulgrave, then Master-General of the Ordnance: and early in 1818 he sailed in the 'Isabella,' making his first Pendulum station at Hare Island, in Baffin's Bay, in the spring of 1818. The results of his experiments, then and subsequently, appeared in the 'Philosophical Transactions,' and in a work entitled 'Pendulum and other Experiments,' published in 1825, at the cost of Government, on the recommendation of the Duke of Wellington, who had succeeded Lord Mulgrave as Master-General of the Ordnance.

It was Sir Edward's hope—in which, however, he was disappointed—that a series of Pendulum experiments on the continental surface comprised between the high Canadian latitudes and the shores of the Mexican Sea, should also be undertaken. He has lived, however, to see the same object admirably accomplished on the continent of British India between Cape Comorin and the Higher Himalaya, under the able direction of Colonel Walker of the Royal (Indian) Engineers,—and to take himself a final part in the completion of the series, at the Kew Physical Observatory, by Captain Heaviside, R.E., and the men of the Indian Engineers, employed on that service by Colonel Walker. It may be said without exaggeration that the support given by Sir Edward—as President of the Royal Society—to Colonel Walker's propositions, and the earlier experiments made by himself in the same field, have been among the highest services rendered by any man to science. Among the many Artillery officers who, since the peace of 1815, have sought to make a return to their country by their devotion to physical science, Sir Edward Sabine stands *facile princeps*:—and he has had the satisfaction of living to see, not merely his experiments carried to maturity, but also the inferences, which he did not hesitate to draw with confidence from his own earlier experiments, confirmed by the results of the labours of others. The results of his experiments, which claimed to be sufficiently extensive to justify the conclusion which they were held to establish of the measure of the ellipticity in the northern portion of the globe, have received an increased value since the published results of a similar series in the southern hemisphere by Captain Henry Foster, from the fact of their mutual agreement. [Transactions of Royal Astronomical Society.]

These earlier services of Sir Edward Sabine supplied the ground on which the then Master-General (Lord Vivian) justified,—and on which Sir Robert Peel, as head of the Government, approved,—his nomination to the superintendence of the Magnetic Observatories in 1839, fourteen years after the publication by him of the work mentioned above, 'Pendulum and other Experiments.' It was while he · held this appointment, that he directed the Magnetic Survey of the Globe, in which so many Artillery officers had the good fortune to take a leading part.

APPENDIX C.

TABULAR STATEMENT SHOWING THE DATE OF FORMATION, AND FORMER DESIGNATION, OF EVERY BATTERY OF THE REGIMENT NOW IN THE SERVICE.

N.B.—The reader should look at the explanatory notes before using the Tables.

Battery.	Brigade.	Designation, previous to Introduction of the Brigade System.	When formed.
A	A	A Troop, Royal Horse Artillery	1793
B	,,	B ,, ,, ,, ,,	1793
C	,,	C ,, ,, ,, ,,	1793
D	,,	G ,, ,, ,, ,,	1804
E	,,	K ,, ,, ,, ,,	1857
A	B	D Troop, Royal Horse Artillery	1794
B	,,	E ,, ,, ,, ,,	1794
C	,,	F ,, ,, ,, ,,	1801
D	,,	H ,, ,, ,, ,,	1805
E	,,	I ,, ,, ,, ,,	1805
F	,,	C Troop, Madras Horse Artillery	1816
G	,,	D ,, ,, ,,	1825
H	,,	———— Royal Horse Artillery	1871
A	C	*1st Troop, 1st B{de}, Bengal Horse Artillery	1800
B	,,	1st ,, 3rd ,, ,, ,, ,,	1809
C	,,	2nd ,, 1st ,, ,, ,, ,,	1825
D	,,	2nd ,, 3rd ,, ,, ,, ,,	1825
E	,,	3rd ,, 1st ,, ,, ,, ,,	1826
A	D	A Troop, Madras Horse Artillery	1805
B	,,	B ,, ,, ,, ,,	1809
C	,,	(a)Leslie's Troop, Bombay Horse Artillery	1811
D	,,	3rd Troop, 3rd B{de}, Bengal Horse Artillery	1826
E	,,	2nd Troop, Bombay Horse Artillery	1820
F	,,	5th Troop, 1st B{de}, Bengal Horse Artillery	1838
G	,,	3rd Troop, Bombay Horse Artillery	1824
H	,,	4th ,, ,, ,, ,,	1824

App. C. *Date of Formation, &c., of Batteries.* 471

Tabular Statement—*continued.*

Battery.	Brigade.	Designation, previous to Introduction of the Brigade System.						When formed.
A	F	1st Troop,	2nd B$^{de.}$,	Bengal	Horse	Artillery		1809
B	,,	2nd ,,	2nd ,,	,,	,,	,,		1816
C	,,	3rd ,,	2nd ,,	,,	,,	,,		1825
E	,,	4th ,,	2nd ,,	,,	,,	,,		1857
F	,,	4th ,,	3rd ,,	,,	,,	,,		1858
A	1st	(b)4th Company,	7th Battalion,	Royal	Artillery			1758
B	,,	2nd ,,	1st ,,	,,	,,			×
C	,,	(b)1st ,,	7th ,,	,,	,,			1756
D	,,	4th ,,	2nd ,,	,,	,,			×
E	,,	8th ,,	4th ,,	,,	,,			1771
F	,,	1st ,,	5th ,,	,,	,,			1794
G	,,	5th ,,	8th ,,	,,	,,			1803
H	,,	1st ,,	8th ,,	,,	,,			1803
I	,,			,,	,,			1871
K	,,			,,	,,			1871
2	2nd	3rd Company,	5th Battalion,	Royal	Artillery			1794
3	,,	4th ,,	5th ,,	,,	,,			1794
4	,,	3rd ,,	6th ,,	,,	,,			1799
5	,,	7th ,,	2nd ,,	,,	,,			×
6	,,	6th ,,	1st ,,	,,	,,			×
7	,,	3rd ,,	1st ,,	,,	,,			×
9	,,			,,	,,			1859
2	3rd	5th Company,	9th Battalion,	Royal	Artillery			1806
3	,,	6th ,,	5th ,,	,,	,,			1795
4	,,	4th ,,	3rd ,,	,,	,,			×
5	,,	8th ,,	6th ,,	,,	,,			1800
6	,,	2nd ,,	4th ,,	,,	,,			×
7	,,	6th ,,	3rd ,,	,,	,,			×
8	,,	5th ,,	2nd ,,	,,	,,			×
A	4th	1st Company,	3rd Battalion,	Royal	Artillery			×
B	,,	1st ,,	11th ,,	,,	,,			1848
C	,,			,,	,,			1871
D	,,	8th ,,	3rd ,,	,,	,,			×
E	,,	3rd ,,	11th ,,	,,	,,			1848
F	,,	5th ,,	11th ,,	,,	,,			1848
G	,,	4th ,,	12th ,,	,,	,,			1848

472 *Statement of Date of Formation,* APP. C.

TABULAR STATEMENT—*continued.*

Battery.	Brigade.	Designation, previous to Introduction of the Brigade System.					When formed.
II	4th	4th Company,	11th Battalion,	Royal Artillery			1779
I	,,			,,	,,		1871
K	,,	(b)8th Company,	7th Battalion,	,,	,,		1794
1	5th	5th Company,	5th Battalion,	Royal Artillery			1794
2	,,	(b)7th	,,	7th	,,	,, ,,	1794
3	,,	4th	,,	1st	,,	,, ,,	×
4	,,	7th	,,	1st	,,	,, ,,	×
5	,,	8th	,,	5th	,,	,, ,,	1795
6	,,	2nd	,,	6th	,,	,, ,,	1791
7	,,	A	,,	2nd	,,	Madras Artillery	1812
1	6th	6th Company,	4th Battalion,	Royal Artillery			×
2	,,	8th	,,	12th	,,	,, ,,	1848
3	,,	(b)5th	,,	7th	,,	,, ,,	1778
4	,,	3rd	,,	13th	,,	,, ,,	1854
5	,,	7th	,,	13th	,,	,, ,,	1854
6	,,	8th	,,	13th	,,	,, ,,	1854
7	,,	B	,,	4th	,,	Madras Artillery	1845
1	7th	8th Company,	8th Battalion,	Royal Artillery			1803
2	,,	4th	,,	13th	,,	,, ,,	1854
3	,,	7th	,,	3rd	,,	,, ,,	×
4	,,	1st	,,	4th	,,	,, ,,	×
5	,,	1st	,,	14th	,,	,, ,,	1855
6	,,	2nd	,,	14th	,,	,, ,,	1855
7	,,	2nd	,,	12th	,,	,, ,,	1848
A	8th	2nd Company,	3rd Battalion,	Bengal Artillery			1786
B	,,	4th	,,	6th	,,	Royal Artillery	1799
C	,,	5th	,,	6th	,,	,, ,,	1799
D	,,	2nd	,,	5th	,,	,, ,,	1794
E	,,	2nd	,,	9th	,,	,, ,,	1806
F	,,	6th	,,	6th	,,	,, ,,	1799
G	,,	6th	,,	2nd	,,	,, ,,	×
H	,,	7th	,,	8th	,,	,, ,,	1803
A	9th	7th Company,	5th Battalion,	Royal Artillery			1795
B	,,	5th	,,	4th	,,	,, ,,	×

APP. C. *and former Designation of Batteries.* 473

TABULAR STATEMENT—*continued.*

Battery.	Brigade.	Designation, previous to Introduction of the Brigade System.					When formed.
C	9th	7th Company,	6th Battalion,	Royal Artillery			1800
D	,,	6th ,,	8th ,,	,,	,,	,,	1803
E	,,	8th ,,	9th ,,	,,	,,	,,	1806
F	,,	1st ,,	1st ,,	,,	,,	,,	×
G	,,	1st ,,	9th ,,	,,	,,	,,	1806
1	10th	1st Company,	10th Battalion,	Royal Artillery			1846
2	,,	2nd ,,	10th ,,	,,	,,	,,	1846
3	,,	3rd ,,	10th ,,	,,	,,	,,	1846
4	,,	4th ,,	10th ,,	,,	,,	,,	1846
5	,,	5th ,,	10th ,,	,,	,,	,,	1846
6	,,	7th ,,	4th ,,	,,	,,	,,	1771
7	,,	3rd ,,	2nd ,,	,,	,,	,,	×
A	11th	8th Company,	1st Battalion,	Royal Artillery			×
B	,,	5th ,,	3rd ,,	,,	,,	,,	×
C	,,	1st ,,	6th ,,	,,	,,	,,	1791
D	,,	(b)6th ,,	7th ,,	,,	,,	,,	1778
E	,,	5th ,,	13th ,,	,,	,,	,,	1854
F	,,	6th ,,	13th ,,	,,	,,	,,	1854
G	,,	5th ,,	14th ,,	,,	,,	,,	1855
1	12th	8th Company,	10th Battalion,	Royal Artillery			1846
2	,,	2nd ,,	2nd ,,	,,	,,	,,	×
3	,,	(b)3rd ,,	7th ,,	,,	,,	,,	1758
4	,,	6th ,,	10th ,,	,,	,,	,,	1846
5	,,	1st ,,	12th ,,	,,	,,	,,	1848
6	,,	4th ,,	9th ,,	,,	,,	,,	1806
7	,,	4th ,,	8th ,,	,,	,,	,,	1803
1	13th	2nd Company,	13th Battalion,	Royal Artillery			1854
2	,,	3rd ,,	3rd ,,	,,	,,	,,	×
3	,,	8th ,,	14th ,,	,,	,,	,,	1855
4	,,	5th ,,	1st ,,	,,	,,	,,	×
5	,,	2nd ,,	11th ,,	,,	,,	,,	1848
6	,,	7th ,,	11th ,,	,,	,,	,,	1848
7	,,	2nd ,,	3rd ,,	,,	,,	,,	×
A	14th	8th Company,	2nd Battalion,	Royal Artillery			×
B	,,	3rd ,,	9th ,,	,,	,,	,,	1806

TABULAR STATEMENT—continued.

Battery.	Brigade.	Designation, previous to Introduction of the Brigade System.					When formed.
C	14th	6th Company,	2nd Battalion,	Royal Artillery			1806
D	,,	6th ,,	11th ,,	,,	,,		1848
E	,,	5th ,,	12th ,,	,,	,,		1848
F	,,	4th ,,	14th ,,	,,	,,		1855
G	,,	6th ,,	14th ,,	,,	,,		1855
H	,,	7th ,,	10th ,,	,,	,,		1846
I	,,			,,	,,		1871
K	,,			,,	,,		1871
1 to 7	15th	——————— Royal Artillery					1860
A	16th	2nd Company,	4th Battalion,	Bengal Artillery			1770
B	,,	1st ,,	1st ,,	,,	,,		1786
C	,,	4th ,,	1st ,,	,,	,,		1786
D	,,	4th ,,	3rd ,,	,,	,,		1802
E	,,	3rd ,,	1st ,,	,,	,,		1818
F	,,			Royal Artillery			1862
G	,,			,,	,,		1862
H	,,	2nd ,,	8th ,,	,,	,,		1803
I	,,			,,	,,		1871
K	,,			,,	,,		1871
1	17th	A Company,	1st Battalion,	Madras Artillery			+
2	,,	B ,,	1st ,,	,,	,,		+
3	,,			Royal Artillery			1862
4	,,	D ,,	1st ,,	Madras Artillery			1786
5	,,	A ,,	4th ,,	,,	,,		1845
6	,,			Royal Artillery			1862
7	,,	9th ,, 8th ⎱ then ⎰ 8th ,, 11th		,,	,,		1803
A	18th	2nd Company,	1st Battalion,	Bombay Artillery			1765
B	,,	3rd ,,	1st ,,	,,	,,		1796
C	,,	3rd ,,	2nd ,,	,,	,,		1798
D	,,	4th ,,	2nd ,,	,,	,,		1820
E	,,	1st ,,	3rd ,,	,,	,,		1857
F	,,	2nd ,,	3rd ,,	,,	,,		1857
G	,,	D ,,	3rd ,,	Madras Artillery			1806
A	19th	2nd Company,	1st Battalion,	Bengal Artillery			1758
B	,,	1st ,,	2nd ,,	,,	,,		1802

APP. C.   *and former Designation of Batteries.*   475

TABULAR STATEMENT—*continued.*

Battery.	Brigade.	Designation, previous to Introduction of the Brigade System.	When formed.
C	19th	4th Company, 2nd Battalion, Bengal Artillery	1802
D	,,	4th ,, 5th ,, ,, ,,	1818
E	,,	2nd ,, 6th ,, ,, ,,	1842
F	,,	3rd ,, 6th ,, ,, ,,	1842
G	,,	7th ,, 14th ,, Royal Artillery	1855
A	20th	A Company, 3rd Battalion, Madras Artillery	†
B	,,	B ,, 2nd ,, ,, ,,	1812
C	,,	C ,, 2nd ,, ,, ,,	1812
D	,,	D ,, 2nd ,, ,, ,,	1809
E	,,	C ,, 1st ,, ,, ,,	1786
F	,,	B ,, 3rd ,, ,, ,,	1806
G	,,	C ,, 3rd ,, ,, ,,	1811
1	21st	1st Company, 1st Battalion, Bombay Artillery	1748
2	,,	——————————————— Royal Artillery	1862
3	,,	2nd ,, 2nd ,, Bombay Artillery	1768
4	,,	4th ,, 1st ,, ,, ,,	1802
5	,,	4th ,, 3rd ,, ,, ,,	1857
6	,,	——————————————— Royal Artillery	1862
7	,,	1st ,, 2nd ,, ,, ,,	×
1	22nd	2nd Company, 5th Battalion, Bengal Artillery	1760
2	,,	——————————————— Royal Artillery	1862
3	,,	1st ,, 5th ,, Bengal Artillery	1786
4	,,	3rd ,, 2nd ,, ,, ,,	1802
5	,,	3rd ,, 3rd ,, ,, ,,	1802
6	,,	——————————————— Royal Artillery	1862
7	,,	,, ,,	1862
1	23rd	1st Company, 4th Battalion, Bengal Artillery	1749
2	,,	4th ,, 4th ,, ,, ,,	1763
3	,,	1st ,, 3rd ,, ,, ,,	1778
4	,,	2nd ,, 2nd ,, ,, ,,	1802
5	,,	1st ,, 6th ,, ,, ,,	1842
6	,,	——————————————— Royal Artillery	1862
7	,,	3rd ,, 4th ,, Bengal Artillery	1786

[NOTES TO APPENDIX C.

NOTES TO APPENDIX C.

* Formed from the Horse Artillery galloper guns raised at different periods between 1760 and 1800, and attached to Regiments of Cavalry. It first served as a distinct troop with Sir David Baird's Division of the Army that fought in Egypt under Sir Ralph Abercrombie in 1801.

(a) Extract from G. O. by G. G. of India, dated Agra, 11/4/43 :—" The 1st Troop " of the Bombay Horse Artillery shall hereafter, *for ever*, be denominated Leslie's " Troop of Horse Artillery; and shall, in addition to all other decorations or " inscriptions upon its appointments, bear *the eagle*."

(b) The 7th Battalion was formed from the Royal Irish Artillery. G. O. 1/4/01.

✕ Two Companies of the 1st, 2nd, and 3rd Battalions of Royal Artillery were formed in 1771. The remaining Companies of these three Battalions and the first six Companies of the 4th Battalion were formed at different periods from 1716 to 1757. Their identity with those Batteries now in the Service cannot be traced.

+ Date of formation unknown, but these Batteries are mentioned in G. O. dated 19/3/1800.

N.B.—The Companies of the 11th and 12th Battalions are in almost every case shown as existing only since 1848. But as they were—in many instances—already existing as the 9th and 10th Companies of other Battalions before that year, they are really entitled to an earlier date, if it could be accurately traced in each case.

G. E. WYNDHAM MALET, CAPTAIN R.A.

PRESENT DESIGNATION OF THE OLD FIELD BATTERIES.

Before the introduction of the Brigade system, Companies of Artillery were made Field Batteries periodically; and on receiving the necessary horses, guns, &c., they assumed the letter, or number, borne by the Company from which they respectively received the equipment. The Table given below shows the Companies which were Field Batteries at the date of the introduction of the Brigade system. Some of these had become Field Batteries since the Crimean war,—and bore the letters, which distinguished other Batteries, during that campaign.

Letter Designa-tion.	In 1859.		Now.		Letter Designa-tion.	In 1859.		Now.	
	Compy.	Battⁿ.	Battery.	Brigade.		Compy.	Battⁿ.	Battery.	Brigade.
A	2	8th	H	16th	X	8	1st	A	11th
B	8	3rd	D	4th	Y	2	3rd	7	13th
C	6	7th	D	11th	Z	5	4th	B	9th
D	3	8th	8*	13th					
E	1	3rd	A	4th	Numeri-cal desig-nation.				
F	3	11th	E	4th					
G	7	8th	H	8th	—				
H	5	11th	F	4th	No. 1	5	1st	4	13th
I	7	6th	C	9th	2	2	5th	D	8th
J	5	3rd	B	11th	3	4	14th	F	14th
K	2	13th	1	13th	4	7	14th	G	19th
L	1	1st	F	9th	5	4	6th	B	8th
M	7	5th	A	9th	6	5	14th	G	11th
N	8	7th	K	4th	7	8	14th	3	13th
O	6	8th	D	9th	8	6	14th	G	14th
P	4	12th	G	4th	9	3	3rd	2	13th
Q	5	12th	E	14th	10	7	10th	H	14th
R	5	6th	C	8th	11	6	6th	F	8th
S	8	9th	E	9th	12	2	9th	E	8th
T	3	9th	B	14th	13	5	13th	E	11th
U	6	2nd	G	8th	14	6	13th	F	11th
V	1	6th	C	11th	15	3	14th	D†	14th
W	1	11th	B	4th	16	1	9th	G	9th

* Reduced February 1, 1871. † Reduced March 1, 1863.

477*

The tables in Appendix C were prepared before the recent remodelling of the Regiment, and must be modified by the reader in accordance with the following changes in designations of Batteries occasioned by the new organization.

ROYAL HORSE ARTILLERY.

A Battery	A Brigade	has become	A Battery	
B „	A „	„	B „	
C „	A „	„	C „	
E „	B „	„	D „	
A „	B „	„	E „	
B „	B „	„	F „	} A Brigade.
C „	B „	„	G „	
D „	A „	„	H „	
D „	B „	„	I „	
E „	A „	„	K „	
A „	Dep. H.A.	„	Dep. „	

A Battery	C Brigade	has become	A Battery	
B „	C „	„	B „	
C „	C „	„	C „	
D „	C „	„	D „	
E „	C „	„	E „	
A „	D „	„	F „	} B Brigade.
B „	D „	„	G „	
C „	D „	„	H „	
D „	D „	„	I „	
E „	D „	„	K „	
Newly formed	. . . . . .	Dep. „	

A Battery	E Brigade	has become	A Battery	
B „	E „	„	B „	
C „	E „	„	C „	
D „	E „	„	D „	
E „	E „	„	E „	
A „	F „	„	F „	} C Brigade.
B „	F „	„	G „	
C „	F „	„	H „	
D „	F „	„	I „	
E „	F „	„	K „	
B „	Dep. H.A.	„	Dep. „	

* Reduced in 1879.

Changes in Designations of Batteries — App. C.

FIELD ARTILLERY.

A Battery	1st Brigade	has become	A Battery	
B „	1st „	„	B „	
C „	1st „	„	C „	
D „	1st „	„	D „	
E „	1st „	„	E „	
F „	1st „	„	F „	
G „	1st „	„	G „	
A „	9th „	„	H „	} 1st Brigade.
B „	9th „	„	I „	
C „	9th „	„	K „	
D „	9th „	„	L „	
E „	9th „	„	M „	
F „	9th „	„	N „	
G „	9th „	„	O „	
A „	Dep. „	„	Dep. „	

A Battery	4th Brigade	has become	A Battery	
B „	4th „	„	B „	
C „	4th „	„	C „	
D „	4th „	„	D „	
E „	4th „	„	E „	
F „	4th „	„	F „	
G „	4th „	„	G „	
A „	18th „	„	H „	} 2nd Brigade.
B „	18th „	„	I „	
C „	18th „	„	K „	
D „	18th „	„	L „	
E „	18th „	„	M „	
F „	18th „	„	N „	
G „	18th „	„	O „	
C „	Dep. „	„	Dep. „	

A Battery	8th Brigade	has become	A Battery	
B „	8th „	„	B „	
C „	8th „	„	C „	
D „	8th „	„	D „	
E „	8th „	„	E „	
F „	8th „	„	F „	
G „	8th „	„	G „	
H „	8th „	„	H „	
A „	14th „	„	I „	} 3rd Brigade.
B „	14th „	„	K „	
C „	14th „	„	L „	
D „	14th „	„	M „	
E „	14th „	„	N „	
F „	14th „	„	O „	
G „	14th „	„	P „	
No. 2 „	Dep. „	„	Dep. „	

App. C.   *Occasioned by the New Organization.*   479*

FIELD ARTILLERY—*(continued).*

A Battery	11th Brigade	has become	A Battery	
B ,,	11th ,,	,,	B ,,	
C ,,	11th ,,	,,	C ,,	
D ,,	11th ,,	,,	D ,,	
E ,,	11th ,,	,,	E ,,	
F ,,	11th ,,	,,	F ,,	
G ,,	11th ,,	,,	G ,,	
A ,,	16th ,,	,,	H ,,	} 4th Brigade.
B ,,	16th ,,	,,	I ,,	
C ,,	16th ,,	,,	K ,,	
D ,,	16th ,,	,,	L ,,	
E ,,	16th ,,	,,	M ,,	
F ,,	16th ,,	,,	N ,,	
G ,,	16th ,,	,,	O ,,	
No. 1 ,,	Dep. ,,	,,	Dep. ,,	

A Battery	19th Brigade	has become	A Battery	
B ,,	19th ,,	,,	B ,,	
C ,,	19th ,,	,,	C ,,	
D ,,	19th ,,	,,	D ,,	
E ,,	19th ,,	,,	E ,,	
F ,,	19th ,,	,,	F ,,	
G ,,	19th ,,	,,	G ,,	
A ,,	24th ,,	,,	H ,,	} 5th Brigade.
B ,,	24th ,,	,,	I ,,	
C ,,	24th ,,	,,	K ,,	
D ,,	24th ,,	,,	L ,,	
E ,,	24th ,,	,,	M ,,	
F ,,	24th ,,	,,	N ,,	
G ,,	24th ,,	,,	O ,,	
B ,,	Dep. ,,	,,	Dep. ,,	

A Battery	20th Brigade	has become	A Battery	
B ,,	20th ,,	,,	B ,,	
C ,,	20th ,,	,,	C ,,	
D ,,	20th ,,	,,	D ,,	
E ,,	20th ,,	,,	E ,,	
F ,,	20th ,,	,,	F ,,	
G ,,	20th ,,	,,	G ,,	
A ,,	25th ,,	,,	H ,,	} 6th Brigade.
B ,,	25th ,,	,,	I ,,	
C ,,	25th ,,	,,	K ,,	
D ,,	25th ,,	,,	L ,,	
E ,,	25th ,,	,,	M ,,	
F ,,	25th ,,	,,	N ,,	
G ,,	25th ,,	,,	O ,,	
Newly formed	. . . . . .		Dep. ,,	

GARRISON ARTILLERY.

2 Battery	2nd Brigade	has become		1 Battery		
3 ,,	2nd ,,	,,		2 ,,		
4 ,,	2nd ,,	,,		3 ,,		
5 ,,	2nd ,,	,,		4 ,,		
6 ,,	2nd ,,	,,		5 ,,		
7 ,,	2nd ,,	,,		6 ,,		
9 ,,	2nd ,,	,,		7 ,,		
1 ,,	22nd ,,	,,		8 ,,		
2 ,,	22nd ,,	,,		9 ,,		
3 ,,	22nd ,,	,,		10 ,,	} 7th Brigade.	
4 ,,	22nd ,,	,,		11 ,,		
5 ,,	22nd ,,	,,		12 ,,		
6 ,,	22nd ,,	,,		13 ,,		
7 ,,	22nd ,,	,,		14 ,,		
1 ,,	17th ,,	,,		15 ,,		
2 ,,	17th ,,	,,		16 ,,		
3 ,,	17th ,,	,,		17 ,,		
4 ,,	17th ,,	,,		18 ,,		
7 ,,	Dep. ,,	,,		Dep. ,,		

A new battery formed in 1879 was called 19th Battery 7th Brigade.

2 Battery	3rd Brigade	has become		1 Battery		
3 ,,	3rd ,,	,,		2 ,,		
4 ,,	3rd ,,	,,		3 ,,		
5 ,,	3rd ,,	,,		4 ,,		
6 ,,	3rd ,,	,,		5 ,,		
7 ,,	3rd ,,	,,		6 ,,		
8 ,,	3rd ,,	,,		7 ,,		
1 ,,	5th ,,	,,		8 ,,		
2 ,,	5th ,,	,,		9 ,,		
3 ,,	5th ,,	,,		10 ,,	} 8th Brigade.	
4 ,,	5th ,,	,,		11 ,,		
5 ,,	5th ,,	,,		12 ,,		
6 ,,	5th ,,	,,		13 ,,		
7 ,,	5th ,,	,,		14 ,,		
1 ,,	6th ,,	,,		15 ,,		
2 ,,	6th ,,	,,		16 ,,		
3 ,,	6th ,,	,,		17 ,,		
4 ,,	6th ,,	,,		18 ,,		
5 ,,	6th ,,	,,		19 ,,		
3 ,,	Dep. ,,	,,		Dep. ,,		

Occasioned by the New Organization.

GARRISON ARTILLERY—(continued).

6 Battery	6th Brigade	has become	1 Battery	
7 "	6th "	"	2 "	
1 "	10th "	"	3 "	
2 "	10th "	"	4 "	
3 "	10th "	"	5 "	
4 "	10th "	"	6 "	
5 "	10th "	"	7 "	
6 "	10th "	"	8 "	
7 "	10th "	"	9 "	
1 "	13th "	"	10 "	9th Brigade.
2 "	13th "	"	11 "	
3 "	13th "	"	12 "	
4 "	13th "	"	13 "	
5 "	13th "	"	14 "	
6 "	13th "	"	15 "	
7 "	13th "	"	16 "	
1 "	7th "	"	17 "	
2 "	7th "	"	18 "	
4 "	Dep. "	"	Dep. "	

3 Battery	7th Brigade	has become	1 Battery	
4 "	7th "	"	2 "	
5 "	7th "	"	3 "	
6 "	7th "	"	4 "	
7 "	7th "	"	5 "	
1 "	15th "	"	6 "	
2 "	15th "	"	7 "	
3 "	15th "	"	8 "	
4 "	15th "	"	9 "	
5 "	15th "	"	10 "	10th Brigade.
6 "	15th "	"	11 "	
7 "	15th "	"	12 "	
1 "	12th "	"	13 "	
2 "	12th "	"	14 "	
3 "	12th "	"	15 "	
4 "	12th "	"	16 "	
5 "	12th "	"	17 "	
6 "	12th "	"	18 "	
5 "	Dep. "	"	Dep. "	

GARRISON ARTILLERY—(*continued*).

7 Battery	12th Brigade	has become	1 Battery	⎫	
5 ,,	17th ,,	,,	2 ,,	
6 ,,	17th ,,	,,	3 ,,	
7 ,,	17th ,,	,,	4 ,,	
1 ,,	21st ,,	,,	5 ,,	
2 ,,	21st ,,	,,	6 ,,	
3 ,,	21st ,,	,,	7 ,,	
4 ,,	21st ,,	,,	8 ,,	
5 ,,	21st ,,	,,	9 ,,	
6 ,,	21st ,,	,,	10 ,,	⎬ 11th Brigade.
7 ,,	21st ,,	,,	11 ,,	
1 ,,	23rd ,,	,,	12 ,,	
2 ,,	23rd ,,	,,	13 ,,	
3 ,,	23rd ,,	,,	14 ,,	
4 ,,	23rd ,,	,,	15 ,,	
5 ,,	23rd ,,	,,	16 ,,	
6 ,,	23rd ,,	,,	17 ,,	
7 ,,	23rd ,,	,,	18 ,,	
6 ,,	Dep. ,,	,,	Dep. ,,	⎭

A new battery was formed in 1879 as 19th Battery 11th Brigade.

October, 1879.

INDEX.

"A" BATTERY, A BRIGADE. | ANTRIM.

"A" Battery, A Brigade (A Troop), i. 396. (*Vide* A Brigade.)
—— Battery, B Brigade (E, afterwards D, Troop), i. 399.
——, 1st Brigade (4 Company, 7th Battalion), i. 422.
——, 4th Brigade (1 Company, 3rd Battalion), i. 220.
——, 9th Brigade (9 Company, afterwards 7, 5th Battalion), i. 409.
——, 11th Brigade (8 Company, 1st Battalion), i. 177, 208.
——, 14th Brigade (10 Company, afterwards 8, 2nd Battalion), i. 183.
"A" Brigade, R.H.A.—A (Chestnut) Troop, now "A" Battery, ii. 34, 76, 79, 89, 91, 99, 100, 257, 275, 276, 277, 325, 355, 373, 376, 378, 380, 381, 418.
—— "B" Battery (formerly B Troop, R.H.A.), ii. 34, 38, 40, 76, 79.
—— "C" Battery (formerly C Troop, R.H.A.), ii. 35, 44, 76, 79.
—— "D" Battery, i. 401; ii. 225.
Abbott, Charles, i. 179.
——, Edward, i. 173, 176.
Abercromby, B., ii. 218.
——, P., ii. 85.
——, Sir Ralph; in Flanders, ii. 60, 61, 65, 69.
——, ——, expedition to the Helder, ii. 90, 96, 97, 99, 100.
——, ——, in Egypt, ii. 104, 108, 111, 116, 121, 127, 128.
Aboukir, ii. 112, 126, 127.
Abson, George, i. 259.
Academy, Royal Military, i. 13, 19, 108 to 121, 243. *Vide* Cadet Company.
Ackland, General, ii. 207, 208.
Adair, R. B., i. 409.
——, Mr., Paymaster R.A., ii. 82.
Addams, James, i. 257; ii. 186, 188, 189.
Adjutant-General, R.A., Deputy, ii. 5, 6, 92, 136.
—— Assistant, ii. 5.
—— Deputy Assistant, ii. 5.
Adjutants of Battalions or Brigades, ii. 6, 12, 25.

Adjutants of Woolwich Garrison. *Vide* Brigade Major, R.A.
Adour River, Operations at, ii. 192, 193, 382, 383.
Adye, J. P., i. 172, 176, 326; ii. 141, 144, 160.
——, Mortimer, i. 222.
——, R. W., i. 180, 411; ii. 140, 146.
——, S. G., i. 408; ii. 106, 108, 132, 230, 234, 416, 421, 424.
Agents, R.A., Regimental. *Vide* Paymasters.
Albuera, ii. 280, 293, 294, 297, 298.
——, proportion of Guns to Troops at, ii. 412.
Alcabon, repulse of Spanish by French Troops at, ii. 254.
Alexandria, ii. 122, 126, 127 to 130, 138.
Algabaria Nuova, affair at, ii. 245.
Algesiras, expedition to, ii. 193, 281, 283.
Alkmaar, ii. 97, 98, 100.
Allowances, Contingent, ii. 26.
——, Good Service. *Vide* Pensions.
Almaraz, storming of, ii. 321.
Almeida, ii. 275, 285.
Alms, Chas. G., i. 421, 423; ii. 154.
Alost, defeat of French at, ii. 64.
Alten, Baron, ii. 294, 296.
America—Braddock's Expedition (1755), i. 158.
American War of Independence, i. 164, 297 to 381.
——, 2nd War, ii. 187, 188, 195, 323, 592, 410, 411.
——, South, Expedition, ii. 168.
——, Transport of Artillery, ii. 178, 401.
Amiens, Peace of, ii. 104, 135, 138.
Anderson, George, i. 188.
——, J. R., i. 400.
——, W., ii. 234, 431, 438.
——, W. C., i. 174.
Andrews, R., i. 421.
Annapolis (Port Royal, Nova Scotia), i. 71 to 78, 105.
Anson, A. E. H., i. 179.
Anstruther, General, ii. 207 to 209.
Antrim Militia, ii. 76.

Antwerp, Expedition to, ii. 224, 231, 416.
Appendices, i. 426 to 443; ii. 444 to 447.
Arabin, Frederick, i. 254; ii. 143, 261.
Arbuckle, B. H. Vaughan, i. 417.
Arbuthnot, C. G., i. 181, 403, 414.
——, John, i. 177; ii. 74.
——, Hon. W., i. 401, 422.
Arentschild, Colonel (Portuguese Artillery), ii. 244, 252, 269, 276, 387.
Ariaga, Major (Portuguese Artillery), ii. 296, 331, 353, 364, 375, 377.
Armagh Militia, ii. 76.
Armstrong, James, i. 174; ii. 105.
——, R. S., i. 254; ii. 394.
Army, command of, Artillery Officers for, ii. 52, 53, 89.
——, Pay of, ii. 71, 79.
—— of Reserve. *Vide* Reserves.
—— of Occupation in France, ii. 441.
Arsenal, Manufacturing Departments, ii. 15, 137.
——, Royal, i. 16.
Arthur, L., ii. 74.
Artificers and Engineers, i. 38–9.
——, Company of, ii. 2, 3.
——, Establishment per Battery in 1813, ii. 342, 343.
Artillery, earliest records of the use of, i. 36–7.
——, Distribution of, in 1797, ii. 84, 85; in 1798, 86; in 1810, 262, 270.
——, East India Company's, ii. 130. *Vide* also Indies, East.
——, field, i. 37–8.
——, horse, i. 37.
——, History of. *Vide* History.
—— in England, infancy of, i. 35 to 44.
——, Loyalty Loan, ii. 72.
—— officers, precedence of, i. 105, 137–8–9, 155.
——, Precedence of, ii. 3, 4, 41.
——, Royal Irish. *Vide* Irish Artillery.
—— of the Guard, ii. 52.
——, command of in the Field, 52.
——————, Expedition to the Helder, ii. 88, 90.
—————— in Egypt, ii. 104, 106, 109.
—————— in the Peninsula, ii. 196, 346.
—————— in the 2nd American War, ii. 394.
—————— at Waterloo, ii. 412, 424.
——————, General Officer of R. A. first employed, ii. 89, 90.
——, Officers of, for Army commands, ii. 52, 53, 89.
——, Pay of, ii. 71.
——, Director-General of, ii. 83, 137.
——, Inspector of, ii. 83, 137.
——, claim to bells in towns captured, ii. 167, 237.

Artillery (*continued*), to pay £40 for each field-piece captured, ii. 175, 176.
—— matériel and transport should devolve upon Artillery control alone, ii. 121.
—————— in Egypt. *Vide* Egypt.
—————— in South America. *Vide* America.
—————— in Peninsula. *Vide* Peninsula.
——, comparison of Horse, Field, and Garrison, ii. 45, 51, 52, 86, 268.
——, complete separation of ditto deprecated, ii. 52, 301, 391.
——, misapplication of, by the Duke of Wellington, ii. 276, 335, 336, 354, 419.
——, Marine. *Vide* Marine Artillery.
——, proportion of Guns to Troops, ii. 412.
—— with Army of Occupation in France, ii. 441.
Askwith, W. H., i. 407.
Assistant Adjutant-General, R.A. *Vide* Adjutant-General, R.A.
—— Woolwich Garrison, ii. 83.
A Troop. *Vide* "A" Battery, A Brigade.
Auchmuty, Sir S., ii. 170.
Augmentations, i. 82, 97, 104, 106, 152, 154, 169, 218, 251, 405 to 425; in 1786, ii. 3; 1787, 2; 1791, 2; 1793, 27 35; 1803, 138, 139; 1806, 150; 1808, 185; 1812, 322.
Augustus, of Prussia, H.R.H. Prince, ii. 439, 440.
Aylmer, Henry, i. 176.

Badajoz, 1st Siege, ii. 260, 280, 287, 289, 290, 291.
——, 2nd Siege, ii. 298, 299 to 305.
——, 3rd Siege, ii. 305, 307, 314, 316, 317.
Bagot, Mr. John, ii. 138.
Bagwell, Colonel, Tipperary Militia, ii. 77.
Baird, Sir David, in Egypt, ii. 108, 130.
——, at Copenhagen, ii. 161, 162.
——, with expedition to Cape of Good Hope, ii. 168.
——, at Corunna, ii. 211, 215, 218, 219.
Baker, G. W., ii. 188.
——, W., ii. 74.
Baltic, ii. 96.
Baltimore, battle of, ii. 395.
Band, Regimental, i. 209; ii. 2.
Bank of England, ii. 70.
Baring, Major, ii. 427.
Barker, Sir George R., i. 416.
Barlow, E., ii. 74.
Barnes, John, i. 411.
——, Joseph, i. 225.

Barnes, Samuel, ii. 186.
Barnett, W. T., i. 262.
Barossa, battle of, ii. 68, 190, 193, 280, 281, 283, 284.
Barreiros, Capt. (Portuguese Artillery), ii. 305.
Barry, W. W., i. 256.
Bastard, J., ii. 145.
———, J. S., i. 182.
Bastia (Corsica), ii. 68.
Bates, Henry, i. 225, 409.
Battalion (or Brigade), Reliefs. *Vide* Reliefs.
——— Guns, ii. 55, 59, 76, 78, 94, 95, 99, 107.
Battering Train for Ciudad Rodrigo, ii. 309, 310, 311.
———, for sieges in France in 1815, ii. 439, 440, 442.
Battery (or Company), the unit—for reliefs, ii. 135—for promotion of N. C. O, ii. 342.
——— *esprit*, i. 4, 170, 206.
Battle-Axe Company (2 Battery, 5th Brigade), i. 418–19.
Bayley, F., ii. 148, 277, 396.
Bayly, Z. C., i. 180, 414.
Baynes, C., i. 414; ii. 141, 143.
———, G. M., ii. 186, 431.
———, H., ii. 141, 255, 432, 435.
Bayonne, siege of, ii. 193, 383, 389.
"B" Battery, A Brigade (B Troop), i. 398.
———, B Brigade (F, afterwards E, Troop), i. 400.
———, 1st Brigade (2 Company, 1st Battalion), i. 173.
———, 8th Brigade (4 Company, 6th Battalion), i. 414.
———, 9th Brigade (5 Company, 4th Battalion), i. 259.
———, 11th Brigade (5 Company, 3rd Battalion), i. 223.
B Brigade, "A" Battery, ii. 91, 430.
———, "B" Battery, ii. 430, 436.
———, "C" Battery, ii. 170.
———, "D" Battery. *Vide* "I" Troop, R.H.A.
Beane, George, i. 223, 399.
———, at Corunna, ii. 215, 220.
———, at Vittoria and San Sebastian, ii. 345, 348, 353.
———, at Orthes and Toulouse, ii. 384, 385, 388.
———, at Waterloo, ii. 418, 424, 426, 431, 432.
Beckman, Sir Martin, i. 45, 57, 92.
Beckwith, General, ii. 260.
Bedingfeld, F., ii. 186.
Beer Money, ii. 71, 72.
Beevor, R., i. 223; ii. 57, 132, 219.

Belford, General Wm., i. 115, 125, 127–8, 132–3, 152; ii. 13.
Belgians at Waterloo, ii. 421.
Belgium, ii. 414.
Bell, Sir William, i. 223, 396.
———, ii. 261, 388, 425, 435.
Belleisle, ii. 108, 112.
———, siege of, i. 227 to 240.
———, list of Artillery officers at, i. 229.
Bells, in towns, &c., captured, lien on by R.A., ii. 167.
———, privilege withdrawn, ii. 237 to 240.
Belson, G. J., i. 172; ii. 257, 325.
Benezet, W. H. C., i. 417.
Benn, Anthony, i. 181.
———, Piercy, i. 222.
Bennett, Lieut. Henry, i. 125; 127.
Bent, Henry, i. 220, 422.
———, W. H., i. 175.
Bentham, Wm., i. 179, 223, 413; ii. 57, 106, 271.
Beresford, D. W. Pack, i. 177.
———, G. J., i. 176.
———, Marshal, in South America, ii. 169, 170, 180.
———, in the Peninsula, ii. 243, 246, 250, 251, 252, 286, 287, 288, 291, 293, 296, 298, 369, 383, 385, 387.
———, his capacity, ii. 293.
Bergen-op-Zoom, siege of (1747), i. 134.
———, ii. 64, 66, 98, 99.
Berners, W., ii. 145.
Bettesworth, J., i. 421.
Bidassoa, passage of the, ii. 374, 375.
Biddulph, M. A. S., i. 179.
Bingham, Charles Cox, i. 226, 256, 413, 416; ii. 74.
Birch, R. H., i. 180, 181; ii. 186, 271.
Bissett, Daniel, i. 180, 414.
Blachley, Charles, i. 220, 398, 399.
———, Henry, i. 423.
———, H. B., ii. 332, 362.
Blackheath, reviews of Artillery on, i. 266.
Bladensburg, battle of, ii. 395.
Blake, General, ii. 294.
Blomefield, Sir Thomas, i. 174, 177, 188, 315, 379; ii. 83, 137, 151, 158, 159, 165, 167.
Bloomfield, Benjamin Lord, i. 398, 411, 415.
Bloomfield, Sir John, i. 223, 400, 406.
———, at San Sebastian, ii. 362, 364.
———, at Waterloo, ii. 425, 431, 434, 435, and Appendix.
Blucher, Marshal, ii. 419.
Blumenbach, Lieut. King's German Artillery, ii. 388.
Boag, James, i. 179, 274; ii. 57, 61.
Board of Ordnance, i. 1, 9, 10, 19, 23 to 28, 137. *Vide* Ordnance Board.

Boats, flat-bottom, for transport of Artillery, ii. 125.
Boddy, Bombardier, R.A., i. 366.
Boger, T., i. 175; ii. 58, 63, 105, 143.
Bogue, R., i. 394, 404; ii. 390.
Bois-le-duc, ii. 64.
Bolton, S., ii. 153.
——, at Copenhagen, ii. 160.
——, at Waterloo, ii. 420, 424, 425, 428, 431, 432.
Bomb-vessels, ii. 54, 58, 74, 82, 85, 109.
Bonaparte, Napoleon, at siege of Toulon, ii. 67.
——, contrasted with Wellington in use of Artillery, ii. 336.
——, rupture of Treaty of Amiens by, and hostilities resumed, ii. 138.
——, war in Spain and Portugal, ii. 195.
——, his designs against England, ii. 158, 224.
——, Walcheren, ii. 228, 232.
——, Peninsular campaigns, ii. 270 to 387.
——, his abdication, ii. 388.
——, escape from Elba, ii. 412.
——, events of the 100 days, ii. 412, 413, 414, 420.
——, at Waterloo, ii. 420, 423.
——, Joseph, ii. 195, 253, 329, 350, 352.
Bonnell, Andrew, i. 432.
Boon Service, for Waterloo, ii. 433.
Boothby, J. G., i. 416.
Bordeaux, entry of Allies into, ii. 385.
Borgard, Lieut.-General Albert, i. 22, 61, 79, 104, 157, 431.
——, Memoir of, i. 83 to 100.
——, Regimental Orders by, i. 141.
——, Withers, i. 124.
Borthwick, General, ii. 314, 316, 318.
——, William, i. 175, 263, 400.
——, William, i. 225; ii. 56, 106, 107, 132.
Bounty (recruiting) in 1787, ii. 2.
Bourbons, restoration of, ii. 388.
Bourchier, D. M., i. 221.
——, ii. 276, 314, 319.
Bousfield, William, i. 61, 104, 431.
Bowater, George, i. 176, 416.
Bowes, General, ii. 206, 208.
Bowyer Fort, capture of, ii. 410.
Boxtel, action at, ii. 64, 66.
Bradbridge, J., i. 260, 292.
Braddock's Expedition in America (1755), i. 158.
Brady, Chas. J., i. 262; ii. 67.
——, Thomas, i. 175–176.
Brandling, J. J., i. 399, 404, 415.
Brandreth, T. A., i. 177, 400; ii. 147, 215, 220, 345, 387.
Brandywine, battle of, i. 319.

Braun, Capt. (Portuguese Artillery), ii. 296.
Breda, ii. 54, 64.
Bredin, Andrew, i. 261; ii. 140, 157, 186, 211, 269, 309, 310.
Bremen, ii. 65.
Brereton, Sir William, i. 223.
——, at San Sebastian, ii. 362, 364.
——, at Orthes, ii. 385.
——, at Waterloo, ii. 430, 432, 434, 437.
Breton, J. F., ii. 429, 430.
Brett, S., ii. 194.
Brettingham, R. W., i. 423.
Brevet to 2nd Captains R. A., ii. 356.
Bridge, Cyprian, i. 222, 261; ii. 394.
Brigade-Major, R.A., at Head-quarters R.A., ii. 5, 6, 83.
—————————————, in the Field, ii. 90, 107, 314, 353, 375, 424, 435.
Bridges, E. J., ii. 143, 190, 191, 192, 193.
Brietzche, Lieut., i. 229.
Brigade system established (1859), i. 3.
Briscoe, John, i. 220, 410, 423.
Brittenstein, George, i. 432.
Broadbridge, Thomas, i. 124; ii. 57.
Brock, General, ii. 392, 393.
Brome, J., at Copenhagen, ii. 160, 162.
——, at Walcheren, ii. 230, 231.
——, at Waterloo, ii. 433, 440.
——, Lieut.-Colonel Joseph, i. 263.
Brooke, Colonel, 44th Regt., ii. 395.
Brooklyn (Long Island), battle of, i. 308.
Broome or Brome, Lieut.-General Joseph, i. 124, 127, 130, 182, 221, 266.
Brough, R. S., i. 177, 431.
Broughton, S. D., i. 180.
Brown, Colonel, Commandant of Monte Video, ii. 177.
——, S., ii. 142.
Browne, Lieut.-Colonel George, i. 431.
——, St. John T., i. 257.
——, T. G., i. 409; ii. 433.
Brownrigg, Major, i. 162.
Bruce, Sir J. R., ii. 431.
Bruges Canal, destruction of, ii. 88.
Brune, General, ii. 96, 97, 98.
Brussels, ii. 420.
B Troop. *Vide* "B" Battery, A Brigade.
Buchanan, J. F., i. 188.
——, G. J. L., i. 175.
Buckner, Richard, i. 408, 409; ii. 144, 230, 231, 352, 361, 368, 378.
Buenos Ayres, ii. 166, 168, 169, 171.
Buffalo City, destruction of, ii. 393.
Bull, Robert, i. 401.
——, at Fuentes d'Onor, ii. 32.
——, at Talavera, ii. 259.
——, at Busaco and Torres Vedras, ii. 269, 277.

Bull, Robert (*cont.*), at Barossa, Badajoz, Albuera, and Ciudad Rodrigo, ii. 284, 285, 319.
——, at San Sebastian, ii. 325, 338.
——, at Bidassoa, ii. 374.
——, at Waterloo, ii. 424, 425, 430, 432, 434, 435.
Bullock, Lieut. Edward, i. 124.
Bunker's Hill, battle of, i. 302.
Burgos, siege of, ii. 321, 323, 330, 331, 332, 335 to 337.
——, blockade of, ii. 350.
Burgoyne, Sir John, R.E., ii. 336, 397, 406.
Burn, R., i. 223.
Burnaby, C. H., i. 422.
——, R. B., i. 416 ; ii. 431.
Burrard, Sir H., ii. 159, 161, 208, 210, 211.
Burrows, A. G., i. 258.
Burslem, J. G., ii. 108, 128.
Burton, John, i. 254.
——, J. C., ii. 186.
Busaco, ii. 262, 274, 276, 277, 278.
Bussman, Capt., King's German Artillery, ii. 272.
Butler, James, i. 180, 244, 400 ; ii. 35.
Butts, William, i. 254, 258 ; ii. 186, 261.
Byfleet, camp at (1756), i. 150–1–2.
Byng, General, ii. 437.

Caddy, William, i. 261 ; ii. 74.
Cadet Company, i. 15, 110 ; ii. 24, 27, 263.
Cadets, i. 13, 106–7, 110 to 121.
Cadiz, Expedition to (1702), i. 93 ; in 1801, ii. 114, 123.
—— defence of, in 1810–12 ; ii. 68, 190, 193, 194, 273, 280, 284, 330.
Cairnes, R. M., summary of his services with No. 4 Company, old 10th Battalion, ii. 186, 189 to 192.
——, at Copenhagen, ii. 160.
——, in the Peninsula, ii. 341, 343, 345, 346, 353, 377, 382.
——, organisation and equipment of his Battery, ii. 341 to 343.
——, at Waterloo, ii. 430, 432, 436.
Cairo, ii. 124, 126, 129, 130, 131.
Calcutta, i. 178.
Calvi (Corsica), ii. 68.
Cambray, siege of, in 1815, ii. 440.
Camden, battle of, i. 367.
Camels in Egypt, for Artillery Transport, ii. 117.
Cameron, A., i. 416.
Campbell, Alex., i. 127, 220.
——, A. M., ii. 160.
——, Dugald, i. 180 ; ii. 107, 108, 128.
——, F. A., i. 173, 177.
——, Fredk., i. 406 ; ii. 105.
——, General, ii. 255.

Campbell, H. A. B., i. 406.
——, P., ii. 230, 244, 269.
Camperdown, ii. 73.
Canada, i. 18, 303–4–5.
——, annexation of, to United States, ii. 392, 411.
——, system of R.A. reliefs in, ii. 135.
——, American invasion of, ii. 392, 393.
Cannon, early construction of, i. 35–6.
—— first used in the field, i. 35.
——, tables of, in the reign of Charles II., i. 46.
Cape of Good Hope, R.A. in, ii. 85, 138.
——, expedition to, in 1806, ii. 168.
——, system of R.A. reliefs in, ii. 135.
"Car" Brigade, ii. 205, 211.
Carey, W. R., i. 257 ; ii. 106, 143, 271.
Carlisle, i. 128.
——, Robert, i. 244.
Carmichael, Lewis, i. 226, 417.
——, in Egypt, ii. 107.
——, in South American War, ii. 170.
——, in 2nd American War, ii. 395, 396, 398, 400, 401, 404, 407.
——, in the Peninsula, ii. 377, 379.
——, at Waterloo, ii. 439.
—— *Vide* also ii. 146, 186.
Carncross, Sir Joseph, i. 406 ; ii. 236, 352, 383, 384, 385.
Carriages in Egypt, ii. 118, 119.
Carronades, employment of, in Egypt, ii. 115, 116, 123.
Carter, John, i. 176, 244, 420.
Carterell, S. S., ii. 74.
Carthagena, attack on (1741), i. 123.
——, expedition to, ii. 193.
Carthew, R., i. 134, 407 ; ii. 106, 211, 215, 230, 269.
Cater, T. O., i. 180, 256 ; ii. 283, 433.
Cathcart, Lord, ii. 161.
Catholic Disabilities Bill, ii. 77.
Cator, John F., i. 421.
——, Sir William, i. 396 ; ii. 193, 381.
Cavalry, 3-pr. guns with, in Egypt. *Vide* Guns.
——, Capture of Dutch Fleet by, ii. 67.
—— in Egypt, ii. 129.
—— in the Peninsula, ii. 207, 245, 348, 383, 386.
—— at Corunna, ii. 212, 216.
—— at Walcheren, ii. 225.
—— in 2nd American War, ii. 395.
——, at Quatre Bras and Waterloo, ii. 421, 422, 428.
Cayenne, capture of, ii. 260.
Cawnpore, ii. 142.
Cazal Nova, ii. 284.
"C" Battery, A Brigade (C Troop), i. 398.
——, B Brigade (G, afterwards F, Troop), i. 400.

2 I 2

"C" Battery *(continued)*, 1st Brigade (1 Company, 7th Battalion), i. 421.
——, 8th Brigade (6 Company, afterwards 5, 6th Battalion), i. 415.
——, 9th Brigade (9 Company, afterwards 7, 6th Battalion), i. 416.
——, 11th Brigade (1 Company, 6th Battalion), i. 413.
Ceylon, system of R.A. reliefs in, ii. 135.
Chalmers, J. A., i. 256; ii. 141.
Chalmers, John, i. 158.
Chamberlain, Sir Henry, i. 414.
Chamberlayne, J., i. 406; ii. 157.
Changes in the designation of troops and companies, i. 439.
Chaplains, ii. 11, 18, 19.
Chapman, Richard, i. 175, 223.
Chapman, S. R., ii. 232.
Charleroi, capture of, ii. 63.
Charles II., royal warrant of, i. 426.
Charles, J. N., ii. 244.
Charlestown, siege of, i. 361.
Charleton, Thomas, i. 179, 182; ii. 186.
Charlton, George, i. 125, 127, 175.
——, George, i. 173.
Chatham, Lord, ii. 138, 223, 225, 230, 231.
Chesney, F. R., i. 261.
Chester, John, i. 173, 226, 398; ii. 186.
Chestnut Troop. *Vide* "A" Battery, "A" Brigade.
Chevenix, Major, i. 162.
Chevrons for N.C.O., ii. 137.
Christie, H. P., i. 422.
——, J., ii. 396.
Cintra, convention of, ii. 196, 210, 211.
Ciudad Rodrigo, sieges of, ii. 274, 275, 305, 307, 309, 312 to 315.
Clairfayt, General, ii. 62.
Clare, Militia, ii. 76.
Clarke, Christopher, i. 176.
——, R., ii. 153.
Clason, A. J., i. 409.
Clausel, General, ii. 329, 330.
Cleaveland, R. F., i. 6, 261, 422; ii. 105, 108.
——, Lieut.-General Samuel, i. 124, 127, 188, 189, 207, 301-2-3, 319, 378.
Cleeve, William, i. 176, 224, 425; ii. 261.
——, Capt., King's German Artillery, at Albuera, ii. 296, 297.
——, at Badajoz, ii. 300, 302.
——, at Quatre Bras, ii. 421.
——, at Waterloo, ii. 424.
Clement, J. A., i. 424; ii. 144.
Clerk, Henry, i. 410.
Clerk or Conductor of Stores, ii. 110.
—— of the Cheque, ii. 10.
—— of the Deliveries, i. 17, 18.
—— of the Ordnance, i. 17.

Clibborn, W., ii. 153, 157, 261.
Clifford, Miller, i. 174.
Clinton, General, ii. 324.
Close, J. M., ii. 153, 193.
Clothing issues, ii. 11, 22, 399.
Clyde, Lord, ii. 142.
Coa, crossing of the, ii. 275.
Coast Brigade (invalid companies), i. 40, 167, 268, 349.
Cobbe, George, i. 172, 177, 222, 400; ii. 186.
Cobourg, Prince of, ii. 59.
Cochrane, Admiral Sir A., ii. 397.
Cockburn, C. V., ii. 153.
——, John, i. 356.
——, J. P., i. 177, 415, 422, 424; ii. 143, 156, 160.
Cocks, P. R., i. 414.
Coffin, G. C., i. 259; ii. 143.
Coimbra, ii. 276, 278.
Colburne, Roger, i. 432.
Colclough, George, i. 172, 407.
Colebrooke, J. R., i. 182.
——, P. W., i. 416.
——, Sir William, i. 174.
Cole, General Sir Lowry, ii. 294, 295, 312, 384.
Coles, G., ii. 425, 434.
Collier, William, i. 179, 256; ii. 68.
Collington, J. W., i. 172.
Collins, Captain, i. 364.
Collyer, Admiral Sir George, ii. 361.
——, E., ii. 160.
Colonels-Commandant, ii. 4, 5, 11 to 15, 151.
Colonies, paucity of Artillery in, in 1790, ii. 94.
Colquhoun, J. W., i. 416.
Colville, Sir Charles, ii. 440.
Command of Army in the Field, Artillery Officers for, ii. 52, 53, 89.
—— of Artillery. *Vide* Artillery.
Commandant, Woolwich, ii. 82, 136.
Commissariat. *Vide* Stores and Supply Department.
Committee on Inventions, ii. 15; Ordnance Select, 83.
Commons, House of, i. 2, 69, 381.
Company of Artillery, strength and pay of (1720), i. 104. (1716), 434.
——, loss of, in the Doddington (1755), i. 158.
Company, R.A., the unit (for reliefs) ii. 135 (for promotion of N.C.O.) 342.
Compton, Sir William, i. 44, 45.
Concannon, J., ii. 74.
Condé, blockade of, ii. 59, 60.
Congreve, Sir William, i. 307.
——, in Flanders, ii. 56, 57, 60, 61, 62.
——, Staff Appointments, ii. 83, 137.
Connel, J. J., ii. 300, 319.

Connell, A. F., i. 177.
Conrade, George, i. 432.
Contingent Allowances. *Vide* Allowances.
Cookson, C. N., i. 181.
——, George, i. 400, 409.
——, G., in Flanders, ii. 57.
——, in Egypt, ii. 106, 110, 127, 130, 132.
——, at Copenhagen, ii. 160, 162, 166.
——, at Corunna, ii. 212, 215, 217.
——, at Walcheren, ii. 225, 230.
Coote, Sir Eyre, ii. 88, 89, 96.
Copenhagen, siege of, ii. 158, 162 to 164.
Cornelius, R. L., i. 258.
Cornwallis, Lord, ii. 73.
Corps d'élite, ii. 48, 49.
Corsica, ii. 68.
Corunna, battle and retreat, ii. 195, 211 to 221.
——, proportion of guns to troops at, ii. 412.
Costa, Lieut., of Portuguese Artillery, ii. 364.
Cotton, Sir Stapleton, ii. 325.
Coupère, General, ii. 148.
Courts-martial, i. 133; ii. 14.
Cowper, J. T., ii. 152.
Cox and Co., Paymasters, R.A., ii. 82.
Cox, William, i. 182.
Coxwell, E., ii. 160.
Cozens, W., ii. 193.
Cradock, Sir J., ii. 243.
Craufurd, R. E. F., i. 221.
Crawford, A. F., i. 406; ii. 396, 398.
——, George, i. 413.
——, George, Major, ii. 394.
——, George, Lieut., ii. 430, 432.
——, H., ii. 154, 215, 395, 399.
——, General, in South America, ii. 170.
——, at Roliça, ii. 206. At Vimiera, 208.
——, at Talavera, ii. 257. At the Coa, 275, 276.
——, at Busaco, ii. 277.
——, W. J., i. 417.
Crawley, J., ii. 396, 399, 401.
Crimea, ii. 140, 232.
Crofton, E. W., i. 423.
——, R. H., i. 180, 423.
Cromie, M. T., ii. 431, 432.
Cruttenden, C., i. 183, 261, 423; ii. 153, 154.
——, E., ii. 144, 394.
C Troop. *Vide* "C" Battery, "A" Brigade.
Cubitt, H. F., ii. 160.
——, Thomas, i. 254, 258; ii. 143.
Cuesta, General (Spanish), ii. 245, 253.
Culloden, battle of (1746), i. 128.
Cumberland, Duke of, i. 132-3, 152.
Cuppage, Burke, ii. 156, 431.

Cuppage, William, i. 172, 274, 399; ii. 35, 109.
Curry, Sir Edmund, i. 263, 421; ii. 106, 129, 144.

Dacres, Sir Richard J., i. 406.
Dadson, J. N. P., ii. 142.
Daendels, General, ii. 96.
D'Aguilar, C. L., i. 400, 417.
Dalrymple, Sir Hew, ii. 210, 211.
Dalton, Charles, i. 173, 175; ii. 156, 232.
——, Charles J., i. 174.
Daniel, Captain, King's German Artillery, ii. 387.
——, J., ii. 394.
Dansey, C. C., i. 404, 416.
——, in the Peninsula, ii. 319, 332, 334, 362, 364, 375.
——, at Waterloo, ii. 430, 432, 436.
Darby, Joseph, i. 423; ii. 153, 160, 220.
D'Arcy, Colonel, ii. 165.
——, Joseph, i. 179.
Dartmouth, Lord, i. 11, 12, 13, 14, 31, 44, 47.
Davers, W., ii. 74.
Davies, Thomas, i. 379.
Davis, Thomas, i. 183.
Day, J., ii. 188, 378, 430, 432.
"D" Battery, A Brigade (H, afterwards G, Troop), i. 401.
——, B Brigade, (I, afterwards H, Troop), i. 401.
——, 1st Brigade (4 Company, 2nd Battalion), i. 180.
—— 4th Brigade (8 Company, 3rd Battalion), i. 225.
——, 8th Brigade (2 Company, 5th Battalion), i. 406.
——, 11th Brigade (6 Company, 7th Battalion), i. 423.
Deacon, C. P., at San Sebastian, ii. 361, 364.
——, in second American War, ii. 395, 396, 398, 399, 404.
——, Henry, i. 174.
Deal, James, i. 124.
De Butts, Lieutenant, Royal Engineers, ii. 68.
De Ginkle, Hon. C., ii. 56.
Denmark, capture of Fleet, ii. 158, 165.
——, siege of Copenhagen, ii. 158, 160.
Dennis, J. B., i. 421.
——, W., ii. 362.
Depeyster, J., ii. 57, 60.
Deputy Adjutant-General, R.A. *Vide* Adjutant-General, R.A.
Deputy Assistant Adjutant-General. *Vide* Adjutant-General, R.A.
De Rettberg, Captain, King's German Artillery, ii. 318, 319.

De Rinzy, G. A. F., i. 224.
De Rottenburg, General, ii. 189.
Deruvijnes, F. L., i. 224; ii. 74.
——, H., ii. 74.
Desaguliers, Lieut.-General T., i. 125, 127, 134, 152, 185, 228; ii. 13.
——, Lieut., i. 313.
Desborough, J., i. 175.
Desbrisay, George, i. 183; ii. 141.
——, Thomas, i. 183.
——, Theo., i. 221.
Des Etans, L. P., i. 432.
Designation of troops and companies, changes in the, i. 439.
Detroit, fort, capture of, ii. 392, 393.
Dettingen, battle of, i. 125.
Devereux, Hon. G. T., i. 407.
De Watterville, General, ii. 189.
De Winton, T., ii. 156.
Dexter, Lieut., i. 133.
"Diadem," Her Majesty's Ship, ii. 110.
Dick, F., i. 176.
Dickens, C. R., i. 414; ii. 144.
Dickenson, E., i. 263; ii. 144.
Dickinson, R., ii. 186, 272.
Dickson, A., i. 174, 175.
——, Sir Alexander, i. 400, 415.
——, in South America, ii. 168, 170, 176, 178.
——, with the Portuguese Artillery, ii. 251, 287, 289, 294, 297, 339, 340.
——, Circumstances under which he commanded the R.A. in the Peninsula, ii. 253, 298, 309, 321, 346.
——, at Olivença, ii. 288.
——, at sieges of Badajoz, 1st, ii. 289, 291, 292, 294, 296; 2nd, 298, 300, 305; 3rd, 316, 318.
——, at Albuera, ii. 294, 297, 298.
——, at Ciudad Rodrigo, ii. 309, 311, 314, 316.
——, at Salamanca and Burgos, ii. 321, 326, 327, 330, 332, 334, 335, 336, 347, 350.
——, at Vittoria, ii. 351, 352, 353, 355.
——, at San Sebastian, ii. 339, 361, 362, 366, 371, 373.
——, crossing the Pyrenees, ii. 379, 380.
——, passage of the Adour, ii. 382, 383.
——, entry into France and battle of Toulouse, ii. 385, 388.
——, in second American War, ii. 396, 397, 398, 399, 400, 403, 406, 407, 410.
——, at Waterloo, ii. 414, 415, 421, 424, 435.
——, at the subsequent siege operations, ii. 433, 438, 439, 440, 442.
——, his opinion of driver officers, ii. 385.
——, Peninsula records, ii. 287.

Dickson, Sir A. (cont.), his character, ii. 51, 168, 176, 287, 311, 347, 391, 442.
—— Vide also, ii. 186.
——, summary of the services of his company, ii. 189.
——, Sir C., ii. 287.
Dilkes, General, ii. 282.
Director General of Artillery, ii. 83.
Discharges by purchase, ii. 267.
——, other modes of, ii. 2, 137.
Discipline, Duke of Wellington on, ii. 250, 251.
——, personal element in, ii. 389.
Distribution of Royal Artillery (1727), i. 105. (1782), 389; (1797), ii. 84, 85. (1798), 86. (1812), 322.
Dixon, F. M., i. 183, 223, 292.
——, G. W., i. 224, 399; ii. 225.
——, William, i. 180; ii. 186, 225, 233, 237, 240.
——, W. H. M., i. 222.
Dodd, Thomas, i. 182, 424; ii. 271.
Domville, J. R., i. 173.
——, J. W., i. 221.
Donegal Militia, ii. 76.
Douglas, Sir Howard, i. 421.
——, Robert, i. 223, 225, 338, 354, 380, 405, 406; ii. 144.
——, Robert, i. 413.
——, Robert, C.B., in the Peninsula, ii. 327, 345, 353, 361, 376, 377.
—— Vide also, ii. 143, 157.
——, R. S., i. 179.
Douglass, J., ii. 98.
Douro, passages of the, in 1809, ii. 242, 245, 246; 249.
——, in 1813, ii. 345, 349.
Dovers, John, i. 226, 244.
Downing, J., i. 223.
Downman, F., i. 175, 176, 398.
——, Sir Thomas, i. 174, 398, 399.
——, in Flanders, ii. 57, 63.
——, at Corunna, ii. 215, 218.
——, in the Peninsula, ii. 338, 339.
Dowse, John, i. 258.
——, Lloyd, ii. 177.
Dragoons, ii. 67, 122, 165.
——, 12th, ii. 379. 14th Light, 395. 15th Light, 100, 113. 16th, 379. 20th Light, 169. 21st Light, 169.
Drawbridge, C., ii. 232.
Dress, ii. 178, 399.
—— of Gunners, &c., in the reign of William III., i. 59.
—— of Royal Artillery (1741), i. 140, 154. (1768-70), 242. (1772), 265. (1799), 412.
—— of Royal Irish Artillery, i. 167.
Drew, R. R., ii. 157.
Drills, Artillery, infantry and militia taught, ii. 76, 77.

Drills, field day in 1788, ii. 22, 23; in 1795, 76.
Driver Corps, formation and organization, ii. 30, 32, 58, 136, 267, 342, 385, 415.
——, establishment and pay of, in 1801, ii. 136. 1803, 139. 1806, 151. 1807, 185. 1810, 265, 343. In the Peninsula, 308. 1812, 322.
——, in Flanders, ii. 58.
——, expedition to the Helder, ii. 91, 92, 267.
——, expedition to Spain and Portugal, ii. 204, 222.
——, at Corunna, ii. 217.
——, at Barossa, ii. 283.
——, in second American War, ii. 398.
——, R.A., gunners for, at Waterloo, ii. 415.
——, with army of occupation, ii. 441.
——, discipline of, ii. 342, 415.
——, abolition of, ii. 342, 385.
Drivers, i. 38, 128-9.
Drosier, E. W., i. 223.
Drummond, Duncan, i. 207, 221, 244, 405; ii. 83, 137, 187, 394.
——, Percy, i. 176, 222.
——, P., at Copenhagen, ii. 160.
——, P., at Corunna, ii. 211, 215.
——, P., in Walcheren, ii. 225, 230.
——, P., at Waterloo, ii. 424, 437.
—— P., *Vide* also ii. 143, 146.
D Troop, i. 399; ii. 35, 38.
Dubourdien, S., in the West Indies, ii. 261
——, at Vittoria, ii. 353.
——, at San Sebastian, ii. 345, 361, 364, 365.
—— *Vide* also ii. 140.
Dubreton, French governor of Burgos, ii. 334.
Dumaresq, W. L., i. 410.
Dumouriez, General, ii. 55.
Dunbar, James, i. 181, 220.
Duncan, Alexander, i. 400, 423.
——, at Toulon, ii. 67, 68.
——, on the staff, ii. 83.
——, in Egypt, ii. 108, 128, 132.
——, defence of Cadiz, ii. 280.
——, at Barossa, ii. 190, 283.
——, John, i. 226; ii. 67, 68.
——, Admiral Lord, ii. 73, 96.
Dundas, General, ii. 66, 67, 97, 99.
——, W. B., i. 261; ii. 154, 193, 314, 316, 319.
Dunkirk, siege of, ii. 60.
Dunlop, F., i. 424.
Dunn, Wm., i. 396, 400, 407; ii. 186, 194.
Du Plat, Chas. T., i. 254.
Dupuis, Sir John E., i. 399; ii. 144.
D'Urban, General, ii. 329.
Durdero, Joseph, i. 432.
Durham, Lieut. Richard, i. 127.

Durnford, P., i. 256, 413.
——, G., i. 261; ii. 152, 177.
Dutch fleet, captured by cavalry, ii. 67.
——, retention by the English, ii. 101.
Du Vernet, A., i. 221; ii. 74.
Dyas, Richard, i. 415, 424; ii. 186.
Dyer, Sir John, i. 175, 183.
——, at San Sebastian, ii. 361, 368.
——, at Passage of the Bidassoa, ii. 374, 375.
——, at Orthes, ii. 383, 384.
——, at Toulouse, ii. 387.
—— *Vide* also ii. 141.
Dyneley, Thomas, i. 257, 398, 399.
——, at Copenhagen, ii. 160.
——, at Ciudad Rodrigo, ii. 314, 315, 316.
——, at Salamanca, ii. 330.
——, at Waterloo, ii. 430.
—— *Vide* also ii. 153.
Dysart, R., i. 222.
Dyson, John, i. 421.

Earliest records of the use of Artillery, i. 36, 37.
Early construction of cannon, i. 35, 36.
Eastaff, Mr., Commissary of Horse, ii. 57
East India detachment, i. 157-8, 411.
East Indies, i. 136. *Vide* Indies.
"E" Battery, A Brigade (K Troop), i. 403.
—— B Brigade (1st Rocket, afterwards I, Troop), i. 404.
—— 1st Brigade (8 Company, 4th Battalion), i. 261.
Ebro, River, passage of the, ii. 350.
Edwardes, D. J., ii. 430.
Edwards, Sam. D., i. 226; ii. 74.
Egan, Chas., i. 177, 222, 414, 416.
Egmont-op-Zee, ii. 99, 100.
Egypt, ii. 104 to 133.
——, strength of R.A. for the Expedition, ii. 105, 108.
——, battalions R.A. for, ii. 105.
——, difficulties of Artillery transit, ii. 112 to 121, 124 to 126.
——, ordnance captured in, ii. 127.
——, "Sphynx" and "Egypt" worn by troops, ii. 132.
Elba, escape of Bonaparte from, ii. 412.
Elgee, C. W., i. 414.
——, J. L., i. 416.
——, W., i. 257; ii. 192, 331, 332.
Eligé, J. P., ii. 92, 98, 147, 324.
Elliott, W. G., i. 394, 404, 408; ii. 37, 244.
——, W. H., i. 259.
Ellis, P., ii. 140.
Ellison, J. T., ii. 186.
Elwyn, Thomas, i. 256; ii. 152.

Engineers and Artificers, i. 38, 39.
——, Royal, relation of Royal Artillery to, i. 121.
——, relative precedence to R.A., ii. 3.
——, Services of, ii. 165, 169.
England, Lieut., in South America, ii. 177.
——, at San Sebastian, ii. 362, 364.
——, P. V., i. 422. *Vide* also ii. 141.
Equipment of R.H.A. *Vide* Horse Artillery.
—— of a Field Battery in 1813, ii. 343.
Erie, Lake, actions at, ii. 393, 394.
Erskine, Sir J., ii. 83.
——, Sir W. E., ii. 61, 285.
Espana, General (Spanish), ii. 329.
Esprit de corps, i. 4, 170, 206.
Essen, Count, ii. 99.
Establishment of the Royal Regiment of Artillery, i. 61, 79-82, 383-391, 436.
——, supernumeraries to regimental, ii. 1.
——, of R.A. augmentations. *Vide* Augmentations.
—— of R.A. reductions. *Vide* Reductions.
——, of R.H.A. *Vide* Horse Artillery.
——, in 1783—1791, ii. 1, 2; 1794, 58. 1802, 136; 1803, 139; 1805, 151; 1807, 185; 1810, 262, 270; 1812, 322; 1813, 343; 1819, 442.
E Troop (afterwards D). *Vide* "A" Battery, B Brigade.
Evans, C. R. O., i. 408.
——, Jas., i. 421; ii. 232.
——, Mark, i. 423.
——, Robert, i. 414; ii. 105.
Eveleigh, Hen., i. 221, 398; ii. 215, 218.
Eyre, Joseph, i. 179, 424.
8th Battalion :—
——, No. 1 Company, or H, 1st Brigade, ii. 140.
——, No. 2 Company, or H, 11th Brigade, ii. 141.
——, No. 3 Company, or 8, 13th Brigade, ii. 142 (note).
——, No. 4 Company, or 7, 12th Brigade, ii. 143.
——, No. 5 Company, or G, 1st Brigade, ii. 143.
——, No. 6 Company, or D, 9th Brigade, ii. 144.
——, No. 7 Company, or H, 8th Brigade, ii. 144.
——, No. 8 Company, or I, 7th Brigade, ii. 145.
——, No. 9 Company, or 7, 17th Brigade, ii. 146.
——, No. 10 Company, ii. 146.
——, *Vide* also ii. 139.
——, its records, ii. 138.
8th Brigade, E Battery, ii. 153, 431. H Battery, ii. 144.

11th Battalion, formation, ii. 185.
——, No. 8 Company, or 7, 17th Brigade, ii. 146.
11th Brigade, A Battery, ii. 194. D Battery, ii. 277, 310. H Battery, ii. 141.
11th Regiment, ii. 88.
82nd Regiment, ii. 207, 282.
85th Regiment, ii. 396, 405.
87th Regiment, ii. 66, 282.

Faddy, Peter, i. 260.
Fage, Edward, i. 224, 372, 411.
Fairlamb, John, i. 181.
Falkirk, battle of (1746), i. 128.
Famars, ii. 59, 60.
Fane, General, ii. 206, 208, 348.
Farquharson, John, i. 127.
Farrell, J. S., i. 421.
Farrington, Sir Anthony, i. 244, 378; ii. 83, 90, 101.
——, Charles, i. 133.
——, H. M., i. 174.
Fauquier, H. T., ii. 105.
"F" Battery, 1st Brigade (1 Company, 5th Battalion), i. 406.
——, 8th Brigade (7, afterwards 6, Company, 6th Battalion), i. 416.
——, 9th Brigade (1 Company, 1st Battalion), i. 172.
Fead, George, i. 182, 261, 411.
——, J. F., i. 182; ii. 186.
——, R., ii. 57, 61, 131.
Fenwick, Benjamin, i. 176, 183; ii. 143.
——, T., ii. 56, 59.
——, W. Y., i. 258.
Ferguson, Captain, i. 190, 244.
——, General, 206, 208, 209.
Ferrol, expedition to, ii. 106, 107, 121.
Field, G. T., i. 409.
Field Artillery, i. 37, 38, 166-7.
—— compared with Horse Artillery, ii. 45-6, 48, 86, 268, 417.
——, progress of, ii. 47, 244, 248, 249, 268, 309, 341, 412, 417.
—— Battery, i. 37.
——, Battery equipments in 1813, ii. 343.
Field-day in 1788. *Vide* Drills.
Field Officers R. A., duties of, in 1783, ii. 15, 92.
Field Train department, establishment of, in 1810, ii. 265.
Fifers, first in the British Army, i. 136.
Finch, M., General, ii. 161.
Firemaster, i. 17.
Fireworker, i. 17.
Fisher, E. H., i. 421.
——, Sir G. B., i. 175, 221, 399, 400.
——, appointed to R.H.A., ii. 36.
——, in Portugal, ii. 269.

Fisher, Sir G. B. (*continued*), in command of R. A., in the Peninsula, ii. 343.
——, resignation of the command, ii. 346, 347.
——, appointed commandant of Woolwich, ii. 36.
——, R. R., i. 413.
Fitzgerald, C. L., i. 408.
Fitzmayer, C. H., i. 225, 422; ii. 143.
——, Sir James W., i. 225; ii. 145.
Fitzroy, A. C. L., i. 261; ii. 146.
Flanders, campaigns in (1743-4-5), i. 124-5-6. (1746-7-8), i. 130-136.
——, Expedition to, ii. 54, 57, 88.
Fleet, Dutch, captured by cavalry, ii. 67.
——, Danish, capture of, ii. 165.
Fletcher, Sir Richard, R.E., at Badajoz, ii. 289, 291, 293, 298, 304.
——, at Albuera, ii. 298.
——, at Ciudad Rodrigo, ii. 309.
Fleurus, battle of, ii. 64.
Flight, Thomas, i. 124, 127.
Flude, T. P., i. 416, 422.
Flushing, expedition and siege, ii. 224, 225, 228, 229, 241.
——, rockets first used as a siege weapon at, ii. 164.
Fogo, James, i. 177.
Fontenoy, battle of, i. 127.
——, officers of Artillery present at, i. 127.
Foot, G., ii. 431.
Forbes, G. H. A., i. 173.
——, T. J., i. 262; ii. 156.
——, W. H., ii. 154.
Ford, A., ii. 142 (note).
——, C., ii. 396, 408.
Forde, M. B., i. 254.
Foreign Artillery, Royal, ii. 262, 266, 322.
—— *Vide* also German Legion.
Forge, carriage of, in the Peninsula, ii. 249.
Forster, George, i. 177, 183.
——, H., ii. 160, 430, 432.
Fort du Quesne, battle of (1755), i. 159.
Fortescue, J. C. W., i. 424.
"Foudroyant," H. M. Ship, ii. 116.
Fox, C. J., ii. 150.
Foy, Edward, i. 208, 222, 244.
—— General (French), ii. 328.
——, Nat., i. 403, 413; ii. 36, 57.
Foz d'Arouce, action at, ii. 285.
Framingham, Sir H., i. 260.
——, at Talavera, ii. 255.
——, at Busaco, ii. 269.
——, at Badajoz, ii. 280, 298, 305, 318.
——, at Ciudad Rodrigo, ii. 309.
——, at Salamanca, ii. 324.
France, expeditions to coast of (1757), i. 190.

France (*continued*), war with, ii. 27, 96, 286 to 391; resumed, 412; ended, 438.
——, army of occupation in, ii. 441.
——, invasion of Ireland, ii. 77.
Francklin, Thos., i. 172, 181; ii. 160, 225.
——, C. T., i. 225
Fraser, Hon. D. M., i. 423
——, G. B., i. 422.
——, Wm., i. 180, 258.
Frazer, Sir Augustus, i. 400.
——, expedition to the Helder, ii. 92, 99.
——, in S. America, ii. 168, 170, 175, 176 to 178, 180, 184.
——, in command of R. H. A. in the Peninsula, ii. 338, 339.
——, at Vittoria, ii. 345, 350, 352, 353, 356.
——, at San Sebastian, ii. 361, 364, 368.
——, passage of the Bidassoa, ii. 375.
——, passage of the Adour, ii. 383.
——, at Nivelle, ii. 378.
——, at Toulouse, ii. 388.
——, at Waterloo, ii. 414, 416, 421, 424, 425, 427, 435.
——, his diaries, ii. 181, 416.
——, his character, ii. 51, 176, 178, 184, 353-4, 391, 427.
——, General, ii. 218.
——, H., ii. 145, 272.
Freeling, S., i. 172.
Freer, J. H., i. 415.
Freeth, R. K., i. 180.
Freire, General, ii. 374.
Frere, J. H., ii. 186.
——, Mr., ii. 253.
Fritzlar, capture of (1761), i. 215-16.
Frost, James, i. 175.
Fry, Oliver, i. 177.
F Troop (afterwards E). *Vide* "B" Battery, B Brigade.
Fuentes d'Onor, ii. 32, 285.
Fuller, J. T., ii. 160.
Furneaux, William, i. 181.
Fyers, Peter, i. 226; ii. 160, 230.
1st Battalion or Brigade, R.A., No. 2 Company or B Battery, 1st Brigade, ii. 57, 58, 63.
—— G. Battery, ii. 143. "H" Battery ii. 140, 309.
—— *Vide* also ii. 105, 134, 135.
4th Battalion or Brigade, No. 1 Company, ii. 61. No. 4 Company, ii. 58. No. 5 Company, ii. 58. D Battery, ii. 218.
—— *Vide* also ii. 105, 134, 135, 209.
5th Battalion or Brigade, No. 4 Battery, ii. 58. No. 5 Battery, ii. 309, 315.
—— *Vide* also ii. pp. 59, 74, 105, 132, 134, 135.
14th Battalion or Brigade, formed, ii. 185. B Battery, ii. 153. C Battery, ii. 155.

4th Regiment, ii. 395, 399.
5th Regiment, ii. 312.
40th Regiment, ii. 98.
43rd Regiment, ii. 209, 257, 404, 408.
44th Regiment, ii. 395, 399.
45th Regiment, ii. 256.
47th Regiment, ii. 282.
48th Regiment, ii. 255, 256.
49th Regiment, ii. 88.
50th Regiment, ii. 209.
52nd Regiment, ii. 257, 428, 429.
54th Regiment, ii. 170.

Gahan, Daniel, i. 179, 183.
Gambier, Gloucester, i. 180; ii. 142.
Gamble, Thomas, i. 415; ii. 272.
Gardiner, Sir Robert, i. 399, 423.
———, at Corunna, ii. 218.
———, in Walcheren, ii. 225.
———, at Badajoz, ii. 318, 319.
———, at Burgos, ii. 332.
———, at Salamanca, ii. 348.
———, at Vittoria, ii. 353.
———, at Orthes, ii. 383, 384.
———, at Toulouse, ii. 386, 387.
———, at Waterloo, ii. 414, 423, 424, 430.
———, return to England, ii. 442.
——— *Vide* also ii. 146, 194, 345.
———, as a Horse Artillery officer, ii. 51.
———, his character, ii. 39.
———, H. L., i. 399.
Gardner, Hon. H., i. 406, 408, 409.
———, Hon. W. H., ii. 36, 186.
———, Lieut. A. B., i. 6.
———, W. B., i. 179.
———, W. H., i. 181, 257, 404.
Garrison Artillery. *Vide* Siege Artillery.
Garstin, R. L., ii. 155.
———, Robert, i. 180.
"G" Battery, 8th Brigade (7, afterwards 6, Company, 2nd Battalion), i. 182.
Geary, Henry, i. 407.
———, in Flanders, ii. 57.
———, in Irish Rebellion, ii. 78.
———, in expedition to the Helder, ii. 92.
———, at Roliça, ii. 207.
Gelmuyden, Peter, i. 432.
Genoa, ii. 108.
George I., royal warrant of, i. 432.
——— III., royal warrant of, i. 438.
German Legion at Copenhagen, ii. 161, 165, 167.
———, Services in the Peninsula, ii. 203, 262, 271, 272.
———, at Corunna, ii. 211.
———, at passage of the Douro, ii. 244.
———, at Talavera, ii. 255.
———, at Badajoz, ii. 288, 289.
———, at Albuera, ii. 296.
——— at Ciudad Rodrigo, ii. 316 318.

German Legion (*continued*) at Salamanca, ii. 326.
——— at Nivelle, ii. 377.
——— at Orthes, ii. 384.
——— at Toulouse, ii. 387.
——— at Quatre Bras and Waterloo, ii. 421, 422, 424, 427.
———, strength of, in 1810, ii. 203, 266, 269; 1812, 322, 327.
———, distribution in the Peninsula, ii. 308, 345.
Germany, campaigns in (1759-62), i. 206-217.
Gertruydenberg, ii. 54.
Gessenins, Capt., German Legion, ii. 269.
Ghent, Treaty of, ii. 411.
Gibbon, Edward, i. 431.
Gibbs, Major-General, ii. 399, 400, 407.
Gibraltar, i. 67, 105, 124, 178.
———, Company of Artificers for, ii. 3.
———, defence of (1727), i. 102.
———, Expedition for Egypt, ii. 106, 107.
———, force of R.A. in 1797, ii. 85. 1810, ii. 271.
———, great siege of (1779-83), i. 271-290.
———, Loyalty Loan, ii. 72, 73.
———, reliefs of R. A., system of, ii. 134.
Gilbert, James, i. 423.
———, W. R., i. 400.
Gillespie, Captain, i. 244.
Gilmore, C., ii. 186.
Gilmour, Charles, i. 416, 421.
Giron, General (Spanish), ii. 374, 377.
Givet, bombardment and capture of, ii. 440.
Gizeh, ii. 124, 126.
Glanville, F. R., ii. 146.
Glasgow, George, i. 173, 263; ii, 394.
———, G. M., i. 182, 417.
Gleig, A. C., i. 221.
Glover, Edward, i. 432.
Glubb, Fredrick, i. 410.
———, in Portugal, ii. 269.
———, at Ciudad Rodrigo, ii. 309, 310, 315.
———, at Badajoz, ii. 318.
———, at Almaraz, ii. 321.
———, at Salamanca, ii. 330.
———, at Burgos, ii. 331.
———, at San Sebastian, ii. 340.
Godby, C. H., i. 176, 181.
———, J., i. 222.
———, R., ii. 186, 193, 218, 271.
Godfrey, Charles, i. 256, 274, 403, 415; ii. 36, 88, 89.
———, J., i. 222.
Godwin, Wm., i. 263, 272.
Gold, Chas., i. 406, 424; ii. 236, 424, 434.
Goll, J. D., i. 175.
Goodenough, H. P., i. 260.
Goodyear, Major, i. 136.
Gordon, C., ii. 392.

Gordon, C. E., i. 175.
——, Fred., i. 182, 222, 414.
——, H. W., i. 180.
——, John, i. 220.
——, W. A., ii. 186, 261.
Gore, John, i. 225.
Gossett, Arthur, i. 222.
Gostling, Charles, i. 408; ii. 142.
——, William, i. 176.
Gowen, Lieut., i. 229.
Graham, A. H., i. 256.
——, G. M., ii. 186.
——, Sir Thomas, in Walcheren, ii. 228.
—— ——, at Barossa, ii. 280, 281, 282, 283, 284.
—— ——, at Salamanca, ii. 345, 346.
—— ——, at passage of the Esla, ii. 349.
—— ——, at passage of the Ebro, ii. 350, 351.
—— ——, at San Sebastian, ii. 363, 366, 367, 369.
—— ——, at Waterloo, ii. 414.
Grant, General Colquhoun, ii. 436.
——, D., i. 417.
——, E. F., i. 401.
——, H. P., i. 416.
——, J., ii. 232.
——, J. E., i. 180, 422, 425.
——, Wm., i. 174, 177.
Grantham, Thomas, i. 183.
Graydon, George, i. 172.
Greatley, Thomas, i. 408; ii. 140, 218, 220.
Greece, ii. 131.
Greene, D. S., i. 180.
——, W., i. 261.
——, in Walcheren, ii. 232.
——, at Burgos, ii. 332.
——, at San Sebastian, ii. 361.
——, at Nivelle, ii. 377. *Vide* also ii. 156, 186.
Green Park, review in, i. 157.
Greenwood, Mr., Paymaster R.A., ii. 82.
——, W., ii. 140.
Gregory, R., i. 222.
Greville, H. L. F., i. 413.
Griffin, J. H., ii. 141.
Griffiths, Fred., i. 221, 398; ii. 155, 225.
——, F. A., i. 222.
Grimes, R., ii. 314, 319.
Grosvenor, Major-General, ii. 161, 228.
Grouchy, Marshal, ii. 423.
Groves, George, i. 180, 229, 288.
Grumley, Lieut. J., i. 274.
G Troop (afterwards F). *Vide* "C" Battery, B Brigade; and ii. 36, 38, 40.
Guadaloupe, i. 165, 179; ii. 74.
Guard, Artillery of the, ii. 52.
Guards, Her Majesty's, ii. 50, 59, 60, 78, 88, 98, 148, 165, 246, 255, 282, 428, 441.

Guildford, battle of, i. 368.
Gun-boats, ii. 78.
Gunner Governor of New York, the, i. 325 to 347.
Gunners, i. 11, 17, 18, 38, 434.
——, mounted on limbers, in Egypt, ii. 118, 119.
——, as drivers, at Waterloo, ii. 415.
Guns, General Lawson's remarks on, ii. 121 to 126.
—— 3 prs.; with Cavalry in Egypt, ii. 118, 124, 128.
—— —— in 2nd American War, ii. 399.
—— —— in pursuit of Soult, ii. 248, 376, 379, 382.
——, R.A. to pay £40 for each field-piece captured, ii. 175, 176.
——, howitzers used as mortars, ii. 302.
——, brass, at siege of Badajoz, ii. 305, 306.
——, 18-pounder brigade, ii. 383.
—— (British), proportion to men, ii. 412.
—— Battalion. *Vide* Battalion Guns.
Guybon, Robert, i. 431.
Gyns, substitute for, in Egypt, ii. 120, 125.

Hadden, J. M., i. 179, 315, 399; ii. 35, 83.
Hall, General (American), ii. 392.
——, Wm., i. 256.
Hamilton, A. G. W., i. 182.
——, F. S., ii. 144.
——, Richard, i. 226, 262, 292.
Handcock, Hon. R. F., i. 177.
Hanoverian Artillery, ii. 424.
Hanwell, Joseph, i. 408.
Harding, John, i. 405, 407.
——, at Copenhagen, ii. 160, 166.
——, in Portugal, ii. 200, 211, 212, 213.
——, at Corunna, ii. 215, 216, 218, 220.
——, R., ii. 353, 362, 430.
Hardinge, R., i. 225; ii. 362, 364, 430.
——, Colonel, ii. 296.
Hardy, T. P. B., i. 172.
——, W. N., i. 407.
Hare, Thomas, i. 261.
Harison, N. E., i. 416.
Harris, John, i. 415; ii. 271.
Harrison, A. R., ii. 145.
——, T. J., i. 174, 183.
Hartman, Sir J., K.G.A., in Portugal, ii. 211, 269.
——, at Albuera, ii. 297, 298.
——, at Vittoria, ii. 352.
——, at San Sebastian, ii. 364, 368.
——, at passage of the Bidassoa, ii. 375.
——, at Nivelle, ii. 376.
——, at Quatre Bras and Waterloo, ii. 421, 424, 435.
Harvey, W. H., ii. 188, 431, 432.
Hastings, F. W., i. 423.

Haultain, F., i. 421.
Havannah, expedition to (1762), i. 188.
Havelock, General, ii. 142 (note).
Hawker, E., ii. 300, 302, 305.
——, James, i. 254.
——, in South America, ii. 176, 177.
——, at Badajoz, ii. 291; Albuera, 296, 297.
——, at Ciudad Rodrigo, ii. 313.
——, at Cambray, ii. 440.
—— Vide also ii. 140, 154.
Hawkins, A. C., i. 261, 425.
Hay, David, i. 174, 244.
——, General, ii. 381, 389.
——, Quartermaster-Sergeant, ii. 179.
——, R. J., i. 407.
"H" Battery, 4th Brigade (9 Company, 4th Battalion, afterwards 4 Company, 11th Battalion), i. 262.
Head-quarter Office, R.A., ii. 4, 5, 92.
Hearsley, Surgeon's mate, ii. 57.
Heaven, Joseph, i. 221.
Heise, King's German Artillery, ii. 269, 421, 424.
Heitland, W. E., i. 423.
Helder, expedition to the, ii. 78, 89 to 92.
——, its object, ii. 95.
Hennis, W. H., i. 179.
Henry, C. S., i. 396.
Herman, General, ii. 97.
Heron, B. R., ii. 155, 261, 362, 364.
Heyman, H., i. 424.
Hickman, H., i. 414; ii. 141, 272.
Higgins, T. G., i. 396; ii. 153.
Hill, B. E., ii. 396.
——, J., ii. 143.
——, Sir Rowland, in Portugal, ii. 206.
—— ——, at Vimiera, ii. 208.
—— ——, at Molinos, ii. 313.
—— ——, at Almaraz, ii. 321.
—— ——, at Ciudad Rodrigo, ii. 345.
—— ——, at Salamanca, ii. 348.
—— ——, passage of the Esla, ii. 349.
—— ——, at Nivelle, ii. 377.
—— ——, at the Nive, ii. 380.
—— ——, Orthes, ii. 383, 385.
Hind, Robert, i. 158, 172, 229.
Hinks, J., ii. 429, 430.
Hislop, Major, i. 158, 178.
History of the Royal Artillery, its scope, ii. 129.
——, regimental, functions of a, ii. 371, 372.
Holcombe, F., ii. 153.
——, H. F., i. 414, 415, 416; ii. 155, 310, 314, 316, 318–9, 330.
——, W., ii. 107.
Holcroft, Wm., i. 222, 263; ii. 88, 89, 160, 394.
Holland, ii. 54–5, 64–5, 91, 101 to 103, 414.

Holman, Capt.-Lieut., i. 104.
Hooke, B. D., ii. 57.
Hook, James, i. 261.
Hope, A. W., i. 423; ii. 186.
——, Edward, i. 257, 292.
——, F., ii. 178.
——, Robert, i. 259; ii. 131, 140, 146.
——, Sir John, ii. 218–19, 230, 376-7, 381–2, 389.
Hopeke, J. H., i. 431.
Horndon, W. H., i. 398.
Hornsby, J. R., i. 176, 223.
Horse Artillery, Royal, i. 37, 393 to 404; ii. 30 to 53, 76, 78, 268.
——, detailed equipment of troop, in 1793, ii. 34; at Waterloo, ii. 419.
——, A, B, C, D E and F Troops raised, ii. 24, 35.
——, establishment, 1793, ii. 35; 1801, 130–1; 1794 to 1804, 35–6, 147.
——, establishment in Egypt, ii. 118, 119; in 1810, 264; 1812, 322; 1815–16, 38; 1854 to 1856, 39, 40.
——, pay, ii. 264.
——, G, H, I, K, L, M Troops raised, ii. 36.
——, Rocket Troop. Vide Rocket Troop.
——, depôt, ii. 37.
——, dress, ii. 42 to 44.
——, armament, ii. 44 to 46, 99, 249, 340, 418.
——, Precedence, ii. 41.
——, officering of, ii. 50 to 53. Selection for, ii. 42, 434.
——, comparison with Field Artillery, ii. 45.
——, comparison with siege, ii. 51, 268.
——, first foreign service of, ii. 90.
——, in the Peninsula, ii. 249, 268, 284, 301, 307–8, 319, 325, 338, 348.
——, gunners in Egypt mounted on limbers, ii. 118, 119.
——, employed as siege Artillerymen, ii. 301, 325.
——, at Waterloo, ii. 416, 417, 421. Reductions, ii. 38.
Horses of Cavalry unsuited to Artillery, ii. 122, 198.
—— for Militia guns, ii. 78.
—— for Artillery on service, ii. 198, 203, 212–13, 267–8, 340, 374, 382, 385, 399, 417.
Hosmer, Thomas, i. 173, 174.
Hospital, regulations and stoppages, ii. 16, 17.
Houat, island of, ii. 110.
Hough, H., ii. 332, 362.
Houghton, William, i. 257.
House of Commons, i. 2, 69, 381.
Houston, General, ii. 228.
Howdell, Thomas, i. 224, 244.

Howe, Lord, ii. 90, 102.
Howitzers, brigade of, ii. 321, 323, 324 326, 327, 331, 333.
—— used as mortars, ii. 302.
—— at Waterloo, ii. 425
Howorth, Sir E., i. 226, 315, 381, 398.
——, appointed to R.H.A., ii. 35.
——, in the Peninsula, ii. 244, 267, 269.
——, passage of the Douro, ii. 246, 247–8.
——, at Talavera, ii. 255, 259.
——, at Busaco, ii. 278.
——, resignation of command, ii. 309.
H Troop (afterwards G). *Vide* "D" Battery, A Brigade, and ii. 36, 435.
Huddlestone, W. O., i. 254, 303; ii. 57.
Hughes, Thomas, i. 104, 105.
——, P. J., ii. 154–5, 269, 283.
——, T. S., ii. 88, 89.
Hunt, A., i. 223.
——, R. B., i. 408; ii. 160.
Hunter, G. J., ii. 187.
Hussars, 15th (King's), ii. 100.
Hussey, Wm., i. 127.
Hutchesson, T., i. 223.
Hutchins, H., ii. 362.
Hutchinson, Assistant-Surgeon, ii. 218.
——, General, ii. 128.
Hutton, Henry, i. 405, 407; ii. 186.
Huy, siege of (1694), i. 92.
Hyde, G. H., i. 262, 413.
Hyde Park, camp at (1723), i. 101–2.

"I" Battery, 1st Brigade (2 Company, 7th Battalion), i. 421.
Ilbert, C., i. 408; ii. 88.
'Inconstant,' H.M.S., ii. 110.
India (East Indies), i. 136.
Indies, East, early employment of Artillery in, ii. 2, 32, 74, 108, 130.
——, Mutiny of, 1857–9, ii. 142, 421.
——, West, R.A. in, ii. 74, 105, 134, 260, 261.
Infancy of Artillery in England, i. 35 to 44.
Infantry, instruction of, in Artillery drills, ii. 76.
——, services of, in conjunction with R.A.; in the American (2nd) War, ii. 395, 402, 407, 410.
—— in Egypt, ii. 129.
—— at Copenhagen, ii. 161.
——, in the Peninsula, ii. 208, 246, 282, 295, 312, 317, 336, 349, 353, 373, 383, 426, 429, 441.
—— at Walcheren, ii. 225.
Ingilby, Sir W. B., i. 223, 398, 406; ii. 314, 430.
Innes, Alex., i. 323.
——, G., ii. 154.
——, John, i. 220, 244, 307, 323, 357.

Innes, P., i. 178.
Inspector of Artillery, ii. 83, 137.
Institution, Royal Artillery, i. 7, 270.
Invalid Battalion, ii. 2, 16, 17, 22, 59, 264, 270.
Invalid Companies — Battalion — (Coast Brigade), i. 40, 167, 268, 349.
Inventors and Inventions, ii. 15, 83.
Ireland, French invasion of, ii. 77.
Irish Artillery, Royal, history of the, i. 160 to 168, 417.
——, ii. 24, 38, 39, 76, 78 to 81.
—— incorporated as the 7th Battalion, ii. 134.
—— Rebellion, ii. 70, 72, 75 to 77, 79, 138.
Irwin, Fred., i. 226, 292.
Italy, expedition to, ii. 108.
——, R.A. in, ii. 147, 244.
I Troop (afterwards H). *Vide* "D" Battery, B Brigade; ii. 36, 44, 45, 425, 435.
——, Rocket Troop merged into, ii. 39.

Jackson, D., i. 422.
——, H. G., i. 177, 407; ii. 394.
——, W. R. E., i. 223, 425.
Jago, D., ii. 431.
James, George, i. 180, 256; ii. 191.
——, Thomas, i. 308, 339, 378.
Jameson, Assistant-Surgeon, ii. 92, 101.
J'ans, T. R., ii. 56.
Jeffreys, Josiah, i. 223, 244.
Jena, battle of, ii. 150.
Jenkinson, George, i. 177, 403; ii. 257, 356, 383–4.
Jerusalem, ii. 131.
'John,' Ordnance ship, ii. 110.
Johnson, Lieut. E., i. 127.
——, G. V., i. 398, 399.
——, Thos., i. 220.
Johnstone, J. W., ii. 314, 332, 362, 364.
——, Wm., i. 226, 337.
Jones, Capt.-Lieut. N., i. 158.
——, J. E., ii. 155.
——, Richard, i. 175, 399, 409.
——, Thomas, i. 229, 304, 315.
——, W. D., i. 224.
Jourdan, Marshal, ii. 360.
Judgson, Thos., i. 396; ii. 89 to 91, 99 to 101.
Judice, Lieut., Portuguese Artillery, ii. 364.
Junot, Marshal, ii. 206, 207, 208.

Kaye, W. L., ii. 157.
"K" Battery, 4th Brigade (9 Company 7th Battalion), i. 425.
Keane, Charles, i. 177.

Keane, Major-General, ii. 395, 397, 399, 407-8.
Keats, Admiral Sir Richard, ii. 283.
Keith, F. M., i. 257.
——, Lord, Admiral, ii. 104, 108, 111, 115.
Kendall, R., i. 260.
Kennedy, G. R. H., i. 425.
Kenny, Assistant-Surgeon, ii. 191.
Kettledrums in the field, i. 14, 59, 126.
Kettlewell, J. W., i. 177, 225, 417.
Kilkenny Militia, ii. 76.
Kindersley, N., i. 229.
King, C., ii. 394.
——, Robert, i. 176.
——, R. T., i. 179.
——, at Corunna, ii. 218.
——, in 2nd American War, ii. 188, 189.
Kirby, Stephen, i. 175, 176, 410, 421, 423; ii. 105.
Kirkduin, capture of the, ii. 96.
Klundert, capture of, ii. 54.
Knatchbull, T., i. 222.
Knox, Francis, i. 182; ii. 92, 101.
——, Lieut. Wm., i. 127.
Koehler, G. F., i. 172, 257.
——, in Flanders, ii. 67, 68.
——, in Egypt, ii. 130, 131.
——, on the Staff, ii. 83.
Kray, General, ii. 61.
K Troop. *Vide* "E" Battery, A Brigade; and ii. 36, 38, 40.
Kuhlmann, Major, K.G.A., ii. 421, 424.

Laboratory, Royal, ii. 137.
Laborde, General, ii. 206, 207.
Lacy, R. J. J., i. 407, 424.
——, T., ii. 57.
Lake, General, ii. 60, 78.
——, N. T., i. 404, 410.
Lambert, Bisby, i. 292-3.
——, General, ii. 404, 409-10.
Landen, battle of (1693), i. 92.
Landmarks, i. 60 to 62.
Landrecy, sieges of, in 1793, ii. 62.
——, in 1815, ii. 438-9.
Lane, H. B., i. 182.
——, in Egypt, ii. 107. South America, ii. 177.
——, in Portugal, ii. 269. At Busaco, ii. 277.
——, passage of the Adour, ii. 383.
——, in 2nd American War, ii. 395, 396, 398-9, 401, 406.
—— *Vide* also ii. 145.
Lannoy, engagements at, ii. 60, 63.
La Peña, General (Spanish), ii. 206, 207.
La Plata, ii. 170.
Latham, W., ii. 300, 301, 319.
Laval, General (French), ii. 282.
Law, J. S., i. 180.

Lawlor, P. W., i. 173.
Lawrence, Capt., R.M.A., ii. 398, 401.
Lawson, Barclay, i. 175.
——, D., ii. 433.
——, Robert, i. 174, 260, 396.
——, Robert, *Capt.*, R.A., in Flanders, ii. 57.
——, in Egypt, ii. 105.
——, in the Peninsula, ii. 211, 345.
——, at Ciudad Rodrigo, ii. 315, 316.
——, at Vittoria, ii. 353.
—— *Vide* also ii. 144.
——, Robert, *Lieut.-Gen.*, R.A., appointed to the 1st Troop of R.H.A., ii. 34.
——, his commands, ii. 95, 104.
——, in Egypt, ii. 104 to 108, 128, 132.
——, MSS. details of ordnance, carriages, &c., ii. 116 to 127.
——, as Colonel-Commandant, ii. 186.
——, his character, ii. 128.
Laye, F., i. 257; ii. 57.
Leake, Richard, i. 45.
——, W. M., i. 175.
——, in Turkey, ii. 131.
—— *Vide* also ii. 141, 186.
Leathes, H. M., ii. 429, 430.
Lee, Lieut., i. 188.
Lefebure, George, i. 399.
——, in Flanders, ii. 57.
——, in Portugal, ii. 259, 260, 268, 269.
——, at Albuera, ii. 296, 297, 298.
——, at Ribera, ii. 329 (foot-note).
Lefroy, J. H., i. 261.
Le Geyt, W., ii. 74.
Legg, Lieut., in Flanders, ii. 65.
Leghorn. *Vide* Italy.
Leipsic, ii. 37, 38, 390.
Leith, Alexander (killed at Havannah, 1762), i. 127, 188.
Lemoine, Edmund, i. 292, 411, 413.
——, John, i. 176, 256, 303.
——, at Toulon, ii. 67.
——, in Egypt, ii. 105, 128, 132.
——, in Italy. At Maida, ii. 147 to 149.
——, in Sicily, ii. 272.
——, William, i. 180, 406; ii. 431.
Lempriere, Henry, i. 414.
——, W. C., ii. 396, 401.
Lennox, A. F. F., i. 176.
Lethbridge, T. A., i. 407.
Levinge, G. C. R., i. 398; ii. 146.
Lewis, C. H., ii. 261.
——, George, i. 225, 272; ii. 92.
——, Jonathan, i. 126-7-8, 131, 156.
——, Thomas, i. 224.
Lexington, battle of, i. 301.
Lieutenants-General of Ordnance, i. 13, 15, 16, 17.
Light, Sir Henry, i. 174, 177, 424.
——, H., ii. 230, 234.
—— Dragoons. *Vide* Dragoons.

Ligny, battle of, ii. 420.
Limerick City Militia, ii. 76.
Lincelles, engagement at, ii. 60.
Lindsay, George, i. 421.
——, John, i. 127.
Linières, General, ii. 170-1, 180.
Lisbon, Duke of Wellington in, ii. 206, 242, 273.
——, force of R.A. in, ii. 211, 269.
Lloyd, General, ii. 82, 83, 136.
——, James, i. 173.
——, Vaughan, i. 180.
——, William, i. 175, 176, 181; ii. 154.
——, W. J., in Walcheren, ii. 188.
——, at Waterloo ii. 188, 421-2, 424, 431-2, 434, 437.
—— *Vide* also ii. 186.
Locke, W. E., ii. 143.
Loison, General, ii. 206, 277.
Long Island (Brooklyn), battle of, i. 308.
——, Major-General, ii. 329.
Longley, J., i. 422; ii. 142.
Lopez, Lieut. (Portuguese Artillery), ii. 305.
Lord, M., ii. 160.
Lots, drawing of, ii. 95.
Louis, Mathew, i. 396, 400; ii. 154, 430, 434, 436.
Louisbourg, i. 128.
——, siege of (1758), i. 194 to 205.
Love, J., ii. 314, 319, 324.
Lovell, C. N., i. 422.
——, Lieut., i. 309.
Low, John, i. 421.
Loyalty Loan, ii. 72.
L Troop, i. 403; 36, 38.
Lucknow, ii. 142 (note).
Ludlow, Sir George, ii. 161.
Lundy's Lane, battle of, ii. 394.
Lyon, H., ii. 160, 163.

Maberly, E., i. 183.
Macartney, A., ii. 234.
——, Viscount, ii. 27.
Macbean, Alexander, i. 400, 413; ii. 362.
——, Archibald, i. 124.
——, Forbes, i. 6, 126, 127, 131, 134, 177, 190, 209 to 217, 242, 378.
——, Forbes (jun.), i. 177, 225, 407.
——, F., Col., ii. 431.
——, F., General, ii. 3.
Macdonald, Alexander, i. 256.
——, A. (*M.-Gen.*), in R.H.A., ii. 36.
——, expedition to Ferrol, ii. 106 (in Records as McDonald).
——, in Walcheren, ii. 225.
——, at Salamanca, ii. 325, 327, 330 (note).
——, at Waterloo, ii. 424, 435, 436.
—— *Vide* also ii. 41, 143.

Macdonald, A. (*Lt.-Gen.*), in the Peninsula, ii. 257 (as J., in Records).
——, at San Sebastian, ii. 362, 364.
——, in South America, ii. 169, 171.
——, at Waterloo, ii. 434.
——, R., ii. 155. At Orthes, ii. 385.
——, at Waterloo, ii. 430, 432, 434.
——, Robert, i. 399.
Macdougal, Major, ii. 407, 408.
Macfarlane, Brigadier, ii. 161.
Mackenzie, Alex., i. 226.
——, R., ii. 74.
Mackonochie, J., ii. 178, 187, 394.
Maclachlan, J., ii. 143, 186, 187.
Maclean, George, i. 225; ii. 145 (McLean in Records).
——, Sir Joseph, ii. 83, 90, 101.
Macleod, Sir John, i. 183, 364, 368, 380, 398.
——, in R.H.A., ii. 34, 51.
——, as Brigade-Major and D.A.G., R.A., ii. 5, 6, 33, 92 to 94, 104, 135-6, 268, 280, 415.
——, in Walcheren, ii. 223, 225, 231, 237.
——, his character, ii. 5 to 7, 92 to 94.
Madeira, ii. 262.
Madrid, ii. 214, 253.
Maestricht, capture of, ii. 65.
Magnetical Survey. *Vide* ii. Appendix B.
Mahon, Port, ii. 109.
Maida, battle of, ii. 147, 150.
Mainwaring, G., ii. 190, 362.
——, B. J., ii. 193, 194, 283.
Maitland, C. D., ii. 234.
——, E., ii. 142 (note).
——, General, ii. 421, 441.
——, Richard, i. 127, 187.
Major, regimental, rank of, ii. 25.
——, brevet of, ii. 356.
Malgere, La, Fort (Toulon), ii. 67.
Malines, engagement at, ii. 64.
Maling, W. E., i. 182; ii. 160, 220.
Mallett, J., ii. 186, 193.
Malta, capture of, ii. 73, 109, 138.
——, expedition for Egypt, ii. 105, 111
——, force of R.A. in, in 1810, ii. 271.
Manilla, siege of (1762), i. 188.
Manley, D., i. 221.
Mann, Gother, i. 410, 425; ii. 57.
Manners, Charles, i. 179.
——, R., at Walcheren, ii. 188.
——, at Barossa, ii. 283.
——, at San Sebastian, ii. 362.
——, at Waterloo, ii. 431, 432.
Marabout Tower (Egypt), effect of Artillery fire on, ii. 129, 130.
Marchaud, General (French), ii. 277, 278.
Marchiennes, attack on, ii. 61.
Mare (Mace), James, i. 127.
Margesson, P. D., i. 408.

Marienbourg, siege of, ii. 438, 439.
Marine Artillery (Royal), ii. 398, 404, 405.
Markland, George, i. 260.
Marlborough, Chas., Duke of, i. 33, 169.
——, John, Duke of, i. 14, 32, 63, 66, 79.
Marlow, B., i. 263.
——, J., ii. 186, 188.
Marmont, Marshal, ii. 245, 304, 307, 312, 326 to 329.
Marmorice, ii. 113.
Marquois, Lieut., i. 367.
Marriott, T. B. F., i. 221, 263.
Marsh, Henry, i. 226.
——, Nat., i. 124, 127.
Marston, M. C., i. 408.
Martin, D. N., ii. 285.
——, P., i. 179, 411.
——, Wm., i. 244.
Martinique, i. 165, 178, 419.
——, capture of, ii. 74, 260 (note).
——, contributions to the Loyalty Loan, ii. 72, 73.
Mason, R., i. 127.
Massena, Marshal, ii. 270, 276, 278, 284.
Massey, George, i. 414; ii. 155.
Masson, Thos., i. 423; ii. 106.
Master of the Ordnance, duties of the, i. 41.
Masters-General of the Ordnance, i. 9, 11, 13, 14, 15, 19, 28 to 34; ii. 225, 356.
—— in Ireland, i. 160, 162.
Master-Gunner of England, i. 40, 45, 60.
Master-Gunners, i. 40, 41, 106, 434.
Mathias, G., ii. 186, 261.
Matthews, J., i. 224.
Mauberge, siege of, ii. 438, 439.
Maude, F. C. (V.C.), ii. 142 (note).
——, G. A., i. 404; ii. 44.
Maunsell, J. E., ii. 431.
Maxwell, A. M., i. 220.
——, Stewart, i. 254.
——, S., in Egypt, ii. 107.
——, in the Peninsula, ii. 345.
——, at Orthes, ii. 383.
——, at Toulouse, ii. 388.
—— *Vide* also ii. 154.
May, Sir John, i. 173, 398.
——, in R.H.A., ii. 51.
——, at Copenhagen, ii. 160, 162.
——, at Corunna, ii. 244.
——, with Portuguese Artillery, ii. 252, 269.
——, at Busaco, ii. 278.
——, at Ciudad Rodrigo, ii. 310, 314, 316.
——, at Badajoz, ii. 319.
——, at Salamanca, ii. 324.
——, at Burgos, ii. 350.
——, at Vittoria, ii. 353, 354.
——, at San Sebastian, ii. 361, 364, 366.

May, Sir John (*continued*), passage of the Bidassoa, ii. 375.
——, at Toulouse, ii. 388.
——, at Quatre Bras, ii. 421.
——, at Waterloo, ii. 434, 435.
—— *Vide* also ii. 154.
Mayo, North, Militia, ii. 76.
McCulloch, Lieut., i. 133.
McDowell, General, i. 6.
McKenzie, Alex., i. 182, 220.
McLachlan, Alex., i. 181.
McLean, G., ii. 145.
——, Sir Joseph, i. 224.
McLeod, Sir John. *Vide* Macleod, Sir John.
——, Wm., i. 127, 133, 226.
Meadows, P., ii. 146, 160.
Medical Department, Ordnance, ii. 15–17, 79.
Mediterranean, R. A. in, 1810, ii. 270, 271.
Mee, C. H., ii. 143.
Meek, Mr., Clerk of Stores, ii. 57.
Meëlman, Lieut., ii. 435.
Menou, General, ii. 130.
Mercer, A. C., i. 399, 408.
—— at Waterloo, ii. 422, 424, 428, 430, 434, and Appendix A.
——, return to England, ii. 442.
Meredith, David, i. 411, 414; ii. 105, 108.
Messina, ii. 148.
Messing on board ship, ii. 26.
Mess-room, establishment of Royal Artillery, i. 391.
Meyrick, Mr., Paymaster, R.A., ii. 82.
Michell, E. T., i. 257, 398; ii. 283.
——, Sir John, expedition to the Helder, ii. 92.
——, expedition to Egypt, ii. 105, 108.
——, passage of the Bidassoa, ii. 375.
——, at Nivelle, ii. 377.
——, at Orthes, ii. 383.
——, in 2nd American War, ii. 395, 396, 398–9, 401, 404, 406, 409.
——, in the Netherlands, ii. 439.
—— *Vide* also ii. 154.
Michelson, Borgard, i. 126, 127, 130, 133.
——, George, i. 124.
Middleton, W. A., i. 6, 400.
Military Society, formation of, at Woolwich (1772), i. 268–9.
Militia, Volunteers to R.A., 1799, ii. 74.
——, discharges of ditto, ii. 136 (note).
——, battalion guns with, ii. 76, 94.
——, horsing of ditto, ii. 77–8.
Millar, William, i. 182, 222, 259, 411, 415; ii. 36, 105 (Miller in Records), 146, 186.
——, James, i. 405, 406; ii. 105.
Miller, Colonel F., i. 3, 41.
——, William, i. 221.

Milman, G. H. L., i. 259.
Minden, battle of (1759), i. 206 to 217.
Miners, company of (raised 1756), i. 159.
Minnies, George, i. 107.
Minorca, i. 69, 94, 124.
——, defence of (1782), i. 291 to 296.
——, capture of, ii. 73.
—— as head-quarters of R.A. in the Mediterranean, ii. 109.
——, expedition for Egypt, ii. 105, 108, 109.
Moira, Lord, ii. 58, 64.
Molesworth, A. O., ii. 160, 433.
——, R. C., i. 414.
Money, Captain, R.N., ii. 401.
Monmouth, battle of, i. 322.
Monro, F., ii. 362.
Montague, W., ii. 433.
Monte Video, ii. 168, 170.
Montressor, H. W., i. 413.
Monveaux, engagement at, ii. 63.
Moor, H. R., i. 176, 223.
Moore, G. A., ii. 188.
——, Jonas, i. 45.
——, Sir J., ii. 211, 213-14, 216, 218-20.
Morales (Spain), affair at, ii. 45.
Morgan, E., i. 406.
——, H., i. 173; ii. 362.
Morocco, adventures of Bombardier Turner in, i. 244 to 250.
Morris, C. H., i. 220, 422.
——, H. J., i. 182, 417.
Morrison, William, i. 260.
——, expedition to the Helder, ii. 92.
——, at Gibraltar, ii. 271.
——, in the Peninsula, ii. 205, 340.
——, at San Sebastian, ii. 361, 367.
——, passage of the Bidassoa, ii. 375.
——, at Nivelle, ii. 377.
—— *Vide* also ii. 141.
Mortars, howitzers used as, ii. 302.
——, General Lawson's remarks on, ii. 125.
Mosse, C., ii. 156, 375, 377, 380.
Moubray, E., i. 413.
Mountain batteries, ii. 376, 379, 382.
M Troop, i. 404; ii. 36, 38.
Muckell, Captain-Lieut., i. 203, 229.
Mudge, Wm., i. 175; ii, 92, 132.
Mules, for artillery draught; in Egypt, ii. 126.
——, in the Peninsula, ii. 343.
Mulgrave, Fort (Toulon), ii. 68.
Mundy, P. H., i. 223, 401, 415.
Munro, A., in Walcheren, ii. 232.
——, in 2nd American War, ii. 396, 407, 410.
—— *Vide* also ii. pages 140, 156.
——, W., ii. 105, 332.

VOL. II.

Murray, Colonel, ii. 164.
Musgrave, Sir Christopher, i. 16, 31.

Namur, siege of (1695), i. 92.
Napier, C. F., i. 417, 423.
——, C. G., i. 182.
——, ——, at Waterloo, ii. 420, 428, 431, 432.
Napoleon Bonaparte. *Vide* Bonaparte.
Navy, Royal, in connection with R.A.: exped. to the Helder, ii. 88. To Egypt, ii. 104, 107, 115, 121.
——, at Copenhagen, ii. 162. In South America, ii. 169.
——, in 2nd American War, ii. 401.
——, bomb vessels, ii. 85.
——, discontent and mutiny, ii. 70, 71.
——, strength in 1799, ii. 73-4.
Nedham, W. R., i. 263.
Negroes, employment of, in the Field, ii. 408.
Neill, General, ii. 142.
Nelson, Admiral, Lord, ii. 68, 73.
Netherlands (1794), i. 165.
Nevett, C. H., i. 179.
Neville, Chas., i. 182, 424.
Newfoundland, ii. 124, 128, 190.
Newhouse, Chas., i. 225.
——, in Flanders, ii. 67. Exped. to Egypt, ii. 105. Siege of Copenhagen, ii. 160, 162, 163.
New Orleans, expedition to, ii. 392, 410.
Newton, H. P., i. 173, 177, 401.
——, L., ii. 74.
——, L. H., i. 177, 220.
New York, the Gunner Governor of, i. 325 to 347.
Ney, Marshal, ii. 275, 278, 420.
Niagara, i. 420.
——, Fort, capture of, ii. 393.
Nicholls, O., ii. 92, 101.
Nicolls, W. D., i. 414.
——, attempt on Ferrol, ii. 107.
——, in South America, ii. 175, 177.
—— *Vide* also ii. 152.
Nicopolis, action at, ii. 127.
Nightingale, General, ii. 206, 208.
Nile, battle of the, ii. 73.
——, operations on the, ii. 124, 126, 128.
Nimeguen, siege of, ii. 65.
Ninety-Six, battle of, i. 368.
Nive, river, passage of the, ii. 380.
Nivelle, battle of, ii. 192, 377. Proportion of guns to troops in, ii. 412.
Nivion, Captain, ii. 271.
Nixon, M. D., i. 183.
Non-commissioned officers, proportion to gunners, ii. 136. Chevrons for, ii. 137.
Northall, John, i. 124, 127.
Nutt, G. F., ii. 105, 108.

2 K

9th Battalion: formation, ii. 151. Its records, ii. 140, 152.
——, Nos. 1 to 10 Companies, with their present designations; and the succession of Captains, ii. 151 to 157.
9th Brigade "B" Battery, ii. 58. "D" Battery, ii. 144. "E" Battery, ii. 157. "G" Battery, ii. 152.
9th Regiment, ii. 207, 282.
93rd Regiment, ii. 395, 408, 409.
95th Regiment, ii. 257, 396, 408.

O'Brien, H. H. D., i. 421.
——, L., i. 423.
——, N., Assistant-Surgeon, ii. 257 (note), 259.
O'Connell, R., i. 224.
Officers, Artillery, reduced through Peace of Versailles, ii. 1.
——, conduct of, between 1783 and 1792, ii. 13.
——, employment on Army Staff of, ii. 82, 83.
——, interchange between Horse, Field, and Siege Artillery, ii. 50 to 53.
——, for command of an army in the Field. *Vide* Artillery.
——, for ditto of Artillery. *Vide* Artillery.
——, pensions to widows, ii. 83, 84.
Ogilvie, J. F., ii. 156, 168, 169, 170.
O'Hara, Augustus, i. 368.
Oldfield, Anthony, i. 262.
——, Richard, i. 3.
Olivença, investment of, ii. 288.
Oliver, N. W., i. 181, 261, 398; ii. 154, 232.
Ommaney, M. R., ii. 74.
Onslow, P. V., ii. 430.
——, Sir Henry, i. 172.
Oporto, operations at, ii. 245, 246, 247.
Ord, F. W. C., i. 407.
——, H. G., i. 408; ii. 430.
——, R. H., at Vittoria, ii. 353.
——, ——, at San Sebastian, ii. 362.
——, ——, passage of the Bidassoa, ii. 375.
——, ——, at Toulouse, ii. 388.
——, Thomas, i. 127, 158, 194.
Orders, Regimental (1743 to 1756), i. 141 to 150. (1758–9), i. 191–3.
Ordnance, Clerk of the, i. 17.
——, Hon Board of, i. 1, 9, 10, 19, 23 to 28, 137; ii. 8 to 11, 74, 82, 109, 176, 196.
——, Lieuts.-General of, i. 13, 15, 16, 17.
——, Masters-General of, i. 9, 11, 13, 14, 15, 19, 28 to 34; ii. 137, 356.
——, matériel and transport should devolve upon the Artillery alone, ii. 121.
——, Select Committee, ii. 83.

Ordnance, Storekeeper of, i. 17.
——, Surveyor-General of, i. 17.
——, Tables of, in the reign of Charles II., i. 46.
——, Treasurer of the, i. 19.
Orlebar, J. R., ii. 160.
Ormsby, J. W., i. 223, 225, 415.
Orthes, battle of, ii. 383 to 385.
——, proportion of guns to troops in, ii. 412.
Ostend, expedition to, ii.. 88, 188.
Otway, Charles, i. 224; ii. 154.
Outram, Sir James, ii. 142 (note).
Owen, H., i. 409.
Owen, W. (H. in Records), ii. 141, 269.
Oxen, for Artillery draught, ii. 126, 203, 342.
100th Regiment, ii. 78.

Pack, General, ii. 171–2, 191.
Paget, Lord, ii. 100, 219, 228.
——, L. G., i. 398, 399.
Pakenham, Sir E., at Salamanca, ii. 327.
——, in 2nd American War, ii. 397, 399, 400–1, 403, 405.
——, his death, ii. 407.
——, W., ii. 435.
Palliser, H., ii. 362, 396.
Pallisser, Henry, i. 259.
Palmer, G. G., i. 259.
——, R., i. 224; ii. 154.
Pampeluna, blockade of, ii. 191–2, 355, 360, 373.
Paris, R.A. in, ii. 438.
——, Peace of, ii. 441.
Parker, Sir E. G., i. 224.
——, Sir J. E. G., ii. 155, 430, 433.
——, J. B., in Walcheren, ii. 232.
——, at Vittoria and San Sebastian, ii. 345, 353, 361, 364.
——, at Waterloo, ii. 432.
Parliamentary Returns, ii. 87.
Parry, Simon, i. 174, 181.
Pascoe, P., at Burgos, ii. 332.
——, at San Sebastian, ii. 361.
——, at Vittoria, ii. 353.
——, passage of the Bidassoa, ii. 375.
—— *Vide* also ii. 142.
Paterson, Thomas, i. 181, 183; ii. 160, 162.
Pattison, General: i. 6, 117, 124, 134, 152, 301, 320, 325 to 347; disputes with the Board, ii. 9.
——, his command in America, ii. 89.
——, Leonard, i. 126, 127.
——, M., ii. 74.
——, Thomas, i. 124, 127, 128, 131, 156.
Patullo, D., ii. 186.
Paul, A., i. 182.
Pay of the R.A. in 1810, ii. 262.

Pay of the Army, ii. 71, 79.
——— Lists, i. 40, 42, 48, 53, 58, 60, 62, 64, 116.
Paymasters, R.A., Regimental,' ii. 79, 82.
Payne, William, i. 182, 259.
———, W. S., i. 263.
Paynter, D. W., ii. 141.
Pearse, A. T. G., ii. 83.
Pedley, H., i. 133.
Peirce, H., ii. 143, 153.
Pendlebury, James, i. 431.
Peninsular War, force of R.A., ii. 267-8–9, 307, 342, 345.
———, nature of Sieges, ii. 306.
———, conclusion of, ii. 389, 390.
Pennycuick, J. F., i. 172.
Pensions to widows of officers, ii. 83, 84.
———, Good Service, to officers, ii. 356.
Peronne, capture of, ii. 441.
Pester, Hen., i. 399; ii. 144, 283.
Petitt, James, i. 82.
———, J. F., i. 432.
Petley, J. C., i. 173; ii. 156.
Phelps, S., ii. 188, 431.
Philadelphia, retreat from, i. 322.
Philippeville, siege of, ii. 438, 439.
Philippon, Governor of Badajoz, ii. 307, 308.
Phillips, R. F., ii. 362.
———, William, i. 134, 185, 207 to 217, 244, 315, 369 to 373, 378; ii. 89.
Phillott, Henry, i. 406; ii. 57, 261, 394.
Phillpotts, A. T., i. 396; ii. 156.
Pichegru, General, ii. 62 to 65.
Pickard, H. W., ii. 188, 189.
Pickering, W. H., i. 220.
Picton, Sir Thomas, ii. 312, 384, 421.
Piegri, General, ii. 148.
Pigou, A. C., i. 182.
Pike, Thomas, i. 127.
Pilkington, R., ii. 236.
Pillage, or Prize, ancient law of, ii. 240.
Pitt, William, ii. 150.
Pombal, action at, ii. 284.
Pondicherry, siege of (1748), i. 136.
Pontoon Train, ii. 339, 343, 344, 345, 349, 382, 385, 386, 387.
Poole, Henry, i. 180, 258.
———, W. S.; ii. 431, 432.
Popham, Admiral Sir Home, ii. 88, 164, 168, 169, 335.
Portugal, R.A. in, i. 190, 242.
——— (Artillery Services), *Expedition to*, in **1808**: its object, ii. 195–6.
———, its composition, ii. 202–3.
———, Artillery equipment, ii. 196.
———, attitude of the Board of Ordnance, ii. 196 to 202.
———, horses, ii. 198, 203, 212–3.
———, "Car" Brigade, ii. 205.

Portugal (*cont.*), force of R.A. in, ii. 204.
———, shortcomings of the Store Department, ii. 197, 205.
———, plan of the Campaign of 1808, ii. 206.
———, Roliça, ii. 206.
———, Zambugeira, ii. 207.
———, Vimiera, ii. 208.
———, Convention of Cintra, ii. 210, 211.
———, command of the Army, ii. 195, 208, 211.
———, command of the Artillery, ii. 196, 211.
———, march to Salamanca, ii. 211.
———, Corunna, ii. 214 to 221.
———, *Campaign of* **1809**: ii. 243.
———, command of the Troops, ii. 244.
———, command of R.A., ii. 244.
———, Artillery equipment, ii. 244.
———, draught, ii. 244.
———, plan of the Campaign, ii. 245.
———, plan of Algabaria Nova, ii. 245.
———, passage of the Douro, ii. 246–7.
———, French retreat out of Portugal, ii. 247–8.
———, Salamonde, ii. 248.
———, mobility and equipment of Field Artillery, ii. 248.
———, *Campaign of* **1810**.
———, retreat to Portugal, ii. 257.
———, Artillery matériel, ii. 259.
———, casualties, ii. 259.
———, plan of Campaign of 1810, ii. 260, 270.
———, force of Artillery, ii. 269.
———, Home Policy, ii. 273, 286.
———, combat of the Coa, ii. 275.
———, Artillery fire, ii. 276.
———, Busaco, ii. 277. Torres Vedras, ii. 279.
———, French evacuation of Portugal, ii. 284.
———, conduct of the R.A. in the pursuit, ii. 285.
———, Fuentes d'Onor, ii. 285.
———, Badajoz, First Siege, ii. 289 to 293.
———, Second Siege, ii. 299 to 304.
———, Third Siege, ii. 316 to 320.
———, Albuera, ii. 294.
———, *Campaign of* **1811**: ii. 307.
———, force of R.A., ii. 308.
———, command of R.A., ii. 309.
———, Ciudad Rodrigo, ii. 309 to 316.
———, Siege Train, ii. 309 to 311.
———, Almaraz, ii. 321.
———, pursuit into Spain, ii. 321.
———, *Campaign of* **1812**: retreat to Portugal, ii. 338.
———, its plan, ii. 339, 345.
———, Artillery, ii. 339.
———, Pontoon equipment, ii. 339.
———, re-entry into Spain, ii. 339.

2 K 2

Portuguese Troops, command, ii. 243, 293.
——, incapacity of Beresford, ii. 293.
—— Artillery, command, ii. 243, 244, 251, 287, 310.
——, equipment, ii. 252.
——, strength, ii. 269, 310.
——, re-organisation, ii. 279, 339, 345–6.
——, operations, ii. 287–8.
——, at Badajoz, ii. 289, 305.
——, at Albuera, ii. 297.
——, at Ciudad Rodrigo, ii. 316.
——, character of the officers, ii. 252.
——, of the troops, ii. 251, 274, 277.
Poulden, R. M., ii. 152.
Power, Francis, i. 410, 416.
——, James, i. 425.
——, Sir Wm.; at Ciudad Rodrigo, ii. 314, 315, 316.
——, at Badajoz, ii. 319.
——, at Burgos, ii. 330, 331, 332.
——, at San Sebastian, ii. 361.
——, W. G., i. 410, 421.
Poynter, B. L., ii. 396.
Precedence of Royal Artillery. *Vide* Artillery.
Press-gang, ii. 137.
Prevost, Sir Geo., ii. 189, 260, 395.
Price, Assistant-Surgeon, ii. 218.
——, E., i. 400, 423.
——, R. Blackwood, i. 175.
Princetown, action at, i. 313.
Pringle, George, i. 410; ii. 232, 431.
Pritchard, W., ii. 74.
Proctor, Colonel, ii. 393.
Promotion in R.A. of officers, ii. 25, 27.
——, of non-commissioned officers, ii. 342.
Prussians at Waterloo, ii. 420, 422, 423, 428–9.
—— in the Netherlands, ii. 439.
Pufflech, action at, ii. 64.
Pulteney, Sir Jas., ii. 96 to 99, 107, 121.
Pym, R., ii. 143, 148, 272.
Pyne, R., ii. 146.
Pyrenees, battle of the, ii. 192.

Quarter-masters, ii. 12, 25, 136.
Quatre Bras, ii. 45, 420, 421.
Quayle, John, i. 174.
Queen's County Militia, ii. 76.
Quiévrain, action at, ii. 59.

Raglan, Lord, i. 11, 16.
Ramsay, A., ii. 396, 402.
——, John, i. 181.
——, P., ii. 58.
——, Wm. Norman, i. 177, 401, 403.
——, passage of the Bidassoa, ii. 375; in Egypt, ii 107; in Portugal, ii. 259.

Ramsay, Wm. Norman (*continued*), at Fuentes d'Onor, ii. 32, 285.
——, at Vittoria, ii. 338, 353, 358.
——, at Nivelle, ii. 377, 379.
——, passage of the Nive, ii. 380, 382.
——, at Bayonne, ii. 381.
——, at Waterloo, ii. 415, 424, 426, 427, 430, 432, 434, 436.
——, as a Horse Artillery officer, ii. 32, 33.
——, placed in arrest by the Duke of Wellington, ii. 359, 360.
——, his character, ii. 357, 360, 415, 427.
——, his death, ii. 427.
Ramsey, George, i. 222; ii. 205.
——, J., ii. 92.
Ramsgate, ii. 94.
Rank, local, to R.A. officers with foreign troops, ii. 252, 253.
Rashell, Thomas, i. 432.
Rations, in connection with the soldier's pay, in 1796 to 1799, ii. 71, 82.
——, disputes with the Board, ii. 107.
Rawlinson, S., ii. 234.
——, S. J., i. 409.
Rawnsley, R. B., i. 261.
——, R. * B., ii. 152, 157. (* A. B. in Records.)
Rayner. *Vide* Raynes.
Raynes, W. A., i. 182.
——, at Copenhagen, ii. 160. (Spelt Rayner in the Records.)
——, expedition to Cadiz, ii. 190.
——, at Vittoria, ii. 191.
——, at River Adour, ii. 192.
——, at Tarifa, ii. 193.
——, at Seville, ii. 194.
Raynsford, E., ii. 105.
——, R. T., in Portugal, ii. 203, 211.
——, at Corunna, ii. 215.
——, at Badajoz, ii. 300–1.
Records, regimental, centralisation, desirability of, ii. 140, 152.
——, Peninsular, ii. 287, 325, 351.
Recruiting in 1803, ii. 139; 1805–6, ii. 150, 151; 1809, ii. 267; 1812, ii. 322.
Redinha, action at, ii. 284.
Reductions, after Peace of Versailles, ii. 1, 2, 38.
——, after Treaty of Amiens, ii. 135 to 137.
——, after Waterloo, ii. 442.
Reeves, John, i. 274.
Regiment of Royal Artillery, first establishment of, i. 61.
——, history of. *Vide* History.
——, permanent establishment of, i. 79 to 82.
——, growth of, i. 104, 106, 131–2, 157.
——, establishment of, in 1782, i. 383 to 391.

Regiment of Royal Artillery, strength of. *Vide* Establishment.
Regimental *esprit*, i. 170, 206.
—— Orders (1743 to 1756), i. 141 to 150. (1758–9), i. 191-2-3.
Regnier, General, ii. 148.
Reid, F. (Road in Records), ii. 218.
——, John, i. 221, 315.
Reille, General (French), ii. 351.
Reilly, W. E. M., i. 421.
Reliefs of R.A., system of, in 1803, ii. 134, 135.
Renny, Colonel, ii. 408, 409.
Repository, Royal Military, foundation of, i. 351.
Reserve, Army of, ii. 139.
Restoration and Revolution of 1688, i. 45 to 59.
Retirement, ii. 26.
Rettberg, Capt., King's German Artillery. *Vide* De Rettberg.
Returns, Parliamentary, ii. 87.
Revolution, ii. 28, 54.
Rey, F., i. 176.
Reynell, Samuel, i. 409; ii. 271.
Rhodes, Isle of, ii. 113, 121.
Riall, General, ii. 187.
Richards, James, i. 105.
Richmond, Duke of, ii. 7, 33.
Riddell, C. J. B., i. 416.
Riding Establishment, ii. 185, 265.
Rimmington, S., i. 261.
Riou, P., i. 409; ii. 92.
Ritchie, J., ii. 140, 152.
Robe, Thos. Congreve, i. 183.
——, Sir William, i. 183, 262.
——, in Flanders, ii. 56.
——, R.A. Regimental School, ii. 82.
——, Helder expedition, ii. 90, 101.
——, at Copenhagen, ii. 160, 162, 166.
——, in Portugal, ii. 196.
——, at Roliça, ii. 207.
——, at Vimiera, ii. 208 to 210.
——, succeeded in the command, ii. 211.
——, in Lisbon, ii. 244, 269.
——, pursuit of Soult, ii. 248.
——, in command of Driver Corps, ii. 267.
——, Badajoz, ii. 319.
——, Salamanca, ii. 332.
——, Burgos, ii. 336.
——, rewards, ii. 340.
——, W. L. (son of the above), at Burgos, ii. 332.
——, Mountain Battery, ii. 376, 379, 382.
——, at Nivelle, ii. 378, 379.
——, Adour, ii. 382.
——, at Waterloo, ii. 376, 430, 432.
Roberton, Archibald, i. 174; ii. 57, 68.
Roberts, G. F., ii. 186.
—— John, i. 353.

Roberts, Wm., i. 408.
——, at Barossa, ii. 190, 193.
——, at Cadiz, ii. 269.
——, at Seville, ii. 194. *Vide* also ii. 186.
Robertson, L. B., ii. 145.
Robinson, S., i. 261.
——, W., ii. 74.
Robison, Chas., i. 183.
——, J. S., i. 261; ii. 152.
Rochfort, George, i. 374.
——, Expedition to (1757), i. 190.
Rockets at Copenhagen, popular error, ii. 164.
——, first use of, as a siege weapon, ii. 164, 225.
—— at Flushing, ii. 229.
—— in the Peninsula, ii. 376.
—— in 2nd American War, ii. 409.
—— at Waterloo, ii. 416-17, 438.
—— at Leipsic, ii. 390.
——, Duke of Wellington on employment of, ii. 376, 416, 417.
Rocket Troop, 1st: formed, ii. 36-7, 382.
——, 2nd : formed, ii. 37.
—— at Orthes, ii. 383.
—— at Leipsic, ii. 37-8, 390.
—— in 2nd American War, ii. 395, 399, 406, 410.
—— at Waterloo, ii. 37, 416, 438.
—— reduced, ii. 37-8.
—— became I Troop, ii. 39.
Rocket troops, i. 393-4, 404.
Rocroy, siege of, in 1815, ii. 439, 440.
Roe, Marcus, i. 180.
Rogers, David, i. 243.
——, Henry, ii. 372, 406.
——, John, i. 172; ii. 74.
——, R. E. H., i. 417.
——, Thomas, i. 221.
——, at Quatre Bras, ii. 421, 422.
——, at Waterloo, ii. 424, 426, 431, 437.
Roliça, battle of, ii. 195, 201, 206.
Rollo, J., ii. 107.
Romer, R. C., i. 422.
——, R. F., i. 222.
Roncoux, battle of, i. 131.
Rooke (Rook in Record), C., ii. 105.
——, William, i. 108.
Rosetta (Egypt), bombardment of, ii. 128.
Ross, battle of, ii. 76.
——, Major-General, ii. 395.
——, Patrick, i. 261.
——, Sir Hew D., i. 16, 396.
——, retreat from Talavera, ii. 257, 259–60.
——, in Portugal, ii. 269.
——, combat of the Coa, ii. 276.
——, at Busaco, ii. 277.
——, pursuit of Massena, ii. 284–5.
——, Badajoz, ii. 319.
——, Salamanca, ii. 325, 335.

Ross, Sir Hew D. (*continued*), at Vittoria, ii. 345, 353, 355–6.
——, at Bidassoa, ii. 375.
——, at Nivelle, ii. 377–8.
——, at Nive, ii. 381.
——, return to England, ii. 383.
——, at Orthes, ii. 383–4.
——, at Waterloo, ii. 418, 424, 426, 430.
——, Peace, ii. 442. *Vide* ii., Appendix A.
Rosslyn, the Earl of, ii. 162.
Rotton, Guy, i. 414.
Roubaix, engagement at, ii. 63.
Rowan, H. S., i. 263.
Rowland, G. T., ii. 154.
Royal Arsenal, i. 16.
—— Artillery Institution, i. 7, 270.
—— Horse Artillery, i. 37, 393.
—— Irish Artillery, History of the, i 160 to 168.
—— Military Academy, i. 13, 19, 108 to 121.
—— Military Repository, i. 351.
—— warrants, i. 426 to 438.
Roza, General (Portuguese), ii. 346.
Rozières, Capt. (Portuguese Artillery), ii. 364.
Rudyerd, S., i. 424; ii. 188, 431.
——, W. C., ii. 57.
Ruffin, General (French), ii. 282.
Russell, H. C., i. 415.
Russia; expedition to the Helder, ii. 96, 97, 98, 99.
——, French invasion of, ii. 323, 339.
Royal Artillery. *Vide* articles "Artillery," "Horse Artillery," "Irish Artillery," "Foreign Artillery," "Siege Artillery." "Establishment," and "History."

Sabine, Sir Edward, i. 244, 413.
——, Magnetic Survey. *Vide* ii., Appendix B.
——, Peninsular Records, ii. 339.
——, in 2nd American War, ii. 395.
Salamanca, Sir Jno. Moore's march to, ii. 211.
——, battles at, ii. 321 to 330, 341 and 347.
——, proportion of guns to troops in, ii. 412.
Salamonde, affair at, ii. 248.
Salmon, G., i. 411, 416; ii. 106.
Sandham, Chas. F., i. 226, 261.
——, at Copenhagen, ii. 160.
——, at Quatre Bras, ii. 421.
——, at Waterloo, ii. 424, 426, 431. *Vide* also ii. 146.
——, Geo. i. 175.
Sandilands, P., i. 222, 400, 406, 425; ii. 430, 434.
San Sebastian, sieges of, ii. 338, 355, 360 to 372.

San Sebastian, R.H.A. employed as siege artillerymen, ii. 325.
Sappers and Miners, ii. 292.
'Sappho' frigate, ii. 192.
Saratoga, Convention of, i. 316–17; ii. 20.
Sardinia, Royal Artillery engaged by the king of (1744), i. 242.
Saunders, Wm., i. 182, 400; ii. 300, 305, 433.
——, W. B., i. 398, 406.
Savage, J. M., i. 177.
Schalch, Andrew, i. 176, 411, 416.
——, A. O., ii. 57, 157, 170.
——, A. O. W., i. 261.
——, Jacob, i. 181, 292, 296; ii. 186.
——, J. A., i. 223.
Scheldt, expedition to the, ii. 226, 227.
Schlundt, J. L., i. 431.
——, J. S., i. 431.
Schomberg, Duke de, i. 31, 55, 56, 59.
School, R. A. Regimental, ii. 82.
Scotland, march of Artillery in, i. 95–6.
——, Rebellion in, i. 128.
Scott, Alex. J., i. 175, 323.
——, C. F., i. 176.
——, David, i. 172, 176.
——, George, i. 175, 176, 399.
——, H. A., ii. 153, 186 (in Record as H. Scott).
——, P. F. G., i. 223, 408.
——, Thomas, i. 182; ii. 257.
——, William, i. 257; ii. 140, 143, 231.
Scriven, S., ii. 261.
Secretary of State for War, i. 2, 6, 105, 381.
Senegal, i. 186.
Seven Years' War (1756–1763), i. 184 to 193.
Seville, capture of, ii. 194, 330.
Seward, E., ii. 186.
——, Thomas, i. 261, 274; ii. 107.
Shafts, General Lawson's observations on, ii. 124.
Shakspear, G. B., i. 222.
Shand, Alex., i. 180, 319.
Sharpin, W., ii. 431.
Shaw, C., ii. 362.
Sheaffe, General, ii. 393.
Sheldrake, John, i. 177, 220.
——, Colonel, ii. 212.
Shenley, W., ii. 186, 193, 269.
Shepherd, R., ii. 422.
Sheppard, Edmund, i. 180, 259, 406; ii. 186, 187.
Sherbrooke, General, ii. 246.
Sherrard, Daniel, i. 432.
Shone, T. A., i. 180, 408.
Shrapnel, Henry, i. 173; ii. 57.
Shrapnel's spherical case (and shell) in the Peninsula, ii. 210, 277, 278, 327.

Shuttleworth, A., i. 183, 259, 303.
Sicily, Garrison of R.A. in, ii. 147, 205, 271-2, 330.
Siege Artillery :—gunners as drivers at Waterloo, ii. 415.
——, compared with Horse and Field Artillery, ii. 51.
——, Horse Artillery employed as, ii. 301, 325.
Sillery, C. D., i. 423.
Silva, Lieut. (Portuguese), ii. 364.
Silveira, General (Portuguese), ii. 345.
Simmons, T. F., ii. 261.
Simpson, J., expedition to the Helder, ii. 88, 89.
——, action of Zyp, ii. 92, 97.
——, T., i. 173.
Sinclair, J., ii. 140, 160, 218.
——, J. S., i. 262, 414 ; ii. 156, 424, 431.
Singleton, J., i. 413.
Skerrett, Colonel, ii. 190, 194.
Skinner, W. T., i. 416, 421.
Skyring, George, i. 260.
——, in Portugal, ii. 205, 211, 215.
—— Vide also ii. 141.
——, William, i. 411, 413.
Slade, H., i. 408 ; ii. 362.
Smith, Charles, i. 220.
——, F., i. 223, 257.
——, G. (R.A. Drivers), ii. 272, 314.
——, J. F. S., i. 409 ; ii. 90, 101.
——, J. L., i. 407.
——, J. W., i. 400.
——, in the Peninsula, ii. 340, 345.
——, passage of the Esla, ii. 348.
——, at Vittoria, ii. 353.
——, at San Sebastian, ii. 361, 364, 366, 368.
——, passage of the Bidassoa, ii. 374.
——, at Nivelle, ii. 377.
——, at Waterloo, ii. 424, 425, 430, 436.
——, at Cambray, ii. 440.
——, return to England, ii. 442.
—— Vide also ii. 154, 156.
——, Lieut., at Waterloo, ii. 430.
——, Major-Gen. Sir John, i. 176, 380. In the West Indies, ii. 74. Gibraltar, ii. 271.
——, R., i. 127.
——, Thomas, i. 127, 244.
——, W. P., i. 181.
Smyth, E., ii. 271.
——, H. A., i. 262.
——, W., ii. 57.
Smythe, W. J., i. 413.
Solignac, General, ii. 209.
Somerset, Lord Edward, ii. 383.
Somerville, Mark (afterwards Lord), ii. 160.

Soult, Marshal, in Portugal ; 1809, ii. 216.
——, at Corunna, ii. 219.
——, at Algabaria, ii. 245.
——, at the Douro, ii. 247.
——, in Spain ; retreat from Portugal, ii. 247.
——, march to Portugal, ii. 253, 257.
——, at Albuera, ii. 298.
——, retreat, ii. 298, 304.
——, at Badajoz, ii. 291, 307.
——, raises the siege of Cadiz, ii. 330.
——, at Toulouse, ii. 386-7.
——, his loyalty, ii. 389.
——, at Bayonne, ii. 389.
Sowerby, James, i. 226.
Spain, War in (1704-10), i. 93-5.
——, expedition to Ferrol, ii. 107.
——, insurrection against Joseph Bonaparte, ii. 195.
——, expedition of 1808, force of R.A. in, ii. 204.
——, Home policy, ii. 242.
——, Wellington's difficulties, ii. 254.
——, passage of the Douro, ii. 245.
——, Alcabon, ii. 254.
——, Talavera, ii. 254.
——, his retreat from Spain, ii. 257, 321, 330.
——, battle of Albuera, ii. 295.
——, Ciudad Rodrigo and Badajoz, ii. 307 to 320.
——, Salamanca, ii. 327.
——, entry into Madrid, ii. 329.
——, siege of Cadiz raised, ii. 330.
——, Burgos, ii. 335.
——, retreat from, ii. 338.
——, passage of the Douro, ii. 345 ; of the Esla, ii. 349 ; of the Ebro, ii. 351.
——, Vittoria and San Sebastian, ii. 352 to 371.
——, passage of the Bidassoa, and entry into France, ii. 374.
Spanish troops, equipment of, ii. 211, 242.
——, command-in-chief of, ii. 341.
——, at Corunna, ii. 217.
——, at Talavera, ii. 255.
——, at Albuera, ii. 295.
——, at Bidassoa, ii. 341, 371, 374.
——, at Nivelle, ii. 377.
——, at Toulouse, ii. 387.
——, character of, ii. 250, 254, 257, 295, 341.
Spearman, A. Y., i. 181, 408-9 ; ii. 58 83.
——, C., ii. 431, 432.
Speer, R. A., ii. 396, 400, 404.
Spellen, J. W., i. 173, 175 ; ii. 261.
Spencer, George, i. 432.
——, Hon. R. C. H., i. 399.
——, Major-General, ii. 161-2, 206.

'Sphynx.' Vide Egypt.
Spicer, William, i. 221; ii. 168.
Spiller, G., ii. 145.
Sproule, F. M., i. 405, 408; ii. 108, 132.
St. Amand, battle of, ii. 59.
St. Clair, J., ii. 261.
——, James P., i. 174, 407, 424.
St. Domingo, capture of, ii. 74. Subscriptions of R.A. to the loyalty loan, ii. 72.
St. Helena, local Artillery, ii. 169.
St. John, J. H., i. 262, 413.
St. Julian (Egypt), Fort, ii. 126, 128.
St. Lucia, i. 165.
——, capture of, ii. 74.
St. Malo, i. 190.
Stace, H. C., i. 421.
——, Mr. Commissary, ii. 416.
Stackpoole, G., ii. 74.
Staff; employment on, of R.A. officers, ii. 82, 83, 353.
Standish, D., i. 176.
Stanway, Henry, i. 176, 223; ii. 362.
Steenkirk, battle of (1692), i. 91.
Stehelim, Brigadier-General, ii. 260, 261.
Stehelin, Benjamin, i. 221, 410.
——, Edward, i. 180, 182, 244.
Stephens, Edward, i. 179.
——, James, i. 133.
——, J. M., i. 180, 259.
Sterling, Admiral, ii. 169.
Stewart, P. D., i. 179; ii. 160.
——, W., i. 225, 424.
——, General, ii. 294, 295.
Stillwater, battle of, i. 315.
Stocks, the (Government), ii. 70.
Stokes, W. J., i. 413.
Stone, H., ii. 251.
Stoney Point, attack on, i. 353.
Stopford-Blair (in Records as Stopford), ii. 177, 431.
Stopford, W. H., i. 221.
Stoppages, hospital. Vide Hospital.
—— on board ship. Vide Messing.
Store and Supply Department. Expedition to Egypt, ii. 110. To Portugal. ii 199, ii. 243. To Walcheren, ii. 237. Siege equipment for the Peninsula, ii. 205, 249, 367. In Spain, ii. 248, 343. In Portugal, ii. 260, 310. In South America, ii. 403.
Stores for an expeditionary force, ii. 199.
——, proportion of, for battery in 1813, ii. 343.
——, General Lawson on, ii. 121.
Story, R. W., i. 177, 183; ii. 261, 362.
Stow, Harry, i. 416, 422.
Strachey, S. (killed at Havannah, 1762), i. 127, 128.
Strange, H. F., ii. 146.

Strangways, T. F., i. 404.
——, at Leipsic, ii. 390. At Waterloo, ii. 430, 432.
Stranover, Lieut. Chas., i. 124, 127, 131.
Straps, foot, use of, at Monte Video, ii. 178.
Straton, Lieut.-General, i. 163.
Straubenzee, Thomas V., i. 175, 226.
Strength of Regiment, R.A. Vide Establishment.
Stuart, Sir John, ii. 147, 148.
Sturgeon, H., ii. 108, 128.
Suchet, Marshal, ii. 386.
Suckling, R. G., ii. 58, 74.
Summerville, John, i. 221.
Sumpter, W., i. 124.
Surat, capture of (1763), i. 187.
Surveyor-General of the Ordnance, i. 17, 45.
Swabey, W., ii. 160, 431.
Sweden, expedition to, ii. 203.
Sweeting, H. L., i. 416.
Symons, T. B., i. 172.
Sympher, Major, King's German Artillery, at Albuera, ii. 296, 297. At Ciudad Rodrigo, ii. 315-16.
——, at Salamanca, ii. 327. Vittoria, ii. 353.
——, San Sebastian, ii. 368. Nivelle, ii. 376, 377. Orthes, ii. 383-4.
——, Waterloo, ii. 424.
Sympson, James, i. 221.
2nd Battalion (or Brigade), ii. 105, 132, 134, 135. No. 4 Battery, ii. 310, 316. No. 7. Battery, ii. 58.
6th Battalion (or Brigade), ii. 74, 105, 110.
7th Battalion (or Brigade), Royal Irish Artillery incorporated as, ii. 134.
——, No. 1 Battery, ii. 145. No. 3 Battery, ii. 440. No. 4 Battery, ii. 58, 61, 296, 388.
17th Brigade, 7th Battery, ii. 146, 300, 301, 318.
7th Regiment, ii. 282, 404, 408.
17th Regiment, ii. 98.
60th Regiment, ii. 256.
67th Regiment, ii. 282.
71st Regiment, ii. 169, 180.

Talavera, battle of, ii. 254 to 260.
——, proportion of guns to troops in, ii. 412.
Talbot, ii. 190, 191, 193.
Tarifa, siege of, ii. 193.
Tarragona, siege of, ii. 361.
Taylor, A. J., i. 256, 396; ii. 152.
——, J., i. 172, 222; ii. 140, 186.
——, prisoner with the French, ii. 216.
Teesdale, H. G., i. 396; ii. 152.
Tentage, proportion of, in 1813, ii. 343.

'Terror,' bomb-vessel, ii. 58.
Terrott, Charles, i. 174.
———, expedition to the Helder, ii. 92, 101. In Walcheren, ii. 225. Claim to church bells, ii. 140.
Thomas, H. J., i. 220, 398.
Thompson, H. T., in Egypt, ii. 105, 132.
———, G., at Busaco, ii. 277, 285. At Ciudad Rodrigo, ii. 310, 314.
———, name spelt Thomson in Records.
Thomson, Alfred, i. 175, 415.
———, G., i. 423.
———, H. T., i. 180.
Thorndike, D., i. 261.
Thornhill, Robert, i. 421; ii. 186, 211, 215, 219.
Thornton, C. W., in Flanders, ii. 56, 60.
———, Colonel, in 2nd American War, ii. 405, 408.
———, Sir C. W., i. 261.
Thring, J. E., i. 183.
Tiffin, William, i. 226.
Tilsit, treaty of, ii. 158.
Tipperary Militia, ii. 77.
Tireman, H. S., i. 257.
Tobago, capture of, ii. 74.
Tobin, J. W., i. 173; ii. 153, 154.
Tomkyns, R., i. 408; ii. 187.
Tone, Wolfe, ii. 77.
Torres Vedras, ii. 207, 260, 262 to 279.
Torriano, C., i. 225, 244.
Toulon, siege of, ii. 67.
Toulouse, battle of, ii. 386 to 388.
———, proportion of guns to troops in, ii. 412.
Tovey, Abram, i. 207, 229, 272.
———, Jacob, i. 127.
Tower of London, i. 1, 12, 17, 60; ii. 94.
Townsend, J., ii. 430.
———, S. P., i. 257.
Trafalgar, ii. 68.
Traile, P., i. 223, 337, 364.
Trains of Artillery in 1544–48, and 1618–28–39. i. 42, 43, 44.
——— in June, 1685 (Sedgemoor), i. 48.
——— to resist the invasion of 1688, i. 52.
——— for Marlborough's campaigns, i. 63 to 70.
Transport of Artillery in Egypt. *Vide* Egypt.
——— in South America. *Vide* America.
——— and matériel should be under sole Artillery control, ii. 121.
Trant, Colonel (Portuguese), ii. 207.
Travers, J. F. E., i. 258.
Trelawney, Edward, i. 261, 398, 399.
———, H., i. 183, 410, 423.
Trelawny, H., ii. 105.
Trevor, E., i. 182; ii. 431.
Trichinopoly, battle of, ii. 32.
Trigonometrical Survey, ii. 132. App. B.

Trinidad, capture of, ii. 74
Troisvilles, engagement at, ii. 62.
Trotter, Thomas, i. 254.
———, in Flanders, ii. 57, 63, 90, 101.
———, in South America, ii. 177.
Troughton, F., ii. 394.
Truscott, R., i. 223; ii. 218, 220.
Tucker, J., ii. 261.
Tuite, H. M., i. 254.
Tulloh, Alexander, i. 175, 423.
———, at Badajoz, ii. 319. In command of the Portuguese Artillery, ii. 346.
———, at Vittoria, ii. 353. At Nivelle, ii. 377. At the Nive, ii. 381.
Tupper, G. le M., i. 396.
Turkey, professional and scientific expedition to, ii. 130–1.
Turkish Artillery, ii. 130.
Turks, in Egypt, ii. 104, 111, 121, 128.
Turner, Bombardier (in Morocco), i. 244 to 250.
———, George (afterwards Sir George), i. 225, 261, 400. ii. 157, 160. South America, ii. 168. At Orthes, ii. 383–4. At Toulouse, ii. 388.
———, George E., i. 416.
———, James, i. 413.
———, John, i. 263, 401.
———, N., ii. 269.
———, W. A., ii. 261.
Tylden, J., ii. 153.
Tylee, A., i. 224.
Tyler, Charles, i. 421.
3rd Battalion (or Brigade), ii. 105, 132, 135, 417. No. 2 Battery, ii. 154. No. 4 Battery, ii. 431.
10th Battalion, *old*, formed, ii. 185. Services of each Company to 194 and 280.
———, reduced, ii. 185.
———, *present*, formed, ii. 185.
12th Battalion, or Brigade, ii. 154, 185. No. 7 Battery (formerly 4–8 Battalion), ii. 143.
13th Battalion, or Brigade, ii. 185. No. 7 Battery, ii. 431. 8th Battery, formerly 3rd Company, 8th Battalion, ii. 42 (note).
3rd Regiment, ii. 246.
21st Regiment, ii. 395, 399.
23rd Regiment, ii. 88.
28th Regiment, ii. 282.
29th Regiment, ii. 78, 207, 246.
33rd Regiment, ii. 66.
37th Regiment, ii. 187.
38th Regiment, ii. 169.

Unett, G. W., i. 224, 425.
———, at siege of Copenhagen, ii. 160, 162.
———, in the West Indies, ii. 261.

Unett, G. W. (*cont.*), at Cambray, ii. 440.
——, R. W., i. 425.
Uniform of Artillerymen, i. 59, 140-1, 154, 265, 412.
Unit of Artillery—the Battery, ii. 135, 342.

Val, battle of (1747), i. 133.
Valenciennes, siege of, ii. 55, 60.
Van Straubenzee, Thomas, i. 175, 226.
Vans, David, i. 226.
Vaudamme, General, ii. 100.
Vaughan, T. L., i. 322.
Vaux, capture of, ii. 61.
Venloo, capture of, ii. 65.
Vernon, H. A., i. 224.
Verplanks, action at, i. 354.
Versailles, Peace of, reduction of officers consequent on, ii. 1.
'Vesuvius,' bomb-vessel, ii. 58.
Victor, Marshal, ii. 245, 249, 281-2, 284.
'Victory,' H.M.S., ii. 67, 68.
Vigo, bombardment of (1719), i. 96
Vimiera, battle of, ii. 208 to 210.
——, conduct of R.A. in, *ibid*.
——, Captain Skyring's Company, ii. 205.
Vinegar Hill, battle of, ii. 76.
Viney, James (afterwards Sir James), i. 424; ii. 211, 217.
Vinicombe, E. C., ii. 186.
Vittoria, French retreat to, ii. 350.
——, battle of, ii. 352 to 356.
——, official R.A. report of, ii. 351.
——, distribution of Artillery in, ii. 352-3.
——, arrest of Ramsay, ii. 358 to 360.
——, proportion of Guns to Troops at, ii. 412.
Vivian, Colonel, ii. 383.
Vivion, J., ii. 146; 180.
Volunteer Forces (British), necessity for discipline, ii. 250.

Waal, the, operations on, ii. 65.
Wadsworth, General (American), ii. 393.
Waggons, Gen. Lawson's remarks on, ii. 124.
Walcheren, expedition to, ii. 223 to 241.
——, description of Walcheren, ii. 223-4.
——, object of the expedition, ii. 224.
——, its place in R.A. history, ii. 195, 223.
——, R.A. in, ii. 187, 188, 225 to 227.
——, distribution of R.A., ii. 228.
——, rockets, ii. 229.
——, ammunition expended, ii. 229.
——, ordnance captured, ii. 235.
——, Supply Department, ii. 237.
——, results, ii. 237.
——, claim to bells, ii. 237 to 241.

Walcot, E. Y., i. 400.
——, E. T. (E. Y. in Records), ii. 430, 436.
Walker, C., i. 425.
——, E., i. 224.
——, F., i. 403, 420, 423; ii. 65.
——, J. G., i. 409.
——, P., i. 261.
——, W. H., i. 222; ii. 88, 89.
——, P. W. (P. H. in Records), ii. 153.
Wall, Adam, i. 422; ii. 215, 440.
Wallace, P. M., i. 256; ii. 232.
Waller, C., in Flanders, ii. 57.
——, in Walcheren, ii. 225.
——, in Portugal, ii. 346-7; superseded in the command, ii. 346.
Walsh, B. T., i. 416, 421, 422; ii. 170, 172.
——, Edward, i. 406.
——, L. E., i. 172.
Walton, Joseph, i. 181, 244, 292.
Warberg, battle of (1760), i. 214-15.
Warburton, G. D., i. 414.
Ward, A., ii. 430.
——, J. H. *Vide* Wood, J. H.
——, F. B., i. 223, 396.
Warde, Brigadier, at Copenhagen, ii. 161.
——, F., ii. 156, 430.
——, Sir E. C., i. 7, 398.
——, Sir Francis, i. 401.
Warrants, Royal, i. 426.
Warren, the (afterwards the Royal Arsenal), i. 16, 118, 145, 147.
Washington, capture of, ii. 395.
——, George, i. 159, 299, 365.
Waterloo, ii. 412 to 442.
——, circumstances preceding, ii. 412-13.
——, strength of the French Army, ii. 423.
——, command of R.A., ii. 414-15.
——, force of Artillery, ii. 414-15, 417, 424, 430 to 433.
——, drivers, ii. 415, 417.
——, Store Department, ii. 416.
——, Rocket Troop, ii. 37-8, 416-17, 436, 438.
——, equipment and armament of Field Artillery, ii. 245, 417.
——, equipment and armament of Horse Artillery, ii. 417, 418-19, 423.
——, tactics, ii. 420, 422, 423, 425, 426, 428.
——, Quatre Bras, ii. 421.
——, the battle, ii. 425 to 429.
——, reserve Artillery, ii. 424, 426.
——, Norman Ramsay, ii. 427, 434.
——, proportion of guns to troops, ii. 412.
——, ammunition expended, ii, 426, 438.

Waterloo (*continued*), boon service, ii. 433. *Vide* Appendix A.
——, conduct of the Artillery, ii. 434 to 438. *Vide* also Appendix A.
——, No. 2 Company, 10th Battalion, ii. 188.
——, No. 9 Company, 3rd Battalion, ii. 417.
——, I Troop, ii. 428, 435.
——, 52nd Regiment, ii. 429.
——, reductions of Artillery after. *Vide* Reductions.
Waters, Colonel, ii. 246.
Watson, A., i. 407; in Flanders, ii. 56, 59.
——, in South America, ii. 169, 170.
——, Jonas (killed at Carthagena, 1741), i. 61, 82, 103, 104, 123, 431.
Webber, W., ii. 431, 432.
Webdell, Phillip, i. 244.
Weetman, Agar, i. 173.
Weller, F., i. 410; ii. 145.
Wellington, Arthur, Duke of, i. 10.
——, first under fire, ii. 66.
——, at siege of Copenhagen, ii. 161, 162, 163, 164.
——, **1808**. Expedition to Portugal, ii. 195-6, 205.
——, at Roliça, ii. 206.
——, superseded, ii. 202, 208.
——, Vimiera, ii. 208.
——, recall to England, ii. 211.
——, **1809**. Resumes command, ii. 242.
——, his opinion of the troops, ii. 243.
——, invades Spain, ii. 245.
——, passage of the Douro, ii. 246-7.
——, at Abrantes, ii. 249.
——, remarks on the Spanish Government and Army, ii. 250.
——, remarks on the Portuguese, ii. 251.
——, remarks on discipline, ii. 251.
——, Home policy, ii. 253, 270, 286.
——, his difficulties, ii. 254.
——, Talavera, ii. 254-5, 260.
——, retreat to Portugal, ii. 257.
——, at Badajoz, ii. 260.
——, occupies Torres Vedras, ii. 260, 274.
——, **1810**. At Celorico, ii. 275.
——, retreats to Coimbra, ii. 276, 278.
——, Busaco, ii. 274, 276 to 278.
——, retreats to Torres Vedras, ii. 278-9.
——, defeats Massena, ii. 284.
——, Fuentes d'Onor, ii. 285.
——, **1811**. Advances into Spain, ii. 289.
——, on the battle of Albuera, ii. 298.
——, Badajoz, 1st siege, ii. 289.
——, Badajoz, 2nd siege, ii. 301, 304.
——, at Elvas, ii. 307.
——, at Pontalagree, ii. 307.
——, Ciudad Rodrigo, ii. 312.

Wellington, Duke of (*cont.*), **1812**. Siege of Ciudad Rodrigo, ii. 312 to 316.
——, 3rd siege of Badajoz, ii. 316 to 318.
——, at Salamanca, ii. 323.
——, the battle of Salamanca, ii. 326 to 329.
——, enters Madrid, ii. 329, 330.
——, siege of Burgos, ii. 330 to 335.
——, retreats to Portugal, ii. 338.
——, **1813**. Preparation, ii. 339, 341.
——, as Commander-in-Chief, ii. 341.
——, re-enters Spain, ii. 345.
——, at Salamanca, ii. 347-8.
——, passage of the Esla, ii. 349.
——, pursuit of Soult, ii. 349.
——, crossing the Ebro, ii. 351-2.
——, Vittoria, ii. 351 to 355
——, places Norman Ramsay in arrest, ii. 357 to 360.
——, siege of San Sebastian, ii. 360 to 371.
——, passage of the Bidassoa, ii. 374 to 375.
——, enters France, ii. 376.
——, Nivelle, ii. 377 to 379.
——, Nive, ii. 380.
——, **1814**. Passage of the Adour, ii. 382.
——, Orthes, ii. 383 to 385.
——, Toulouse, ii. 386-7.
——, peace, ii. 389.
——, **1815**. Events of the 100 days, ii. 412 to end.
——, the Army in Belgium, ii. 414-15.
——, the Army at Brussels, ii. 416, 420.
——, Quatre Bras, ii. 420-1.
——, Waterloo, ii. 422 to 429.
——, entry into Paris, ii. 438.
——, Army of Occupation, ii. 441.
——, command of the Artillery, ii. 298, 309, 346.
——, his handling of Artillery, ii. 276, 335, 354.
——, his general tactics, ii. 306, 336, 354, 423.
——, contrasted with Napoleon, ii. 336.
——, publication of his letters, ii. 270.
——, on the conduct of R.A., ii. 357 and Appendix A.
——, his character, ii. 66, 69, 202, 209, 245, 249-50, 254, 270, 286, 335.
Wells, F., ii. 186, 188, 434.
Weluwe (expedition to Flanders), ii. 66.
West India Regiments in 2nd American war, ii. 395, 396, 399.
West Indies. *Vide* Indies.
—— (1741), i. 123. (1793-6), i. 165.
Weston, F., ii. 188, 319, 396.
Wexford, battle of, ii. 76, 78.
Wheatley, Colonel, ii. 282.
Whinyates, Sir E. C., i. 177, 394, 401 404.

Whinyates, Sir E. C. (*cont.*), appointed to Rocket Troop, ii. 390.
——, in 8th Battalion, ii. 145.
——, expedition to the Helder, ii. 92.
——, siege of Copenhagen, ii. 160.
——, at Ribera, ii. 329 (note).
——, at Waterloo, ii. 390, 416–17, 422, 424, 426, 430, 432.
——, return to England, ii. 442.
——, as a Horse Artillery officer, ii. 51.
——, as Commandant of Woolwich, ii. 37.
——, his character, ii. 37, 51, 390.
White Plains, battle of, i. 310.
Whitelock, General, in South America, ii. 170 to 182.
——, his incapacity, *ibid.*
——, dual government, ii. 175.
Whitty, J., i. 413.
Whitworth, Lord, ii. 138.
——, F., i. 220.
——, Sir Francis, ii. 90, 101.
Widows of officers, pensions to, ii. 83, 84.
Widows' Pension Fund, i. 155.
Wilford, E. C., i. 257, 413.
——, E. M., i. 222.
Wilgress, Edward, i. 407.
——, E. P., ii. 170, 172.
Wilkinson, Christopher, i. 409; ii. 153, 269.
Wilks, John, i. 226.
William III., royal warrant of, i. 429.
Williams, Edward, i. 315, 405.
——, Griffith, i. 175, 244.
——, Henry, i. 414.
——, Sir William F., i. 406.
——, W., ii. 144, 396.
——, T. G. T. (in Record as T. G.), at Vittoria, ii. 362.
——, at San Sebastian, ii. 364.
——, in 2nd American war, ii. 396.
Williamson, Commissary and Paymaster, ii. 57.
——, Edmund, i. 431.
——, George, i. 188, 194, 200, 243.
——, John, i. 174.
——, J. S., i. 408.
——, at Waterloo, ii. 424.
——, in Sicily, ii. 272.
—— *Vide* also ii. 144.
Williamstadt, siege of, ii. 54.
Willington, Bailey, i. 274, 411.
Willis, Browne, i. 409.
——, Lieut., ii. 300.
Wills, B., ii. 244.
Wilmot, Edward, i. 225, 398, 410.
——, in Walcheren, ii. 230, 231.
——, in Portugal, ii. 211, 215.
——, at Corunna, ii. 218.
——, F. Eardley, i. 416.
——, H. R. Eardley, i. 407.
Wilson, A. R., ii. 160.

Wilson, General, ii. 374.
——, George, i. 171; ii. 57.
——, James, i. 260.
——, J. A., i. 181.
——, Ralph, i. 181, 323.
——, R. G. B., i. 177, 414.
——, Sir Robert, ii. 244, 344.
——, Sir Wiltshire, i. 172, 257, 259.
——, expedition to the Helder, ii. 88, 89.
——, in Flanders, ii. 57.
Winter, James, i. 173, 175, 244, 262.
Witham, Abraham, i. 182.
Wittman, W. (assistant surgeon), ii. 131.
Wolfe, General James, i. 197-8, 200, 205.
Wood, Charles, i. 259.
——, Sir David E., i. 224, 400.
——, Sir George A., i. 396, 398, 416; in Egypt, ii. 132; in Walcheren, ii. 225; in the Peninsula, ii. 211; at Corunna, ii. 215; in command of Artillery at Waterloo, ii. 412, 414 to 417, 422, 424, 432, 434, 435, 437–8; with the Army of Occupation, ii. 441; in old 10th Battalion, ii. 186. (As E. A. in Record.)
——, J., i. 222, 408.
——, J. H., at Vittoria, ii. 362.
——, in 8th Battalion (as Ward), ii. 145.
——, Ralph, i. 432.
Woodward, Edward, i. 292.
Woodyear, L., ii. 353, 354.
Woolcombe, P. J., at Barossa, ii. 190, 283.
——, R., at Fuentes d'Onor, ii. 285.
Woolsey, O'B. B., i. 407.
Woolwich, Commandant of. *Vide* Commandant.
——, Garrison Adjutant, or Brigade-Major, or Assistant Adjutant-General, ii. 83.
——, i. 13, 16, 47, 105, 140, 264.
——, Battalion or Brigade Headquarters concentrated at, ii. 135.
Worsley, E. V., i. 261.
Worth, F., ii. 74.
——, Lieut. John, i. 127.
Wragge, A. R., i. 181, 414.
Wright, A., siege of Copenhagen, ii. 160.
——, C. J., i. 179.
——, F., i. 408.
——, H. R., i. 425.
——, Jesse, i. 173-4-5.
——, J., in Flanders, ii. 56, 59, 60, 63.
——, at Corunna, ii. 220.
——, at Waterloo, ii. 430.
——, Robert, i. 179, 182, 262; ii. 271.
Wulff, George, i. 181, 261, 292.
Wyatt, H., ii. 186.
——, S., ii. 186.
Wylde, W., ii. 143, 186.
Wynne, C. R., ii. 155.

Yorke, Capt.-Lieut., i. 242.
York, the Duchess of, ii. 82.
———, H.R.H. the Duke of, in Flanders, ii. 55 to 65.
———, as Commander-in-Chief, ii. 71, 78.
———, expedition to the Helder, ii. 90, 95 to, 101.
——— (Upper Canada), capture of, ii. 393.
York, Lieut., i. 315.

——— Town, capitulation of, i. 375.
Young, Brooke, i. 257, 409; ii. 74.
———, C. C., i. 400; ii. 143.
———, G. R. C., i. 423.
———, W. B., i. 423.
Younghusband, Charles, i. 222, 259.

Zuyder Zee, ii. 97.
Zyp, action of, ii. 97.

1st Battalion. History, &c., i. 169.
1 Battery, 5th Brigade, i. 408.
———, 6th Brigade, i. 260, 303-4.
1 Company, 1st Battalion. *Vide* "F" Battery, 9th Brigade.
———, 2nd Battalion. *Vide* 7 Battery, 21st Brigade.
———, 3rd Battalion. *Vide* "A" Battery, 4th Brigade.
———, 4th Battalion. *Vide* 4 Battery, 7th Brigade.
———, 5th Battalion. *Vide* "F" Battery, 1st Brigade.
———, 6th Battalion. *Vide* "C" Battery, 11th Brigade.
———, 7th Battalion. *Vide* "C" Battery, 1st Brigade.
2nd Battalion, i. 169, 178.
2 Battery, 2nd Brigade, i. 407.
———, 5th Brigade, i. 418, 424.
———, 12th Brigade, i. 179.
———, 13th Brigade, i. 221.
2 Company, 1st Battalion. *Vide* "B" Battery, 1st Brigade.
———, 2nd Battalion. *Vide* 2 Battery, 12th Brigade.
———, 3rd Battalion. *Vide* 7 Battery, 13th Brigade.
———, 4th Battalion. *Vide* 6 Battery, 3rd Brigade.
———, 5th Battalion. *Vide* "D" Battery, 8th Brigade.
———, 6th Battalion. *Vide* 6 Battery, 5th Brigade.
———, 7th Battalion. *Vide* "I" Battery, 1st Brigade.
3rd Battalion, i. 218.
3 Battery, 2nd Brigade, i. 407.
———, 3rd Brigade, i. 408.
———, 5th Brigade, i. 174, 207.
———, 6th Brigade, i. 423.
———, 7th Brigade, i. 224.
———, 12th Brigade, i. 422.
3 Company, 1st Battalion. *Vide* 7 Battery, 2nd Brigade.
———, 2nd Battalion. *Vide* 7 Battery, 10th Brigade.
———, 3rd Battalion. *Vide* 2 Battery, 13th Brigade.
———, 4th Battalion. *Vide* 8 Battery, 2nd Brigade.
———, 5th Battalion. *Vide* 2 Battery, 2nd Brigade.
———, 6th Battalion. *Vide* 4 Battery, 2nd Brigade.
———, 7th Battalion. *Vide* 3 Battery, 12th Brigade.
4th Battalion, i. 251, 301.
4 Battery, 2nd Brigade, i. 414.
———, 3rd Brigade, i. 222.
———, 5th Brigade, i. 176.
———, 7th Brigade, i. 252-254.
———, 13th Brigade, i. 175-207.
4 Company, 1st Battalion. *Vide* 3 Battery, 5th Brigade.
———, 2nd Battalion. *Vide* "D" Battery, 1st Brigade.
———, 3rd Battalion. *Vide* 4 Battery, 3rd Brigade.
———, 4th Battalion, i. 257.

4 Company, 5th Battalion.   *Vide* 3 Battery, 2nd Brigade.
————————, 6th Battalion.   *Vide* "B" Battery, 8th Brigade.
————————, 7th Battalion.   *Vide* "A" Battery, 1st Brigade.
————————, 11th Battalion.   *Vide* "H" Battery, 4th Brigade.
5th Battalion, i. 405.
5 Battery,   2nd Brigade, i. 182.
————————,   3rd Brigade, i. 417.
————————,   5th Brigade, i. 410.
5 Company,   1st Battalion.   *Vide* 4 Battery, 13th Brigade.
————————,   2nd Battalion.   *Vide* 8 Battery, 3rd Brigade.
————————,   3rd Battalion.   *Vide* "B" Battery, 11th Brigade.
————————,   4th Battalion.   *Vide* "B" Battery, 9th Brigade.
————————,   5th Battalion.   *Vide* 1 Battery, 5th Brigade.
————————,   6th Battalion.   *Vide* "C" Battery, 8th Brigade; also i. 415.
————————,   7th Battalion.   *Vide* 3 Battery, 6th Brigade.
6th Battalion, i. 410.
6 Battery, 2nd Brigade, i. 176.
————————,   3rd Brigade, i. 256.
————————,   5th Brigade, i. 413.
————————,   10th Brigade, i. 261.
6 Company,   1st Battalion.   *Vide* 6 Battery, 2nd Brigade.
————————,   2nd Battalion.   *Vide* "G" Battery, 8th Brigade; also i. 181.
————————,   3rd Battalion.   *Vide* 7 Battery, 3rd Brigade.
————————,   4th Battalion.   *Vide* 1 Battery, 6th Brigade.
————————,   5th Battalion.   *Vide* 3 Battery, 3rd Brigade.
————————,   6th Battalion (formerly 7 Company).   *Vide* "F" Battery, 8th Brigade.
————————,   7th Battalion.   *Vide* "D" Battery, 11th Brigade.
7 Battalion (formerly Royal Irish Artillery), i. 163-168, 417.
7 Battery,   2nd Brigade, i. 174.
————————,   3rd Brigade, i. 223.
————————,   10th Brigade, i. 180.
————————,   13th Brigade, i. 221.
————————,   21st Brigade, i. 179.
7 Company,   1st Battalion.   *Vide* 4 Battery, 5th Brigade.
————————,   2nd Battalion (formerly 8 Company).   *Vide* 5 Battery, 2nd Brigade.
————————,   3rd Battalion.   *Vide* 3 Battery, 7th Brigade.
————————,   4th Battalion.   *Vide* 6 Battery, 10th Brigade.
————————,   5th Battalion (formerly 9 Company).   *Vide* "A" Battery, 9th Brigade. *See* also i. 409.
————————,   6th Battalion (formerly 9 Company).   *Vide* "C" Battery, 9th Brigade. *See* also i. 416.
————————,   7th Battalion (formerly 8 Company).   *Vide* 2 Battery, 5th Brigade. *See* also i. 424.
8 Battery,   2nd Brigade, i. 257, 303-4.
————————,   3rd Brigade, i. 181.
————————,   12th Brigade, i. 252, 263.
8 Company, 1st Battalion.   *Vide* "A" Battery, 11th Brigade.
————————,   2nd Battalion (formerly 10 Company).   *Vide* "A" Battery, 14th Brigade. *See* also i. 182.
————————,   3rd Battalion.   *Vide* "D" Battery, 4th Brigade.
————————,   4th Battalion.   *Vide* "E" Battery, 1st Brigade.
————————,   5th Battalion (formerly 10 Company).   *Vide* 5 Battery, 5th Brigade. *See* also i. 409.
————————,   6th Battalion (formerly 10 Company).   *Vide* 5 Battery, 3rd Brigade. *See* also i. 416.
————————,   7th Battalion (formerly 9 Company.)   *Vide* "K" Battery, 4th Brigade. *See* also i. 424.
9 Company,   2nd Battalion, i. 183.
————————,   3rd Battalion, i. 226.
————————,   4th Battalion.   *Vide* "H" Battery, 4th Brigade.
————————,   5th Battalion.   *Vide* "A" Battery, 9th Brigade.

9 Company, 6th Battalion.   *Vide* "C" Battery, 9th Brigade.
————, 7th Battalion.   *Vide* "K" Battery, 4th Brigade.
10 Company, 2nd Battalion.   *Vide* "A" Battery, 14th Brigade.
————, 3rd Battalion, i. 226.
————, 4th Battalion.   *Vide* 8 Battery, 12th Brigade.
————, 5th Battalion.   *Vide* 5 Battery, 5th Brigade.
————, 6th Battalion.   *Vide* 5 Battery, 3rd Brigade.
————, 7th Battalion, i. 425.

LONDON:
PRINTED BY WILLIAM CLOWES AND SONS,
STAMFORD STREET AND CHARING CROSS.

www.ingramcontent.com/pod-product-compliance
Lightning Source LLC
Chambersburg PA
CBHW031947290426
44108CB00011B/708